150

$7 500.$

A GUIDE
TO THE
ARCHAEOLOGICAL
SITES
OF THE
BRITISH ISLES

A GUIDE
TO THE
ARCHAEOLOGICAL
SITES
OF THE
BRITISH ISLES

Courtlandt Canby

A HUDSON GROUP BOOK

Facts On File
New York • Oxford

A Guide to the Archaeological Sites of the British Isles

copyright © 1988 by Courtlandt Canby

Library of Congress Cataloging-in-Publication Data

Canby, Courtlandt.
    A guide to the archaeological sites of the British Isles /
Courtlandt Canby.
        p.   cm.
    "A Hudson Group book."
    Includes indexes.
    ISBN 0-8160-1570-8
    1. Great Britain—Antiquities—Guide-books. 2. Ireland—
Antiquities—Guide-books. 3. Excavations (Archaeology)—Great
Britain—Guide-books. 4. Excavations (Archaeology)—Ireland—Guide-
books. 5. Historic sites—Great Britain—Guide-books. 6. Historic
sites—Ireland—Guide-books. I. Title.
DA90.C36 1988   88-25068
914.1'04858—dc19   CIP

British CIP data available on request

Printed in the United States of America

10 9 8 7 6 5 4 3 2 1

CONTENTS

Introduction

The story of the first 40,000 years or so of human habitation in the British Isles—from the first evidences of Stone Age man in these islands up into the period of the first recorded history—is a fascinating one. But it is all too little known. And the further back one delves into this huge and misty span of time, the less is known about the lives and activities of these prehistoric people—except through the findings of archaeology. However, even archaeology, dealing as it does solely with material remains, can give us only hints and surmises of what went on. Nevertheless, archaeology is all we have for the earliest periods. Even as we move up into the early historic period it continues to play a significant role in supplementing and enriching the often meager written records.

As an aid in understanding this long and fruitful span of years, this Guide offers an up-to-date and comprehensive description of the most important archaeological sites in the British Isles, both prehistoric and early historic—and many lesser sites as well. The listing is alphabetical under countries, for the Guide is twofold in its purpose. It is intended as a reference book for the stay-at-home; but it can be equally useful as a field manual for the interested traveler. The student, no doubt, will also find it invaluable; and so will even the occasional scholar or archaeologist seeking information outside of his chosen field.

Every attempt has been made to make the Guide as accurate as possible, but it is written primarily for the layman and thus avoids most scholarly terminology.

The time limits of the Guide run from the Paleolithic up to the beginnings of modern history. In England a convenient cutoff date is provided by the Norman Conquest of 1066 AD; in Scotland and Ireland it is the Early Christian and Viking periods, roughly up into the 12th cent. AD. (The Irish section includes both Northern Ireland and the Republic in one cultural area; similarly, Wales is covered as part of England.) I have made no attempt to include every surviving archaeological site or monument in the three areas; there are, for example, over 3,000 known Iron Age hill forts in England, over 600 megalithic tombs in Scotland and some 1,200 in Ireland as well as possibly 40,000 ring forts and cashels and countless Early Christian monastic sites. The choice has been difficult, and many will quarrel with my decisions; but in general I have tried to include most sites or monuments of any importance, or at least representative examples of every kind of field monument within the described period. The emphasis is on those sites that seem to me interesting or important and/or worth visiting because there is something to see there. Now and then, however, I have included a site or monument that has been destroyed, because of its importance in the archaeological record.

The unusual alphabetical rather than geographic listing of sites within countries in this Guide makes it easy for the stay-at-home to look up any given entry by name—as in an encyclopedia. However, the method does throw together a variety of sites from many different periods and places—a megalithic tomb in Cornwall, for example, may be listed alphabetically next to an Anglo-Saxon church in Sussex. Various aids have been provided to minimize this difficulty. The sites are extensively cross-referenced—by type, by location, by period. And each site is located with reasonable precision, by county and usually by nearest town. (In Scotland the sites are listed under both the old counties and the new, larger regions, because the latter are too large to be useful in pinpointing a location.) One can therefore use the appendix, which includes geographical locations, to find out, for instance, what sites of interest may lie in or around a given town or city the traveler is visiting.

For the traveler who does not have access to the detailed Ordnance Survey maps, I can happily recommend the Reader's Digest *Book of the Road*, a set of fine maps covering all three areas in one volume. Almost all of the towns and even the villages mentioned in the site locations can be found on these maps.

The term "archaeology" is used in its widest and loosest context in the Guide. Thus an archaeological site or monument may be defined as one where excavation or analysis has made a significant contribution to the elucidation of the site's structure, plan, purpose and place in the history of ancient cultures. The archaeological contribution in this sense can be important all the way up to the early historic period—that often-cited "Anglo-Saxon church," for instance. And of course the archaeological contribution extends well beyond this into the medieval period and, lately, the monuments of the Industrial Revolution—though the latter two are not included in this Guide for lack of space. Because modern archaeology has immensely broadened its scope and refined its techniques in recent years, the aforementioned excavation or analysis of today may embrace a wider range of disciplines than mere digging. There has been a healthy infusion into modern archaeology of methods borrowed from many related disciplines—anthropology, sociology, economics, geology and geography, architecture and environmental studies. More attention is now paid, for instance, not only to the usual material remains excavated, but also to pollen analysis, animal bones, evidences of clearances and agricultural practices and settlement patterns in order to reconstruct the original environment of a site, thus placing it more securely in its wider historical context.

Today's excavations are no longer the treasure hunts of old—tearing apart a barrow to see what antiques of value are in it—but are generally larger and more inclusive in order to analyze a site in all its aspects. This applies even to the proverbial Anglo-Saxon church, where the analysis or excavation calls upon different disciplines to elucidate its date and structural history. Not only are the excavations larger and more inclusive—up to the huge urban excavation projects in *London* or *York*—but there are also examples of the re-creation of ancient sites (in a discipline called Experimental Archaeology) in order to isolate the problems and solutions encountered and adopted by the ancient peoples themselves. See for instance *Butser Hill* in England or *Ballyvourney* in Ireland.

There are also problems of interpretation, touched upon in my prefaces for each region: To what extent, for example, were marked social changes noted in the archaeological record the result of "invasions" of a new people with a new culture, as used to be widely assumed, or were they the result of indigenous developments influenced by new ideas, rather than people, coming from the outside—in other words, new fashions, new cults? An example is the mysterious Beaker Folk, known primarily from their distinctive pots. Were they a "people" or a fashionable cult?

New methods of dating, in particular radiocarbon dating, have helped greatly in elucidating such problems. No longer are the megalithic monuments of Europe considered as indebted to the similar constructions of Mycenaean Greece; new dating has shown them to be considerably older than the monuments of the Mediterranean.

And in the new archaeology the now traditional cultural periods—the Old and New Stone Ages, the Bronze Age, the Iron Age—are now downplayed in favor of continuous development, which often yields "periods" rather different from the old arbitrary divisions, for example the grey area between the Neolithic and Bronze Ages, the one sliding into the other. However, in this Guide I have used the old divisions for convenience, while attempting to convey at the same time some feeling for the new concept of often continuous flow.

Radiocarbon and other new methods of dating have joined the old determinants of age and culture—stratification, the evidence of the finds, including styles and motifs in pottery and other objects—to bring greater precision into the interpretive process. But we are dealing here with vast reaches of time, and even the new dating methods are only approximate at best and depend for any accuracy on a variety of random considerations that cannot always be controlled. Then there is the question of calibration of radiocarbon dates: reconciling a raw radiocarbon date with tree ring sequences recently built up. This has pushed back the radiocarbon dates for the prehistoric by some 500 years or so, depending how far back they are in time. Since this Guide is written for the layman, I have used dates only to give the reader a general idea of comparative chronology. The strict accuracy of any date is not that important considering the huge spans of time we are dealing with. However, I have tried to use calibrated rather than raw radiocarbon dates where possible, generally following a consensus from my sources for the dating of each site.

My sources are so various and for the most part easily available—other archaeological guides for particular areas, tourist guidebooks, magazine articles, newspaper clips and so forth, as well as occasional scholarly books for certain sites and for background—that I do not feel it necessary to list them all here. For this Guide is above all a synthesis of easily available materials in one overall volume. It breaks no new ground; and in this, I suggest, lies its value for the average reader. However, I must acknowledge the invaluable help in writing the prefaces of Timothy Darvill's up-to-date synthesis, *Prehistoric Britain* (New Haven and London, 1987), for England, Wales and Scotland; of Graham and Anna Ritchie's *Scotland: Archaeology and Early History* (London, 1981), for Scotland; and for Ireland, up-to-date material from the Archaeology Department of the University College of Cork, specifically through my son-in-law, Michael Monk.

I have mentioned the names of the archaeologists involved in various sites only if they already have some general reputation. The names of the others, no matter how worthy they may be, would mean little to the average reader.

Finally, I must acknowledge the unfailing help and encouragement of Kate Kelly, best of editors. Without her the task of getting this book off the ground would have been immeasurably more difficult.

England and Wales

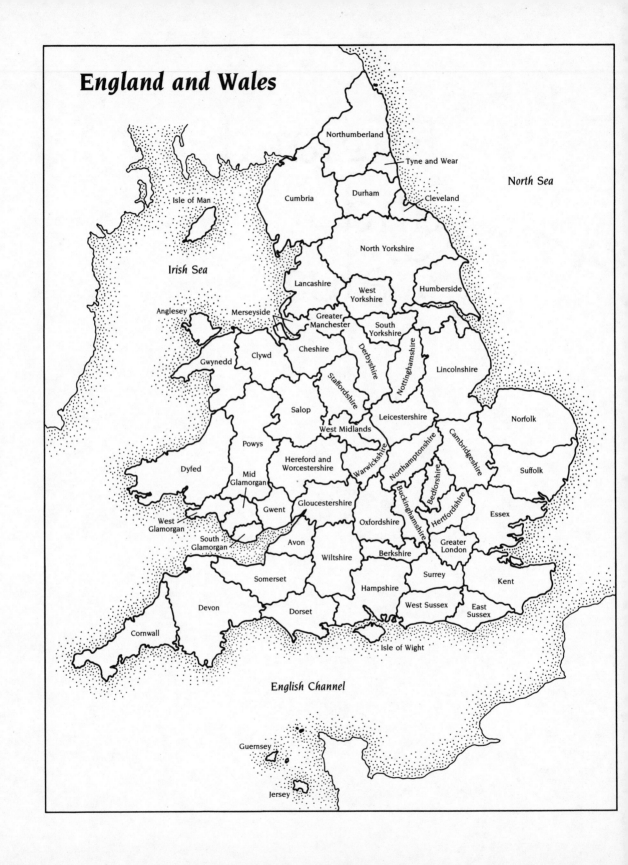

England and Wales

Northumberland

Tyne and Wear

North Sea

Durham

Cleveland

Isle of Man

Cumbria

North Yorkshire

Irish Sea

Lancashire

West Yorkshire

Humberside

Anglesey

Merseyside

Greater Manchester

South Yorkshire

Gwynedd

Clywd

Cheshire

Derbyshire

Nottinghamshire

Lincolnshire

Salop

Staffordshire

Leicestershire

Norfolk

West Midlands

Powys

Hereford and Worcestershire

Warwickshire

Northamptonshire

Cambridgeshire

Suffolk

Dyfed

Mid Glamorgan

Gwent

Gloucestershire

Buckinghamshire

Bedfordshire

Hertfordshire

Essex

West Glamorgan

South Glamorgan

Avon

Oxfordshire

Wiltshire

Berkshire

Greater London

Somerset

Hampshire

Surrey

Kent

Devon

Dorset

West Sussex

East Sussex

Cornwall

Isle of Wight

English Channel

Guernsey

Jersey

Preface:
The Archaeology
of England
and Wales

Though only a part of a relatively small island, England has a rich past, both in history and prehistory. This beneficent island with its mild climate and abundant natural resources has been for thousands of years, ever since the glaciers withdrew, a crossroads of people and ideas from all of northern and western Europe, from Scandinavia to Iberia—and from the Mediterranean lands too, especially just before and during the Roman occupation. Often sparked by influences from abroad, the earlier peoples of England developed a complex series of cultures that have left their mark all over the land. In parts of Cornwall, for example, most of the present field boundaries date from prehistoric times, and many withered heaths and barren uplands are in large part the result of over-exploitation thousands of years ago. Then there are the countless megalithic tombs and hill forts and, from later periods, numerous Roman forts and villas and Anglo-Saxon churches that have survived to speak to us of their times. During the last 25 years or so the investigation of these survivals has been the subject of intensive archaeological efforts.

With massive development and rebuilding during the last quarter-century, the opportunity for archaeology has become both urgent (as key sites disappear under bulldozers) and far-reaching. For instance, as one town or city after the other is redeveloped the archaeologists are now allowed to carry out important digs on cleared sites before rebuilding starts (see *London; York*.) Hence many of the current digs are "rescue" operations, some necessarily hasty, some meticulous. And while the opportunities multiply, the discipline of archaeology itself, especially in England, has met the challenge by growing in scope and expertise until English archaeology has become perhaps the best, if not the most innovative, in the world. In the meantime public interest in archaeology (and hence the possibility of funding) has also increased remarkably. For instance, while there has long been an interest in English prehistory dating back to the anti-quarians, as well as in Roman forts and other sites, the rich complexity of the prehistoric period in particular has really been a revelation of recent archaeo-logical endeavors—and the work continues unabated. Much of the progress is owing to the new dating methods, especially radiocarbon dating. Dating prob-lems have been discussed in the Introduction. Suffice it to say here that with the intense recent archaeological activity, over 5,000 radiocarbon dates are now available for England.

England as viewed here includes the whole island (with the exception of Scotland and its islands)—Wales and the outlying islands off England: the Isle of Man, the Scilly Isles, the Channel Islands. The entries in this book embrace the most important sites—and many lesser sites of some interest—ranging from the earliest Paleolithic caves down to approximately the Norman Conquest of 1066. This is judged to be the prime archaeological period in the sense already proposed in the Introduction. Any listing of archaeological sites is of course bound to be at best an interim report on a rapidly developing and widening subject. And this includes even the Roman and post-Roman periods; for new Roman forts are still being identified and more sites of early Anglo-Saxon set-tlements and graveyards discovered. New light is being thrown even on the elusive Dark Ages, and the surviving Anglo-Saxon churches of a later period are being studied more intensively.

The Early Stone Age

In the Paleolithic period Britain lay at the outermost limits of the spread of the early hominids, our remote ancestors, who may have reached it around 500,000 BC—rather late in the perspective of human evolution. But as the gla-ciers advanced and retreated during the later ice ages Britain alternately became a peninsula of Europe or an island; scant evidence of early man's presence has survived, and these mostly scatterings of tools. Only a few of the better-known and representative Paleolithic sites have been included in this guide, since there is usually little to see. The two earliest human tool kits have been designated the Clactonian and Acheulian, as in the lowest levels of *Swanscombe* and of *Kent's Cavern*, *Boxgrove* and *Hoxne* respectively. The earliest human remains include the Swanscombe Man skull fragments, possible Neanderthal remains at *Pontnewydd* in Wales, and authentic Neanderthal remains in *Jersey* at La Cotte de Saint-Brelade. Of modern man (Homo sapiens) the famous "Red Lady of Paviland" (see *Goat's Cave*) is the oldest complete burial known.

The final advance of the glaciers over England came at the time of the fa-mous painted caves of France and Spain, so only a mere handful of bones incised with similar designs are known from England. About 12,000 to 10,000 BC southern Britain again became available for occupation, and another indus-try, the Cresswellian (see *Cresswell Crags*), indicates the renewed presence of Pa-leolithic man (see, for example, *Kent's Cavern* again and *Hengistbury Head*).

We now reach the borders of the period traditionally called the Mesolithic (Middle Stone Age) when groups of hunter-gatherers occupied seasonal camps, mostly on open sites, hunting, fowling, fishing with tiny flints called microliths, and gathering edibles. The type site is the well-known *Star Carr* in Yorkshire, occupied about 7500 BC. As time went on and the population increased these hunter-gatherer bands began to settle down the year around in one place, leading to significant changes in the exploitation of food sources after about 7500 BC. The stage was set for the first deliberate domestication of grains and farm animals and the introduction of pottery—the so-called Neolithic Revolution.

The Neolithic

Farming was in full swing in Europe by about 4500 BC and reached England some 500 or more years later, mostly, it is presumed, through the gradual spread of farming ideas from the continent, leading to imitation in Britain. There must, however, have been at least some farming colonists from abroad—though probably never an "invasion"—to bring in the domesticated grain seeds and, for example, the sheep that are not native to England. The earliest farming communities grew up along the coasts and in the river valleys while hunter-gatherer groups were still living on the island, and there is some evidence of early clearing of woodlands and forests. By about 3500 BC farming settlements had spread widely, some about the size of villages (see *Carn Brae* and *Crickley Hill*). The demand for flint for sharp tools and certain stones for polished stone axes led to primitive mining operations, and the products as well as other artifacts were traded over long distances (see *Cissbury Ring* in Sussex, *Penmaenmawr* in Wales and the *Pike of Stickle Axe Factory* in Cumbria). Heavy stone monuments (megaliths) began to appear, as well as long earthen barrows, some covering stone burial chambers. These were both tombs and ancestral shrines of a sort, symbolizing for the community that built them a pride in the unity and continuity of their community.

A larger type of enclosure called a causewayed camp also appears in this period, some very large indeed—the type site is Windmill Hill near *Avebury*—others far smaller, but most consisting of a non-defensive ring of ditches interrupted by causeways. About 50 of these hill structures are now known. Probably they were at first seasonal gathering places for ritual festivals, trading exchanges and ceremonies connected with the dead (an example at *Hambledon Hill* appears to have been a vast necropolis), but later some at least became fortified enclosures, like *Hambledon Hill* and *Crickley Hill*. For warfare, it is now known, had already set in with a vengeance, as soon as people had settled down and when ownership of land became something worth fighting over. There is the massive defensive wall at Carn Brae and stark reminders of enemy attack at both Hambledon Hill and Crickley Hill.

Several thousand early megalithic tombs still survive around the country. These massive constructions can claim to be the earliest stone architecture in northern Europe, antedating those of the Mediterranean, including the Great Pyramids of Egypt, by many years. They began to appear around and before 3000 BC, each marking the ownership of a farming community's land and their claim to it through an ancestor cult. Most were built for collective burials—again for the community as a whole rather than the individual—though there is evidence that those who were chosen for such burial were often the more privileged sort. Their remains, whether cremated or not, were deposited in the tombs in jumbles of bones over and over again during a period of up to 500 years. The entombed bones were often disarticulated skeletons all piled in together, along with a few grave goods. Many of the earliest tombs, especially in the eastern regions, consisted of wooden mortuary chambers eventually covered by a long mound. Later most tombs were of stone, inside and out.

There were, in general, a number of types of tomb, each perhaps representing a different local burial cult—round cairns or mounds covering a cist burial; portal tombs in the W. like those of Ireland, with a single large capstone over the burial, supported on upright stones and possibly never covered by a mound; the simple passage tombs of Wales, a stone burial chamber approached by a passage running into the mound or cairn, as well as larger passage tombs like that at La Hougue Bie on *Jersey*, and finally, variations of a rectangular stone burial chamber, faced with some kind of facade and covered by a long mound.

In time many of the tombs were enlarged and elaborated. Several earlier tombs might be encased in one larger mound (see *Dyffryn Long Barrow* in Wales), or a new, larger tomb might be built over the old one (see Wayland's Smithy under *White Horse*). Regional groups of similar tomb types developed, such as the Cotswold-Severn group (see *Hetty Pegler's Tump*), these often with open courts in front embraced in stone horns, used for burial rituals. A special, late group of entrance tombs is found mostly on the *Scilly Isles*, with a few in Cornwall.

In the years after 3000 BC there seems to have been a widespread breakup of society, especially in the southern half of England, perhaps owing to population pressures and the wearing out of arable and pasture land, but more likely caused by the replacement of the earlier small farming communities, with their ancestor cults, by a more stratified society, with emphasis on rank and the individual, and leading eventually to the formation of chiefdoms. In any case, much land apparently went out of use, many of the megalithic tombs were blocked up or abandoned—for instance, the well-known, huge gallery tomb at West Kennet (see *Avebury*), which was blocked up about 2500 BC or later—and the causewayed camps were largely deserted. Worked bone and flint objects became cruder and new forms of pottery were introduced. Single graves rather than communal tombs began to appear, and the prevailing burials were more and more under round barrows rather than long mounds.

In fact, circular monuments became the vogue—not only barrows but ring cairns (a burial within a circular ditch and bank), circular henges and eventually stone circles. All of these monuments might be called the product of a wish for the display of power and prestige, and were built with incredible outputs of labor. Other types of ceremonial monument developed, generally associated with the rings and henges. Long mounds (bank barrrows) of great length (see *Maiden Castle* in Dorset) and the cursus monuments (see *Stonehenge*) were both apparently ritual processional constructions, and certainly not for burial or defense.

Henges, found only in the British Isles, were circular enclosures surrounded by a bank with a ditch *inside* it, thus not for defense, and usually with one or two entrances. Sometimes there was a circle of pits inside the bank. The flat space inside the henge was usually empty (one can envisage the processions and frenzied ceremonies that took place inside these enclosures!). The henges come in all sizes, but a few in southern England were enormous (see *Woodhenge* and *Marden*) and, though still ritual enclosures, contained within them huge, circular timber buildings, probably roofed, and show evidence of occupation, probably by the priestly caste that directed the arduous labor that went into building them. One of the earliest henges is at *Arminghall*, and the best known, of a very special type, is *Stonehenge*. Much larger and a bit earlier is the impressive henge at *Avebury*. Contemporary with these monuments were huge man-made hills like Silbury Hill, close to *Avebury*—with no burial apparent in it.

Eventually the circular henge idea led to the building of large stone circles, which culminated in the Early Bronze Age. Some were erected inside the henge banks, as at Avebury and Stonehenge, others were built anew, for example *Castlerigg* in Cumbria and *Stanton Drew* in Avon. At the center of the latter—as also at Avebury and *Arbor Low* in Derby—was a U-shaped setting of stones called a cove, probably a focus for rituals. Associated with the large circles were stone rows and alignments and numerous single standing stones—the straight alignments perhaps taking the place of the cursus monuments and long mounds of the past as processional ways. There seemed to be a new interest in the siting of astronomical events—for instance the rising and setting of the sun and moon—using the stones of these monuments in order to mark the timing of rituals and the change of seasons, so important for an agricultural society. But this feature has been grossly exaggerated by speculative writers; similar practices have been noted among early agricultural groups all over the world.

By the end of the Neolithic and the beginning of the Bronze Age Stonehenge had nearly reached the final form we see today; and both Stonehenge and Avebury, as venerated sacred centers, were surrounded by the developed round burial barrows of the dead, like the burials around a Christian cathedral. These barrows were of many types—bowl, bell, disc, saucer and pond barrows (see for instance the Lambourn barrows under *White Horse*)—and were usually grouped in cemeteries that often included earlier Neolithic long barrows. Some of the barrows around Stonehenge covered richly-furnished burials of the so-called Wessex Culture, burials that seem to indicate the development of a warrior aristocracy complete with daggers and other objects of copper, bronze and gold. The Neolithic slump by this time was over, and new clearances, especially in the uplands, have been noted by archaeologists.

We have now reached the so-called Beaker period, a relatively short interval centering around 2000 BC and named for the distinctive tall beakers found in the graves of this time. Whether there was an actual invasion of Beaker Folk from their center in the continental Lowlands, or some infiltration of such people from the continent, is not known. More likely, it is now thought, there was a package of ideas, characterized by the beaker vessels representing a new cult, that became the latest fashion as trade and contact with the continent increased. In any case the Beaker period, in which metals first appear (copper, bronze and gold), ushered in the Early Bronze Age, which was characterized by many new developments in society and methods in technology. Curiously enough, it was not long before this that the production and export of fine flints from mines such as those at *Grimes Graves* had reached its peak. It was the Beaker Folk, or adherents of the cult, who built much of the later aspects of the great ritual centers at Avebury and Stonehenge. Along with the beakers at this time, another new type of pottery is often found in the burials, that of the Food Vessel people. Again, these vessels were probably not the product of an invading people but merely representative of still another fashionable cult with its attendant practices.

The Bronze Age

In the usual convention, the Bronze Age in England runs roughly from 1500 BC to 600 BC or, more traditionally, from 2000 to 700 BC, though there was actually little break from what went before. Fine metalwork and more sophisticated weapons—rapiers, spears and, later, swords—appear, usually strongly influenced by continental models. At first metalworking was sporadic, probably carried out by roving smiths, but soon more communities got into the act, implying a complex system of distribution for the raw materials required for working bronze, copper, tin and lead. By 650 BC smiths were already using iron, but only sparingly and for forgings, not castings. From the evidence of bronze harness gear found at sites, the horse, and possibly wagons, became more important after about 1000 BC—though when the horse first appeared in England is not known (possibly as early as the Beaker period). Much of the metalwork we have was recovered from buried hoards and later from lakes, rivers, ponds and bogs where it was thrown as votive offerings, presumably for a water cult.

Again there was a marked expansion of land use and settlement, best seen in the uplands today, such as at Dartmoor, Bodmin Moor and Ilkley Moor (all in the W. and N.) where more traces have survived. Bounded "Celtic" fields appear and round houses of wood, then later of stone, scattered about or in settlements, closed and open. However, these little settlements are also found in many parts of England, for instance at Itford Hill in Sussex. Also widely found are piles of burned stones, called Fulachta Fiadha in Ireland, identified as communal cooking places where meat was boiled in troughs of water heated by hot stones.

The megalithic impulse continued to produce great ceremonial and burial areas such as the large stone circles with standing stones as at Stanton Moor, Derby, the Merry Maidens in Cornwall, Long Meg and her Daughters in Cumbria and the impressively tall standing stone at Rudston in Humberside. There are also many mounds or cairns covering cremation burials (See Blawearie Cairn). The last touches were given to Stonehenge, probably earlier in the Bronze Age. But the stone circles gradually disappeared and burials seemed to grow less and less important to these people as the organization of society and beliefs changed. Many cremated remains were inserted into older monuments and even at the base of standing stones in the W., while flat cremation cemeteries became common. Even these disappeared after about 600 BC. The ashes were usually buried in characteristic Bronze Age urns, hence these cremation cemeteries are often called urnfields. The Urnfield Culture was already widespread in Europe.

Possibly environmental factors played a part in the changes in society and its practices. After about 1000 BC there is evidence for a slow change in the climate, with attendant soil exhaustion under population pressures, and again an abandonment of upland areas in particular, as well as a shift from the small Celtic fields to larger areas, often called ranch boundaries. Curiously enough, in this period the widespread production of salt from seawater became common— just possibly because the salt was required for grazing animals and to salt down meat. Settlements were more generally enclosed, often with heavy ramparts, and in the case of a few upland areas such as the Welsh Marches and elsewhere, hilltop settlements were defended by the same ramparts—the beginnings of the famous English hill forts, far more typical of the Iron Age. A large settlement of this period has recently been uncovered at Flag Fen in Cambridgeshire.

By the early 7th cent. BC Crickley Hill in Gloucestershire was encircled by stone ramparts laced with timbers for added strength, and Mam Tor in Derby, formerly an open Bronze Age hilltop settlement, probably received its first defenses, as did Breiddin Hill in the Welsh Marches. With the need for defense came new weaponry, especially fine swords based on European models, round metal shields and much horse gear. With the first hill forts, the new weapons, evidence of a wealthy warrior aristocracy dominating ever wider areas, and an emphasis on display, fighting, feasting and horsemanship, we begin to glimpse the emergence of the so-called Celtic society, which probably had its origins in the widespread Urnfield Culture of Europe. Presumably there was a uniform Indo-European language that later developed into the various branches of the Celtic tongue.

The Iron Age

England's landscape is dominated even today by a multitude of defended hilltops, the hill forts, mostly the product of the Iron Age and conventionally dated from after about 650 BC. Over 3,000 hill forts of different types have been identified, especially in a broad belt running across southern England from the E. and up along the Welsh border into northern Wales. A less visible characteristic of the Iron Age is the increasing contact with, and influences from, Celtic Europe and particularly the Mediterranean world right up to the Roman invasion of 43 AD. (Of course, many aspects of the Celtic way of life persisted in the more remote and rural areas of Roman Britain right through the Roman occupation.) The numerous hill forts of the pre-Roman period speak of constant, bitter internecine warfare for which the contentious and undisciplined Celts were famous; for this was a period of unrest and tension in England, perhaps again as a result of increasing population pressures on limited resources.

The term "hill fort" covers many different types, varying in size and function. Some are very large but were thinly populated, defended enclosures, so far inadequately investigated, and perhaps used as stock enclosures or storage places; but the majority were smaller and were in effect densely occupied hilltop villages, heavily defended in a dangerous age—as for instance the forts along the Welsh border, such as Credenhill Camp. Recent excavations have clearly demonstrated that the old idea of hill forts as merely places of periodic refuge is quite untenable. Even The Wrekin, for instance, far up on top of a mountain in Shropshire, was inhabited, in spite of being hard to reach. Among these village forts a number of types may be discerned: the defended hilltop, the promontory fort (a headland defended at the neck as at Trevelgue Head in Cornwall), or large castle-like forts overlooking the sea. The usual early hill fort (7th to 5th cents. BC) was well-defended, usually with a single circuit of ramparts, faced with stone and often laced with timbers, and with gatehouses and strong outworks defending the entrances—or in the W. a pair of guard chambers.

Around the 4th cent. many of the early hill forts were abandoned, like Crickley Hill, leaving fewer but stronger fortresses that dominated a whole region. Those in northern Wales (see Tre'r Ceiri) were defended largely by a single, heavily-built stone wall, but in the central part of the hill fort zone the ramparts were often doubled or tripled, the outworks becoming more complex and a new type of sloping glacis-style rampart replacing the older timber-laced walls—all designed to take advantage of or counteract the effects of slingers. Danebury in Hampshire is one of the most meticulously excavated of these developed hill forts. Probably typical of the larger forts, it was not only a defended village but also an elaborate storage center for grain from the whole region, a manufacturing center for a variety of local products, a center for the exchange or redistribution of local as well as imported luxury goods, a ritual center and the power center of the local chiefdom. Danebury was abandoned about 100 BC, but other hill forts, such as the impressive *Maiden Castle* in Dorsetshire, continued to be strengthened and elaborated right up to the Roman conquest of 43 AD. *Maiden Castle* was one of some 20 forts belonging to the stubbornly-resisting Durotriges that were taken, one by one, by the Roman general Vespasian as he fought his way westward. Still other forts in the far W. and Wales only fell, or were abandoned, well into the Roman period. See, for example, *South Cadbury Castle*.

The major hill forts were not alone in the landscape. Around them, and in some way perhaps dependent on these central forts, were some lesser forts, many settlements, open or enclosed, and individual defended farmsteads such as *Little Woodbury* in Wiltshire or Staple Howe (see under *Great Driffield*). Outside the major hill fort zone these villages and farmsteads were the rule and actual large hill forts were rare (examples are *Wandlebury* in Cambridgeshire and *Mam Tor* in Derbyshire). There were also many larger farmsteads, mini-hill forts with multiple ramparts belonging to an extended family, like the ring forts of Ireland. At Wetwang Slack in Humberside (see *Great Driffield*) a dense Iron Age settlement of over 80 round houses has been found and there were lake settlements such as *Glastonbury* and Meare. In the far southwest a new type of defended village developed in the 2nd cent. BC, clusters of courtyard houses as at the well-known *Chysauster* as well as at *Carn Euny* (both in Cornwall).

The working of iron only became widespread after the middle of the 1st millennium BC, though fine bronze objects, especially horse harness fittings, continue to appear among the archaeological finds. In the manufacture of luxury goods continental models were closely followed (some were also imported) and horse harness parts, swords, daggers, shields and parade gear were beautifully decorated with the lovely, flowing, curvilinear La Tène styles of the late continental Iron Age. Luxury imports included not only weaponry but also vases and drinking and feasting items imported from the Mediterranean civilizations. In Cornwall and Devon European materials were exchanged for the export of tin. In general, however, imports from the continent for some reason slowed down in the 3rd cent. and only picked up again, quite briskly, during the 1st cent. BC—perhaps as Rome's expansion brought the "civilized" areas closer to England. A trading port on the S. coast, *Hengistbury Head*, became extremely active, importing, exporting and redistributing foreign and locally manufactured goods.

In the 1st cent. BC, marked by Caesar's two incursions into England in 55 and 54 BC, the southeastern part of the country underwent a rapid change in social and political organization. The importation of many foreign goods seemed to indicate an attempt to imitate the Roman way of life, as it was known from Gaul just across the Channel, and large tribal areas developed under kings who began to mint their own coins. Supposedly in this century the Celtic Belgae (following Caesar's account) invaded from Belgium, taking over many of the southern hill forts—though scholars today tend to minimize the invasion theory in favor of a marked increase in the importation of coins and other goods from nearby Gaul. Eventually many of the southeastern hill forts were abandoned and tribal settlements called oppida developed from the Gallic versions. They were divided internally and defended by long linear dikes and contained scattered groups of buildings—a commercial center, a religious center and so forth. *Colchester* (Camulodunum) is a good example. In other parts of the country life went on much as before, particularly in those areas farthest from the southeastern sector, while both in the oppida and the zones closest to the SE fine Celtic metalwork with La Tène-style designs reached its height.

Celtic religion embraced many fantastic gods and goddesses, mostly connected with nature, which in the Celtic beliefs was infused on every hand with spirits, both evil and benign. Much of the worship, under the direction of the Druid class, was in the open and has thus left few traces except for the occasional sculpture of a deity or the like. A veneration for water and the throwing of votive objects into lakes, bogs and streams continued—much to our benefit. At *Bath* the Celtic deity Sulis, presiding over a sacred spring, was conflated in Roman times with Minerva. There was certainly human sacrifice, as attested to by Caesar, and the well-known cult of the severed head, at its grisly height in southern Gaul, is hinted at in the hill fort of *Bredon Hill* where the excavators found six skulls in the remains of a wooden gateway after an attack—enemy heads which had been displayed above the gate. And at *Danebury* human skulls were found in pits. Here too what seems to have been a central shrine within the fort was discovered.

Burials were as before minimized, and skeletons have been found thrown into pits and ditches while the occasional cremation burial has turned up—and inhumation graves in the W. An exception is in North Yorkshire and Humberside where the Arras culture, probably representing recent immigrants from the continent, is marked by huge cemeteries of burial barrows, some of them chariot graves of both men and women (see *Great Driffield*). In the last years of the millennium burials apparently again became important. Richly-furnished graves and cemeteries are found around the southeastern oppida, and in the neighboring zones warrior graves and well-furnished graves of wealthy women have been found.

Finally, in 43 AD the Romans successfully invaded and eventually took over the country (see *Richborough*). The southeastern zone was quickly captured and *Colchester* was set up as the first capital of the province; but thereafter the conquest was slow and difficult, probably more difficult than the Roman chroniclers suggest, since a strong military presence had to be maintained in England throughout the occupation. Wales was finally subdued after a long struggle with the Silures in the S., and in northern England there was also stout resistance (see *Stanwick* in Yorkshire). In the SE all the oppida became Roman centers of one kind or another, and elsewhere new tribal capitals were established on the Roman town pattern near the old central hill forts (see *Dorchester* and *Wroxeter*). Romanization gradually took place, including superb communication by road and water, though pockets remained, particularly outside the southeastern sector, in which the old Celtic way of life continued through the whole period much as before.

The Roman Period

The Roman occupation lasted nearly 400 years, a period of much growth and consolidation but also of one crisis after another, usually caused by disaffected natives or coastal attacks from the barbarians. Near the very beginning, around

60 AD, the tenuous Roman hold on the countryside was almost broken when in the inevitable native backlash Queen Boudicca of the Iceni revolted and burned the fledgling Roman towns at *Colchester*, *St. Albans* and *London*. But there were rewards for those like Cogidubnus of the Atrebates, who remained faithful to Rome through these perilous early years; he was given his great palace at *Fishbourne*. Much later, when an imperial pretender, Albinus, denuded the country of troops, the province had to be pacified all over again, largely by the Emperor Septimius Severus in person from 208 to 211 AD.

The 3rd cent. was undoubtedly the most peaceful and prosperous interval in the whole period, though in the later years the coasts began to be menaced by the raids of the early Saxons. Then in 367 a deadly, concerted attack by the Scottish Picts, Irish Scots and Saxons again nearly destroyed the province. It was rescued by the general Theodosius, only to founder for the last time in 410 when the troops were withdrawn in a time of troubles for the empire as a whole. Thereafter the Roman way of life in Britain gradually disappeared, though there is tenuous evidence, for instance at *St. Albans* and *Wroxeter*, that organized urban life lingered on in places well into the 5th cent.

Throughout this tumultuous period the military was all-important in maintaining a measure of security in the province. The basic unit of course was the legion (about 5,200 men), divided into cohorts and centuries. The legionnaires built their own camps, on a standard model, and in peacetime carried out all sorts of engineering tasks—building the famous Roman roads (see *Blackstone Edge*; *Holtye*; and Wade's Causeway under *Cawthorn*) and bridges (though contractors may have later taken their place). At times the troops were even miners (see *Charterhouse*; *Dolaucothi*). The auxiliary units were lightly armed native troops, often made up of skilled horsemen, archers or the like. The quarters of both were the famed "playing card"-shaped camps of different sizes and functions. Hundreds of these have been excavated or are known, and more are being spotted all the time by avid Romanists.

The legionary fortresses were large permanent camps of around 50 acres, forming the principal focus of the island's defenses (see, for instance, *Caerleon*: *Chester*; *Lincoln*; *York*). In the standard plan a grid of streets filled the camp's interior, entered from four gates, one on each side of the ramparts. At the center was the courtyarded *principia*, the camp headquarters, which included a basilica, legionary shrine and treasury. Beside it was the *praetorium* or commandant's house. Long barrack blocks for the troops filled most of the rest of the interior along with workshops, granaries, stables and other buildings. The camp's communal bathhouse, as well as the earthen amphitheater (see *Caerleon*), lay outside the gates, and usually a *vicus* or civilian settlement for the soldiers' families and others grew up around the camp. The *vicus* often developed later into a town, like *Cirencester*, or even a city, like *Exeter* or *York*—the latter becoming the military and administrative capital of northern England.

The smaller auxiliary or semi-permanent camps followed the same general plan, as did even the practice camps (see *Cawthorn*) and the marching camps (see *Rey Cross* in Durham), for the troops on campaign carried their tools with them and built a camp for themselves each night, protected by earthen ramparts and palisades. All the camps of whatever size started out with earth and clay ramparts and gates, and towers, breastworks and internal buildings of timber, with a deep ditch surrounding them. All the numerous camps established by the general Agricola during his northern campaign in the 1st cent. AD were of this nature. Eventually most of the more permanent camps gained stone-faced ramparts and masonry buildings inside.

During the last centuries of the occupation heavy projecting bastions were added to the walls to accommodate the large artillery pieces. The best examples of these are in the magnificent *Saxon Shore* fortresses set up along the SE shores of the island in the late 3rd and 4th cents. to watch for and repel Saxon raiders. The finest of these is *Portchester* in Hampshire. Even later a system of signal stations was built by Count Theodosius along the E. Yorkshire coast after the Great Barbarian Conspiracy of 367 AD (see *Huntcliff*, *Scarborough Head*). Fine examples of all kinds of fortifications, forts, fortlets, milecastles, roads, even an occasional *vicus* can be seen today along the magnificent *Hadrian's Wall* in northern England, which for much of the period was the northern boundary of Roman Britain.

The fleet, known in the earlier period as the *Classis Britannica*, was an important branch of the military structure (see *Dover*). It was used for transport and in conjunction with various campaigns and later became the seaward defense and the eyes and ears of the military in the period of coastal raiding; and it was used to patrol the Channel—for example, under the usurper Carausius, commander of the Channel fleet, who briefly ruled his own empire in Britain and Gaul in the late 3rd cent. AD.

The towns and cities of Roman Britain were modeled on those of the empire as a whole. Most had a forum, temples, the basilica, town houses, perhaps arches and fountains, the municipal baths with a simple channel aqueduct to supply the water (see *Dorchester*), and an amphitheater and ramparts, usually of earth, later perhaps rebuilt in stone. Many towns began as the *vicus* of a fort, like *Manchester*, others as posting stations (*mansiones*) on a Roman road (see *Wall* in Staffordshire or *Great Casterton* in Leicestershire); still others were established as the *civitas* of a local tribe, like *Silchester*, or were built over the site of a tribal capital as at Verulamium (*St. Albans*). The larger cities, again like Verulamium, were given the rank, in the Roman system, of a *municipium* under a charter. Only a few cities attained the highest rank as *colonia*—Colchester, Lincoln, Gloucester, York and probably *London*—whose inhabitants were all Roman citizens (until all provincials became citizens in 212 AD). The inhabitants of the lesser settlements were usually all Romanized Britons.

In the larger places the town houses were adorned with mosaics and painted walls as in any Roman city (see the Painted House in *Dover*). The baths were sometimes large and elaborate establishments. Fine examples can be seen at *Bath*, *Leicester* and *Wroxeter*, and a few towns even boasted theaters—an example is on view at Verulamium (*St. Albans*). By the 2nd cent. most cities were defended by earthen ramparts, though stone was preferred thereafter if it could be afforded. The magnificent stone wall of *London* was the earliest, built in the late 2nd cent. It enclosed what had become the capital of the province. Provincial examples of stone walls can be seen at *Silchester* and in *Caerwent* in Wales, and in *Lincoln* part of a town gate still survives and is in use. During the troubled 4th cent. great bastions, like those of the *Saxon Shore* forts, were added to many of the walls. Of course numerous semi-Romanized small settlements with at least some of these features were scattered here and there, especially in the outlying areas of the country. Typical of these are *Ancaster* in Lincolnshire and *Carmarthen* in Wales, though there is little to see at either site.

Country villas, along with forts, are probably among the most visible and enduring relics of Roman Britain and are much visited by tourists. They do indeed afford a precious glimpse into the daily lives of the wealthier classes—almost all Romanized Britons. The best villas, like B*ignor* and *Chedworth*, are found in the southern, most Romanized part of the country, where one can also visit Cogidubnus's great palace-villa at *Fishbourne* near Chichester, a very early and magnificent example of an elaborate villa. Most of the villas began as simple farmhouses set on considerable land. As time went on they were elaborated or rebuilt by successive owners into larger, corridor villas—the rooms all in line as at the villa in *Newport* on the Isle of Wight—or into even more elaborate court-yard villas, with one or more courts centering as many as 65 rooms. Much of this elaboration took place in the 4th cent. as the towns and cities began to decay and the landowners took refuge in their villas. A fine example of a villa that survived, with many alterations, from about 60 AD into the 5th cent.—the entire period of the occupation—is *Lullingstone* in Kent. But from first to last the villa, of whatever size, was a country farm-estate, almost entirely self-sufficient, with its farmyard, barns, fields, orchards and woodland.

As the more important villas grew in size they gained not only new rooms but also mosaic floors in the principal rooms, painted walls, hypocausts for underfloor heating, private bath suites and graveyards; and many, like Lullingstone again, were adorned with fine marble busts, painted murals and other art objects. Some of the late mosaic floors, like the Orpheus mosaic at *Littlecote* in Wiltshire, or the huge *Woodchester Mosaic* in Gloucestershire (also an Orpheus mosaic and now on display in an accurate replica), were among the finest of the art in northwestern Europe. Of course, among the lesser folk life went on in the countryside much as it had before the Roman invasion. A revealing example of such a native setttlement of the Roman period, hardly changed at all, with its round house, storage pits and palisade, was excavated in the late 19th cent. at *Woodcuts* on Cranborne Chase in Dorset. It bears close comparison to the reconstructed, pre-Roman, Iron Age farmstead at B*utser Hill* in Hampshire (about 300 BC).

Religion in Roman Britain, as elsewhere in the empire, was a mixture of native cults, native gods often conflated with Roman deities, and here and there the formal Roman religion, represented for instance by the grand classical-style temple dedicated to the Emperor Claudius in early *Colchester* and destroyed by Boudicca. Another of the rare classical-style temples was that at B*ath*, dedicated to the local god Sulis and probably conflated with the Roman Minerva. Among the square, provincial-style Romano-Celtic temples were those at *Dean Hall*, Gloucestershire, *Maiden Castle*, Dorset (again probably dedicated to Minerva) and *Jordan Hill*, also Dorset, the latter two both 4th cent. Much larger was the elaborate healing sanctuary dedicated to the local god Nodens at *Lydney Park*, Gloucestershire, with its own bath suite and guesthouse for the pilgrims.

The soldiers stationed in England, particularly the auxiliaries who hailed from all parts of the empire, brought along their own gods. The soldiers' favorite everywhere was Mithras, the Persian god, and in *London* a small Mithraeum has been discovered, its foundations now on view. Another can be seen at the fort of Carrawburgh on *Hadrian's Wall*. Some Thracian troops from Bulgaria erected two small shrines at Scargill near B*owes* in Durham, dedicated to a god of hunting, Silvanus—for they loved hunting. In one a magnificent collection of altars was found. The spread of Christianity in Britain after Constantine the Great has been occasionally documented. In early excavations at *Silchester* a small apsidal building near the forum was uncovered and is generally considered to have been a church.

More dramatic was the discovery of a late-4th-cent. Christian chapel in one wing of the large villa at *Lullingstone*, possibly the earliest such chapel in Europe. Its reconstructed wall paintings with Christian themes are now in the British Museum. Of equal interest is the great Orpheus mosaic that floored a series of rooms at one side of the villa at *Littlecote* in Wiltshire, now interpreted—on the basis of its architecture and the iconography of the mosaic—as a cult center for the Orphic mystery religion. It is dated from the years when the Emperor Julian the Apostate briefly returned the empire to paganism from Christianity. He encouraged in particular the popular mystery cults such as Orphism. The Littlecote shrine lasted only about 10 years, then was turned into a dwelling.

Burials in the Roman period were always just outside the town or city, and a number of large Romano-British burial mounds have been excavated, revealing interesting grave goods (see *Bartlow Hills* and *Mersea Mount*, both in Essex, and *Harpenden* in Hertfordshire). At *Keston* in Bromley, just S. of London, a cemetery was discovered, probably that of a neighboring villa. It contained a large and elaborate mausoleum surrounded by lesser burials.

The Dark Ages and After

Though the English Dark Ages, after the collapse of Roman law and order, was a chaotic period that left behind few physical remains, even here probing archaeologists have managed to throw a bit of light into the darkness of this obscure age. The story of the Saxons, for one thing, provides a bridge between the Roman and the later Saxon hegemonies in England. For the earliest Anglo-Saxons (roving Germanic tribes from the northern coasts of Holland and Germany), while raiding the shores of Roman Britain for years, also came to England during the late empire period as federates and mercenaries and soon started settling down in their own communities. For example, possible Saxon mercenary burials have been found in Roman cemeteries at *York*, and at *West Stow* a rare pagan Saxon settlement has been excavated. It was inhabited from about 400 AD up to the coming of Christianity around 650. At *Mucking* in Essex the sunken huts, a hall and many burials of these early Saxon settlers have also been uncovered. Most fascinating was the discovery of an incredibly rich treasure in the ship burial (or cenotaph) of an early East Anglian king at *Sutton Hoo* in Suffolk, dating from the 7th cent. Discovered somewhat earlier, a well-furnished chieftain's burial mound of about the same date was investigated at *Taplow*, again revealing a treasure of grave goods. By this time the Anglo-Saxons were in England to stay.

What of the Romano-British survivors who for a time fought off the invading Saxons? The struggle is enshrined in the legends of King Arthur and his Camelot, his "capital"—which may have been discovered at the famous dig at *South Cadbury* in Somerset. Also *Castle Dore* may have been the base of King Mark of Cornwall—and of Tristan and Isolde—while at *Dinas Emrys* traces of an even earlier 5th-cent. occupation have been found, associated with Arthur's predecessor, Vortigern. Finally, at *Tintagel Head* the remains of a Celtic monastery of this period have been excavated; for the Dark Ages saw both the survival here and there of late Roman Christianity as well as its official reintroduction into the pagan Saxon world when the Pope sent St. Augustine to *Canterbury* where he converted the pagan king Ethelbert in 597 AD. The baptism probably took place in the little church of St. Martin, which still survives at Canterbury.

One by one the new Anglo-Saxon kingdoms—East Anglia, Wessex, Mercia, Northumbria, Kent—were converted to Christianity. The 7th-cent. church of one of the early missionaries to the East Saxons, St. Cedd, survives today in the middle of the Roman fort at *Bradwell-on-Sea* in Essex. Each kingdom had its day: Northumbria, then Mercia under its great king, Offa, in the late 8th cent. (see *Offa's Dyke*), and finally Wessex under Alfred and his successors. By the 650s Northumbria, with its capital at *York*, had become Christian and the fusion of Latin, Celtic and Saxon strains brought about a rich cultural Renaissance, with powerful centers at the twin monasteries of *Monkwearmouth* and *Jarrow*, the latter the home of the Venerable Bede, as well as at *Lindisfarne* monastery, creator of the famous illuminated Lindisfarne Gospels, now in the British Museum. Lindisfarne's renowned St. Cuthbert is buried at *Durham*, where Bede also lies. The missionary Wilfrid founded more monasteries at *Ripon* and *Hexham* where the splendid 7th-cent. crypts of the churches can be seen today.

An outstanding example of Northumbrian art is the tall *Bewcastle Cross* in Cumbria, probably erected by or under the learned King Aldfrith of Northumbria. In the 8th cent. another scholar of *York*, Alcuin, was sent to head the schools of no less than Charlemagne the Great. Finally, at *Glastonbury* in Somerset excavations at the ruins of the medieval abbey uncovered an interesting sequence of earlier foundations from an older monastery at the site.

Among the many Anglo-Saxon churches surviving today parts of a few may date back to the 7th cent., such as at *Brixworth* in Northamptonshire and possibly *Stow* in Lincolnshire and *Wing* in Buckinghamshire, while *Escomb* in Durham is an almost perfect little 7th cent. church built out of reused Roman stones. Most of the earliest churches were built of wood and have disappeared, but a remarkable survival of the type still exists at *Greensted* in Essex. Dating to about 850 AD, its nave is enclosed by walls of heavy upright timbers side by side. Anglo-Saxon royal "palaces"—a central great hall with attendant buildings—have also been discovered. The Northumbrian palace of *Yeavering* was occupied during the 6th and 7th cents., and a royal palace of Wessex at *Cheddar* (9th-10th cents.) was well known to the great King Alfred, whose bustling Wessex port of Hamwih, recently excavated at *Southampton*, was the commercial outlet for the royal capital at *Winchester*, just inland. By this time the Danish Vikings had overrun eastern England, taking *York* in 866 and making a surprise attack on Wessex in 878. Fighting back, King Alfred and his sons set up fortified *burhs* along the line of the Viking advance, and the earthen remains of these defenses can be seen at *Cricklade*, *Warham* and *Wallingford*. More Anglo-Saxon defenses have been excavated and reconstructed in *Hereford*.

After a stalemate between Vikings and Saxons England was divided, the Danes in the northeast (the Danelaw), and the Saxons, or English, in the SW., and by the time of the Norman conquest the English had prevailed (*York* fell in 954 AD), absorbing the Anglo-Scandinavian areas to create the beginnings of modern England. Up until the Conquest Anglo-Saxon culture flourished unabated, leaving behind as its most visible testament hundreds of its austere stone churches, so different from the Norman—many, of course, overlaid by later work. Both *Oxford* and *Cambridge*, for instance, possess fine Anglo-Saxon church towers. Among the many churches included in this guide, a few can be singled out.

There is the little reconstructed chapel at *Bradford-on-Avon*, the beautiful tower at *Barton-on-Humber*, the massive church at *Braemore* in Hampshire, the tower at *Earl's Barton* in Northamptonshire, elaborately decorated with stripwork. All these date from the 10th cent. From the next cent. comes the remarkably unspoiled, simple tower and church at *Rothwell* in Lincolnshire and the historically interesting church at *Bosham* in Sussex, once an Anglo-Saxon port from whence Harold of England sailed on his fateful voyage to meet with William the Norman. The church was probably built by Edward the Confessor, king of England, who owned the manor—which was possibly also held by King Canute before him.

The Viking presence in England has left many reminders, especially in the N.—in the language, the place names, the arts of the time and in many more subtle ways. For example, a number of high crosses survive, dating from the 9th to 11th cents.—see the cross at *Halton* in Lincolnshire and the *Middleton Crosses* in Yorkshire—in which the fusion of Scandinavian with Celtic and Saxon art forms produced masterpieces of design. For more visible examples of the Viking way of life one must visit the *Isle of Man*, once a Norse kingdom and still independent under the British crown. Here are a profusion of "Manx" crosses, some Viking halls and ship burials, and the fascinating excavation at Peel Castle. The island still retains vestiges of its long Scandinavian occupation, for instance in the annual proclamation of its laws from Tynwald Hill.

Not much was known about the Vikings in England itself until the recent large-scale excavation of Viking *York* (Jorvik) and another site in *Lincoln*, complemented by the similar excavation of Viking *Dublin* in Ireland. These excavations, with others in Scandinavia, have led to a dramatic reappraisal of the Vikings' contribution to early medieval civilization—not as the well-known, early and ferocious raiders but as settlers, traders, and artisans, as well as skilled seafarers and explorers. The extensive excavations in York, culminating in the Coppergate dig (1976–81), revealed the astounding remains of the 10th-cent. Jorvik, a city of some 10,000 and one of the most important commercial centers of Europe at the time. The Coppergate site and its finds have been enshrined for all to see in the innovative Jorvik Viking Center, now one of the most popular tourist attractions in all of Europe.

ABINGER COMMON
(Surrey)

The remains of a rare Mesolithic pit dwelling and work place, preserved under a shelter on the grounds of Abinger Manor a few miles E. of Guildford and N. of Holmbury. Only 10 by 14 ft., the pit shows two postholes (for a shelter?), a probable sleeping ledge and a hearth. Excavated by Louis Leakey in 1950, it yielded over a thousand worked microliths of flint. There is a small site museum. See also *Star Carr*.

AILCY HILL
(North Yorkshire)

See *Ripon*.

ALDBROUGH
(North Yorkshire)

The scant remains of the Roman town of Isurium Brigantium, just E. of Boroughbridge, about 15 mi. (24 km.) NW of *York*. Isurium was the tribal town of the Brigantes during the Roman period, who came from the huge hill fort of *Stanwick*. Beginning as a station of the ninth legion, Isurium became a small Brigantian-Roman township of some 55 acres, but a prosperous one as attested by the numerous mosaics found at the site. Originally protected behind earth ramparts, it was given stone walls in the 3rd cent. and angle bastions were added in the 4th. There is not much to see—a stretch of the walls behind the local museum, a few stones from the north gate. Of the many mosaics found, some were reburied, two are on view on the site, others are in the Leeds museum.

ALDERNEY

One of the smaller *Channel Islands*. A small fort called the Nunnery on the W. side of Longis Bay, now in private hands, is traditionally of Roman origin, with four bastions, part-fallen into the sea. It may have been a late fort of the *Saxon Shore* type. Surface finds indicate an extensive Roman settlement, unexcavated, on nearby Longis Common. Finds are in the St. Anne's museum. See also *Guernsey*.

ALFRED'S CASTLE
(Berkshire)

See *White Horse*.

ALMONDBURY
(West Yorkshire)

Impressive Iron Age hill fort of the Brigantes, possibly held by the famous Queen Cartimandua; partly disfigured by a medieval castle. It lies in Huddersfield's outskirts, 2 mi. (3 km.) SE. Excavations have indicated a long elaboration of the defenses from as early as the 8th–7th cents. BC, ending up with two and three lines of ramparts and ditches. The latest rampart was of stone laced with timbers, and there was an elaborate gateway. The fort was destroyed by fire, possibly about 500 BC, and abandoned. See also *Stanwick*.

AMBLESIDE
(Cumbria)

See *Hardknott Castle*.

ANCASTER
(Lincolnshire)

The scant remains of a fortified Roman posting station and town on Ermine Street on its way toward *Lincoln*, 5 mi. (8 km.) N. of Grantham. This natural gap in the Lincoln Edge was also commanded in earlier times by the Iron Age fort of *Honington*. The defenses, enclosing nine acres, were of stone, with a ditch and bastions (3rd–4th cents. AD) and can best be seen as mounds and ditches in the area known as Castle Close opposite the church. The town, known as Causennae, straggled for a mile along the Roman road, and excavations at its center

Arbor Low, a classic henge circle set in a magnificent site in Derbyshire's Peak District. The surrounding bank and the internal ditch, gouged from hard limestone, are shown with some of the 56 stones of the circle. Presumably, all the stones were once upright. (Photo: the author.)

revealed mosaics and vaults as well as many small finds. The remains of an Iron Age settlement, an earlier Roman fort and a late Roman cemetery lie under the modern cemetery, where two Roman coffins may be seen. Finds are in the Grantham museum and at Lincoln and Nottingham universities.

ANDERIDA

See *Pevensey*.

ANGLESEY (Gwynedd)

See *Barclodiad y Gawres, Bryn Celli Dhu, Din Lligwy*.

AQUAE SULIS

See *Bath*.

ARBOR LOW (Derbyshire)

Stone circle set on a high hillside with magnificent views of the Peak District, 5 mi. (8 km.) SW of Bakewell. Over 50 massive stones survive, all now fallen, enclosed within an earthen bank of about 250 ft. in diameter, with a ditch inside it. There are entrances N. and S. and traces of an earthen avenue leading off S. toward Gib Hill, on which stands a huge, round Bronze Age barrow. Excavations in the barrow found no burials. At the center of the circle is a U-shaped cove of four stones, now also fallen. A cist and round barrow were built later into the circle. All of this indicates that Arbor Low was a henge, a ceremonial meeting place built along the lines of *Avebury* to the S. and other henges. It probably dates from the Late Neolithic or Early Bronze Age. Excavated in 1901–2, the skeleton of a man with no grave goods was found beside the cove, probably a human sacrifice. Finds from the circle and Gib Hill are in Sheffield's city museum. See also *Minning Low*.

ARMINGHALL (Norfolk)

Only a slight depression and bank here remain of a most important Neolithic henge site of about 3250 BC. The site is 1.5 mi. (2.3 km.) S. of Norwich, off a minor road to Caistor St. Edmund. Discovered from the air in the 1920s, the site was excavated and identified as one of the earliest henge monuments of the Late Neolithic, comparable to *Avebury*, *Marden*, *Mt. Pleasant* and *Woodhenge*. It was unusual in that it had two rings of ditches with a bank in between, 120 ft. in diameter, and a single entrance from the S.—enclosing a ceremonial center consisting of an oval of massive timber uprights (probably not roofed), whole trees set about 10 ft. apart. Henges seem to have been communal centers for social and religious purposes.

ARRAS
(Humberside)

See *Great Driffield*.

ARTHUR'S STONE
(Hereford and
Worcester)

Neolithic long barrow near Dorstone, about 10 mi. (16 km.) W. of Hereford. Only the huge capstone, split but intact, supported on nine small stones, remains. It lies on top of a ridge above the Golden Valley. Though unexcavated, one can see the bizarre entrance passage that bends almost at right angles before reaching the burial chamber. See *Maen Ceti*.

AVEBURY
(Wiltshire)

One of the most impressive prehistoric sites in all of Europe, a henge monument that ranks with *Stonehenge* (some 18 mi. S.), and is considerably larger and somewhat older—though much destroyed. Encircled by rolling chalk downs spotted with numerous burial barrows in this sacred area, Avebury lies 6 mi. (9.5 km.) W. of Marlborough and contains within its outer ring, enclosing almost 30 acres, much of the entire village of Avebury with its pub, its main street and grazing fields. In the recent past many of the huge unshaped stones of the ring, dragged from the surrounding downs, were broken up or buried by heedless farmers or religious fanatics, so that now only 76 remain of over 600 in the complex. Some stones were almost 25 ft. high and weighed up to 60 tons. Sporadic early excavations of the site were succeeded in the 1930s by a meticulous restoration by Alexander Keiller so that of the 98 original stones of the outer circle, about 30 are now standing, mostly on the W. side, with the heaviest at the four original entrances. The stone circle is enclosed within a colossal bank 18 ft. high, irregular in shape, with a ditch inside it 70 ft. wide and once an incredible 30 ft. deep, cut down into the chalk. In the interior of the henge were two smaller stone circles once made up of some 60 more stones, each circle larger than Stonehenge itself. At the center of the southern circle, the best preserved, stood another stone (the obelisk), now marked in concrete, and a curious rectangle of small boulders (the "Z" stones). Only a few stones of the northern ring survive. It had a smaller circle inside it (long disappeared), and at its center was a cove of three huge stones, two of which remain.

Once, two stone-lined processional avenues issued from the W. and S. entrances. Only one stone remains standing of the western (Beckhampton) avenue, but sections of the southern Kennet Avenue, 50 ft. broad, have been restored, its opposing stones diamond and pillar shaped, suggesting male and female forms, and thus possibly a fertility cult. The Kennet Avenue led in a few miles to Overton Hill, formerly crowned by a double stone circle called the Sanctuary, destroyed in the 18th cent. Excavations here enabled the archaeologists to identify these circles but also to reveal the postholes of three successive, preceding, circular wooden structures, each larger than the last and all probably used for mortuary purposes. The stone rings of the fourth phase, built by Beaker folk about 2300 BC, along with the avenues, closely followed the ground plan of

Avebury, its bank, vast ditch (once 30 ft. deep), and the stones of the outer circle; also a close view of some of the larger stones. With Stonehenge, Avebury is one of the most impressive of England's Neolithic henge monuments. (Photo: the author. Photo: courtesy of English Heritage.)

phase III. This site (the positions of the stones and earlier postholes now marked out prosaically in concrete) may have been the earliest shrine at Avebury, and the sequence of round buildings of tall oaken posts succeeded by stone rings suggests a development pattern for these communal henges, borne out by the recent discoveries of other early wooden henges (see *Arminghall, Marden,* and *Woodhenge*).

Avebury proper probably began with the building of the two inner stone

Two views of the extraordinary man-made mound of Silbury Hill, close to Avebury circle. An elaborate—but rather embarrassing—dig into the great hill, widely viewed on television, found nothing in the interior. But the dig did clarify the complex engineering of the mound. (Photo: the author. Photo: courtesy of the British Tourist Authority, New York.)

circles (possibly a third was started but never finished) about 2600 BC, followed about 2300 BC by the erection of the outer circle, the avenues, and the stone circles of the Sanctuary. By this time the Beaker folk, ushering in the Bronze Age, were established here. They buried some of their dead at the foot of the stones, and apparently sacrificed a girl at Sanctuary IV. The enormous Silbury Hill, the largest man-made mound in Europe, which rises dramatically 130 ft. high a mile S. of Avebury, follows much the same chronology as that of Avebury

The West Kennet gallery grave near Avebury; the interior and the entrance. This large communal tomb lay under an immense barrow originally 340 ft. long. (Photo: courtesy of Michael Holroyd, London. Photo: the author.)

proper. Excavations found no burial at its center but showed that it had been built in three phases, again starting about 2600 BC, and was carefully engineered with horizontal layers to prevent slippage. Its purpose is still a matter of conjecture. It has been estimated that Silbury Hill may have required up to 18 million manhours to build. In fact the time and labor put into all the Avebury monuments with only the crudest tools, including antler picks to dig Avebury's huge ditch and bank, staggers the imagination. What impelled this enormous effort? Much study has gone into the possible religious, geometrical and astronomical aspects of Avebury as well as the evidence for ancestor and burial cults. What is really needed is more careful excavation at the site.

The probable origin of the henges, both of wood and stone, lies in the so-called Neolithic causewayed camps, communal meeting places that have been discovered in a number of localities in England. The most famous and probably largest example is Windmill Hill, a mile NW of Avebury, dated at about 3500 BC (see also *Knap Hill*.) Here a triple ring of ditches, interrupted by causeways, circled the hill, enclosing about 24 acres. Remnants of the ditches may still be seen. These camps were not defensive, for excavation in the ditches uncovered many animal bones, the skeletons and scattered bones of people, pottery from distant parts, and ritual balls and phallic items of chalk, along with other debris. This suggested only brief periods of occupation—for communal feasting, fairs, and mortuary rituals by people from the whole region.

Selected human bones may well have been taken to Windmill Hill for mortuary ceremonies from chamber tombs like the enormous West Kennet gallery grave (a Cotswold-Severn type) not far off and close to Silbury Hill, for this tomb was in use contemporaneously with Windmill Hill. Last excavated in 1955–56, it contained over 40 disarticulated skeletons of adults and children from generations of burials. Its inner gallery, 40 ft. long, with four side chambers and one at the end, lay under a barrow originally 340 ft. long, and was entered through a heavy concave facade of large sarsen stones. The tomb was filled with rubble and sealed with massive stones by Beaker people about 2500 BC or later. It is now accessible to tourists and well-lighted. Material from Avebury and the sites around it is displayed in two fine museums, one in Avebury village, the other in nearby *Devizes*.

AVELINE'S HOLE
(Somerset)

See *Cheddar*.

AYLESFORD
(Kent)

Village close to Maidstone and a few miles S. of Chatham in the Medway valley, center for a number of interesting sites. In the village itself, N. of the church, (Sir) Arthur Evans excavated an important Iron Age cemetery in 1890 that has been identified as belonging to the Belgic invaders from France, mentioned by Caesar in his *Gallic Wars*, and dated 75 BC or later. The cremation burials were in pedestalled urns and were richly furnished with bronze vessels, brooches and pottery in the late Iron Age La Tène style.

An isolated cluster of megalithic chambered tombs (most of this type are in the West) is grouped around Aylesford. The best known is Kit's Coty House, 2 mi. (3 km.) NE, three ponderous uprights and a capstone 11 ft. long, all that remains of the rectangular burial chamber. Its original long barrow has been plowed out. This tomb of about 3500 BC was excavated in 1910, yielding the bones of many adults, children and babies. Nearby is another tomb, Lower Kit's

Coty; and closer to Aylesford, on the road to Chatham, are the Countless Stones, a group of fallen megaliths marking the ruins of another tomb. A few mi. to the W. and 1 mi. (.6 km.) NE of Trottiscliffe across the Medway the four sides of a burial chamber may be seen at the Coldrum Stones. The capstone is missing.

BACON'S HOLE
(West Glamorgan)

See *Goat's Cave*.

BADBURY RINGS
(Dorset)

Huge Iron Age hill fort on a round hill crowned by dense woods, with a triple ring of banks and ditches, 3.5 mi. (5.6 km.) NW of Wimborne Minster, 6 mi. (9.6 km.) SE of *Blandford Forum*. Though never excavated, Bronze Age burial mounds near it indicate early occupation. The first two rings are Iron Age, the third, weaker ring probably 1st cent. BC. There are entrances on the W. and E. The fort was undoubtedly taken in the Roman invasion of 43 AD; later it marked the junction of four Roman roads, and a small settlement grew up nearby. The bed of Ackling street is clearly visible running across the NW end of the outer rampart, part of an 8-mi. (13-km.) stretch of the Roman road.

BALLYDOOLE SHIP
BURIAL

See *Isle of Man*.

BANKS EAST, BANKS
BURN
(Cumbria)

See *Hadrian's Wall*.

BANT'S CARN

See *Scilly Isles*.

BARBURY CASTLE
(Wiltshire)

See *White Horse*.

BARCLODIAD Y GAWRES
(Gwynedd)

Neolithic passage tomb on the SW coast of Anglesey island, Wales, 12 mi. (19 km.) S. of Holyhead and 2 mi. (3.25 km.) N. of Aberffraw. Well-restored by the state in 1952-53, this remarkable tomb has a passageway 20 ft. long and a burial chamber up to 12 ft. across with three shallow subsidiary chambers off it. It was discovered that five of the massive stones held pecked designs on them—zig-zags, lozenges, spirals—reminiscent of *New Grange* and other passage tombs in IRELAND. The tomb is dated to the Late Neolithic, about 2500–2000 BC. It is now protected by a dome (the capstone is missing) and an iron grille at the entrance. See also *Bryn Celli Dhu*.

BARNACK
(Cambridgeshire)

Site of a Mercian monastery and of quarries of stone much prized in Anglo-Saxon times and later. The church of St. John the Baptist, though much rebuilt, has an interesting tower, its lower stages all of 10th cent. or later Anglo-Saxon work, with typical pilaster strips and round and triangular-headed windows. Three earlier carved panels, perhaps from crosses, are set into the wall, each surmounted by a bird. Four openings, pierced in different designs, suggest Danish influence (Barnack was in the Danelaw), and there is an original sundial in the S. wall. The huge tower arch inside is also Saxon work. So probably is a fine statue of Christ in Majesty in the north aisle.

**BARTLOW HILLS
(Essex)**

Romano-British burial barrows, largest and best-known in England, now much overgrown. They lie on the Essex-Cambridgeshire border, 10 mi. (16 km.) SE of Cambridge off the Colchester road. Originally there were seven to eight barrows. Only four are left, the largest 45 ft. high. These were tombs of influential Romano-British families and probably date to the 2nd cent. AD. Excavations in 1832 and 1840 found a rich array of grave goods, most of which are now lost. Barrow 3, the largest, yielded, for instance, a wooden chest filled with glassware, a bronze-fitted folding stool and an enameled bowl. Barrow 4 is inaccessible across a railway line. The surviving finds are in a small museum in Bartlow and in the Saffron Walden museum. See also *Harpendon*; *Keston*; *Mersea Mount*.

**BARTON-ON-HUMBER
(Humberside)**

One of the finest of Anglo-Saxon monuments, St. Peter's stands just S. of the end of the Humber bridge. The tower, the first two stages of 10th-cent. date, the top 11th-cent., is a fine example of Saxon stripwork against plaster, with double and triangular-headed windows, and original doorways N. and S. The tower arches dominate the inside. A small western annex is all that is left of the original church.

The Saxon tower and annex of Barton-on-Humber, one of the finest Anglo-Saxon survivals in England, showing the characteristic stripwork, narrow windows and heavy original doorway. (Courtesy of Philip Dixon.)

BATH
(Avon)

Lovely city known today as the elegant watering spa of Jane Austen and Beau Nash. In Roman times Aquae Sulis was an equally elegant spa unlike any other in Roman Britain and probably in all of northern Europe. Today the gracious Georgian buildings and its famous Roman bath make it a prime tourist spot in Britain. The present 18th-century spa buildings center around the Roman Great Bath, a rectangular pool (40 ft. by 83 ft.) now open to the air but otherwise complete with its original lead flooring, pavement, steps and recesses. Some of the original lead pipes are visible, and there are 12 great piers that once supported a barrel roof over 50 ft. high. The remains of a complex of smaller baths around the Great Bath, including a graceful circular pool, have long been on view as part of the excellent Roman Baths Museum. The actual hot springs, still pouring out a vast gush of water at 120°F., are hidden beneath the medieval King's Bath.

The center of the Roman spa was the temple of Sulis/Minerva, now inaccessible under a main street just outside the baths. But owing to cellar probes and earlier finds much is known about it. It was the classical type, rare in England, with four columns in front, steps climbing to the podium, two small shrines on either side, and a steep pediment with a magnificent gorgon's head, very Celtic in feeling, at its center, flanked by two very classical winged victories. In 1727 a fine gilt-bronze head of Minerva from the temple turned up near the site. Both sculptures are now in the museum.

A series of daring underground excavations under Barry Cunliffe began in 1978 to explore parts of the large temple precinct beneath the famous 18th-cent. Pump Room, which had to be shored up for the purpose. At all stages the excavations were open to the public. They began with the draining of the King's Bath and removal of its increasingly unstable floor to reveal, under the tumbled

The Great Bath of the Roman bathing establishment at Bath, Avon, showing the heavy piers that once supported a high barrel roof. On next page, two close views emphasize the Roman detail around the original pool, and a Roman lead pipe, discovered in its original trough. (First photo: courtesy of British Tourist Authority, New York. Other photos: the author.)

remains of a massive vaulted roof, the lead-lined, polygonal reservoir, the settling tank and a large drain built by the Romans to contain and periodically clean the hot spring itself—a masterpiece of hydraulic engineering. Numerous offerings—curses engraved on pewter, many with Celtic names, metal vessels, some 15,000 coins covering the entire Roman period—were dredged out of the reservoir.

Further excavations from 1981 into 1983 uncovered much of the paved temple precinct, and a section of the much-worn lower steps leading up to the temple itself. At the center of the precinct the great sacrificial altar has been reconstructed and three of its highly decorated corners replaced. Nearby the excavators found a statue base dedicated by an augur, an important temple functionary who read the future from the entrails of sacrificed animals. The diggers found, too, the heavy 3rd-cent. buttresses that stabilized the vault over the spring and the ceremonial entrance to the spring, its pediment carrying the head of the sun god Sol. This was tastefully balanced across the precinct with the four seasons ornamental facade featuring the moon goddess, Luna. The precinct now forms an underground extension to the museum.

The excavations also showed that the main bath buildings were still in use long after the Romans left, though increasingly swamped in a sea of mud as the drainage system clogged up. They collapsed only in the 8th cent. AD. Of the Roman town around the baths practically nothing survives, although archaeological soundings here and there continue.

BATTLESBURY AND SCRATCHBURY (Wiltshire)

Two Iron Age camps commanding fine views, about 1 mi. (1.6 km.) apart on the western edge of Salisbury Plain. They dominate the Wylye valley a few mi. E. of Warminster, some 15 mi. (24 km.) due W. of *Stonehenge*. Battlesbury has double ramparts with a weak third one on the N. side. Rescue excavations in 1922 dug into nine pits with Iron Age remains, and a mass burial was found in quarrying outside the NW entrance. This probably represented a massacre, by Romans or other enemies. Scratchbury is a contour fort with a single bank and ditch, three entrances, and a smaller, earlier earthwork inside it (about 350 BC). There are two small barrows inside the fort, both excavated. On its slopes are exceptionally well preserved Anglo-Saxon strip fields. A third Iron Age camp, Bratton Castle, lies about 10 mi. (16 km.) due N., 5 mi. (8 km.) from Westbury. Its ramparts are single on the N., doubled on the more vulnerable E. and S. A long barrow lies inside the fort. Both fort and barrow have been subjected to sporadic excavations.

BEACON HILL (Hampshire)

Iron Age hill fort commanding a wide view over Hampshire, at Kingsclere, 5 mi. (8 km.) SE of Newbury. An hourglass-shaped contour fort with a rampart, ditch and bank, it has an entrance on the SE protected by an elaborate inturn and outerworks, much like that at *Maiden Castle* (Dorset) and thus dated probably about 100 BC. About 20 depressions within the unexcavated fort represent hut sites. Surprisingly, on the SW side is the tomb of Lord Carnarvon of King Tut fame, who lived nearby. Another hill fort, Ladle Hill, about a mile to the W., is an unfinished fort, throwing light on how these forts were built. The ditches of its single rampart had been dug only in sections, as if by different work gangs, when the work stopped, the top soil piled inside ready to be used for the bank. Two earlier Bronze Age barrows lie outside the fort.

BEDD YR AFANC	See *Newport* (Dyfed).
BELAS KNAP **(Gloucestershire)**	Neolithic chambered tomb, reconstructed and under state care, about 2 mi. (3.25 km.) S. of Winchcombe. Dated roughly about 3000 BC, it is the best known example of some 50 "Cotswold-Severn" type of megalithic tombs in the Gloucester-Cotswold region. The barrow has a "false entrance" at the higher and broader end (about 60 ft. wide here) facing on to a horned court in front. Behind it the cairn stretches back about 178 ft. in a trapezoidal shape with four small burial chambers opening into the mound at the sides and rear. The tomb cannot now be entered. See also *Hetty Pegler's Tump* and *Nympsfield*.
BELSTONE **(Devon)**	See *Dartmoor*.
BENWELL **(Tyne & Wear)**	See *Hadrian's Wall*.
BERWICK DOWN **(Wiltshire)**	See *Woodcuts*.
BEWCASTLE CROSS **(Cumbria)**	Magnificent Northumbrian cross (late 7th cent. AD Anglian work) in a remote village churchyard near the Scottish border, about 18 mi. (29 km.) NE of Carlisle. The shaft alone survives, standing 14½ ft. high, and is richly carved on three sides with interlace work, scrolls and chevrons, with runic inscriptions on the N. and S. and animals amongst the scrolls on the E. Three figures are carved in panels on the W. side, one of Christ. The little church and the cross sit within the visible ramparts of a hexagonal Roman fort, an outlier of *Hadrian's Wall* to the S. The ruins of a medieval border castle sit on one corner. See also *Ruthwell Cross* (SCOTLAND).
BIGBURY **(Kent)**	Iron Age settlement and fort on a hill overlooking *Canterbury*, 2 mi. (3.25 km.) to the E. It is bisected by the Chaucerian Pilgrims' Way. The damaged ramparts of the rectangular fort enclosed a late Iron Age Belgic settlement, excavated several times after 1900, which yielded a remarkable quantity of iron objects—horse gear, ploughs, sickles, adzes. The settlement was overrun by Caesar's legions in his invasion of 54 BC.
BIGNOR ROMAN VILLA **(West Sussex)**	One of the best-known Roman villas in England, 5 mi. (8 km.) SW of Pulborough and about 14 mi. (22.5 km.) from Chichester, close to the village of Bignor. Excavated after 1811, its principal rooms with hypocausts and mosaics have been somewhat restored and preserved under thatched huts; the rest was covered over again. The situation, overlooking the Roman Stane Street, was a pleasant one. Recent excavations have shown that there was an Iron Age and early Roman period of occupation on the site, the main building being of timber. The villa proper was built at the end of the 2nd cent. AD as a simple corridor house. After a fire it was rebuilt in stone, and by the early 4th cent. had grown into a large courtyard villa with a number of outbuildings set into an agricultural estate of about 4½ acres. It was not destroyed but seems simply to have declined into the early 5th cent. when it was abandoned. Bignor is known for its six fine mosaic floors, mostly of the 4th cent., including geometric mosaics in two rooms

and along a corridor fully 80 ft. long, and its figured mosaics, the prize being the famous mosaic of Ganymede and the Eagle. There are also dancing girls, a head of winter, Venus with winged cupids playing gladiatorial games, and a fine Medusa. One of the rooms contains a small museum.

BINCHESTER ROMAN FORT (Durham)

The large Roman fort of Vinovia, 1.5 mi. (2.3 km.) due N. of Bishop Auckland. Excavations have gone on here sporadically for centuries, the latest from 1977 into the 1980s; today the ramparts to the N. and E. are still visible. The fort's long history began with the timber buildings of a 1st cent. Agricolan fort, abandoned in 122 AD. It was reoccupied about 160, with at least three other building phases until the Roman withdrawal. The grandest site here is the hypocaust (heating) system, the best preserved in Britain, discovered in the 19th cent. and now preserved under a shed. The remains include a concrete floor and several fine arches; it was probably part of the bath suite of the 4th-cent. commandant's house. Other rooms are being prepared for display. Of the once extensive settlement S. of the fort nothing is now visible. See also *Escomb*; *Piercebridge*, nearby.

BIRDOSWALD (Cumbria)

See *Hadrian's Wall*.

BITTERNE (Hampshire)

See *Portchester*.

BLACKPOOL BRIDGE (Gloucestershire)

A preserved stretch of paved Roman road connecting *Lydney* on the W. side of the Severn with the inland Forest of Dean Roman iron mines around Weston-under-Penyard. The stretch is found parallel to a side road off the Lydney-Colesford road. Though only 8 ft. wide, it is well built with stone kerbs and boasts the remains of a road junction leading off to a former bridge over the nearby stream.

BLACKSTONE EDGE (West Yorkshire)

The finest stretch of paved Roman road in Britain, cresting the moorland on the borders of West Yorkshire and Greater Manchester, near Rochdale, 7 mi. (11.25 km.) W. of Ripparden. It was an early Roman main road (later bypassed by an easier route over the steep moors) from the fort at *Ilkley* to *Manchester*. It can be seen above Littleborough near the top as the road climbs the hill. It is 16 ft. wide, surfaced with heavy paving stones and kerbs, and with a central depressed channel, probably to hold the brake poles of carts (the channel is much worn on the steeper sections).

BLANDFORD FORUM (Dorset)

Delightful 18th-cent. town, a convenient center for a large number of interesting antiquities. Along the road running NE to Salisbury over Cranborne Chase, which for a time in its middle course is built on the bed of the Roman road, are numerous barrows, both long and round, including bowl, bell and disk types. Of these the Pimperne long barrow is one of the largest in Dorset, measuring 350 ft. by 90 ft. It lies off the road to the NW, 3.5 mi. (5.6 km.) NE of Blandford and is unexcavated. Another Neolithic long barrow, the Wor, lies at 10 mi. (16 km.) NE on the same side of the road. It has been much excavated and is almost leveled, though the ditch has now been cleared. At 12.5 mi. (20 km.) the two Thickthorn long barrows, E. of the road, have been dated to the Neolithic. They lie near the southern end of the impressive Dorset Cursus, one of a number in Dorset and Wiltshire (see *Stonehenge*), that runs for 6 mi. (9.6 km.) roughly parallel to the road on the E. side. About 300 ft. wide, it is bounded by banks and an external ditch, and involved the moving of about 6½ million cubic ft. of earth! It dates from about 2490 (± 100 years) bc. These strange Neolithic monuments may have been associated with long barrows, perhaps as ceremonial processional ways. Near the eastern end of the Cursus, Bokerley Dyke, a 3-mi. barrier of ditch and bank, cuts across the road. It has been proved to be late Roman (4th-5th cents.), erected perhaps as a barrier against raiders from the W. and N.

Of the many monuments in the area we should mention those at Knowlton, off a country road E. of Blandford. There are round barrows here, and there were four Bronze Age henge circles, only one of which survives, its banks cut by two entrances. At its center, where perhaps a stone or timber circle stood, is a ruined 12th-cent. church. Two Iron Age hill forts close together, Hod Hill and Hambledon Hill (3 to 4 mi. NW of Blandford), and Badbury Rings, 6 mi. (9.6 km.) SE, are treated elsewhere.

BLAWEARIE CAIRN
(Northumberland)

Bronze Age cairn about 9 mi. (14.5 km.) NW of Alnwick, NE of Old Bewick in an area rich in prehistoric monuments: other cairns, two hill forts (one a double fort), Bronze Age rock carvings and the Devil's Causeway, a Roman road running from Hadrian's Wall in the S. to Berwick. First excavated by Canon Greenwell in the 1860s, the large cairn—about 40 ft. in diameter and enclosed within a heavy stone kerb—was re-excavated with great care by the local authorities from the early 1980s to 1987 with the help of students from a number of high schools. It was investigated in detail along with the immediate area around it in which other, smaller cairns were found. It was developed in four stages, beginning with a circular wall surrounding a central open space with a burned spot at the center, and later an oval stone-lined pit dug into it. The finds included cremation urns from a number of stone cists, and flint knives, a jet and shale necklace, pottery sherds and amber beads. The site has been prepared for public viewing with five open cists of various types visible. The finds are in the Greenwell Collection at the British Museum, London.

BODMIN MOOR
(Cornwall)

This bleak and bare plateau exhibits some of the finest prehistoric monuments in Cornwall. The first, Trevethy Quoit, 3 mi. (4.75 km.) N. of Liskeard, is a magnificent portal dolmen, a Neolithic burial chamber—seven huge stones (one fallen) supporting an immense sloping capstone 11 ft. long. The covering mound has disappeared. The chamber is divided into a small antechamber and a larger central chamber, entirely closed except for a small hole in the huge stone block that separates them, just large enough to pass a body through. About 2 mi. (3.25 km.) NE and 4.5 mi. (7.25 km.) N. of Liskeard is a very different site, three fine Bronze Age stone rings, close together and all in line—the Hurlers—the central ring, about 135 ft. in diameter, larger than the other two, with 17 standing stones and a small stone near the center. The other rings are less complete. All the stones are carefully shaped and set so that the tops are level. Two tall stones, the Pipers, stand W. of the central circle. The whole is in state care. On the summit of the hill above the hurlers is an immense round barrow. From it in the 19th cent. came a Bronze Age treasure including a gold cup that, as treasure trove, ended up in the dressing room of George V! It only reached the British Museum in the 1930s. The nearby Stowe's Hill is crowned by the remains of a stone fort, probably Bronze Age.

Trevethy Quoit, a dramatic Neolithic portal dolmen or tomb on Bodmin Moor, Cornwall. Were this tomb and others like it really covered by a mound, as often stated? One wonders why the ancients would want to hide such striking monuments under piles of earth. (Courtesy of British Tourist Authority, New York.)

There are at least half a dozen stone rings on Bodmin Moor. The Nine Maidens lies 3 mi. (4.75 km.) N. of Stowe's Hill. This was an alignment, not a ring, of nine stones (three fallen). Well to the W. of the Hurlers and 6 mi. (9.6 km.) NE of Bodmin lie the Trippet Stones, a ring of 12 stones standing out of a possible 26, dated probably around 2300 BC. In legend they are supposed to be petrified dancing girls, suggesting ancient fertility rites. Less than a mi. to the E. are the Stripple Stones, an irregular much-ruined ring of about 150 ft. diameter enclosed by a bank with an inner ditch and, originally, 28 stones set in a circle inside that. One large stone stands at the center and three others farther out. The monument is a rare western example of a henge monument, combined with a stone ring. To the N. the highest peak of the moor, Rough Tor, is encircled by a much-ruined fort with hut circles within it as well as down the slopes, possibly Neolithic. S. and SW of Rough Tor lie two more stone rings of very small stones, Stannon and Fernacre, also associated with hut circles.

BOKERLEY DYKE
(Hampshire)

See *Blandford Forum.*

BOSCAWEN-UN
(Cornwall)

Or Nine Maidens, stone circle on private land, about 1 mi. (1.6 km.) across the gorse off the road from Penzance to Sennen and Land's End (5 mi. W. of Penzance). Here are 19 large standing stones, one of quartz, the rest of granite, with another near the center, now leaning but once taller than a man. This impressive circle, now restored, is about 80 ft. in diameter. There is a gap or entrance on the W.

BOSHAM
(West Sussex)

Now a sailing center about 4 mi. (6.5 km.) W. of Chichester, Bosham was a bustling port in Anglo-Saxon times, part of the manor of Bosham held by Edward the Confessor and, by tradition, Canute before him. The church, Holy Trinity, stands close to the harbor. Here the grave of a young girl, probably Canute's daughter, was opened in 1865. Later King Harold left Bosham for his ill-fated meeting with William the Conqueror in Normandy, and a stylized depiction of the church can be seen in the Bayeux Tapestry. The nave, chancel arch and West Tower are all of 11th cent. Saxon work, with later windows in the three-storied tower. The interior is dominated by the magnificent chancel arch, probably the work of the pious Edward the Confessor.

**BOWES
(Durham)**

Some interesting Roman sites, though there is now little to see. Just W. of the village of Bowes in the far south of the county are the overgrown remains of the Roman fort of Lavatrae, dating from an Agricolan fort of 78 AD into the 4th cent. Over four acres in extent, the fort guarded the entrance to Stanmore Pass leading westwards. The final ramparts, after two rebuildings, consisted of a stone wall nearly 8 ft. thick. The rampart mounds can still be seen in the S. and W. while in the NE the church, cemetery and Norman castle have cut into the remains. In the 2nd and 3rd cents. the garrison, in typically Roman style, consisted of Spanish Vettones, then of Thracians from Bulgaria under a commander from Parma, Italy. A few mi. S. of the fort, on Scargill Moor, the Thracians, fond of hunting, erected two rustic shrines to the appropriate god, Silvanus, one rectangular, one round, of which little is left to see now. Parts of many altars were found. The best altar is preserved in the Bowes Museum at nearby Barnard Castle, erected by the officer from Parma. Lavatrae was part of a signal system leading over Stanmore Pass, possibly as far as Carlisle and *Hadrian's Wall*. One of these signal stations was at Bowes Moor, 4 mi. (6.5 km.) W. of Bowes village, where the mounds of the ramparts can be seen (of turf, once 10 ft. thick, with a V-shaped ditch outside). On the summit of the pass, 2 mi. (3.25 km.) W., is the marching camp of *Rey Cross*.

**BOXGROVE
(West Sussex)**

Important Paleolithic site about 4 mi. (6.5 km.) NE of Chichester. Probably the earliest Acheulian find in Britain, the many-layered site, in a gravel quarry, is currently being excavated (1987), turning up many flints and much paleoenvironmental evidence. See also *Hoxne; Kent's Cavern*.

**BRAAID VIKING LONG
HOUSE**

See *Isle of Man.*

**BRADFORD-ON-AVON
(Wiltshire)**

Well-known small Anglo-Saxon chapel of St. Lawrence. Apparently it was all built at once and is entirely 10th-cent. work, though it may have stood on the site of a small church reported to have been built in the 8th cent. by St. Aldhelm, who also founded a monastery here that has disappeared. The chapel early fell into disuse and was rebuilt (and disguised) as a cottage and a school until the mid-19th cent., when its antiquity was recognized and it was later restored. The chapel is notable for the great height of its walls, of fine ashlar masonry, and of the interior, and for the elaborate decoration of strip work and arcades on the outside in the late Saxon style. The simple plan includes a small nave (only 25 ft. long) and chancel, and one surviving porticus to the N. The present altar is made up of Saxon decorated stones unearthed near the church. The "Bradford Angels" can just be seen high above the chancel arch—fine pieces of carving that probably once flanked a missing rood lower down the wall.

The well-known chapel of St. Lawrence in the pretty town of Bradford-on-Avon; a late Saxon masterpiece noted for its arcading and fine ashlar masonry. The original building was lost under later additions until the last century when it was "discovered" and restored. (Courtesy of Michael Holford.)

BRADING ROMAN VILLA (Isle of Wight)

One of four known villa sites on the island (see *Newport Roman Villa*), excavated in the 1880s, a courtyard villa of the 4th cent. (though habitation on the site goes back to the 1st), lying about 1 mi. (1.6 km.) SW of Brading. The main block of 13 rooms (the west wing) and a well and hypocaust of the north wing are preserved under roofs, the rest reburied. The interest here lies in the mosaics, partly preserved in four rooms; crude in execution, their subject matter, allegorical and symbolic, is unusual. There is a small site museum and a guidebook is available.

BRADWELL-ON-SEA (Essex)

The badly ruined Roman fort of Othona, one of the 3rd-cent. *Saxon Shore* forts, is on a promontory among the lovely marshes along the Essex coast, about 10 mi. (16 km.) due E. of Maldon, but much farther by back roads. The line of ramparts may best be seen on the S. side though now only 4-5 ft. high. The E. side has been washed into the sea. Straddling the line of the western ramparts is the ancient little chapel of St. Peter-on-the-Wall, undoubtedly the original church built by St. Cedd, a missionary from *Lindisfarne*, in the mid-7th cent. AD as a center for converting the East Saxons. The church is built largely of reused materials from the fort. It was and is a center of pilgrimage. Only the nave still stands, though the apse and porch have been traced.

BRAEMORE (Hampshire)

Large and handsome Anglo-Saxon minster, substantially late-10th-cent. work. The nave, central tower and southern porticus as well as other details belong to the period, and the timber structure atop the tower is thought to have been copied from the Saxon original. An enigmatic inscription (before 1020) runs over the arch leading into the S. porticus. It shows traces of the original red paint.

BRANCASTER ROMAN FORT
(Norfolk)

See *The Saxon Shore.*

BRANE CHAMBERED TOMB
(Cornwall)

See *St. Just.*

BRANTINGHAM
(Humberside)

See *Hull.*

BRATTON CASTLE
(Wiltshire)

See *Battlesbury.*

BRECON
(Powys)

Center for a number of sites in Wales. In Brecon itself the Brecknock Museum has a good general collection of antiquities. About 4 mi. (6.5 km.) to the E., in the Usk valley, the chambered long barrow of Ty Illtud lies on the end of a ridge. It has a sloping capstone intact, and a probable forecourt. Inside it one can glimpse the rectangular chamber. Puzzling decorations and inscriptions on the uprights may be medieval. Mounting a footpath a mi. or two W. of Brecon one reaches a hill fort, the Crug (or Pen-y Crug), on an isolated hilltop. It may have been the predecessor of Brecon itself. There are three, sometimes four, earth ramparts and an entrance on the S. Three mi. (5 km.) W. of Brecon off the main road is the major Roman fort of *Brecon Gaer.* Moving W. on the main road to the village of Trecastell, the Roman road, now a mere track, veers off S. then W. about 4 mi. (6.5 km.) steeply up the side of the Usk valley to several stone circles and the ramparts of two superimposed Roman marching camps, close together, about 12 mi. (19 km.) W. of Brecon. The camps at Y Pigwin, 1,350 ft. high and in a desolate area, were probably built in the early Roman campaigns in Wales (1st cent.). The larger and earlier could hold a legion; the smaller lies askew over it and is only a few years younger. Just short of the camps on this highest part of the moor are the two Mynydd-bach Bronze Age circles of small stones, part of a group of seven in the region. One has 15 stones left, the other five. Roughly S. and SE a few miles lie two more Bronze Age circles, at Nant Tarw, and the better known, more complete circle of *Cerrig Duon*—respectively 13 and 12 mi. (21 and 19 km.) W. of Brecon.

BRECON GAER
(Powys)

Major Roman fort at the intersection of at least five Roman roads; 3 mi. (4.75 km.) W. of *Brecon.* Best approached from the village of Battle, it lies 1 mi. (1.6 km.) S. on a farm (permission required). The fort, almost nine acres in size, was excavated by Sir Mortimer Wheeler in 1924–25. Today three gates, an angle turret, and a stretch of the wall still standing 10 ft. high are visible. The remains of the S. gate are the most rewarding. Originally built in turf and timber about 80 AD, when it was garrisoned by a force of 500 Spanish Vettones cavalry, the walls and principal buildings were rebuilt in stone about 140 AD. An extensive settlement outside the N. gate and a small bathhouse were added (not visible). It was only intermittently occupied after the end of the 2nd cent.

BREDON HILL
(Hereford and
Worcester)

Iron Age promontory hill fort, SE of Worcester and 3 mi. (4.75 km.) NE of Tewkesbury. High up on the N. end of the massive Bredon Hill two lines of ramparts defend the promontory (difficult of access). Excavators of the 11-acre camp in 1935–37 found that the single wooden gate with an inturned passage at the rear had been destroyed in a fierce fire, probably by a Belgic attack on this late Celtic fort shortly before the Roman conquest. A number of skeletal heads (six) were found in the gate's ruins, probably those enemies that had been displayed on the gate in the Celtic manner. The smaller fort of Conderton Camp (3 acres) occupies a southern spur of Bredon Hill. In use at the same time as the big fort, it was at first an outlying cattle enclosure for the latter, and later became a subsidiary 2-acre fortlet and village of about a dozen round huts. It was hastily deserted, probably before the final attack on the big fort.

BREEDON-ON-THE-HILL
(Leicestershire)

The church of St. Mary and St. Hardulph—on a commanding hill above the village, situated within an Iron Age hill fort, about 5–6 mi. (8–10 km.) NE of Ashby de la Zouch—is on a very ancient site. A monastery was founded here in the late 7th cent. about the time of the conversion of pagan Mercia, and there may have been a pagan shrine on the site before that. Excavations E. of the church have revealed traces of the early Christian cemetery. The nave of the present church may be Anglo-Saxon, but of greater interest is the profusion of early sculpture within the church—elaborately carved 8th-cent. friezes from the former monastery built into the walls, figure panels, including the "Breedon Angel" built into the ringing room of the tower, and three 9th-cent. carved cross shafts.

BREIDDIN HILL
(Powys)

"The Breiddin"; Iron Age hill fort on a promontory overlooking the Severn and *Offa's Dyke*, 6.5 mi. (10.5 km) NE of Welshpool. On the top of a hill over 1,000 ft. high, it was defended on the vulnerable S. and E. sides by doubled ramparts, with a funneled entrance on the SE. The site was also occupied in Bronze Age times. Substantial Iron Age rectangular houses were erected in the late centuries BC, succeeded by round huts, and the latest ramparts were built with masonry facings. The fort was abandoned until late Roman times, when it was refortified. See also *Old Oswestry*; *The Wrekin*.

BRENT KNOLL
(Somerset)

Isolated Iron Age hill fort, 6 mi. (9.6 km.) S. of Weston-super-Mare. It rises spectacularly from the Somerset levels. Its single defensive rampart and ditch and its entrance are still well defined, though the interior was quarried in the Middle Ages. There is evidence of reoccupation in Roman times.

BRISTOL
(Avon)

The City Museum and Art Gallery in this large city contains a fine collection of archaeological materials from the region—Bronze Age, Iron Age and Roman, and including the finds from the *Cheddar* caves. To the E. of the city, at 3.5 mi. (5.6 km.), rises the Iron Age hill fort of Cadbury Camp (391 ft. high) with a fine panoramic view both E. and W. The 7-acre camp is in good condition with double ramparts (three at the weakest point). Bristol was not a Roman town, but at Sea Mills, a western suburb, was the Roman port of Abonae—possibly at first a naval port, later a commercial ferry port. Today only the foundations of one small courtyard house are visible. The remains of a number of villas around Bristol are known. At King's Weston, about 2 mi. (3.25 km.) NW of Sea Mills, six

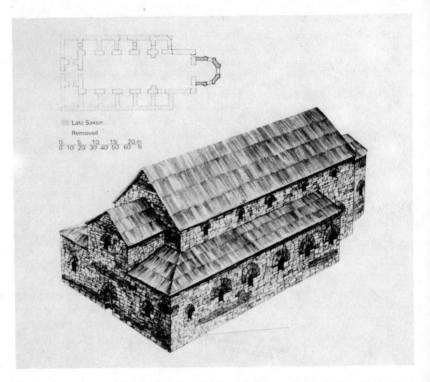

Late Saxon
Removed
0   5   10   15   20 m
0 10 20 30 40 50 60 ft

A reconstruction, following archaeological soundings, of the probable
appearance of the great Anglo-Saxon
church at Brixworth, Northamptonshire, once thought to be a remarkable survival from the 7th cent. It is
agreed today, however, that only the
existing nave is 7th cent. The rest,
though still Anglo-Saxon, is later. A
shrine in the eastern apse may have
been dedicated to St. Boniface, an
early Saxon missionary to the heathen
Germans, who was long revered here.
(Courtesy of Equinox [Oxford] Ltd.)

rooms of a Roman villa (two houses) were excavated in 1948–50 and are now
on display under protective roofs, with mosaics and a small museum. To the SE
of Bristol, at Keynsham, 17 rooms of a palatial 30-room courtyard villa, with
about 10 mosaics, were excavated in 1922–24. Only part of the N. corridor is
now visible in a cemetery, and some of the mosaics are preserved in a museum
at the Keynsham headquarters of Cadburys, along with the foundations of a
small Roman House.

BRIXWORTH
(Northamptonshire)

Imposing Anglo-Saxon church of All Saints, 7 mi. (11.25 km.) N. of Northampton.
Once hailed as one of the most important 7th-cent. monuments surviving in
England, its status has been clarified by careful study and excavation in recent
years—though aside from the tradition little is known of its history. The tradition states that it was part of a monastery founded in the 7th cent. in pagan
Mercia to convert the kingdom. Its sheer size, in Anglo-Saxon terms, its heavy
stone fabric and reused Roman materials would support that assertion, and
excavations have indeed uncovered slight evidence of a monastery around it—
an outer defensive ditch and Anglo-Saxon graves. The monastery may have been
destroyed in a Danish raid in 870 AD. Only the church's nave is now considered
7th cent. The aisles, perhaps the upper part of the nave, and a tower (once the
W. porch) were added later, perhaps around 850 but still in Anglo-Saxon times.
A curious sunken ambulatory or crypt around the eastern apse, of the same later
date, uncovered in 19th-cent. alterations, may possibly have been used by pilgrims revering a bone of St. Boniface, the famous 8th-cent. missionary to the

Germans, that traditionally belonged to the monastery. All in all Brixworth is a most impressive building, and continued excavations may reveal more of its history. See also *Wing*.

BROOM HILL
(Hampshire)

Interesting Mesolithic site, E. of Braishfield, 3 mi. (4.75 km.) N. of Romsey. Meticulously excavated by an amateur, Michael O'Malley of Romsey, over a 10-year period in the 1970s, the site yielded a wealth of materials from a camping site of early hunter-gatherers who lived here, according to a radiocarbon date, about 8,500 years ago. The remains of four pit dwellings were uncovered and the finds included over 100,000 skillfully worked flints, mostly microliths—axes, adzes, borers, awls, engraving tools, projectile points. Bead and shell ornaments and colored ochres, probably used for body painting, with pestles for crushing them, were found in the pits, and curious slate "knives"—the stone from distant Cornwall—possibly gifts. Probably there is little to see at the site today. See also *Star Carr*.

BROUGH-ON-HUMBER
(Humberside)

See *Hull*.

BRUNTON
(Northumberland)

See *Hadrian's Wall*.

BRYN CADER FANER
(Gwynedd)

See *Moel Goedog*.

BRYN CELLI DHU
(Gwynedd)

One of the finest prehistoric monuments in Wales, a large passage grave not far from the Menai Straits on Anglesey, 4 mi. (6.5 km.) SW of the Menai bridge, With *Barclodiad y Gawres* on Anglesey's southern coast it is a rare example of a passage tomb, more common in Scotland and Ireland, especially in the *Boyne Valley* (IRELAND). Excavated in 1925–29 and splendidly restored under its mound encircled with heavy kerb stones, it is considered late Neolithic since it is built over an earlier henge circle with 14 upright stones, which seem to have been scattered and disfigured by the later tomb builders, and a ritual pit at the center. The 27-ft. passage, defined in its inner part by heavy megalithic uprights, leads into a single polygonal chamber 8 ft. in diameter and 6 ft. high. In the chamber stands a round, deliberately smoothed monolith, probably phallic, which suggests that the monument was as much a temple as a tomb. At the end of the chamber was found a slab incised with wavy lines and spirals, associated with the earlier henge, and reminiscent of Irish tombs. It is now in Cardiff, but a replica stands outside the tomb. Outside the passage was a forecourt, and just inside it a low bench, probably for offerings.

About a mi. NE on the grounds of Lord Anglesey's house, not far from Menai bridge, stand two other monuments. Plas Newydd is a Neolithic tomb of large uprights and a massive capstone over two adjacent chambers, one larger than the other. The mound has disappeared. Closer to the Straits the megalithic tomb of Bryn yr Hen Bobl lies under a large mound with a small single chamber under it and a funnel-shaped forecourt outside the entrance. Beyond this is a curious, man-made large terrace. Fully excavated in 1929, the tomb yielded Neolithic tools and pottery and the remains of over 20 burials.

BRYN YR HEN BOBL
(Gwynedd)

See *Bryn Celli Dhu* above.

BURFORD DOWN
(Devon)

See *Dartmoor*.

BURGH CASTLE
(Norfolk)

The Roman Garriannonum, a fine example of one of the late Roman forts of the *Saxon Shore*, a defensive system to hold off raiding pirates. It lies in a marshy area 3 mi. (4.75 km.) W. of Great Yarmouth at the confluence of the Yare and Breydon Water. The Roman town at *Caister-by-Yarmouth* is nearby. Oblong in shape, covering about 5 acres, the fort's three landward walls still stand in places to the original height of 15 ft. Of rubble faced with flint and tiles, they lean perilously outward, pulled down by the weight of the heavy rounded bastions, six of which were added later. Remaining examples of the bastions show the sockets for the huge revolving catapults placed on their tops. The fourth, western wall has slipped down the cliffs. The entrance gate is marked by a gap on the E. Built about 275 AD, the fort was destroyed in the mid or late 4th cent.

BURROUGH HILL
(Leicestershire)

One of the finest of a number of Iron Age hill forts in the area, about 7 mi. (11.25 km.) S. of Melton Mowbray at Burrough-on-the-Hill. A trapezoidal fort of about 12 acres, it has a massive rampart faced with dry stone on the E. and ramparts and ditches on the other sides, with very steep slopes. On the SE is a massive inturned entrance about 147 ft. long, with large stone guard chambers possibly built by the Coritani, who were late owners. Sporadic excavations in the interior uncovered numerous storage pits with debris from the 2nd cent. BC into the Roman period, but strangely, no hut remains.

BURRINGTON COMBE
(Somerset)

See *Cheddar*.

BURTON FLEMING
(Humberside)

See *Great Driffield*.

BURY HILL
(Hampshire)

Iron Age hill fort, just SW of Andover and 4 mi. (6.5 km.) N. of *Danebury* hill fort. A strong circular fort on a spur, much overgrown, it dates to the period of the Belgic incursions from Europe just before the Roman conquest. An earlier, single rampart fort was rebuilt at this time with doubled ramparts, as was shown by the excavations in the 1930s.

BUTSER HILL
(Hampshire)

A broad hill at the end of the South Downs rising 890 ft. above the London-Portsmouth road. A Hampshire Country Park, it is 2.5 mi. (4 km.) S. of Petersfield near the Sussex border. Here on Little Butser Hill, sited amidst barrows and ancient dikes, is an experimental farm, The Butser Ancient Farm Project, an ongoing attempt to recreate as far as possible a Celtic Iron Age farm of about 300 BC in order to solve archaeological problems of the period. It is also an open air museum, accessible to the public. Several thatched round houses of wattle and daub, one quite large, have been built within an enclosure with palisade and ditch. Early forms of cereal are cultivated with implements similar to those of the period, and primitive forms of farm animals are raised. Related activities include pottery-making, metal-smelting and charcoal burning.

BUTTERDON HILL
(Devon)

See *Dartmoor*.

BYWELL
(Northumberland)

Charming hamlet on the Tyne River, 12 mi. (19 km.) W. of Newcastle, once a place of importance. Two churches stand here side by side, both of Anglo-Saxon origin (they belonged to adjoining estates) and recently restored. Little is left of the period in St. Peter's, but its size and the treatment of the remaining windows and doors indicate that it was a major church, undoubtedly the church in which Egbert was consecrated bishop of *Lindisfarne* in 802 AD. St. Andrew's, at the entrance to Bywell Hall, still has a notable Saxon tower, built in two periods, and part of the old nave wall. The church at Ovingham, 3. mi. (4.75 km.) NE of Bywell, has a very similar Anglo-Saxon tower.

CABURN, THE
(East Sussex)

Or Mt. Caburn, an important Iron Age hill fort, about 2 mi. (3.25 km.) SE of Lewes, near Glynde, crowning a bare hilltop 490 ft. high. It has a long history of excavations into the 1930s, beginning with General Pitt-Rivers in the 1870s. The Caburn was occupied by a substantial community from about 500 BC for some three centuries. About 150 BC the fort was built with a single bank and ditch; just before the Roman invasion of 43 AD this was strengthened with chalk, the entrance rebuilt, and a new flat-bottomed ditch dug around the outside. To no avail, for the fort was attacked, the gate burnt by the Romans and the whole abandoned. See also nearby *Itford Hill*.

CADBURY CAMP
(Avon)

See *Bristol*.

CADBURY CASTLE
(Somerset)

See *South Cadbury*.

CAER DREWYN
(Clwyd)

Fine Iron Age hill fort at Corwen, just N. across the river from the town. It has one of the best preserved stone ramparts in Wales, crowning the hill. With a deep inturned entrance, it compares with *Tre'r Ceiri*, and apparently dates from the Roman period. Four earlier phases of construction have been noted; an annex on the N. is all that is left of the earliest earthwork. There are traces of round huts within the fort.

CAER GAI
(Gwynedd)

Roman fort on a hill above a broad valley near the SW end of Lake Bala, less than a mi. N. of Llanuwchllyn. The fort, covering about 4 acres, was excavated in 1965. It began with a turf rampart of about 78 AD. This was revetted in stone in the 2nd cent. In this period it was garrisoned by the First Cohort of Nervii, auxiliary cavalry from Belgium, as we know from a statue base dedicated to Hercules found in 1885 in a little shrine outside the NE gate (now in *Cardiff*). The fort was occupied until about 130 AD. The buildings inside were of timber, in three phases. Today a farm covers the northern corner but the rampart and ditch, with some masonry showing, can be seen on the SW and SE sides, with the entrance gap in the SW. Two practice camps are known nearby. See also *Tomen y Mur*.

CAER GYBI
(Gwynedd)

Few travelers taking the ferry from *Holyhead* harbor to Dublin realize they are looking at a tiny Roman naval fort on a cliff to the N. of the harbor. Three-sided, covering about an acre, the fort's wall still stands up to 15 ft. high on the N. and W., with the rampart walk still visible, and two of the round projecting bastions may be seen. The original S. gate has been repeatedly rebuilt. The fort, which owes its preservation to the church of St. Gybi standing in its interior, is late Roman, probably built by Count Theodosius in the 4th cent. in a vain attempt to stand off Irish raiders and protect the Roman fleet.

CAERHUN
(Gwynedd)

See *Penmaenmawr*.

CAERLEON
(Gwent)

The Roman legionary fortress of Isca, 3 mi. (4.75 km.) NE of Newport. First built around 75 AD, the 50-acre fort, headquarters of the 2nd Augustan Legion, was used as a springboard, with *Chester* to the N., for the conquest of Wales in the late 1st cent. At first its ramparts were of earth, its buildings timber, but starting about 100 AD, as an inscription proves, it began to be rebuilt in stone, though some barracks were still of wood. Occupation was reduced after about 120 AD and it was abandoned, except perhaps for a small military unit, when the garrison moved out, probably in the early 4th cent. Inside the conventional rectangular fort were 64 long barracks buildings arranged in pairs facing each other. The headquarters building of stone (the church now covers part of it) measured 89 ft. by 210 ft., and a recent discovery was an impressive bath building inside the fort with hypocaust rooms and marble-stepped plunge baths, now on display.

Excavations in available areas of the fort within the modern village that overlies it have taken place since 1926. Today however only an area in the NW corner of the fort is still visible. Here is a stretch of the rampart with large

The amphitheater of the legionary fortress of Isca at Caerleon, Wales. It lay outside the walls of the 50-acre fort, of which little is now visible. Built at about the same time as the Colosseum at Rome (around 80 AD), it was probably used only for military exercises and displays. The visible banks, backed by masonry walls, once held timber seats. (Courtesy of British Tourist Authority, New York.)

communal ovens built up against it, a cookhouse, an angle tower, and the great drain of a latrine nearby. The foundations of a barrack block may be viewed— 12 double rooms and a more spacious suite at the end for the centurion. The amphitheater outside the fort walls (with a small bath suite nearby), the finest in Britain, was excavated by Sir Mortimer Wheeler in 1926–27 and restored. It dates from about 80 AD, and unlike its contemporary in Rome, the Colosseum, was primarily used for military exercises and displays along with the usual diversions. Its earth bank was contained within masonry walls, with the usual entrance gaps, and held timber seats. Waiting rooms for gladiators and others may be seen, one with stone benches, and stairs that led up to the seats. There seems to have been an extensive vicus or settlement between the fort and river. An excellent little site museum stands near the church. It shares the finds with the *Cardiff* museum. See also *Usk*.

CAERNARVON (Gwynedd)

Site of the great Edwardian castle on Menai Strait opposite Anglesey, a strategic spot earlier used by the Romans whose auxiliary fort of Segontium is sited on a hill overlooking the river and the castle. Excavated by Sir Mortimer Wheeler in 1920–23, the fort is now open to the public, the outline of its rectangular ramparts, which cover 4¼ acres, clearly visible, although the main road cuts diagonally through it. The sparse remains of the three gates are visible; and on the inland side of the road the foundations of barrack buildings, a workshop, a 2nd-cent. granary, and the commandant's house and *principia* or headquarters have been marked out in the turf. The commandant's house shows rooms grouped around a courtyard, and the *principia* a courtyard, an assembly hall (later divided) and other rooms to the rear, with a strong room under the military chapel. Recent excavations on the river side of the main road have uncovered a bath house within the fort, now on display. Remains of an extensive settlement around the fort and of a Mithraeum outside it have been found. Nothing is now visible. The fine explanatory museum stands beside the main road.

Segontium began as an earth and timber fort of about 78 AD, holding an auxiliary regiment of 1,000 men, partly mounted (in the early 3rd cent. these were German Sunici), and was rebuilt in stone several times into the 4th cent. Its life ended in 383 AD when Magnus Maximus withdrew its garrison in his attempt to become emperor. Along the riverfront a rectangular building, called Hen Waliau, its wall still standing 19 ft. high, may be seen. It was probably a 3rd-cent. stores-compound for transshipments along the waterways.

CAERSWS (Powys)

Roman military center and forts on the Severn at its confluence with the Carno River, about 7 mi. (11.25 km.) W. of Newtown. Part of the military system set up for the conquest of Wales in 78 AD, it lay at the focus of five roads to other forts. Excavations in the early 1900s and in 1966–67 of the principal fort of Mediomanum (7.6 acres) showed that it began with a clay and turf rampart and timber buildings, and in two later periods of reconstruction all was rebuilt in stone except the barracks. The SW corner now lies under a railway and the external bath building under a railway shed. There was a civilian settlement outside the fort. Both fort and settlement were occupied until after 400 AD. A few ditches on a spur above the Severn NE of the main fort mark the site of an earlier fort of 9.3 acres built during the first penetration of Wales from *Wroxeter* in the mid-1st cent. AD.

The impressive 3rd-cent. Roman walls of Venta Silurum at Caerwent, the market town and capital of the Welsh Silures. The bulging bastions were added to the walls in the 4th cent. to hold the heavy artillery of the time. (Photo: the author.)

CAERWENT
(Gwent)

Small Roman town of Venta Silurum, with impressive ramparts, one of two known in Wales (see *Carmarthen*). It was established by the Romans in the late 1st cent. AD as the market town and capital for the unruly Silures, recently subdued. It lies off the Severn estuary 5 mi. (8 km.) W. of Chepstow and not far from the large fort of *Caerleon* to the W. The circuit of walls, originally of earth, rebuilt in stone in the 3rd cent., with heavy polygonal bastions added in the 4th, encloses a roughly rectangular area of about 44 acres. They are best preserved on the southern side, and of the four gates the S. gate, having been blocked up in the dangerous 4th cent., is the most complete today. Continuing excavations since the late 19th cent. in the interior, now holding the village of Caerwent, revealed the usual grid of streets tightly packed with houses and public buildings. There was a forum and a basilica, a fine bath building, shops, houses (some substantial) and a small Romano-British temple. Only the latter is visible today, with part of an insulae of houses and shops, excavated in 1947. Two interesting inscriptions are preserved in the church, but there is no site museum. The finds are divided between the Newport museum and the National Museum at *Cardiff*.

The complex Iron Age fort of Llanmelin overlooking Caerwent, excavated in 1930–32, may have been the tribal capital of the Silures, or at least one of their major centers, before the founding of Venta. Slowly developed into a major citadel with two lines of ramparts, the inner one of heavy drystone construction, and an elongated annex on the SE, presumably for livestock, it was abandoned at the Roman conquest.

CAER Y TWR
(Gwynedd)

Iron Age fortifications on the rocky summit of Holyhead Mtn. on Holy Island off Anglesey, just west of *Holyhead*. A drystone wall, still 9 ft. high in places, encloses where necessary an area of 17 acres with a rampart walk still visible on the N. and W. where the fort is strongest. The other sides are protected by sheer cliffs. Most notable is the northeastern entrance with its flanking walls. A half mile farther down the slope is a group of stone-built huts at Ty Mawr, mostly round.

Some 20 still survive out of the original 50 known. They were apparently occupied by native Celts in the late Roman period, for coins and crude pottery of the period, as well as mortars, spindle-whorls and other debris, were found in the excavations.

**CAISTER-BY-YARMOUTH
(Norfolk)**

Or Caister-on-Sea; about 3 mi. (4.75 km.) N. of Great Yarmouth, site of a Roman port, once occupied in the Rhineland trade in pottery and glassware. Founded about 125 AD, it was originally separated from the fort of *Burgh Castle* to the S. by an estuary, now silted up with the town's harbor. The ramparts, originally of clay with a palisade, then rebuilt with a 10-ft.-thick flint wall, enclosed about 30 acres. Just inside the S. gate excavations in the 1950s discovered the foundations of a seamen's inn. Part of this building and of the town wall, with the S. gate, have been preserved. About 150 Saxon burials (7th–8th cents. AD) and the site of two huts were also uncovered in the excavations.

**CAISTOR
(Lincolnshire)**

As its name implies, there was a fortified Roman town at this village about 10 mi. (16 km.) SE of Brigg. Only the slight remains of its 4th-cent. walls survive—a stretch of rubble wall and the core of some bastions along the S. side of the churchyard, and another stretch beside the grammar school grounds. See also *Horncastle.*

**CAISTOR-BY-NORWICH
(Norfolk)**

Roman capital of the former Iceni, the tribe led by Boudicca in her famous revolt of 60 AD. The Iceni were settled in Venta Icenorum some 10 years later. The site lies 3 mi. (4.75 km.) S. of Norwich Castle on a minor road. Romanization was apparently very slow, because it was only in about 125 AD that the native huts along the grid of streets were replaced by Roman-style houses, and a bath suite, forum and basilica built. A pottery industry also developed. Much later, probably in the 3rd cent., heavy walls of concrete, flint and brick with ditch and bastions were built around a restricted area, reducing the town size to about 35 acres. Two temples were built at the same time. Today all of the remains are under cultivation, but the impressive ramparts and ditch still surround the area. A Saxon cemetery was uncovered S. of the walls. The finds from a number of excavations can be seen in the Norwich Castle museum.

**CALLEVA ATREBATUM
(Hampshire)**

See *Silchester.*

**CAMBRIDGE
(Cambridge)**

Renowned for its medieval and modern university, Cambridge has a few sites left from earlier times. The most impressive is St. Bene't's (short for Benedict's), a Saxon church in the middle of the university area, with its fine Anglo-Saxon tower, probably late 10th cent. It shows three stages separated by string courses, and double belfry windows on all four sides. Inside, the splendid tower arch is decorated with strange beasts. Cambridge's ford over the Cam was once the site of an Iron Age settlement and a Roman walled river port with a bridge over the river. The site is now marked by the castle mound built by William the Conqueror. These remains are being investigated by a university team. In the larger region around Cambridge the sites include a defensive system of dikes facing SW, starting with the 7 mi. (11 km.) Devil's Ditch, which cuts across the Icknield Way just SW of Newmarket to the NW. Parts of this huge mound and ditch still far surpass *Offa's Dyke* in size. Below it, moving SW, is Fleam Ditch, then the

Brent and Bran ditches SE and S. of Cambridge. The system may have been built to stem the Anglo-Saxon advance in the 5th cent. AD, but is more likely to have been an East Anglian defense of the 7th cent. against the encroachment of the Mercians. Cambridge's University Museum of Archeology and Anthropology has varied displays from Britain and around the world.

CAMULODUNUM
(Essex)

See *Colchester*.

CANTERBURY
(Kent)

Ancient city, the cradle of Christianity in England, earlier a Roman town built over an oppidum of the Belgic Cantiaci. As revealed postwar by numerous small excavations at World War II bomb sites, Roman Durovernum Cantiacorum was a crowded town with the usual forum and basilica, theater and two bath suites. Some of the finds are on view, notably part of a large house lying under Butchery Lane where one can see a mosaic-paved corridor, a room with a hypocaust, and a small site museum. In the Dane John pleasure gardens in the S. of the city is an 80-ft.-high Roman burial mound. Of the Roman walls, built at the end of the 4th cent., rather late, little is to be seen, but the medieval walls, of which

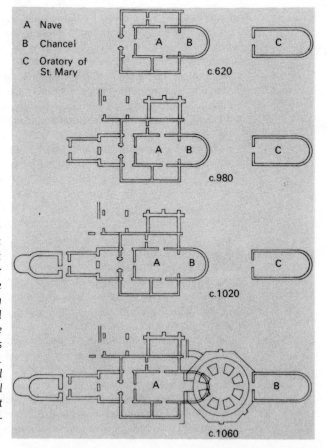

Schematic evolution, during the Anglo-Saxon period, of the monastic church of St. Peter and St. Paul at Canterbury. Its foundations, after excavation, are now on view. The original church was built in the early 7th cent. by St. Augustine, who had been sent from Rome to convert the pagan king of the Kentish Angles (about 597 AD). In the 11th cent. Bishop Wulfric built his octagonal rotunda over St. Augustine's chancel (B). Later the Normans built a great cruciform church on the site. (Courtesy of Equinox |Oxford| Ltd.)

fine stretches survive, were built on their foundations. In 1977 it was discovered that the N. wall of St. Radigund's church was actually part of the Roman wall, stills standing to its full height of 29 ft.

The glory of Canterbury is its great medieval cathedral and its early Christian predecessors. Of the latter the most interesting is the little church of St. Martin on a hill to the E. of the city. There is convincing evidence that its chancel and part of the nave, built with Roman brick, belonged to the original St. Martin's where, according to Bede's *History*, St. Augustine—sent to convert the "angelic Angles" of Kent by Pope Gregory around 597 AD—probably baptized their king, Ethelbert. His queen, Bertha, was a Christian from France who was reported to have worshipped in St. Martin's, so the building may well have been a Roman Christian church belonging to Durovernum, and thus perhaps the oldest church in northern Europe in continuous service.

Augustine also built a cathedral, lost under the present one, and a monastic church, St. Peter and St. Paul, E. of the walls, which has been excavated and is on view within the ruins of the great Norman cruciform church built later on the site. Here Augustine and his successors and Ethelbert and his queen were buried. In the visible foundations one can see a part of Augustine's church and how its chancel was replaced in the mid-11th cent. by Bishop Wulfric's octagonal rotunda and crypt. Farther E. are the standing ruins of St. Pancras of the early 7th cent., which may have begun as a pagan temple. Canterbury's Royal Museum, High Street, contains interesting finds from the city and its region. Numerous excavations continue to date.

CAPEL GARMON
(Gwynedd)

Neolithic chamber tomb in the upper Conway valley, 2 mi. (3.25 km.) E. of Betws-y-Coed, about a mi. S. of Capel Garmon. Here is a well-maintained barrow grave of the Severn-Cotswold type, 140 ft. long under a wedge-shaped mound. It has a horned forecourt in front leading to a false portal, but the actual antechamber and two side chambers are entered through a passage on the S. side.

CARDIFF
(South Glamorgan)

Large city, once a Roman military station and today home of the splendid National Museum of Wales, one of the great museums for antiquities of all sorts. The medieval Cardiff Castle nearby was built largely on the foundations of a strong, early-4th-cent. Roman fort, comparable to the *Saxon Shore* forts of the E. and S. coasts with its massive walls, bastions and gates. It was the successor to the earlier fort at *Caerleon*. Excavations have shown that the fort, built to combat sea raiders from Ireland, replaced two previous forts of timber and turf. In the 19th cent. Lord Bute reconstructed the N., E. and part of the S. walls and gates of the fort in a reasonable semblance of the Roman original. The North gate is particularly fine. Two notable Neolithic gallery graves lie SW of Cardiff off the A-48 amid a concentration of megalithic mounds and monuments. Both are of the Severn-Cotswold type, with wedge-shaped cairn, drystone walling and a horned forecourt. At Tinkinswood, 7 mi. (11.25 km.) from Cardiff, the chamber is covered by a single, massive 40-ton capstone (some 15 by 22 ft.) on five uprights. It was excavated in 1914, yielding the remains of some 50 burials. About a mile farther SE is St. Lythan's. It has lost almost all its cairn, leaving the megalithic structure bare.

THE CARLES
(Cumbria)

See *Castlerigg Stone Circle*.

CARLISLE
(Cumbria)

See *Hadrian's Wall.*

CARL WARK
(South Yorkshire)

Impressive ancient hill fort high on the moors 4.5 mi. (7.25 km.) SW of Sheffield, close to the Derby border. Three sides fall off steeply; on the W. and S. sides the earthen rampart is strengthened by a facing of heavy stones. Long thought to be Iron Age, it is now assigned to the Dark Ages, just after the Roman period, because of the excellent condition of the stonework.

CARMARTHEN
(Dyfed)

Excavations here from 1968 on have uncovered evidence of an urban settlement on the northern outskirts of Carmarthen, one of two Roman towns known in Wales (see *Caerwent*). Moridunum was the tribal capital of the Demetae. Timber buildings of the 2nd cent. AD with evidence of iron and bronze working were found, succeeded by stone houses with mosaic floors and hypocausts, occupied into the 4th cent. The earlier town walls were of clay and turf with a ditch, later rebuilt in stone. Of all this there is little to see; only the western half of the oval amphitheater is preserved, made of turf strengthened with timbers, the oval once holding timber seats. More is to be seen of Moridunum in the Carmarthen Museum at Abergwili .5 mi. (1 km.) to the E.

CARN BRAE
(Cornwall)

Conspicuous hilltop with three summits, 1.5 mi. (2.6 km.) SW of Redruth, between it and Camborne and close to the N. Cornish coast. This moorland site was occupied from Neolithic into medieval times and carries a ruined castle and a modern monument on two summits. There are also the remains of an Iron Age hill fort and of Bronze Age occupation. Of most interest however is the low eastern summit where excavations from 1970 to 1973 by Roger Mercer uncovered indisputable evidence of a rare walled Neolithic farming settlement of the late 4th millennium BC (radiocarbon dates embraced 3109 to 2687 BC). The straggling, irregular Neolithic walls were built (with vast labor) of huge stones, with a ditch in front. Inside was jumbled evidence of many post-supported huts and shelters, surely the oldest in Britain, and storage pits, middens, hearths and quantities of Neolithic pottery, flints and stonework indicating intensive occupation by several hundred people. It is possible that all the walls around the castle here could be Neolithic. Outside the walls were pockets of rudimentary fields, and evidence from the village itself indicated widespread trade—pottery from the Lizard in southern Cornwall, or fragments of polished flint axes from Wessex. The community was burned and destroyed by hostiles armed with bows and arrows—over 700 flint arrow tips were found on the site.

CARNEDDAU HENGWM
(Gwynedd)

See *Dyffryn Long Barrow.*

CARN EUNY
(Cornwall)

Well-known Iron Age village, 5 mi. (8 km.) SW of *Penzance* on Land's End. The well-preserved ruins, in state care, are of a number of interlocking stone courtyard houses of the 1st cent. BC surrounding a large curving fogou, a specifically Cornish type of stone-walled underground chamber, probably for communal food storage. This one, 66 ft. long with a stone-walled entrance passage, has its roof of massive slabs still intact and a circular chamber, once roofed in corbelled stone, off to one side. The stone-built village was preceded by one of timber-built houses, perhaps dating to 400 BC; the village was occupied into the Roman period. See also the ancient villages of *Chysauster* nearby and *Din Lligwy* in Wales.

**CARN FADRUN
(Gwynedd)**

Iron Age hill fort and village on the Caernarvon (Lleyn) peninsula, inland near Nevin (Nefryn) above Garn village. The site is on an isolated hill, the ramparts of heavy dry-stone masonry encircling it. Round hut foundations are associated with an earlier enclosure; many of these, unusually, are scattered on the slopes outside the walls. A second, larger enclosure, probably from the Roman period, is associated with semi-rectangular hut foundations. Another similar fort, probably earlier, Garn Boduan, lies 3 mi. (4.75 km.) from Carn Fadrun, 1 mi. (1.6 km.) S. of Nevin. Again it has an outer and inner rampart, and about 170 round hut foundations. Estimates of the population here vary from 400 people to as many as 700. The best-known of these stone-defended village-forts is *Tre'r Ceiri*, a few mi. NE.

**CARN GLUZE
(Cornwall)**

See St. *Just*.

**CARN LLECHART
(Glamorgan)**

Bronze Age circle and tomb in the hills above Rhyd-y-Fro in the Swansea valley, inland from Swansea about 8–10 mi. (13–16 km.) Here is an impressive ring, fully 60 ft. across, of large standing slabs set close together, with a rectangular burial cist, also of slabs, in the center. This fine monument belongs to a type more common in Scotland.

**CARN LLIDT
(Dyfed)**

See St. *David's Head*.

**CARRAWBURGH
(Northumberland)**

See *Hadrian's Wall*.

**CARREG SAMSON
(Dyfed)**

See *Newport*.

**CARVORAN
(Northumberland)**

See *Hadrian's Wall*.

CASHTAL YN ARD

See *Isle of Man*.

CASTELL COLON (Powys)

Roman auxiliary fort sited by the River Ithon 1.5 mi. (2.6 km.) N. of Llandridod Wells. Excavated 1911–13 and 1954–57, the fort was shown to have gone through four phases. A 5-acre fort holding 1,000 men was built during the conquest of Wales (75–78 AD), then revetted in stone in the middle of the next cent. By the end of that century or later it was reduced by half to a square fort of 3.6 acres. It was then completely rebuilt in the 3rd or 4th cent., after periods of abandonment in between. Today banks and ditches and the foundations of the central buildings may be seen, with an unusually large bath house to the S. outside the fort.

**CASTELL DINAS
(Powys)**

See *Ty Isaf*.

CASTELL HENLLYS
(Dyfed)

Iron Age hill fort N. off the road between Cardigan and Fishguard, near Meline. The site, in the Pembrokeshire Coast National Park, was occupied through Roman times. It is being reconstructed with round houses and other buildings, set on original foundations, as a tourist attraction. Training in field archaeology is also available.

CASTELL ODO
(Gwynedd)

Iron Age hill fort near Aberdaron at the end of the Lleyn peninsula, Caernarvonshire. Careful excavations (1958–59) have established an Iron Age sequence for the region. The fort began as an undefended settlement of 9–10 round houses, later enclosed in two banks and ditches. The whole was burnt and abandoned, then later rebuilt with some stone on the outer bank. It was destroyed by the Romans about 78 AD, but huts continued to be built on the ruined site.

CASTLE-AN-DINAS
(Cornwall)

Name of two Iron Age forts. 1. The fort, 2 mi. (3.25 km.) SE of St. Columb Major, is a magnificent round fort damaged by a modern mine. It has two massive rings of stone-built ramparts, with ditches, and traces of a third ring in between. A few round hut sites are visible around a pond, the ancient water supply. 2. It lies in the middle of Penwith peninsula, a few mi. N. of Penzance, on the left of the Penzance-St. Ives road. Affording a fine view, the fort has three lines of stone-built ramparts and ditches, though marred now by a modern tower. It was probably built to defend the Iron Age village of *Chysauster* nearby.

CASTLE DORE
(Cornwall)

Small Iron Age hill fort 2.5 mi. (4 km.) N. of the picturesque little seaport of Fowey. Much overgrown, it shows two lines of ramparts and ditches and an elaborate defended entrance on the E. Excavations in 1935–36 have shown that

The great stone circle at Castlerigg in the Lake District, over 100 ft. across with 38 of its stones surviving. The circle, obviously the site of impressive ceremonies in the Neolithic period, may be one of the earliest on the island. The wide entrance on the N., flanked by two larger stones, may be seen at the rear. The tumble of stones on the eastern side of the interior is unexplained. (Courtesy of English Heritage.)

it belongs to two periods, the 1st cent. BC, with nine or more roundhouses associated with it, and a reoccupation in the post-Roman Dark Ages, giving credence to its traditional association with King Mark (Cunomorus) and the Tristan and Isolde legend. Three rectangular buildings were discovered from this period, perhaps the "palace" of King Mark. Two mi. (3 km.) S. at a crossroads an authentic 6th cent. memorial stone stands 6 ft. high and on it a Latin inscription reads "Here lies Tristan son of Cunomorus."

CASTLERIGG STONE CIRCLE (Cumbria)

Or "The Carles," one of the finest monuments of the Lake District, set in the midst of a wide mountain landscape on Chestnut Hill, 1.5 mi. (2.6 km.) E. and above Keswick. The ring of 38 stones (originally 42) is over 100 ft. across, with an entrance on the N. flanked by two larger stones. Keats undoubtedly had it in mind when he wrote ". . . like a dismal cirque/ of Druid stones, upon a forlorn moor. . . ." There are traces of a cairn or cairns in the interior, of an outer ditch, and up against the eastern stones a mysterious rectangle of stones, so far unexplained. The circle, probably Neolithic, may be among the earliest in England.

CASTOR (Cambridgeshire)

See *Water Newton*.

CATEL MENHIR

See *Guernsey*.

CAT'S HOLE (West Glamorgan)

See *Goat's Cave*.

CAWFIELDS (Northumberland)

See *Hadrian's Wall*.

CAWTHORN (North Yorkshire)

Roman practice camps, about 4 mi. (6.5 km.) N. of Pickering, E. of Cropton village at the southern edge of North York Moors National Park. The four camps here, all of the early 2nd cent., are considered practice legionary camps built by the men of the 9th Legion. The more substantial two (B and D) may have later been occupied, since the complex lies on the Roman road to Whitby called Wade's Causeway. There is evidence that D was the latest, the others earlier, A the earliest of all. Camp D is the best preserved, while the ramparts of B still stand 10 ft. high above its outer ditch. Excavations revealed turf buildings inside camps A and B and a system of roads within the latter. A 1.25 mi. (2 km.) stretch of Wade's Causeway, 16 ft. wide, is exposed on Wheeldale Moor to the N., 3 mi. (4.75 km.) SW of Goathland. It shows the heavy slab foundations, kerb stones and culverts of the road—one of the finest excavated sections in Britain.

CERNE ABBAS GIANT (Dorset)

Huge figure cut into a chalk hillside of the Downs above the village of Cerne Abbas, 8 mi. (13 km.) N. of *Dorchester*. Wielding an enormous knotted club and with large erect phallus, the 180-ft.-high figure probably dates from the early Roman period and represents a local fertility god in the guise of Roman Hercules. Remarkably, this ancient fertility figure was regularly cleaned and maintained by the local people until recent times. See also *White Horse*; *Wilmington Long Man*.

CERRIG DUON
(Powys)

Bronze Age stone circle, 12 mi. (19 km.) W. of Brecon and 7 mi. (11.25 km.) SW of Sennybridge on the W. side of the River Tawe near its source. It is a humble ring of 20 small, low stones (possibly eight more are missing) with one gigantic 6-ft. outlier, Maen Mawr (the Big Stone) to the N. An avenue of small stones leads toward it from the NE. Just SE is Saeth Maen, a rare six-stone alignment.

CERRIG Y GOF
(Dyfed)

See *Newport*.

CHALBURY
(Dorset)

Iron Age hill fort S. of *Maiden Castle* and Dorchester, overlooking Weymouth Bay at Bincombe. A single rampart, revetted with stone slabs inside and out and with a ditch, protected this settlement, which was abandoned in the early Iron Age. Some 70 depressions in the interior represent round huts and pits. Two huts have been excavated, one stone, one wood, with human remains scattered on the floor of the latter. There are two round barrows within the fort and a fine view from the top. Around the fort prehistoric field systems are clearly visible.

CHALLACOMBE STONES
(Devon)

See *Dartmoor*.

CHANCTONBURY RING
(West Sussex)

Small but conspicuous Iron Age hill fort on the Downs near Washington, about 2 mi. (3.25 km.) W. of Steyning. A grove of beeches crowning the top obscures its single bank and ditch of the early Iron Age, excavated in 1977. In 1909 a rectangular Romano-British temple of flint and mortar was discovered at the center of the fort. Cross dikes running E. and W. protect the approaches to the fort. See also *Cissbury Ring*.

CHANNEL ISLANDS

See *Alderney*; *Guernsey*; *Jersey*.

CHARTERHOUSE
(Somerset)

Area of Roman lead-mining in the Mendips, N. of *Cheddar* Gorge. In 49 AD, only six years after the invasion, lead was already being exploited here by the Roman military, as a lead pig from the site attests. It was primarily used to extract silver. Around the site mounds are the only indication of several Roman buildings. The most conspicuous survival is the amphitheater, whose oval banks still stand about 15 ft. high. There are extensive mining remains in the region, many of them undoubtedly Roman, others later. Numerous finds from the area are in the Taunton and *Bristol* museums.

CHASTLETON
(Oxfordshire)

Iron Age hill fort a few mi. W. of Chipping Norton, commanding the River Evenlode in the Cotswolds, just within Oxfordshire. Roughly circular, its walls were built of stone, with two entrances. Minor excavations in 1928–29 dated the fort to the early Iron Age, but found no house foundations. It may have been a cattle enclosure.

CHEDDAR
(Somerset)

8 mi. (13 km.) NW of Wells. The limestone of the Mendip Hills, running NW from Wells, is seamed with gorges and there are many caves in the hillsides. Of these Wookey Hole, just W. of Wells, beloved of tourists, has little of archaeological interest though it is a spectacular ravine ending in the cavern itself, where the River Axe issues from underground. Of most interest along the ravine is Hyena Den, a small cave that, in the mid-19th cent., yielded tons of Ice Age

animal bones mixed with implements and hearth remains of Paleolithic hunters. Equally spectacular (and tourist-ridden) is the Cheddar Gorge itself, about 6 mi. (9.6 km.) NW of Wookey Hole. Over 2 mi. (3.25 km.) long, its sides are pitted with caves of which the most important is Gough's Cave, inhabited by late Ice Age man for thousands of years. The Cheddar Gorge Museum at its mouth exhibits a fine collection of Paleolithic implements and the skeleton of Cheddar Man, dated about 8000 BC. Many other caves, both in the gorge and beyond it, were frequented by Paleolithic man, notably Aveline's Hole in Burrington Combe to the N., which has yielded rich human deposits. See also *Cresswell Crags*; *Goat's Cave*; *Hengistbury Head*; *Jersey*; *Kent's Cavern*; *Pontnewydd*.

In Cheddar town itself meticulous excavations have uncovered a palace complex of the Anglo-Saxon kings of Wessex, including Alfred himself. An often-rebuilt, timber long hall, with outbuildings, formed the nucleus. It was protected against flooding by an elaborate drainage system. A new West hall, built after 930 AD, with stone chapel and farm buildings, was protected by a palisade and ditch. See also *Charterhouse*.

CHEDWORTH ROMAN VILLA (Gloucestershire)

One of the finest villas in Britain, first excavated in 1864 and well-preserved. It is still being excavated and conserved, and is open to the public. A Cotswold villa near Northleach, it is the most rewarding of the many found around *Cirencester*, 8 mi. (13 km.) to the S. It lies in a pleasant wooded valley by a spring and was occupied from about 120 to 400 AD. It developed through four separate phases into a large courtyard style villa with a garden court and a larger farmyard courtyard. The mosaics, from the Cirencester workshop, are outstanding, especially those of the four seasons in the dining room. The largest of the bath suites is one of the most complete in England. A nymphaeum once covered the spring and from its remains came the chi-rho symbols indicating that a late owner was a Christian. The foundations of a square pagan temple have been found SE of the villa. In fact Chedworth seems to have been a long standing religious center. There is an on-site museum and shop, and guidebooks are available.

CHESTER (Cheshire)

Present county capital, founded in a strategic situation by the Romans as the legionary fortress of Deva. The fort was constructed between 76 and 79 AD, probably on the site of a much smaller fort. The first version of the fortress, covering 60 acres, was of earth, with earth and timber defenses. This was rebuilt in stone about 100 AD. Deva was garrisoned by the 20th Legion almost throughout its span, and was extensively rebuilt early in the 4th cent. It was probably abandoned about 376 AD. Extensive excavation has been carried on for many years, including much rescue work—and still continues. This has resulted in a patchwork of small sites in the city, many on private property or visible under modern buildings. These include fine stretches of the N. and E. walls, angle towers, remnants of the *principia* (headquarters building), hypocausts, columns etc. The visitor may be confused, but most of the layout of the fort has now been determined. Outside the fort's perimeter part of the wall of the Roman quay on the River Dee has been found, and one half of the legionary amphitheater laid bare in excavations since 1960. This was of stone, with wooden seats, built over an earlier amphitheater of timber, and was the largest in Britain, holding 8,000 spectators. The visitor can see the curving arena wall with steps, entrances on the N. and E., and a small shrine of Nemesis (Fate). The local finds are gathered in the excellent Grosvenor Museum, with its special emphasis on the Roman army. Recent excavations in Saxon Chester, which was made a fortified town or *burh* in 907 AD, have revealed widespread occupation and local industries and substantial timber buildings, both within the area of the Roman fort and in a section to the S., close to the river.

CHESTERHOLM
(Northumberland)

See *Hadrian's Wall*.

CHESTERS
(Northumberland)

See *Hadrian's Wall*.

CHEW GREEN
(Northumberland)

Roman camps in the midst of the Cheviot Hills N. of Alwinton, a few mi. from the Scottish border. The camps lie within the vast Redesdale artillery range, on the Roman Dere street running up from *High Rochester*, and served as staging areas for troops moving into Scotland and as patrol posts. The earthworks of four camps are clearly visible but are so intricately overlaid as to be impossible to unscramble except by experts. The earliest and largest, designed to hold a legion, is Agricolan of about 80 AD. The smaller camps belong to various phases in the 2nd cent. See also *Woden Law* in Scotland.

CHICHESTER
(West Sussex)

See *Fishbourne*.

CHUN CASTLE
(Cornwall)

Small but memorable Iron Age hill fort commanding Land's End, just outside St. Just and 5 mi. (8 km.) NW of Penzance. Its double circuit of drystone walls, faced with granite and still standing 8 ft. high, the ditches in front of each and elaborate staggered entrance on the SW, must have made it all but impregnable. Inside, about a dozen hut foundations have been found, and rectangular ones from a later Dark Ages reoccupation, the latter obviously connected with the tin trade—tin and iron slag were found in the interior, and a furnace. Close to the fort on the W. side is a fine, massive chambered tomb, Chun Quoit, with its huge capstone still in place on four uprights.

CHUN QUOIT
(Cornwall)

See *Chun Castle* above.

CHYSAUSTER
(Cornwall)

Best example, meticulously excavated and restored, of some 20 Iron Age courtyard villages in Cornwall and Devon. It lies 7 mi. (11.25 km.) N. of *Penzance*. Occupied from the late Iron Age into the Roman period, its inhabitants were undoubtedly concerned with the tin trade, and the village may have been protected by the hill fort of *Castle-an-Dinas* (2) 1 mi. (1.6 km.) away, for it was undefended. Eight house complexes of a peculiar nature lie mostly along a street with terraced gardens behind. The heavy oval wall of each house encloses an open courtyard, approached by a covered passage from the outside, with rooms and store rooms built into the thickness of the wall facing inwards. The rooms were corbelled in stone or thatched, usually paved, and some with hearths and covered drains. A *fogou*, a subterranean storage room, lies at the end of the village. Grinding querns and much pottery and domestic debris were recovered from the houses. See *Penzance*.

Chysauster in Cornwall, a courtyard village from the late Iron Age-early Roman period. Some of the oval courtyards of the eight house-complexes of the village may be seen, with a bit of its paved "street" on the right. The inhabitants were undoubtedly workers in the traditional tin industry of Cornwall, which supplied the valuable ore to many lands. (Courtesy of English Heritage.)

CIRENCESTER
(Gloucestershire)

Site of a large Roman town, Corinium, the Romanized capital of the Dobunni, placed at the junction of five Roman roads. Of the town itself little is to be seen today in the smaller modern town except the mounds of the walls here and there. These enclosed about 240 acres and were eventually of stone; so too was the amphitheater, with wooden seats, whose mounds, still 27 ft. high, can still be seen outside the walls. Excavations have revealed a basilica (now marked out on the ground), a forum, town houses, shops and the grid of streets, and a wealth of materials now on display in the excellent Corinium Museum, where the ancient town comes alive. Here are reconstructed rooms and a number of mosaics from the well-known Corinium workshop that supplied them to the surrounding area (see, for instance, *Chedworth Roman Villa* and *Woodchester*).

CISSBURY RING
(West Sussex)

Iron Age fort, one of the largest in the country, near Findon 3 mi. (4.75 km.) N. of Worthing and not far from *Chanctonbury Ring*. The oval fort is surrounded by a single massive rampart and ditch enclosing about 60 acres, with entrances on the S. and E.—an incredibly huge job of work for the period. It was occupied from about 260 BC into the 1st cent. AD, then abandoned after the Pax Romana had set in. Under the fort on the SE part of the hill a series of depressions mark the site of one of the largest Neolithic flint-mining operations in Britain, comparable to the better known *Grimes Graves* in Norfolk. The mines here, dated at about 3600 BC and long abandoned when the fort was built, were laboriously dug down through the chalk up to 40 ft. deep to extract the prized flint nodules, using antler picks and shoulder blade shovels. There were over 200 such mines here, some with extensive lateral tunnels. General Pitt-Rivers first excavated the mines in the 1860s and 1870s, finding two skeletons, one of a girl who had apparently fallen down a shaft to her death. In this South Downs area not far from Cissbury three more groups of mines have been found that in the Neolithic period supplied all of southern England with flint.

CLAUSENTIUM
(Hampshire)

See *Portchester*.

CLAYDON PIKE
(Gloucestershire)

Extensive series of excavations by an Oxford group since 1979 of Thames-side settlements from the 3rd cent. BC through the Roman period; 2 mi. (3.25 km.) W. of Lechlade and 10 mi. (16 km.) E. of Cirencester. The sites include villages, cemeteries, temples, roads and fields.

COCKLEY CLEY
(Norfolk)

Iron Age village of the Iceni (Boudicca's tribe) privately reconstructed on the original site by the owner as a small open air museum. The village, in the middle of East Anglia, lies at Weeting, 3 mi. (4.75 km.) SW of Swaffham. There is also an early Anglo-Saxon church of about 620 AD on the site. See also *Caistor-by-Norwich*.

COELBREN
(West Glamorgan)

Good example of a small Roman fort of earth and timber (500 cavalry or 1,000 infantry) covering 5.2 acres. It was abandoned about 150 AD. The fort lies at the very top of West Glamorgan on the Powys border, 1 mi. (1.6 km.) SE of Coelbren village on the Roman road from *Neath* to *Brecon Gaer* forts. The earthen ramparts (highest on the N.) can be traced and the positions of three gates. The towers, gates and buildings were of timber. The finds from excavations in 1904 are in the Swansea museum.

COETAN ARTHUR
(Dyfed)

See *St David's Head*.

COLCHESTER
(Essex)

Historic first capital of Roman Britain. Previously it was, as Camulodunum, one of the largest tribal capitals in southern England, first under the Trinovantes and later (about 10 AD) under Cunobelin (Cymbeline) of the expanding Catuvellauni. As such it was a prime target of the invading Romans in 43 AD. Emperor Claudius was brought in for the kill, and thereafter a new town, Colonia Claudia Victricensis, the first colony in Britain, was established in the old tribal capital. As a symbol of imperial power a huge classical temple to Claudius (a type very rare in England—see *Bath*) was built and the colony began to expand from an original legionary fortress (this has recently been identified under the western part of the modern town). Then in Boudicca's revolt in 60 AD the enraged natives burned the undefended town, besieged the survivors in the temple for two days, then massacred them all. The huge masonry base of the temple (80 by 105 ft.) can still be seen under the Norman castle built on top of it. The visitor will note the superiority of the Roman masonry compared to the Norman work above it. The castle now houses a fine museum of Roman finds from Colchester and the region.

The city's first walls were thrown up only by the early 2nd cent. and were of stone (unusual for such an early date). Fine stretches survive and they can be traced around the entire circuit enclosing 108 acres—over an hour's walk. Parts of the massive main Balkerne Gate are still visible, partly under an inn. It had two central carriageway arches flanked by two pedestrian arches and bastions (one still stands 20 ft. high). The original tribal capital was a sprawling settlement, an oppidum, a kind of promontory fort covering about 15 sq. mi. (24 sq. km.) protected by massive linear earthworks with an industrial area on the river, a temple section, and an agricultural section inland. Much of this has been deduced recently from occasional digs, aerial photographs, and the scant remains around Colchester. Excavations in and around the Roman town have uncovered a number of fine houses with mosaic floors, and much evidence of the fury of Boudicca's sack in thick deposits of burned debris found in the western sector.

COLDRUM STONES
(Kent)

See *Aylesford*.

COLONIA CLAUDIA VICTRICENSIS
(Essex)

See *Colchester*, above.

COLONIA LINDUM
(Lincolnshire)

See *Lincoln*.

CONDERTON CAMP
(Hereford and Worcester)

See *Bredon Hill*.

COMBE HILL
(East Sussex)

A rare Neolithic causewayed camp (communal meeting place) a few mi. N. of Eastbourne, near Jevington. There were two concentric rings of ditches and banks here, the inner ring broken by at least 16 causeways, but excavations in 1949 found no evidence of any interior structures. Though partly demolished by a quarry, the rings can still be traced. In the area are many Bronze Age round barrows and a long barrow. See also *Avebury* (Windmill Hill).

CORBRIDGE
(Northumberland)

See *Hadrian's Wall*.

CORINIUM
(Gloucestershire)

See *Cirencester*.

COUNTLESS STONES
(Kent)

See *Aylesford*.

CREDENHILL CAMP
(Hereford and Worcester)

By far the largest of the Iron Age hill forts of the Welsh Marches, about 2 mi. (3.25 km.) W. of Hereford and just N. of the Wye River. These facts suggest that it may have been the capital fort of Iron Age Herefordshire. Limited excavations in 1963 gave indications that Credenhill—like some of the other Marcher forts (see *Croft Ambrey*, *Herefordshire Beacon*, *Midsummer Hill*, *Sutton Walls*, and the *Wrekin*)—had been intensively occupied for a long period of some 500 years by stable and prosperous farming groups, until the Romans in 48 AD systematically destroyed that way of life. The fort is circled by a single rampart and ditch with two entrances, and the discovery of a number of rectangular and square four-post huts, set in three regular rows and several times rebuilt, suggests occupation over the whole hill by as many as 4,000 people in a planned settlement over a long time.

CRESSWELL CRAGS
(Derbyshire)

Dramatic limestone ravine between Chesterfield and Worksop, about 5 mi. (8 km.) SW of the latter. Along its sides are 20 caves occupied intermittently by Paleolithic man over a period of perhaps 50,000 years—from Neanderthal man through the Upper Paleolithic to what is known as Cresswellian man (about 13,000 to 11,000 years ago) who lived in a period at the end of the Paleolithic roughly contemporary with the French Magdalenian. The Cresswellians engraved crude art on bone (a human figure, a horse's head), somewhat reminiscent of French portable cave art. Excavated since the 19th cent., the caves are now closed by iron grilles for protection but can be inspected from without. There is a visitors' center. See also *Cheddar Gorge; Goat's Cave; Hengistbury Head; Jersey (La Cotte de Brelade); Kent's Cavern; Pontnewydd*.

CRICKLADE
(Wiltshire)

Small town on the upper Thames, 6 mi. (9.66 km.) NW of Swindon. Cricklade was originally one of the Anglo-Saxon *burhs* or fortified strong points instituted by the Wessex kings to stem the Viking advance. Still visible here are the remains of an earthen rampart with outer ditch, probably built by Edward the Elder, son of Alfred the Great. See also *Wallingford; Wareham*.

CRICKLEY HILL
(Gloucestershire)

Large Iron Age and Neolithic hill fort and settlement, a promontory fort on a steep-sided spur of the Cotswolds 4 mi. (6.5 km.) S. of Cheltenham on Birdlip road, 7 mi. (11.25 km.) from Gloucester. This 7-acre site, excavated annually by Philip Dixon since 1969, is a richly rewarding site. Occupation began with a Neolithic, undefended causewayed camp, or meeting place, of about 3500 BC—two lines of ditches interrupted by causeways with stone banks behind them, often rebuilt. In the late Neolithic this was reorganized into a defensive drystone wall with a timber stockade behind it and two entrances—all burned in an attack of about 2500 BC, leaving over 200 arrowheads behind. Later a long mound—a processional way?—was built over the ruins, then the hill was abandoned until perhaps 700 BC when Iron Age people fortified an area twice as large with a drystone wall and ditch, building large rectangular houses (and square storage huts) along a road inside the double-gated entrance. This too was burned and destroyed, but was soon rebuilt by a new group with a heavy hornwork in front of the entrance and a large round house, and smaller round huts, inside it. About 500 BC the site was again burned and abandoned, then in the Dark Ages finally saw a village inside a palisaded enclosure. There is a site museum and guides are available.

CROFT AMBREY
(Hereford and Worcester)

Iron Age hill fort in the Welsh Marches, just NE of Mortimer's Cross on the Ludlow road near Croft Castle. The triangular fort with strong multiple defenses has been extensively excavated, revealing steady occupation from about 650 BC until it was burned and destroyed by the Romans in 48 AD. Like many other Marcher forts (see *Breiddin, Credenhill, Herefordshire Beacon, Midsummer Hill, Old Oswestry, Sutton Walls.* and the *Wrekin*), its interior was crammed with small square huts regularly laid out along streets or paths, probably housing 500 to 900 people. In its 700 years of occupation some huts were rebuilt over and over on the same site, and the gateposts at the SW gate were replaced 20 times! The small finds indicated that the community was stable and self-sufficient: bones of cattle, sheep and pig, spindle-whorls and loom weights, evidence of iron smelting, bronze working and pottery making, and granaries, carbonized grain, querns and sickles. A circular mound from a late period is thought to have been a sanctuary.

CRUG, THE
(Powys)

See *Brecon*.

CRUTHER'S HILL

See *Scilly Isles*.

DANEBURY
(Hampshire)

Major excavation of an important Iron Age fort in the Wessex chalklands, about 3 mi. (4.75 km.) NW of Stockbridge. The well-preserved fort on a tree-covered hill, the most important in its region, was densely occupied by a planned settlement, indeed an early town, throughout much of the Iron Age, from the 7th–6th cents. BC down to about 100 BC; and the excavation, carried out seasonally from 1969 by Professor Barry Cunliffe of Oxford for the Hampshire County Council, was a model of its kind. The site was planned to eventually become a public amenity. A deliberate program of research and excavation, designed to answer many questions about life in the Iron Age, the project brought all the resources of modern archaeology to bear on the social and economic aspects of the period. Hitherto the excavation of most hill forts had concentrated upon the defenses, but here the interior of the fort received equal, and most meticulous, attention to illuminate as far as possible the life lived in the settlement itself. Thousands of postholes and pits were uncovered and countless finds of all kinds recorded.

The site seems to have begun as a religious center in the Bronze Age. The earliest find was that of a Beaker period (early Bronze Age) burial of about 2500–2300 BC, but between 1000 and 500 BC a series of ritual pits were dug into the hillside with dog bones in some of them and posts then set on top of the bones. The building of the oval fort, enclosing about 12 acres, with a single massive rampart and ditch and the beginnings of a substantial settlement, is dated about 550 BC. Thereafter the defenses were rebuilt and enlarged, a cattle enclosure was thrown out to the S., the western gate closed up and the eastern entrance elaborated. About 400 BC the east gate was destroyed (and perhaps the whole fort), which led later to a massive strengthening of the defenses; the ditch was deepened, the rampart enlarged to 60 ft. wide (today it rises up to 16 ft. high) and the east gate further elaborated with complex outer hornworks. Probably much later a weak second ditch and bank were constructed around the hill. About 100 BC more strengthening took place, probably against the invading Belgae, but shortly thereafter the fort was destroyed and abandoned. After the invasion of 43 AD the defenses were briefly refurbished against the Romans, but to no avail.

In the early days of the fort the settlement consisted of round huts in the interior, but there was already evidence of planning. Throughout most of its life a road ran from E. to W. through the settlement. N. of it were numerous storage pits, probably for grain, with dwellings and refuse pits to the S. of it. Later two more subsidiary roads were laid down and lined by small rectangular structures, probably above-ground granaries, while round wattle-sided huts were built up against the ramparts. The roads were surfaced with flint, the earliest metaled roads known. A group of rectangular buildings at the center of the fort may have served a religious function. Curious burials were found—bodies dumped unceremoniously into pits, others dismembered and various parts, such as skulls, thrown into other pits—suggesting ritual cannibalism or killings for auguries. Evidence for industrial activity was also uncovered—pottery, bronze and iron working, basketry, weaving, wood and leather crafts. Raw materials and fine

Looking out across the heavy Iron Age rampart of Danebury hill fort to the fertile Hampshire countryside around it. Another view focuses on the meticulous excavations of the interior, shown in progress in 1974. The huge inner rampart, up to 60 ft. across at the base and still standing some 16 ft. high, enclosed about 13 acres crammed with huts and granaries along well-defined roads. (Photos: the author.)

Mediterranean goods were imported and worked up for redistribution, perhaps to supply the entire region as well as the settlement itself, which was largely self-sufficient with its farm animals and the growing of wheat and barley. The planning, industrial areas and large storage facilities suggest control by an elite under a powerful leader who dominated the region.

DANE'S DYKE
(Humberside)

See *Great Driffield*.

DANE'S GRAVES
(Humberside)

See *Great Driffield*.

DARTMOOR
(Devon)

High granite tableland, over 300 sq. mi. (559 sq. km.) in extent, NE of Plymouth, now a National Park. It is peppered with a remarkable number of Bronze Age monuments (the lowlands at that time being inhospitable)—stone circles, often in association with burial mounds and cists, numerous stone alignments (over 60 are known, with single, double and triple lines, and often of unusual length), and settlements marked by hut circles; 1,350 of these monuments are known. Neolithic survivals are almost unknown.

Starting at the N. end of the moor and moving down the E. side, then across the middle and finally into the southern sector, some of the better-known monuments are as follows.

First, the Nine Stones circle at Belstone, E. of Okehampton. Much better known and the finest circle in Dartmoor is the large open circle at Scorhill at Gidleigh, 5 mi. (8 km.) W. of Chagford. Of its tall pointed stones, originally about 36, 23 are still standing, with an especially tall one at the NW. A mi. or two farther E., on Shovel Down W. of Kestor Rock, are the first of the stone rows: three or four double rows, a single row, the stones all rather low, and several tall standing stones. The rows converge on cairns of various sizes, one cairn with a triple row of stones around a cist. In the area around Kestor Rock more than two dozen hut circles are scattered about, their field systems delineated by lines of upright stones. Round Pound here is an exceptionally large hut circle within a walled enclosure. Across the moor to the SW, 3 mi. (4.75 km.) W. of Postbridge, the well-known circles of Grey Wethers—two large circles roughly 100 ft. across, the southern one slightly larger—stand side by side in desolate moorland. The stones, about 3 ft. high, were carefully reconstructed in the late 19th cent. About 1 mi. E. at Fernworthy is another more obscure circle. About 2 mi. (3 km.) E. of it again is another stone row at Metherall.

Back on the E. side of the moor again, we find one of the best of the Bronze Age walled settlements, Grimspound, S. of Shapley and about 2 mi. (3 km.) E. of Postbridge. Around four acres were enclosed within a substantial wall, with the entrance on the E. and two dozen hut circles in the interior, some obviously storage huts or the like. The dwellings have hearths and sleeping benches and there are cattle pens inside the walls and traces of field systems outside them.

W. across the valley are the Challacombe stone rows, three of them ending at a triangular stone on the S. Six more hut circles at Foales Arrishes, about 2 mi. (3 km.) SE of Widecombe, set amidst Celtic and medieval field systems, are very well preserved. The wall around them has long since vanished. Moving SW and W. across the center of the moor there are some fine Bronze Age burial cists between Postbridge and Two Bridges. W. again on the Tavistock road just beyond Merrivale Bridge is a bewildering sample of every kind of monument on both sides of the road, some easily accessible—a stone circle, three stone rows, two of them double and one of those over 800 ft. long, cairns, burial cists, standing stones, and hut circles and enclosures.

In the southern sector of the moor above Plymouth, roughly around and S. of Sheepstor is another area rich in monuments—the valleys of the Plym, Yealm and Erme rivers. Around the head of the Plym River four stone circles around each other can just be discerned. The Yellowmead Down circles represent the kerb stones of a ruined burial cairn at the center, restored in 1921. The three center circles are graded in height toward the outside, and the stones of the inner circle, 21 still standing, are set close together. At Down Tor, 4.5 mi. (7.25 km.) ENE of Yelverton, a row of at least 174 stones leads uphill to a stone circle surrounding a wrecked cairn, the stones of the row increasing in height as they approach the circle, as if in honor of some great person buried there.

The so-called Drizzlecombe Antiquities 2 mi. (3.25 km.) SE of Sheepstor, include a number of barrows, one quite large, stone rows accompanied by two sizable standing stones, and two enclosures with hut circles inside. South of Yellowmead, at Ditsworthy Warren, there are more hut circles, a burial cist and stone rows, including a tall standing stone nearly 18 ft. high. Farther S. at Trowlesworthy Warren are a number of hut compounds, a circle and stone rows. At Legis Tor are four more close-built hut compounds of varying Bronze Age dates.

Moving E. to the upper Erme River valley at Stall Moor, a row of small stones runs over 2 mi. (3 km.) across the Erme to end in a circle. Still on the Erme, at Burford Down, are more rows associated with cairns and circles. Finally, on the SE edge of the moor at Butterdon Hill is one of the longest rows on Dartmoor, starting at a small round cairn.

This is just a small selection of the surviving monuments that constitute a tribute to the astounding activity of these Bronze Age people on Dartmoor long ago.

DEADMEN'S GRAVES
(Lincolnshire)

See *Skegness.*

DEAN HALL
(Gloucestershire)

Romano-British temple, discovered in 1984 on a hillside above Dean Hall at Littledean, overlooking the great bend of the Severn River at Newnham, and excavated by the University of Manchester. The temple, built around a spring-head, is on private land and is dated roughly to the 2nd–3rd cents. AD. It went through two phases, first a rectangular room with entrance on the E. and an apse in the western wall; this was later reconstructed and widened, a new wall with statue niches taking the place of the apse, and side corridors or ambulatories around the central room. The spring source under the central cella was given a covered drain. Puzzling circular postholes in the cella may be of later date, or perhaps supporting a small central pool. Another statue niche was at the western end of the S. wall.

DEERHURST
(Gloucestershire)

Anglo-Saxon church in a tiny, peaceful village 3 mi. (4.75 km.) S. of Tewkesbury. St. Mary's was formerly attached to a major monastery in this once important settlement. It was originally built in the 9th cent. AD as a very large church.

Careful studies have shown that it went through six major rebuildings, ending up with a nave and chancel surrounded by side chapels—and all two stories high. The nave survives, with the sanctuary arch in its E. wall; the chancel is ruinous and is now blocked off. The church's most prominent feature is the 10th-cent. tower.

There is a fine 9th-cent. font, and vigorous carvings of beasts' heads, as well as of a Virgin Mary just inside the W. door. In the surviving SW wall of the chancel is the well-known carving of the Deerhurst Angel, dating from the reign of Alfred the Great (9th cent.). Close by to the SW is Odda's chapel, now in state care. It was dedicated, according to an inscription now in Oxford, by Earl Odda, a kinsman of Edward the Confessor, in 1056. It had a nave and chancel; the chancel arch survives within it.

DENTON
(Tyne and Wear)

See *Hadrian's Wall*.

DEVA
(Cheshire)

See *Chester*.

DEVIL'S ARROWS
(North Yorkshire)

Three colossal Bronze Age standing stones in line, in the southwestern suburbs of Boroughbridge, 7 mi. (11.25 km.) NE of Harrogate. The stones, which were dragged from over 6 mi. (9.6 km.) away, stand in an impressive N-S line, 200 and 370 ft. apart, all curiously fluted at the top by weathering. One is 18 ft. high, the others 22 ft. high. Undoubtedly they represent the remnants of a Bronze Age religious center. See also *Rudston*.

DEVIL'S DITCH
(Cambridgeshire)

See *Cambridge*.

DEVIL'S DYKE
(Hertfordshire)

See *Wheathampstead*.

DEVIL'S DYKE CAMP
(West Sussex)

Iron Age fort near Poynings, overlooking Brighton from the NW, a famous view spot over the South Downs. A massive wall and ditch, now cut by the modern road, defends a bold chalk headland, with weaker ramparts on the sides. Traces of a large settlement in and around the fort seem to date from the late (Belgic) Iron Age. See also nearby *Hollingbury*, *Whitehawk*.

DEVIZES
(Wiltshire)

This small town boasts one of the finest archaeological museums in Britain, containing displays of materials from the Neolithic through the Roman period from the Wiltshire area—for instance, the finds from the West Kennet chambered tomb (see *Avebury*). About 4 mi. (6.5 km.) NE of Devizes one can see long stretches of the Wansdyke on both sides of the road. This stupendous 50-mile defensive boundary line, running roughly E. and W., consists of a high bank with a ditch on the northern side. It is assigned either to the Dark Ages period when Ambrosius, and later King Arthur, were withstanding the first incursions of the Anglo-Saxons up the Thames valley, or perhaps to the Anglo-Saxons themselves in the late 6th cent., as a defense of the emerging kingdom of Wessex against the British. Another good stretch of the Wansdyke can be seen near *Avebury*.

DICKET MEAD VILLA
(Hertfordshire)

See *Welwyn*.

DINAS EMRYS
(Gwynedd)

Hill fort or fortified homestead associated with Arthurian legends, on a crag in a site of great beauty, 1.5 mi. (2.3 km.) NE of Beddgelert just S. of the Snowdonia mountain mass. Here are the scant remains of an area fortified with two principal ramparts and occupied from the Early Iron Age right through the Roman period and into the 5th cent. AD. It is associated in legend both with Vortigern and Ambrosius Aurelianus (Emrys in Welsh means Aurelianus), those shadowy predecessors of King Arthur. Excavations around an artificial pool built inside the fort in the 1st cent. AD show that the structures bordering it belonged to the Roman period. There was also evidence of a 5th-cent. occupation (in Vortigern's time), including bits of pottery imported from the classical world, similar to the finds at *South Cadbury* of the same period. Traces of terraced field systems and round huts are discernible outside the fortifications.

DIN LLIGWY
(Gwynedd)

Ancient fortified homestead near Anglesey's NE coast, about 10 mi. (16 km.) N. of the Menai Bridge, between the villages of Llanallgo and Moelfre. At this charming site the strongly-built remains of two circular and four rectangular stone huts, their walls still standing up to 6 ft. high, are enclosed within a heavy, five-sided wall. Excavated in 1905, the site appears to have been the "castle" of a local chieftain of the 4th cent. AD—a far cry from the luxurious Roman villas in England in the same period! The round huts may be older; the rectangular buildings were used as iron workshops (or as a gatehouse). They compare with the ancient houses of *Carn Euny* and *Chysauster* in Cornwall.

Nearby is the Din Lligwy chambered tomb from the Neolithic. Its enormous 28-ton capstone rests on short uprights, giving it the appearance of a table. This is because the burial chamber under it is a natural fissure in the rock. Remains of 30 individuals were found in the tomb in 1908, with pottery.

DITSWORTHY WARREN
(Devon)

See *Dartmoor*.

**DOLAUCOTHI GOLD
MINES**
(Dyfed)

Roman gold-workings, unique in Britain, SE of the village of Pumpsaint, between Llandovery and Lampeter. Though somewhat confused by medieval and modern workings, much of the complex Roman mining installations can still be traced. Open-cast mining and shafts were employed, one of the latter 145 ft. deep, in which fragments of a wooden water-wheel used to drain it were found (now in the *Cardiff* National Museum). Three aqueducts—simple channels in the hillside, one 7 mi. (11.25 km.) long, with associated reservoirs and sluices—brought quantities of water to the site to wash out the ore. The workings were probably operated by the military with the help of civilian managers. There were several Roman forts in the neighborhood, and the remains of a small fort (5.6 acres) were excavated in the 1970s beneath Pumpsaint. Seven buildings were located and the finds indicated that it was occupied from 75 to 150 AD. See also *Charterhouse* mines.

DOLL TOR
(Derbyshire)

See *Stanton Moor*.

DORCHESTER
(Dorsetshire)

The Roman Durnovaria, provincial capital of the Durotriges tribe. They had been moved here by the Romans after the capture of their great hill fort, Maiden Castle, about 2 mi. (3.25 km.) away, by Vespasian about 44 AD. Little is left of the Roman town. Parts of the ramparts, built in the 2nd cent. AD and faced with stone about 300, can be traced on the W. and S. sides of the present town, and a town house of the 4th cent. AD, L-shaped and with a mosaic, lies exposed at Colliton Park. The public baths have been found and excavated, but nothing can now be seen. On the SW edge of the town stand the high banks of the impressive Roman amphitheater, known as Maumbury Rings, with a diameter of about 350 ft. It was once an early Neolithic henge circle (see Avebury), considerably adapted by the Romans and in the 17 cent. used as an artillery platform during the English civil wars. Excavated between 1908 and 1913, it proved to be a single entrance henge with an internal ditch in which, the excavators found, some 45 pits had been dug and filled with bones and tools, probably by way of offerings during the construction of the henge.

At Poundbury to the NW of the town a large Christian cemetery has been excavated. It seems to have grown out of a private graveyard of a Roman villa, and was centered on the grave of a man and two children, obviously important people, and finally included some 4,000 graves and several small rectangular mausoleums, one at least decorated with wall paintings. It went out of use by the end of the 4th cent., indicating that Dorchester may have had an early pocket of Christians in late Roman Britain. Also from Poundbury one can see the remains of a 12-mi. (19 km.) chalk-cut aqueduct channel that supplied Durnovaria with water. It circles gradually around the hills toward the town to maintain an even flow—a fine piece of engineering. The best of Durnovaria, however, can be seen in the excellent Dorset County Museum, which displays much prehistoric material from Dorset, the finds from Maiden Castle, mosaics from Durnovaria (suggesting that there may have been a flourishing mosaic school in the town) and much else.

That the Dorchester area was heavily settled from Neolithic times onwards has been shown by recent (1987) excavations in advance of the building of a new by-pass road S. of the town. One of the principal finds was that of a Neolithic causewayed camp, a tribal gathering place, to the SE. The circular monument, about 300 ft. across, was dated to about 3000 BC. One half of it lies under the grounds of the Thomas Hardy house; but the other half, before destruction, yielded two burials under stones, as well as flints, pottery, tools, animal bones and the antler picks used in digging the ditch. At the center was found the remains of a later Neolithic round house enclosed within another ring ditch. A Bronze Age, defended farmstead of about 1000 BC, N. of Maiden Castle, was also uncovered, consisting of a round house from an earlier Bronze Age period within the later enclosing ditch. A Late Iron Age trackway, field systems and the traces of rectangular timber buildings were also found and N. of them a Romano-British cemetery, with about 20 burials, dating up to about 400 AD, the end of the Roman occupation. Also discovered was a rare barrow in a square enclosure.

DORSET CURSUS
(Dorsetshire)

See Blandford Forum.

DOUGLAS

See Isle of Man.

DOVER
(Kent)

Entering Dover harbor today one can clearly see the Roman lighthouse tower in the grounds of the medieval castle on the headland, reminding one that Roman Dubris was a chief port for Britain, as it still is today, and headquarters of the *Classis Britannica*, the fleet whose continental base was at Boulogne. A rescue excavation in Dover in 1970 in advance of road building discovered quite unexpectedly the remains of an early-2nd-cent. fort, identified from roof tiles as the headquarters of the *Classis*. It lay beneath the later *Saxon Shore* fort that was known to be in Dubris but had not hitherto been found. The earlier fort covered at least two acres and contained at least 14 major buildings and a settlement or *vicus* around it. One of the houses of this *vicus* was uncovered 12 ft. underground and is preserved as the public Painted House Museum, in which one can also see finds from Dubris and part of the walls and a later bastion from the Saxon Shore fort. The rest of both forts has been reburied under the new road, which was raised to preserve them for posterity.

Of the Painted House one complete room, a corridor, and parts of four other rooms have been preserved. All the walls of the main room, still standing up to 4 to 6 ft. high, were preserved under fill from the later fort and all are painted with colored bands and decorated panels—the most extensive example of Roman painted plaster preserved in Britain. The underfloor heating system can also be glimpsed in the room. On view also are considerable remains of a bath building. The lighthouse over the eastern side of the harbor stands close to the Saxon church of St. Mary-in-Castro, built of Roman brick and badly restored. The lighthouse was one of a pair; the other, on the opposite side of the harbor, is now rubble. Originally it stood 80 ft. high, octagonal on the outside, with eight stepped stages up to the lantern, square on the inside. Of its present 69 ft., 43 are Roman, the rest medieval.

DOWN TOR
(Devon)

See *Dartmoor*.

DRIFFIELD
(Humberside)

See *Great Driffield*.

DRIZZLECOMBE
ANTIQUITIES
(Devon)

See *Dartmoor*.

DRUID'S CIRCLE
(Gwynedd)

See *Penmaenmawr*.

DUGGLEBY HOWE
(North Yorkshire)

Or Howe Hill. Huge, round, late Neolithic burial mound, 6 mi. (9.6 km.) SE of Malton, one of the largest in northern Britain and comparable in size and date to Silbury Hill in the S. (see *Avebury*), though the latter seems to contain no burials. Once nearly 32 ft. high, Duggleby now measures about 20 ft. in height and 120 in diameter. About half the mound was excavated in 1890. At its center was an 8-ft.-deep pit dug into the chalk and another shallower grave in which there had been crouched burials of 10 adults and children, with some Neolithic pottery and artifacts. A mound of chalk rubble covered the burials and in this and in the outer parts of the mound 53 cremation burials were found. These remains, if all buried at once as is thought, suggest ritual sacrifice. Among a number of other, similar huge round mounds in the same region is Willy Howe, about a dozen mi. (19 km.) slightly NE of Duggleby near Burton Fleming, Humberside. It is very similar in size (148 by 23 ft. high), except that no burials were found in it. See also *Great Driffield* in this area.

DURHAM **(Durham)**	The great Norman cathedral that rises so nobly above the river here is the last resting place of St. Cuthbert, Bishop of *Lindisfarne*, who died in 687 AD. Many years later the monks of Lindisfarne, threatened by Viking raids, fled with his body, eventually ending up at the future site of Durham in 995 to build a "white church" over the river, of which no trace survives. Also here, in the Galilee Chapel in the cathedral, is the body of the Venerable Bede, the historian, which has lain here since 1370. He died at *Jarrow* in 735 and his body was brought to Durham in 1022. St. Cuthbert now lies in a vault behind the high altar. When his grave was opened in 1827 a remarkable collection of objects was found within it and is now on display in the cathedral treasury. They include the restored wooden coffin in which the saint's body was brought from Lindisfarne, its sides decorated with carvings, and inside the coffin his portable altar, an ivory comb and his 7th-cent. gold and garnet pectoral cross, remarkably similar to the garnet jewelry found at *Sutton Hoo*. Pieces of rich embroidered vestments may have been presented to the saint's shrine by King Athelstan when he visited it in 934. In the former monk's dormitory W. of the cloisters over 70 pieces of early religious sculpture from all over the north are displayed, including some replicas (for instance, the *Bewcastle Cross*).

DUROBRIVAE
(Kent)

See *Rochester*.

DUROVERNUM
CANTIACORUM
(Kent)

See *Canterbury*.

DURRINGTON WALLS
(Wiltshire)

See *Woodhenge*.

DYFFRYN LONG BARROW
(Gwynedd)

The barrow lies at Dyffryn Ardudwy—behind the school and close to the sea— 5 mi. (8 km.) N. of Barmouth along the coast of Cardigan Bay. Carefully excavated and restored in 1961–62, the barrow proved to have covered two separate tombs, the oldest a portal tomb of a type common in Ireland—two tall portal stones topped by a single slanting capstone, and covered by a round cairn of pebbles. From pottery found at the entrance this tomb seems to date as far back as 3000 BC. A later, rectangular chamber was built to the E. and its long barrow was built to take in the earlier tomb. Pottery from the later Neolithic and Early Bronze Age came from the second tomb, and it was formally closed in prehistory. The barrow is in state care. Inland from Tal-y-bont, about a mile S. of Dyffryn on the coast, two more long barrows lie side by side on a hillside at Carneddau Hengwm—as difficult of access as Dyffryn is easy. The southern barrow is the largest, about 200 ft. long, and seems again to be of two different periods, the eastern chamber again a portal tomb much like that at *Pentre-Ifan* S. of Cardigan (see *Newport*, Dyfed). A second small chamber in the center is approached by a short passage from the N. side. The northern, smaller barrow again has a chamber, possibly two, at the E. end and another at the center, now roofless. Close by are the remnants of two stone circles, both set together on a raised platform.

EARLS BARTON
(Northamptonshire)

Outstanding Anglo-Saxon church tower of All Saints in the center of the village of Earls Barton, between Northampton and Wellingborough, 4 mi. (6.5 km.) SW of the latter. The church as a whole and the top parapet of the tower is Norman or later; however, the substantial tower is 10th-cent. Anglo-Saxon and is well-known for its elaborate, even exuberant stripwork decoration in four stages, with double round-headed windows, triangular-headed windows and five narrow pillared openings at the belfry stage. The stripwork may owe something to timber prototypes.

EBORACUM
(North Yorkshire)

See *York*.

EDDISBURY HILL FORT
(Cheshire)

Or Castle Ditches, on private property 11 mi. (17.75 km.) E. of Chester, near Delamere village; very difficult to find. However, here is a quite substantial Iron Age oval fort with double ramparts enclosing 11 acres. It has an elaborate in-turned entrance, originally built of timber-laced stone in the 1st cent. BC and equipped with guard chambers. The hill was occupied as far back as about 600 BC. In the 3rd cent. part of it was fortified with a single rampart and the rest was built in the 1st cent.; but despite these defenses the fort was destroyed by the Romans from nearby *Chester* (the 20th Legion) in the early years AD. It was reoccupied in Anglo-Saxon times (10th cent.) by Queen Aethelflaed, Alfred's daughter, as a defensive point against the infiltration of Norse Vikings from Ireland.

EGGARDON HILL FORT
(Dorset)

Magnificent Iron Age hill fort on a high promontory overlooking the west country from the final westward point of the chalk of southern England. It lies 5 mi. (8 km.) NE of Bridport, N. of Askerswell. Three ramparts and ditches, widely spaced in the outer sections, enclose the fort, and its entrances are staggered. Numerous hollows inside seem to have been storage pits, and there are remains of what appear to be two Bronze Age barrows.

ELISEG'S PILLAR
(Clwyd)

Famous Welsh monument, 2 mi. (3.25 km.) N. of Llangollen, with an intriguing history. A damaged cross shaft stands 8 ft. high on a low barrow, its inscription no longer legible. But as copied in the 17th cent., it is a dedication by Prince Cyngen of Powys, who died in Rome in 854 AD, to his great-grandfather, the 8th-cent. king of Powys who was the most deadly opponent of Offa, the great Saxon king of Mercia. *Offa's Dyke*, only a few mi. E. of the monument, was built by the king to mark the border between Saxon England and British Wales.

EOFORWIC
(North Yorkshire)

See *York*.

ESCOMB
(Durham)

Simple, austere Anglo-Saxon church, 2 mi. (3.25 km.) W. of Bishop Auckland, which has survived almost intact, except for the porch and windows, from the 7th cent. AD—probably the earliest and best-preserved of all Saxon churches. It is largely built of fine ashlar stone blocks robbed from the nearby Roman fort

The charming little Anglo-Saxon church of Escomb in Durham county, one of the few dating from the 7th cent. The large, well-shaped stone blocks visible in the wall were robbed from the nearby Roman fort of Vindovia at Binchester. (Courtesy of Philip Dixon.)

of Vindovia at *Binchester*, and its chancel arch in the interior was lifted entire from some building in the same Roman ruin. The church has a plain nave and square chancel, and high up on the S. exterior wall is an early Saxon sundial decorated with a carved serpent. Excavations in 1968 on the site of a former N. porticus turned up fragments of Saxon colored window glass. The church's present porch has a small display.

**EXETER
(Devon)**

Principal town of Devon, the Roman Isca Dumnoniorum or administrative capital of the Dumnonii. The street grid in the old city follows the Roman pattern, and since World War II, when there was heavy German bombing, excavations where possible have revealed some of the remains of Isca, though nothing worth preserving. Isca began with a legionary fortress of about 38 acres, parts of which have been identified as well as a legionary bath in the cathedral close, excavated in 1971–77. The massive 3rd-cent. city wall, overlaid by medieval work here and there, can be traced around much of its circuit. Finds from the Roman city, as well as prehistoric materials from nearby *Dartmoor*, are exhibited in the Rougemont House Museum.

FALDOUET DOLMEN

See *Jersey*.

**FERNACRE
(Cornwall)**

See *Bodmin Moor*.

FERNWORTHY
(Devon)

See *Dartmoor.*

FFRIDD FALDWYN
(Powys)

Iron Age hill fort overlooking Montgomery on its E. just inside Wales, partially excavated in 1934–39. There was occupation on this high promontory in the Neolithic period, but the first fortification, a double palisade around the summit, dates from the 3rd cent. BC. This was replaced by ramparts reinforced with timbers, a third line of defense, and a bridged entranceway—all of which was burned at some point, vitrifying the stone. In the 1st cent. BC the fort, entirely rebuilt, reached its greatest complexity with another rampart, faced with stone, a ditch, and elaborate entrance works on the E. and W. The approach of the Romans in the 1st cent. AD led to hasty repair work, but the fort was soon abandoned.

FIGSBURY RINGS
(Wiltshire)

Rather typical Iron Age hill fort on a chalk promontory with a fine view, 4 mi. (6.5 km.) NE of *Salisbury*, 1 mi. (1.6 km.) E. of Winterbourne Dauntsey. A single rampart and ditch enclose about 15 acres; however, well within this circuit is a curious single ditch with no bank—either a fort quarry, a cattle enclosure or perhaps the remains of an earlier henge or causewayed camp. Speculation is rife.

FISHBOURNE ROMAN
PALACE
(West Sussex)

Opulent Roman palace, 1.5 mi. (2.6 km.) W. of Chichester, the largest and most remarkable Roman structure in Britain. It was excavated for eight seasons from 1961 by Barry Cunliffe after its accidental discovery in 1960. It is now open to the public. The excavator was astonished to find that this palatial structure, covering 10 acres, its four wings enclosing a garden courtyard, was built as early as the years immediately following 75 AD when Britain, still being subdued, was very much a frontier province. For here was a splendid display of long corridors, colonnades, and suites of rooms luxuriously decorated with painted walls, stucco work and magnificent mosaic floors, of gardens, statues and fountains, all constructed by skilled craftsmen especially imported from the continent and Italy itself, working in the latest styles with expensive imported materials from abroad. The marbles, for example, came from France, Spain, Italy, Greece and Turkey. In size and grandeur the palace was comparable to the imperial palaces of the period on the Palatine Hill in Rome, and was not to be equaled in Europe outside Italy until the 3rd and 4th cents. AD.

It now seems almost certain that the palace was built for the aging Cogidubnus, the client king of the Atrebates, who had been staunch allies of Rome since about 15 BC and had greatly facilitated the Roman conquest in its early stages. There is simply no other candidate. Moreover, an inscription from a temple of Neptune and Minerva, found in Chichester in 1723 (and now in the town's assembly rooms) names Cogidubnus as "king and legate of the emperor in Britain." It is very likely, though not proved, that the young Cogidubnus had spent some time in Rome as an exile and may have been brought back by the Romans during the invasion of 43 AD.

After the initial invasion the site of Fishbourne, on an inlet from the sea, became (as the excavations showed) a military supply base for Vespasian's conquest of the West, equipped with long timber storage buildings, two of which have been excavated. The nearby harbor has been located, though not dug to date, and presumably the road from it led to a fort to the E., now buried under

Chichester. When the armies moved on, the site became a civilian area with streets and a number of buildings, one of which was a substantial timber house with painted plaster walls and a verandah. In the late '60s this was replaced by a luxurious stone-built country house with a colonnaded garden, painted walls, mosaic floors and a bath suite. It can be supposed that this mansion, and also its timber predecessor, had also been built for or by Cogidubnus whose capital city, Noviomagus Regnensium, now Chichester, was rising nearby. (The Regnenses were the southern Atrebates.)

At some time after 75 AD the present palace was being constructed, incorporating the former mansion into its SE corner. It was designed to impress, not only with the wealth Cogidubnus had gained by serving Rome but also with the might of Rome itself. The visitor from Chichester entered through a spacious colonnaded entrance hall in the E. wing beyond which, across a pool and the garden, could be glimpsed the apsed audience hall or "throne room" in the W. wing, entered by steps up to a portico. The owner's apartments and the former bath suite occupied the S. wing, which had colonnades on both sides, the outside one looking down over another garden to the water. More living apartments flanked the entrance hall in the E. wing, and the N. wing grouped a series of sumptuous rooms into suites around two colonnaded private apartments. These were for important guests. At the E. end of the wing was an enormous hall with aisles. All the rooms were sumptuously decorated with inlaid marbles, painted walls, stucco friezes and mosaic floors—perhaps 60 of these originally, though few survive today.

The great central garden, originally 250 ft. by 320 ft., was laid out with paths and box borders in formal patterns, varied with trees, shrubs and fountains. The excavated northern half of the garden (most of the southern half of the palace is lost under the modern road and village) has been replanted following the lines of the original bedding trenches, which were exposed, along with the lead water pipes, in the excavation, thus restoring what is said to be the only formal garden known in Europe outside Italy.

Today only the northern wing, tastefully preserved under a sleek modern building, is open to the visitor, who enters it through a small but most informative museum. Of the visible mosaics at the site, only about half survive from the original palace. Though these are mostly geometric they must have been laid at vast expense by craftsmen imported from Italy, long before there were any workshops in Britain. After Cogidubnus' death, probably at the end of the century, the palace was rebuilt, with two new bath suites—suggesting that it had been subdivided into a number of separate apartments—more hypocausts for heating (the original builders did not know the British climate!) and new mosaics. The best of these, from the mid-2nd cent. AD, include two fine figured mosaics, the Shell and Dolphin. In the 3rd cent. another, inferior, mosaic floor was laid down. Then, sometime toward the end of that century, the palace was utterly destroyed in a fierce fire, set by accident or possibly by pirate raiders.

Of Roman Chichester little is left, except for the displays in the local museum. Some of the Roman bastions, added to the town walls in the 4th cent., are still visible, as well as the remains of an earthen amphitheater outside the walls. Noviomagus was a "new town" by definition. A large pre-Roman oppidum lay on the Selsey peninsula to the S.; and to the N. of Chichester the Chichester Dykes, miles of linear earthworks still somewhat visible, protected the town. The *Trundle* hill fort, just N. of Chichester, represents an earlier period of Iron Age occupation.

FISHGUARD
(Dyfed)

See *Newport*.

FIVE KNOLLS
(Bedfordshire)

Group of seven round barrows of different types, the finest such cemetery in the Chilterns, on Dunstable Down about 3 mi. (4.75 km.) W. of Dunstable. Among them three bell barrows lie together inside a ditch. The most northerly of the group, excavated in 1928, yielded a strange assortment of burials: a crouched female with late Neolithic knife, the first occupant, a later cremation burial, 30 or more Anglo-Saxon skeletons laid out in rows, hands tied behind their backs (presumably massacred by their British foes) and several later criminals hanged at some nearby gallows. The finds are in the Luton museum.

FLAG FEN
(Cambridgeshire)

Bronze Age lake village. A remarkable discovery in the fens near Peterborough in 1982 of a well-preserved plank and timber walkway, about 263 ft. long, and subsequently of the timbers of a large house, has led to a major, long-term excavation at Flag Fen. It is already open to the public and is ultimately intended to become an important tourist attraction in future years, comparable to the Jorvik Viking Center in *York*. This will include a visitor center with changing exhibits, guided tours, and, probably later, reconstructed Bronze Age and Iron Age houses. The first phase, with the exhibition center, was opened in July 1987 for English Heritage. The site was originally a large artificial island in a lagoon, over two acres in size, connected to the mainland by the walkway and containing a group of buildings belonging to the Late Bronze Age, around 1000 BC. The first house discovered, its wall timbers and roof supports well-preserved in the moist conditions, is now on display. It was a rectangular long house over 65 ft. in length, with partitions inside and abundant pottery and food remains scattered in the floor. There was evidence of bronze working at the site and indications of two more houses have now been found.

FOALE'S ARRISHES
(Devon)

See *Dartmoor*.

GARN BODUAN
(Gwynedd)

See *Carn Fadrun*.

GARTON SLACK
(Humberside)

See *Great Driffield*.

GELLIGAER ROMAN FORT
(Mid Glamorgan)

Under a field just W. of Gelligaer church, about 6 mi. (9.6 km.) NW of Caerphilly, lies a Roman fort of the 2nd cent. AD. Though there is little to see now except for the mounds of the ramparts excavated in 1899–1901, the dig did bring to light the complete foundations of a model fort of 3.7 acres, solidly built of long-lasting masonry with stone ramparts, angle towers, fortified gates and the normal barracks, granaries, commandant's quarters and streets within. It was built and then occupied for most of the 2nd cent., then reoccupied in the late 3rd or early 4th cent., when an annex was built to the SE that included the regimental baths. An investigation of a rectangular earthwork to the W. of the fort, no longer visible, showed that it was a larger, predecessor fort (6 acres)—a marching camp or temporary fort of the 1st cent. campaigns. The finds and plans of the Gelligaer fort are well set forth in *Cardiff's* National Museum. On nearby Gelligaer

Common to the N. a number of practice camps can be traced, as well as some 15 Bronze Age cairns.

GIANT'S CASTLE.   See *Scilly Isles*.

GIANTS' HILLS   See *Skegness*.
(Lincolnshire)

GIB HILL   See *Arbor Low*.
(Derbyshire)

GLASTONBURY   Noted early Christian center and medieval shrine, haunted by legends of King
(Somerset)   Arthur, who was traditionally buried here, and by folk memories of the earliest years of Christianity in England. The ruins of its great abbey lie under the steep Glastonbury Tor. The Tor itself was found in 1965 to be the site of early chapels and a Dark Ages settlement (6th cent. AD). The first monastery was founded at Glastonbury as early as 600 AD and excavations at the abbey in the 1950s were able to trace an interesting sequence of buildings, the earliest crudely constructed of wattle and daub. The first stone construction was that of King Ine of Wessex, built in 705, a church with flanking chapels, each with painted plaster walls and chipped stone floors. Finally, under Bishop Dunstan in the 10th cent., when the monastery had become one of the richest and most important in England, there was a complete rebuilding and enlargment of the complex. From this period dates the rare Anglo-Saxon glass furnaces uncovered at the site.

Glastonbury is equally well known for its famous Iron Age lake villages, excavated between 1892 and 1907—Glastonbury Village about a mi. (1.6 km.) N. of the present town, and Meare Village, 3.5 mi. (5.6 km.) to the NW. Both villages, built for protection on artificial platforms of logs and brushwood in the marshes, were occupied from the 3rd cent. BC up to the Roman period and were found to contain an extraordinarily wide variety of organic materials well-preserved in the damp conditions—baskets, wooden tubs, wheel spokes, iron tools with hafts, dugout canoes, as well as pottery, iron currency bars and bone-work, which indicated large-scale production of woolen textiles (as did the extensive remains of sheep skeletons). Glastonbury Village contained some 60 round huts with clay and wood floors, surrounded by a palisade. Nothing is to be seen at the site today, but many of the finds are preserved in the Tribunal Museum in modern Glastonbury and others are displayed in the Somerset County Museum in Taunton Castle. Other similar materials preserved in the peat of the Somerset Levels may be seen in the Somerset Levels Museum, 1 mi. (1.6 km.) S. of Westhay beyond Meare, in an area still being excavated.

GLOUCESTER   Cathedral and county city, its inner streets still following the grid plan of Roman
(Gloucestershire)   Glevum, a colony based on an initial fort, then a major provincial city that survived into the 5th cent. AD. Much Roman material from the city and region can be viewed in the city museum (including Romano-British and 9th cent. Christian sculpture); close to it the Roman and medieval East gates are displayed. Excavations from 1975 to 1978 at the site of Oswald's Priory (909 to 1643 AD), just N. of the cathedral (marked by several medieval arches) uncovered about 500 graves and much early Christian and medieval material. Its ground plans are now laid out for view.

GOAT'S CAVE
(West Glamorgan)

Or Goat's Hole, a cave washed by the tide, at Paviland on the end of the Gower peninsula, W. of Swansea. Here in 1823 Dean William Buckland, first professor of geology at Oxford, found remains of mammoth, wild horses, hyenas, cave bears, rhinoceros, along with flint and stone tools and objects of ivory and bone, as well as a human skeleton covered with red ochre and wearing a necklace of ivory amulets. This being long before Darwin's day, the dean decided the skeleton was that of a Romano-British lady, thereafter dubbed the "Red Lady of Paviland" and the animal bones had been washed in by the Flood! Recent investigations have shown that the "lady," now in Oxford's University Museum, was probably a Paleolithic hunter of the Cro-Magnon type about 25,000 years old, carbon-dated rather insecurely to 16,510 bc, and the animal bones including mammoth, belonged to the earlier Aurignacian period some 10,000 years before him. This is, to date, the oldest burial known in Britain. Other Paleolithic cave dwellings on the peninsula are Bacon's Hole, Long Hole and Cat's Hole, the latter belonging to the British Creswellian period (see *Creswell Crags*). See also *Cheddar*; *Hengistbury Head*; *Jersey* (La Cotte de Brelade); *Pontnewydd*.

GOLDSBOROUGH
(North Yorkshire)

See *Scarborough Head*.

GORS FAWR
(Dyfed)

Stone circle, 10 mi. (16 km.) S. of Cardigan and a few mi. N. of Mynachlog-ddu in Pembrokeshire, just S. of the Preseli Mtns. This impressive ring, typical of others in Wales, is made up of low boulders in a circle 76 ft. across. They are graded in height toward the S., and 16 survive. Roughly to the N. and well outside the circle are two taller standing stones, their astronomical purpose, if any, not clear.

GOSFORTH CROSS
(Cumbria)

High cross in the Gosforth churchyard, 12 mi. SE of Whitehaven, one of the finest Anglo-Scandinavian sculptures in England. Gosforth lies in an area that was settled by Vikings from Ireland in the 10th cent. and the cross shows influences from the Irish high crosses. The elegant tapering shaft, rounded in the lower part, squared towards the middle where sculptured panels begin, is of red sandstone and is 14½ ft. high on a stepped base. It probably belongs to the early 10th cent. The lower part is decorated in typical Viking Borre-style ring-chain patterns. The panels of jumbled figures and interlaced serpents show scenes from Scandinavian mythology. The only Christian motif, aside from the cross itself, is a Christ crucified on one face. Inside the church is a collection of early carved stones found on the site, many again showing Scandinavian motifs. See also *Halton*; *Middleton Crosses*.

GOUGH'S CAVE
(Somerset)

See *Cheddar*.

GRAIG LWYD AXE
FACTORY
(Gwynedd)

See *Penmaenmawr*.

GRASSINGTON
(West Yorkshire)

See *Ilkley*.

GREAT CASTERTON
(Leicestershire)

Roman town a few mi. NW of Stamford, off the main road. Here was an early fort and a posting station on Ermine Street, later a settled area around a walled town of about 15 acres that now lies under and to the E. of the village. An impressive stretch of the defenses is visible to the NE, consisting of a huge flat ditch 60 ft. wide and the mounds of the rampart behind it, dating from a reconstruction after 354 AD, probably on the orders of Count Theodosius. The wall was equipped with rectangular bastions to hold catapults shooting across the ditch. Excavations in the 1950s showed that the first wall was built in the late 2nd cent. with a series of V-shaped ditches in front of it, and the outlines of the early temporary fort were discovered from the air in 1959 just E. of the village. Even farther E. a substantial, mid-4th-cent. villa was excavated (now filled in). The villa had been burned later in the century; but life probably continued inside the walled town into the 5th cent.

GREATCHESTERS
(Northumberland)

See *Hadrian's Wall.*

GREAT DRIFFIELD
(Humberside)

Or Driffield, about 28 mi. (45 km.) E. of *York*, a convenient center for a remarkable group of late Iron Age sites on the Yorkshire chalk wolds; of great archaeological interest though there is little now to see on the ground. In the wold area alone several thousand Iron Age graves of a special type are known, singly, in small groups, or in large cemeteries of several hundred barrows. Many were spotted from the air. Excavation has shown that these are crouched inhumation burials under a small mound enclosed within a square ditch—which is the most obvious feature from the air. Of these a few here and there are richly furnished chariot burials, obviously of the elite, though not all of warriors; for a number are of women. The chariot burials strongly suggest European parallels, and indeed it is thought that these people, probably the Parisi from France, were recent Celtic migrants from the continent, probably in the 4th cent. BC.

Their culture is now known as the Arras culture from the first group of barrows excavated, mostly around 1815, at Arras W. of Market Weighton, about 15 mi. (or 24 km.) SW of Driffield. This mid-2nd-cent. cemetery contained at least 100 barrows, though only three are still visible today. Of the chariot burials here, one was of an old man buried with his chariot and two horses, another of a woman with her chariot and an iron mirror, a third of a woman with a rich assortment of jewelry including a necklace of glass beads and a gold ring. Of a similar cemetery called Dane's Graves, about 4 mi. (6.5 km.) N. of Driffield, some hundreds survive out of the original 500 or so. Many of them were opened in the 19th cent., including a chariot burial of a presumed warrior and his charioteer.

In most recent years other cemeteries have been excavated, using modern archaeology methods—the first in the 1970s at a site between Burton Fleming and *Rudston,* W. of Bridlington on the coast and N. of Driffield. Here a sampling of 250 barrows was excavated, each with a few grave goods such as a brooch, pot or bracelet. But the most extensive and richest excavations have been in the long gravel valley leading W. up into the wolds from Driffield through Garton to Wetwang. In 1963 gravel digging began in the valley, which destroyed another cemetery at Garton Slack. Thereafter the archaeologists were busy in advance of gravel digging, uncovering not only barrows but also Roman and Saxon remains. In 1971 Tony Brewster found another chariot burial well E. of Wetwang Slack;

then from 1975 to 1979 his successor, John Dent, opened a total of 446 barrows at Wetwang Slack in one of the largest Iron Age cemeteries excavated in Europe, exploring also house sites (over 80 round houses), roads and field boundaries of the period. But this cemetery contained no chariot burials.

Excavations ceased in 1981, though quarrying continued. Then in 1984, in a dramatic development, three chariot graves were found close together, perhaps of the same family, the two male burials containing weapons—swords, spearheads and a shield. The pattern of these chariot burials was now clear: the body laid N. to S. between the two wheels of the dismantled chariot with the yoke laid along the W. side of the body. Most of the grave goods, including horse bits and the body, were usually found inside the remains of a large wooden box or compartment, and in most cases numerous pig bones were found with the burials. The third and largest burial at Wetwang was that of a young woman and her chariot along with horse bits, a pin made of gold, iron and coral, an iron mirror, and a unique round bronze canister with a chain, dubbed the "bean tin." It was perhaps a ritual object and was decorated, as were the sword scabbards and other objects, with swirling Celtic designs.

In 1985 13 more barrows were excavated at Garton Station a few mi. down the valley, the largest proving to be another chariot burial—the largest Iron Age grave found in Britain. Here the wheels were leaning against the grave walls, the framework of the chariot had been apparently laid over the body, and there was no box. As of 1986, 13 chariot burials had been found in this area alone, only two with weapons, and two more probably of women. The finds from Wetwang Slack and Garton have been displayed in the British Museum.

Moving NE from Driffield to Flamborough Head one finds another Iron Age survival, the Dane's Dyke, a huge bank up to 18 ft. high with a wide ditch on the landward side. It runs 2.5 mi. (4 km.) N. to S. across the Head. Inland from Flamborough Head, a mi. (1.6 km.) SE of Knapton, is an Iron Age farmstead, Staple Howe, originally a large, oval, stone-built hut on a hilltop, protected by a palisade, of about 500 BC. Later this was replaced by two smaller timber-built huts and a granary. Hearths, ovens and the remains of a loom were found in the huts. The site is now on view. See also *Duggleby Howe* and *Rudston*, both in this region.

GREAT PAXTON
(Cambridgeshire)

Substantial Anglo-Saxon church of Holy Trinity, about 3 mi. (4.75 km.) N. of St. Neot's. Only the late Saxon nave arcades and clerestory windows survive in the later fabric, and the original nave is cut short by the later western tower. Nevertheless the arcades are impressively large and the whole nave spacious so that the view down it into the raised chancel (on Saxon lines) must have been awe-inspiring. The columns of the nave piers sport unusual bulbous capitals. Excavations have shown that there was a north transept (and probably a southern one too) and its great entrance arch survives in part. The church stood on a manor held by the pious Edward the Confessor, which may explain its unusual size and splendor.

GREAT WITCOMBE
ROMAN VILLA
(Gloucestershire)

Late Roman courtyard villa, 6 mi. (9.6 km.) SE of *Gloucester*, off the main road to the S. and open to the public. The remains are under sheds. Arranged around three sides of a courtyard, the villa was built about 250–270 AD and much altered thereafter up to about 400. The site is beautiful but treacherous, the hillside being seamed with springs requiring extensive shoring up to prevent the villa from sliding down the hill. Two of the rooms, one octagonal, the other with a basin at the center, have been tentatively identified as shrines to the local water spirits who presumably caused the trouble! There are some good geometric mosaic floors, and from the later period, in the frigidarium of the baths in the SW corner, some crude but spirited mosaics of aquatic animals—fish, dolphins, eels. See also *Chedworth Villa*; *Cirencester*; *Lydney*.

GREENSTED SAXON CHURCH (Essex)

Charming little Anglo-Saxon church at Greensted-juxta-Ongar, 10 mi. (16 km.) W. of Chelmsford, sole relic of the many timber churches in England of Saxon and earlier times. Though the chancel arch is Norman and the chancel dates from about 1500 AD, the nave is a miraculous survival from an earlier period. Its walls are constructed of split oak logs, placed upright and joined together by tongue and groove and morticed at top and bottom into heavy horizontal timbers. This work probably dates as far back as about 850 AD, and the church may have served as one of the resting places for the body of St. Edmund when it was carried from East Anglia to London in 1013 to escape the Danes. Excavations in 1960 showed that there had been an earlier church under the present one.

GREY WETHERS (Devon)

See *Dartmoor*.

GRIMES GRAVES (Norfolkshire)

Famous Neolithic flint-mining area near Weeting, about 5 mi. (8 km.) NW of Brandon in Suffolk where flint-knapping is still carried out. This major ancient industrial area is closely comparable to, though later than, the less well-known

A view of some of the deep galleries open to the public at the Neolithic flint-mining area of Grimes Graves, Norfolk. The galleries, out of which the miners hewed the flint nodules with crude antler picks, were reached by shafts up to 30 ft. deep. (Courtesy of English Heritage.)

mining area at *Cissbury Ring* in West Sussex. At Grimes Graves an expanse of about 34 acres is closely packed with over 360 depressions marking the filled-in shafts and open pits of the ancient miners. Working with antler picks to extract the nodules and baskets to raise them with, they fashioned most of the flints into axes that were widely exported. Some of the shafts were up to 30 ft. deep with radiating galleries at the bottom, and the visitor today can descend one such shaft to view the galleries. In another shallow, disused shaft a remarkable shrine was found—a small, crude chalk statuette of a voluptuous Mother Goddess placed on a ledge, and in front of it a pile of flint nodules and antler picks by way of offerings to propitiate the goddess, with a chalk phallus placed on top of the pile. From under a roof the visitor can now look down into the shrine, which contains replicas of the fertility objects in their original positions. The shafts have been carbon-dated to between 3000 and 2500 BC. The finds, and a reconstruction of a mine, are in the Norwich Castle museum.

GRIMSPOUND VILLAGE (Devon)   See *Dartmoor.*

GUERNSEY   One of the largest of the *Channel Islands*. The main islands abound in Megalithic monuments, in many cases an extension of the rich Neolithic cultures of nearby France at Carnac. On Guernsey there are magnificent passage tombs, many with their covering mounds still intact; and most can be entered. The largest is La Verde in Vale parish in the northern part of the island, 3.5 mi. (5.6 km.) N. of St. Peter Port at the western end of L'Ancresse Common. It is a typical bottle-shaped chambered tomb of the islands, on a hill. There is a short passage under a mound leading into a chamber measuring 33 ft. by 12 ft. and 7 ft. high. The side slabs support a roof of six massive capstones, the largest 16 ft. long by 10 ft. wide.

The next largest is Le Déhus, or L'Autel de Déhus, at Paradis, again in Vale parish near the NE coast 5 mi. (8 km.) N. of St. Peter Port. Again bottle-shaped and lying under its original mound, it is entered by a passage 11 ft. long leading into a burial chamber 20 ft. by 11 ft., with four small side chambers opening into it. Seven huge capstones form the roof and on one of them a human figure is scratched—face, hands and arms, with an enigmatic crescent symbol below it. Le Creux des Faies, another passage grave in St. Peter in the Wood parish just SE of Fort Saumarez, measures 28 ft. by 10 ft. in all, its chamber covered by two large capstones. The view of the rocky western coast from here is magnificent. Finally, the smaller tomb of Le Trepied in St. Peter in the Wood parish, with a fine view over Le Catiorac Point, contains a chamber only 18 ft. by 6 ft., covered by three capstones on 4 ft. uprights. Le Trepied was formerly a famous gathering place for witches.

The menhirs, or standing stones, of Guernsey are equally interesting. Best-known is La Gran'mère du Chimquière, or Great Mother of the Churchyard. Its top is carved into the semblance of a woman with head and shoulders and bared breasts, obviously a fertility figure and probably of the Bronze Age. She once stood in the churchyard of St. Martin de la Bellieuse, 1.5 mi. (2.6 km.) S. of St. Peter Port, and as late as the 19th cent. local people would leave offerings of fruit and flowers in a hollowed stone at her feet. Considered an idol, some pious vicar broke her in half, and she now stands 5 ft. high as one of the gate-posts of the churchyard. Another effigy stone, the Catel Menhir, not as well fashioned, stands 6½ ft. high in the churchyard of the Catel parish church, 2 mi. (3.25 km.) W. of St. Peter Port.

In 1978 a mound on L'Ancresse Common, NW Guernsey, was discovered by chance. It was not far from La Verde and Le Déhus and was thought to be another chambered tomb. But upon excavation from 1979 on it proved to contain a remarkable sequence of remains, quite unique on Guernsey. At the bottom were the postholes and artifacts of a very early Neolithic farming settlement of the early 4th millennium BC. Next on the site came a mortuary structure of two small cists covered with boulders and a single capstone, with a standing stone at one end. From this level came a unique pot of a kind found only at the site of Manio in Brittany. In the late 4th millennium BC a burial mound was erected over this with a kerb of slabs and boulders and a facade of upright slabs at one end and an entrance leading into a burial chamber. This tomb was finally sealed around the mid-3rd millennium, and later a timber building of large posts, surrounded by huge boulders, appeared on the top of the mound, possibly a mortuary house. It was dismantled about 2000 BC. Finally, Gallo-Roman field systems appeared around the mound before all was covered by blown sand.

The Guernsey Museum and Art Gallery, a well-organized modern institution in a public park in St. Peter Port, displays much material found in the chambered tombs, as well as a famous collection of Bronze Age weapons and tools found in *Alderney* island. See also *Jersey*.

GURNARD'S HEAD (Cornwall)

Long rocky promontory off the NW coast of Cornwall's westerly peninsula near *Zennor*, in an area rich in antiquities (see also *St. Ives*). There are a number of chambered round cairns here like that at *Penzance*, but the promontory is known for its Iron Age fort cutting off the headland with a defensive system of two banks and ditches. Archaeological investigation indicated that the main rampart, roughly 180 ft. long, had been built of stone, sloping on the outside and stepped on the inside. It still stands about 6 ft. high in places. In front of it were two ditches cut into the rock, with a rubble bank in between and an apparently unfinished third ditch. In the interior, on the eastern side, remnants of 13 hut circles can still be seen. The pottery here dated from the 1st cent. BC.

HADDISCOE (Norfolk)

The church of St. Mary's with a round Anglo-Saxon tower, perched high above a river 4 mi. (6.5 km.) N. of Beccles, on the Beccles-Yarmouth road. These round church towers are common all over Norfolk, with some in Suffolk too; built mostly in Saxon and Norman times for lack of any local stone better than flint and pebbles. The tower of St. Mary's, of flint, is late Anglo-Saxon except for the medieval parapet, and is divided by string courses into four stages. High up are four narrow double windows with tall triangular heads, and below them small round-headed windows. The tower arch inside is also Saxon, and the nave may be too.

HADRIAN'S WALL (Tyne and Wear/ Northumberland/ Cumbria)

Magnificent Roman stone barrier, built 122–128 AD to delimit Rome's northern frontier in Britain. Running 73 miles from Newcastle-upon-Tyne to Bowness on Solway Firth, it is the finest survival of the long Roman occupation of Britain and the most complex engineering feat of all the *limes* (frontier defense lines) that protected the empire, from North Africa to the Levant to the Danube and Rhine rivers. Over a million yards of stone went into it, reflecting the Roman

A well-preserved stretch of Hadrian's Wall, one of the finest Roman monuments in northern Europe. It runs 73 miles across the hilly country of northern England and can be traversed by the tourist for most of its length. Now largely excavated and consolidated, it is a remarkable surviving tribute to the genius of the Roman military engineers. (Courtesy of the British Tourist Authority, New York.)

genius for organization and engineering. After years of piecemeal excavation and restoration from the 19th cent. to the present, much of the wall, which runs boldly up and downhill through some of the most spectacular scenery in Britain, has now been laid bare as a major tourist site.

When General Agricola was abruptly recalled in 85 AD after he had in effect subdued all of Scotland (see *Inchtuthil* in Scotland), his conquests were given up and the frontier was eventually established, shortly after 100 AD, on the line of Stanegate, a military road Agricola had built across the island, with a few forts on it, in 80 AD. This was the course adopted roughly for Hadrian's Wall. It was not a naturally defensible line, and when there was a dangerous native uprising the Emperor Hadrian came to Britain in 122 AD to see what could be done to improve it. The result was the wall, built not so much as a defense against the northern tribes but rather as an artificial frontier, delimiting the area of Roman dominance and separating the still hostile Brigantes to the S. from the Scottish tribes to the N. Originally it was built of stone westward to the Irthing River, the rest to the Solway Firth of turf; but by 163 AD the turf wall had been rebuilt in stone. The wall was about 20 ft. high with a 6-ft. parapet along the top. At every Roman mile along the wall there was a milecastle, each holding up to 50 soldiers. Between each pair of milecastles were two turrets or watchtowers, about 30 ft. high and built of stone with two stories and a sloping roof. In all some 2,000 auxiliary troops were required to man and patrol the wall. Detachments from all three legions in Britain built the wall but did not necessarily man it.

N. of the wall ran a ditch, about 27 ft. wide and 9 ft. deep, and S. of it, often at some distance, the vallum, a flat-bottomed ditch about 20 ft. wide with level platforms and two heavy banks on either side. The vallum could only be crossed by causeways at certain points, often at a milecastle or fort. Not really a defense, the vallum's purpose was undoubtedly to delimit the wall's military zone and to control the movements of the restless Brigantes to the S. As building progressed there were changes. The wall was to be 10 ft. wide; this was narrowed to 8 ft. later so that both dimensions are found—sometimes an 8-ft. wall was built on 10-ft. foundations! The turf wall was rebuilt at 9 ft. The wall was also extended in the E. from Newcastle to Wallsend, and in the W. a system of forts, smaller forts and watchtowers extended the defenses S. for 40 mi. (64 km.) along the Cumbrian coast (see *Hardknott Castle; Maryport*). Above all it was decided to move the fighting forces from the Stanegate line up to the wall itself, and eventually 16 new forts were built, each holding 500 to 1,000 men. The Stanegate Agricolan forts became supply bases behind the wall.

Only about 17 years after its completion the wall was evacuated and the frontier moved up to the new *Antonine Wall* in Scotland, finished about 145 AD. Here the frontier remained, with one brief interruption, until about 163 when it was permanently moved back to Hadrian's line. During the next centuries the wall was thrice denuded of troops by pretenders to the imperial throne, allowing the barbarians to overrun it with varying amounts of damage. Each time it was repaired, first by Severus, who then carried out his Scottish campaigns (208–211), later by Constantius, father of Constantine, in 306. The great barbarian revolt of 367 destroyed it again, after which it was recommissioned by Count Theodosius in 369–70. But the end was close. More trouble in 383 left the wall only partly defended and by 400 the last Roman troops had left.

The visible remains of the wall are abundant and varied. A quick view of the more interesting sites would start, in the usual E. to W. sequence, with South Shields (Tyne and Wear), well to the eastward of the wall's end. Here was the fort of Arbeia, built by Hadrian to protect the Tynemouth port on the S. side. In 162 an extra granary was added, and for the Severan campaigns of 208–11 the fort became a major supply base with four barracks and no less than 27 granaries. With some alterations the fort was occupied through the 4th cent. The site today, in an industrial area and difficult to find, is being excavated and consolidated. The fort wall, three of the gates, the *principia* and granaries are on display, and there is a small site museum.

Newcastle-upon-Tyne, formerly a station on the wall, whose route has been traced through the city, has a rich display of Roman materials, mostly from the wall, in the University Museum of Antiquities. There is a scale model of the wall and a reproduction of the Mithraeum at Carrawburgh. The museum also displays collections from the prehistoric through the Saxon periods. At Benwell, 2 mi. W. of the city center, the fort of Condercum has been built upon, but a little temple to the Celtic god Antenociticus, only 10 ft. by 16 ft., has been uncovered and preserved with casts of the three altars and a head of the god found there in situ (the originals in Newcastle). Nearby, part of the vallum and the causeway leading over it to the fort, the only causeway now visible, is on view. At Denton, about 1 mi. farther W., there are stretches of the wall, with turret 7b, excavated in 1929, built into one of the stretches.

The first major site is just W. of Corbridge and 2 mi. (3.25 km.) S. of the wall, once the Agricolan fort of Corstopitum on Stanegate (which still bisects the fort), later a supply base and military arsenal. Most of the military remains at Corbridge date from the latter phase (3rd and 4th cents.). There are well-preserved granaries, a vast unfinished storehouse and two military compounds of the arsenal, as well as the shrines of local gods. There was once a sizable town or *vicus* around the base. The small site museum contains the famous Romano-

Celtic sculpture, the Corbridge Lion, shown attacking a stag, as well as a model of the one-time bridge here over the Tyne, whose abutments can still be seen. Another sculptured stone from the site can be seen in the nearby church at Hexham. Along the wall 4 mi. (6.5 km.) farther W. is the exceptionally well-preserved Brunton turret 28b in a stretch of wall, just N. of Low Brunton.

Close by on the W. is the fort and the bridge abutment at Chesters. The abutment of the bridge over the North Tyne (the river has changed its course) is now on dry land. A massive affair, it is a tower 22 ft. square at the end of the wall, which once crossed the river here, its purpose to guard the river and bridge. It was built over the remains of a pier of an earlier bridge and included in it a watermill. The fort of Cilurnum lay across the river to the W. Largely excavated in the 19th cent., it was a cavalry fort with an impressive headquarters building and three of its gates opening N. of the wall for quick sorties. The wall seems to have been completed *after* the fort. The *principia*, quite well preserved, featured arcades around its interior courtyard and is notable today for the barrel vault of the 3rd cent. strong room under it, entered from the regimental chapel. Next to the *principia* on the E. is the commandant's house with a private bath suite and hypocausts. Several towers of the defenses as well as all four gates can be visited and a number of buildings, including some barrack blocks and part of a stable. Outside the walls near the river is the fort's commodious bath house, one wall still standing 10 ft. high, notable for its size, its latrine and the seven niches for holding the bathers' clothes. The Clayton Memorial Museum here shows a model of the fort and has a fine collection from this and other sites.

About 3 mi. (4.75 km.) farther W. was the late-built fort of Bricolitia at Carrawburgh, only a mound now marking the site. (Just E. of it is a dramatic stretch of the vallum.) Fortunately the fort's temple of Mithras, outside it to the W., came to light in 1949 and was excavated the next year. It is now 36 ft. long. Originally constructed after 205 AD, it was soon doubled in size and thereafter several times refurbished. Destroyed by the Picts in 297, it was then completely rebuilt, only to be smashed to pieces early in the 4th cent., presumably by Christians. Three fine altars were discovered in it at the end of the nave, contributed by military prefects, and many other broken statues, tiny altars and inscriptions. These finds, now in the Newcastle museum where they stand within a full-scale replica of the Mithraeum, are reproduced in concrete at the site along with the low benches for the worshipers along the sides of the nave. In a well just to the N., all that remains from a shrine of the water nymph Coventina, a rich haul of coins and other offerings was found. There is a site museum.

Traveling W. 4 mi. (6.5 km.) one comes to the well-known Housesteads site, the Roman Vercovicium, an infantry fort of five acres once housing about 800 men. Dramatically built on a sloping site rising to precipitous cliffs, it is the tourists' favorite, and beyond it both to the E. and the W. the wall snakes up and down along the rocky crests of the ridge, leading on the W. to Milecastle 37 with its stone barrack building and fine N. gate. There is much to see in the fort—all four gates (the W. is the best), the commandant's house, some poor remains of the *principia*, two granaries, barrack blocks, a long storage building against the N. wall where the remains of turret 36b are exposed (built before the fort), internal towers along the fort's wall and another storage building with a bath suite at one end. Of special note is the hospital, the only visible example in Britain, and the beautifully built latrine in the SE corner, fully flushing. Outside the S. gate lay an extensive settlement. Three houses here have been left

The solidly built latrine in the SE corner of the five-acre fort of Virco-vicium at Housesteads on Hadrian's Wall. The flushing channels can be seen running under the site of the wooden seats on either side. (Courtesy of English Heritage.)

exposed, including one where murdered bodies were found secretly buried under the floor. There is a small site museum.

At Chesterholm, S. of Housesteads on the line of the old Stanegate defense system stood the fort of Vindolanda, excavated in the 1930s. It also had a *vicus* or civilian settlement around it, and in a deliberate attempt to find out more about such settlements extensive excavations were undertaken by the Vindolanda Trust in recent years, exposing a *mansio* or posting inn and a bath suite. Most notable however, and widely reported, was the recovery, remarkable in the local wet conditions, of masses of well-preserved organic materials from the houses of the *vicus*—domestic rubbish of all kinds, many items of leather, particularly shoes, and especially wooden writing tablets that have thrown much light on the day-to-day life in such a settlement. Excavation of the fort itself, newly rebuilt in the early 3rd cent. and several times rebuilt in the 4th cent., revealed an Agricolan and an Antonine fort beneath the later one. Of the latter one can see the N. and W. gates, part of the fort's walls, and the headquarters. Moreover reconstructions on the site have recreated stone and turf sections of the wall, a turret, and a wooden milecastle gate. There is also a museum.

Between Chesterholm and Birdoswald, about 10 mi. (16 km.) to the W., are a number of lesser sites. A few mi. to the W., back on the wall, one reaches its highest point at Winshiels (1,230 ft. high) with superb views and milecastle 40—

built of small stones more easily transportable to this remote area. There is also a good stretch of the wall to the W. Moving on to Cawfields, about 5 mi. (8 km.) beyond Housesteads, one can see first the mounds of a small early wall fort just E. of Haltwhistle Burn before coming on milecastle 42. Both gates of the milecastle are built of massive masonry, and that of the S. gate still stands 6 ft. high. At the end of the restored wall running E. is a curiosity. The wall climbs a hill so steep that its courses are laid almost at right angles to the slope of the hillside—a tribute to Roman engineering! About 1 mi. (1.6 km.) farther on the younger fort of Aesica (about 128 AD) at Greatchesters is much overgrown and ruinous. It lies entirely S. of the line of the wall and is notable for its W. gate and a bath suite S. of it fed by a 6-mi. channel aqueduct. At Walltown, about 3 mi. (4.75 km.) W., one of the finest stretches of the wall runs westward from turret 45a. To its E. lies turret 45b. N. of the main road in this region is an interesting, private Roman Army Museum at Carvoran House, opened in 1981, with models, reconstructions and audiovisual displays. At Willowford above Gilsland is another bridge abutment, where the wall crossed the Irthing River; and a complex series of structures covering three periods, with a fine stretch of the wall, incorporating turrets 48a and b, running down to it. Here are the remains of piers, culverts, a tower, and a paved river emplacement for a millwheel.

On the other side of the Irthing, 2 mi. (3.25 km.) to the W., is the fort of Camboglanna at Birdoswald on a promontory overlooking a bend of the river. Here the defenses are perhaps the best-preserved of all the forts—the main S. and E. gates (the latter is the finest), internal towers, an angle tower and a postern gate. The fort, originally built on the old turf wall, shows rebuilding into the 4th cent. Fine stretches of the later stone wall (farther N. than the turf wall) can be seen on the E., with milecastle 49, and to the W. with turret 49b. About 4 mi. (6.5 km.) farther on at Banks are two final sites: E. of the village at Banks East are the imposing remains of turret 52a with the stone wall on either side of it. W. of the village at Banks Burn is milecastle 53, with a fine length of the wall running westward from it. From here to Bowness there is little of the wall left to see. Stanwix fort, buried under a northern suburb of Carlisle, was the largest fort on the wall and headquarters of its commander, garrisoned by a 1,000-man cavalry regiment. Across the river at Carlisle was the flourishing Roman town of Luguvalium. Probes in the 1980s have produced substantial remains of a fort here, just S. of the Castle and probably built by Agricola about 79–80 AD as part of his Stanegate line, as well as timber and stone Roman houses in the area of the Lanes and Blackfriars street. The existence of a major legionary fortress underneath the town is a possibility, though so far no evidence has turned up. Carlisle's Tullie House Museum houses, with other exhibits, another rich collection of Roman finds, mainly from the wall.

HALLIGYE
(Cornwall)

The finest example of a *fogou* in Cornwall (see also *Chysauster*), near Trelowarren at the base of the Lizard peninsula. The site was a fortified Iron Age homestead or settlement, with double ramparts. The subterranean *fogou*, running in part under the inner rampart, was T-shaped and 54 ft. long, its sides and roof made of heavy slabs. It was used either for cold storage or for refuge. A low block of stone just inside one of the entrances would have caused any hostile intruder to stumble—if the *fogou* actually was used as a refuge. A light is needed to explore it. Its dates may be 1st cent. BC into the 3rd cent. AD.

HALTON
(Lancashire)

The Sigurd cross stands in the quiet churchyard of Halton village, about 3 mi. (4.75 km.) NE of Lancaster. It is a fascinating reminder of the period in the early 11th cent. when the pagan sagas of the Scandinavian settlers in the region still vied with Christianity for attention. For on one side of the weathered shaft three lively panels depict episodes in the life of Sigurd, later a hero of Wagner's *Ring*, while on the other side is a Christian cross and two figures. Inside the church is an interesting collection of mostly earlier Anglian cross fragments and other carvings, some also showing Scandinavian influences. See also *Gosforth Cross*; *Ripon*.

HAMBLEDON HILL
(Dorset)

Magnificent Iron Age hill fort, 6 mi. (9.6 km.) NW of *Blandford Forum*. With its close neighbor, Hod Hill, a mi. or two to the SE, these are among the finest and largest forts in southern England, bearing comparison only with *Maiden Castle* near Dorchester. At Hambledon, a stronghold of the Durotriges, the northern spur of the long, sinuous chalk hill is edged by massive earthworks, two banks and ditches, enclosing 31 acres. These are doubled on the vulnerable SE side, and there were originally three entrances protected by elaborate outer hornworks. The fort was apparently built in three stages from the 3rd cent. BC to close to the Roman conquest, finally taking in an additional large section to the S. Though unexcavated, a few hundred hut circles can be detected in the fort's interior.

The Iron Age fort is only the most visible survival at Hambledon Hill. The site is also known for the remarkable Neolithic remains excavated there, dating very roughly from as far back as 3000 BC, in the period of the very first farming people. Traces of a causewayed camp on the hill had long been noted. A survey in the 1960s led Roger Mercer to a full-scale excavation for over a half-dozen years from 1974—revealing a remarkable story. The causewayed camp indeed proved to be an enclosure around the domed central summit of the hill, lying mostly outside the Iron Age fort. Within its 19 acres the hilltop had been riddled with pits, each containing a selection of what were assumed to be offerings—imported pottery, red deer antlers. More amazing were the contents of the interrupted ditches of the enclosure (see Windmill Hill in *Avebury*). Skulls had been deliberately placed at the bottom of one ditch. Two child burials were found in niches; then the ditches were gradually filled up over a long period with fragments of human bone and other materials, repeatedly recut, then filled again. In short, it appeared that here was a vast necropolis to which the dead were brought from all around and exposed until the flesh had gone. Much of the remaining skeletal material found its way into the ditches; and over half the bones were of children; the mortality rate was high. The skeletons of more notable people were perhaps assembled and moved into the many long barrows that dot the region. One such plowed-down barrow, 208 ft. long, dominates the hill at the highest point just S. of the enclosure, and another lay to the N. Excavations showed that the former belonged roughly to the same period as the camp.

This was not all. Meticulous surveys revealed that the enclosure was the center of a vast Neolithic fortified camp of some 90 acres covering the whole hill, with complex gateways, ramparts and outworks reinforced with timber. In its SE corner, on the Stapleton spur, another, smaller, 2-acre causewayed enclosure was excavated, and here the finds were very different, suggesting that this may have been an enclosed village of the same period—much like *Carn Brae* in

Cornwall, also excavated by Mercer. If it was a village, it ended in violence, all burned. The skeleton of a young man, possibly carrying a child, was found here in a ditch with a leaf-shaped arrowhead deep in his chest. The finds from Hambledon are in the Dorset County Museum, Dorchester. See also *Crickley Hill* and *Whitehawk Camp.*

Hod Hill is far larger and far younger than Hambledon. It is an Iron Age hill fort developed in four phases from the early Iron Age, as excavations in 1951–58 revealed. Roughly rectangular, its 50 acres are enclosed by two huge ramparts and ditches, reduced to one in the W. where the Stour River ran below it. Originally there were two gates with outer hornworks (three others now visible are later), and a flint-paved walk along the top of the main rampart. In the interior were hundreds of hut circles; after plowing, only a few survive, in the SE sector. This then was a major oppidum, a town. After the Roman invasion of 43 AD the fort was besieged and humbled by Vespasian in his western campaign and the inhabitants removed. Iron ballista bolts, for which the local sling-stones found piled here in large numbers were no match, were concentrated around a large house in its own enclosure—obviously that of the chief. Later the Romans built a fort of about 7 acres in the NW sector which was in use for six or seven years thereafter.

HAM HILL (Somerset)

Very large, L-shaped Iron Age hill fort of some 200 acres, about 5 mi. (8 km.) due W. of Yeovil, S. of Stoke-sub-Hamdon and W. of Montacute. Its size suggests that it was a late oppidum of the Durotriges. It dominates the region from a bold limestone outcrop from which the famous Ham stone has been quarried since Roman times, and which quarrying has destroyed some of the fort. Defended by double and occasionally triple banks and ditches, it seems to have been occupied throughout most of the Iron Age. Traces of a large Roman building have been found in the SE, possibly a villa or a small fort, since the site yielded Roman military equipment as well as Iron Age pottery, chariot fittings, and a bronze bull's head. The finds are in the Taunton Museum.

HAMWIC (Hampshire)

See *Southampton.*

HARDKNOTT CASTLE ROMAN FORT (Cumbria)

Small Roman fort of Mediobogdum guarding the western end of Hardknott Pass on a remote and dramatic site high in the mountains. Built under Trajan, its walls with four gates—three with double portals—enclose about three acres. The fort has been carefully consolidated, and inside one may see the foundations of the *principia* and of two granaries. A small bath suite lies S. of the fort and to the NE a parade ground that had to be excavated in part from the mountainside to make it level. Following the route of the Roman road 9 mi. (14.5 km.) down the pass to the coast, one comes on the Roman fort of Glennaventa, just S. of Ravenglass. This four-acre fort guarded a Roman port that was essentially an outlying unit of the *Hadrian's Wall* defensive system running down the Cumbrian coast. There is little to see of the fort, cut through by the railroad, but its bathhouse is well-preserved, with walls standing 12½ ft. high. In the other direction from Hardknott, E. over the passes for about 8 mi. (13 km.), was the larger fort of Galava looking down over Lake Windermere from the outskirts of the present Ambleside. A Hadrianic stone foundation built over an earlier clay and timber fort, it was excavated in the early 20th cent. and its two gates, towers and interior buildings can be seen but are much overgrown.

**HARPENDEN ROMAN
MAUSOLEUM
(Hertfordshire)**

A rare stone-built mausoleum (most are earthen tumuli) just S. of Harpenden, about 5 mi. (8 km.) N. of St. *Albans*. It is in private grounds, though accessible. At the center is a circular foundation with a wall around it 100 ft. square, and an external ditch. Indications from an excavation in 1937 suggest that the circular structure may have been as much as 20 ft. high and contained within it an altar facing a statue standing in an alcove. Fragments of the statue were uncovered, as well as two cremation burials of about 130 AD inside the enclosure. There may have been other burials nearby. See also *Bartlow Hills; Keston; Mersea Mount*.

**HEMBURY CASTLE
(Devon)**

An attractive Iron Age hill fort of some seven acres, 3.5 mi. (5.6 km.) slightly NW of Honiton. The hill has a long history, for like *Hambledon Hill, Maiden Castle* and *The Trundle* it began life as a Neolithic causewayed camp (see Windmill Hill in *Avebury*). Probably reoccupied in the early Iron Age, it was fortified as a stronghold of the Dumnonii, with two ramparts and ditches in its final form, and entrances to the NE and W. with inturned defenses. Finally, about 50 BC, perhaps under Belgic control, a double bank and ditches bisected the fort, the southern half used as a cattle pound, the northern for habitation. It was abandoned about 70 AD and a Roman fort, traces of which have been found, built within it. Excavations in 1930–35 found a curving Neolithic ditch crossing the middle of the fort, and evidence of a Neolithic gate and a large hut circle under the later western entrance. Another remnant of a Neolithic palisade was discovered under the NE gate, as well as many typical Neolithic artifacts. Radiocarbon dates indicate a very early Neolithic occupation of between 4200 and 3900 BC, possibly the earliest known in England.

**HENGISTBURY HEAD
(Dorset)**

Site of two important recent excavations, one of a late Iron Age settlement, the other of two adjacent hunting camps of Upper Paleolithic and Mesolithic people. Hengistbury Head juts out eastward into the Channel near Bournemouth, enfolding Christchurch Bay. Massive Iron Age double dikes and a ditch still cut off about a square mile of the Head, which is dotted with earlier Bronze Age barrows. The Iron Age settlement here was first excavated in 1911–12, but has been intensively reexcavated and studied by Barry Cunliffe in a major project beginning in 1980. Even in its early Iron Age phase (8th to 6th cents. BC) the settlement was one of the largest in Britain. However, there was little cross-Channel contact until after the Roman capture of southern France in 123 BC. The settlement then became a unique port of entry for goods from the continent, and in its most flourishing period after about 100 BC may have controlled the foreign trade for all of southern England. Its imports included wine from the Mediterranean, pottery from northern France, coins, lumps of purple glass for making beads and ornaments. In return it appears that Hengistbury exported tin from Cornwall, copper and lead, woolen cloth, corn, hides and slaves. The site was ideal for this trade—easy to defend, with good sea approaches and a sheltered harbor, and abundant natural resources. Moreover it commanded the rivers Avon and Stour leading into the interior. Hengistbury was also a manufacturing center in its own right, producing shale and glass ornaments, pottery and possibly coins, as well as working bronze and iron and extracting salt. It is possible that Hengistbury's trade also first brought the potter's wheel and the lathe into southern England, revolutionizing its technology. Altogether a remarkable site.

Hengistbury Head also boasts, on Warren Hill, which dominates the Head, one of the largest Upper Paleolithic sites in Britain, unfortunately on the unstable cliffs facing the sea (and rapidly being washed away). The open-air settlement or hunting camp is more than 11,000 years old. Farther W. along the top of the cliff a Mesolithic camp over 9,000 years old also yielded significant information. Specialists from many disciplines have been studying the Paleolithic camp, which was also investigated in 1957 and 1968–69, and was reopened in 1981. There are no organic remains here, but a large assemblage of flint tools—cores and flakes and blades, many of which have been fitted together again by experts studying the knapping techniques of the ancient hunters. Excavation on the Mesolithic camp, which had long been known, was begun in 1980. The site, dated by thermoluminescence to the 8th millennium BC, featured large numbers of finely made microlith points, which have been studied for their use as tools as well as for archery. See also *Cheddar; Creswell Crags; Goat's Cave; Jersey; Kent's Cavern; Pontnewydd.*

HEREFORD (Hereford and Worcester)

Cathedral town, founded in the late 7th cent. AD as an Anglo-Saxon frontier fortress on the Welsh border. Excavations from 1966 have uncovered the Saxon defensive wall, now reconstructed for display as an example of a Saxon town defense rare in England. The City Museum and Art Gallery has some Roman material from the hamlet of Castra Magna (or Magnae) at Kenchester, 5 mi. (8 km.) to the W., where little is to be seen—though the town plan has been identified from the air.

HEREFORDSHIRE BEACON (Hereford and Worcester)

Fine example of an Iron Age contour fort on a narrow ridge in the Malvern Hills, 4 mi. (6.5 km.) NE of Ledbury, one of the large forts of the Welsh Marches. Now a tourist attraction for its splendid views, it is a long and sinuous hill with a medieval motte crowning its highest point. The motte is at the center of the original, small, 3rd-cent.-BC fort of the earlier Iron Age. The massive ramparts, ditch and counterscarp of the later 1st cent. BC fort run around the entire hill, enclosing 32 acres with four defended entrances. There are faint traces of numerous hut circles within the fort, and from these the Iron Age population of the fort has been estimated at from 1,500 to 2,000 people. For other Marcher forts, see *Breiddin Hill; Credenhill; Croft Ambrey; Midsummer Hill; Old Oswestry; Sutton Walls; The Wrekin.*

HETTY PEGLER'S TUMP (Gloucestershire)

Whimsically named, Neolithic chambered tomb, probably the best-known of the Cotswold-Severn group of some 50 megalithic tombs in the area. Hetty's, in state care, lies on the very edge of the escarpment overlooking the Severn flats to the W., near Uley, 5.5 mi. (9 km.) SW of Stroud. Despite hard usage in the 19th cent. and considerable reconstruction, the tomb is remarkably complete, with both covering mound and interior chambers. It measures 123 ft. by 85 and is up to 10 ft. high, with a narrow forecourt and a 22-ft.-long passage (a light is needed to inspect the inside). A pair of chambers open off each side (the N. ones are closed) with a fifth chamber at the end of the passage. The entrance, though inaccurately reconstructed (the large stone is out of place) is imposing. At least 24 burials were found in the tomb in early excavations, and two more in the forecourt. See also from the same group: *Nympsfield*, about 1 mi. (1.6 km.) N., and *Belas Knap*, considerably farther to the NE.

A reconstruction of the great 7th-cent. monastic basilica of Wilfrid, Bishop of York, at Hexham, Northumberland, based on archaeological explorations on the site in 1908–10, just before the present Hexham parish church was built there. The noble crypt of Wilfrid's church, however, survives underneath the church; it is built from Roman stones robbed from the nearby Roman fort at Corbridge, part of the Hadrian's Wall complex. Wilfrid had spent some time in Rome and his magnificent basilica, on Roman models, was about 100 ft. long and 65 ft. wide, with four aisles. (Courtesy of Equinox [Oxford] Ltd.)

HEXHAM
(Northumberland)

The parish church of St. Andrew's here is notable for the survival, below its crossing, of the Anglo-Saxon crypt of St. Wilfrid's great 7th-cent. basilica. It was built by the ambitious archbishop of York as part of a monastery between 627 and 678 AD. The walls of the crypt, one of the finest to survive in England, are built of stones robbed from the nearby Roman fort of Corstopitum at Corbridge, part of the Hadrian's Wall complex, and incorporate numerous Roman inscriptions, an altar, and the well-known relief from the tomb of a Roman cavalry standard bearer. Within the church at Hexham is a fascinating museum of Saxon sculpture, notably the cross-shaft called Acca's Cross with its lovely vine-scroll decoration, the best of Northumbrian artistry. It was probably donated to the monastery by one of Wilfrid's successors, Acca, whose grave is also here. The stone "Frith Stool," possibly 9th cent., may have been a sanctuary chair for those fleeing the law. The copper-gilt chalice is one of only five Anglo-Saxon chalices known. See also Ripon for another crypt built by Wilfrid.

HEYSHAM
(Lancashire)

In this village, part of the seaside resort of Morecombe, are rare survivals of an early Christian center. Most striking are the lonely ruins of St. Patrick's Chapel standing boldly on a promontory above the wide sweep of Morecombe Bay. The stone building is probably 9th cent. and the rock-cut graves around it most likely 10th cent. Just below the promontory stands the parish church of St. Peter with Anglo-Saxon elements—the W. wall, parts of the other walls, a blocked W. doorway very similar to a door in the chapel above. Inside the church a hogback tombstone shows strange carved friezes on its sides: scenes of a stag hunt that may depict part of the Viking Sigurd myth (see also Halton), probably carved by a local Anglo-Scandinavian sculptor. In the churchyard a section of a cross-shaft shows another odd scene, probably meant to depict a biblical tale. The decoration indicates a 9th-cent. date.

HIGH ROCHESTER
(Northumberland)

Substantial Roman fort, just off the main road from Newcastle to Edinburgh, about 5 mi. (8 km.) N. of Otterburn. The stone-built remains of Bremenium on the Roman Dere Street leading into Scotland can be found at the Hamlet of

High Rochester just above Rochester itself, and are the most impressive of any fort above *Hadrian's Wall*. After the Roman withdrawal from Scotland Bremenium was the most northerly garrisoned outpost in Britain in the 3rd and 4th cents. The fort was founded by Agricola, rebuilt in stone by Lollius Urbicus of the *Antonine Wall* in 139 AD, twice again rebuilt in the 3rd and early 4th cents., and abandoned about 343 AD. The emphasis was on massive stonework—catapult emplacements on the N. and W. sides, and a multiple ditch system to keep the enemy at a distance. Today the most striking survival is the W. gate with the bases of its heavy flanking towers. The huge stones of an interval tower and three superimposed bits of the wall of different periods at the NW angle can also be seen. Of the Roman tombs lining Dere Street outside of the fort only the circular base of one survives; it is difficult to find. Most of the fine inscriptions found at the site, as well as an amusing crude relief of a braided Celtic Venus bathing with her handmaids, are in the University Museum, Newcastle. A few others are to be seen in Durham cathedral. See also *Chew Green* for the Roman forts to the N. on the border.

HIMSBURY HILL FORT
(Northamptonshire)

See *Northampton*.

HOLKHAM
(Norfolk)

See *Warham*.

HOD HILL FORT
(Dorset)

See *Hambledon Hill*.

HOLLINGBURY HILL FORT
(East Sussex)

Remains of an Iron Age fort in the midst of a golf course up behind Brighton. The fort, square with rounded corners, was excavated in 1931. It was apparently occupied only in the early Iron Age, up to about 250 BC. The real interest of the excavation lay in its careful study of the construction of the fort's single rampart—now called the Hollingbury type of rampart. It consisted of two rows of heavy upright timbers tied together with cross-beams, forming a breastwork that was then filled with chalk rubble. After the excavation a section of the rampart was reconstructed—and is now itself somewhat crumbling. There was a flat-bottomed ditch in front of the rampart, and of the two gates, the western was defended by inturned ends of the rampart; the eastern proved to have had two massive oaken gateposts. Inside the fort are faint indications of an earlier enclosure and four bowl barrows. Nearby sites include *Devil's Dyke Camp* and *Whitehawk*.

HOLTYE ROMAN ROAD
(East Sussex)

Interesting stretch of ancient road 4.5 mi. (7.25 km.) E. of East Grinstead just S. of the modern road to Tunbridge Wells; uncovered in 1939 and now fenced in. This was part of the road, here 15 ft. wide, that ran from London to Lewes. It was just N. of the iron-smelting area of the Sussex Weald and was surfaced with iron slag, which had become rusted into a hard surface. Traces of the tracks of heavy iron-working carts could be seen on the road when first exposed.

HOLYHEAD
(Gwynedd)

See *Caer Gybi; Caer y Twr; Trefignath Chambered Tomb*.

HONINGTON CAMP
(Lincolnshire)

Iron Age hill fort with multiple ramparts of a type rare in these parts, commanding a natural gap in the limestone Lincoln Edge, about 5 mi. (8 km.) N. of Grantham. About 3 mi. (4.75 km.) to the E. is the site of the Roman settlement and posting station at *Ancaster*. The fort is roughly rectangular, with two lines of heavy ramparts, ditches and counterscarp on all sides, and an entrance on the E. It has not been excavated to date.

HORNCASTLE
(Lincolnshire)

Roman town buried under the modern market center of Horncastle, on the wolds about 18 mi. (29 km.) due E. of *Lincoln*. Little is left except bits of the walls, probably built (like those of *Caistor* far to the N.) around 350 AD when Saxon pirates were threatening the coast. Among fragmentary stretches of the walls, one can be seen within a library on Wharf Road, another in St. Mary's churchyard, and the core of a bastion off Lawrence Street. Also see *Ancaster*.

HOUSESTEADS
(Northumberland)

See *Hadrian's Wall*.

HOVINGHAM
(North Yorkshire)

All Saints church in the charming village of Hovingham in the Vale of Pickering, about 8 mi. (13 km.) N. of Malton. Its stately tower, late Anglo-Saxon in date, has three stages separated by string courses, double belfry windows with rounded heads and an elaborate western door. There must have been an earlier church on the site, for a reused cross-shaft is built into the church above the northern belfry window, a cross above the western door, and inside the church is a much-worn frieze, once also built into the tower. It is over 5 ft. long and a superb piece of work. Probably 9th cent., it shows figures in eight arched panels above a vine-scroll ornamentation entangled with birds and beasts.

HOWE HILL
(North Yorkshire)

See *Duggleby Howe*.

HOXNE
(Suffolk)

Paleolithic site, 3 mi. (4.75 km.) NE of Eye near the Norfolk border. Here, in the bed of a prehistoric lake, a record of the flora and fauna of the so-called Hoxnian interglacial period (about 200,000 to 300,000 years ago) has been found in abundance during a number of excavations, the latest in 1974–78. At the top of the lake deposits a layer of animal bones and teeth of temperate period animals was found, mostly horse, and mixed with these the Acheulian handaxes and flakes of very early man. The fragmentary animal remains may represent the food remains of these very early people. See also *Boxgrove*, and *Pontnewydd* in Wales.

HULL
(Humberside)

Officially Kingston upon Hull. The city's Archaeological and Transport Museum has broad collections of prehistoric, Roman and Saxon materials. (It is planned to move them later to a new Central Museum.) The Roman displays include the crude mosaics from *Rudston* as well as the varied and important finds from the Roman settlement of Petuaria at Brough-on-Humber about 10 mi. (16 km.) upriver from Hull. There is little to see on the actual site today. The museum also owns some fine mosaics from Brantingham, just N. of Brough.

HUNSBURY HILL FORT
(Northamptonshire)

See *Northampton*.

**HUNTCLIFF SIGNAL
    STATION
(Cleveland)**

Walking along the cliff top eastward from the resort town of Saltburn-by-the-Sea, one comes upon part of the Roman signal station overlooking Tees Bay from a sheer cliff. The rest has been washed into the sea, but enough has been left to understand the original structure. A ditch, 28 ft. wide, surrounded the station. The entrance, leading over it, pierces a heavy rectangular wall and goes across a paved courtyard up to the remaining wall of the central tower, which was originally 50 ft. square. At each corner of the wall were projecting bastions for artillery emplacements. Between entrance and tower was a 14-ft.-deep well. In it were found the remains of 14 bodies, adults and children, probably the garrison of the station dumped into the well after it had been reduced by marauding pirates (Anglo-Saxon?) in the 4th cent. or later. See also *Scarborough Head*.

**HURLERS, THE
(Cornwall)**

See *Bodmin Moor*.

**HUTTON MOOR
(North Yorkshire)**

See *Thornborough Moor*.

**ICKLINGHAM
(Suffolk)**

See *West Stow*.

**ILKLEY
(West Yorkshire)**

The town is built on a civilian settlement that grew up around the small, 3½-acre Roman fort of Olicana, covered now by the parish church and the manor house. The fort, an Agricolan foundation, was later reoccupied and given its stone wall under Severus. A 68-ft. stretch of the fort's W. wall can now be seen behind the Manor House Museum, which displays many Roman finds. The fort managed to survive throughout the Roman period, being rebuilt for the last time by Count Theodosius. There are three fine Anglian crosses in All Saints churchyard, and opposite St. Margaret's church to the S. is a Bronze Age stone, the Panorama Stone, brought down from the moors. It is carved with the usual cup-and-ring design and ladder patterns. Up along the northern and western edges of Ilkley Moor to the S. of the town are more such incised stones, the largest concentration in the British Isles. Some 40 are to be found on Ilkley and on the moors adjoining it to the E. and W., as well as some eight Bronze Age stone circles, most of them actually the kerbs of destroyed burial cairns, and hut sites, cairns and enclosures. It reminds one of the profusion of Bronze Age sites on *Bodmin Moor* and *Dartmoor* in Cornwall and Devon. The best-known of the circles is the large Twelve Apostles, a true Bronze Age circle about 50 ft. in diameter of which 12 stones survive, set on a bank. Many more field boundaries and hut circles are to be found on the moors N. of Grassington.

**INGLEBOROUGH
(North Yorkshire)**

Striking mountain, over 2,300 ft. high, the site of a Brigantian hill fort. The mountain rises N. of Clapham and NE of Ingleton. The crags at the top are reinforced with a heavy single wall, about 12 ft. thick, made of large blocks and slabs with rubble filling. Quarrying here unfortunately damaged the wall. Inside, on a plateau of about 15 acres, many hut circles are visible, suggesting that this was an oppidum, a town, as well as a fort of refuge.

INNISIDGEN CARN

See *Scilly Isles*.

ISCA FORT
(Gwent)

See *Caerleon*.

ISCA DUMNONIORUM
(Devon)

See *Exeter*.

ISLE OF MAN

Island in the Irish Sea midway between England and Ireland and even closer to Scotland. Only 33 mi. (53 km.) long, it is a crossroads of history and richly endowed with archaeological sites of great interest. Raided and then settled by Vikings in the 9th cent., it became an independent Norse kingdom, and even today it is constitutionally independent in the United Kingdom under the crown. Its early Viking and Viking-Christian survivals are as impressive as any in Britain, and in a thousand-year-old Scandinavian tradition the laws are proclaimed each year on July 5 (Midsummer day) from Tynwald Hill near St. Johns—an artificial mound on the site of the ancient Viking meeting place—in English and Manx, the Gaelic-Scandinavian local language. The island is dotted with known or excavated archaeological sites ranging from the prehistoric through the Viking; and many others have been discovered in an aerial survey of parts of the island in 1979–83.

Typical of the Viking sites is the large bow-sided long house at Braaid, 4 mi. (6.5 km.) W. of Douglas, sited next to pre-Viking round houses, both marked by stones on the ground. On a hill at Ballydoole, near the SE coast and the Ronaldsway airport, is the well-known Viking ship burial in the corner of a church graveyard that also has an early chapel. Excavation here also substantiated a Dark Ages occupation. But the most intriguing Viking remains are the many elaborate 10th-cent. "Manx" stones and crosses (nearly 30 are known) decorated with Scandinavian ornament, mythological scenes and, often, runic inscriptions—while at the same time displaying some Gaelic elements. These stones are found usually in recent churches built at the sites of a number of early Christian chapels, or Keeills. Latex copies of many of these are shown in the Manx Museum, Douglas. Many of the crosses show a Viking Borre-style ring chain ornamentation closely related to that found in NW England (see *Gosforth Cross*), and others have panels depicting episodes from the sagas.

For example, in the church at Kirk Michael, near the W. coast 6 mi. (9.6 km.) NE of Peel, one of the up to a dozen crosses on display shows elaborate ring-chain decoration and a runic inscription by the Viking artist: "Gaut made this and all in Man." At Kirk Andreas, about 4 mi. (6.5 km.) NW of Ramsey, one of the stones depicts a scene from the popular Sigurd legend (see also *Halton* and *Ripon*). Under a shed in the churchyard at Maughold parish church on the E. coast Maughold peninsula, just S. of Ramsey, is the best collection of Manx crosses on the island. In the churchyard here the remains of four pre-Viking, early Christian Keeills have been found, probably monastic cells. Eight more Manx crosses are on display in the Jurby parish church, overlooking the W. coast near Jurby airport.

Peel Castle and its recent excavation offer something from every period treated here, including remains from 6000 BC. It is a fascinating site. The roofless medieval castle and adjoining cathedral are situated on St. Patrick's Isle guarding the narrow Peel harbor and connected to the mainland by a causeway. On the Isle too is an earlier ecclesiastical group (10th–11th cents.) of St. Patrick's church and the earlier St. Patrick's chapel—both again roofless—and an Irish-style round tower, one of only three outside Ireland. After exploratory excavations on the isle in 1982 proved exciting, turning up, for instance, a hoard of 41 Viking silver coins of Sitric Silkbeard of Dublin, and a mass of undated prehistoric flints, an ambitious five-year program was begun in 1983. In that year a pre-Viking cemetery with heavy stone "lintel graves" and two 8th-cent. cross slabs, possibly that of a Celtic monastery on the site, was excavated. From the Norse-Viking period came a timber building of about 1150, probably belonging to the fortress of the kings of Man. In 1984 part of a pagan Norse cemetery of the 10th cent. was discovered, with at least four burials, one of a woman of some standing, "The Pagan Lady of Peel," buried with her domestic possessions and jewelry in a church graveyard.

The Manx Museum, Library and Art Gallery in Douglas contains small but valuable collections of finds from many of the sites described here, including the Dublin Viking coin hoard from Peel, Norse weapons and jewelry and a model of a Viking warship.

ISLES OF SCILLY

See *Scilly Isles*.

ITFORD HILL
(East Sussex)

Small Bronze Age settlement, site of some 11 to 13 round huts, near Beddingham, about 2 mi. (3.25 km.) SE of Lewes, occupied around 1000 BC. Excavated in 1957, the banks and hollows of the site are still visible. The huts were inside a number of palisaded paddocks, the largest hut, boasting a porch, inside its own paddock. No huts had fireplaces and the roofs were thatched. Field systems around the settlement were indicated by low banks, and in a pit in the settlement a quantity of carbonized barley was found. Above the village to the N. a burial mound contained 17 cremations. There were numerous flint flakes here too, from flint-knapping operations. The Iron Age fort of *The Caburn* is close by the site. See also *Flag Fen*.

JARROW
(Tyne and Wear)

St. Paul's church on the S. bank of the Tyne River near the Tyne tunnel, close to South Shields. The church is a remnant of the famous monastery of Jarrow founded by the energetic Northumbrian Benedict Biscop and dedicated in 684 AD, about 10 years after he founded its sister monastery of *Monkwearmouth* on the Wear River about 6 mi. (9.6 km.) to the S. Here at Jarrow the Venerable Bede, renowned early historian, spent most of his life. Only the chancel of St. Paul's dates from the original foundation and may have been a chapel attached to Biscop's larger basilican church nearby. The present tower joining chancel and nave is also Anglo-Saxon but later, built probably after the Danish Vikings sacked the monastery in 794 AD. The early monastery buildings, between the church and the ruins of the later medieval monastery to the S., have been excavated and their walls are now marked out on the grass. There were two main buildings, one quite substantial and possibly two-storied. The finds are displayed in the Bede Monastery Museum in Jarrow Hall N. of the church, which also contains informative exhibits on the early British church as a whole. Interesting fragments of pre-Conquest sculpture may be viewed in the N. porch of the church.

JERSEY

Largest of the *Channel Islands*, only 16 mi. (25.75 km.) from the French coast. Like *Guernsey* it is rich in early sites. Perhaps the most remarkable, and most ancient, are the Neanderthal period finds at the La Cotte headland in SW Jersey. Three narrow ravines in the towering granite headland of La Cotte de St. Brelade have produced an exceedingly rich collection of finds from the Middle Paleolithic period, surpassing in quantity and variety all the Old Stone Age finds in Britain itself. It began about 1911 with the discovery of the fossilized teeth of Neanderthal Man, the only physical remains so far found in Britain. By the 1920s the site had yielded thousands of worked flints, hammerstones, human bones and animal remains of mammoth, wooly rhinoceros, deer, elk, horse and birds. The work went on, at first by a dedicated retired schoolmaster, then by teams from the University of Cambridge, right into the mid-1980s. The later excavations turned up two deliberate piles of mammoth and rhinoceros bones, the fruits of the hunt, as well as other finds, but concentrated more on an analysis of the extreme changes in climate and landscape at the site and the human adaptation to these conditions. Apparently occupation began some 250,000 years ago when Jersey was a peninsula attached to the mainland (no other such finds have been found in the other islands), then continued intermittently over thousands of years after it became an island. Changes in the tool kits of these early men provided an insight into their adaptation to the climate and landscape changes—the flint-rich beach, once at the edge of the ravines, receding 5 or 10 mi. (8 to 16 km.) away as the land was raised. (See also *Pontnewydd* in Wales.)

Excavation at another interesting site at La Moye, across the bay westwards from La Cotte, begun in 1981, has turned up part of an extensive Bronze Age settlement, dated by its pottery to 1650–1500 BC: a stone-revetted retaining wall with three small circular structures built against it, and a large rectangular structure of rubble and boulders with a possible bed enclosure in its interior. But surely Jersey's most noteworthy site is the famous megalithic tomb of La Hougue Bie, about 3 mi. (4.75 km.) NE of St. Helier in Grouville parish, finest in the islands and one of the largest and best in all of Britain. This huge, well-lighted Neolithic passage grave lies under a 40-ft.-high mound crowned by a medieval chapel—thus capturing it for Christianity! Its passage, 32 ft. long, leads into an oval chamber 30 ft. by 12 ft. with small side chambers on the N., S. and W. When excavated—though it had been robbed by Viking pirates—the bones of eight people, two of them women, were found. Around the mound is the Jersey Museum—actually a complex of different museums, one containing extensive displays of prehistoric materials.

There are other megalithic tombs on the island: the Faldouet Dolmen near Gorey on the E. coast, 4.5 mi. (7.25 km.) NE of St. Helier, a fine bottle-shaped passage grave; Le Couperon on the NE coast 8 mi. (13 km.) from St. Helier, with a splendid view over Rozel Bay, a rare gallery grave 45 ft. long and very narrow, with 20 low uprights supporting seven capstones, and a heavy kerb around it. On the western side of the island is the passage grave of Les Monts Grantez, inland from the NW coast of St. Ouen Bay, and La Sargente at the bottom of the bay with its fine corbelled roofing.

N. of this tomb the bold 200-ft.-high Pinnacle Rock juts upward above the sea at the end of a land bridge on the extreme northwestern coast, and below it are the lonely remains of the only indisputably Roman structure on the islands, excavated in 1930–36. Roman pottery and a coin were found within the rectangular, concentric walls. It is now considered to be a Gallo-Roman temple, sited near a spring. On the land bridge here are two ramparts of a promontory fort, and inside them the excavators found the remains of a Neolithic settlement—hearths, pottery, tools of flint bone and stone and the bones of domestic animals. Above this were the remains of later settlements: pottery, arrowheads, polished stone axes and a bronze axe from the period of the ramparts, more remains dating from the Late Bronze Age to the Late Iron Age, and finally a Roman layer yielding an iron blade, bronze rings, sherds and a Roman coin.

JEWRY WALL
(Leicestershire)

See *Leicester*.

JORDAN HILL
(Dorset)

Romano-Celtic temple, 2.5 mi. (4 km.) NE of Weymouth, near Overcombe, not far from *Maiden Castle* where a similar temple has been found. Now only a square foundation on the ground (247 ft. square), the temple was excavated in 1843 and 1932 and is now in state care. Capitals and bases of Tuscan columns found in the excavations indicate that it was a building of some pretension. At the SE corner a curious pit was found, filled up with 16 distinct layers separated by flat slabs, each layer containing ashes and the bones of a bird, with a Roman coin— probably the remains of burnt offerings ritually buried after a ceremony. Nearly a hundred human burials were found around the temple—like a parish church today! The coins indicated the temple was in use in the 4th and into the 5th cent. AD.

JORVIK
(North Yorkshire)

See *York*.

JURBY CHURCH

See *Isle of Man*.

KANOVIUM ROMAN FORT

See *Penmaenmawr*.

KENCHESTER ROMAN
TOWN
(Hereford and
Worcester)

See *Hereford*.

KENT'S CAVERN
(Devon)

Famous Paleolithic cave in the eastern outskirts of Torquay, two main chambers and radiating galleries, now well-lighted, with display cases at the entrance. A fine sequence of human and animal remains found here ranges in date from about 100,000 BC to 8000 BC. When it was first excavated in the 1820s, the mix of human remains with extinct animals such as mammoth, rhinoceros, cave bear, hyena and lion, was denounced as a hoax and downright blasphemous. Not until Darwin's ideas had gained some acceptance after 1858 was further intensive excavation carried out. Over 1,200 artifacts of flint, bone and antler, including an ivory baton, a sewing needle and three harpoons, were uncovered. The earliest implements belonged to the period of Neanderthal man, though no human remains were found. Later finds belonged to the Upper Paleolithic— Solutrean and Cresswellian types. The bulk of the finds are in the Torquay museum with some in the Natural History Museum, London. See also *Boxgrove*; *Cheddar*; *Cresswell Crags*; *Goat's Cave*; *Hengistbury Head*; *Jersey*; *Pontnewydd*.

KESTON
(Greater London)

Roman cemetery, 3.5 mi. (5.6 km.) S. of Bromley on the southern edge of Greater London. As late as 1815 the main tomb here was still under its tumulus. Excavated in 1828 and three times thereafter the remains, now only a few ft. high, were reexcavated and consolidated in 1967 and can now be visited (with permission of the owners). The central, circular stone tomb, once an imposing 20 ft. to 30 ft. high, was reinforced by six external buttresses, probably to hold the mound or tumulus in place. A smaller tomb next to it was rectangular and was probably the origin of a much-traveled sarcophagus—removed from the site in the 19th cent., shattered by a German bomb at its new location, reconstructed and now returned to the site! Another small, tile-built tomb between two of the buttresses was only discovered in later excavations and can now be viewed below a trap door. Inside was a lead casket containing a cremation burial. Twelve other ordinary burials were found on the site. Perhaps the whole was the private cemetery for the master and servants of a Roman villa whose site is nearby. See also *Bartlow Hills*; *Harpenden*; *Mersea Mount*; *Orpington*.

KESTOR
(Devon)

See *Dartmoor*.

KEYNSHAM
(Avon)

See *Bristol*.

KINGSCOTE
(Gloucester)

See *Woodchester Mosaic*.

KING'S WESTON
(Avon)

See *Bristol*.

KIRK ANDREAS

See *Isle of Man*.

KIRK MICHAEL

See *Isle of Man*.

KIT'S COTY HOUSE
(Kent)

See *Aylesford*.

KNAP HILL
(Wiltshire)

Neolithic causewayed camp sited boldly above the Vale of Pewsey at Alton Priors, about 6 mi. (9.6 km.) E. of *Devizes* and an equal distance S. of *Avebury* where the much larger and better known causewayed camp of Windmill Hill is located. But Knap Hill was the first to be recognized for what it is and has now been radio-carbon-dated at about 3500 BC. Six or seven ditches broken by causeways can still be discerned. Some Beaker pottery of about 2200 BC was left on the hill after the camp had long been disused.

KNOWLTON CIRCLES
(Dorset)

See *Blandford Forum*.

LA COTTE DE BRELADE

See *Jersey*.

LADLE HILL
(Hampshire)

See *Beacon Hill*.

LA GRAN'MÈRE DU
CHIMIQUIÈRE

See *Guernsey*.

LA HOUGUE BIE	See *Jersey*.
LAMBOURN BARROWS (Berkshire)	See *White Horse*.
LA MOYE	See *Jersey*.
L'ANCRESSE COMMON	See *Guernsey*.

LANYON QUOIT
(Cornwall)

Much visited, Neolithic chambered tomb, 3.5 mi. (5.6 km.) NW of Penzance at Madron on the road to Morvah. Today it is a striking monument about 5 ft. high, though before it collapsed in 1815 and was badly reconstructed it was reputedly much taller. An enormous capstone almost 19 ft. long rests on three uprights. The original 90-ft.-long barrow can still be traced. The chamber was probably at the N. end. See also *Penzance*.

LA SARGENTE	See *Jersey*.
LAVATRAE ROMAN FORT (Durham)	See *Bowes*.
LA VERDE	See *Guernsey*.
LE COUPERON	See *Jersey*.
LE CREUX DES FAIES	See *Guernsey*.
LE DÉHUS	See *Guernsey*.

LEDSHAM
(West Yorkshire)

Part Anglo-Saxon church in the rural hamlet of Ledsham, once in the forest of Elmet, 4 mi. (6.5 km.) N. of Ferrybridge, NW of Castleford. The nave walls of the original, small, 7th- or 8th-cent. church survive. Above the S. door are traces of an amazing Anglo-Saxon doorway, fully 14 ft. high and only 2 ft. wide! The two lower stories of the tower are also Saxon. The S. tower doorway with its elaborate floral decoration is an 1871 reconstruction, but it may have followed the original design.

LEGIS TOR (Devon)	See *Dartmoor*.

LEICESTER
(Leicestershire)

Once the tribal capital of the Coritani and then the Roman city of Ratae Coritanorum, the city's Roman remains are well worth seeing. On St. Nicholas Street close to St. Nicholas' church and the river is the Jewry Wall, a massive masonry survival from the former *palaestra* or exercise hall of the city's 2nd-cent. Roman baths. Over 70 ft. long and 24 ft. high, with tile-bonding courses and four recessed arches on the back side, the wall is reminiscent of the similar survival (the "Old Work") and baths at *Wroxeter* in Salop. In front of the Jewry Wall the foundations of part of the baths and of a Roman town house have been laid out for viewing, after excavations in 1936–39. The Jewry Wall Museum adjoining the Wall exhibits Roman materials, including the charming peacock mosaic pavement from a Roman town house and two stretches of elaborately painted wall plaster from another house, discovered in 1958.

LES MONTS GRANEZ

See *Jersey*.

LETOCETUM
(Staffordshire)

See *Wall Roman Station*.

LE TREPIED

See *Guernsey*.

LIDDINGTON CASTLE
(Wiltshire)

See *White Horse*.

LINCOLN
(Lincolnshire)

A small city with a long history, Lincoln was the Roman Colonia Lindum and also an important Viking and medieval center. Extensive excavations, especially after 1972—many of the rescue variety—have uncovered bits and pieces of this long history. And urban excavation in advance of redevelopment continues on a large scale. The city began as a legionary fortress of about 42 acres, built around 61 AD on the plateau above the Whitam River where it flows through a gap in the Lincoln Edge to the sea. Scant finds indicate that for at least two centuries earlier there had been a native settlement along the river below the plateau, at Brayford Pool. On the plateau, where now stands the magnificent cathedral and the castle the only remains of the original fortress, uncovered in excavations on the site of St. Paul in the Bail, were of the *principia* or headquarters, a large building.

After the army left the walls of the fortress served for a time to enclose the new veterans' town of Lindum Colonia, laid out about 90 AD. Parts of these walls, rebuilt in stone in the 2nd cent. and then extended down to the river to enclose another 56 acres, have long been known, especially the famous Newport Gate—the inner section of the legionary N. gate, which when built probably had a second story. Traffic still flows under the 16-ft.-wide arch, and one of the two pedestrian passages survives on one side. One of the towers and the remains of the E. gate of the fortress were excavated in 1959–60, and some of it has been left exposed in front of the East Gate Hotel. This gate, with its two central arches, may have been the main entrance. The fort's W. gate, next to the castle, was uncovered in 1836, collapsed, and was again buried. In 1970 it was reexcavated and consolidated. The massive S. gate of the lower town was discovered in 1971. Other small sections of the ruined wall, and the great ditch in front of it, are to be seen here and there.

Of the numerous Roman buildings excavated from time to time none is to be seen today. Some Roman houses were found in the lower town, and four traders' houses S. of the city outside the walls on Ermine Street, the main Roman road, were excavated in 1977. When the medieval St. Mary's Guildhall was being renovated in 1981 it was discovered that its west range had been built on top of Ermine Street, complete with ruts and all! Some of the timber-revetted waterfront on the river at Brayford Wharf was also discovered.

But the most interesting finds were back in the area of St. Paul in the Bail. Excavations in 1978–79 discovered that Hadrianic public buildings and a forum had been built over the site of the former *principia*. The "Bailgate Colonnade," long known and now marked out on the modern street, was undoubtedly part of this Hadrianic complex, as well as the impressively tall "Mint Wall," excavated to its foundations in 1980, that probably underpinned an immense public building. The excavations also uncovered the remains of a very early church, built over the forum courtyard, with some early graves. In one of them a lovely bronze hanging bowl of the early 7th cent. was discovered. The church was probably that built by Bishop Paulinus of York in Lincoln in 628 AD, as Bede tells us. Radiocarbon dates from the graves suggest the possibility of an exceedingly rare Christian community here as early as the 5th to 6th cents. AD.

But Lincoln had shrunk after the Roman withdrawal and really revived only with the coming of the Viking settlers in the 9th cent. By the 10th cent. it was once more a flourishing city, a trading center of some 5,000 to 8,000 people. Timber buildings and new streets excavated at the Flaxengate site in the lower town revealed much small-scale industrial activity—glass and copper-working, textiles—and evidence of extensive trade from the Baltic and as far as China. Finally, from the late Anglo-Saxon period two churches, each with very similar late Saxon towers, stand less than a half mi. (1 km.) apart in the suburb of Wigford S. of the city. A foundation stone built into St. Mary-le-Wigford was inscribed on a reused Roman tombstone. The other, St. Peter-at-Gowts, stands farther S. The City and County Museum displays local finds.

LINDISFARNE
(Northumberland)

Holy Island, renowned seat of early Christianity at the monastery founded in 634 AD by St. Aidan from Iona in SCOTLAND, and briefly home of the saintly Cuthbert after 685, and his original burial place. Lindisfarne was also a center of learning and the arts during the golden days of Northumbria (see York) and here the glorious Lindisfarne Gospels were produced about 700 AD (now in the British Museum, London). After repeated Viking raids in the 8th and 9th cents. the monks fled, carrying with them Cuthbert's body, and eventually ended up at Durham. Lindisfarne, accessible by car across a causeway only at low tide from Beal, is now shared by the ruins of the Norman abbey and a tiny castle. Nothing of the original monastic buildings has survived, though soundings have uncovered a fascinating collection of carved stones and crosses from the Anglo-Saxon and Danish periods, now displayed in the Lindisfarne Monastery Museum next to the abbey ruins.

LITTLECOTE ROMAN VILLA
(Wiltshire)

On the Kennet River, 3 mi. (4.75 km.) W. of Hungerford, in the park close to Littlecote House, in itself a gem of early Tudor architecture and now the center of a tourist park. The villa, in a valley rich in Roman remains, is known for its great Orpheus mosaic, discovered in 1727 then covered up again. Rediscovered in 1977, it was excavated from 1978 and fully restored with the help of a colored engraving and a tapestry, both made from it when it was first exposed. The excavators found that it lay in a former Roman barn of the villa, rebuilt in about 360 AD into a separate building next to the main villa house, with an entrance vestibule, an enclosed court, a small bath suite beyond it, and next to it a barrel-vaulted room opening onto an inner chamber with three apses and a tower overhead—both rooms paved with the mosaic. Thought by some to have been a warm-weather dining room, the plan of these rooms is more reminiscent of Christian churches, particularly Byzantine churches of the 6th cent.; moreover the mosaic, about 28 ft. by 41 ft., displays a complex scheme of pagan mythological figures and symbols typical of the Orphic cult, which had many resemblances to early Christianity. In the mosaic and in the building itself the shell design is used to represent the rays of the sun—a typically Orphic concept.

Now, 360 AD was the year of the accession of the Emperor Julian the Apostate, who in his three-year reign attempted to return the empire to paganism and encouraged the mystery cults like Orphism, with its worship of the sun god, Helios. It is therefore most likely that this was a cult center for the Orphic mysteries. The cult center lasted less than 10 years, when the villa was demolished and the house-temple turned into an ordinary dwelling. From the earliest days of the Roman occupation and for almost 400 years thereafter, the villa itself went through six rebuilding phases. It is now planned to reconstruct the villa house as a museum-center for the site.

LITTLE WOODBURY
(Wiltshire)

See *Salisbury.*

LLANMELIN FORT
(Gwent)

See *Caerwent.*

LODGE PARK
(Gloucestershire)

One of the finest of the Gloucestershire long barrows in the Cotswolds, unexcavated to date but seemingly quite undamaged. It lies just behind the 17th-cent. Lodge Park House, between Aldsworth and Eastington. Its mound is turf-covered and the whole is 150 ft. long, rising in height to the SE where two upright stones and a lintel stone can be seen showing through. See also *Belas Knap; Hetty Pegler's Tump; Nympsfield.*

LONDON

The Roman Londinium, sited on the first possible crossing of the Thames above its estuary and always a hub of communications. According to the latest findings it was founded by the Romans as a commercial port as late as 50 to 55 AD, a number of years *after* the initial invasion of Britain in 43 AD, which, it is now thought, probably crossed the Thames in the Westminster area farther up the river. The invasion troops were on the way to capture *Colchester*, which became the first capital of the province. There is no evidence of any previous native settlement at Londinium, whose site and size roughly corresponded with modern London's inner core, called The City. However, across the river at Southwark on the South Bank there may have been such a settlement. London was so perfectly sited as an international port and communications center that after its founding it grew with astonishing speed and was already a flourishing commercial city when Queen Boudicca's (or Boadicea's) hordes burned its timber buildings in the disastrous native revolt of 60 AD, leaving a layer of debris and ashes that has been uncovered in many of the archaeological sites in the City today. (An example can be seen in the All Hallows site described below.) Quickly rebuilt, London entered a boom period that lasted until about 125–130 when much of it was again destroyed in another disastrous fire (the "Hadrianic fire").

By this time London had become in effect the capital of the province, though just when it officially superseded Colchester is in doubt. London's first basilica and forum, with a small classical temple, had been built, and there were public baths, timber wharves along the river, and on the bank above the river at Cannon Street the large governor's palace with a garden court, a huge pool, state rooms and its own bath suite—of which nothing is now visible. A small 12-acre fort of the early 2nd cent. lay in the NW corner of the city. (It was only discovered after World War II.) The fort was probably used just by the governor's bodyguard; but the city, as befitted a bustling commercial center, was unwalled. Toward the end of the 1st cent. the forum and basilica were replaced by a truly grandiloquent city center on Cornhill with an enormous enclosed forum, and along its N. side a new and splendid basilica that was the longest Roman building N. of the Alps at that time—a fitting symbol of London's prosperity.

After the Hadrianic fire, however, a relentless decline set in and even depopulation, as the developing cities of Roman Britain cut into London's trade and markets just as it was trying to recover from the fire. Actually, London seems to have been in transition from an open commercial city to the very different administrative and military capital of the province, a city with a smaller population perhaps, but with grand public buildings, monuments and luxurious town houses set in gardens with fine mosaic floors and painted rooms. The remains of sophisticated sculpture, elaborate monuments, a triumphal arch—all built into the 4th-cent. bastions and river wall and there discovered by the archaeologists—attest to the splendor of 3rd-cent. Londinium. The visit of the Emperor Septimius Severus about 208 AD may have hastened the transition.

Around 200 AD an immense wall, 2 mi. (3.25 km.) long and enclosing 330 acres of the city, was built—one of the earliest and certainly the largest city wall in Britain. It incorporated the old fort in its NW corner. In the 4th cent. these defenses were refurbished with massive bastions built along the eastern side of the wall circuit, and a heavy new wall was built along the river front (apparently in two stages). At the other end of London Bridge the suburb of Southwark, as excavations since 1945 have shown, followed much the same pattern as Londinium. Sited on the then-sandy islands S. of the Thames, it grew into a settlement of over 30 acres, then languished as London did, and in the 4th cent. may have been virtually abandoned. Then came the Roman withdrawal from Britain (409 AD) and Roman life in London gradually withered away.

Innumerable random finds and excavations from the 19th cent. to the present—many of the later ones as rescue operations in advance of redevelopment—have gradually filled in the story of Roman London. Since the 1970s the pace has accelerated. Burrowing in bomb sites, private cellars, car parks, or wherever rebuilding was taking place, bits and pieces of the story have been found. Put together, the whole enterprise amounts to one of the largest urban excavation projects in the world. While many of the finds, along with Roman materials from all over England and elsewhere are to be seen in the British Museum, the bulk of the more recent finds are lodged in the admirable Museum of London N. of the street called London Wall in Aldersgate. The museum also carried out many of the recent digs.

Among visible sites the pathetic remnants of the great wall, which determined the shape of inner London right into the 16th cent., have long been the chief attraction. Its six ancient gates are all gone but are preserved in the names Aldgate, Cripplegate, Bishopsgate, Ludgate and the rest. Only the foundations of one lesser gate, that of the W. gate of the old fort, are preserved, with a guardroom, underground near the Museum of London. In the eastern City the sites of 13 of the possible 20 bastions added to the wall in the 4th cent. have been located, and one, excavated in 1979–80, has been preserved in Emperor House, Vine Street.

The wall was built with a rubble and mortar core, faced with ragstone brought by barge from Kent, and bonded with tile courses for strength. One of these barges with its load was discovered sunk in the Thames in 1962. Outside the wall ran a deep V-shaped ditch. The principal visible wall sites, usually topped by medieval work, cluster around Tower Hill and the London Museum areas, and to date so many sites have been discovered that an official "do-it-yourself" London Wall Walk with descriptive plaques was inaugurated in 1984 between the two.

The finest stretch of the wall is undoubtedly that in the Wakefield Gardens just N. of Tower Hill, 50 ft. long. The Roman lower section, with four bonding courses of tile, rises 14½ ft. high; above this it is medieval. At one end are the foundations of a turret. Built into a late bastion near here, fragments of a famous inscription were found, part of the tomb of Julius Classicianus, the procurator sent to Britain in 61 AD to help restore order after Boudicca's revolt. Casts of the inscription are set into a modern wall here. The actual inscription, reconstructed, is in the British Museum, with a cast in the Museum of London. Just E. of the Tower is another 10-ft.-long stretch and another bastion (rebuilt in the 13th cent.) in the ruins of the Wardrobe Tower. A late discovery (1976–77) just S. of the Tower, is part of the massive 4th-cent. river wall, built of reused stones and reinforced with timbers. This is attributed to Stilicho, the great Vandal general in charge at Rome at the time. Again N. of the Tower, in a courtyard behind Midland House in Cooper's Row, is another stretch of the Roman wall 13 ft. high and again topped by medieval masonry.

Moving N. and W. further stretches of the wall may be seen on the N. side of the churchyard of All Hallows on the Wall, and in a car park under the eastern end of London Wall street. Farther W. in St. Alphage's churchyard N. of London Wall, now a garden, the remains are mostly medieval, but the Roman part shows two walls built against each other, that of the old fort and against it the thicker wall of 200 AD with medieval topping. We are now in the London Museum area, and S. of St. Giles Cripplegate church, now part of the Barbican development, some of the old fort wall shows again, but most of the work is 13th cent., including the two bastions. The striking, hollow bastions along the line of the wall that can be seen from a window of the museum are again 13th cent. S. of London Wall street along Noble Street the reinforced wall of the old fort at its lower corner can be seen again, with the foundations of two of its turrets. Finally, N. of Newgate Street in the yard of the General Post Office is a curved stretch of the western wall where it turns southwards, with a medieval bastion (appointment required).

Within the walls not much of Roman London survives. Of the many magnificent houses of its most prosperous period an interesting relic is that on Lower Thames Street near Billingsgate and the waterfront. Discovered in several phases and excavated in 1969–70, parts of this substantial 3rd cent. mansion, and especially its private bath suite with hypocausts and mosaic floors, are on view beneath a modern building. Surprising evidence from coins and an Anglo-Saxon brooch indicate that life went on here until the house fell into ruins about 500 AD. In the crypt of All Hallows Barking W. of Tower Hill the walls and tesselated floors of another house can be viewed, along with the Roman finds, a model of Roman London about 400 AD, and burned debris left from Boudicca's earlier assault. Another red tesselated pavement of a house can be seen under St. Brides, Fleet Street, outside the Roman walls to the W. Other mosaics are to be seen in the Bank of England (permission required) and in the British Museum and the Museum of London, especially the fine 3rd-cent. floor from Bucklesbury House in the latter.

A sensational find of 1953–54 was the small temple of Mithras in a redevelopment site on Walbrook, the only temple found in London, though an inscription notes a temple of Isis in the city. The foundations of the Temple of Mithras have since been reassembled 60 yds. W. of its original position, off Queen Victoria Street. The basilican plan of the temple is quite clear—nave and aisles with a sanctuary in the apse at the end. In the excavation a cache of superb marble sculptures was found buried under the sanctuary, doubtless to conceal them from outraged Christians in the 4th cent.—heads of Mithras himself, the soldiers' favorite, of Mercury, Minerva, Bacchus and Serapis and other objects. Similar sculptures—one of Mithras slaying the bull—were found nearby in the 19th cent. before the temple was discovered, and both sets are now united in the Museum of London.

Of the recent major excavations in London, those along the waterfront have aroused great interest. In 1974–75 the massive timber quay constructed in the late 2nd or early 3rd cent. for a half mi. along the waterfront as part of London's renewal in this period, was glimpsed in digs at the Seal House, New Fresh Wharf and Old Custom House sites. Then a dig in Pudding Lane from 1979 to 1982 uncovered not only about 200 ft. of the first major Roman quay—made of stout oaken beams during the earlier boom of about 70 to 100 AD—but also the remains of two warehouses behind it, open in front and encased in stone walls on the three landward sides. These buildings may have had two stories, topped by tiled roofs; their floors were made of wooden planks. Even more exciting was the discovery of a large timber structure that may have been a pier of Londinium's London Bridge. After tracing two converging roads on the other bank at Southwark, it now appears that the bridge probably crossed just downstream from the medieval one.

An even more ambitious excavation in the parking lot of the old Billingsgate Market from 1982 to 1983, involving a coffer dam to hold back the earth around the site, worked down 28 ft. through medieval and Saxon levels to uncover more of the second great Roman timber quay. Ancient infilling behind the quay produced among other finds well-preserved Roman leather shoes, including a delicate lady's sandal with gilded decorations. But the fragmentary nature of these remains contrasted with the loads of red Samian tableware from Gaul and mixing bowls from the Rhineland uncovered in the infill behind the aforementioned quay stretches at the Old Custom House, Seal House and New Fresh Wharf sites. The Billingsgate dig was watched by thousands from a specially-constructed viewing gallery and was featured on the BBC/TV.

Perhaps the most interesting of all the major excavations was that of London's great civic center, completed in September 1986, with its forum and basilica on top of Cornhill, from early on the center of London's life. To date, the results of this most recent excavation are not yet in. Since the 19th cent. it had been known that extensive and massive Roman walls lay beneath the Leadenhall Market area, and later the site was definitely identified as the center, especially when by 1977 a cable tunnel along Gracechurch Street had burrowed through the remains of the great forum and the basilican hall. We now know that the whole complex covered an entire insula, nearly 8 acres.

The forum, enclosed by colonnades and shops on three sides and with an ornamental pool at the center, was bordered on the N. by the huge basilica, 500 ft. long—as large as St. Paul's today, and longer than any building in Rome itself, with the exception of the Basilica Ulpia. Its great central nave, with a tribune at one end and aisles and offices along the sides, served as a combined law court and town hall—and undoubtedly as a business center as well. That much is known; many details remain to be filled in by the excavations at the new Leadenhall Court redevelopment site, which covers the entire E. end of the basilica—notably, such details as the date of its construction, which is now cautiously described as between 90 and 120 AD. The project began with the discovery early in 1985 of three phases of earlier timber buildings beneath the basilica, reached by perilously digging down through the basement of a standing house, and finally of the earliest timber-framed buildings found in London. Buildings N. of the basilica were also investigated, and finally the basilica itself was tackled.

The latest and most exciting discovery has been the remains of London's ancient amphitheater, a stone-built oval found deeply buried under the site of the new Guildhall Art Gallery in a rescue excavation begun in July 1987. The arena, apparently extending under the Guildhall, was the largest in Britain.

What happened to London after the Romans left? According to the Anglo-Saxon Chronicle its walls sheltered Britons fleeing from the Saxons in the mid-5th cent. Thereafter and until the mid-9th cent. little is known about London. Finds of the mid-Saxon period within the walled city are negligible and no remains of Saxon buildings have been found there. By contrast, from the 9th cent. on, especially after Alfred the Great had retaken the city from the Danish Vikings in 886, there is abundant archaeological evidence for a dramatic revival of the walled city and its trade. For example in the area of the Billingsgate excavations a group of 9th-cent. Saxon timber houses was uncovered in 1981 at the southern end of Pudding Lane, sited close to the bridge and waterfront; and these houses were enlarged and added to in the 10th cent., indicating increasing prosperity. These were only a few of over 40 Saxon buildings, mostly of the 10th cent., found in recent excavations.

Yet there is ample documentary evidence for a large international trading center at London in the 7th and 8th cents., not least Bede's description of it as an "emporium of many nations coming by land and sea." Where was this port? There is recent and convincing evidence, reinforced by further excavation, to show that this Saxon trading settlement lay to the W., *outside* the walled town on the gravel strip along the Thames shore, now the Strand and Fleet Street in the Aldwych area, where the ships could be pulled up on the "strand." While not deserted, the old walled city of "Lundenburh"—as contrasted with the trading center of "Lundenwic"—was reserved for ecclesiastical and royal purposes. In 886 King Alfred, it is stated, "rebuilt the City of London in a splendid manner, and made it fit for habitation." London's rebirth thereafter was rapid, and continued without a break even under the brief dominance of the Danes under Cnut and his successors. From this latter period comes the lovely St. Paul's Stone, a Viking memorial relief runestone of a dragon in the elaborate Scandinavian Ringerike style of the 11th cent., found in St. Paul's churchyard in 1852 and now in the Museum of London. See also *Keston; Orpington.*

LONG HOLE
(West Glamorgan)

See *Goat's Cave.*

LONGHOUSE
(Dyfed)

See *Newport.*

LONG MAN OF WILMINGTON (East Sussex)

See *Wilmington Long Man*.

LONG MEG AND HER DAUGHTERS (Cumbria)

One of the largest and most important of Bronze Age rings, an impressive 350 ft. across. In state care, it can be found near Little Salkeld, about 6 mi. (9.6 km.) NE of Penrith. Originally it had nearly 70 stones in an oval ring, of which only 27 still stand; these are about 10 ft. high. Many others have fallen. Two of the heaviest boulders mark the E. and W. sides and four other huge portal stones emphasize the entrance on the SW. These main stones are Long Meg's daughters; she herself, a witch in legend, stands outside the SW entrance, a tall thin stone 12 ft. high aligned exactly on the midwinter sunset as seen from the middle of the ring. Long Meg, unusually for these parts, is decorated with some cup and ring marks, spirals and circles more commonly found in Scotland and Ireland. Records indicate that there may have been two cairns at the center of the ring, long since vanished. The very size of the ring suggests a major religious gathering place for hundreds of people at a time.

LUGUVALIUM (Cumbria)

See *Hadrian's Wall*.

LULLINGSTONE ROMAN VILLA (Kent)

About 6 mi. (9.6 km.) S. of Dartford and 1 mi. (1.6 km.) SW of the village of Eynsford. Lullingstone is one of the most rewarding villas uncovered in England, not so much for its architecture—though it is well-preserved, with some walls

The central mosaic (early 4th cent.) in the reception room of Lullingstone Roman villa in Kent, known for its mosaics, among the finest in Britain, and its unusual wall paintings, some Christian. The subject of the mosaic is Bellerophon on his horse Pegasus spearing the lion-like Chimaera. Dolphins fill the corners and outside them are depictions of the four seasons. The villa's life spanned over 300 years. (Courtesy of English Heritage.)

still standing 8 ft. high—as for the discoveries found in it, covering a period of over 300 years. The remains are now protected under a roof and the finds are well-displayed in showcases. Known since the 18th cent., it was finally excavated over a 12-year period, beginning in 1949. The first house on the site, built of flint and mortar, was begun about 60 AD. A century later a new owner added a bath suite at the W. end and a series of cult rooms at the other. One of these, with a water tank at its center, was dedicated to water spirits, with paintings of nymphs, now much damaged, on its walls. The owner also possessed two fine busts in Greek marble of his ancestors—now with the wall paintings in the British Museum. The villa was suddenly deserted about 200 AD and lay derelict for some 50 years until reoccupied by a family that sealed off the cult rooms and made other changes. In the early 4th cent. a pair of mosaic floors was laid in the reception room and the adjoining apsidal dining room, the one showing Bellerophon spearing the chimaera with the four seasons at the corners, the other Europa and the Bull. The figure work here is very fine, the geometric parts rather clumsy. From this period come the remains of a temple-mausoleum behind the villa, next to a small, very early (1st cent.), round pagan temple. By about 360–70 the occupying family were Christian, for they converted the E. end of the villa into a Christian chapel, one of the earliest known in Europe. On its walls were a frieze of six praying figures, almost Byzantine in their formal frontality, and a large Chi-Rho Christian monogram within a wreath. The fragments of the paintings, reconstructed, are now in the British Museum, with copies at Lullingstone. The villa was burned, either by accident or an attack, in the early 5th cent. AD.

LUNT ROMAN FORT (Warwickshire)

Important Roman site, unique in Britain, a strangely-shaped small (4.5 acre) fort near Baginton just S. of Coventry, incorporating inside its unexpectedly sinuous ramparts, on the E. side, a circular *gyrus*, an equestrian exercise ring, 107 ft. in diameter. This was possibly for cavalry training, or perhaps for a group of military horse-breakers and trainers. The fort was initially constructed about 60 AD and occupied, with some changes, for about 20 years—with a period of reoccupation two centuries later. Preliminary excavations in 1960 were followed from 1966 on by the experimental reconstruction, by the Coventry Corporation, of two stretches of turf and timber rampart, the eastern gate, a granary (now a museum and interpretive center), and the *gyrus* (1978). The whole is open to the public as an educational venture and among other activities there are periodic displays by the Ermine Street Guard, an amateur group devoted to the exact recreation of a unit of the Roman army—uniforms, weapons, standards and all.

The stretches of reconstructed ramparts (1966 and 1970), built of turves with a palisaded walkway and crenellations on top, and the eastern gate, prefabricated of timbers in 1970 and erected by army engineers in just two days, give a good idea of what all the Roman forts in Britain were like before most were rebuilt in stone. It was found that after 13 years (1983) the ramparts had to be rebuilt and the timbers replaced, though the gate was still sound. Excavations on the W. side of the fort continue and there were plans in 1985 to reconstruct more of the ramparts and, if possible, all the interior buildings, beginning with the headquarters building. The Lunt compares with the reconstruction of Viking Jorvik at *York* as one of the two most imaginative and interesting archaeological displays for the public in England.

LYDNEY
(Gloucestershire)

A most interesting site on a high promontory with magnificent views over the Severn valley, 8 mi. (13 km.) NE of Chepstow, off the main road to Gloucester. Here was an Iron Age hill fort, Roman iron mines and a late Roman pagan temple, excavated by Sir Mortimer Wheeler in 1928–29, the remains now much overgrown and not much to look at. The site is part of a private deer park and permission is required to visit it. The temple complex was once a cult center of importance with a large temple, guest house and bath suite, built shortly after 364 AD and dedicated to the Celtic god Nodens—most surprising in the closing years of the empire when Christianity was already in the ascendant. The rectangular temple, of unusual design, measured 60 by 80 ft. Its cella, divided into three small sanctuaries at one end, was surrounded by a wide corridor with seven curious alcoves or "chapels" along its outer wall, each fronted by a mosaic. The elaborate bath suite N. of the temple, some of which is still visible, was fed by a water tank and conduit. Apparently Nodens was a water god and above all a healing god, for many small bronze votive figures of dogs, often associated with healing in antiquity, were found in the excavations, and facing the temple on the W. was a long, narrow suite of cubicles opening onto a verandah, probably for patients who slept there overnight in hopes that the god would visit them with a cure—a common practice at ancient healing shrines. According to reports, the main mosaic in the temple, now destroyed, was dedicated by the commanding officer of a naval depot, probably somewhere nearby on the Severn estuary. Finally, a large hotel for pilgrims (130 by 160 ft.), with many rooms around a courtyard, lay NE of the temple. It is no longer visible.

The sanctuary complex was built into an Iron Age promontory fort of the 1st cent. BC with ramparts defending the NE end of the spur. During the Roman period and into the 3rd cent. AD the inhabitants dug iron mines. The most impressive of these is now under the bath suite and can be entered with care. It descends to a depth of 15 ft. and runs for 50 ft. under the ramparts. The pick marks of the miners can still be seen in its walls. The finds from the excavations are housed in a private museum in Lydney Park.

LYMPNE CASTLE
(Kent)

Or Stutfall Castle, one of the late Roman *Saxon Shore* forts built in the late 3rd cent. to withstand coastal raiders. The much-tumbled remains of the polygonal fort of Portus Lemanis, covering 11 acres, overlooks Romney Marsh, 1.5 mi. (2.6 km.) from the present coastline, just S. of Lympne. Excavations in 1977 turned up an altar and other finds that indicated there had been an earlier 2nd-cent. naval station here, though no trace of it has been found on the ground.

MAEN CETI
(West Glamorgan)

Unusual Neolithic chambered tomb, close to another tomb, *Parc Cwm*, on the Gower peninsula W. of Swansea, 1 mi. (1.6 km.) NE of Reynoldston; also known as Arthur's Stone (the mighty king is supposed to have thrown it down here). Two irregular burial chambers are covered by a huge, 25-ton glacial boulder as capstone, resting now on nine small uprights. The stone circle surrounding it appears to be the remains of a ring cairn. See *Goat's Cave*, also on the Gower peninsula.

MAIDEN CASTLE
(Cheshire)

Promontory fort in Bickerton Hill, about equidistant between Wrexham and Nantwich in southern Cheshire. Although only about 1½ acres in size, the fort was protected by elaborate double walls on the SE side; cliffs protect the other sides. The outer wall is probably the oldest, built earlier in the Iron Age and later strengthened with a new stone facing and palisade. The inner wall, possibly 1st cent. BC, was of *Murus Gallicus* construction, common on the continent—faced with stone on both sides, tied together with heavy beams, and filled with rubble in between. The beams were burned and the stone vitrified, suggesting a possible Roman attack. The 50-ft., inturned entrance passageway through both walls narrowed from 16 ft. wide to half that and was paved with cobbles, still showing the ruts of cart wheels. See also *Eddisbury*.

MAIDEN CASTLE
(Dorset)

Magnificent Iron Age hill fort, less than 2 mi. (3.25 km.) S. of Dorchester, un-equalled in the country for the complexity of its massive multiple defenses—though *Hambledon Hill* NE of Dorchester bears some comparison. The famous excavations by Sir Mortimer Wheeler from 1934 to 1938, widely reported in the news, showed that the eastern of its two knolls was occupied as early as about 3000 BC by a Neolithic causewayed camp with two concentric rings of ditches (see Windmill Hill in *Avebury*)—in this respect also comparable to Hambledon Hill. Later on in the Neolithic period, when the camp had been abandoned, a curious ritual structure of parallel ditches delimiting a mound many hundreds of ft. long was erected along the top of the hill (no longer visible). Its construction was accompanied by ritual burials of children and of a cannibalized human body.

Thousands of years later (about 350 BC) the same knoll was ringed with a simple Iron Age rampart and ditch, with entrances on the E. and W. Some hundred years later the defenses were extended to the whole hill—about 45 acres—and the entrances were elaborated. In another 100 years the final remodeling of the defenses and entrances began, leaving the huge bank, ditches and incredibly elaborate gate systems we see today, with platforms for slingers and multiple ditches and banks to hold the enemy at a distance. The final defense system may have been the work of Venetic invaders from France in the late 1st cent. BC—as suggested by Sir Mortimer—refugees from Caesar's campaign in Brittany, for the Venetii were great sailors and famous for their use of that new weapon, the sling. In fact Sir Mortimer found a cache of some 22,000 sling stones at the eastern entrance, gathered from a beach about 8 mi. (13 km.) away.

We now enter recorded history with the successful siege and capture of the fortress by the Roman general (later emperor) Vespasian around 44 AD, after the initial Roman invasion of 43 AD. Of the defenders, women as well as men, massacred after the assault, 38 were hastily buried by the survivors at the eastern gate, though each was provided with a last meal. Among the grievously wounded a Celtic warrior was found with a Roman iron bolt embedded in his spine. This clinching evidence can be found, with other finds, in the Dorchester museum today.

About 20 years later the inhabitants of the hill were moved to the new Roman town of Durnovaria, now *Dorchester*. Late in the 4th cent. a Romano-Celtic temple was built on the hill—a square cella and verandah, the interior paved with simple mosaics, and a small priest's house adjoining it. Its foundations may be seen today. A major new excavation of Maiden Castle began in July 1985, preceded by a renovation of its deteriorating ramparts by 100 unemployed youths. The new excavation, launched with much fanfare, is open to the public with guided tours. It seeks to substantiate the assumed dates for the fort's phases,

Maiden Castle, Dorset, the great Iron
Age hill fort of the Durotriges, finest
in England. It lies close to Dorchester. The aerial view brings out the
massive, late Iron Age, multiple fortifications and the complex eastern
entrance gate (foreground) that was
stormed by the Roman troops under
the future Emperor Vespasian about
44 AD. In the background lies
Dorchester, Roman Durnovaria, the
eventual home of the fortress's inhabitants. A striking, closer view looks
out over the enormous ramparts of
the hill fort. (Photo: courtesy English
Heritage. Photo: the author.)

to investigate the density of occupation within the fort, and to answer other such questions.

MALTON
(North Yorkshire)

Outside this market town on the Derwent River lay the rather large, 8-acre Roman fort of Derventio, surrounded by a substantial civilian *vicus*. Just a few banks of the fort can now be seen, but excavations have shown that it began as an Agricolan fort of about 79 AD and was several times rebuilt in stone into the 4th cent. Under it lay a far larger camp of some 22 acres, probably dating from about 71–72 AD and built by part of the 9th Legion. The *vicus* was partly excavated in 1949–52 in advance of redevelopment. The best of Derventio is to be seen in the town museum in the old town hall.

MAM TOR
(Derbyshire)

Largest hill fort in Derby, high up in the Peak District near Castleton and about 10 mi. (16 km.) due W. of *Carl Wark* over in South Yorkshire. Excavations from 1965 to 1969 showed that the ramparts were eventually faced with stone; there were inturned entrances N. and S. Two Bronze Age round barrows lie within the circuit and there are hut circles on the hilltop. Radiocarbon dates from the interior suggest a puzzling Middle Bronze Age occupation, though the defenses, undated, are undoubtedly later.

MANCHESTER
(Greater Manchester)

Famous industrial and commercial city, originating in a Roman fort on the ancient military road between *Chester* and *York*. The fort, whose site has long been known, was founded during the Agricolan campaigns of 77–78 at the confluence of the rivers Medlock and Irwell, in a section now called Castlefields near the center of the modern city. It held an auxiliary garrison of nearly 500 men, and a substantial *vicus* or civilian settlement grew up around it. Once lost to sight, parts of the fort have now been excavated and reconstructed in the course of redevelopment, and now form part of Britain's first urban heritage park along with several museums and heritage trails. Excavations began in 1972 and the first phase of the reconstruction was opened in 1983. It now comprises a section of the fort's wall with inner and outer ditches, the North gate, and the stone foundations of several houses of the *vicus* outside the fort's walls as well as a number of roads—all as they were in the prosperous period of 200–250 AD when the original turf and timber fort had been rebuilt in stone.

MAN, ISLE OF

See *Isle of Man*.

MARDEN HENGE
(Wiltshire)

Largest of the many impressive Neolithic henge monuments discovered or excavated in recent years in the British Isles. Three of the four largest are close to the Avon River in Wiltshire and are no more than 30 mi. (48 km.) from each other: *Avebury* to the N., Marden 8 mi. (13 km.) to the S. of it, and Durrington Walls (with *Woodhenge* as an annex) 10 mi. (16 km.) still farther S., lying only 2 mi. (3.25 km.) NE of *Stonehenge*—a rather different kind of monument. The fourth is Mt. Pleasant, near the Dorset coast just SE of *Dorchester* and some 60 mi. (97 km.) SW of Stonehedge. Little is visible at Mt. Pleasant, although its great oval enclosure (900 by 1,200 ft.), on a hilltop with one entrance on the SE, has been traced. It was excavated in 1970, revealing the postholes of a huge 130-ft. wide circular building in the interior. These enormous Late Neolithic henges, dated to the 3rd millennium BC, were apparently religious and ceremonial gathering places, enclosed within huge banks with a wide ditch usually inside the bank (and thus not defensive) and timber structures, some quite large, in their interiors. They had either one or two entrance passages crossing the ditch on causeways. Avebury alone has stone circles as well as other features. Stonehenge is a unique variation on the henge theme. Each of these enormous henges would have required untold man-hours to build.

The village of Marden in the Vale of Pewsey, about 6 mi. (9.6 km.) SE of *Devizes*, sits inside an enormous oval henge that enclosed 35 acres within its bank and ditch—most of which has been plowed away. The meandering Avon forms its boundary on the S. and W. sides, and the two entrance causeways, unlike the other henges, are at right angles to each other on the N. and E. sides. Exploratory excavations in 1969 at the northern entrance and inside it showed that the ditch was over 50 ft. wide but very shallow. Visitors to the shrine had dropped antler picks, sherds of Neolithic grooved ware, animal bones and flint tools into the ditch, and inside the entrance the scant remains of a circular timber structure about 32 ft. across were discovered—all very similar to the previously excavated Durrington Walls (see *Woodhenge*). A great mound, over 20 ft. high, used to stand inside the enclosure but was destroyed early in the 19th cent. Unlike Durrington Walls, no Beaker pottery from the end of the Neolithic period showed up at Marden, which indicates that it may have gone out of use much earlier.

MARTINHOE
(Devon)

Along the N. Exmoor coast of Devon, facing the Bristol Channel, are the remains of two early Roman fortlets or signal stations, obviously built to keep an eye, in conjunction with the Roman fleet, on the still rebellious Silures in Wales across the Channel. Martinhoe, partly collapsed into the sea, is about 4 mi. (6.5 km.) W. of Lynmouth; Old Burrow Walls lies E. of Lynmouth at Glenthorne, close to the Somerset/Devon border. Excavations of both in the 1960s showed that Old Burrow was the earliest, built about 48 AD as a temporary fort in the early years of the conquest, with its garrison living in tents, and abandoned about 52 AD when the Silures (and Caratacus) had been defeated. It was succeeded by Martinhoe, built about 58–60 AD and abandoned about 75 when the legionary fortress at *Caerleon* in Wales superseded it. Martinhoe held about 65 to 80 troops under a centurion, living in timber barracks. Both fortlets had the same plan, an outer circular rampart with entrance from the landward side and an inner square enclosure with entrance on the seaward side to make things difficult for the enemy. Today all that is to be seen are the mounded lines of the double ramparts. The finds from Martinhoe are in the Athenaeum Museum, Barnstaple; of Old Burrow in the Taunton museum.

MARYPORT ROMAN FORT
(Cumbria)

The only visible remains of a series of forts and watchtowers built down along the Cumbrian coast to protect the western approaches to *Hadrian's Wall*. The 5.75 acre fort of Alauna lies N. of the town of Maryport, overlooking the sea. Only the platform and the openings of the four gates can be seen today. Excavations in 1967 determined four building periods in stone from the 2nd cent. through the 4th. A large parade ground lay S. of the fort, with a tribunal, the whole quaintly known as Pudding Pie Hill in later years. N. of it was an extensive civilian settlement that has been excavated, revealing the foundations of the usual houses, shops and so forth. Here lay the original, earlier parade ground, and in 1870 a remarkable discovery was made here of 17 altars with inscriptions, in mint condition, buried in pits (apparently Roman altars were periodically replaced in a kind of renewal ceremony), revealing much information about the earlier garrisons of the fort—units from Spain, Dalmatia, the Rhine and else-where. In the 1970s the altars were in a private collection at Netherall Lodge, and may eventually be tranferred to a new museum in the vicinity.

MAUGHOLD CHURCH

See *Isle of Man.*

MAUMBURY RINGS
(Dorset)

See *Dorchester.*

MAYBURGH
(Cumbria)

Huge Neolithic henge, at Eamont Bridge, just S. of Penrith. There is only one entrance, and no ditch; nevertheless the enormous area of the henge is sur-rounded by a massive bank of heaped-up earth and cobbles as high as a small house. At the center only one stone still stands of the four reported by Stukeley in the 18th cent.

MEARE VILLAGE
(Somerset)

See *Glastonbury.*

MELANDRA CASTLE
ROMAN FORT
(Derbyshire)

Small Roman fort, 5 acres, called Ardotalia, built about 78 AD to command a road over a pass in the High Peak district leading from Brough to nearby *Man-chester.* It lies less than 2 mi. (3 km.) NW of Glossop. Its defenses, reinforced in stone about 100 AD, are in very good shape. Excavations in the 1960s and '70s uncovered the *principia,* timber barracks and a small bathhouse outside the fort. There was a civilian settlement around the fort, including a large *mansio* or inn.

MEN-AN-TOL
(Cornwall)

Curious megalithic monument near Madron, NW of *Penzance,* a long, thin stand-ing slab with a perfectly circular hole at its center, large enough to pass a child through—which used to be done as a cure for rickets! It may have been a "port-hole" partition in the burial chamber of a lost Neolithic tomb, though this is by no means certain.

MEONSTOKE
(Hampshire)

Mid-Saxon settlement and cemetery, currently (1987) under excavation, located 12 mi. (19 km.) E. of *Winchester,* close to Exton. The village is unusual in that it was sited close to a Roman settlement.

MERRIVALE BRIDGE
(Devon)

See *Dartmoor.*

MERRY MAIDENS
(Cornwall)

One of the most perfect Bronze Age stone rings in Britain, a true circle 80 ft. across, consisting of 19 evenly-spaced stones, each about 4 ft. high. It lies 1.5 mi. (2.6 km.) SE of St. Buryan, about 4 mi. (6.5 km.) SW of Penzance, and is named for the usual story of maidens turned to stone for dancing on the Sab-bath—possibly a memory of prehistoric dance-rituals on the site. Two stones appropriately called the Pipers, about 14 and 15 ft. high and aligned on the circle's center, stand about 400 yds. to the NE. Another stone, closer on the W., is called the Fiddler. These stones suggest possible astronomical sighting lines.

MERSEA MOUNT
MAUSOLEUM
(Essex)

Romano-British tumulus on Mersea Island, just after the causeway to the island reaches it, about 7 mi. (11 km.) S. of *Colchester.* With a diameter of 100 ft. and 22 ft. high, this imposing barrow, probably late 1st cent. AD, is the best of many such barrows found in Essex. Thanks to a concrete tunnel into its center, built after the excavations of 1912, the burial chamber can be inspected. This was about 20 inches high and built of brick and tiles. It contained a glass bowl with the ashes, sealed in a lead casket (now in the Colchester museum). See also *Bartlow Hills; Harpenden; Keston.*

METHERALL
(Devon)

See *Dartmoor.*

MIDDLETON CROSSES
(North Yorkshire)

In Middleton church, 1 mi. (1.6 km.) W. of Pickering, with its late Saxon W. tower and nave, are three interesting Anglo-Danish wheel crosses of the 9th or 10th cent., and fragments of others, typical of a region that was under strong Scandinavian influences. The most famous cross depicts what appears to be a Viking warrior in a conical helmet, surrounded by his weapons—battle-axe, sword, shield and spear. Being on a cross, he was possibly a recently converted pagan warrior, though there are other interpretations. On the reverse is a crude dragon, reflecting the earlier Scandinavian Jellinge style. Another cross depicts a hunting scene with a dog, with another dragon on the reverse. See also *Gosforth Cross; Halton.*

MIDSUMMER HILL CAMP
(Hereford and
Worcester)

One of the Iron Age hill forts of the Welsh Marches, a few mi. E. of Ledbury at Eastnor and not far S. of the *Herefordshire Beacon* fort. Excavated from 1965 to 1970, Midsummer Hill proved to have been, like the other Marcher forts, intensively occupied in a planned village by a stable agricultural population for about 500 years until it was conquered and the huts burned, like *Croft Ambrey*, by the Romans in 48 AD. Again like Croft Ambrey a sequence of 17 successive S. gates was uncovered, the earliest radiocarbon-dated at 470 BC. Inside the fort about 250 terraces held huts arranged in lines along streets. The huts were oblong at the beginning and each was rebuilt on the same spot from four to six times. Many of these thatch-roofed, timber-framed houses were barns, the others dwellings with hearths. It is estimated that the village housed a population of between 500 and 2,500 people in a largely self-sufficient farming community, though there was some evidence of iron-smelting and bronze-working on the hill. See also *Breiddin Hill; Credenhill; Old Oswestry; Sutton Walls; The Wrekin.*

MINNING LOW
(Derbyshire)

Largest of a group of Neolithic communal chambered tombs in the Peak District, near Ballidon W. of Matlock on the Roman road that runs southeasterly from Buxton. It is not far from the stone circle of *Arbor Low* to the NW. The much-ruined, 10-ft.-high mound measures about 120 by 140 ft. and contains at least four burial chambers, one centrally placed—obviously the earliest and original part of the mound—and another to the S., both with their capstones still in place. Passageways with drystone walls lead into both. Nothing was found in the cairn when cleared out in 1851, for it had long before been robbed.

MITCHELL'S FOLD
(Shropshire)

Bronze Age circle about 16 mi. (26 km.) SW of Shrewsbury, W. of A488 near Chirbury, some 5 mi. (8 km.) NW of Lydham. It is difficult to find but is boldly sited on a mountainside with superb views toward Wales. The circle, about 75 ft. across, once contained 16 or more stones from 2 ft. to 6 ft. in height, of which about half are still standing.

MOEL GOEDOG
(Gwynedd)

Several monuments on a remote Bronze Age trackway that starts at Llanbedr, about 3 mi. (4.75 km.) S. of Harlech near the coast of Cardigan Bay in old

Merionethshire. These trackways, used by the metal traders, were marked by standing stones, and one finds a variety of cairns, circles and standing stones of the Bronze Age along them, as well as Iron Age forts and hut circles. At Moel Goedog a short way along the trackway there is a small circular Iron Age fort with double ramparts, undoubtedly palisaded in its day (4th to 3rd cents. BC). Near it are two groups of hut circles, probably contemporary, and to the SW two Bronze Age ring cairns, the internal mounds gone but a ring, sometimes doubled, of standing kerb stones around each, backed by another ring of small stones.

One cairn was excavated and restored in 1978. Under one of its 12 kerb stones was found an offering in an urn, of charcoal and bits of human bone. Inside the circle nine pits, randomly placed and dug apparently over a very long period, were filled some with pure charcoal, two others with bits of human bone again. Only one contained a true cremation burial. These offerings of charcoal and bone are common in Wales and also in Scotland. A few miles farther along the trackway another similar ring cairn, Bryn Cader Fader, dramatically dominates a ridge with a circle of 15 long, sharp stones angling out like teeth or a crown of thorns.

MONKWEARMOUTH (Tyne and Wear)

The remnants of the great monastery founded here by Benedict Biscop in 674 AD. In a grimy area of factories and developments stands St. Peter's church, a companion to St. Paul's church about 6 mi. (10 km.) N. on the Tyne, on the site of Benedict's sister monastery of *Jarrow*, founded about 10 years later, where the Venerable Bede spent most of his life. St. Peter's is on the N. bank of the Wear River close to the bridge to Sutherland on the other bank. Only the lower part of its W. tower seems to date from the founding of the monastery or shortly thereafter, along with bits of sculpture under the tower. The upper part of the tower is probably 10th cent. Originally a porch rather than a tower, one can see the line of the original roof embedded in later masonry in the third stage of the tower, and the doorway pillars with carvings of entwined birds attest to the once magnificent building.

Benedict, an energetic Northumbrian, introduced Latin Christianity to the North with his two monasteries, which became great centers of learning (see also *York*). He also brought masons and glaziers from France to build and adorn his church, thus reintroducing European building methods that had not been seen here since the Romans left. The beautifully illustrated, vellum *Codex Amiatinus*, the oldest known complete Latin Bible, now in Florence, Italy, was apparently produced in the workshops of this monastery. Excavations S. of the church in 1962 have uncovered early Saxon buildings and fragments of colored glass from Benedict's French glaziers, but nothing is now to be seen here. The glass is now in the Sunderland Museum and there is an information center in the modern chapter house and some displays in St. Peter's itself. See also *Durham*.

MOUNT CABURN (East Sussex)

See *Caburn, The*.

MOUNT PLEASANT HENGE (Dorset)

See *Marden Henge*.

MUCKING
(Essex)

Remarkable site on a gravel terrace overlooking the N. bank of the lower Thames, just S. of Stanford le Hope across the river from Gravesend. A long series of excavations here has revealed occupations from the Iron Age through the early Saxon period. Beginning as a rescue operation in advance of gravel digging, Mucking became an archaeological training ground for thousands of students well into the 1970s. The excavations uncovered the ramparts of a round Iron Age fort on the site, with many later Iron Age hut remains (over 100) in its silted-up ditches, Belgic sheepfolds (about 1st cent. AD) and Roman field systems probably belonging to a villa nearby. Of most interest, however, were well over 100 sunken huts (*grubenhausen*) of the earliest Saxon period, and one large hall—a rare find from a little-known era. There were also two Saxon cemeteries of the 5th to 7th cents. AD, one of which contained over 700 graves, now completely excavated. The finds included vessels of pottery, wood and glass, knives, weapons and military gear, beads and bronze brooches. See also *West Stow* for another Saxon village of the period.

MYNYDD-BACH
   TRECASTELL CIRCLES
(Powys)

See *Brecon*.

NANT TAWR CIRCLES
(Powys)

See *Brecon*.

NEATH ROMAN FORT
(West Glamorgan)

The main road from Swansea bisects the remains of this fort just before Neath. It was discovered bit by bit just after World War II in the course of development in a heavily industrialized area. Nidum fort was built in a strategic position on the estuary of the Neath River and commanded the main E-W road as well as a cross road leading N. to *Brecon Gaer* near *Brecon* and other forts. Presumably there was an early Flavian fort on the site. Bits of the clay ramparts of the second phase of about 80–85 AD have been discovered, as well as of the third phase, a reoccupation after a hiatus about 120–125 AD, when the 5.8-acre fort was rebuilt in stone. It was abandoned shortly thereafter, though a *mansio* or inn may have continued on the site. The SE and SW gates of the stone fort, uncovered in 1949, are in state care and may be viewed in a housing estate.

NEVERN
(Dyfed)

See *Newport*.

NEWCASTLE UPON TYNE
(Tyne and Wear)

See *Hadrian's Wall*.

NEWPORT
(Dyfed)

There are many interesting sites clustered around Newport and Fishguard bays on the Irish Sea and inland. Among them is an eccentric megalithic tomb, without parallel, Cerrig y Gof, W. of Newport itself. It is a roughly circular mound rather damaged by 1811 excavations, with five burial cists set radially around the perimeter. Only one still has its capstone, though others are lying about. At St. Brynach's church at Nevern, 2 mi. (3.25 km.) W. of Newport, there are a number of interesting early Christian stones. In the churchyard a great cross of about 1000 AD, decorated with interlace panels, stands 13 ft. high. Its inscriptions are no longer readable, but another cross nearby, of about 500 AD, shows inscriptions in Latin and Ogam. There are more stones inside the church. Inland, near the headwaters of the Nevern River on the northern slopes of the Preseli Mtns. (whence, it is thought, came the bluestones for early *Stonehenge*) stands the imposing skeleton of a portal tomb, Pentre Ifan, 1.5 mi. (2.6 km.) N. of Brynberian. Excavated and conserved, it is now in state care. Three uprights, tall and thin, precariously—and dramatically—support a 17-ton capstone. With its semi-circular facade and forecourt, its tall portal stones and long tapering mound (now marked out on the ground), it is closely related to a type of Neolithic court cairn found in Northern Ireland and SW Scotland, as well as in N. Wales (see *Dyffryn Long Barrow*). Along the sides of the cairn, about 130 ft. long, mysterious lines of stones and two pits were found. It is thought that the tomb was constructed in two phases, the facade added later to the original portal tomb. A mi. or more along the slopes of the Preselis, in the parish of Meline, Bedd-yr-Afanc is an undated, wedge-shaped gallery grave, over 30 ft. long, in the center of a large mound. It has affinities with a common tomb type in southern Ireland.

Among the many monuments around Fishguard Bay and S. of Strumble Head a fine tomb, Carreg Samson, or Longhouse, is near the coast in the parish of Mathry. Its seven uprights define a polygonal burial chamber and only three of them support the huge heavy capstone, about 15 ft. long by 9 ft. There is no trace of a cairn. The tomb is in state care.

NEWPORT ROMAN VILLA (Isle of Wight)

A corridor villa in Newport itself, the main building only excavated in 1926–27. It is in care of the local council and a shed covers a few of its 14 rooms. These have tessellated floors and in one case, surprisingly, a fireplace against the wall of the largest room. The W. wing is a well-preserved bath suite. The villa was probably built during the 2nd or 3rd cent. AD over an earlier structure. See also *Brading Roman Villa*.

NINE LADIES (Derbyshire)

See *Stanton Moor*.

NINE MAIDENS (Cornwall)

See *Bodmin Moor*.

NINE MAIDENS (Cornwall)

See *Boscawen-Un Stone Circle*.

NINE MAIDENS (Cornwall)

Stone row, the only one in Cornwall, N. of St. Columb Major near the road to Wadebridge. A row of nine standing stones, six still upright, run irregularly along a line about 350 ft. in length. There are also many round barrows in the area.

NINE MAIDENS (Cornwall)

See *St. Just*.

NINE STONES (Devon)

See *Dartmoor*.

NINE STONES (Dorsetshire)

Small elliptical stone circle just S. of the main road, W. of Winterbourne Abbas, near *Dorchester*. There are indeed nine upright sarsen stones here, the two tallest on the N. side of the circle. The monument, enclosed in railings, is in state care.

NORMANTON DOWN
   BARROW GROUP
(Wiltshire)

See *Stonehenge*.

NORTHAMPTON
(Northamptonshire)

Midlands industrial city with a very long history, though little of the earlier city
survives. Just to the S. of the city, W. of Hardingstone, the Iron Age hill fort of
Hunsbury with its overgrown ramparts and hut sites, revealed by earlier quarrying, indicates prehistoric exploitation of the site in farming, weaving and metal-
working. Less than a mi. to the N. on Briar Hill recent excavations revealed an
even earlier Neolithic causewayed camp. Nothing of it now remains.

   There was an important Saxon settlement at Northampton, and the local
archaeological unit, responding to extensive redevelopment after 1965, found
evidence of its origins in a number of early, pagan Saxon, sunken huts in the
city. The explorations culminated in 1981–82 with the excavation just E. of the
old Norman church of St. Peter's of a series of Anglo-Saxon royal (Mercian)
halls, the first a timber structure of the late 7th cent. AD, almost 100 ft. long,
with annexes at either end and, possibly, nine bays in the interior, the whole
roofed in a single span. Early in the next century it was replaced by an even
larger (123 ft. long) stone-built hall, unique in England, later increased to 142
ft. by the addition of two rooms. W. of it and running under the present St.
Peter's was another stone structure, undoubtedly an early church, and here there
were five large basket-lined bowls—mortar mixers—dug into the earth; they
were used in building these important structures, obviously the center of an
influential royal and ecclesiastical establishment. The hall was demolished in
the 9th cent. when Northampton became part of the Viking Danelaw. In the early
Middle Ages it became a prosperous large city. Northampton's Museum and Art
Gallery contains a large archaeological collection, including the Iron Age finds
from Hunsbury Hill.

NORTH ELMHAM
(Norfolk)

Little village, once the seat of the Saxon bishopric of East Anglia, from 956 to
1075 AD. The excavated ruins of the 10th-cent. Saxon cathedral, in state care,
lie behind the present church, some of its flint-rubble walls still standing. Placed
within a later medieval, moated manor house, the cathedral was only 100 ft.
long, with an aisleless nave, transept and shallow apse as well as two small
towers. It has been assumed that North Elmham also held one half of the earlier
7th-cent. divided see before the Viking raids, but though excavations on the site
have indicated timber structures below the 10th-cent. ruins, nothing as early as
the pre-Viking period has appeared. That the Saxon settlement here was an
important one is shown by a sequence of timber buildings, huts and halls excavated at the N. end of the village.

NORTH LEIGH ROMAN
   VILLA
(Oxfordshire)

In the Cotswolds 3 mi. (4.75 km.) N. of Witney (and actually in East End village,
not in North Leigh). After its 4th-cent.-AD remodeling this was a very large villa
with rooms on three sides of a courtyard, the entrance on the fourth, and two
sets of baths. It began in the 2nd cent. as a single small building with detached
bath house, to which wings and floors of simple mosaics were later added before the final remodeling. The main room of the late villa, with its hypocaust for
heating perfectly preserved, is now the showpiece. It is floored with a sophisticated and elaborate geometric mosaic, much like that at *Chedworth* villa, designed by craftsmen from *Cirencester*. The rest of the villa is disappointing. Excavated in 1813–16 and again before World War I, it has been neglected, but is

now being reexcavated and consolidated. Many outbuildings, unexcavated, have been discovered from the air by crop marks on the SW side of the hill.

NYMPSFIELD LONG BARROW (Gloucestershire)

Neolithic chambered tomb of about 3000 BC, on the western edge of the Cotswold escarpment, about 4 mi. (6.5 km.) SW of Stroud, one of about 50 similar tombs clustered on the high ground of the Cotswolds, all belonging to the "Cotswold-Severn" type. At 90 by 50 ft. Nympsfield is the smallest of the better-known tombs of this group, which includes *Belas Knap* and *Hetty Pegler's Tump*, the latter only one mi. (1.6 km.) to the S. Excavated at least three times, the latest in 1974, it is now consolidated and open to the public, though its chambers have lost their capstones and most of the mound has gone. The entrance, this time through the horned facade of the forecourt, leads into an antechamber and a gallery, with chambers to the right and left and one at the end. Some 20 to 30 burials were found in various excavations, and evidence of elaborate funeral rites with burnings in the forecourt. The finds are in the Stroud and Gloucester museums.

OFFA'S DYKE

Renowned barrier, huge bank and ditch that runs from "sea to sea" and still marks the boundary between the English and the Welsh. It was constructed in the late 8th cent. AD at the orders of King Offa, greatest king of Anglo-Saxon Mercia, as a border barrier to control Welsh raiding rather than as a fully garrisoned frontier. With a bank up to 10 ft. high, probably topped by a palisade in certain areas, and a deep ditch on the Welsh side, it ran for 149 mi. (240 km.) from the Bristol Channel E. of Chepstow to Prestatyn on the Irish Sea W. of Chester. Only about 80 mi. (130 km.) of it were man-made; the rest of the frontier of that time was probably protected by impenetrable forests; and in its northern parts it may have incorporated some of an earlier Mercian barrier, Wat's Dyke, dating from the early 8th cent.

The official Offa's Dyke Path, opened in 1971, roughly follows the entire route, crossing the Dyke now and then. A fine stretch of the Dyke and ditch may be seen close to the southern end as it reaches the Bristol Channel across the Wye from Chepstow (Gwent), and again about 5 mi. (8 km.) N. across the Wye from Tintern Abbey. Farther N. the Offa's Dyke Riverside Park in Knighton (Powys) preserves a good section. W. of Clun in Shropshire it can be viewed again N. and S. of the Clun River, and it passes close to the Iron Age hill fort of *Breiddin Hill* 6.5 mi. (10.5 km.) NE of Welshpool in Powys. A long stretch runs S. across the Chirk River from Chirk Castle in Clwd. Some of the earlier Wat's Dyke may be seen running by the hill fort of *Old Oswestry* just N. of Oswestry in Shropshire. See also *Eliseg's Pillar*.

OLD BLOCKHOUSE

See *Scilly Isles.*

OLD BURROW WALLS (Devon)

See *Martinhoe.*

OLDBURY CASTLE (Wiltshire)

See *White Horse.*

OLDBURY HILL (Kent)

Large, Late Iron Age hill fort with Paleolithic caves, W. of Ightham near Sevenoaks. A single line of Belgic ramparts, doubled at vulnerable points, surrounds the hill. Excavated in 1938, it was found that the hill was first fortified about

100 BC, then, either about 50 years later or before the advance of the Romans in the '40s AD the ramparts were heightened and given a sloping glacis in front, as well as a wide ditch in the continental style (Fécamp), and the NE gate was strengthened. All of this was probably done by the Belgic invaders from the continent. This NE gate, with a cache of slingstones found near it, was burned down in an attack, probably Roman. The southern gate has been damaged by a new road. On the side of the hill two small caves, excavated in 1890 and 1938, yielded very early Middle Paleolithic Mousterian flints of Neanderthal Man, a rare find in Britain.

OLD OSWESTRY
(Shropshire)

One of the more complex and substantial hill forts along the border of Wales, on a hill just N. of Oswestry. Excavated in 1939, it probably dates from the mid-3rd cent. BC and was abandoned after the Roman conquest. In between there were four major rebuildings of the defenses, involving especially the complex outworks of the W. gate, mostly in stone, and two small enclosures on either side of the hill, possibly cattle pens. The final act was the construction of the huge double outer ramparts enclosing all the earlier defenses; at the end there were as many as seven ramparts and ditches in places. A group of circular timber huts on the hilltop predated any defenses. Later similar huts were built on the hill in stone. For other forts of the Welsh Marches see *Breiddin Hill*; *Credenhill*; *Croft Ambrey*; *Herefordshire Beacon*; *Midsummer Hill*; *Sutton Walls*; *The Wrekin*.

OLD SARUM
(Wiltshire)

See *Salisbury*.

OLD WINCHESTER HILL
(Hampshire)

Iron Age hill fort high up over the Meon valley E. of Meonstoke, with great views, about 12 mi. (19 km.) SE of *Winchester*. The oval fort has a single circuit of ramparts, with inturned entrances on the E. and W. There are and were up to a dozen earlier barrows both inside the fort and outside its entrances.

OLD WORK, THE
(Shropshire)

See *Wroxeter*.

OLIVER'S CASTLE
(Wiltshire)

See *White Horse*.

ORPINGTON
(Greater London)

A great many chance finds and a number of excavations of Roman artifacts and sites in the London borough of Bromley in southern London have suggested an extensive settlement in and around the Cray River valley. This would include the Roman cemetery and possible Roman villa at *Keston* to the S. of Bromley as an outlier, and the more central Roman finds at Orpington. For instance, a Roman building with red tessellated floors, occupied from about 80 AD into the 4th cent., built over an Iron Age hut, was excavated in 1954–57 W. of Orpington station. Part of it has been consolidated and is on view in a bank. In 1971–78 two rooms (and part of a third) of a bath house were excavated in Orpington itself and are now visible under a large shed. Finds from the site suggest intensive occupation of the area from the 2nd cent. to about 370 AD. A Saxon cemetery, unusually encroaching on the Roman occupation area, was also excavated. The finds from both sites are in the Borough of Bromley Museum.

OTHONA ROMAN FORT
(Essex)

See *Bradwell-on-Sea*.

OVERTON SANCTUARY
(Wiltshire)

See *Avebury*.

OVINGHAM SAXON
CHURCH
(Northumberland)

See *Bywell*.

OXFORD
(Oxfordshire)

University city. A prominent remnant of Anglo-Saxon Oxford is St. Michael's, the tower alone surviving just inside what was once the N. gate of the medieval walled city. It now stands at the head of the very commercial street known as Cornmarket. Of solid, late Saxon rubble construction, the tower shows fine double windows on the fourth and fifth stories and a blocked door on the W. side. Nothing Saxon survives inside. Oxford's famous museum is of course the Ashmolean, a museum of art and archaeology with outstanding collections from all over the world.

PARC CWM CHAMBERED
TOMB
(West Glamorgan)

Or Parc-le-Breos Cwm, a fine specimen of the Severn-Cotswold type of Neolithic tomb (see *Hetty Pegler's Tump*). In state care, it is to be found in the middle of the Gower peninsula, beyond Swansea, at Penmaen, not far from the *Maen Ceti* tomb. A wedge-shaped cairn about 75 ft. long once covered a gallery, entered from a deeply indented horned forecourt at one end. Off the gallery were four thin-walled burial chambers, two on each side. The chambers have long ago lost their capstones. The forecourt and cairn are neatly lined with drystone walling. Excavations in 1896 recovered the scattered bones of about two dozen skeletons, for this was a long-used communal tomb. In 1960–61 it was reexcavated and consolidated. Also on the Gower peninsula is the *Goat's Cave* Paleolithic site.

PAVILAND
(West Glamorgan)

See *Goat's Cave*.

PEAK DISTRICT

See *Sheffield* (South Yorkshire) and in Derbyshire: *Anbor Low*, *Minning Low* and *Stanton Moor*.

PEEL CASTLE

See *Isle of Man*.

PEN DINAS
(Dyfed)

Iron Age hill fort just S. of Aberystwyth, its twin peaks overlooking Cardigan Bay from a site rising between two rivers. Excavations from 1933 to 1937 showed that its life had covered the last three cents. BC, the N. summit being fortified first, then the southern summit with a more substantial stone-faced rubble wall and two gates N. and S. Finally in the 1st cent. BC the two forts were united by walls built in the saddle between, and a new gate there, several times rebuilt. There is evidence, despite extensive ploughing, of round huts in the interior.

PENMACHNO
(Gwynedd)

See *Penmaenmawr*.

PENMAENMAWR
(Gwynedd)

Town on the northern coast of Wales and a mountain behind it, grotesquely quarried away for its volcanic rock, destroying in the process a fine hill fort. However, there are still sites on its slopes worth seeing. Prehistoric people also valued this stone, and at the eastern end of the mountain are the remains of the Neolithic Graig Lwyd Axe Factory, excavated in 1920. Here the slopes are still littered with the axes, adzes and picks, mostly unfinished or discarded, that were produced here on a large scale as roughouts and exported widely in Britain. (See also the Neolithic flint mines of *Cissbury Ring*, *Grimes Graves* and *Pike of Stickle Axe Factory*). There is now nothing more to see of this very ancient industrial site. A half mi. (1 km.) farther up the mountain, on a prominent site in the desolate moorland, stands the well-known Bronze Age Druid's Circle, a somber monument with 10 of its 30 original stones standing upright on a low circular bank. The stones are up to 6 ft. high and two of the tallest mark the entrance gap on the SW. Around it there is another ruined circle and a ring cairn, and an ancient trackway passes close to the main circle. It was excavated in 1958, and at and near the center were found a number of cremation burials under scattered stones, two of the burials children—surely ritual sacrifices.

Moving E. to Conway and then some 5 mi. (8 km.) up the Conway River valley one comes to the Roman fort of Kanovium at Caerhun, the church and its churchyard located in the NE corner of its ramparts, which are still clearly visible, particularly around the churchyard. Excavations from 1926 to 1927 uncovered its interior buildings, now once again grassed over. It was an earth and timber fort of the late 1st cent. AD, rebuilt in stone about 150 AD. After a major destruction in about 200 AD, the fort was sporadically occupied again into the 4th cent. The excavations also found an external bath house and evidence of an extensive settlement around the fort and between it and the river, where there was a dock and jetty.

Over 10 mi. (16 km.) S. down the Conway valley is the Neolithic chambered tomb of *Capel Garmon*. S. again about 5 mi. (8 km.) up a tributary of the Conway, the little church at Penmachno holds a number of early Christian inscribed stones of much interest, one datable to the 6th cent. AD.

PENNANCE MEGALITHIC
TOMB
(Cornwall)

Just SW of Zennor, also called the Giant's House, a small Neolithic gallery grave in better condition than most in Cornwall. Its mound measures 25 ft. in diameter. It is not far from *Zennor Quoit* and *Gurnard's Head*. See *St. Ives*.

PENTRE IFAN
(Dyfed)

See *Newport*.

PEN Y CRUG HILL FORT
(Powys)

See *Brecon*.

PENZANCE
(Cornwall)

See in this area *Boscawen-Un*; *Carn Euny*; *Castle-an-Dinas*; *Chysauster*; *Lanyon Quoit*; *Men-an-Tol*; *Merry Maidens*.

PETUARIA
(Humberside)

See *Hull*.

PEVENSEY
(East Sussex)

Impressive ruins of the *Saxon Shore* fort of Anderida, 4 mi. (6.5 km.) N. of Eastbourne, probably built in the 4th cent., very late in the series of these forts.

The Roman fortress of Anderida (Pevensey Castle), East Sussex, one of the late Saxon Shore forts ringing the S. and E. coasts of Britain. Very well preserved, the fort's massive bastions, jutting out from the wall, are clearly visible. In the foreground is the main gate flanked by towers, and inside the circuit is a later Norman castle. Anderida, once next to the sea, now lies over a mile inland. (Courtesy of English Heritage.)

Once washed by the sea, which gave it a harbor, it now stands on a bluff over the marshes more than a mi. inland. Its circuit of walls, unusually oval in shape, encloses about 9 acres; they are 12 ft. thick and in places rise up to 28 ft. They are surprisingly complete although missing in the S. and for a stretch on the N., and from them project the massive semicircular bastions characteristic of the period, closely spaced. Ten still stand, one on the N. wall nearly at full height, with an artillery embrasure. To the W. is the massive arched main gate flanked by bastions and two guardrooms. A Norman keep, built by the half brother of William the Conqueror, with a later bailey around it, occupies the SE corner. Excavation of the interior many years ago found nothing but the foundations of timber huts. Anderida, as recorded in the Anglo-Saxon Chronicle, was the scene of a pitiful massacre of British defenders by a Saxon horde in 491 AD.

PIERCEBRIDGE ROMAN FORT
(Durham)

Roman Dere Street, running N. from York, crosses the Tees River at the site of this fort, about 6 mi. (10 km.) W. of Darlington, which embraces within its 10.75 acres most of the village of Piercebridge. The fort was built about 300 AD, presumably on or near earlier forts. Its NE corner, with a sewer and latrine, has been left exposed after excavations in 1934. More excavations in the 1970s uncovered a barrack block and internal bath house and discovered the stone piers of the Roman timber bridge over the Tees, now left exposed (the river has changed course). The mounds of the ramparts can also be seen around the village. Another Roman road, branching off southwestward, leads past the marching camp of *Rey Cross*. See also *Binchester*; *Stanwick*.

PIKE OF STICKLE AXE FACTORY (Cumbria)

The site lies 9 mi. (14.5 km.) W. of Ambleside, 2 mi. (3.25 km.) up a difficult climb beyond the end of the minor road that strikes up into the Langdale Pikes in the Cumbrian Mts. On the steep slopes below Pike of Stickle Neolithic man around 3000 BC roughed out the volcanic rock into axe heads that were carried all over Britain. Many for instance have been found in Wessex. The site, littered with broken implements, flakes and discarded axes, is very similar to the Graig Lwyd axe factory in northern Wales (see *Penmaenmawr*).

PIMPERNE LONG BARROW (Dorset)

See *Blandford Forum*.

PINNACLE, THE

See *Jersey*.

PLAS NEWYDD (Gwynedd)

See *Bryn Celli Dhu*.

PONTNEWYDD (Clwyd)

Upper Paleolithic cave, about 5 mi. (8 km.) S. of Rhyl in the Elwy River valley near its juncture with the Clwyd River. Finds, rare in Britain, of extremely ancient hominids were made here in excavations from 1978 to 1981. Although the cave had been excavated in the 1870s and later, the new dig exploited hitherto untouched side passages, turning up not only the stone tools but also the actual remains of a band of early Paleolithic hunters. These included fragments of upper and lower jaws, teeth and a vertebra of these creatures, dated by a battery of modern methods to about 250,000 BC (see also *Hoxne*). Thus they were either extremely early Neanderthal types or a pre-Neanderthal species of early man. See also *Cheddar*; *Cresswell Crags*; *Goat's Cave*; *Hengistbury Head*; *Jersey*; *Kent's Cavern*.

PORTCHESTER (Hampshire)

Finest of the late Roman *Saxon Shore* forts and the most westerly, standing almost complete, still at the end of a promontory jutting out into Portsmouth Harbor to the W. of Portsmouth. Portus Adurni, as it was called, is one of the most impressive surviving Roman buildings in Britain. The walls, enclosing a square of nine acres, still stand about 18 ft. high, with a fine Norman castle in the NW corner and a Romanesque church in the opposite corner. And 14 out of the original 20 semicircular bastions along the walls survive. These are hollow, but probably contained wooden floors supporting light artillery. The two main gates, however, were rebuilt in medieval times, the posterns blocked and the walls refaced and the battlements added. The sea still washes the eastern side as it did in Roman times, making it easier to visualize the fort as it used to be. The fort was built under Carausius in the late 3rd cent. AD, abandoned when his revolt was crushed, then reoccupied about 340 until perhaps 370 AD.

Well to the W., on a promontory in a bend of the Itchen River in Southampton itself, the site of Clausentium at Bitterne, just E. of the Northern Bridge, was once a 1st cent. Roman port, later fortified, that may have briefly succeeded Portchester. It is now marked only by some ditches, a bit of the stone rampart across the promontory, and the remains of a small bath house among a group of modern flats. Apparently there was a port and a small settlement with bath house here in the late 4th cent., protected by the stone rampart.

PORTH HELLICK DOWN

See *Scilly Isles*.

PORTUS ADURNI
(Hampshire)

See *Portchester*.

POUNDBURY
(Dorset)

See *Dorchester*.

PUMPSAINT
(Dyfed)

See *Dolaucothi*.

QUARLEY HILL
(Hampshire)

Early Iron Age hill fort, about 6 mi. (10 km.) W. of Andover, close to an ancient track that runs on SE about 5 mi. (8 km.) to *Danebury*. Excavations have shown that this oval fort, with a single rampart built without timber reinforcing, and with a V-shaped ditch, was constructed about the 5th to 4th cents. BC on a hilltop site where ancient boundary ditches, Bronze Age or Early Iron Age, converged. At first there was a palisaded enclosure here, then the ramparts were constructed and two gates—but they were never finished.

RAMSBURY
(Wiltshire)

Village on the Kennet River, about 4.5 mi. (7.25 km.) NW of Hungerford, that was once, from 909 to 1058 AD, the see of the Bishop of Winchester and a considerable Anglo-Saxon settlement, until the see was merged once more into that of Sherborne. (The see of Sherborne was then moved in 1070 to Old Sarum; see *Salisbury*.) Excavations in the village have found nothing either of the settlement or of its cathedral church, and the period is represented here only by a collection of carved stones, chief of which is the great 11th-cent. cross-shaft ornamented with vigorous dragons in the Viking Ringerike style (England was then under a Danish king) with wheel and knot patterns on the sides. It is similar to the St. Paul's Stone of the same period (see *London*). There are also two fine tombstones of the period, decorated with patterns of foliage.

RATAE CORITANORUM
(Leicestershire)

See *Leicester*.

RAUNDS
(Northampton)

Interesting series of excavations into the origins of the large village of Raunds, about 9 mi. (14.5 km.) SE of Kettering. Beginning as a rescue excavation by the County Council in a field in the northern outskirts of the village in 1977, the first project lasted for five years and uncovered a sequence, stretching into the 15th cent., that included faint traces of Saxon occupation in the 6th or 7th cents. and postholes of at least three 8th-cent. timber buildings, which were replaced by a ditched enclosure with four buildings. In late Saxon times a large wooden hall, probably the manor house of an estate, dominated the area. Of the same period were the stone foundations of the first of two superimposed churches. By the 12th cent. the present village church had taken over and a new manor house replaced the old one. The cemeteries of the two earlier churches were completely excavated, the 367 burials, some with crude carved headstones, revealing much about the health and burial practices of the late Saxon population. In 1986, with the Raunds Area Project, the County Council opened a new and major excavation into the manor houses and Saxon origins of the village. Close to Raunds is the *Stanwick Roman Villa* excavation.

RAVENGLASS
(Cumbria)

See *Hardknott Castle*.

RECULVER
(Kent)

One of the late Roman forts of the *Saxon Shore*, on the N. coast of Kent, 3 mi. (4.75 km.) E. of the city of Herne Bay. Regulbium guarded the northern end of the Wantsum Channel—now completely silted up—that bounded the Isle of Thanet, the easternmost promontory of Kent, making it into an island. Its later sister fort of *Richborough* near the E. coast to the SE of Reculver, guarded the southern end of the channel. About half of the fort has been washed into the sea in recent centuries, leaving the two tall towers of the ruined 12th-cent. church in its midst—still a sailors' landmark and perilously close to the cliff edge, though the cliffs have now been consolidated. The fort, originally enclosing about eight acres, had rounded ends and no bastions, suggesting that it was earlier than Richborough—perhaps about 220 AD. Within the fort the street grid, barracks, houses and the *principia* have been located, though nothing is now visible. The walls have now deteriorated mostly to rubble, though the E. gate, excavated in 1967, can be seen. The church in the interior was enlarged from a very early Anglo-Saxon church, founded by a priest called Bassa as a monastery within the fort in the 7th cent.—like that of St. Cedd in the Saxon Shore fort of *Bradwell-on-Sea* in Essex. Bassa's church, excavated in 1927, is now outlined in white on the ground. Later enlarged, it became a parish church and was wantonly destroyed—all but the towers—by a misguided clergyman in 1805.

REGULBIUM
(Kent)

See *Reculver*, above.

REPTON
(Derbyshire)

A town about 7 mi. (11 km.) S. of Derby off the road to Burton-on-Trent, once an important ecclesiastical center of Anglo-Saxon Mercia, now the site of the part-Anglo-Saxon church and ancient crypt of St. Wystan's. It is known that Repton had a monastery, established before 700 AD, and that at least two kings of Mercia, Aethelbald and Wiglaf, were buried in the church's crypt, which seemed to have been built as a royal mausoleum. So too was Wiglaf's grandson, St. Wystan, who was murdered in 850. His tomb in the crypt became a place of pilgrimage before the town was taken by a Danish-Viking army, which wintered in Repton in 873–74. The church and crypt survived, though the monastery seems to have been destroyed or withered away thereafter. The present chancel of the church is 9th-cent. Anglo-Saxon work, and stairs, well-worn by pilgrims, lead down from it into the noble 8th-cent. crypt. Its four pillars, decorated with spirals boldly incised on the shafts, uphold eight arches. Recesses on the four sides doubtless held the royal tombs.

The long-standing Repton Project under Professor Martin Biddle of Oxford has been carrying out a program of excavation and analysis at Repton, investigating the church and, in its vicinity, the remains of the monastery, a burial ground and other features. Discovered in 1976 were earthwork defenses undoubtedly erected by the Danish army in 873—the first Viking fortifications discovered in England—and in 1982 a mass burial of at least 150 bodies, almost all men, the bones bearing the cuts of battle. This no doubt was the consequence of an actual battle between Saxons and Vikings at Repton.

REY CROSS MARCHING CAMP (Durham)

Roman marching camp large enough to hold a legion, nearly 1,500 ft. high at the summit of Stanmore Pass, 2 mi. (3.25 km.) W. of the *Bowes* moor signal station. The main road to Brough passes through the fort. The finest example of such a camp in Britain, it was probably the temporary quarters for the 9th Legion during the Brigantes campaign in 72–73 AD. The ramparts, quarried away in the W. and with another gap in the N., are still impressive, enclosing 20 acres. Built of limestone, they are 20 ft. wide and still stand over 6 ft. high in places. No less than nine gates of the original 11 or 12 can be identified by the external defensive walls guarding each one. See also *Piercebridge*.

RIBCHESTER ROMAN FORT (Lancashire)

The small cavalry fort of Bremetennacum in the village of Ribchester, 8 mi. (13 km.) NE of Preston. The best of it is in the small museum on the site; behind the museum one can see the front ends of two granaries and the site of the N. gate. The fort was built in the 1st cent. AD, probably under Agricola, its clay ramparts and ditch enclosing 5½ acres. It was rebuilt in stone under Trajan in the early 2nd cent. and occupied through the 4th cent., garrisoned at different times by cavalry units of Sarmatians from the Danube and Asturians from Spain. The museum contains an interesting collection of inscriptions and carved stones, including one dedicated to Caracalla on which the name of Geta, the brother he murdered in 212, is all but erased. The magnificent Ribchester cavalry parade helmet, found here in the 18th cent., is in the British Museum, with a replica here.

RICHBOROUGH ROMAN FORT (Kent)

One of the forts of the *Saxon Shore*. It guarded the southern end of the Wantsum Channel, now silted up, that made the Isle of Thanet into an island. Its earlier sister fort of *Reculver* guarded the northern end of the channel. Rutupiae, once on a natural harbor, now lies 1.5 mi. (2.3 km.) NW of Sandwich, well inland on the Stour River, which, with a railroad, has cut off the eastern side of the fort. However, its mighty walls, which once enclosed five acres, still stand up to 25 ft. high on the other three sides.

Richborough was not only one of the more important Saxon Shore forts but is also of particular interest because inside it one can find remains that cover the entire history of Roman Britain. For it was here that the Roman invasion force of 43 AD first climbed ashore on a small peninsula on which the later fort stood, defending it with a double line of ditches to protect their beachhead. A section of these ditches, the earliest evidence of the Roman presence in Britain, has been preserved just inside the W. gateway of the fort, with a causeway crossing over them. The peninsula then became a supply base for the armies and a commercial port. About 85 AD, when Britain had been largely subdued, the timber buildings of the port were demolished and a huge four-sided triumphal arch was erected as a propaganda gesture to mark the entry to Roman Britain, as well as the start of Watling Street, which led to *London* and westward beyond it.

The arch, clad in white imported marble and ornamented with bronze statues, stood on a massive cross-shaped foundation that can be seen today dominating the center of the fort. Later the arch, neglected, became a signal tower, and when Saxon pirates became active, it was surrounded by a triple defensive ditch, now excavated and open to view, with the original cruciform foundations. Later in the 3rd cent. all was leveled and the fort built on the site, with bastions and round corner towers. Today the foundations of some of the 2nd- and 3rd-cent. structures, including those of an inn, a block of shops and a Saxon church to boot, can be seen inside the fort, and there is a small museum by the entrance filled with interesting finds from the site. A depression across the road outside marks the local amphitheater.

RIDGEWAY, THE
(Oxfordshire)

See *White Horse of Uffington*.

RIPON CATHEDRAL
(North Yorkshire)

Medieval cathedral of Ripon, NW of *York*, built on the site of St. Wilfrid's Anglo-Saxon abbey church, dedicated by him in 672 AD. The crypt belongs to Wilfrid's church (his other church, at *Hexham*, has a similar crypt). At Ripon the glittering gold and silver objects of the cathedral treasury are displayed in a special recess in the crypt. Ripon also possesses a fragment of a cross, discovered in 1974, that portrays the Scandinavian saga of Sigurd, similar to that at *Halton*—both testimony to the strong Viking influence in the region long after Wilfrid's day. Extensive recent excavations on Ailcy Hill, a huge mound just E. of the cathedral, have discovered that it was a large graveyard of the 7th-10th cents. with many skeletons but few grave goods. See also *Gosforth Cross; Middleton Crosses*.

RISINGHAM
(Northumberland)

Roman fort of Habitancum, an outpost of the *Hadrian's Wall* system, on Dere Street N. of Corbridge. The fort's mounds, ditches and bits of stonework lie on a farm a half mi. (1 km.) W. of the main road near West Woodburn, about 16 mi. (26 km.) N. of Corbridge on the wall. Habitancum was a permanent fort founded by Lollius Urbicus of the *Antonine Wall* (SCOTLAND) in the mid-2nd cent., then massively rebuilt in stone, with polygonal towers guarding the S. gate, in the early 3rd cent. It was occupied into the 4th cent. Two inscriptions from the fort, one long enough to cover an entire wall, can be seen in the Newcastle upon Tyne museum.

ROCHESTER
(Kent)

The Roman town of Durobrivae, strategically sited on the Roman Watling Street where it crossed the Medway River SE of *London*. Of its ancient circuit of stone walls, the SW corner survives near the E. bank of the river, standing 10 ft. high in Eagle Court, a public garden. It is topped here by medieval work. Another stretch of the walls forms the lower part of the bailey of the famous Norman castle on the river. This Rochester is not to be confused with the fort of *High Rochester* in Northumberland.

ROCKBOURNE ROMAN
VILLA
(Hampshire)

See *Salisbury*.

ROLLRIGHT STONES
(Oxfordshire)

A number of prehistoric monuments of different periods here are dominated by the only Bronze Age stone circle in Oxfordshire, in a long-standing sacred site in the foothills of the Cotswolds. It breasts a ridge about 3 mi. (4 km.) NW of Chipping Norton. Until quite recent years many local folk legends and traditions clustered around the stones, suggesting memories of healing powers, fertility rites and the importance of the midwinter and midsummer solstices, and giving the stones their present picturesque names. The circle, called the King's Men, and a tall misshapen outlying stone, the King Stone, recall the legend of a king and his men turned to stone by a witch. About 77 gnarled, weathered and pock-marked limestone monoliths, many of them just stumps and others wrongly re-erected, form a circle about 100 ft. across. Beyond a field to the W. the so-called Whispering Knights are actually the side slabs of a denuded earlier Neolithic burial chamber, with the capstone askew. The King Stone, across the road from the circle and thus in Warwickshire, may be the remnant of another burial chamber, or perhaps a marker stone associated with the circle. Unexcavated to date, all three monuments are enclosed within ugly iron railings.

ROTHERLEY
(Wiltshire)

See *Woodcuts.*

ROTHWELL
(Lincolnshire)

A simple and elegant, late Anglo-Saxon church in a little village in the Wolds NW of *Lincoln,* about 2 mi. (3.25 km.) SE of *Caistor.* The rectangular tower typical of Lincolnshire, is topped by a medieval parapet but is otherwise entirely Anglo-Saxon. It shows two stages, with narrow windows below and paired windows around the belfry stage, and an austerely beautiful W. doorway. Inside, the once-narrow nave has been opened out by Norman arches, but the tower arch is original.

ROUGH TOR
(Cornwall)

See *Bodmin Moor.*

ROUND POND
(Devon)

See *Dartmoor.*

RUDSTON
(Humberside)

In the churchyard of this village, about 6 mi. (10 km.) due W. of Bridlington, stands the tallest monolith in England, a Bronze Age standing stone 25½ ft. high and at the base 6 ft. by over 2 ft. thick, tapering toward the top. The grit-stone of which it is composed must have been dragged to the site from more than 10 mi. (16 km.) away. A smaller stone also stands in the churchyard near the sandstone slabs of a burial cist. Obviously the church was sited on a pre-historic sacred place in an attempt to Christianize it. Several Neolithic cursuses lead toward the monument (see *Blandford Forum*). See also *Devil's Arrows, Great Driffield.*

   Near Rudston the site of a 4th-cent. Roman villa, one of many identified in the region, has yielded a number of mosaic floors now on display in the Hull museum. One is a ludicrous but interesting attempt by a not-very-gifted local artisan to portray a naked Venus—worth seeing!

RUTUPIAE
(Kent)

See *Richborough Roman Fort.*

SAETH MAEN
(Powys)

See *Cerrig Duon.*

ST. ALBANS
(Hertfordshire)

This small city above the Ver River resonates with the memory of its illustrious predecessor, Verulamium, third largest city in Roman Britain. Its very name, St.

The huge Norman abbey of St. Albans. Roman bricks and tiles, robbed from the nearby Roman city of Verulamium, can clearly be seen, reused in the lower walls. Verulamium became one of the largest cities in Roman Britain. (Photo: the author.)

Albans, derives from that of a Roman soldier and Christian martyr. Its great early Norman abbey church is largely built of brick and tile robbed from the site of the ancient city, and Verulamium itself lies under the green and open park and playing fields W. of the present city. Much of the 200-acre site lying within the ancient walls has been excavated in the 1930s by two famous archaeologists, Sir Mortimer Wheeler and Dame Kathleen Kenyon, and by Sheppard Frere from 1955 to 1961 and by others subsequently; but considering this and the availability of the site, there is surprisingly little to see. Much of it has been grassed over again, with a few foundations preserved and other sites marked out on the turf. The opulence and splendor of the city at its height can best be appreciated in the excellent site museum, containing models of the town and the Roman gate, some of the most elegant mosaics in Britain, painted wall plaster, inscriptions, burials, and objects of daily life from the excavations.

In Prae Woods W. of the Roman city, the mounds and ditches of the original Iron Age settlement or oppidum here, first capital of the Catuvellauni before they moved to *Colchester,* can be seen. Like Colchester, it was protected by long linear earthworks. The original Roman nucleus lay under and around St. Michael's church. About 50 AD the Roman town was laid out and was created a self-governing *municipium*; but this timber-built town was utterly destroyed, like London and Colchester, by vengeful Queen Boudicca in her revolt of 61 AD. Verulamium took a long time to recover, but a basilica and forum were dedicated in 79 AD (a corner of the basilica complex is marked out W. of the museum). Thereafter the town flourished and its growth seems scarcely to have been halted by a fire in 155 AD. After the fire the theater was built, now one of the principal sites, lying NW of the museum.

The theater's stage building, orchestra and banks that held timber seats are clearly visible. In its earliest phase it was an almost circular type of theater—as opposed to an amphitheater—known from Gaul and rare in Britain. This is the only known example that can be visited. Used for drama, spectacles, cockfights, it was often rebuilt until the later years of the city, when it was neglected and used for the town dump. Beside the theater a line of early timber-built shops, destroyed by Boudicca, has been marked out on the grass. The shops were later rebuilt in stone. Here too was a substantial stone house with the apse of a little shrine belonging to it still visible. Near the museum the foundations of part of the bath suite belonging to a large (200 ft. by 130 ft.) house can be seen under a shelter, with a heating hypocaust under a mosaic floor.

About 200 AD the city was supplied with a circuit of walls of flint with tile courses; a fine stretch of it, standing up to 10 ft. high, survives, with bastions and a 30-ft.-wide ditch in front of it. At one end of this stretch the site of the elaborate London Gate is marked out. It had two pedestrian and two vehicle passages, with guard chambers. Large town houses continued to be built in Verulamium into the 4th cent., and evidence from one house, built anew about 380 AD, indicates that organized urban life continued in this civilized city as late as the middle of the 5th cent., long after the legions had left the island.

ST. CATHERINE'S HILL
(Hampshire)

See *Winchester.*

ST. DAVID'S HEAD
(Dyfed)

Westward-facing peninsula of southern Wales, its headland cut off by a substantial Iron Age stone rampart running N-S, with an entrance, making it into a promontory fort. There are traces of ditches inland of the rampart, and boundary walls of large enclosures, probably for cattle. Inside the fort, excavated in 1898, are the round foundations of seven huts, and others are among the enclosures outside it. Of the many chambered tombs in the vicinity, Carn Llidi lies behind the fort. Its two chambers are partly cut into the rock that, with the uprights, supports the roofing slabs. At the very end of the headland, Coetan Arthur has a round cairn and a possible passage leading to the chamber, which has collapsed. The venerable cathedral of St. David's S. of the Head possesses a number of carved and inscribed stones, some of them crosses of the 9th and 10th cents. For more monuments E. along the N. coast of the peninsula, see *Newport* (Dyfed).

ST. IVES
(Cornwall)

See *Gurnard's Head; Pennance Megalithic Tomb; Zennor Quoit.*

ST. JUST
(Cornwall)

Convenient center for visiting a few of the many monuments of Cornwall that lie nearby. The Brane chambered tomb is about 2.5 mi. (4 km.) SE of St. Just and SW of Sancreed. It is the best example in Cornwall, out of four known, of a particular type of late Neolithic tomb found in abundance in the *Scilly Isles*. These "entrance graves" consist of a round cairn held up by heavy kerbstones, with a short entrance leading directly into the chamber. The well-preserved Brane tomb is covered by two large capstones. A mi. (1.6 km.) to the W. of St. Just on Cape Cornwall is the remarkable Bronze Age cairn of Carn Gluze, excavated in 1874. It began as a huge T-shaped pit dug down 7 ft. into the rock with steps leading down into it—obviously for ritual purposes, for no burials were found in it. Around it were four cists covering miniature Bronze Age urns. All of this was then covered by a great corbelled dome, double-walled and still 10 ft. high, which had been sealed; but not until another cist was built under it. Two more cists, empty, were found outside it. Finally a massive oval wall, nearly 5 ft. high, was constructed around the whole monument. A final Neolithic burial chamber of the entrance grave type was found between the dome and the outer wall, to the SW. Burned human bones and sherds were uncovered under its floor.

Just N. of St. Just in the direction of Morvah is the Iron Age fort of *Chun Castle*. A mi. and a half (2.3 km.) to the NE are the Tregeseal stone circles, on open moorland. Only two stones belonging to one of them survive, but the other shows 16 of the original 20 stones neatly arranged around the circle. Finally, one of the many Nine Maidens sites is also a stone circle. Known additionally as Boskednan, it lies 5 mi. (8 km.) NE of St. Just and 1.5 mi. (2.3 km.) SE of Morvah off the road to Madron. It is very difficult to find. Seven of its stones are still standing out of the original 19. See also *Carn Euny*.

ST. LYTHAN'S TOMB
(South Glamorgan)

See *Cardiff*.

ST. OSWALD'S PRIORY
(Gloucestershire)

See *Gloucester*.

SALISBURY
(Wiltshire)

Ancient cathedral town, actually dating only from the 13th cent. when the see of nearby Old Sarum was moved down into the valley to form, with its cathedral, the nucleus of Salisbury. For the antiquarian-minded the Salisbury and South Wiltshire Museum here is worth a visit. It contains a fine prehistoric and Roman collection, particularly of the antiquities of nearby Salisbury Plain, including models of *Stonehenge*. Its collection supplements the holdings of the *Devizes* museum, also in Wiltshire.

Old Sarum, Salisbury's parent, is about 2 mi. (3 km.) N. of Salisbury on the road to Stonehenge. Conspicuous on this commanding headland are the Norman motte and inner ramparts of a medieval castle. In the interior the outlines of the old cathedral are marked on the turf, its stones robbed in 1331 to build the glorious new one in Salisbury. However, the massive outer earthen rampart and its ditch belong to an earlier Iron Age hill fort on the headland, and there was likely some Roman occupation of the site as well.

Among sites to be visited around Salisbury is the Rockbourne Roman villa (Hampshire), about 8 mi. (13 km.) S. of the city and 3 mi. (4.75 km.) NW of Fordingbridge. By the 4th cent. this huge villa, possibly the main building on an imperial estate, had grown into a large courtyard villa with bath suite and many farm buildings around it. In excavations from 1956 to 1976 over 70 of its rooms were located. It has been backfilled and grassed over for preservation, though a hypocaust, a mosaic of more than average quality and other remains have been left on view. The contents of the site museum are more interesting than the site itself. Of interest, too, is the site of Little Woodbury, about 1 mi. (1.6 km.) S. of Salisbury and still in Wiltshire, though now visible only from the air. This was a classic excavation (1938–39) that exhaustively studied an Iron Age farmstead occupied probably from the 4th cent. BC for at least 300 years. A central round house, 45 ft. in diameter and several times rebuilt, was surrounded by granaries, silo pits, drying racks and working areas, all enclosed within a timber stockade.

SAMSON ISLAND

See *Scilly Isles*.

SANCTUARY, THE
(Wiltshire)

See *Avebury*.

SANDBACH CROSSES
(Cheshire)

Two battered 9th-cent. Mercian crosses standing in the market place of this small town, just W. of the M6 motorway and about 5 mi. (8 km.) NE of Crewe. They have been standing here since the 16th cent. or earlier and are now in state care. Smashed by religious zealots in the 17th cent., they were reconstructed and replaced in 1816. Their tall, tapering shafts are richly decorated with vine scroll, interlace and triangular ornamentation and numerous panels portraying Christian and biblical scenes and figures. Of Mercian Anglo-Saxon workmanship, their decoration shows elements of Northumbrian design.

SAXON SHORE, THE

A group of strong fortresses built along the SE shores of Roman Britain in the 3rd and 4th cents. AD to protect the island from the increasingly dangerous raids of early Saxons and other pirates. The forts, which stretched from the Wash and Norfolk around to the Isle of Wight, were usually built on harbors and river mouths and were used as bases by the Roman fleet. There is evidence that a number of similar forts guarded the opposite shores on the continent and, in the earlier period at least, were under the same command as those of England. The system was in charge of a Count of the Saxon Shore (one incumbent was killed in the great barbarian raids of 367–68). Of these magnificent forts, with their massive walls and out-jutting bastions, nearly a dozen are known and some of them are among the most impressive Roman ruins in Britain. The forts described here include *Bradwell-on-Sea*, *Burgh Castle*, *Dover*, *Lympne Castle*, *Pevensey*, *Portchester*, *Reculver*, and *Richborough*. Nothing worth seeing is left of the fort at Brancaster in Norfolk, and the fragments of a Roman fort under Carisbrooke Castle on the *Isle of Wight* may have been part of the system. Various outliers such as *Cardiff* Castle were built at about the same time.

SCARBOROUGH HEAD
(North Yorkshire)

One of the late Roman signal stations on the high headlands of the eastern Yorkshire coast, built by Count Theodosius, who restored control in Britain after the concerted barbarian attacks of 367–68. Five of these stations are known, all built on the same model: a square defensive wall about 100 ft. across, with circular bastions at the corners to carry artillery, a ditch outside the wall, a single inturned entrance over a causeway, and in the middle of the internal courtyard a square tower, built probably of timber on a strong masonry base, about 100 ft. tall. From its top the garrison could watch for enemy attack from the sea—especially the Picts, who had learned to bypass *Hadrian's Wall* by sea in their horsehide curraghs—and thus give warning to the Roman fleet or the garrison at *York* in the interior—signaling by torch-semaphore, or even by trumpet. Most or all of these stations met violent ends, probably in the early 5th cent., as attested at *Huntcliff* and Goldsborough.

The Scarborough station, excavated in 1919, can be entered only through the medieval castle on Castle Hill. It stands on the cliff edge, its foundations marked out in concrete, the rest obscured by medieval constructions and part of it washed into the sea. At Goldsborough, 5 mi. (8 km.) N. of Whitby, the complete plan of the station was revealed after its discovery in 1918; now, unfortunately, it is covered over again by a mound. In the SE corner the skeletons of two men were discovered lying face down, one covering the bones of a huge dog at his throat, the other with his skull cleft by a swordcut and then smashed by a heavy blow. In the well three skulls were found, one of an old man, another of a young woman—dramatic testimony to the end of Roman Britain.

SCARGILL
(Devon)

See *Dartmoor*.

SCARGILL SHRINES
(Durham)

See *Bowes*.

SCILLY ISLES, THE

Archipelago of about 150 islands, islets and rocks 28 mi. (44 km.) SW of Land's End in Cornwall. The islands are no longer identified with the Arthurian "Lyonesse"—geological evidence is against it. Only five of the islands are inhabited. Archaeologically, they are known for the extraordinary number of megalithic tombs on them, including at least 50 of the entrance grave type, a few of which are also found in Cornwall (See *St. Just*). There are, for instance, three times as many chambered tombs crowded onto the mere 3,500 acres of these islands as there are in the whole of Cornwall. This can be explained in part by the known fact that the principal islands once formed a single island (possibly as late as medieval times) with a rich plain at the center—now drowned under the sea—where the ancient people lived, building their tombs on the hills, which now form the separate islands. The Scillys may also have known an exceptionally powerful cult of the dead in ancient times. The chambered tombs seem to date from around 2000 BC, on the borders of the Bronze Age, and show many features in common with the megalithic tombs of Brittany in France. Many were in use over a long period; and to the expert eye there is much evidence of the houses and field boundaries of the people who built the tombs—buried under sand dunes, exposed on cliff edges, visible off shore at low tide, or now permanently under the waters

Best known and one of the largest of the entrance tombs is Bant's Carn on the NW coast of St. Mary's island, now in state care. Its oval cairn, covering over 40 ft., is held together by the usual kerb of heavy stones, and in this case another, outer wall encircles the area. The chamber, entered by the short entrance characteristic of the type, is covered by four capstones. The excavator in 1899 found four piles of cremated human bone inside it, and some pottery that indicated use of the tomb for over 500 years, into the Bronze Age. Nearby on the downs is an Iron Age village of about a dozen well-built huts with small gardens, much like those of *Chysauster* in Cornwall, apparently occupied through the Roman period and possibly even later. On the NE coast one finds two more entrance tombs. The upper Innisidgen Carn, the best preserved on the islands, is much like Bant's in plan, with five capstones; the lower one near the sea is partly covered in sand. On Porth Hellick down on the E. coast is a group of five tombs, one of which, excavated in 1899, is well preserved with a long open-air passage leading into the chamber, which has four capstones. It too was occupied, or reoccupied, in the Late Bronze Age.

On St. Martin's Island are four more tombs on the three knolls of Cruther's Hill. On the small island of Samson, the whole of it a nature preserve and in state care, a large number of tombs top the N. and S. hills (at least eight more are on tiny Bryher Island nearby). Running down from them to the Samson flats in between the two hills and on into the sea are visible boundary walls of the ancient people. More of these are to be seen on the southern part of White Island just off St. Martin's. Of the Iron Age, besides the village described above, there are only the remains of two promontory forts, the Giant's Castle on the extreme SW of St. Mary's, defended by three ramparts and ditches, and Old Blockhouse (also a 17th-cent. fort) on Tresco Island.

SCORHILL CIRCLE
(Devon)

See *Dartmoor.*

SCRATCHBURY
(Wiltshire)

See *Battlesbury.*

SEA MILLS
(Avon)

See *Bristol.*

SEGONTIUM ROMAN
FORT
(Gwynedd)

See *Caernarvon.*

SEGSBURY HILL FORT
(Oxfordshire)

See *White Horse.*

SHEFFIELD
(South Yorkshire)

The Sheffield City Museum holds the rich Bateman collection of 19th-cent. finds from prehistoric, Romano-British and Anglo-Saxon tombs and barrows of the nearby Peak District, one of the richest archaeological landscapes in Britain. See also *Arbor Low; Stanton Moor.*

SHOVEL DOWN
(Devon)

See *Dartmoor.*

SIGURD CROSS

See *Halton.*

SILBURY HILL
(Wiltshire)

See *Avebury.*

SILCHESTER ROMAN
TOWN
(Hampshire)

Site of the Romano-British town of Calleva Atrebatum, 10 mi. (16 km.) SW of Reading, 6 mi. (9.6 km.) NW of Basingstoke. Deserted at the end of the Roman period, Calleva is now under open farmland, with only a medieval church and a farm within its 107 acres. Built over the pre-Roman capital of the Atrebates, it was polygonal in shape and the walls, shorn of their outer facing but still stand-

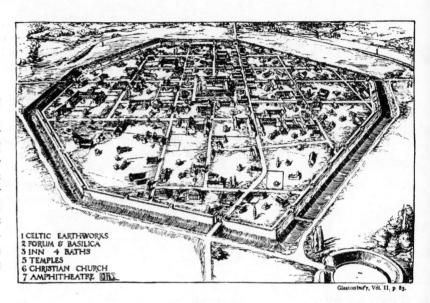

1 CELTIC EARTHWORKS
2 FORUM & BASILICA
3 INN 4 BATHS
5 TEMPLES
6 CHRISTIAN CHURCH
7 AMPHITHEATRE

Glastonbury, Vol. II. p 83.

A reconstruction plan of the small Roman city of Calleva Atrebatum, now Silchester in Hampshire, after excavations in the 19th cent. had revealed most of its details. The entire polygonal circuit of the 3rd-cent. walls can still be traced, though the interior is now once again under cultivation. The amphitheater outside the walls has been reconstructed. (From Marjorie Quennel: Everyday Life in Roman Britain, *by permission from B. T. Batsford Ltd.)*

ing up to 15 ft. high, can be traced around their entire circuit, notably the S. wall, restored and in state care. Heavy earthworks beyond the walls, once thought to be "Celtic," probably belonged to an earlier, more ambitious defensive plan that was subsequently abandoned. The present walls were rebuilt in stone in the 3rd cent. AD, and had four gates; the remains of the S. and N. gates are the best-preserved. Calleva was the focus of seven Roman roads. The town itself was completely excavated in 1864–78 and 1890–1909, unfortunately without regard to chronology or stratification. There were small follow-up excavations up to 1961; but the whole area is now under cultivation. Recently there has been some investigation of the pre-Roman oppidum here.

Nevertheless the complete plan of this Roman city was recovered, with forum, basilica, baths, many houses, a hotel and three square temples (two under the church) and a fourth, octagonal temple. The most remarkable find was of a small apsidal building near the forum, almost certainly a Christian church, probably of the 4th cent. AD, the oldest public church known in Britain. The amphitheater outside the walls is being excavated for public display. There is a small site museum here, but the varied finds of the many excavations, including a notable set of woodworking tools, well-preserved, are displayed in the Reading museum.

SKEGNESS
(Lincolnshire)

On the wolds behind Skegness on the Lincolnshire coast there are numbers of Neolithic long barrows, mostly unexcavated and in poor condition. However, of two barrows called the Giants Hills, near Skendelby, 2 mi. (3.25 km.) NE of Partney, one has been excavated. More than 200 ft. long, it was found to have been erected over a platform of chalk blocks inside an enclosure of split timbers, and on the platform lay eight bodies, one of a child. Radiocarbon dates indicated a span of 3500 to 2700 BC for the barrow. The other barrow here is hardly visible. A mi. (1.6 km.) farther NE in the direction of Claxby two more long barrows, called Deadmen's Graves, lie on a ridge, one about 160 ft. long and the other 173 ft. Neither is excavated. The largest and longest of all the barrows lies to the N. near Swaby, W. of Alford. It is 257 ft. long and still 7 ft. high at one end. However, it is much damaged.

SOMPTING
(West Sussex)

Unusual Anglo-Saxon church tower, outside this village 2 mi. (3.25 km.) NE of Worthing, with a remarkable "Rhenish style" helmet-shaped roof, apparently original. The rest of the church of St. Mary's is later work, though there are interesting bits of Anglo-Saxon sculpture built into the interior walls of the later church. The tower shows round-headed and triangular-headed Saxon windows, and is divided into upper and lower stages by a string course ornamented with a curious fluted design. From it vertical string courses run up each side of the tower. In the inside the capitals upholding the tower arch are richly decorated.

SOUTHAMPTON
(Hampshire)

The large modern seaport of Southampton had two important predecessors, the Roman port of Clausentium, E. of the city center across the Itchen River (see *Portchester*), and the Anglo-Saxon port of Hamwic or Hamwih, once a bustling, crowded town with streets laid out in a grid pattern behind a busy port. It traded mostly with Rouen across the Channel. The remains of Hamwic have been excavated in a long-term project centering on the St. Mary's district, E. of the medieval town center and W. of the Itchen. Apparently Hamwic, after the Roman period, was one of the earliest such commercial towns to grow up in northern Europe. Its port was first recorded in 720 AD, and it flourished, probably as the port for Alfred's capital, *Winchester* (just inland), until at least 850 AD. The excavations have uncovered the remains of its timber buildings, its streets, pits and wells, and a wealth of finds that document thriving industries in the working of iron, bronze, glass, pottery and leather. Southampton's Museum of Archaeology, housed in the medieval God's House tower, is nearby. It displays prehistoric, Roman, Saxon and medieval finds.

SOUTH BARRULE
MOUNTAIN

See *Isle of Man*.

SOUTH CADBURY CASTLE
(Somerset)

Magnificent hill fort with an interesting history. It rises just W. of South Cadbury village, about 9 mi. (14.5 km.) NE of Yeovil. This prominent hill, conspicuous on the Somerset levels, is notable for its circuit of four heavy ramparts. It has persistently been associated in legend with King Arthur's Camelot. Intensive and well-publicized excavations by Leslie Alcock from 1966 to 1970, beset by fervent Arthur-watchers, did indeed identify a reoccupation and strengthening of the Iron Age hill fort on a substantial scale around 500 AD, the right time for Arthur. The postholes of a square timber-built tower/gatehouse were uncovered, and the remains of a fair-sized timber hall on the crest of the hill. Around the hilltop ran a drystone wall of the same period, 16 ft. thick, reinforced with heavy timbers and a wooden breastwork at the top, and reused Roman stones and tiles mixed into the rubble of its filling. All over the hill sherds of pottery of a type imported from France and the Mediterranean at this time indicated, with the other evidence, that a powerful chieftain, important enough to command the arduous labor suggested by the substantial remains, had used the fort as his headquarters. This chieftain just could have been the legendary Arthur.

The hill was first occupied as early as 3300 BC in the Neolithic period. Finds from the Bronze Age and early Iron Age (6th cent. BC) followed, the first modest defenses dating from the 5th cent. About 400 BC new defenses, revetted in front with limestone slabs, were constructed and the earlier ditch dug down deeper right into the rock. By 200 BC all four ramparts with their ditches and elaborate entrances had been built and the interior was crowded with timber huts, both round and rectangular, and storage pits, making the hill one of the major de-

King Arthur's Camelot? The dramatic hill fort of South Cadbury, with a long history running from the Neolithic to the 11th cent. AD. Well-publicized excavations did reveal a timber hall, a timber gatehouse and tower and a heavy wall from an occupation about 500 AD, the right time for Arthur—or at least for some other, powerful Dark Ages chieftain. The photograph clearly shows the four massive ramparts and ditches of the earlier Iron Age fortress. (Courtesy of British Tourist Authority, New York.)

fended settlements of the period. The defenses were strengthened again in the 1st cent AD as the Romans approached, and a wooden shrine with a wide veranda was erected on the hill. This teeming fortified town, now occupied by the Durotriges (see *Maiden Castle*), was bypassed by the Roman invaders of the early 1st cent. AD, but for some reason was violently destroyed by the Romans about 70–80 AD. The bones of men, women and children, their corpses gnawed by scavenging animals, were found at the entrance where they had been cut down and left to rot.

A last brief occupation of the hill came around 1010 AD when Ethelred the Unready, harried by the advancing Danes, turned it into a fortified *burh*, building a massive stone wall on the "Arthurian" foundations inside the old defenses and setting up a mint in the town. The fort was probably destroyed and deserted under his successor in 1016, Cnut the Dane. The finds from the excavation are in Taunton's Somerset County Museum.

SOUTH SHIELDS
(Tyne and Wear)

See *Hadrian's Wall*.

STALL MOOR
(Devon)

See *Dartmoor*.

STANNON (Cornwall)	See *Bodmin Moor*.

STANTON DREW
(Avon)

Much-ruined Late Neolithic religious center, comparable to but smaller than *Avebury* in Wiltshire; about 7 mi. (11 km.) S. of Bristol and 10 mi. (16 km.) W. of Bath. This complex of three stone circles, two avenues, a cove and an outlying standing stone should be impressive, but in its ruined state it is not of much interest for the visitor. It lies in low pastureland between Stanton Drew church and the Chew River. The great circle, 365 ft. across, is one of the largest in Britain. Of its 30 odd stones, however, only three still stand, the rest are fallen. Close to it the NE circle, 100 ft. across and oval in shape, has only four of its huge gnarled stones still standing out of the original eight. Short avenues converge from each circle toward the river. Off to the SW is another oval circle, 140 ft. across. All its 12 stones have fallen. To its W., close to the church and pub, is the cove, a U-shaped setting of three large stones, the back one fallen. The SW circle and cove are on private land, the rest is in state care. Various alignments have been traced, with possible astronomical significance. A straight line extended from the cove passes through the centers of the principal and NE rings; another from the SW circle passes through the great circle to the outlying stone called Hautville's Quoit, across the river. Originally about 10 ft. high, the stone has been broken off. As with many other circles, local legends here suggest a fertility background. The monument, curiously, is unexcavated to date, but can probably be dated to about 2600–2500 BC.

STANTON MOOR
(Derbyshire)

Sacred Bronze Age burial ground in the Peak District on a desolate plateau closely covered with monuments—about 70 burial mounds or cairns, a few stone circles and a standing stone, all a few mi. S. of Bakewell between Stanton-in-the-Peak and Birchover. Many of the cairns have been excavated by the Heathcote family, yielding numerous cremation burials with grave goods such as urns, a battle-ax, a bronze awl, flint tools, incense cups. One large round barrow has been left open for inspection. There are also a number of ring cairns in the area, three of them close to the small circle called the Nine Ladies, one of two circles on either side of the burial area, three-quarters of a mi. (1.2 km.) apart to the NE and SW. About nine low stones sit here on a low bank, with two entrances and an outlying stone, the King Stone, to the SW. Originally there was a small cairn in the center of the ring. The other circle, Doll Tor, with six stones (four still standing) is even smaller. Excavated by the Heathcotes in the 1930s, it yielded various grave goods from about half a dozen cremation cairns in it, including a faience bead imported from the Middle East in a female cremation at the center. These and other finds from Stanton Moor may be seen by appointment in the Heathcotes' private museum in Birchover. The famous henge-circle of *Arbor Low* is about 5 mi. (8 km.) to the W. of Stanton Moor.

STANWICK HILL FORT
(North Yorkshire)

Largest Iron Age hill fort and tribal center in Britain, with about 6 mi. (10 km.) of ramparts, i   SW of Darlington and about 3 mi. (5 km.) from *Piercebridge* Roman fort. The short and violent last years of Stanwick fort are chronicled in history, largely by the Roman historian Tacitus, and have been dramatically confirmed on the ground by the excavations of Sir Mortimer Wheeler in 1951–52. Stanwick became the capital of Venutius, king of the huge northern tribe of the

Brigantes, when he broke with Rome and prepared for his revolt of about 50 AD. Until the revolt the Brigantes had been favored clients of Rome. When Cartimandua, famous queen of Venutius, refused to join the revolt, king and queen went to war. Cartimandua may have retreated to the old Brigantian fort of Almondbury. Eventually most of the Brigantes flocked to Venutius, now ensconced in Stanwick, forcing the Romans to come to the rescue of their loyal ally, the queen. Between 71 and 74 AD the Roman governor, Cerialis, attacked Stanwick, now grown to enormous size, and with his disciplined troops quickly overcame Venutius and crushed his revolt.

Stanwick developed from a strong central hill fort of the early 1st cent. AD called the Tofts, which quickly developed into a major settlement, an oppidum like *Colchester*. At the site, S. of Stanwick church, hut circles have been found within its perimeter. Under Venutius an additional 130 acres to the N. was added to the fort about 50–60 AD and strongly fortified with a flat-bottomed ditch about 40 ft. wide, cut into the rock, and a huge rampart faced with stone behind the ditch. Part of this ditch, excavated and restored, is now on view to visitors NE of Forcett village. When excavated, a well-preserved sword with wooden scabbard and a skull bearing sword slashes were found in it, testimony to the final drama. As more Brigantes rallied to Venutius, the fort was again enlarged about 69 to 72 AD to its final, huge 747 acres with the addition of another 600 acres to the S., defended by another bank and ditch. This work was never finished, probably because of the Roman attack. The whole immense fort, still under excavation, is now on view, though sometimes difficult to visualize as a whole because of the trees and low hills at the site. The Brigantes were later moved to the Romanized town of *Aldbrough*.

STANWICK ROMAN VILLA (Northamptonshire)

Current (1987) excavation of a Roman villa that has mosaic pavements along with outbuildings and satellite farms—the first time such a villa-estate has been excavated as a whole. The site is W. of Stanwick village (and to the W. of Wellingborough) and only a few mi. SW of the excavations at *Raunds*.

STANWIX FORT (Cumbria)

See *Hadrian's Wall*.

STAPLE HOWE (Humberside)

See *Great Driffield*.

STAR CARR (North Yorkshire)

Famous Mesolithic site, a seasonal camp of hunter-gatherers of about 9,500 years ago, 5 mi. (8 km.) S. of *Scarborough* in the Vale of Pickering. Although the site is not worth a visit, its classic excavation by Graham Clarke in 1949–51, published in 1954, was of great archaeological importance. The camp had been set up on a platform of brushwood, stones and clay on the margins of what was a lake in Mesolithic times, dated about 7500 BC, and the continuing damp conditions had preserved much of the organic material, wood, bone and antler. Four or five families of a culture possibly originating in Denmark had used the site from time to time for hunting, plant-gathering and fowling. A great variety of flints were uncovered, many unfinished—core axes, adzes, burins and microliths in many forms including saws, awls and scrapers. These were the earliest worked flints of the type found in England. Elk and deer antlers were used for spear points, skin-working tools, mattocks and fasteners. Remarkable antler headdresses—21 of them were found—were used either for hunting or for ritual purposes. The earliest wooden paddle, with a long narrow blade, had survived. Ornaments were made of amber, teeth and shale. These finds are displayed in Scarborough's small Rotunda Museum. For another Mesolithic site, see also *Broom Hill*.

STONEA GRANGE (Cambridgeshire)

Site of a large and unusual Roman tower in the lonely fen country, about 4 mi. (6.5 km.) SE of March, excavated by the British Museum from 1981. Here are the massive foundations of what appears to have been a great stone tower, measuring about 56 ft. by 65 ft.—the stones all brought from near Peterborough, some 30 mi. (48 km.) away—possibly three stories high with an apse on one side and a portico on the other. It was lavishly decorated inside, as fragments of painted wall plaster, of mosaics and of columns, as well as quantities of window glass, suggest. A furnace to one side indicates that it was heated. A large drain led from it to a huge pit in which much interesting debris was found, such as bits of wooden furniture and planks, preserved in the wet conditions. Around the tower was a large complex of stone and timber buildings and a number of wells.

What was the purpose of such a remarkable complex, miles from any other substantial constructions? The excavators have suggested that it was the deliberately showy administrative and military headquarters of a large imperial estate in Hadrian's time, sited deliberately in the midst of the lands of a branch of the Iceni tribe as a political focus for the group and the possible center for a town. A very similar great tower of the same period (135–145 AD) still stands near Anguillara just N. of Rome in Italy. If the purpose was to create a focus for free native landowners (a pet idea of Hadrian's), it did not work. Though the tower was modified after it was built with a large attached hall and other rooms, the whole was deliberately dismantled about 200 AD, and in the late Roman period the site was used for a farm settlement, and finally a Saxon village (a number of foundations of wooden houses, one set within palisades, have been found). There is also evidence of earlier Bronze Age and Iron Age occupation on this unusual site.

STONE-BY-FAVERSHAM (Kent)

Roman building encased within a ruined medieval church, 100 yds. N. of the Roman Watling Street, now the main road to *Canterbury*, 1.5 mi. (2.3 km.) W. of Faversham. The Roman walls of a square building with typical tile courses can clearly be seen in the chancel of the church, with the sill and door socket of its entrance in the chancel's W. wall. Excavated in 1947, the building proved to be of the 4th cent. AD and was undoubtedly a Christian martyrium, or memorial chapel, in a late Roman cemetery—much like the martyrium that formed the nucleus of St. Peter's in Rome. It probably lay outside the Roman town of Durolevum, thought to be located in or near the nearby village of Ospringe.

STONEHENGE (Wiltshire)

Certainly the best-known archaeological monument in Britain and perhaps in Europe. 2.5 mi. (4 km.) W. of Amesbury and not far from *Salisbury*. The stone circle has been the subject of countless publications since the 17th cent. and victim, too, of innumerable far-out speculations on its builders and its purpose—not the least of which is the Druidic curse, fastened on it by William Stukeley in the 18th cent. and unfortunately still prevalent. The Druids of course were thousands of years later than Stonehenge. Stonehenge, it has been sug-

A *close view of the famous Stone-henge circle emphasizes the heavy horizontal lintels that distinguish the monument from the many other large stone circles. They once tied together all the huge sarsen upright stones, giving the circle and its central tri-lithon a uniquely harmonious char-acter. Stonehenge was the central temple in a huge sacred area dotted with burial mounds and other mon-uments from over a thousand years of prehistoric history. (Courtesy of English Heritage.)*

gested, was built by the Phoenicians, conjured up by Merlin, was a Roman tem-ple, the tomb of Boudicca or—more lately—the focus of invisible ley lines puls-ing with energy, or an astronomical observatory on a par with Mt. Wilson. Its age and development over at least 1500 years have now been defined by more accurate radiocarbon dates, but its purpose is still the subject of hot debate. A sober consensus today is that the monument was the center of a vast Neolithic and Bronze Age cemetery and at the same time a temple to the dead and to the gods of the sky and of the agricultural seasons.

Visited by some 600,000 spectators a year, frequented by hippies and modern pseudo-Druids, the monument was until recently in danger of irreversible dete-rioration. Now at last it has been taken in hand by the English Heritage Com-mission and beginning in the 1980s the whole tourist operation will be restruc-tured to preserve the circle and to present it properly in the context of the wide range of other monuments on the high desolate chalklands of Salisbury Plain. For the Plain here was holy ground for centuries and centuries, and Stonehenge in its midst was the focal point of over 300 burial mounds and other monu-ments. Moreover Stonehenge is architecturally unique among megalithic mon-uments. These two facts now govern the commission's plans.

The monument probably began as a Neolithic mortuary structure—made of wood on this stoneless plateau, like nearby *Woodhenge* and Durrington Walls—in which the dead were exposed for eventual burial in the many venerable long barrows that from earlier times had hallowed the area. Any trace of such a structure has been destroyed by later building. About 2800 BC (the Late Neo-lithic) the Grooved Ware people constructed a ditch and internal bank about 320 ft. in diameter around the center (making the monument into a henge; see *Avebury*) and erected a monolith about 15 ft. high, the Heel Stone, outside the single NE entrance to mark the position of the midsummer rising of the sun. Inside the bank a ring of 56 ritual pits—called the Aubrey Holes after an early antiquary and now marked out in white chalk—were dug for an unknown purpose. Later they were gradually filled with cremated human bone fragments, charcoal and domestic debris like flints, bone pins and maceheads. At least 30 other cremation burials have been found in and around the monument, witness to its continuing mortuary character. This then was probably the original Stonehenge.

Around 2200 BC (Phase II), when those enterprising newcomers called the Beaker Folk first appeared, the monument whose ruins we contemplate today began to take shape. Over 80 bluestones, weighing up to four tons each, were with enormous labor dragged, rafted and brought to the site from the far-off Preseli Mtns. in Wales, then were erected one by one in a double circle around the center (they are now marked on the ground as the Q and R holes). The Heel Stone was surrounded with a low ditch and bank, and two more, about 70 ft. apart, delimited the avenue that led from the entrance in a wide curve down to the Avon River; probably the avenue was first used to drag the bluestones on rollers up to the monument from rafts on the river. The bluestone circles were never completed; around 2100 BC the stones were taken away and stored. Perhaps the Beaker People had been driven out by the natives at this time and their work dismantled.

In Phase III, around 2000 BC—probably when the Wessex culture first appeared, an early Bronze Age society of chieftains, warriors and herdsmen—the grandiose monument we know today was built. About 80 huge sarsen stones, weighing 20 to 30 tons apiece, were dragged 24 miles (39 km.) from the Marlborough Downs near Avebury, and the tallest of them (up to 17 ft. high) were erected around the center in a horseshoe of "trilithons"—five pairs of uprights, each capped by a lintel—which opened toward the entrance, with the tallest stones at the back. An outer circle 100 ft. across of 30 sarsens up to 13 ft. high, with a continuous topping of lintels, enclosed the trilithons. It is these lintels that give Stonehenge its distinctive and unique character. Moreover all the stones were carefully worked into shape and smoothed with the crudest of tools, and the lintels, which must have been raised with enormous difficulty on timber cradles, were held on the uprights by crude mortice and tenon joints, left protruding on one stone and dug into the other. These techniques may well have stemmed from a long tradition of woodworking in these parts on slightly earlier monuments such as Woodhenge. The old entrance to the henge now received two tall gate stones (the survivor, fallen today, is erroneously called the Slaughter Stone), and just inside the old ditch a rectangle of four "station stones," possibly for astronomical sightings, was erected. Two survive, one fallen. The so-called North and South barrows may mark the site of the other two.

At some point the bluestones were returned to the site, and an oval was erected inside the trilithons, later converted into a horseshoe of 19 bluestones. Earlier holes had been dug for a double circle of the remaining bluestones outside the sarsen circle (the Z and Y holes), but they were never erected. Instead, perhaps around 1550 BC, the remaining bluestones were formed into a circle inside the sarsen ring—a few survive today—and a 12-ft.-high sandstone monolith, also from Wales, was erected at the center of the site (now fallen, it is mistakenly called the Altar Stone). This is the history and plan of the monument; for the visitor it is often difficult to distinguish the different elements in the present clutter of surviving stones, many fallen. A visit to the Salisbury and South Wiltshire Museum in *Salisbury* with its models of Stonehenge at different periods and prehistoric finds from Stonehenge and elsewhere, would help to clarify the picture.

In the 1950s faint carvings were first detected on many of the sarsens, especially of axes, but also daggers and possibly "boats of the dead," a very common prehistoric symbol. The axes and daggers were at first thought to reflect Mycenaean influences from the Aegean civilizations of Greece, but recent corrected or "calibrated" radiocarbon dates show that even Stonehenge III is far too early for any such influences. These are obviously ritual carvings denoting the complex meanings built into the monument—the sky gods (the axe is a solar symbol), the round of the seasons, and the presence of the dead. Of course there are astronomical alignments connected with the monument, especially the Heel Stone, but nothing to show that it was an observatory in the modern sense. These sightings merely enabled the priestly caste, who must have presided here, to mark the feast-days celebrating the all-important seasons of the year for these farmer-herders.

Another curious ritual monument just N. of Stonehenge is the Cursus (see also the Dorset Cursus under *Blandford Forum*), a long narrow area like a race track, nearly 2 mi. (3.25 km.) long, marked off by a bank and ditch about 100 ft. across, that may date from the earlier phases of Stonehenge. It could have been used for processions or for funeral games, since it ends on the E. at a Neolithic long barrow covering the burial of a child.

Most of the other sites on Salisbury Plain are barrows, 303 round barrows and 25 long barrows. The later Bronze Age round barrows are often strung out in lines starting at an earlier Neolithic long barrow (like the Cursus), indicating the continuing veneration accorded over hundreds of years to those venerable temple-tombs to the dead. The barrows occur in groups or cemeteries of differing sizes all over the area, the largest such concentration in England: the Lake, Winterbourne Stoke, Normanton Down, Wilsford, Cursus, and Snail groups, the latter inaccessible on a military firing range. The best of these groups contain every type of round barrow—bowl, bell, pond, disk, etc. The Normanton Down group, closest to Stonehenge, contains many burials of Wessex chieftains, especially the Bush Barrow, opened in 1808, that covered the remains of a chieftain surrounded by rich grave goods and weapons, including objects of gold, amber, faience and bone and with a gold plaque on his chest. These and other finds are in the British Museum, with copies in the *Devizes* museum.

STONEY LITTLETON LONG BARROW (Avon)

A fine example of an early Neolithic chambered tomb of the Severn-Cotswold group, 5 mi. (8 km.) S. of Bath, 3 mi. (4.75 km.) NE of Radstock. Opened in 1816, it was carefully restored in 1858 as what was then considered a "perfect specimen of Celtic antiquity." It is 107 ft. long and 54 ft. wide under its mound. Built of drystone walling, a large entrance passage between horns leads through a low passage 48 ft. long into the main chamber, with three pairs of side chambers and one at the end. The roof is corbelled. See also *Hetty Pegler's Tump*.

STOW ANGLO-SAXON CHURCH (Lincolnshire)

Huge "Mother Church of Lindsey," about 10 mi. (16 km.) N. of *Lincoln*, 4.5 mi. (7.25 km.) N. of Saxilby; St. Mary's dominates the little village of Stow. The nave and chancel are Norman, but the massive arches of the central crossing inside and the transepts are Anglo-Saxon work, probably of the early 11th cent. when a prosperous college of canons was founded here. However, the church is on the site of an earlier church built by King Ecgfrith of Northumbria for his queen, St. Etheldreda, in 674 AD and some of the lower work may date from that period. If so, the church was an unusually large one from the beginning. In the present N. transept an original Saxon window and a narrow doorway survive, and another window with palmette decoration can be found in the S. transept.

STOWE'S HILL
(Cornwall)

See *Bodmin Moor*.

STRIPPLE STONES
(Cornwall)

See *Bodmin Moor*.

STUTFALL CASTLE
(Kent)

See *Lympne*.

SUTTON HOO
(Suffolk)

Royal cemetery of the early Anglo-Saxon kings of East Anglia, high on a headland over the Deben estuary, across from Woodbridge and NE of Ipswich near the eastern coast of Suffolk. On private land; permission is required to visit the site. In 1938 three of the 11 burial mounds here were excavated, yielding some grave goods. Then in 1939, on the eve of World War II, the largest and tallest mound, the king's mound, was opened up with astonishing results. It was a magnificent ship burial, the ship itself decayed but traceable through its surviving nails. It was about 85 ft. long with 38 oars. The bottom of the ship and the wooden burial chamber amidships held undoubtedly the richest treasure ever found in Britain—but no trace of a body. The mound was therefore probably a cenotaph or memorial to the king, and it is now generally agreed that it belonged to Raedwald, an early king of East Anglia and *Bretwalda* or overking of the early Saxon kingdoms, who died about 652 AD. It is known that he was a late convert to Christianity and may even have reverted to paganism, for although there are Christian objects in the treasure, the whole burial is essentially a pagan one.

The treasure, meticulously restored after many years of work and on view in the British Museum, included a great gold buckle, straps, a purse lid, a sword pommel and harness, and other objects of gold intricately inlaid with garnet and colored glass, a 6-ft.-long iron standard and whetstone scepter, a shield, a gilt-bronze helmet of Swedish type with face mask, iron spears and battle-axes, a great Byzantine silver dish, a lyre, a pair of silver Christian spoons inscribed "Saul" and "Paul," silver bowls, drinking horn mounts, hanging bowls, and a purseful of Merovingian coins that clinched the date. The mound was reexamined in 1966–70, and from about 1984 on new surveys and excavations have been exploring the site's long series of settlements and cemeteries, back to the Neolithic. The finds from this later work are in the Woodbridge museum.

Intensive study of the finds has caused a reappraisal of the great Anglo-Saxon poem of *Beowulf*, belonging to the same period, and its minute descriptions of fabulous treasures, hitherto thought to be merely literary exaggeration. The scholars point in particular to a description of Beowulf's burial when his companions "built a barrow on the headland—it was high and broad, visible from afar to all seafarers . . . They buried rings and brooches in the barrow . . . They bequeathed the gleaming gold, treasure of men, to the earth. . . ." Perhaps the poem was written in East Anglia? And could the author have been at Raed-wald's burial? See also *Taplow*.

SUTTON WALLS (Hereford and Worcester)

One of the Iron Age hill forts along the borders of Wales, this one disastrously halved by a gravel quarry filled with toxic waste, about 4 mi. (6.5 km.) due N. of Hereford. It was occupied in the early Iron Age, but ramparts and a V-shaped ditch were only constructed around the hill about 100 BC and enlarged 75 years later. Like the other hill forts in the area it apparently fell victim to the inexorable Roman advance, in 48 AD; the skeletons of some two dozen of its inhabitants, victims of the attack, some with battle wounds and others decapitated, were found thrown into the ditch outside the eastern entrance and covered over as the defenses were pulled down. See also *The Breiddin; Credenhill; Croft Ambrey; Herefordshire Beacon; Midsummer Hill; Old Oswestry; The Wrekin.*

SWANSCOMBE (Kent)

Rich Paleolithic site on the ancient gravel terraces of the lower Thames, SE of London and just W. of Gravesend, under excavation for many years. Here in the Barnfield Pit, now a nature reserve, three fragments of the fossilized skull of the earliest man found in Britain were unearthed in 1936 and 1955 from the upper levels of the site, which also produced thousands of Acheulian handaxes and remains of extinct animals such as the European elephant and rhinoceros. The lower levels yielded an even earlier flake industry. Swanscombe man, it seems, was actually a young woman about 250,000 years old. She belonged to an immediate precursor of modern man, an archaic type of Homo sapiens. The finds are in London's Natural History Museum in South Kensington.

SWINSIDE (Cumbria)

An almost perfect circle of 52 close-set slate stones, around 85 ft. across, set in a meadow 5 mi. (8 km.) N. of Millom near the head of the inlet known as Duddon Sands. Its close counterpart lies at *Ballynoe* in Ireland, only some 80 mi. (128 km.) across the sea from whence would have come traders on their way inland to the Lake District. The circle at Swinside, also known as Sunken Kirk because of a local legend of the Devil, was excavated in 1901 with the discovery in its interior of nothing more than one piece of charcoal and a fragment of human bone. Of the 32 stones still standing, a thin upright at the N. is the tallest. An entrance at the SE is framed by two portal stones.

TAPLOW (Buckinghamshire)

Imposing Anglo-Saxon burial mound, in an old churchyard on the grounds of a Victorian mansion in Taplow, about 1 mi. (1.6 km.) E. of Maidenhead on the Thames. The mound, still about 15 ft. high and 80 across at the base, was opened by the village clerk in 1883 and yielded the richest early Anglo-Saxon treasure known before the discovery of the *Sutton Hoo* treasure in 1939. The grave was apparently that of an unknown but powerful chieftain or king of the 7th cent. AD named Taeppa, who gave his name to the village (in Anglo-Saxon "Low" means a burial mound). He was buried in a wooden coffin with his sword, two shields, spears and a knife, and an array of rich possessions including a great gold buckle inset with garnets and lapis lazuli, clasps of gilded bronze, a mead bucket, mead horns with silver-gilt terminals, rare glassware, bone playing pieces, a harp, and a bronze bowl from Egypt. A profusion of gold threads in the grave may have come from a decayed tunic or baldric. These finds are in the British Museum.

THICKTHORN LONG BARROW (Dorset)	See *Blandford Forum*.

THORNBOROUGH MOOR HENGES (North Yorkshire)

Three very large henge monuments of an unusual design (see *Avebury*), about 6 mi. (10 km.) N. of *Ripon* near West Tanfield. These are the best-preserved of at least six henges in an area N. of Ripon and between the Ure and Swale rivers that was obviously once of great sanctity. Three more lie about 5 mi. (8 km.) to the SE: around Hutton Moor, where there is one, while the other two are nearby, at Cana and Nunwick. All these henges are accompanied by numerous round barrows, a sure sign of sacred ground. The Thornborough henges are in a line about half a mi. (1 km.) apart; the northern (being among trees) is the best preserved; the other two are damaged by ploughing and quarrying. All are on the same pattern, with entrances on the NW and SE. The central henge, excavated in 1952, was about 800 ft. in diameter with a bank constructed of large boulders, originally coated with white gypsum crystals. The usual ditch lay inside the bank, well separated from it and about 65 ft. wide, but there was also another ditch outside the bank. Under this central henge the excavators found the remains of an earlier cursus (see *Stonehenge*) about a mi. (1.6 km.) long and already out of use when the henge was constructed. Obviously great concourses of people gathered in this sacred area for many centuries.

TINKINSWOOD CHAMBERED TOMB (South Glamorgan)

See *Cardiff*.

TINTAGEL HEAD (Cornwall)

Famous scenic headland in NW Cornwall, 15.2 mi. (25 km.) SW of Bude, near Boscastle, legendary birthplace of King Arthur. The story dates from the 12th-cent. chronicler Geoffrey of Monmouth, who may have drawn on earlier traditions. The headland is crowned by the ruins of the 12th-cent. castle of Henry I's bastard son. Excavations here by Radford in the 1930s found the remains of a possible Celtic monastery of the Arthurian period on the seaside below the castle, consisting of buildings, a church and a graveyard. The site was identified by the presence of sherds of "Class A" fine red tableware imported from the eastern Mediterranean, which were also found at *South Cadbury*, considered by some to be Arthur's Camelot. Radford went on to excavate at two other sites with Arthurian associations—King Mark's *Castle Dore* and *Glastonbury*. The monastery at Tintagel seems to have been occupied from about 500 to 850 AD, and included individual cells for about 30 monks, a scriptorium, bath house and corn-drying kiln, as well as the church and graveyard.

TOMEN Y MUR (Gwynedd)

Roman auxiliary fort in an isolated, lonely spot, 900 ft. high, with superb views, 4 mi. (6.5 km.) S. of Ffestiniog in Wales. Founded by Agricola about 78 AD, it was a 4.2-acre fort with earthen ramparts topped by palisades. Excavations in 1962 indicated that perhaps around 120 AD the fort was reduced in size to 3.3 acres and given stone fortifications. It was abandoned by the mid-2nd cent. From the Norman motte built over one of the ramparts one can see the grassy mounds that reveal the whole complex—the ramparts, a small oval amphitheater outside the walls to the E. (unusual in such a small fort and perhaps a reward for such a remote posting), one and possibly two practice camps outside the fort, and the sites of the bath house, associated settlement and parade ground. A road led SE to the fort of *Caer Gai*. Inscriptions retrieved from the fort may be seen in the Segontium museum in *Caernarvon*.

TOWLESWORTHY WARREN (Devon)

See *Dartmoor*.

TRECASTELL CIRCLES (Powys)

See *Brecon*.

TREFIGNATH CHAMBERED TOMB (Gwynedd)

A so-called segmented cist tomb, rare in these parts, on Holy Island SE of *Holyhead*—just S. of the main bridge from Anglesey to the island. Excavations in 1977–79 showed that the tomb had been elaborated over a long period, starting with a simple stone tomb under a small round cairn, now at the W. end. A larger chamber faced by two 7-ft.-tall portal stones and a forecourt was added to this, and finally a third chamber was built into the forecourt, with its own forecourt of drystone masonry before it. The whole cairn (now disappeared) was edged with drystone walling. The eastern chamber with its portal stones and a double capstone over it is the best preserved. The whole has been consolidated and restored by the state for public viewing. No burials were found in the excavations.

TREGEARE ROUNDS (Cornwall)

Typical, round, Iron Age Cornish hill fort between *Bodmin Moor* and the coast, about 2.5 mi. (4 km.) N. of St. Kew, N. of Wadebridge, lightly excavated in 1904 and dated at about 100 BC. Its two concentric circles of heavy earthen ramparts and ditches lie on the slope of the hill, the outer rampart almost 53 ft. across and 9 ft. high. The entrance on the SE leads up from a stream through a hollow way, protected by an annex.

TREGESEAL CIRCLES (Cornwall)

See *St. Just*.

TRE'R CEIRI (Gwynedd)

"The town of the giants," probably the most spectacular stone-built, Iron Age hill fort in all of Britain. Long and narrow, the fort crowns the SW summit of the triple Yr Eifl peaks overlooking Caernarvon Bay; over 1,500 ft. high, on the NW coast of the Lleyn peninsula. It is approached by a steep climb up from Llanaelhaearn and commands extensive views. A stronghold of the Ordovices, it was certainly occupied in the late Iron Age and throughout the Roman period, when the ramparts and numerous stone huts in the interior were mostly built. The ramparts, of skillfully piled up loose stone, are remarkably well preserved, still standing in the N. up to 12 ft. high, with ramps leading up to a wall walk behind parapets. There are five gates, the principal ones in the SW and W, and three small posterns. The main ramparts form a single line, though in the NW a second rampart runs well down the slope from the main one. The interior is crowded with stone-built huts, 150 of them, some round and presumably earlier, others D-shaped, as well as the rectangular huts of the Roman period. On the slopes are numerous enclosures that may have been sheep and cattle pounds—stock-raising under difficulties! See also *Caer Drewyn*.

TREVELGUE HEAD
(Cornwall)

Fine example of a promontory fort on Cornwall's NW coast overlooking Newquay, 1 mi. (1.6 km.) to the N. No less than six ramparts protect the fortress, four on the landward side and three on the headland side of a deep chasm across the promontory, now crossed by a modern bridge. The site was occupied for over 800 years, as excavations in 1939 showed, from the Bronze Age through the Roman period and probably into the Dark Ages. There was metal-working here in the Bronze and Iron Ages, and a number of stone-based huts of the later period were also found—one a large circular house 46 ft. across occupied from 200 BC to 120 AD. Also on the headland and within the fort are two round Bronze Age barrows.

TREVETHY QUOIT
(Cornwall)

See *Bodmin Moor*.

TRIPPETT STONES
(Cornwall)

See *Bodmin Moor*.

TRISTAN STONE
(Cornwall)

See *Castle Dore*.

TRUNDLE, THE
(West Sussex)

Major Iron Age hill fort, beautifully sited with wide views. It overlooks Goodwood Racecourse, 4 mi. (6.5 km.) N. of Chichester (see *Fishbourne*). Within its octagonal single rampart and ditch, enclosing 12½ acres, a smaller Neolithic causewayed camp of about 3000 BC was discovered (see Windmill Hill in *Avebury*). Excavated in 1929, the camp proved to have two rings of ditches and a subsidiary ring, with internal banks crossed by a series of causeways, the inner ring 380 ft. in diameter, the outer 950 ft. across. During the Iron Age the hill seems to have been reoccupied about 500 BC and the fortifications constructed about 320 BC. It became the capital of the Regni, the southern section of the Atrebates. Of the two inturned gates, E. and W., only the eastern one was excavated, showing at least three phases of rebuilding, the last about 100 BC. A massive new entrance with a bridge over it to carry a wall walk was in the course of construction, but was never finished, for at this time the Belgae from Europe invaded the area and probably destroyed the fort, which in any case was abandoned. The Belgae settled the area with open towns, probably at Selsey Bill S. of Chichester and certainly at Chichester itself, which became, under the Romans, Noviomagus, the New Town. To protect their settlements the Belgae probably erected the long lines of earthworks still visible on the plain N. of Chichester.

TWELVE APOSTLES
(West Yorkshire)

See *Ilkley*.

TY ILLTUD
(Powys)

See *Brecon*.

TY ISAF CHAMBERED
TOMB
(Powys)

A Severn-Cotswold type of Neolithic long barrow (see *Hetty Pegler's Tump*), 4 mi. (6.5 km.) S. of Talgarth in Wales, the best-known of the Black Mtns. group of long barrows closely related to those of the Cotswolds. Careful excavation of the tomb, almost 100 ft. long, in 1938 found that it was held together within double drystone walls forming a horned entrance with a forecourt at the larger, northern end, curving out from a false entrance. Two burial chambers were entered by short passages on either side, and at the end of the barrow there was a third, rectangular chamber containing a Bronze Age cremation. Crushed bones (of 17 individuals in the western chamber) and skeletons, totaling at least 33 burials, were found in the chambers, along with Neolithic pottery, polished axes and flint arrowheads. Finally, between the rear and middle chambers was a separate oval cairn, its drystone walls set at a curious angle to the rest, the whole apparently engulfed within the later long barrow. Its passage led into a tripartite chamber containing more bones and Neolithic pottery. The barrow was back-filled after excavation so that today only the tops of the uprights are visible.

The Iron Age hill fort of Castell Dinas looms over Ty Isaf on the N., set on a high spur commanding the pass to Talgarth. Massive double ramparts guard the southern side, with an oblique entrance in the N., and inside it there is the motte of a Norman castle. A cross wall divides the fort into two sections.

TY MAWR
(Gwynedd)

See *Caer y Twr*.

TYNWALD

See *Isle of Man*.

UFFINGTON CASTLE
(Oxfordshire)

See *White Horse*.

USK
(Gwent)

Small town on the Usk River, built over the site of the early legionary fort (and town) of Burrium. This fort was the immediate predecessor of the legionary fortress at *Caerleon*, which lies 8 mi. (13 km.) due S. of Usk. Complex excavations in two parts of the fort and underneath the small Norman castle of Usk, from 1967 to 1975, filled in the story of Burrium, which was occupied by elements of the 2nd Augustan Legion for pacification campaigns among the local tribes, in both the Claudian and Neronian periods. The low-lying site was subject to flooding, which undoubtedly prompted the move to the site of Caerleon. The original fort at Usk (of the Roman invasion period) covered 10 acres, defended by a stout earthen rampart and ditch. About 55 AD, during the reign of Nero, a far larger fortress of about 50 acres was constructed; part of its E-W road was cleared in excavations, with barracks and granaries. This was destroyed about 60 AD; then from about 66 to 70 a final fort was built before the military moved out about 75 AD. Part of the principal street, lined with colonnades and compounds, and indications of the principal buildings, workshops, offices and stores were uncovered, as well as five pairs of granaries and a timber building used for iron-working. Civilians continued to live on the site of the abandoned fort during the 3rd and 4th cents., as graves and rubbish from pits indicate. Undoubtedly there is little left to see from the excavations today.

VENTA BELGARUM
(Hampshire)

See *Winchester*.

VENTA ICENORUM
(Norfolk)

See *Caister-by-Norwich*.

VENTA SILURUM
(Gwent)

See *Caerwent.*

VERULAMIUM
(Hertfordshire)

See *St. Albans.*

VINDOLANDA
(Northumberland)

See *Hadrian's Wall* (Chesterholm).

VINOVIA
(Durham)

See *Binchester Roman Fort.*

VIROCONIUM
(Shropshire)

See *Wroxeter.*

WADE'S CAUSEWAY
(North Yorkshire)

See *Cawthorn.*

WALL ROMAN STATION
(Staffordshire)

Remains of a Roman posting station, 2 mi. (3.25 km.) SW of Lichfield. It lay on Watling Street, the principal Roman road that ran across the country from *London* to the city of *Wroxeter*, close to Shrewsbury and close to the borders of Wales. The station, which undoubtedly started as a military post, with a *mansio* or inn and a bath suite, grew into the prosperous little town of Letocetum covering about 20 to 30 acres and provided with walls, probably in the 4th cent. The site has been despoiled in the last few cents. and little is known of the town itself, but excavations from 1912 to 1914 uncovered the bath suite and what was probably the inn. The latter was covered over again but has now been reexcavated; the bath suite, consolidated, was left exposed and is now open to view. An elaborate complex of cold and hot rooms with well-preserved hypocausts for underfloor heating, the structure went through several phases of expansion from the 1st cent. on. What one sees now is mostly the final, 4th-cent. structure and constitutes the most complete bath suite on view in Britain. The whole is in state care and there is a small site museum, which also contains finds from an excavated, Roman-period farmhouse at nearby Shenstone.

WALLINGFORD
(Oxfordshire)

Town commanding a crossing of the Thames, 12 mi. (19 km.) SE of Oxford. Wallingford was one of the fortified *burhs* set up by Alfred the Great and his son Edward the Elder to foil the invading Danish Vikings. The remains of the mighty ramparts are still visible around the town except on the Thames side—a bank, originally faced with timber and still 10 ft. high, and a ditch 5 ft. deep. Excavations showed that the ramparts date from the 9th or 10th cent. AD. Similar defenses of other *burhs* can also be seen at *Cricklade* and *Wareham.*

WALLTOWN
(Northumberland)

See *Hadrian's Wall.*

WANDLEBURY
(Cambridgeshire)

Remnants of the double ramparts and ditches of one of the few Iron Age hill forts in East Anglia, about 4 mi. (6.5 km.) SE of Cambridge. The round fort in a wooded area was partly destroyed by 18th-cent. landscaping, but the ramparts, enclosing about 15 acres, are still visible in part. Excavations in 1955–56 determined that the outer rampart, once faced with timber on both sides, and its accompanying flat-bottomed ditch, were constructed in the 5th cent. BC to protect an already flourishing settlement. In the next cent. the rampart was rebuilt and a new inner rampart, with V-shaped ditch, added to it. By about 250 BC the camp had been abandoned.

WANSDYKE
(Wiltshire)

See *Devizes*; *White Horse*.

WAREHAM
(Dorset)

Ancient town just W. of Poole Harbor. In Anglo-Saxon times it was a settlement of some note with an important nunnery, carrying on a brisk cross-Channel trade. Alfred the Great made it one of his *burhs*, fortified against Danish attacks with high earthen banks on three sides of the town—the southern side lying along the Frome River. The remains of the great banks, particularly along the W. side, are the best-preserved of the *burh* fortifications surviving (see also *Cricklade*; *Wallingford*). Beside the N. gate of Wareham's old ramparts stands the little 10th-cent. church of St. Martin's, part of the nave and the chancel, tall and narrow, betraying its Saxon origin. Lady St. Mary church, across the town to the S., stands on the site of the large Anglo-Saxon church belonging to the nunnery, built around 700 AD and only destroyed in the 1840s. In turn this early Saxon church had replaced an even earlier British church going back to the 6th cent., as attested by some of the early inscribed grave monuments found on the site. These can be seen inside the present church.

WARHAM
(Norfolk)

Pleasingly symmetrical, small hill fort, the finest in Norfolk, about 1 mi. (1.6 km.) SE of Wells-next-the-Sea, in the N. of the county. Its double ramparts and ditches, enclosing only 3½ acres, are mathematically laid out, forming almost a perfect circle. Another less-impressive fort with a single rampart lies at Holkham about 3 mi. (4.75 km.) to the NW. Excavations of the fort at Warham in 1914 and 1959 turned up some Roman period material, but little else. Both forts may have been built by the Iceni to guard against the advancing Belgae in the late Iron Age.

WATER NEWTON
(Cambridgeshire)

The Roman town of Durobrivae, E. of the present village of Water Newton, about 5 mi. (8 km.) W. of Peterborough. This 44-acre town, which grew up where the Roman Ermine Street crossed the Neve River, was the center of Britain's most industrialized area, the pottery industry of the Neve valley. Here in the late 2nd through the 4th cents. the imitation Samian ware, the decorated tableware of the Roman empire, was produced in numerous large kilns. After the larger pottery industries of Gaul were no longer operative, the local version produced here supplied most of Britain with its wares, called Castor wares. The Gallic industries (and some in Tunisia and Germany as well) had in turn replaced the original Samian or Arretine ware of Italy itself. The local British version was named Castor for the factories there, just across the river from Durobrivae on its N. bank. Castor has been excavated, yielding many kilns, comfortable houses with mosaic floors belonging to the managers, and the less pretentious houses of the workers. Nothing is to be seen at Castor today, and at Durobrivae only the immense mounds of its ramparts, best seen along the main road, are visible. Here one can also see the line of Ermine Street leading up to the town's

E. gate. In 1974 and 1975 rich hoards turned up at Water Newton, one containing perhaps the earliest-known group of Romano-Christian silver found to date. Both are in the British museum.

WAT'S DYKE
(Shropshire)

See *Offa's Dyke*.

WAYLAND'S SMITHY
(Oxfordshire)

See *White Horse*.

WELWYN
(Hertfordshire)

Roman bath house. The Dicket Mead villa, just E. of the old village of Welwyn and a few mi. N. of Welwyn Garden City was excavated in 1937. Though nothing of the villa except its bath house is visible today, the excavators found two long buildings about 300 yds. apart within an enclosure. At the end of one of the buildings the small bath house was excavated in 1970–71 and is now consolidated and preserved inside a concrete vault entered by a tunnel leading under the motorway, which was built across its site. Dating to about 250 AD, it has three rooms, each about 8 ft. square. Details of the villa and the finds from both excavations are displayed in the vault along with the remains of the bath house.

WEST KENNET LONG
BARROW
(Wiltshire)

See *Avebury*.

WEST STOW
(Suffolk)

Remarkable find of an early pagan Saxon village, about 6 mi. (10 km.) NW of Bury St. Edmunds. The site is just W. of the village. Excavated in its entirety from 1965, some of its houses have been reconstructed from the evidence provided by the excavations and can now be visited. The village was settled around 400 AD when the Saxons were first entering and settling in England and occupation continued until at least 650 AD, at the beginning of the Christian period. It lay close to a more substantial area of Romano-British settlement. For instance, at Icklingham to the W. a Romano-British church complex has been uncovered. Apparently some six family groups occupied the Saxon village, which had about 80 structures. Six of these were large timber-built halls with thatched roofs, earthen floors and walls of upright split logs set close together—like the surviving walls of the Saxon church at *Greensted*, Essex. Most of the rest were smaller sunken-floor huts or *grubenhausen*, probably used as workshops or for storage.

The village's cemetery nearby was also excavated, yielding varied grave goods, domestic and other objects, for these were pagan burials. The finds from village and cemetery gave a vivid picture of some 250 years of the life of these early immigrants. They grew cereals in fields around the village, hunted, spun and wove wool, kept sheep, pigs, cattle, dogs and cats, wore amber jewelry and bronze brooches, and by the late 6th cent. boasted a master potter in the village whose wares have been found all over the area. The finds are in the Ipswich museum. See also *Mucking* in Essex where early Saxon houses were also found.

WEST TUMP LONG
BARROW
(Gloucestershire)

Concealed today in the beech trees of Buckle Wood near Brimpsfield, about 6 mi. (10 km.) S. of Cheltenham, the barrow was excavated in 1880. Nearly 150 ft. long and tapering back from a false entrance and horns at the larger end, it was held together within drystone walls and contained one large burial chamber entered through a passage from the S. side. Here were found the jumbled bones of at least 20 individuals and the complete skeleton of a young woman and her baby, either the first or the last burial. Four more skeletons lay in front of the false door. See also *Hetty Pegler's Tump*.

WETWANG
(Humberside)

See *Great Driffield*.

WHEATHAMPSTEAD
(Hertfordshire)

A Belgic settlement here, about 4 mi. (6.5 km.) NE of St. *Albans*, was defended against the advancing Romans by massive banks and ditches, still visible today. The defense on the W. side, called today the Devil's Dyke, was a truly enormous construction, a ditch a quarter of a mi. (.5 km.) long, almost 40 ft. deep and 120 ft. wide. It is still impressive today. These were probably the defenses built by the chieftain Cassivellaunus of the Catevellauni when attacked by Julius Caesar in 54 BC. The tribe later moved their capital to St. Albans and then to *Colchester*.

WHEELDALE MOOR
(North Yorkshire)

See *Cawthorn*.

WHITBY
(North Yorkshire)

Coastal town dominated by the dramatic ruins of medieval Whitby Abbey on a cliff 200 ft. above the sea. N. of the abbey ruins (12th–13th cents.) are many traces of the original abbey, founded by St. Hild in 657 AD for monks and nuns, which became a center of Northumbrian learning (see *York*). It was destroyed by the Danish Vikings in 857 AD. The famous Synod of Whitby, held here under the aegis of the king of Northumbria in 664, brought the Celtic churches of northern England into conformity with the practices of Rome.

WHITEHAWK CAMP
(Sussex)

Remains of a Neolithic causewayed camp, just E. of Brighton (see Windmill Hill in *Avebury*). The camp was a big one, with four circuits of ditches (the third one cut the deepest) and causeways across them. Little is left of the ditches, since suburbiana and one end of the Brighton racecourse have destroyed most of the remains; however, excavations in the 1930s uncovered the usual remarkable story of these early ceremonial gathering places (see for instance *Hambledon Hill*). In the ditches, along with a litter of potsherds, flints and food bones, human burials were found and other bodies thrown unceremoniously into them. Moreover, in the litter around a hearth positive evidence of cannibalism was found—five human brain pans, all of young people or children, charred from the fire. The excavators also uncovered evidence that there may have been fences along the tops of the banks, with wooden gates at the causeways. Two Iron Age camps, *Devil's Dyke Camp* and *Hollingbury*, are also to be seen nearby around Brighton.

WHITE HORSE OF
UFFINGTON
(Oxfordshire)

Famous chalk figure of a horse cut in the turf above the Vale of White Horse on the crest of the Berkshire Downs, 6.5 mi. (10.5 km.) W. of Wantage. It is one of the principal sites on the Ridgeway, the lovely prehistoric trackway that leads SW across the countryside. A large stretch of the original Ridgeway, running along high ground, is now an official walking path leading from Streatley on the Thames in Berkshire westward to Overton Hill just above *Avebury* in Wiltshire, a distance of some 40 mi. (64 km.).

The White Horse, close to the Ridgeway path, is by far the oldest of the many white horses cut in the chalk of southern England, mostly in the last three centuries AD. Traditionally associated with King Alfred, it is on the contrary almost certainly an Iron Age tribal symbol, probably of about 100 BC (on the analogy of Iron Age coins of that period marked with very similar schematic horse figures). It was presumably cut by the Celtic tribesmen who built the hill fort of Uffington Castle close by on the other side of Uffington Hill. The horse, suggesting rather than depicting the animal, is 374 ft. long and was lovingly maintained by the local people, with elaborate festivities, until recent centuries. It is now in state care.

The finest and most interesting stretch of the Ridgeway begins with another Iron Age hill fort E. of the White Horse, that of Segsbury (Oxon.) near Letcombe Bassett, above Wantage. Like the 8-acre Uffington Castle this fort, though far larger (about 26 acres), is protected by a single bank and ditch, the rampart once faced with massive sarsen stones.

Moving on W. about a mi. (1.6 km.) from the White Horse one comes to the well-known megalithic tomb called Wayland's Smithy (probably named for its association with the White Horse, for in Scandinavian mythology Wayland, the smith of the gods, owned a white horse). The tomb, 185 ft. long, stands near the Ridgeway in a grove of trees. It is an early outlier of the Severn-Cotswold group of graves (see Hetty Pegler's Tump) and has been radiocarbon-dated between 3700 and 3400 BC. Originally covered by a mound of chalk held in by a stone kerb, its wider end was faced with a facade of huge sarsen stones and an entrance passage leading into a cruciform set of three burial chambers. Skeletons of eight people were found in one chamber. Excavations also showed that originally there had been a wooden mortuary chamber on the site under a long barrow into which 14 bodies had been piled. The wooden structure was then closed and the larger stone tomb built over it so that nothing of the original is now visible.

On the slopes of the downs S. of Uffington are a number of interesting sites, principally the fine barrow cemetery called Lambourn Seven Barrows (there are

The frowning double ramparts of Barbury Castle, an Iron Age hill fort and one of the many prehistoric sites to be seen along the ancient pathway known as the Ridgeway. Like many of the hill forts, Barbury actually enclosed a village, as crop marks of hut circles and storage pits, seen from the air, attest. (Photo: the author.)

actually some 50 in the larger group). It lies about 2 mi. (3.25 km.) N. of Lambourn village in Berkshire. Here are one Neolithic long barrow and numerous Bronze Age round barrows of all types and sizes, the most accessible group right beside the road. About 4 mi. (6.5 km.) due W. (still in Berkshire) is the striking Iron Age hill fort of Alfred's Castle, defended by a single rampart except on the SE where an extra ditch guards an original entrance. W. again and back on the Ridgeway, which now curves SW into Wiltshire, is another Iron Age hill fort on the left of the pathway, about 4 mi. (6.5 km.) SW of Swindon. Liddington Castle, an oval fort with a single rampart, ditch and counterscarp, has been excavated and produced mainly pottery of the Early Iron Age (6th-5th cents. BC) but also some Romano-British wares and a few sherds of about 500 AD, which could substantiate the legend that King Arthur defeated the Saxons here in the famed battle of Mons Badonicus.

About 5 mi. (8 km.) farther on is another Ridgeway hill fort, Barbury Castle, again an oval fort strongly defended by doubled ramparts and ditches and with one of its two entrances inturned. From the air, numerous hut circles and storage pits are visible in the interior as crop marks. The Ridgeway now descends Hackpen Hill toward *Avebury*. Nearby two more hill forts are worth seeking out, Oldbury Castle about 3.5 mi. (5.6 km.) W. of Avebury, and Oliver's Castle farther to the SW and about 4 mi. (6.5 km.) NW of Devizes. Between the two forts the Wansdyke crosses the route (see *Devizes*).

WHITLEY CASTLE ROMAN FORT
(Northumberland)

A very striking fort with multiple defenses, comparable only with *Ardoch* in Scotland. On private property, it lies about 2 mi. (3.25 km.) NW of Alston on the former Roman road called Maiden Way that runs straight N. some 12 mi. (19 km.) to *Hadrian's Wall* near Greenhead. Though no stonework shows, the multiple ditches that defend the fort on its low hill are clearly visible, especially on the most vulnerable SW side where up to seven ditches mount up to a strong rampart at the top. The fort apparently dates to the 2nd cent. AD.

WILLOWFORD
(Northumberland)

See *Hadrian's Wall*.

WILLY HOWE ROUND BARROW
(North Yorkshire)

See *Duggleby Howe*.

WILMINGTON LONG MAN
(East Sussex)

One of the three indisputably ancient chalk-cut figures in southern England (see also *White Horse* and the *Cerne Abbas Giant*). The figure, doubtfully restored in 1874, stands 312 ft. high on a hillside in the South Downs near Wilmington, over 5 mi. (8 km.) NW of Eastbourne. He is long and thin and stands frontally, his hands grasping long staffs on either side. They are far taller than he is. He could date any time from the Iron Age through the Romano-British period into Saxon times—but no later. He may have been a representation of the pagan god, Woden.

WINCHESTER
(Hampshire)

Cathedral city known for its prestigious boys' public school, chief town of Hampshire with a long and special history. The capital of Saxon Wessex since 519 AD and of King Alfred and many of his successors, it developed on the ruins of what was once the fifth largest city in Roman Britain. Venta Belgarum, as its Roman name implies, was founded even earlier as the capital town of the Romanized Celtic Belgae, who had previously invaded southern England from the continent. Undoubtedly the earliest settlement at Winchester was *not* the hill fort called *Old Winchester Hill* about 12 mi. (19 km.) SE of the city, but the rounded St. Catherine's Hill that rises above the Itchen River just S. of Winchester center. A classic excavation here in the 1920s showed that an open settlement had been established on the hilltop around 500 BC. It was fortified some 100 years later with a single rampart, ditch and counterscarp and a single entrance on the NE. The defenses were rebuilt several times before the whole was destroyed and abandoned about 50 BC. Undoubtedly the attackers were the Belgae, who then founded their settlement across the river at the site of modern Winchester. The defenses are still visible around the hilltop, with the ruins of a medieval chapel inside them and a maze, probably of the 18th cent., built by and much frequented by the boys of Winchester College below the hill.

Very little remains of Roman Venta Belgarum and its early successors; remnants of the Roman and Belgic ramparts around the city and numerous finds on view in the City Museum, along with other materials from Winchester's region. With intensive redevelopment after World War II, however, excavations began in 1953 on a number of sites N. of the cathedral and have continued into the 1980s—always open to the public, with site tours and lectures—culminating in the current dig at The Brooks, Britain's largest excavation, in the heart of the Roman and medieval city. So far a number of fine Roman townhouses have been discovered. The earlier excavations, of which little is visible today, included exploration of the Roman defenses, discovery of sections of a Roman road and of the site of the Old Minster, built over the Roman forum, and the ecclesiastical and royal buildings that clustered around it, one of them St. Mary's Abbey, a Benedictine nunnery occupied from 905 AD to 1539.

The Old Minster, founded by King Cenwalh of Wessex about 648, was the core of old Winchester. It was the earliest Saxon cathedral, which first the kings of Wessex and then those of England used for coronations, burials and services. From the 970s the original church was greatly enlarged, and around it were the royal palaces and buildings, the nunnery, and the New Minster, an abbey founded by King Alfred and actually built by his son Edward in 903. It was later moved outside the city. Meantime the Old Minster was replaced and torn down in 1093–94 and the present cathedral took over, begun in 1079 and consecrated in 1093.

WINDMILL HILL
(Wiltshire)

See *Avebury*.

WING
(Buckinghamshire)

Large Anglo-Saxon church, possibly very early in date, in the village of Wing, about 3 mi. (4.75 km.) SW of Leighton Buzzard. The church of All Saints shares with that of *Brixworth* in Northamptonshire several characteristics that suggest a possible 7th-cent. date for both—a basilican plan, an apse, and a chancel with a crypt beneath it. The large seven-sided chancel displays an interesting pattern of stripwork and arches on the outside, with round-headed windows. The stripwork, as well as the piers and barrel roof of the octagonal crypt, probably date from a 10th-cent. rebuilding of both chancel and crypt. In the interior the great nave arches and chancel arch are Saxon, as is certainly the whole plan of the church. Nothing however is known of its early history, though in the 10th cent. it did house a shrine and relics.

WINSHIELS
(Northumberland)

See *Hadrian's Wall.*

WINTERBOURNE STOKE
BARROW GROUP
(Wiltshire)

See *Stonehenge.*

WOODCHESTER MOSAIC
(Gloucestershire)

Largest and one of the finest Roman mosaics ever found in Britain. The story of its discovery is bizarre. Now reburied in the churchyard at Woodchester, about 2 mi. (3.25 km.) S. of Stroud, it was known as early as 1695 and was uncovered no less than eight times from 1793, the last time in 1973 when it was examined by over 141,000 visitors. The mosaic, made in the famous Corinium workshop at *Cirencester*, dates from about 325 AD. The workshop supplied mosaics for many of the luxurious villas in the region (see for example *Chedworth*). It covered the floor of a splendid dining room in a huge courtyard villa with at least 65 rooms— as occasional soundings have indicated. By 1973, when the mosaic was last uncovered, it had been so damaged by gravediggers, visitors and the weather that it was decided to bury it permanently.

In that year two brothers, John and Robert Woodward, joint owners of a local construction business and with an amateur passion for archaeology, decided to sell their business and devote themselves to making an accurate reproduction of the mosaic for permanent display. Taking hundreds of color slides of the mosaic before it was reburied, they spent 10 years on the project, buying a disused church in Wotton-under-Edge, about 8 mi. (13 km.) S. of Woodchester, as a permanent home for their reproduction. It is now on view there from a gallery, along with an accompanying display that includes finds from the exca-vation of a Roman settlement nearby at Kingscote, now covered up. The mosaic was restored using 1.5 million tesserae especially cut for the job, and filling in the missing parts after a careful study of comparable mosaics of the period.

The Orpheus mosaic (its subject was popular with the mosaic-makers of Cir-encester) is over 45 ft. square. A depression in the center inside an octagon contained a pool fed by a small fountain. Between the octagon and the first circle sits Orpheus playing his lyre, with the birds he charmed in a circle around him and another circle of rapt animals outside that, all realistically portrayed. The damaged Orpheus, as reconstructed, is closely similar to (though not copied from) the Orpheus in the mosaic at *Littlecote* Roman villa. The rest of the mosaic consists of an outer circle and a square area of intricate and elaborate geomet-ric designs, the spandrels between circle and square filled with four pairs of water nymphs on a water-blue background. Four pillar bases, reconstructed in the display, once supported the villa's dining room roof.

WOODCUTS SETTLEMENT
(Dorset)

One of the native settlements of Iron Age and Roman times excavated on Cran-borne Chase in 1884–86 by the pioneer archaeologist, General Pitt-Rivers. In contrast to the luxurious country villas of the Romanized Britons, these farm-steads show how little life of the humbler natives was changed by the Roman occupation. The farmstead on Woodcuts Common, about 2 mi. (3.25 km.) NW of Sixpenny Handley (just W. of the main road from *Blandford Forum* to *Salisbury*), restored by Pitt-Rivers, consisted of a circular bank and ditch (once with a palisade) and within it a large circular hut, built shortly before the Roman invasion of 43 AD, as well as some 80 grain pits, dug at different times, There was no change at all at the farmstead until the late 2nd cent., when some Roman technology was introduced (the use of wall plaster, corn-dryers in a separate enclosure, and two wells, now marked in stone). With few other changes the farm was abandoned during the 4th cent.

A very similar farmstead, also excavated in 1885–86 and restored by Pitt-Rivers, lies close to Woodcuts but across the border in Wiltshire. Rotherley, about 1 mi. (1.6 km.) NE of Tollard Royal, was also built in the late Iron Age and occupied with little change to about 300 AD. Due W. of it about a half mi., and about 1 mi. (1⅔ km.) N. of Tollard, are the earthworks at Berwick Down, including a U-shaped farm enclosure dated to the 1st cent. AD, a Romano-British settlement of rectangular hut platforms inside a two-acre circular enclosure, just to the N., and finally N. again a large circular hut with storage pits of pre-Roman date.

WOODHENGE (Wiltshire)

A small circular henge structure of timber, on Salisbury Plain, 2 mi. (3.25 km.) NE of *Stonehenge*, discovered from the air and excavated in 1926–27. Its concentric rings of posts are now marked on the ground by concrete stumps. It stood just S. of Durrington Walls, one of the four largest henge monuments in Britain (including *Avebury*, *Marden* and Mt. Pleasant). Durrington Walls contained inside its circle two more, similar timber structures—and probably many more, now lost. Its huge perimeter covered over 30 acres of a valley descending toward the Avon River. Today nothing is visible except some denuded traces of its huge bank.

Over 80 of these henge monuments of different sizes are known in England, Scotland and Ireland, all built with an incredible output of labor and in use between the end of the 3rd millennium (Late Neolithic) and the middle of the 2nd millennium BC (the middle Bronze Age). These monuments were apparently public gathering places for both secular and ritual purposes, and are characterized by circular outer banks with an internal ditch, usually with one or two entrances across causeways, and timber structures inside them. Some henges, such as Stonehenge and Avebury, enclosed different types of stone structures—possibly a later development. Whether they were purely secular or purely ritual in purpose, or a combination of both, is still hotly debated. It has been suggested that a priestly caste, responsible for the tremendous organization and labor involved in their construction, may have lived within the larger ones at least, and certainly presided there in the public buildings over the ceremonies of the calendar year.

Excavation at Woodhenge revealed six concentric rings of postholes that had contained massive oaken timbers or masts. These were surrounded by a ditch and outer bank with a diameter of nearly 135 ft. The entrance causeway was in the NE. At the very center of the henge the grave of a three-year-old child was found, her skull cleft open, and buried under a cairn of flints—one of the few clear examples of ritual child sacrifice. It is not known whether the post structure at Woodhenge was open to the sky, or more likely roofed with thatch, leaving an open courtyard in the center, and it is also possible that the six rings represented two successive structures rather than one. The finds from Woodhenge are in the *Devizes* museum.

Both Woodhenge and Durrington Walls were actively in use for around 500 years, from about 2500 BC into the Beaker period, about 2000 BC. Durington Walls was excavated in a rescue operation in 1966–67, in advance of road building across the site. A strip was opened up across the eastern half of the site following the proposed route of the road, which included part of the henge's ditch and the SE causeway entrance. What was revealed was impressive. The huge bank, it appeared, was originally about 9 ft. high and 90 ft. broad. Well within it the ditch, about 50 ft. wide, had been nearly 20 ft. deep. Where the entrance causeway crossed it the ditch was filled with broken pottery, animal bones, antler picks and flint tools thrown into it or lost by people going in and out of the henge. From the site as a whole about 12,000 flints, 440 deer antler picks, 30 bone tools, many animal remains, mostly of pigs, and numerous potsherds were retrieved. The sherds were mostly the special Neolithic Grooved Ware and seem to have been pots used in the rituals and then ceremoniously broken and discarded, a practice also found among the Creek and Cherokee Indians of North America.

Just inside the SE entrance the excavators uncovered the concentric postholes of the larger of the two timber structures found. Apparently there had been two successive buildings on the spot, one 99 ft. wide, the later one 127 ft. across. The final structure showed five rings of postholes, the oaken posts increasing in size and height towards the center, with a sixth ring of shorter posts around the actual center. The entrance to the building facing the causeway was flanked by two of the tallest and heaviest of the posts, each weighing many tons. The whole has been interpreted as a roofed building about 30 ft. high, its roof sloping up toward the open center, with a smaller ring of freestanding posts encircling the open court at the center. Again, very similar council halls were built by the Creek and Cherokee Indians in the 18th cent. Outside the entrance to the building was a platform of chalk and flint rubble on which many fires had been burned, with potsherds, flints, tools and bones scattered all around it. The remains of this building seem to suggest scenes of intense activity in this remote period.

To the N. a second and smaller round timber structure was unearthed, distinguished by an avenue lined with freestanding posts approaching its entrance and screened near the entrance by a fence of closely-spaced posts. The strip nature of the excavation by no means precludes the existence of other round structures of the type within the great circle of Durrington Walls.

WOOKEY HOLE
(Somerset)

See *Cheddar*.

WORLEBURY HILL FORT
(Avon)

Strong Iron Age hill fort, on the northern side of Weston-super-Mare, protected on the N. side by the sea and on the S. and E. by a substantial stone rampart still standing up to 9 ft. high, pierced by an inturned entrance. There are also other entrances on the E. and W. Excavations in the early 1900s found an oval area of the fort, cut off by a wall and filled with 93 deeply-dug storage pits, some still containing charred grain as well as potsherds, slingstones and spindle whorls. A violent end to the fort was indicated by numerous skeletons lying about.

WOR LONG BARROW
(Dorset)

See *Blandford Forum.*

WORTH
(West Sussex)

A fine, large Anglo-Saxon church in the little village of Worth just E. of Crawley New Town, a village once isolated in the great Anglo-Saxon forest of Andredswald. The size of this cruciform church suggests that it may have belonged to a royal hunting estate in the forest. Completely restored in 1871, the church still looks much as it did in the 11th cent. when it was built—except for the Victorian tower. The exterior is pleasingly decorated with broad stripwork (the rubble walls may have once been plastered), there are three sets of double windows in the nave, and the large chancel arch in the interior and the two arches opening into the transepts are original. So are the tall narrow N. and S. doors farther on into the nave.

WREKIN, THE
(Shropshire)

Iron Age hill fort, one of the stronger fortresses of the Welsh Marches, constructed on the craggy top of the Wrekin, a striking isolated peak with extensive views 2 mi. S. of Wellington and 4 mi. (6.5 km.) SE of Telford. The long narrow ridge is fortified with ramparts, single or double depending on the terrain, enclosing about 10 acres with an inturned entrance on the NE. Within this another wall encloses the seven acres of an inner camp with inturned entrances NE and SW. Excavations showed that the fort dated from shortly after 400 BC or later and that settlement was restricted to the inner camp after about 350 BC. Rows of square hut foundations were found between the inner and outer ramparts and may have covered other available areas of the hilltop, as in the other Welsh Marches forts in the region. A settlement such as this on an inhospitable, windy crag dramatizes the overriding need for protection in the turbulent late Iron Age times. In its last days the Wrekin was the tribal center of the Cornovii, who were later moved down to the Roman city of *Wroxeter*, 4 mi. (6.5 km.) to the W. In fact some late, hastily-constructed modifications of the defenses may have been undertaken as the Romans advanced toward Wales. They probably captured the fort about 50–48 BC. See also *Breiddin Hill; Credenhill; Croft Ambrey; Herefordshire Beacon; Midsummer Hill; Old Oswestry;* and *Sutton Walls.*

WROXETER
(Shropshire)

The large Roman city of Viroconium Cornoviorum, the fourth largest in Britain, covering about 180 acres at its most prosperous period in the 3rd cent., finally abandoned, after a long, slow decline, about 500 AD. Since the site was never thereafter heavily reoccupied, it is an archaeologist's dream, affording an opportunity to study in detail the rise and decline of a great Romano-British city. And the opportunity has been seized. After some initial trenching by Kathleen Kenyon in the 1930s, the University of Birmingham initiated a long-term excavation project in the 1960s that has yielded fresh information year after year. The site, 5 mi. (8 km.) SE of Shrewsbury above the Severn River, has long been dominated by a still standing part of the wall of the great bath's basilica, called locally "The Old Work," and it is in this area, with the baths, basilica and a market, that the major excavations have taken place and are on view, accompanied by an excellent site museum. Across the present minor road (once the

"The Old Work," still standing at Wroxeter, the ancient Roman city of Viroconium, fourth largest in Roman Britain, after Verulamium (St. Albans). The Old Work is the remnant of an elaborate gateway between the large baths and basilica and the 240-ft.-long, covered palaestra or indoor exercise hall. With an assist from Emperor Hadrian, the one-time legionary fortress became a magnificent city covering 180 acres, improbably sited in Shropshire near the borders of wild Wales. (Photo: the author.)

Roman Watling Street) that runs through the site the column bases of the forum colonnade can still be seen, exposed in a special cutting.

Viroconium began life with a series of legionary fortresses first established about 56 AD and by the 14th Legion as one of the two bases, with *Gloucester,* used for the conquest of Wales. Later the 20th Legion moved in. The military did not leave until about 89 AD, when the fortress buildings were systematically demolished and the new town of Viroconium laid out, to become the cantonal capital of the Cornovii, whose base had previously been the hill fort on *The Wrekin,* 4 mi. (6.5 km.) to the E. The inhabitants of the new city now consisted of Cornovii, the people of the civil settlement that as usual had grown up around the fortress, and perhaps some retired legionaries. Soundings here and there deep beneath the remains of the later city are now beginning to throw light on the walls and layout of the fortress as well as details of the earliest city on the site.

In Viroconium's early years a number of large public buildings in the Roman fashion were laid out but were never completed and were abandoned about 100 AD. Then at the instigation of Hadrian on his visit to Britain in 122 AD a new building program was begun, and the city was doubled in size. The forum, dated to 129–30 from an inscription, and an adjoining, large civic basilica as well as the great bath establishment were built. These baths were one of the finest in Britain, with a large basilica, an aisled *palaestra* or indoor exercise hall, 240 ft. long by 65 ft. wide, that was in effect a vast antechamber to the baths on its southern side. The entrance from it to the baths and part of the basilica's S. wall still stand as The Old Work today.

Next to the baths was a *macellum* or market place and a large public latrine. Late in the 2nd cent. the town was enclosed within a rampart and ditch, but the city so prospered that in the 3rd cent. a new, much larger circuit of walls, a bank and ditch, was constructed, enclosing the full 180 acres. These years, up to about 250 AD, were the city's most prosperous. Then began the slow decline. The civil basilica and forum were burned down during the reign of the usurper Carausius (286 AD) and were never rebuilt. The baths however were repaired and continued in use until perhaps the period 300-350 AD. After that the bath block and its basilica went out of use, and the basilica was gradually dismantled, starting with the deteriorating roof of the nave. Crude wattle and daub timber structures then appeared on the ruined basilica's floor.

Then a curious thing happened. From meager evidence (and with an insecure chronology) it appears that in the period 350 to around 400 (a coin dated 367 was found in the basilica's rubble), just when Rome was abandoning Britain to its fate, the whole basilica area was cleared (except the Old Work fragment) and some surprisingly substantial buildings were erected on the site, in two stages, the later stage even grander than the first. During the second half of the 5th cent. it appears that a Latin-speaking Christian community occupied the site. Of some 30 timber buildings of the final stage, the largest, built on a platform of rubble on the basilica floor, covered almost the whole area of its nave and boasted a classical-style portico, wings and possibly two or more stories. This was Roman-inspired work translated into timber. So was another building, which appeared to be a timber version of a classical temple with a colonnade in wood. One of the Roman streets crossing from E. to W. was turned into an apparently covered market area, and substantial warehouses and workshops were built E. of the basilica.

If the dates are right, we are now approaching the "King Arthur" period when local rulers were struggling to control the emerging kingdoms of sub-Roman Britain. Perhaps a powerful ruler of this kind now occupied Wroxeter and was responsible for the surprisingly high degree of wealth and labor put into the rebuilding of the basilica area. Others suggest that it may have been at this time an important religious center; still others tend to date the whole back in late Roman times. Nevertheless, the inhabitants, though Romanized, were hardly Roman provincials, for on evidence of human skull fragments found in the rubble from this period they scalped their enemies, cut off their heads and preserved the skulls as trophies—the old Celtic custom of head-worship. Moreover, over 35 crude plaster eyes—and one pair of eyes in gold—were also found in the basilica rubble, suggesting an eye-healing cult at Wroxeter, or perhaps they were talismans to ward off the evil eye. The timber-building complex was deliberately dismantled and abandoned, probably shortly after 500 AD, and possibly in order to move to more easily defended Shrewsbury. Thus Viroconium came to its end. Finds from the site are on display in the Rowley's House museum, a restored 16th-cent. house in Shrewsbury.

YARNBURY CASTLE
(Wiltshire)

Prominent Iron Age fort, about 5.5 mi. (9 km.) W. of *Stonehenge*, on the N. side of the road that leads eastward toward Amesbury. The strong circular fort, on level ground, covered nearly 30 acres and shows two ramparts and ditches as well as traces of a third, outer rampart. There was an elaborate inturned entrance with outworks on the E. side. The fort was built by the invading Belgae about 50 BC around an earlier, smaller Iron Age fort dated by excavation to the 7th to 5th cents. BC. Traces of this earlier fort can still be seen. There was a Roman-period occupation too, for both Belgic and Roman coins have been found in the fort. The outlines of much later sheep enclosures from a large annual sheep fair held here up to 1916 are visible in the interior.

YEAVERING
(Northumberland)

Remarkable site with an Iron Age hill fort, high up on Yeavering Bell, and a Northumbrian palace at its foot; near Old Yeavering in the northern Cheviot hills, 4 mi. (6.5 km.) W. of Wooler. The fort, with a single stone-built rampart and three entrances, encloses the two summits of Yeavering Bell and the saddle between them. There are small crescent-shaped annexes at either end and at the center there are hollows marking the sites of about 130 round huts. The eastern summit, excavated in the 19th cent., proved to have been encircled by a rather earlier wooden palisade. Later excavations found Roman coins and pottery and two rectangular house foundations built on top of earlier round huts, indicating occupation into the Roman period.

   The Anglo-Saxon palace at the foot of Yeavering Bell, first detected from the air and skillfully excavated from 1953 to 1957, dominated the settlement of Ad Gefrin, founded in the 6th cent. AD. It was occupied for about three quarters of a century. Its 20 wooden buildings were often burned and carefully rebuilt, until the whole was destroyed on the collapse of the Northumbrian kingdom about 685 AD. The central building, the great palace, was a timber-built longhouse of Scandinavian and European type, first erected in the early years of the 7th cent., and was closely reminiscent of the hall of Heorot described in *Beowulf* (see also *Sutton Hoo*). Around it were a number of smaller timber halls regularly spaced, a large semicircular open-air grandstand for public meetings, enclosed by timber posts, and a very large timber fort.

   One of the buildings in the village has been identified as a pagan temple, later converted to a Christian church. It is known from Bede's *History* that the missionary Paulinus, after baptizing King Edwin of Northumbria in the wooden chapel at *York* in 627, traveled N. through Northumbria preaching, converting, baptizing in many places including Yeavering, where he stayed for 36 days. He may well have preached in the great timber grandstand. See also *Cheddar* where a similar Anglo-Saxon palace has been discovered.

YELLOWMEAD DOWN
(Devon)

See *Dartmoor*.

Y PIGWIN ROMAN CAMPS
(Powys)

See *Brecon*.

YORK
(North Yorkshire)

Ancient city, famous for its noble York Minster, largest of England's medieval cathedrals, seat of the Archbishop of York, Primate of England, and of a bishopric, early in Saxon times and even in late Roman times when the Bishop of Roman York attended the Council of Arles in 314 AD. Historically, York's two great periods were under the Roman empire, when as Eboracum it was a major military center and capital of the North, and under the Viking settlers in the 9th and 10th cents. AD when it was capital of the kingdom of Jorvik and one of the largest and most active trading centers in northern Europe. In between, as the Anglo-Saxon Eoforwic and capital of the kingdom of Northumbria, though a small town it was briefly one of the most dazzling centers of learning and the arts in Europe.

During the Roman conquest of Britain a garrison was first established here in 71 AD on the site of an early British settlement called Caer Ebrauc. Then as Eboracum, one of the three permanent legionary fortresses in Roman Britain (with *Caerleon* and *Chester*), it boasted a rapidly growing *vicus* or civil settlement. Under the Emperor Severus, who died here in 211 AD, this settlement on the western bank of the Ouse River, across from the fortress, was created a colony, one of only four in Britain, and was laid out anew as the capital of Britannia Inferior. The 50-acre fort, garrisoned by the 9th Legion until its mysterious disgrace in 120 AD, then became the seat of the 6th Legion until the withdrawal of the Roman armies in 410 AD. Its ramparts, at first of clay turf and timber, were rebuilt in stone, with towers, in 107–108, refurbished under Severus, and in the 4th cent. given interval towers and two massive angle towers facing the Ouse. The Emperor Constantius Chlorus died here in 306 AD and his son, Constantine the Great, was proclaimed emperor here in his stead. In late Roman times York became in effect the military capital of Britain as *London* was the administrative capital.

Not much is left of Roman Eboracum, and most of that is within the rectangular bounds of the former fortress. The most visible site is the great multiangular tower in the gardens of the Yorkshire Museum (which contains a rich collection of Roman materials). This was one of the 4th-cent. projecting bastions at the western angle of the fortress walls, and the Roman work, topped by medieval, still stands 19 ft. high with an adjoining stretch of the Roman wall 35 ft. long. Near the eastern angle of the walls, behind the Merchant Taylors' Hall, Aldwark, E. of the Minster, is one of the fortress towers, the Roman work still 9 ft. high with a curving stretch of the wall in front of it. The wall, with medieval work at the top, continues W. almost to Monk Bar. Hypocausts in one room of the fort's 4th-cent. baths can be seen through a glass panel if you go for a pint into the saloon bar of the Roman Bath Inn, a pub in St. Sampson's Square. And under Swingate 150 ft. of a large vaulted stone drain was discovered in 1972. Entry only by permission from the museum.

Most impressive of the remains, however, are those of the fort's headquarters building or *principia*, discovered and excavated in the Minster's undercroft during maintenance work on the cathedral—now beautifully displayed and labeled, along with a fine stretch of painted plaster wall from one of its rooms. Set at a different angle from the Minster, the *principia* was a huge colonnaded building, obviously designed to impress the colonials with the might of Rome. It was comparable in length, though not of course in height, with the Minster itself.

Recent, continuing rescue work by the York Archaeological Trust has revealed other bits of Roman York. For example, in Rougier Street across the river a dig in 1983–84 deep under a car park revealed the waterlogged timber buildings, remarkably well preserved, of the 2nd cent. *vicus*, and above these remains the substantial stone buildings of the later colony, one a very large building. Back on the fortress side of the river again, at Aldwark, a trench dug through the line of the Roman fortress wall enabled its three stages to be studied.

Little is known of the derelict city after the Romans left it until it emerged as the Anglian Eoforwic in later centuries. However, Saxon graves found in the late Roman cemeteries suggested that these earliest Saxon immigrants were probably brought in as mercenary federates of the Romans. Eoforwic became the capital of the Saxon kingdom of Deria, which in the 650s AD was united with Bernicia to the N. to form Northumbria, with its capital at York. The kingdom of Northumbria stretched for much of its history from the Humber in the S. to the Forth in Scotland. Northumbria's golden age did not dawn until Christian missionaries penetrated the area, thus combining European learning with the vigorous Anglian and Celtic arts of the region. Architecture, manuscript illumination, sculpture, metalwork all flourished while schools were founded and the first historical records compiled, notably Bede's great *History* of 731 AD.

In 627 Paulinus, one of the missionaries, baptized King Edwin in his capital of Eoforwic in a small wooden chapel, especially built on or near the present Minster (no trace of it has been found). Paulinus became the first Bishop of York in the period. The powerful cultural centers of the new Northumbrian renaissance included York itself, where the learned Alcuin became Master of the Schools in 767 before joining Charlemagne at Aachen for a similar job; also the monasteries of *Monkwearmouth* and *Jarrow* (Bede's home), founded in 674 and 684 by Benedict Biscop, a Northumbrian nobleman, and *Lindisfarne* on Holy Island to the N. where the famous Lindisfarne Gospels were produced about 700 AD. Wilfrid, another missionary, founded his churches at *Hexham* and *Ripon* in the 670s. A fine example of Northumbrian carving of the period is the great cross at *Bewcastle* in Cumbria.

In York itself, despite extensive excavations, few survivals from the period have been found. Perhaps the "Anglian Tower," built up against the Roman fortress walls in the museum garden belongs to the period. In 1985 the beginnings of a rescue excavation of a priory unexpectedly turned up Anglian materials and postholes of Eoforwic in the 7th to 9th cents. Best of all was the discovery in a pit at Coppergate in 1982 of a magnificent Northumbrian helmet with brass mounts, beautifully ornamented, a fine-meshed chain mail neckpiece, and two inscriptions giving the name of the owner. A highly sophisticated example of Northumbrian craftmanship, it has been dated between 750 and 775, though it may well have been lost or buried at the time of the Viking attack on York.

In 866 a great Danish-Viking army under Ivar the Boneless swept over an already weakened Northumbria and with much slaughter captured York. Ten years later the army decided to "share out the lands of Northumbrians" and were joined by more Scandinavian colonists to form part of the Danelaw, the Scandinavian eastern half of England after the settlement with Alfred the Great. The Danes ruled York until 919, when a Norwegian Viking dynasty took over until 927. After an English interlude until 939, the Vikings returned, and the last Norwegian king, Erik Bloodaxe, was expelled by the English in 954; but York and its region remained largely Scandinavian in speech and race up to and well beyond the Norman conquest—some 200 years in all. From this late Anglo-Saxon period of York comes the tower of St. Mary Bishophall Junior (11th cent.).

After capturing York the Danes thoroughly overhauled and extended the defenses, with turf ramparts and palisades, pulling down part of the Roman wall, as the excavations at Aldwark showed. Jorvik (the Danish name) grew mightily until by the 10th cent. the city had become one of the largest and richest economic centers in Europe. Covering 200 acres and with a population of 10,000 or more, it was a rabbit warren of workshops and merchants' houses. Tapping the rich worldwide network of Viking trade routes, it imported fine goods from Byzantium, Aden, Samarkand, Ireland, the Rhineland, as well as from Scandinavia itself. Jorvik also manufactured and exported many of its own products such as metalwork, leather goods, wooden and pottery bowls, amber and jet jewelry, bone combs and needles, and textiles. Meantime, in Jorvik and all of Northumbria a vigorous Anglo-Scandinavian art style was developing, evident on many of the local products and especially in the carving of crosses—for the Vikings had soon turned Christian. Sculptured cross fragments of the period may be seen in St. Mary's Heritage Center in York, at Castlegate. See also *Gosforth Cross*.

With modern York undergoing rapid redevelopment in the 1970s, the York Archaeological Trust was organized in 1972 and immediately carried out an excavation deep under Lloyd's Bank, discovering the remains of 10 superimposed timber workshops of cobblers and leatherworkers, with shoes, clothes and other items perfectly preserved in the waterlogged conditions. In 1976 the ambitious Coppergate excavation began on four long narrow properties running down to the Foss River in the Coppergate area ("Street of the Woodworkers"). In five years of meticulous excavation the results were astounding. The excavators penetrated to the Roman level, of which very little was left, and no Anglian remains at all in this part of the city. The chief finds were of the timber houses, fences, workshops, pits and thick layers of debris left behind by more than 50 generations of rather messy Anglo-Scandinavian inhabitants of Jorvik. At the project's height about 50 volunteers were digging, supervised by trained personnel. The finds included over five tons of animal bones, about a million potsherds, and some 15,000 small finds such as pan pipes, jet jewelry (a local specialty), textiles, metalwork, combs and wooden bowls—again preserved in the wet conditions. Also two coins and two coin dies from the royal mint. Environmentalists also collected seeds, pollen, bones, grain and insects for study.

The Coppergate excavation proved to only half of the trust's ambitious program. In 1984 the Jorvik Viking Center opened in the basement of the shopping complex that had been built on the Coppergate site. A daring experiment in the reconstruction of the past, it combined the latest museum techniques with more than a dash of Disneyland to recreate Viking York, specifically the Coppergate and a market, as it once looked, smelled and sounded. The visitor to the center today, after orientation on the Vikings, steps into a small electric "time car" with a concealed speaker and is carried through a "time tunnel" into the Coppergate street exactly as it looked on a day in October 948, meticulously recreated with houses, workshops, people and animals. As a result of intense research even the sounds of that far-off time have been recreated. One hears the seagulls around the river port and voices speaking Old Norse. And there are the smells of that ancient street, sweet and foul. At the end of the street is a wharf on the river's edge with Viking ships' prows looming over it, and here concealed voices tell the visitor all about the far-flung trade of the Vikings. A second time tunnel takes him out of the street into an exact reproduction of the Coppergate dig as it looked in 1979, using the actual timbers and other remains carefully replaced on the site, while the hidden sound track discourses on modern archaeological methods. The visitor, descending from the time car, finally enters the Artifact Hall on foot to view the actual, smaller finds from the dig, carefully conserved. In its first year 980,000 visitors were carried through the Jorvik Center, now one of the finest and most exciting archaeological displays in Europe. The

A glimpse of the underground Jorvik Viking Center, a re-creation of a day in Viking York in October of 948 AD. The meticulously excavated Coppergate street has been simulated here, complete with the sounds and smells of the time. Thousands of tourists are now carried through it in electric "time cars," with a mechanically spoken narrative of the sights as they move along. This is modern archaeology at its "Disneyland" best. (Courtesy of British Tourist Authority, New York.)

Yorkshire Museum also exhibits collections of Viking and early Christian materials, with many additional items from the Coppergate project.

ZENNOR QUOIT
(Cornwall)

Neolithic chambered tomb, 5 mi. (8 km.) SE of St. Ives and just N. of Zennor village. Here is a massive megalithic tomb, once covered by a round cairn that has disappeared. Five uprights form the rectangular burial chamber, with the huge capstone, 18 ft. long, now leaning backwards onto the ground over them, the result of treasure-hunters using dynamite in the 19th cent. The entrance is exceedingly narrow and in front of it more uprights form a kind of antechamber. A later excavation discovered Neolithic pottery, flints and cremation burials in the tomb.

SCOTLAND

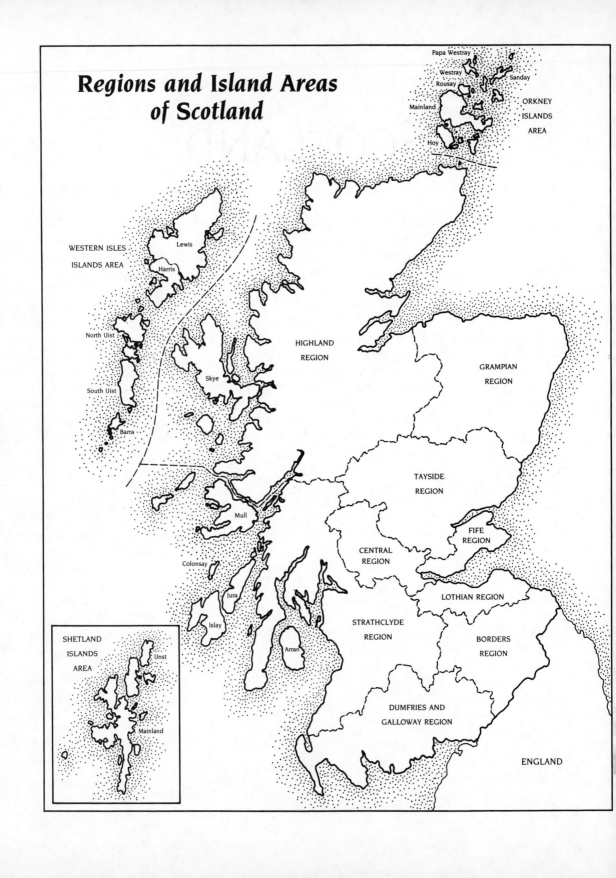

Regions and Island Areas of Scotland

Papa Westray

Westray
Rousay

Sanday

Mainland

ORKNEY
ISLANDS
AREA

Hoy

WESTERN ISLES
ISLANDS AREA

Lewis

Harris

North Uist

Skye

South Uist

Barra

Mull

Colonsay

Jura

Islay

Arran

HIGHLAND
REGION

GRAMPIAN
REGION

TAYSIDE
REGION

FIFE
REGION

CENTRAL
REGION

LOTHIAN REGION

STRATHCLYDE
REGION

BORDERS
REGION

DUMFRIES AND
GALLOWAY REGION

ENGLAND

SHETLAND
ISLANDS
AREA

Unst

Mainland

The Archaeology of Scotland

In general the archaeological sites of Scotland parallel those of England, though of course there are local variations and even whole classes of monuments found nowhere else, such as the tall, handsome broch towers, those marvels of engineering, or the lively, carved symbol stones of the Picts. One might also include the Recumbent Stone Circles of NE Scotland, though rather similar circles are also found in southern Ireland.

Paleolithic man was barred from the area of Scotland by the ice age glaciers, but there are a respectable number of sites that remind us of the presence, rather later than in England, of his successor, the Mesolithic (Middle Stone Age) hunter-gatherer. The sites are found mostly in the W., including the Hebrides—see *Lussa Wood*. The archaeological history of Scotland really begins with the Neolithic period (about 4000 to 2000 BC), and the advent of the first farming communities, complete with domestic animals and pottery.

The Neolithic

Scotland seems to have entered the Neolithic age about as rapidly as England, probably at least in part as a result of a certain amount of immigration by farming people. Again the most visible relics of the Neolithic presence are the megalithic chambered tombs—over 600 are known—found all over the country. Built with enormous labor out of heavy stone uprights (orthostats) and roof slabs, they are divided roughly, as in England, into two main types, the gallery grave and the passage grave. The first has a rectangular elongated chamber, often subdivided and with some kind of a facade in front, the whole covered by a mound of earth, or more usually a cairn of loose stones, with a kerb of heavy stones around it. The passage grave has a long narrow passage of uprights and roof slabs leading into the cairn to the burial chamber inside it.

These monuments were not only tombs but shrines as well, dedicated to the ancestors and symbols of the solidarity of the group that built them. There is plenty of evidence for the elaborate rituals carried out around and in them, including fires and feasting and probably human sacrifice. They were largely

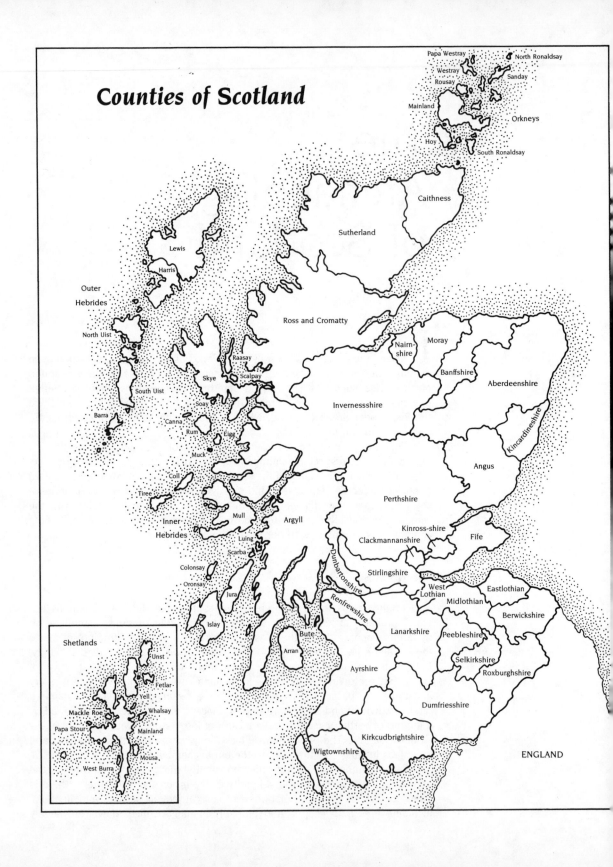

Counties of Scotland

Papa Westray
North Ronaldsay
Westray
Rousay
Sanday
Mainland
Orkneys
Hoy
South Ronaldsay

Caithness

Sutherland

Lewis

Harris

Outer
Hebrides

North Uist

Ross and Cromatty

Nairn-
shire
Moray

Banffshire

Aberdeenshire

Raasay

Skye
Scalpay

South Uist

Soay

Invernessshire

Kincardineshire

Barra

Canna
Rum
Eigg

Muck

Coll

Tiree

Angus

Perthshire

Mull

Inner

Hebrides

Luing

Scarba

Argyll

Kinross-shire

Clackmannanshire
Fife

Colonsay

Oronsay

Jura

Dunbartonshire

Stirlingshire

West
Lothian
Eastlothian

Midlothian

Islay

Renfrewshire

Berwickshire

Lanarkshire

Peebleshire

Bute

Arran

Selkirkshire

Roxburghshire

Ayrshire

Shetlands

Unst

Fetlar

Yell

Whalsay

Mackle Roe

Papa Stour
Mainland

Mousa

West Burra

Dumfriesshire

Kirkcudbrightshire

Wigtownshire

ENGLAND

collective tombs in which the disarticulated bones were interred, often over many hundreds of years, the tombs repeatedly opened for the purpose and finally, as fashion changed, sealed up or abandoned. The sparse grave goods found in the tombs included pottery and flints. An extreme example is the gallery grave of *Isbister* in the Orkneys, in use for about 800 years. A jumble of some 16,000 bones was found in it, representing about 340 people (no complete skeletons were found) and many animals and bird remains, especially the local sea eagle (a totem bird for the group?). Most of the tombs were rebuilt, enlarged, altered over many years. One of the earliest is *Lochhill* near Dumfries, originally (before 4000 BC) an elaborate wooden mortuary structure, later rebuilt in stone under a long cairn, then finally closed—still in the Neolithic period. A good example of a tomb remodeled over a long period is *Achnacreebeag* in Argyll; also the *Mid-Gleniron Cairns* in Wigtownshire.

As in England the tombs fall into groups, both by region and by type. The Clyde Group gallery graves (95 are known) are found along the western seaboard, with a heavy concentration on the island of Arran (see Torrylinn under *Machrie Moor*). They date, with rebuildings, from about 4000 to 2500 BC. These tombs have rectangular burial chambers, often with a number of separate compartments and a horned forecourt in front for ritual purposes. Examples can be found at *Cairnholy*, the *Mid-Gleniron Cairns* and Nether Largie South (under *Kilmartin*). The Clava Group of passage tombs, only 11 of them, are clustered around Inverness, all once covered by substantial cairns and encircled by a ring of standing stones, with the long passage into the cairn always facing SW. The best are the *Clava Cairns* themselves and the outlying *Corrimony*.

Another group of passage graves is called the Orkney-Cromarty-Hebridean, named for the areas where they are found. The tombs show considerable variations, and their dates range from 3000 to 2500 BC. Examples are the *Camster Chambered Tombs* in Caithness, and in the Orkneys a number of large tombs such as *Isbister* (previously mentioned), and on Rousay Island four fine "stalled cairns," so-called because their chambers are divided into a number of stalls or compartments. The huge *Midhowe* cairn here, a veritable mausoleum, had 24 compartments in the long chamber, 12 on each side, while *Taversoe Tuack* is a unique two-storied tomb.

A final group of passage tombs in the Orkneys, called the Maes Howe Group from its finest example, numbers 10 or 11 monuments; all show fewer signs of remodeling and may have been inspired by foreign models. *Maes Howe* itself, one of the finest monuments in Europe, shows close affinities with New Grange in the *Boyne Valley* (IRELAND), and indeed is an architectural and engineering masterpiece. A small local group of heel-shaped passage tombs in the Shetlands should also be mentioned (see, for example, *Vementry*).

Where did the people live who built these magnificent monuments? Fortunately three settlements have been discovered in the Orkneys, all well-preserved under blankets of sand. The earliest, really only a farmstead consisting of two connected structures, is the *Knap of Howar*; somewhat later is the much-excavated and deservedly famous village of *Skara Brae* where not only the houses but also a wealth of finds have been recovered. It was apparently occupied from about 3100 to 2450 BC, when a wild storm drove out the inhabitants, leaving it to the sand. More recently a similar village of eight houses has been excavated at *Rinyo*. The latter two villages seem to have been occupied during the period of the great Maes Howe tombs. In the Shetlands there are many vestiges of house sites of a local type, very different from those of Skara Brae and some at least may date back to the period of the chambered tombs. The best known of these is at the *Ness of Gruting*, while at *Stanydale* a small settlement includes an enigmatic, large, heavily-built oval building that may have been a public meeting hall or even a temple. It seems to be Late Neolithic in date, or possibly Early Bronze Age.

As in England the Late Neolithic saw the beginnings of a new fashion for circular monuments—the henges and stone circles, unique to the British Isles—probably all of them public sanctuaries of some sort. They continued to be built well into the Bronze Age. Henges, which first appeared in the days of the chambered tombs, were circular enclosures with a bank, a ditch inside the bank and one or two entrances; sometimes stone circles were built inside them. The interior space—a prehistoric dance floor—was obviously used for rituals, and sometimes burials too, and occasionally there were stone settings at the center; but in Scotland the larger henges, in contrast to the huge English henges, apparently did not contain timber structures. Two examples of henge sites can be seen at Stenness and the nearby Ring of Brodgar in the Orkneys (see *Stenness Standing Stones*). Both had stone circles; the stones of Brodgar were set up with impressive mathematical accuracy, suggesting the possibility of an astronomical use. Indeed most of the henges and especially the stone rings may have been used for primitive seasonal sightings of the sun or moon, but not too much should be made of this. Another impressive henge monument was at *Balfarg* in Fife (unfortunately, there is little to see there now). It began with the usual bank and ditch and a circle of heavy posts, which seem to have been set up to the accompaniment of an exceedingly bizarre ritual. Later the site was rebuilt with two stone circles.

Though many henges are accompanied by stone circles, most of Scotland's stone circles are not henges. The finest of these numerous stone circles is undoubtedly *Callinish* in the Hebrides, a magnificent circular setting of stones with four processional avenues of stone leading into it. A very different kind of circle can be found at *Cullerlie* in Aberdeenshire, and another, larger one at *Torhouskie* near Wigtown. Many of these circles, particularly those of the Early Bronze Age, are found in groups along with standing stones and stone alignments, Bronze Age cairns, cist burials and even an occasional Neolithic tomb to make up large sacred areas. These areas were cult centers, akin to *Avebury* and *Stonehenge* in England, which had been frequented by people for miles around for many centuries. Such a site can be seen at *Machrie Moor*, a confusing array of monuments on the island of Arran. Another such center is Stennis itself, and around the village of *Kilmartin* in Argyll a variety of monuments date from the Neolithic right through to the Early Christian. Examples of Bronze Age standing stones, which also occur in the sacred areas, include the alignment at *Ballachroy* in Argyll and the huge *Trushel Stone* on Lewis in the Hebrides.

The monumental Recumbent Stone Circles, peculiar to NE Scotland, are cult centers in themselves. Carefully planned, boldly sited with wide views, the stones of these circles—there are some 22 of them—are graduated in height toward the huge flat-topped recumbent stone, always lying in the SW, with its top exactly leveled. They may have developed out of the earlier *Clava Cairns* farther to the W. and generally date from about 2500 to 1700 BC, into the Bronze Age. A ring cairn in the interior of these monuments surrounds an open space with evidence of much ritual burning, and offerings of human bone and broken pottery are found in abundance. That these circles are aligned for astronomical sitings to aid in the ritual cannot be doubted. A fine example of such a circle can be found at *Loanhead of Daviot*. Many of the stones are incised with cup and ring marks, possibly symbols of the sun and moon. These marks are widely found in northern England and in Scotland, while at a few sites geometrical designs are found, simple versions of the rich repertoire of passage grave art in Ireland.

For the archaeologist the presence of tall distinctive pots called beakers in the Late Neolithic burials suggests either the infiltration of a new people with new ways, skilled warriors and archers who ushered in the Bronze Age, or a persuasive cultural fashion adopted from its continental origins (see prefaces to ENGLAND and IRELAND). Whether an invasion by actual Beaker Folk, or a new fashion, the presence of these pots denotes a marked change in society. It was in this period, around 2000 BC, that metals first appeared, and possibly the horse, leading toward a new kind of aristocratic social organization with chieftains, mounted warriors, feasting and warfare, foreshadowing the later Celtic society. About the same time the graves produce another type of pottery, the food vessel, again probably a new cultural fashion.

The Bronze Age

Traditionally the Bronze Age is said to run from about 2000 to 700 BC, indeed a purely artificial division of time as suggested by the overlap between the Neolithic and the Bronze Age megalithic monuments described above. The Bronze Age proper, starting about 1700 BC, is characterized by the abandonment of the old funerary rites and monuments and the development of a more stratified metal-using society with more emphasis on this world's goods and less on burial rituals and monuments. A new form of burial in cists (rectangular stone boxes) under huge round cairns becomes common (see *Cairnpapple* Hill and *Kilmartin*), and inhumation burial gradually gives way to cremation. Eventually, flat cemeteries of cremation burials in distinctive urns developed, closely akin to the Urnfields of Europe. One such cemetery of over 35 people was excavated next to the stone circle at *Loanhead of Daviot*; for the Bronze Age people still revered the old sites.

A marked change in society is indeed indicated by a more belligerent period's increasing use of metal, especially for weapons, ranging from the rare copper flat axes of the Beakers to more technically advanced bronze axes, daggers, armlets and other objects (mostly found in burials or hoards). Heavy necklaces of jet are a Scottish feature of the period, with others of bronze beads, and gold was extensively fashioned into striking ornaments and jewelry. Some Scottish metalwork shows affinities with continental models and especially with Irish work, from where many were imported. As time went on designs and techniques became more sophisticated. Spearheads, dirks and rapiers appear and finally swords, as well as sickles, knives, chisels, razors and horse gear of bronze. From the Late Bronze Age shields and cauldrons of sheet bronze and many more swords have been identified, some of the objects cast into lakes as votive offerings. Iron began to be worked in a primitive fashion, heralding the next period.

Relics of the houses and field systems of Bronze Age man in Scotland are amazingly sparse. There are no Skara Braes. Such uncertainly-dated sites as the *Stanydale* settlement on the Shetlands, with its "temple," or even the *Ness of Gruting* there, could be Early Bronze Age rather than Neolithic. Generally, Bronze Age houses were round and substantially built of stone, with internal posts holding up, presumably, a thatched roof. Such houses and their field systems have been investigated at Tormore and Kirkpatrick on the island of Arran (see *Machrie Moor*) and form the lowest strata of the great multi-period site at Jarlshof in the Shetlands. One of the Jarlshof structures had been a cow stall; another was later used by a Bronze Age smith who left his molds behind. See also *Tofts Ness*.

The Late Bronze Age was a period of social unrest and probably marked the coming of the earliest Celts—perhaps an infiltration rather than an invasion—bringing with them a new language, ancestor of all the Celtic tongues. The abundance of new weapons in this late period, the farmsteads protected by palisades and the earliest hill forts (more typical of the Iron Age) with ramparts strengthened by horizontal timbers (see *Finavon*) mark the uncertain nature of the times.

The Iron Age

A turbulent society is indicated by many aspects of the Iron Age, a period lasting traditionally from 700 or 600 BC into the First Millennium AD. A Celtic warrior society with a ruling aristocracy seems to have been very similar to that of Ireland and England at the time. The elite were given to feasting and fighting, represented by the bronze trumpets, the drinking horns and cauldrons and the slashing swords found in the hoards. All hands farmed and there was much stockraising and cattle raiding (cattle was a measure of wealth), and squabbles between groups based on different hill forts were usual. The Celts have been described as "war mad"; apparently they went proudly naked into battle and, in eastern Scotland at least, rode in horse-drawn chariots (long outmoded in Europe). The hoards too suggest a vigorous amount of foreign trade. Bards and Druids presided at the courts of kings and chieftains, and craftsmen, as elsewhere in the Celtic lands, decorated the armlets, bracelets, mirror backs, horse gear and scabbards with lovely swirling designs in the European Late Iron Age La Tène style, or produced magnificent torcs of gold and silver rings.

As usual hill forts are the dominant feature of the Iron Age landscape of Scotland. Some 1,500 are known, most of them in the southern and eastern parts of Scotland. They are for the most part much smaller than those of England, though two stand out for size: *Traprain Law* and *Eildon Hill North*; and the larger of the two *Caterthuns* is no mean fort. On Eildon Hill North one can count some 300 house sites, implying a dense occupation like the larger English hill forts, and the forming of large tribal centers. Again as in England these hill forts evolved over the centuries. The earlier forts with their timber-laced ramparts were often attacked and their strengthening timbers burned, leaving what Scottish archaeologists call "vitrified forts" (see *Castle Law* and *Finavon*). Many forts started as palisaded enclosures (doubled in the larger examples) then later were girded with stone ramparts and finally, as the Romans approached from the S., became multivallate forts with several circuits of ramparts and elaborately protected entrances. *Hownam Rings* shows just such a long history of elaboration, as does *Woden Law*, both in Roxburghshire. There were also promontory forts—a neck of land cut off by ramparts. The *Barsalloch Point* fort in Wigtownshire or the *Ness of Burgi* in the Shetlands are examples.

Individual farmsteads and small settlements were usually also protected by palisades, and of course there were many undefended sites within a bank and ditch. The houses were generally round and built of wood, though in the SE, perhaps owing to Roman influence, they began to be built of stone. The smaller stone-built forts called "duns," which existed along with the hill forts, were really for the most part fortified homesteads (they would be called "cashels" in Ireland) protected by a circular drystone wall. Most are found in Argyll; an example is *Leccamore* in the Hebrides. Some of these duns, including Leccamore, show galleries, stairs and guard chambers inside their thick walls. Along with a related type called semi-brochs, this seems to link them with the famous brochs of Scotland and suggests, according to one theory, that the broch design originated in such galleried duns in the Hebrides, and specifically on the island of *Skye*, spreading out from there.

Though such duns may have been ancestral to brochs, the two types of fort existed together, for the dun was a very successful and long-lived type of homestead. The brochs—tall drystone towers with galleried walls—were built, on the other hand, only from about 100 BC to 100 AD. These superbly engineered towers, up to some 50 ft. high, were masterpieces of architectural design and were unique to Scotland. Found in western Scotland and the Hebrides, their greatest concentration, however, was in northern Scotland and the Northern Isles. For details on their construction, see the *Broch of Mousa* in the Shetlands, the finest and best-preserved of them all. So uniform is the broch design that it seems likely they were built on order by roving specialists.

There were two main types of broch, those with internal galleries in the walls, entered at ground level—"ground galleried" brochs, found mostly in the Hebrides—and "solid-based" brochs with the galleries higher up within the walls. These latter are most common in the northern areas where many of the brochs also have heavy outlying defenses (see *Broch of Burland*; *Broch of Gurness*; and *Midhowe*). Along with some northern brochs, an apparently earlier form of gateway defense called a blockhouse is found, as at *Clickhimin* and the *Ness of Burgi*, both in the Shetlands. Some later brochs, including *Leckie* and *Torwoodlee* in the S., were built by wealthy families as defenses against the Romans—and were eventually destroyed by them.

Another form of defended stone house, later than the brochs, was the wheelhouse, a few of them built into the older brochs as at *Clickhimin* and *Jarlshof*. These were round houses with heavy drystone walls and stone piers radiating out from the central hearth to form partitions as well as roof supports. In the aisled version there was a space between the piers and the outer walls. Another form of common defended homestead, prevalent throughout the Iron Age and probably beyond, is the "crannog"—also common in Ireland. This was a timber house built on an artificial platform in the midst of a lake, with rooms partitioned off and a central hearth—and usually a causeway to the mainland. A well-excavated example is described under *Milton Loch*.

Finally, a numerous group of underground structures called "souterrains" usually accompanied small settlements during the early cents. AD. They are also found in Ireland and in Cornwall, where they are called fogous. These stone-built undergrounds, usually with a number of passages and chambers, were apparently used for storage, for stabling cattle and perhaps as refuges during an attack. For the Orkneys souterrains see under *Rennibister*; also *Ardestie*, *Culsh* and *Pitcur* for mainland examples.

Scotland and the Romans

The story of the Romans in Scotland is purely a military one, for Scotland was never Romanized. There are no villas, no planned towns (except for an occasional *vicus* found around forts), no temples (except military), though certainly Roman influences and trade helped to coalesce the larger tribes, leading to the later Pictish kingdom.

The story starts with Agricola's brief invasion of Scotland, fortunately documented by his son-in-law Tacitus in his biography. With 20,000 legionnaires and an accompanying fleet, Agricola marched N. in 80 AD, scattering in his wake forts, fortlets and marching camps, all earth-built, both in northern England and Scotland. He bypassed the friendly Votadini in their great hill fort of *Traprain Law* but reduced the forts of the Selgovae at *Woden Law* and *Eildon Hill North*. He pacified southern Scotland with little trouble, gazing longingly over at Ireland from the western shores, then started to build his large legionary camp at *Inchtuthil* as a base for further advances. It has been identified and excavated, though there is little to see there now. Marching northward, he fought a great battle at Mons Graupius (the site is not securely identified) against a coalition of 30,000 troops from northern tribes, and routed the natives—10,000 killed, unmanned chariots racing out of control over the stricken field. He then sent his fleet around the top of Scotland as far as the Orkneys. In effect all Scotland lay at his feet when he was abruptly recalled in 85–86. In the subsequent withdrawal Inchtuthil was dismantled, lock, stock and barrel—or rather timber, stones and nails and much else besides—and the Romans eventually fell back to the Tyne-Solway line, where in the 120s *Hadrian's Wall* was built (ENGLAND).

Once again, in 138 AD under Antoninus Pius, the Romans advanced into and subdued the Scottish Lowlands, eventually building, from 142 AD, the complex turf barrier, the *Antonine Wall*, from the Firth of Forth to the Clyde to mark the new frontier—not as stupendous a construction as Hadrian's Wall farther S. but still impressive in its survivals today, with some 16 forts, and fortlets and signal stations along its line. An outlying forward defense for the Wall can still be seen in the remarkable multivallate *Ardoch* fort. Southwards of the Wall, at *Newstead*, another fort was built close to its predecessor, the hill fort of *Eildon Hill North*, which has yielded a remarkable collection of Roman military gear—though there is nothing to see now at the site. Two other 1st- and 2nd-cents. sites near the English border are of interest. At both sites temporary camps and siege lines had been built close to abandoned Iron Age hill forts and the troops shot bolts and heavy artillery into the derelict camps by way of training (see *Birrens* and *Woden Law*).

After the death of Antoninus Pius in 161 AD the Antonine Wall was finally abandoned, after only about a decade or more in use, and the line withdrawn again to Hadrian's Wall—though patrols ranged far N. of it and some of the northern forts were manned for some time thereafter. In 208 the Emperor Septimius Severus and his sons, after the barbarians had grown rebellious, once again marched into Scotland on a campaign of pacification, establishing more camps and marching camps of a larger size than the earlier ones and rebuilding, for instance, Cramond fort on the *Antonine Wall*. But by 211 the troops had again been withdrawn into England. Thereafter Scotland was mostly neglected, except on a number of occasions when Hadrian's Wall was overrun by barbarians in the 3rd and 4th cents., usually because some would-be emperor denuded the Wall to provide troops for his struggle. As order was restored in each case there were campaigns into Scotland by, for instance, Constantius, father of Constantine the Great, in the early 4th cent., or by Magnus Maximus in 382 AD. But by 410 AD all of Roman Britain had been abandoned as the empire itself was overrun.

A relic of the last days of Roman Britain was found at *Traprain Law*, capital of the Votadini (later Gododdin), a remarkable hoard of over 100 highly decorated pieces of late Roman silver plate, cut up or folded for use as bullion, some with Christian motifs. It had been secreted in a pit during the troubled times of the 5th cent.

Dark Age Scotland

After the debacle of the Roman period the Romanized tribes of Lowland Scotland were left alone in citadels such as *Traprain Law* to build a new life. Another such citadel is the *Mote of Mark* in Kirkcudbrightshire, probably that of a chieftain of the early kingdom of Rheged, where excavators have found a strong 6th-cent. presence. Capital of another kingdom, Strathclyde, was Dumbarton Rock (though no remains of the period have survived). Strathclyde was the only one of the early kingdoms to survive into the early Middle Ages. Lowland Scotland, however, was soon to achieve that mix of Celtic-British, Irish and Anglian that still to a certain extent characterizes it today, while in the northern parts a coalescence of early tribes, both Celtic and non-Celtic, was to create the powerful Pictish kingdom. Around 500 AD those roving pirates from Ireland called Scotti began to settle along the shores of Argyll and its islands, setting up their kingdom of Dalriada whose capital was probably at the dramatic hill fort site of *Dunadd*. The Irish Scotti not only gave their name to modern Scotland but also introduced the Scottish Gaelic, as well as the strange Ogham script (see IRELAND).

Not much later, as the Anglo-Saxons swept over England in the wake of the Roman withdrawal, an Anglian branch in northern England, soon to become Northumbrians, began raiding into Lowland Scotland, taking over the kingdoms of the Gododdin and Rheged; and in the second quarter of the 7th cent. they began settling down amidst the Celtic Britains. A recent excavation at Doon Hill, Dunbar, East Lothian, has uncovered the remains of a 6th-cent. British chieftain's hall and overlying it an Anglian hall of the 7th cent., closely resembling those at *Yeavering* in Northumberland (ENGLAND). Other relics of the Anglian invasion are scarce, except for three later crosses showing in their rich blend of Northumbrian and early Celtic Christian motifs what had taken place. Of the three—the *Abercorn*, *Kildalton* and *Ruthwell* crosses—the latter, with its runic inscription, is a superb example of Northumbrian art of the mid-8th cent. (in itself a mix of Celtic and Anglian). Another blending of Anglian, this time with Pictish art, is shown on the deeply-carved tomb shrine at *St. Andrews*.

The British kingdoms in Scotland, it seems, were converted to Christianity during the 5th cent., and several interesting Christian monuments date from that period, especially the memorial stone of *Catstane* near Edinburgh, of the late 5th or early 6th cent. It bears a Latin inscription, and excavations around it uncovered an inhumation cemetery of long cists, a Christian practice. Two of the *Kirkmadrine Crosses* in Wigtownshire also date to the 5th cent. One of the early Romanized British missionaries, St. Ninian, according to Bede, built a church at *Whithorn Priory*, also in Wigtownshire, and excavations at the priory did indeed uncover graves probably dating from Ninian's 5th-cent. period as well as the foundations of a crude early chapel—most likely 7th cent., but presumably built over Ninian's first church. And on the lonely *Ardwall* island in Kirkcudbrightshire more remains of a Christian community of this and later centuries have been unearthed.

A new chapter opened when the famous and forceful Irish missionary St. Columba and his little band left Ireland in 563 AD and with the encouragement and protection of the king of Dalriada set up the famous monastery at Iona on a remote western island in the Hebrides. A few traces of the early Celtic monastery can be seen there, and two of its fine crosses of about 800 AD closely resemble in their decoration the Irish *Book of Kells*, which may have been illuminated at Iona before being brought to Ireland. Monks from Iona also founded *Lindisfarne* in England in the 7th cent. Two more examples of Early Christian monasteries may be seen on the island of *Eileach na Naoihm* and at the *Brough of Deerness* in the Orkneys. After the Synod of Whitby in England in 664 AD the Celtic churches gradually came into conformity with Roman practices, and in the early 8th cent. King Nechtan of the Picts imported Northumbrian masons to build a Roman-style church at *Restenneth Priory*: part of its fabric is still visible. Finally in 843 the thrones of Dalriada and the Picts were united under Kenneth MacAlpin, king of Dalriada, who moved his capital to Scone and inaugurated the monarchy of a united Scotland. A final importation from Ireland are the two 10th-cent., Irish-style round towers at *Brechin* in Angus and *Abernethy* in Perthshire.

The mysterious Picts are first heard of from Roman historians—as one of the barbarian groups attacking late Roman Britain. Called "Picti," the Painted Ones, possibly for early body-painting, they formed a kingdom that in the 7th and 8th cents., with their substantial navy, was the most powerful in the northern lands. Pictland included all the territory N. of the Forth-Clyde rivers except for Dalriada in the W., which was at times under Pict control. The Picts were in the Northern Isles as well, and in southern Scotland, though for a time they were forced out by the Anglians. The Picts appear to have spoken two languages, one a form of Celtic, the other an ancient non-Indo-European tongue. Their earliest recorded king was Bridei, who may have been converted to Christianity by St. Columba. The saint certainly visited Bridei's court in the 6th cent., exorcising the Loch Ness Monster en route (it was the beast's first recorded appearance). Bridei's citadel was possible at the hill fort of *Craig Phadrig*, though more likely it was the great Pictish fortress of *Burghead* in Morayshire.

The Picts are chiefly known for their famous symbol stones. About 250 survive, found all over Scotland. They were memorial stones, boundary stones, possibly grave stones (no one really knows), vigorously carved with lively birds and animals and scenes of hunting and warfare, as well as an array of strange symbols whose meaning was known only to the Picts. The stones are divided by scholars into: Class I, early; Class II, mostly Christian, for the Picts were converted in the 6th and 7th cents.; and Class III, entirely Christian with none of the symbols. See *Borthwick Mains* (Class I), the *Aberlemno Stones* (Classes I and II), the *Dun Fallandy Stone*, *Fowlis Wester* and *Maiden Stone* (all Class II), and the very late and exceptional *Sueno's Stone* of Class III. Good collections of stones are also found in Edinburgh's National Museum and in the small museums at *Meigle* and *St. Vigean's*.

The Picts were also fine metal-workers, and from the evidence of the hoard of 28 silver pieces found under the floor of an ancient church at St. *Ninian's Isle* in 1958, as well as from other chance finds, they probably wore a great deal of jewelry about their persons, including heavy silver chains of office. All the St. Ninian's pieces—ecclesiastical, horse gear, sword fittings, bowls—were elaborately ornamented in styles derived from many foreign sources. A few typical Pictish house sites have also been excavated, at U*dal* in the Hebrides, *Yarrows* in Caithness, and notably at Buckquoy in the Orkneys (see *Brough of Birsay*) where three successive Pictish houses were found beneath a 9th-cent. Norse Viking farmstead. Pictish burials have been found mostly in the N. where the classic example, in Caithness, is at A*ckergill* with its eight large, kerbed cairns. The end of the Pictish kingdom, already weakened by fighting off increasingly dangerous Viking raids on the N. and W., came when Kenneth MacAlpin ascended the Pictish-Scottish throne in 843. For reasons still obscure the older Pict language, the symbol stones and other aspects of Pictish life soon disappeared under the new Scottish control.

By 800 AD the Viking raids had become severe and by the early 9th cent. extensive Viking settlement had begun, earliest and most extensive in the Northern Isles, as evidence by the farmhouse at Buckquoy. The Vikings sacked Iona many times, finally forcing the monks to flee back to Ireland. They took over the Hebrides, the *Isle of Man* (ENGLAND), and penetrated deeply into Scottish Galloway. In the N. they settled in Caithness and Ross, and turned the Northern Isles into a Scandinavian area (its place names are now mostly Norse-derived), with a powerful Norse earldom in the Orkneys. However, the Scottish kingdom (often called Alba), though harassed, held firm, and the Scots began to move S. into the Lowlands, driving the English (Anglians) for instance out of Edinburgh in the mid-10th cent. In 1018 they absorbed the old kingdom of Strathclyde. The shape of modern Scotland had emerged.

Many examples of the typical Viking longhouse have been excavated, notably at *Jarlshof*. Others have been found at U*dal* in the Hebrides, at the *Brough of Birsay* in the Orkneys, and a Viking farmstead with attendant graveyard has been excavated in *Westness*, also in the Orkneys. In 1986 continuing excavations at *Whithorn Priory* uncovered a 12th-cent. Norse settlement under a cemetery on the site. And so we enter the Middle Ages.

ABERCORN CROSS
(West Lothian/Lothian)

Inside Abercorn church, just W. of South Queensferry, is a fine Anglian (Northumbrian) sculptured cross-shaft of the 9th-cent. AD, set into a modern base. It is decorated in relief on all four sides. Abercorn is a very ancient monastic site and traces of the wall that surrounded the monastery (stone-faced, as excavations in 1967 suggested) can still be seen. There are also fragments of other crosses and two hogback gravestones in the church. See also *Kildalton Cross, Ruthwell Cross.*

ABERLEMNO PICTISH
STONES
(Angus/Tayside)

There are three stones here, about 5 mi. (8 km.) NE of Forfar, carved from the local red sandstone of Angus. These are fine examples of some 250 carved Pictish stones surviving in Scotland. A handsome example of a so-called Class II (middle period) cross slab stands in the churchyard. On one side is a cross in relief, profusely decorated with spirals and interlace, on the other an amusing battle scene. Two others are beside a side road shortly to the NE, a simple Class I (earlier), carved with Pictish symbols, and another Class II stone showing a cross and angels, with a hunting scene on the back.

A Pictish symbol stone in the churchyard at Aberlemno. Carved from the local red sandstone of Angus, it is an early and impressive example of a Class II stone (in the scholars' parlance). Vigorous in execution and as mysterious as the Picts themselves, who dominated much of Scotland from the 7th to 9th cents. AD, the stones are an enigma. Neither their purpose (boundary markers, memorial stones, gravestones?) or the meaning of the complex symbols on them is known, or is ever likely to be known. A military scene, a fine composition, is shown here with various symbols at the top. The back of the stone, profusely decorated with interlace and spirals, bears a cross. (Courtesy of Historic Buildings and Monuments, Scottish Development Dept.)

ABERNETHY
(Perthshire/Tayside)

One of the two round towers, of Irish derivation, in Scotland (see also *Brechin*). It stands 74 ft. high in the churchyard, with a Pictish Class I stone beside it. There is the usual raised doorway, and originally there were six wooden floors in the interior. It is probably 10th cent.

ACHAVANICH STANDING STONES
(Caithness/Highland)

See *Loch Stemster Standing Stones*.

ACHNABRECK
(Argyll/Strathclyde)

See *Kilmartin*.

ACHNACREEBEAG
(Argyll/Strathclyde)

Neolithic chambered tomb in the Lorn district SE of Oban, of interest because several structural phases over a long period were revealed in recent excavations. First there was a small round cairn with burial chamber of heavy boulders. The cairn was then enlarged to accommodate a passage tomb on one side. Finally the tomb was formally closed during the Beaker period by piling boulders into passage and chamber.

ACKERGILL
(Caithness/Highland)

A classic group of Pictish burial mounds, a few mi. NW of Wick. There are seven rectangular cairns, and a circular eighth cairn, made of piled-up stones inside kerbs of upright slabs. In the cairns were burials, sometimes more than one in each, in long cists dug into the sand. They are probably 9th cent. AD.

AIKEY BRAE
(Aberdeenshire/
Grampian)

See *Berrybrae*.

ANTONINE WALL

Substantial remains of Rome's northernmost imperial frontier, some 80 mi. (130 km.) N. of *Hadrian's Wall* (ENGLAND), which it briefly superseded in the 2nd cent. AD. The wall ran 37 mi. (60 km.) across the waist of Scotland, from Bridgeness near Bo'ness on the Forth, well W. of Edinburgh, to Old Kilpatrick on the Clyde, just W. of Glasgow. Unlike Hadrian's Wall it was built of turf on a stone foundation 14 ft. wide and stood about 9 ft. high, tapering up to a 6-ft.-wide walkway (and probably a wooden parapet) along the top. In front of it ran a massive ditch, 40 ft. wide and up to 15 ft. deep, and behind it the Military Way, a service road, paralleled it. There were possibly 18 or 19 forts along the wall (16 are known), spaced about 2 mi. (3.25 km.) apart and mostly defended by turf ramparts, a number of fortlets, and six signalling platforms. To the N. of the eastern stretch, considered more dangerous, were a number of outlying forts, including *Ardoch*.

Tribal unrest, or perhaps imperial vainglory, prompted Antoninus Pius, Hadrian's successor, to order the reoccupation of southern Scotland and the building of the wall. The campaign and the beginnings of the wall were carried out by the governor, Q. Lollius Urbicus, probably in 142 AD. Urbicus, incidentally, came from Algeria where his mausoleum may still be seen in the mountain town of Tiddis. Completed about 145, the wall was only garrisoned (with one interruption) for less than 20 years. Built by detachments from three legions, the completion of each stretch was commemorated by the setting up of a "distance slab." The best of these may now be seen in the Hunterian Museum of

Glasgow University. After the emperor's death (161 AD) the whole campaign—and the wall—was acknowledged a failure, and the frontier was withdrawn to Hadrian's Wall, about 163 AD.

Reviewing the more rewarding sites along the wall, one might start (moving from E. to W.) with the fort at Cramond, well to the E. of the wall and just W. of Edinburgh, which undoubtedly served as a supply port on the Forth for the wall itself. The one standing wall in this pretty village and the fort's buildings marked out on the ground represent a later rebuilding of the fort for the abortive Scottish campaign of the Severan emperors. Moving W. to the wall itself, an impressive stretch of the huge ditch can be seen at Watling Lodge, 2 mi. (3.25 km.) W. of Falkirk. Farther on, about a mile SE of Bonnybridge, is Rough Castle, best-preserved of the forts, excavated in 1903 and 1932–33, with fine stretches of the wall and ditch leading up to it (the wall forms the fort's northern side) and the Military Way, here running through it. The turf ramparts and ditches of this tiny fort (about one acre) are clearly visible and some traces of the stone foundations of the buildings in the interior as well. A few of the signalling platforms can be seen in the vicinity, and N. of the wall and ditch a series of *lilias*, defensive pits with sharpened stakes at the bottom concealed by brush, have been exposed.

Just to the W. at Seabegs Wood (SW of Bonnybridge) a good stretch of the wall, ditch and Military Way are visible, and at Croy Hill about 9 mi. (14 km.) W. of Rough Castle, the highest point on the wall, there is a long stretch of the ditch, about 1.5 mi. (2.3 km.), partly excavated from solid rock—and at the top about 80 ft. was left undug. Even the Romans gave up! Just W. of Croy Hill toward Twechar the ramparts of a fort at Bar Hill (3.6 acres) can be seen, set unusually to the rear of the wall. The remains of the *principia* and a bath house have been preserved here. Finally at Bearsden in the northwestern outskirts of Glasgow a half of a fort was excavated in 1973–81 and parts of the bath house have been preserved, the only stone-built Roman building on view in Scotland.

ARDBLAIR
(Perthshire/Tayside)

Stone circle, bisected by the road running S. from Blairgowrie. Six stones are now set in concrete on either side of the road with the most massive stone, as is usual in these parts, in the SW.

ARDESTIE EARTH-HOUSE
(Angus/Tayside)

E. of Dundee and less than 2 mi. (3 km.) inland from Monifieth, a good example of the some 200 earth-houses discovered in Scotland. Ardestie is a long sunken passage, about 95 ft., walled in stone and paved. It was excavated in 1949–51; the remains of contemporary round huts were found to be associated with it. The roof, of stone slabs or timber, has disappeared. Earth-houses or souterrains were apparently used for cattle and/or storage during the first three cents. AD. Another souterrain at Carlungie, a few mi. NE of Ardestie, excavated at the same time, is U-shaped, about 4 ft. deep and again roofless, with four entrances and eight huts associated with it. Some 8 mi. (13 km.) E. and 5.5 mi. (9 km.) N. of Dundee the roofless souterrain of Tealing can be found at Balgray. It is a shallow trench about 90 ft. long, 5 ft. deep and semicircular in shape. See also *Culsh*; *Pitcur*.

About 1 mi. (1.6 km.) NW of Ardestie stands Laws Hill, crowned by an oval hill fort defended by a rubble wall faced with stone blocks, and with outer ramparts at both ends. The walls were timber-framed and had been burnt in some catastrophe, the stone vitrified, suggesting a date from the 8th to 6th cents. BC. The scant remains of a later broch lie inside it.

ARDOCH ROMAN FORT
(Perthshire/Tayside)

The best preserved fort in Scotland, situated between Crieff, 10 mi. (16 km.) N., and Dunblane, 7 mi. (11.25 km.) SW, on private land. First established by Agricola in the 1st cent. AD, it was refurbished as a permanent legionary base, 7.2 acres at its largest, a forward defense for the *Antonine Wall* to the S; the spectacular lines of ditches and ramparts seen today date from the latter period. The multiple defenses, with two entrances, are best-preserved on the N. and E. sides— no less than five ditches outside the main rampart, once faced with stone. Excavations in 1896–97 uncovered the interior buildings of stone and timber, but nothing is visible today. To the N. and NE are faint traces of a number of overlapping large camps, probably practice camps from different periods.

ARDWALL ISLAND
(Kircudbrightshire/
Dumfries and Galloway)

Important Early Christian site on an island in the Fleet estuary, off the village of Knockbrex W. of Kircudbright, excavated 1964–65. There was a cemetery here, possibly around a shrine, as early as the 5th or early 6th cent. AD. Later a small timber mortuary chapel was built in the cemetery and was replaced by a larger stone chapel in the 8th cent. By about 1000 AD the chapel was in ruins, though burials continued inside it. Traces of the stone-revetted bank around the cemetery can be seen, and an important series of memorial stones and crosses found at the site is in the Dumfries museum. See also *Castle Haven Dun* nearby.

ARDWELL BROCH
(Wigtownshire/Dumfries
and Galloway)

Much ruined and unexcavated Iron Age broch, 4 mi. (6.5 km.) S. of Sandhead on Luce Bay. Situated on a rocky promontory close to the bay, it was defended by a wall and ditch on the landward side. The inner wall and other features can be seen amidst the rubble, and the narrow entrance passages on the sea and landward sides. For brochs, see *Broch of Mousa*.

ARRAN ISLAND
(Inner Hebrides)

See *Machrie Moor*.

AUCHAGALLON
(Inner Hebrides, Arran)

See *Machrie Moor*.

BALBIRNIE
(Fife/Fife)

See *Balfarg*.

BALFARG
(Fife/Fife)

Remnants of an important prehistoric religious center, 6 mi. (9.6 km.) N. of Kirkcaldy, 1 mi. (1.6 km.) NW of Markinch. The site included the enormous henge monument of Balfarg, nearly 200 ft. across, discovered through aerial photography and excavated 1977–78, and to the E. of it the much smaller stone ring of Balbirnie, excavated 1970–71. There may well have been other monuments on the site, now vanished. The excavations uncovered evidence of weird rituals, probably mortuary in nature, that were carried out on the site for a thousand years after the initial building in about 2900 BC.

Balfarg consisted of a circular bank with a ditch inside it, typical of henges (see for instance *Avebury* in England and *Stenness*, in the Orkneys). On the leveled platform inside the bank and ditch 16 huge timber posts, up to five tons in weight and possibly encircled by a palisade, were erected in a circle (their sites now marked by small modern posts), the tallest on the W. side and a pair of the largest outlying posts marking the entrance. Just before all this was constructed some kind of fiery inaugural ceremony, involving numerous, broken grooved-ware pots, burnt wood and cremated human bones took place on the western side (obviously the most sacred direction). The remains were then raked into and around the postholes. Many centuries later two concentric stone rings were set up on the site, again graduated in height towards the W. with a massive portal stone marking the western entrance. The two remaining stones on the site today have long been known. Finally, about 1900 BC a Beaker youth was buried under a 2-ton slab (still visible) accompanied by a flint knife and a late Beaker pot.

The small Balbirnie ring may have been erected with the henge or later. The builders placed cremated bones in the pits holding four of the 10 stones, and at the center of the ring was a small square of stones with more cremated bone around it. Later two stone-lined burial cists were dug inside the ring, and still later a cairn was erected there that contained at least 16 cremation burials. The Balbirnie ring has been moved entire to the SE to make way for the widening of a road. See also *Broomend of Crichie*.

BALLACHROY
(Argyll/Strathclyde)

Row of three tall, narrow standing stones on the Kintyre peninsula, just off the main road running down its W. side, about 15 mi. (24 km.) S. of Tarbert. The astronomical possibilities of the alignment have been discussed by Professor Alexander Thom and others; certainly the stones are lined up with a large megalithic cist, once covered by a cairn, to the SW, and with two smaller cists and a standing stone beyond that. The line as a whole points to the setting of the midwinter sun in 1800 BC—*but* the cairn would have obstructed any such view. More promising is the central stone, which does seem to point to Cora Bheim to the NW, a mountain on the island of Jura 19 mi. (31 km.) away where the sun sets during the midsummer solstice. Among other monuments in the region is the largest cairn in Kintyre, Corriechrevie, about 1 mi. (1.6 km.) N. of Ballachroy above the road on its eastern side.

BALLYMEANOCH
(Argyll/Strathclyde)

See *Kilmartin*.

BALNUARAN OF CLAVA
(Invernessshire/
Highland)

See *Clava Cairns*.

BALQUHAIN
(Aberdeenshire/
Grampian)

See *Loanhead of Daviot*.

BAR HILL
(Dumbartonshire/
Strathclyde)

See *Antonine Wall*.

BARMKIN OF ECHT
(Aberdeenshire/
Grampian)

Complex Iron Age hill fort isolated in difficult moorland country, 14 mi. (22.5 km.) due W. of Aberdeen, just NW of Echt. The ruins of two inner defense circles of stone are tumbled about, with the entrances in each lined up. Three more ramparts, barely discernible today, encircle those two, with five entrances, two of them not in line with the inner two entrances. All these ramparts undoubtedly represent different building periods.

**BARPA LANGASS
(Outer Hebrides, North
Uist Island)**

Neolithic passage grave about 6 mi. (10 km.) SW of Lochmaddy, on the slope of a hill. The huge cairn of stones rises some 14 ft. high from a ring of kerb stones. A ruined forecourt on the E. leads through a 12-ft.-long passage to a large inner chamber, difficult of access, built of massive slabs and roofed with three heavy lintels. Moving toward the W. coast from Lochmaddy, another Neolithic chambered cairn stands on South Clettraval hill, just before Hosta. Much of the Clettraval cairn, close to 100 ft. long, is well preserved. Excavated in 1934, it proved to have a long chamber with five compartments. Built into the W. end of the cairn is an interesting Iron Age wheelhouse, dating perhaps 3,000 years after the cairn—probably 2nd-3rd cents. AD, and the first wheelhouse to be excavated (1946–48). This circular farmhouse of heavy drystone masonry had eight radiating stone piers (two are still visible) to support a timber and thatch roof over the open center with its hearth. Traces of the wall enclosing the farmstead are visible and inside it small buildings, including a horseshoe-shaped hut and a rectangular byre. See also *Jarlshof*; *Kilphedir*.

**BARSALLOCH POINT
(Wigtownshire/Dumfries
and Galloway)**

Iron Age fort on a promontory overlooking Luce Bay, less than 2 mi. (3 km.) S. of Port William. Mesolithic hunter-gatherers camped on the cliffs above an old raised beach along the coast here, and a hearth at Barsalloch yielded a radiocarbon date 4050 ± 110 years bc. The D-shaped fort on the point, facing on to the sea, has impressive double ramparts on the land side with a wide ditch in between.

**BEARSDEN
(Dumbartonshire/
Strathclyde)**

See *Antonine Wall*.

**BERRYBRAE
(Aberdeenshire/
Grampian)**

Stone ring, 7 mi. (11.25 km.) S. of Fraserburgh and 5 mi. (8 km.) NE of Strichen, near the sea in the far NE of Aberdeenshire, a late example of a Recumbent Stone Circle characteristic of this area, excavated and restored by Aubrey Burl in 1975–78. The stones of these curious rings are graded in height toward the SW with the two tallest flanking a huge block, the recumbent, lying on its side, which Burl thinks was aligned on the midsummer full moon. Berrybrae, built on an artificial platform, originally (perhaps around 2000 BC) was encircled with a low oval bank of stone with the nine uprights and the recumbent set on it. A burial ring cairn around the interior space contained three cremation burials— only parts of the skeletons, by way of an offering. Around 1750 BC (confirmed by a radiocarbon date) new people attempted to level the stones, building a bank and low wall over the stumps. Today only the recumbent, one of its flanking stones and another stone are left from the original ring. Other Recumbent Circles within a few miles include Aikey Brae and Loudon Wood, with *Strichen* farther off. See also *Loanhead of Daviot*; *Old Keig*; *Tomnaverie*.

**BIRRENS
(Dumfriesshire/Dumfries
and Galloway)**

Vestiges of the large and important Roman fortress of Blatobulgium, or Birrens, about 1.5 mi. (2.6 km.) NE of Ecclefechan, less than 1 mi. S. of Middlebie. It lay on the main Roman road from Carlisle into SW Scotland. Excavations in 1895– 96 and 1962–67 demonstrated that it had been built in the 1st cent. AD, initially perhaps by Agricola, and had lasted until about 180 AD. The stone-built *principia* and barracks were uncovered (nothing visible today) and numerous inscriptions, now in the National Museum in Edinburgh. Only the six banks and ditches of the ramparts on the N. side can now be seen.

Troops from Birrens built two practice camps on the slopes of the prominent hill of Brunswark 2.5 mi. (4 km.) due N. of Ecclefechan on a minor road. The hill is crowned by the faint vestiges of what was once a major tribal hill fort, abandoned before the Roman camps were built. Excavations in the fort in 1898 and 1966–67 uncovered a number of round hut foundations, and underneath the main rampart evidence of an earlier wooden palisade that has been radiocarbon-dated to 574 BC. Many Roman ballista balls and lead bolts were found inside the native fort, apparently fired at the abandoned ramparts in artillery field practice. In fact, just outside the southern Roman practice camp, which is well-preserved, are three huge flat-topped mounds (locally called "the three brethren") facing the three gateways of the native fort. These were obviously artillery platforms. Gaps in the Roman camp ramparts gave access to these practice platforms. The southern camp includes an earlier fortlet in the NE corner. Traces of a third practice camp may be discerned just to the N. The finds are in the Dumfries museum. See also *Woden Law*.

BIRSAY, BROUGH OF   See *Brough of Birsay*.

BLACKHAMMER
(Orkneys, Rousay)

Neolithic chambered tomb, 1.5 mi. (2.3 km.) W. of Rousay pier, a so-called stalled cairn (divided inside into stalls or compartments by slabs). Excavated in 1936, it is now in state care with a concrete turfed roof over it containing a hole to view the chamber below. The cairn is over 65 ft. long, the walled chamber inside just over 42 ft. long and 6 ft. wide. It is divided into no less than seven stalls, on each side, by six pairs of slabs reaching part way to the roof (some are gone). The entrance, unusually, was on the middle of the southern long side. See also the stalled cairns *Knowe of Yarso*, *Midhowe*, *Taversoe Tuack* and *Unstan* as well as *Rinyo*, all on Rousay.

BONCHESTER HILL
(Roxburghshire/Borders)

Iron Age hill fort on a 1,020-ft.-high hill with wonderful views, rising E. of Bonchester Bridge about 7 mi. (11 km.) SE of Hawick. There are three circuits of ramparts around the hill, and excavations in 1950 indicated that they belonged to successive phases of the fort. The oldest, probably 5th cent. BC, is a stone-faced wall without timber reinforcement encircling the summit of the knoll. Below this are traces of an earthen rampart and finally, below the base of the knoll, an outer ring of earthworks. Some round hut foundations were found inside the latter. The fort was probably occupied up to the Roman conquest.

BORTHWICK MAINS
PICTISH STONE
(Roxburghshire/Borders)

Pictish symbol stone, less than 4 mi. (6.5 km.) W. of Hawick, standing on the lawn of Borthwick Mains farm. Rare in the lowlands, this square stone displays a carved fish and belongs to Class I, earliest of the type, about 6th–7th cent. AD.

BRECHIN
(Angus/Tayside)

About 8 mi. (13 km.) inland, W. of Montrose on the coast, one of two Irish-derived round towers in Scotland (see also *Abernethy*). Once free-standing but now attached to the 13th-cent. cathedral of Brechin, it stands 86 ft. high to the base of the conical roof, which was added in the 14th cent. The narrow doorway, typically Irish in every detail, is raised 6 ft. above ground level and the carvings around it include a crucified Christ with uncrossed legs, two bishops, one holding an Irish crozier, and two grotesque beasts—all Irish in origin. The tower once had seven wooden floors in the interior. It is dated to the 10th or 11th cent. AD, the Viking period, and the need for protection—if that was its purpose—is clear;

for Brechin was sacked by the Danish Vikings in 1012 AD. See also *Caterthuns, The*, a nearby site.

BROCH OF BURLAND
(Shetlands, Mainland)

One of the many brochs or fortified towers dating roughly from the 1st cent. BC to the 1st cent. AD. It is situated on a promontory on the E. coast requiring a walk off the main road running N. towards Lerwick, after passing Loch Brindister. Though unexcavated, the broch was one of the most heavily fortified of its kind, a characteristic of the Shetland brochs, and commands a spectacular cliff site overlooking the sea. The walls on the sea side still stand nearly 10 ft. high. The tower was defended by an inner wall, two shallow ditches beyond it with a rampart in between them, then a massive outer wall of stone nearly 18 ft. thick, guarded by another ditch. The entrance causeway ran through the whole series of defenses to the entrance passage in the broch, which can be entered. See also *Broch of Mousa*.

BROCH OF GURNESS
(Orkneys, Mainland)

Situated on Aikerness about 11 mi. (18 km.) NW of Kirkwall, on the NE coast near Evie, looking toward Rousay Island. The broch is about 1.5 mi. (2.3 km.) from the main road, the last part on foot. Its walls still stand about 15 ft. high, but the site has been cut into on the N. by the eroding sea. It may date from about 100 AD. Excavated in the 1930s, it has the usual features, a narrow entrance passage with door checks and guard cells on either side. In addition there is a gallery running at ground level between the inner and outer walls of the tower, as well as another internal gallery in the wall farther up. This was presumably reached by a ladder, for added defense, and from it a stairway climbs up through the wall. High up around the inner wall there is a ledge, probably used to support a wooden upper floor. The outer defenses of the broch consisted of a wall with three rock-cut ditches in front of it—and unusual bastions on the wall added at a later period. In fact in the Viking period (and perhaps earlier) a settlement grew up in and around the ruined broch, and these remains complicate the site today. To the NE a typical Viking longhouse was built, and outside the broch the grave of a 9th-cent.-AD Viking woman was found, buried in woolen clothes with bronze brooches, a sickle, knife, shears and a necklace. See also *Broch of Mousa*.

BROCH OF MOUSA
(Shetlands)

On the tiny islet of Mousa just off the E. coast of Mainland Island, 14 mi. (22.5 km.) S. of Lerwick, stands the finest and best-preserved of all Scottish brochs. Mousa, now in state care, is difficult to reach (one hires a boat from nearby Sandwick), but to see one of the outstanding architectural monuments of Europe is worth the effort. But first, on brochs in general: These marvels of engineering—almost 500 are known—are a purely Scottish development, perhaps initially in response to the threat of the advancing Roman armies. They were built over a rather short period, roughly from 100 BC to 100 AD, probably in all cases by local chieftains. It seems most likely now that they developed in the Western Isles, specifically on *Skye*, out of the local galleried duns and semi-brochs typical of the Hebridean islands, and from there spread W. and N. into the Northern Isles. So sophisticated is their architecture and so uniform the model that they must have been built by itinerant, professional master engineers who traveled from one place to another on order, refining their designs as they went. Though the design is remarkably uniform everywhere, there are local differences. Those in the Northern Isles are taller than the brochs of the

Finest and best preserved of the Scottish brochs—fortified homestead towers in use for only about 200 years (roughly 100 BC-100 AD)—stands on Mousa, a little islet off the Shetlands' Mainland island. These marvels of engineering, with tapering double-skinned walls up to 50 ft. high, built without mortar, are found in western and northern Scotland and in the Northern Isles. Rooms, galleries and stairways were incorporated within the walls. So uniform is their pattern, despite local variations, that they were probably constructed by roving, highly-skilled builders. Mousa's broch still stands about 43 ft. high. (Courtesy of Historic Buildings and Monuments, Scottish Development Dept.)

A ground plan and section of the Broch of Mousa gives some idea of the sophisticated architectural designing that went into these remarkable towers. Mousa's broch itself is one of the finest architectural monuments of Europe. (From Graham and Anna Ritchie, Scotland: Archaeology and Early History, Thames & Hudson, London, 1981.)

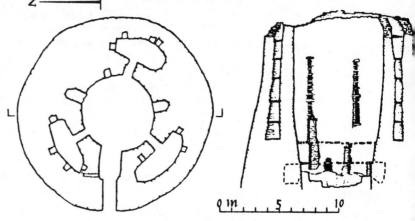

Western Isles, and the former tend to have more and stronger outlying defenses. Again, these with galleries in the walls at ground level may be earlier than those with a solid base and the galleries higher up inside the wall.

The challenge was to create a stable tower, in drystone masonry, tall enough perhaps to overtop the range of fire-bearing missiles, yet stable enough to stand without collapsing. The response was to encase the towers in double-skinned walls with cells, galleries and stairways in the hollow to lighten the load, then to taper the double wall upward to increase the stability, thus achieving heights of some 40 to 50 ft. The typical broch was entered through a lintelled passageway with door checks and bar holes for the doors, and guard chambers on one or both sides. There was a hearth in the interior court, and cells in the walls, corbelled only on the ground level, as well as long galleries and a winding stairway to the top. The two walls were held together by cross-slabs bonding the two. Ledges on the interior walls, the lower one to help support a wooden floor or wooden galleries on posts around the inside perimeter, the higher ledge perhaps to support a roof (its nature can only be guessed at), completed the assembly. The end result was a stable tapering tower, reminiscent of a modern cooling tower, with the perfection and beauty of the perfect fit of form to function.

Mousa is indeed the finest and most sophisticated example of the art of broch building. It still stands some 43 ft. high, its thick dry-stone walls tapering gracefully from 50 ft. wide at the bottom to 40 ft. at the top. The upper walls are lightened by six large superimposed galleries running all around the broch inside its walls, and other cavities. A stairway, its entrance door once reached by a ladder, winds clockwise up through the galleries to the top. The round central courtyard, 20 ft. across, has a hearth in the middle; three large rooms in the thickness of the wall, corbel-roofed, open off it, each equipped with built-in shelves. Access to the courtyard is through a narrow passage, 16 ft. long, with the usual door checks and bar hole. The heavy lintels of its roof were broken away long ago. There are two ledges around the inner wall, 7 ft. and 12 ft. up, the one for a wooden floor or gallery, the other for some kind of a roof. Inside the broch today are the remains of a later wheelhouse (see *Jarlshof*). Indeed, Mousa was still in use, as the Viking sagas tell us; on at least two occasions, the latest in 1153 AD—some 800 to 900 years after its building.

BRODGAR, RING OF (Orkneys, Mainland)	See *Stenness*.
BROOMEND OF CRICHIE (Aberdeenshire/ Grampian)	Scant remains of what was once a large and important prehistoric religious center, on the southern outskirts of Inverurie, E. of the main road. Here was a typical henge circle (see *Balfarg*) about 100 ft. across—a bank and internal ditch, with entrances N. and S. Within the ring was once a circle of six standing stones of which only two survive. Excavations in 1885 uncovered a cist with inhumation burial, probably Early Bronze Age, at the center, several cremation burials, and Bronze Age artifacts. Reports as late as the 18th cent. described a larger circle about 165 ft. N. of the henge circle, now vanished. It had three concentric rings of stone and an avenue of standing stones leading from it to the smaller henge circle and beyond. The early Pictish symbol stone now standing within the henge was moved there in the 19th cent.
BROUGH OF BIRSAY (Orkneys, Mainland)	Small islet, reached only on foot at low tide, on the NW corner of Mainland, about 12 mi. N. of Stromness. Here is a fascinating Dark Ages site offering remains from Pictish Christian to the Norse occupation, well explained in a small site museum on the island. The most visible ruins are the standing walls—nave and apse—of a small 11th-cent. church or cathedral inside its walled enclosure, presumably built by Earl Thorfinn the Mighty of Orkney, who died here in 1065 after a lifetime of raiding and roving in the true Viking spirit. One of the two graves found inside the church could well be his. Beside the church are the remains of what is now thought to be the 12th-cent. palace of Bishop William

of Orkney—four large rooms around three sides of a court. Here and there are traces of an earlier Pictish-Christian church and enclosure, possibly of the 7th cent. AD, the church lying under the church of Earl Thorfinn; and inside the enclosure is the cemetery, both Norse graves, and Pictish graves marked by slabs standing on edge. Here were found an early cross, an Ogham inscription, and the famous Birsay Stone displaying Pictish symbols above a relief of three warriors carrying spears and small square shields. It was found, broken, at the head of a large triple grave, and is now in the Edinburgh National Museum. A replica stands at the site.

A group of small Norse houses were uncovered outside the enclosure, probably those of Bishop William's retainers, and beneath them the remains of a well-built rectangular great hall, undoubtedly that of Earl Thorfinn himself. A number of Norse long houses stood nearby, comparable to those at Jarlshof and evidence of the first Norse settlement of Orkney. The largest is 56 ft. long.

Much evidence has been found on the island of extensive Pict metalworking, and on the mainland opposite Birsay excavations at Buckquoy have uncovered the foundations of three successive Pictish farmsteads of the 7th and early 8th cents. Overlying them, significantly, was a Norse farmstead of the 9th cent. AD, with a brief interruption between the two occupations suggesting that the conquering Vikings drove the Picts from the site. The Pict dwellings were cellular houses on stone foundations, the latest a so-called figure-of-eight house with a round central room containing the hearth.

BROUGH OF DEERNESS (Orkneys, Mainland)	Monastic settlement on a rocky, sea-washed cliff promontory off the eastern end of the Deerness peninsula in far eastern Mainland, 13 mi. (21 km.) E. of Kirkwall and a mile or two N. of Skaill. Access by a single rocky path is difficult. On the flat top of the promontory are the outlines of 19 rectangular buildings in the turf, grouped around the remains of a stone chapel with walls 5 ft. thick. Stretches of the defensive rampart survive and a few earlier hut circles to the SE. The monastery was probably established by Irish monks in the 7th to 8th cents. AD.
BUCKQUOY (Orkneys, Mainland)	See *Brough of Birsay*.
BURGHEAD (Moray/Grampian)	Huge Pictish fortress, about 7 mi. (11 km.) W. of Lossiemouth and the same NW of Elgin, on a promontory over the ocean. The remains were partly destroyed during the expansion of the fishing village of Burghead in the 19th cent. Originally the promontory was defended by three lines of ramparts, and a massive interior wall ran down the promontory, dividing it into a double fort. Today all that is left is part of the massive, timber-reinforced cross wall, and in 1966 the wall was radiocarbon-dated to the 5th or 6th cent. AD, indicating that this was indeed one of the few known Pictish forts. Its symbol seems to have been the bull, for about 2 doz. symbol stones showing bulls were found at the site; a few are in the *Elgin* museum nearby. Burghead shares with *Craig Phadrig* farther W. the possibility of being the capital of the Pictish king Bridei, who was visited at his court by St. Columba. A large rock-cut well can be visited on the site at the base of the remaining wall. It is thought to date from Early Christian times.
BURLAND, BROCH OF	See *Broch of Burland*.

BURNSWARK
(Dumfriesshire/Dumfries
and Galloway)

See *Birrens Roman Fort*.

BUSTA
(Shetlands, Mainland)

Impressive standing stone, probably dating from the Early Iron Age, rising 10½ ft. from a cliff in the NW part of the island, about 4.5 mi. (7.25 km.) NW of Voe. A granite slab, roughly squared, it is the best of the few standing stones on the Shetlands.

CAIRNBAAN
(Argyll/Strathclyde)

See *Kilmartin*.

CAIRNBAN
(Inner Hebrides, Arran)

See *Machrie Moor*.

CAIRNHOLY
(Kircudbrightshire/
Dumfries and Galloway)

Two spectacular chambered cairns of the Clyde group, excavated 1949. They lie above Wigtown Bay near the coast road from Gatehouse of Fleet to Creetown, 4 mi. (6.5 km.) SE of the latter. A farm road leads up the hill inland to the tombs from Kirkdale Bridge. Cairnholy I is the most impressive. Its cairn, originally about 170 ft. long, has gone, and the chamber, divided into two compartments, is much ruined. But in front of it a horned forecourt added later in its development stands out clearly. It is built of narrow upright slabs once filled in with drystone walling. Five fires had been built in front of the tomb during its long period of use during the late Neolithic and early Bronze (Beaker) periods. The dead were cremated and then placed in the chamber. Cairnholy II, up the hill, is of the same design but is shorter, lacks a forecourt and is much dilapidated; but it does have its original capstone over the rear compartment. Both tombs had been blocked up with stones when they went out of use.

CAIRNPAPPLE HILL
(West Lothian/Lothian)

A prehistoric sacred site set appropriately on a high hill with magnificent views over the Forth and as far as Arran Island. It lies about 12 mi. (19 km.) due W. from the outskirts of Edinburgh and 2 mi. (3.25 km.) E. of Torpichen. For at least 1,600 years the hill was a religious-mortuary shrine, and is one of the most important and complex sites in Scotland. Excavated by Stuart Piggott in 1947–48 it is now in state care, has been consolidated and is open to the public, with a small site museum. Its archaeological history began about 2800 BC with an arc of seven pits like the Aubrey Holes at *Stonehenge* (ENGLAND) in which bits of cremated human bones had been placed as offerings. A "cove" of three large upright stones may have stood in front of the arc. Fragments of Neolithic axes from as far away as the Lake District and North Wales were found at this level, suggesting that this cremation cemetery was already a place for meetings, ceremonies and trade as well.

Somewhat later it was turned into a real henge monument (see *Balfarg*, and *Avebury* in England) by erecting an egg-shaped ring of 24 stones, with a ditch and external bank outside the ring and entrances N. and S. (The position of some of the stones is now marked on the ground.) In the interior of the ring stood a cove (the same as the possible earlier one or a new one?) and two early Bronze Age (Beaker) burials, the northern one under a cairn covering a chamber cut into the rock that used one of the cove stones as its western end. The cairn and tomb, reconstructed under a concrete dome, can now be entered from the top.

Shortly thereafter, in a drastic change of plans, a huge Bronze Age burial cairn was erected, 40 ft. across, completely swallowing the northern tomb and using the stones of the old ring as kerb stones. It covered two burials, the most important an inhumation burial of some important chieftain in a stone-lined cist. In time the cairn was doubled in size to 100 ft. in diameter, using material from the old henge bank as fill, and two cremation urn burials were placed in it. Finally four full-length burials, probably early Iron Age, were found on the site. closing its long history as an active shrine.

CALLINISH
(Outer Hebrides, Lewis)

Stone circle, the justly famous "Stonehenge of the North," beautifully sited on a promontory-ridge overlooking Loch Roag, an inlet on the W. coast of Lewis, 13 mi. (21 km.) W. of Stornoway. It is not a large circle, only 37 ft. across, but

The Standing Stones of Callinish on Lewis, Outer Hebrides, one of the most interesting and important of stone circles, next to Stonehenge. The circle of 13 strikingly tall stones surrounds a huge central monolith nearly 16 ft. high. Remnants of four processional avenues (the most complete is to the left) run off roughly in the four cardinal directions, making a cross. Like Stonehenge, Callinish was obviously the central temple in a large religious complex, with six other circles in the vicinity. Much has been made of possible astronomical alignments but with meager results. (Courtesy of British Tourist Authority, New York.)

its 13 striking stones, tall and narrow, averaging 10 ft. high, and its huge central monolith standing almost 16 ft. tall, make it particularly appealing. From this flattened circle an avenue of 19 stones—10 on one side, 9 on the other—runs N. for 270 ft., and single stone alignments run E., S. and W. (with only 4 to 5 stones in each), enhancing the interest of the monument. These may be remnants of three other avenues—planned or built. Squeezed into the circle and between it and the central monolith are the remnants of a Neolithic cairn, its passage and double chamber now open to the sky. When Callinish was stripped of its peat covering in 1857 cremated human bones were found in the chamber. Scholars argue whether the cairn was built before, during or after the construction of the ring, but the consensus seems to be the latter. Another chambered cairn lies just NE of the circle.

Was Callinish an astronomical center? There have been exhaustive studies and much speculation, and many sight alignments have been proposed. The most plausible cites the fact that the avenue points directly toward Mt. Clisham to the S., the highest point on Harris, where the midsummer moon sets; but this could be accidental. It is most likely that Callinish was actually a major religious center, a temple, the avenues used as processional ways, for there are six other stone circles around Loch Roag near Callinish, two of them within site of the monument to the N., making the area a religious complex like Stonehenge. One of these to the S., Cnoc Fillibhir, was a double ring, eight stones of the outer ring surviving and four of the inner, taller ring. Garynahine is a smaller ring of lighter stones with a ruined cairn at its center—perhaps a family shrine. Loch Roag circle, W. of Cnoc Fillibhir, a single ring, is the largest of all.

CAMSTER CHAMBERED TOMBS (Caithness/Highland)

Or Grey Cairns of Camster, a pair of Neolithic burial mounds, among the most interesting of a number in Caithness built, like those of the Orkneys, of flat flagstones. The Grey Cairns lie about 16 mi. (26 km.) down the main coastal road from Wick, then inland due N. about 4 mi. (6.5 km.) from West Clyth. Extensively excavated and restored in the 1970s, the cairns are under state care and are open to the public. The first, Camster Round, a passage grave, is a circular pile of stones, quite intact, about 60 ft. across and 12 ft. high. A narrow passage leads in about 20 ft. to the chamber—a rectangular antechamber giving way to the main chamber, the latter an exceptionally fine round room with a corbelled roof 10 ft. overhead, the rear section separated by projecting slabs. A perspex window now lights the chamber from the top. At the end of its use the tomb was blocked with stones.

Camster Long, about 200 yds. to the N., is an impressive cairn about 228 ft. long overall, one of the largest in Scotland, with large horns at either end. Two chambers have been found in it so far, and there may be more. Both can be entered through passages from the side of the cairn and one is now top-lighted. The northern chamber again has an antechamber and main chamber, divided into three compartments with curving walls, and has a corbelled roof. The other chamber is polygonal. It seems that all these tombs within the long cairn were once separate round cairns, later joined together under the one mound, indicating many centuries of use (see also *Mid-Gleniron Cairns*). The huge hornwork at the NE end of the cairn is actually made up of raised platforms, and on these "stages" ancient burial ceremonies may have taken place, a species of early drama. A set of similar cairns is to be found at *Yarrows*, nearby to the E.

Inland from the coastal road again, 1.5 mi. (2.3 km.) from Mid-Clyth and 9

Camster Round, one of two paired Neolithic passage graves in Caithness. The Gray Cairns of Camster include Camster Long, a huge cairn about 228 ft. long, and Camster Round, both built of flat flagstones. Camster Round, excavated and restored, is almost complete. The forecourt and entrance at the left lead through a 20-ft.-long passage into an antechamber and round central chamber with a high corbelled roof. (Courtesy of Historic Buildings and Monuments, Scottish Development Dept.)

mi. (14.5 km.) SW of Wick, is a curious monument—the Hill o' Many Stanes, 250 stones only a foot or so high arranged in 22 rows on the slope of a hill, the rows fanning out slightly to the S. Its purpose is obscure, but it reminds one of the much larger alignments of *Carnac* in France. If it was an observatory to chart the setting or rising of the moon, as Professor Thom and others believe, it could be one of the more significant Bronze Age monuments of Scotland.

CARLOWAY
(Outer Hebrides, Lewis)

See *Dun Carloway Broch*.

CARLUNGIE SOUTERRAIN
(Angus/Tayside)

See *Ardestie Earth-House*.

CARN LIATH BROCH
(Sutherland/Highland)

A good example of a broch (see *Broch of Mousa*), a little over a mi. (1.6 km.) E. of Dunrobin Castle, on the main coastal road. Its interior was cleared out in the mid-19th cent. and the whole consolidated in 1972. The inner walls stand about 12 ft. high in places. The entrance, with its lintels, door checks, bar hole and one guard chamber is clear, as is the bottom of the winding stair in the wall. Of two deep holes in the floor, one was probably a well. Around the broch are house foundations, presumably from a later period when the broch, no longer used as a fort, centered a settlement.

CASTLE HAVEN DUN
(Kircudbrightshire/
Dumfries and Galloway)

Iron Age galleried dun, or fort, of the 1st cent. BC, rare in these parts. It lies W. of Kircudbright and about 3 mi. (4.75 km.) W. of Borgue overlooking Wigtown Bay. The ivy-clad, ruined fort is D-shaped with the straight wall along the cliffs. Behind it is a secondary wall, probably later. The fort was cleared out in 1905 and somewhat restored. The doorway is on the N. and the main feature is the three galleries inside the wall at ground level, with six doors giving access to the interior. A stairway to the top apparently was built against the inner wall. Nearby is *Ardwall Island*. See also *Broch of Mousa; Clickhimin*.

CASTLE LAW HILL FORT (Perthsire/Tayside)

Or Abernethy hill fort, between Abernethy and Auchtermuchty to the S., on the eastern end of the ridge. Here is a stone-walled hill fort that has been dated by the finds within it to the last century or two BC. Its importance lies in the empty sockets for horizontal beams found in the inner wall-face during explorations in 1896–98. The burning of these reinforcing beams within the walls, either by accident or enemy attack, seems to have been responsible for the many "vitrified" stone fort walls of the Iron Age period found in Scotland, some dating as far back as the 8th cent. BC. See also *Finavon*.

CATERTHUNS, THE (Angus/Tayside)

Two massive hill forts, among the most impressive in Scotland, on either side of the road beyond Little Brechin, 5 mi. (8 km.) NW of Brechin. Of this pair of unexcavated forts, inexplicably only about 1 mi. (1.6 km.) apart, the White Caterthun to the S. is the largest and highest. Five concentric ramparts can be traced here. A wide tumble of stones seems to represent the two massive inner walls, collapsed as their timber reinforcements decayed. The inside wall may have been almost 40 ft. thick. Outside these is another rampart, then two more, much decayed. The Brown Caterthun, much smaller, shows six ramparts, the inner one of stone with one entrance, and five more beyond, the first three (strangely) with nine entrances, the outer two with eight.

CATSTANE, THE (West Lothian/Lothian)

An important Early Christian memorial stone of the late 5th or 6th cent. AD, bearing an inscription in Latin. It stands W. of Edinburgh near Kirkliston. Recent excavations around it (before a runway extension to the airport was built) revealed that the stone presided over a cemetery of regularly laid out, long cist graves of the succeeding centuries. See also *Ardwall Island; Whithorn*.

CHESTERS (East Lothian/Lothian)

One of Scotland's best-preserved Iron Age hill forts, 4 mi (6.5 km.) SW of Dunbar, 1.5 mi. (2.3 km.) SW of the village of Spott. Two massive earthen ramparts, still about 7 ft. high in places and each with its ditch, enclose an interior measuring up to 380 ft. across. Both walls were once stone-faced. Beyond them are faint traces of six more ramparts. Doubtless all were built at different periods, but the fort has not been excavated.

CLACHAIG CAIRN (Inner Hebrides, Arran)

See *Machrie Moor*.

CLAVA CAIRNS (Invernessshire/ Highland)

Just SE of Culloden Battlefield, 6 mi. (9.6 km.) E. of Inverness, three Late Neolithic cairns in line at Balnuaran of Clava. These are the best of a local group of Clava-style cairns found around the Inverness region. Two passage graves with a ring cairn between them stretch SW to NE in line here, all on platforms with stone rings around them. The chambers of the two passage graves are now roofless, and both their passages line up exactly to face SW to the setting of the midwinter sun, suggesting that they were built at the same time. Around the southwestern cairn 10 stones of the original circle remain and 11 stones of the egg-shaped ring around the northeastern cairn. The cairn around both chambers consists of piled-up cobbles held in place by heavy kerb stones. Excavated in 1828 and 1858, the cairns were found to contain fragments of cremated human bone—offerings rather than burials as these cairns seem to have been temples as much as tombs. The much lower ring cairn in the middle, excavated in 1857, has no passage and its central area was never roofed. Of its outer stone circle nine stones remain, and strange cobbled paths lead out from the cairn to three of the stones on the S., E. and NW. The ring stones as well as kerb stones of all three monuments increase in size toward the SW, obviously the sacred direction here. Cupmarks, possibly symbols of the sun or moon, are engraved on a number of the stones of all three cairns. See also *Corrimony*, another Clava cairn.

CLETTRAVAL CAIRN (Outer Hebrides, North Uist)

See *Barpa Langass*.

CLICKHIMIN (Shetlands, Mainland)

Complex prehistoric site, one of the richest and most important in Britain, on a lake promontory on the western outskirts of Lerwick. It is now in state care. Extensive excavations between 1953 and 1957 uncovered structures and varied finds ranging from the late Bronze Age into the Dark Ages. Most visible today on the small promontory, once an islet, is the broch, its walls still standing around 17 ft. high, and outside it the blockhouse, an earlier structure within the tumbled defensive wall around the islet. Earliest of all are the well-preserved remains of a late Bronze Age farmstead (perhaps 700–500 BC) just NW of the broch, built at a period when the little island was undefended, and later occupied by Iron Age people. What happened next is still a matter of controversy. Certainly the islet was fortified with the massive drystone ring wall, with a landing stage at its SE entrance; but whether the freestanding blockhouse just inside the entrance was built at the same time or later, as the fortified entrance of a second series of Iron Age defenses, now gone, is in doubt. The blockhouse (see also *Ness of Burgi*) is a stone-built arc with an entrance passage running through it and two chambers on either side, not reached from the passageway. There are also the remains of an upper gallery and of a staircase at one end. The blockhouse may have had a number of stories. All this took place sometime during the last few cents. BC.

Perhaps in the 1st cent. AD the broch was built on the site, utilizing stones from the previous constructions (see *Broch of Mousa*). It is 65 ft. across at the base and may have stood 40 to 50 ft. high. The 17-ft.-long entrance passage on the W. side leads into a large interior court with two intramural cells off it and a stairway in the wall opposite the entrance, its door raised well above the ground level. Another raised door leads to the galleries in the wall. Unusually, a mural gallery runs clockwise around the broch wall at a slant. The broch may have been maintained as a fort as late as 200 AD, and in the meantime the blockhouse survived, as part of the broch's outer defenses or possibly as a chieftain's house. Later, in more peaceful times, a wheelhouse was built in the courtyard, its radiating piers extending outward from the broch's inner wall (see *Jarlshof*). The wheelhouse may have been occupied up to Viking times (9th cent.). Finally, a stone sunk into the causeway on the islet end is engraved with a pecked pair of footprints, a symbol usually associated with high kings, like the single footprint at *Dunadd* fort, indicating that Clickhimin was indeed the seat of powerful rulers. Finds from Clickhimin can be seen in the Shetland Museum, Lerwick.

CNOC FILLIBHIR
(Outer Hebrides, Lewis)

See *Callinish*.

CORRIECHRIVIE
(Argyll/Strathclyde)

See *Ballachroy*.

CORRIMONY
(Invernessshire/
Highland)

Neolithic passage grave, in state care, one of the best preserved of the *Clava* group, 20 mi. SW of Inverness, 8 mi. (13 km.) W. of Drumnadrochit up Glen Urquhart. Excavated in 1952 by Stuart Piggott, this far eastern outpost of the Clava group has all the same characteristics. Built on an artificial platform, the cairn of rough pebbles and boulders is bordered by a heavy kerb of boulders supporting slabs set on edge. The low passage, oriented toward the sacred SW, leads into a small, roughly circular chamber about 12 ft. across—not now accessible. It was once roofed by a large slab, now set to one side upside down on the cairn, so that one can peer down into the chamber below. The slab is decorated, on its former underside, with many cupmarks, originally seen only by the dead. Around the cairn, again like Clava, is a ring of 11 standing stones. Little was found in the chamber—some charcoal, no cremated bones, only the stain of a single inhumation burial by way of offering. The cairn, like those at Clava, was probably a family shrine as much as a tomb.

CRAIG PHADRIG
(Invernessshire/
Highland)

Iron Age hill fort just W. of Inverness, N. of Upper Leachkin village; once defended by two ramparts. The most recent excavations in 1970–71 indicated that both walls dated from the 4th cent. BC, and both were vitrified, i.e., burned probably by enemy action (see *Castle Law*). The massive inner rampart, now turf-covered but still standing nearly 12 ft. high, was once a rectangular drystone wall reinforced with heavy timbers. The outer rampart, not well-preserved but still visible in places, was similar. The excavations revealed a much later Pictish presence in the fort—imported wares from western France dating from the 5th to 8th cents. AD. Possibly Craig Phadrig may have been the capital of the Pictish king, Bridei; others think it was at *Burghead* farther E.

CRAMOND
(Midlothian/Lothian)

See *Antonine Wall*.

CROFT MORAIG
(Perthshire/Tayside)

Stone circle, 4 mi. (6.5 km.) W. of Aberfeldy near the head of Loch Tay. An interesting early ritual site, excavated in 1965 and now in state care, that went through three distinct phases during its long life. Beautifully sited on a knoll with wide views, the monument lay on the prehistoric trade routes from Ireland across Scotland and has affinities with the Recumbent Stone Circles of Aberdeenshire to the E. (see *Berrybrae*). In the first phase, probably Middle Neolithic (4th millennium BC), a horseshoe-shaped structure of 14 timber posts was set up, its open end facing the sacred SW direction, with a possible porch on the E. This may have been a roofed structure like that at *Woodhenge* in England. Later on the site began to resemble a henge (see *Balfarg*) as an oval of eight standing stones, graded in height toward the SW, was set up on the site with three more stones outlying, and a stone bank was built around the circle, possibly with two entrances. At the SW, again, lay a long recumbent stone like those of Aberdeenshire, liberally cupmarked. Scatters of white quartz, associated with sacred sites, were found inside the oval. In phase three, probably Early Bronze Age, a ring of 12 much larger standing stones was constructed around the oval, with two even larger portal stones outside on the E. Pits at the bases of the portal stones may have contained Beaker burials. Remnants of both the inner and the outer stone circles can be seen today.

CROY HILL
(Dunbartonshire/
Strathclyde)

See *Antonine Wall.*

CULLERLIE
(Aberdeenshire/
Grampian)

Curious stone circle, about 10 mi. (16 km.) W. of Aberdeen (turning S. at Garlogie). Excavated in 1934, it has been reconstructed and is in state care. Eight squat stones form an almost perfect circle, 32 ft. across. Originally the area within the circle had been blackened with many fires, evidence of prolonged ceremonial use, not necessarily connected with burials. Later eight small Bronze Age ring cairns with heavy kerbs were built within the circle, filling most of the space. These have been reconstructed and are now on view. They were apparently used as fire pits to cremate the dead, indicating a change of function for the ring. Charcoal, cremated bone deposits and flint tools were found in six of the cairns.

Of the Bronze Age stone circles in the neighborhood, Sunhoney—a few mi. farther along the main road and just to the N. of it—is a quietly unspoiled ring that gets its lovely name from Sunhoney farm, which owns the land (permission required). Of the original 11 stones on this hill a few have been re-erected. The recumbent stone (see *Berrybrae*), apparently fallen outward, exhibits 28 cupmarks on its outer surface. Inside a central ring cairn were found the usual burnt earth, charcoal and cremated bone. A mi. (1.6 km.) W. again the stones of Midmar Kirk in a graveyard have probably been moved from their original positions. *Barmkin of Echt*, a hill fort, is also in the area.

CULLYCAN
(Banffshire/Grampian)

Or Cullykhan, well-preserved promontory fort, near Pennan on the northern coast. It lies about 9 mi. (14.5 km.) NW of *Strichen* stone circle, and has been radiocarbon-dated at 1186 ± 60 years bc. There is evidence of a later, Pictish occupation.

CULSH EARTH-HOUSE
(Aberdeenshire/
Grampian)

Underground souterrain 2.5 mi. (4 km.) NE of Tarland, a fine example of these numerous Late Iron Age monuments (probably the first few cents. AD), used no doubt for storage. Almost circular, Culsh is still covered by much of its heavy stone lintel roof—and it may be entered. See also *Ardestie; Pitcur*. The *Tomnaverie* stone circle is nearby.

CUWEEN HILL
(Orkneys, Mainland)

One of the *Maes Howe* group of Orkney Neolithic passage tombs, 6 mi. (9.6 km.) W. of Kirkwall on the road leading to Maes Howe. Closer to Kirkwall are two others, *Quanterness* and Wideford Hill. The group, nearly a dozen all told, also includes *Quoyness* on the island of Sanday and the *Holm of Papa Westray* on the islet of that name. The tombs are roughly contemporaneous with the Neolithic village of *Skara Brae* and show affinities with the passage graves of the *Boyne Valley* in Ireland, which may have influenced their construction.

Cuween Hill, a turf-covered circular mound above the Bay of Firth, is about 55 ft. in diameter and covers a rectangular chamber over 7 ft. high with a corbelled roof, with four corbelled side chambers opening off it. To enter the chamber one must crawl along an 18-ft.-long, narrow passage. In state care.

**DEERNESS
(Orkneys, Mainland)**

See *Brough of Deerness.*

**DEVA CRAIG HILL FORT
(Peebleshire/Borders)**

Iron Age fort and settlement on a commanding hill 10 mi. (16 km.) SW of Peebles, about 1 mi. (1.6 km.) SE of Broughton. Two stone walls faced with boulders enclose an area of 190 by 140 ft. and beyond the outer wall on the SW are the remains of a *chevaux de frise*, rare in Britain—not pits containing sharpened stakes as with the Romans but large boulders designed to break up a cavalry charge like modern tank traps. Originally about 200 in all, about half the boulders are still in place. Several groups of hut foundations indicate an open settlement during Roman times or later. The site has not been excavated.

**DUNADD FORT
(Argyll/Strathclyde)**

Dramatic Dark Ages site, thought to be the early capital of the Celtic Scots invaders from Ireland, situated in a strategic location between the Sound of Jura and Loch Fyne, 5 mi. (8 km.) N. of Lochgilphead. The twin peaks of Dunadd rock rise abruptly from the flat valley floor, once a marsh. On the lower peak, 160 ft. above the valley, the Scots established their capital of Dalriada amidst hostile Picts about 500 AD. Here was the birthplace of the modern Scottish nation, since the two, Scots and Picts, were finally united under a king of Dalriada in 843 AD.

The fort was excavated in 1904 and 1929 and among the finds were Gallic

The dramatic rock of Dunadd near the western coast in Argyll. The rock in a sense became the birthplace of modern Scotland, for it was the capital of Dalriada, founded by the invading Celtic Scotti, from nearby Ireland. And it was a later king of Dalriada, Kenneth MacAlpin, who united the Picts and Scots in 843 AD to inaugurate the Scottish nation. (Courtesy of Historic Buildings and Monuments, Scottish Development Dept.)

sherds showing extensive trade between the Scots and the continent. A tiny citadel near the top of the peak, only 40 ft. by 100 ft., was protected by a heavy, 12-ft.-thick drystone wall. It is possible that the citadel began as an Iron Age hill fort. Below this wall lesser walls, undoubtedly built by the Scots, encircle two more enclosures on descending terraces. Inside the fort traces of internal walling, platforms and terraces may indicate the sites of timber halls. On a rocky ridge near the summit a flight of steps in the rock leads to the top, and beside the steps, on a large flat rock, are the famous carvings—a Pict-style boar, an unreadable ogham inscription, a shallow basin and a single footprint, carved. The latter can be associated with the inaugural ceremonies of the kings of Dalriada (see also *Clickhimin*). The boar may be Scottish, carved under Pictish inspiration, or perhaps carved by King Fergus of the Picts, who captured Dunadd in 736 AD. See also *Kilmartin* for other sites in the neighborhood.

DUNAGOIL
(Bute/Strathclyde)

At the bottom of Bute Island, overlooking Bute Bay 2 mi. (3.25 km.) S. of Kingarth, is the Iron Age fort of Dunagoil, investigated in the late 19th or early 20th cent. Sited on a narrow ridge close to the sea, its heavily vitrified wall (the timbers burnt out) encloses an area of some 75 ft. by 300 ft. The finds indicate occupation in the late cents. BC, but the fort itself may date to the 6th or 7th cent. BC. Just to the N., also on the sea, is Little Dunagoil fort, investigated in the 1960s, with the foundations of two Viking (Norse) longhouses near its ramparts. Inland across the road St. Blane's church apparently covers an early Christian monastic site of some importance, for a number of sculptured stones and cross slabs have been found there, some still on the site. Near Kingarth is a stone circle and some standing stones.

DUN AN RUIGH RUAIDH
(Ross and Cromarty/
Highland)

See *Dun Lagaidh*.

DUN ARDTRECK
(Inner Hebrides, Skye)

See *Skye*.

DUN BEAG
(Inner Hebrides, Skye)

See *Skye*.

DUNBEATH BROCH
(Caithness/Highland)

See *Ousedale Broch*.

DUN BORERAIG
(Inner Hebrides, Skye)

See *Skye*.

DUN CARLOWAY
(Outer Hebrides, Lewis)

A broch, despite its name, about 6 mi. (10 km.) NW of *Callinish*, 15 mi (24 km.) W. of Stornoway. It stands, impressively, almost 30 ft. high in parts, on a rocky ridge overlooking Loch Roag inlet on the W. coast. The double wall with internal galleries, the low NW entrance with its massive outer lintel intact, the guardroom and inner court, 25 ft. across, are well exhibited. Four doors open off the court to cells and galleries and the stairway inside the double wall, around which runs a ledge that supported an upper wooden gallery. The broch is almost identical with one at *Dun Dornadilla* (below) far to the E. in northern Scotland. Sell also *Broch of Mousa*.

DUNCHRAIGAIG CAIRN
(Argyll/Strathclyde)

See *Kilmartin*.

DUN DORNADILLA
(Sutherland/Highland)

Another ruined broch, its outer wall still standing over 20 ft. high, 28 mi. (44 km.) SE of Durness, down the eastern side of Loch Hope on a very minor road running S. from the main coastal road. Of the brochs in Sutherland and Caithness this is the best preserved, though the inner wall has fallen and the interior is full of rubble. Noteworthy is the massive triangular lintel over the entrance passage. The whole resembles *Dun Carloway* on Lewis (above).

DUN FALLANDY STONE
(Perthshire/Tayside)

Fine Pictish Class II carved stone just outside the churchyard, 1.5 mi. (2.3 km.) S. of Pitlochry. On the front is a cross, ornamented with bosses and interlace, as well as various beasts and two angels. The back shows enthroned men, a horseman and various Pictish symbols.

DUN FIADHAIRT
(Inner Hebrides, Skye)

See *Skye*.

DUN FLODIGARRY BROCH
(Inner Hebrides, Skye)

See *Skye*.

DUN GRUGAIG
(Inner Hebrides, Skye)

See *Skye*.

DUN GRUGAIG
(Invernessshire/
Highland)

Interesting fort on the W. coast near *Skye*, 3.5 mi. (5.6 km.) SE of Glenelg at the southeastern end of Glen Beag. This D-shaped, galleried dun or semi-broch stands on a cliff over the ravine. Its wall, 14 ft. thick, still rises 8 ft. high on the uphill side and contains, like a broch, an internal gallery, a ledge around the inner wall, door checks and bar hole in the entrance. In fact, such galleried duns or forts are considered the immediate ancestors of the better-built, better-designed Scottish brochs. (See *Broch of Mousa*.)

Farther down the glen toward Glenelg Bay stand two of the best-preserved brochs in Scotland, short of Mousa in the Shetlands. Dun Telve, 1.5 mi. (2.6 km.) SE of Glenelg, still stands almost 34 ft. high on one side. Its sturdy wall, almost 14 ft. thick at the base, once enclosed a courtyard 32 ft. across. Galleries, stairs and rooms were contained within the walls, on which two ledges appear, one to support a floor, the other a roof. A quarter-mile up the glen the walls of Dun Troddan rise 25 ft. high, with a ledge on the wall to support a floor or gallery. Excavations in 1920 exposed a ring of postholes on the floor of the interior, presumably to support the floor or gallery.

DUN HALLIN BROCH
(Inner Hebrides, Skye)

See *Skye*.

DUN LAGAIDH
(Ross and Cromarty/
Highland)

Three-phase fortified site covering almost 2,000 years, on the southern shore of the long inlet called Loch Broom in Wester Ross, 4 mi (6.5 km.) SE of Ullapool. The fort, excavated in 1967–68, stands in a strategic location just N. of Loggie on a rocky ridge over the narrowest part of Loch Broom. Originally there was an Iron Age fort here, its massive wall, vitrified by fire, still visible at the W. end, and its outlying wall, now mere mounds, off the E. end. It was built between the 8th and 6th cents. BC and was abandoned early. Much later an Iron Age chieftain built a massive round dun, with solid walls except for an internal stair, over the ruins of the eastern end of the old fort and its narrow entrance. The dun's entrance faced E., with door checks and a guard chamber. Much later again the dun was somewhat rebuilt in the 13th cent. into a castle with flanking defensive walls on the W. side.

Just S. of Loggie is another dun on a rocky bluff, Dun an Ruigh Ruaidh, excavated in 1968. This proved to be a semi-broch (see *Dun Grugaig*) of the 3rd or 2nd cent. BC, one of the predecessors of true brochs, with a doubled wall around a flattened circle except on the cliff side. Inside the wall are the stairs, a mural chamber and an upper gallery. A ledge runs around the inner wall-face, with postholes underneath at ground level to support a floor. The dun, later used as a dwelling, eventually collapsed in part.

DUN MOR VAUL
(Inner Hebrides, Tiree)

A broch on a rocky knoll overlooking the sea on the island's NE coast, about 4 mi. (6.5 km.) across the island from Scarinish. It was a typical Hebridean broch with a ground-level gallery within the walls, three doors—one leading to the stairway—opening into it from the court, entrance passage with guard chamber, fragments of an upper gallery, and an inner ledge above ground level. In addition the knoll was encircled by a wall while another wall defended the landward access.

The excavation of Dun Mor Vaul in 1962–64 was notable, for the interior of most brochs had been torn up in crude earlier excavations, destroying much information. Here careful excavation of this untouched site identified many occupation levels and made important finds such as carbonized barley and the remains of sheep, cattle and seals, suggesting the economy of the broch dwellers. The discovery of a large central hearth confirmed continuous, rather than occasional, occupation of the broch. Moreover, under it the first pre-broch settlement ever found, radiocarbon-dated about 600–300 BC, was uncovered. The broch was built on top of it, probably in the 1st cent. BC, apparently by an intrusive ruling group perhaps coming, as their pottery suggested, from southern England. The broch lasted until the early cents. AD when it was partly demolished and turned into a farmstead, then later abandoned. See also *Broch of Mousa; Leckie; Skye.*

DUN RINGILL
(Inner Hebrides, Skye)

See *Skye.*

DUN SKEIG FORTS
(Argyll/Strathclyde)

Fortified site on the upper Kintyre peninsula, overlooking the entrance to West Loch Tarbert, just NW of Clachan. Here is a large hill fort, its walls almost all robbed to provide stone for later duns (fortified homesteads) built on the same site. Traces of the original wall are still visible at the N. end. The first of these duns, a large oval, was built at the S. end of the fort. It had been burned out, its walls vitrified; moreover its stones had been robbed in turn to build the final dun, a very small one at the N. end, quite well preserved. Its entrance with door checks and bar hole was at the E. side.

DUN TELVE
(Invernessshire/ Highland)

See *Dun Grugaig.*

DUN TRODDAN
(Invernessshire/
Highland)

See *Dun Grugaig.*

DWARFIE STANE
(Orkneys, Hoy)

The only rock-cut Neolithic chambered tomb in Britain, 3 mi. (4.75 km.) S. of Moness Pier, the visit mostly by foot. This curiosity, in state care, has been carved out of a huge block of red sandstone on the slopes of Ward Hill, fallen from the cliffs above. A narrow passage, $7\frac{1}{2}$ ft. long, leads to a pair of chambers about 5 ft. by 3 ft., on either side at the end, both with sills, and at the end of one a curious stone "pillow." Entrance into the tomb was always difficult, for the living or the dead, since both passage and chambers are less than 3 ft. high! A blocking stone, shaped to fit the entrance, lies just outside it.

DYCE
(Aberdeenshire/
Grampian)

A Recumbent Stone Circle here overlooks Aberdeen airport in a grove on the E. side. (For circles of this type, see *Berrybrae*; *Loanhead of Daviot*.) Just NW of Dyce village there are two Pictish symbol stones in the ruins of St. Fergus church. One is a class I (earlier type) incised with an elephant and other symbols. The other, Class II, sculptured on only one face, displays an ornamented Celtic cross surrounded by a variety of symbols.

EAST BENNAN CAIRN
(Inner Hebrides, Arran)

See *Machrie Moor.*

EASTER AQUHORTHIES
(Aberdeenshire/
Grampian)

See *Loanhead of Daviot.*

EDINBURGH
(Midlothian/Lothian)

Capital of Scotland, famous center of Scottish culture and political life. Finds from many of the sites described here can be found in Scotland's "British Museum," The National Museum of Antiquities, Queen Street. Huntly House, the museum of local and Edinburgh history, displays other prehistoric and Roman finds from nearby sites, for instance, Cramond to the E. of the *Antonine Wall.*

EDINSHALL
(Berwickshire/Borders)

Iron Age hill fort, broch and settlement, in state care, 5.5 mi. (9 km.) N. of Duns and 2 mi. (3.25 km.) NW of Preston. The oval hill fort with double ramparts, each with external ditch, and an entrance to the W., encloses an area of about 240 ft. by 440 ft. It was built, not on the crown of a hill as was usual, but on the slopes of Cockburn Law. The fort must date from pre-Roman times. Then in the 1st or early 2nd cents. AD an unusually large broch (rare in these parts; see also *Torwoodlee Broch*) was built inside the eastern half of the fort. Excavated, its walls still stand about 5 ft. high, displaying the usual entrance with door checks and two guard chambers, three mural cells and the remains of a stairway in one of them (see also *Broch of Mousa*). Finally, an undefended settlement grew up in the western end of the old fort, perhaps in the late 2nd-cent. (Pax Romana) period. Its round hut circles can still be seen.

EILACH-AN-NAOIMH
(Argyll/Strathclyde)

Early Christian monastery site on the southernmost of the Garvellach Islands in the mouth of the Firth of Lorne, N. of Jura. Access only by boat. In this remote spot the three roughly-built beehive huts of stone, a plain rectangular drystone chapel and a grave enclosure, all belonging to a monastery with close parallels in Ireland, are remarkably well preserved, dating from the early days of the Celtic church in Scotland. The circular grave enclosure is traditionally that of the mother of St. Columba, who it is said often visited here. At one end of the grave is a slab incised with a cross of 7th-cent. type.

EILDON HILL NORTH
(Roxburghshire/Borders)

The largest Iron Age hill fort in Scotland, 1 mi. (1.6 km.) SE of Melrose, sited in a strategic area of many crossroads in which its successor, the Roman fort of *Newstead*, was also built. Capital of the Selgovae until the Romans drove them out in 79 AD, the oppidum at its largest covered almost 40 acres on this high hill, 1,327 ft. up, the whole protected by a triple rampart. It is estimated that some 2,300 people lived here. The fortress had grown from two earlier forts, the first encircling just the summit, the next taking in more land from the north slopes. Traces of some 500 crude round huts have been found, and there were perhaps more. A small circular earthwork W. of the summit marks the site of a later Roman signal station. Little else can be seen here today except the indistinct traces of the ramparts and huts. See also *Traprain Law*.

ELGIN
(Moray/Grampian)

The local museum here is of more than usual interest, containing among other holdings fine archaeological collections, notably from the Bronze Age. A few of the Pictish bull slabs from *Burghead* are also here.

ELGINHAUGH ROMAN
FORT
(Midlothian/Lothian)

In one of Scotland's largest excavations, a complete though small Roman fort of the time of Agricola (about 80 AD) was thoroughly investigated in 1986–1987 in advance of redevelopment of the site; it is one of the few Roman forts to have revealed its entire plan. The fort, just N. of Dalkeith near Edinburgh, was sited at the junction of two Roman roads and was first spotted in 1979 through aerial reconnaissance. Most of the plan of the three-acre fort, probably an auxiliary fort housing up to 800 men, was revealed in the excavation; it followed the conventional pattern, though the internal buildings were crammed into the limited space. As usual with the earlier forts in Roman Britain its ramparts were of turf, with ditches outside them, and the gates, towers and buildings of timber. The buildings included the *principia* or headquarters building, possibly with two stories, the *praetorium* or commandant's house, raised granaries, and eight long barrack blocks. The only stone-built structure was probably a workshop, built up against the ramparts as were a series of stone ovens. The fort was occupied for only about 10 years, then was deliberately demolished, as was Agricola's legionary fortress of *Inchtuthil*. The whole excavation has been meticulously recorded and much environmental information preserved in advance of redevelopment. From the air a ditched annex and a possible bath suite had been observed, but lack of funds has precluded their excavation.

FAN KNOWE
(Orkneys, Mainland)

Interesting communal cooking place, in the center of the island, about .75 mi. (1 km.) SE of Dounby. It is typical of many such sites in the Orkneys, Shetlands and Ireland. Though most are undated, evidence from Ireland indicates that they were used in late prehistoric and Early Christian times. The sites are marked by mounds of heat-cracked stones—thrown into pools of water to heat them for boiling food, then discarded—as well as occasional stone basins for the water, and food debris.

FARR STONE
(Sutherland/Highland)

Fine example of an Early Christian cross, still in its original churchyard just E. of Bettyhill in northeastern Sutherland, 22 mi. (35 km.) W. of Thurso. The Celtic cross, probably dated about 850 AD, stands 7 ft. tall and has no Pictish symbols nor even figures, except for two long-necked birds on the base. Even these are intertwined with the elaborate interlace ornament all over the one carved side of the slab. At its center is a typical Celtic wheel cross.

FINAVON
(Angus/Tayside)

Iron Age hill fort, 4 mi. (6.5 km.) NE of Forfar and less than 2 mi. (3.25 km.) S. of Finavon on the road to *Aberlemno*. The tumbled remains of the heavy wall around the top of the hill still stand about 6 ft. high in places. There seems to have been an outlying hornwork at the E. end. The fort was burned out in antiquity, destroying the timber wall reinforcement and vitrifying the stone work. Excavation in 1933–35 found hearths, traces of wooden huts and a rock-cut dry well to the E. Another trench dug behind the wall in 1966 discovered the remains of timber buildings up against the wall. Radiocarbon-dated, these showed that this example of a vitrified fort was built surprisingly early, in the 8th to 6th cents. BC. See also *Castle Law*.

FORRES
(Morayshire/Grampian)

See *Sueno's Stone*.

FOWLIS WESTER
(Perthshire/Tayside)

Two Pictish symbol stones, both Class II, dating probably from the mid or late 9th cent. AD. The first, much weathered, stands in the village square, about 4 mi. E. of Crieff. Of red sandstone and over 12 ft. high, its cross—uniquely—has projecting arms. On the back a crowded scene of symbols, horsemen, soldiers and animals is almost obliterated. Much finer is a slab inside the village kirk, carved on one side only with a wheel cross and interlace and spiral patterns, as well as mythical animals and a number of seated and standing figures, presumably priests.

GARYNAHINE
(Outer Hebrides/Lewis)

See *Callinish*.

GIRDLE STANES
(Dumfriesshire/Dumfries and Galloway)

Two minor stone rings of the Late Neolithic, the Girdle Stanes on the White Esk River and the Loupin' Stanes, close to the first circle, both on private land 11 mi. (17.75 km.) NE of Lockerbie. The Girdle Stanes, a large henge-like circle, must have had up to 40 stones originally, though the river in a change of course has destroyed the western half. Two stones, standing outside the circle to the E., form an entranceway. Two other fallen stones lie on a ridge not far off and may be remnants of an avenue that led N. for .3 mi. (.5 km.) to the Loupin' Stanes, a very different kind of ring and probably later. It is a small flattened circle of 10 very low stones on an artificial platform, with two taller stones at the SW.

GLASGOW
(Lanarkshire/ Strathclyde)

Among the other museums here the Glasgow Art Gallery and Museum has good collections in the Mesolithic, Neolithic, Bronze Age and Iron Age periods. The University of Glasgow's famed Hunterian Museum, founded in 1807, has a notable Roman collection from the *Antonine Wall* and other sites. The 19th-cent. Govan church, W. of central Glasgow and S. of the Clyde, has a remarkable collection of Early Christian carved stones of the 10th and 11th cents. AD, both in the church and outside in the graveyard.

GLEBE CAIRN
(Argyllshire/Strathclyde)

See *Kilmartin*.

GLENELG BROCHS
(Invernessshire/
Highland)

See *Dun Grugaig*.

**GLENVOIDEAN
CHAMBERED TOMB**
(Inner Hebrides, Bute)

One of a number of the Clyde group of chambered tombs on Bute. Glenvoidean is on the island's NW coast, reachable only by a farm road up the W. coast. Excavations from 1963 to 1971 showed that it had gone through a number of structural phases, an early one radiocarbon-dated as far back as about 3700 BC. Apparently three separate early cairns were later joined into the single trapezoidal cairn with a flat facade.

GOVAN CHURCH
(Lanarkshire/
Strathclyde)

See *Glasgow*.

GRAIN EARTH HOUSE,
or Grainbank
(Orkneys, Mainland)

See *Rennibister*.

**GREY CAIRNS OF
CAMSTER**
(Caithness/Highland)

See *Camster*.

GURNESS, BROCH OF

See *Broch of Gurness*.

HILL O' MANY STANES
(Caithness/Highland)

See *Camster*.

HOLM OF PAPA WESTRAY
(Orkneys)

Tiny uninhabited island just off Papa Westray Island to the E., with two tombs. The southern tomb, in state care and protected by a concrete roof, is of the *Maes Howe* type, though very late in the sequence. This immense tomb, opened in 1849, is 104 ft. overall with a central chamber 67 ft. long and 9 ft. high. The chamber is divided into three stalls by substantial walls with portals, and 12 small side chambers with corbelled roofs open off the main chamber. The entrance passage opened into the E. side of the chamber, but access is now by ladder from a manhole in the concrete roof. The walls of the chamber are decorated with some crude designs—zigzags, circles and rectangles—of a type very rare in Scotland though abundant in Ireland. Excavations around the tomb have uncovered house foundations of the *Skara Brae* type, dated about 2000 BC. The northern tomb on the island is much smaller and quite ruinous.

HOWNAM RINGS
(Roxburghshire/Borders)

Hill fort, excavated in 1948, with an interesting and classic sequence of occupations, 8.5 mi. (14 km.) E. of Jedburgh and just E. of Hownam village. Another hill fort, *Woden Law*, is 4 mi. (6.5 km.) S. The fort is at the steep northern end of a plateau. Its first defense was a double palisade, built perhaps as early as the Late Bronze Age (7th or 6th cent. BC). This was replaced by a heavy stone wall circling the hill; then, presumably in the period of the Roman advance northward (43–80 AD), a multivallate defense was built to provide defense in depth, consisting of up to four ramparts and ditches. The stones of the earlier wall were used to build the inner rampart; this and the second still stand about 4 ft. high. The outer ramparts are scarcely discernible today. This system was soon abandoned and, probably during the Pax Romana period, the site became an open settlement with many hut circles visible. Traces to the E. of a rectangular homestead may be post-Roman. Down the hill to the W. is a row of about 16 low stones running E. to W. with traces of other rows. These megalithic alignments may have had astronomical significance.

INCHTUTHIL
(Perthshire/Tayside)

The scant remains of Agricola's great legionary fortress built for his abortive conquest of Scotland in 84–85 AD; 6.5 mi. (10.5 km.) SW of Blairgowrie and 4 mi. (6.5 km.) W. of Meikleour. Aerial surveys and thorough excavation from 1952 to 1965 by Sir Ian Richmond and Dr. St. Joseph have determined the entire layout of the fortress, though little is left to see today. Nevertheless the site is one to stir the imagination. The fort was begun in 83 or 84 while Agricola, having subdued the western and southern tribes, prepared to march with some 8,000 men and naval support against a northern tribal coalition of perhaps 30,000 under Calgacus, the first identifiable name in Scottish history. According to Tacitus, Calgacus addressed his troops in these memorable words: "Here at the world's end . . . we have lived unmolested to this day . . . Now the uttermost parts of Britain lie exposed . . . There are no other tribes to come; nothing but sea and cliffs and these more deadly Romans."

At the battle of Mons Graupius in 84, probably somewhere in Aberdeenshire, the natives were utterly routed. Scotland lay at the mercy of Agricola, who sent his fleet N. around the top of Britain, even to the Orkneys. Unfortunately Agricola was abruptly recalled in 85 because of trouble on the Danube, and his conquest was annulled. In the Roman withdrawal to the line that became the *Antonine Wall*, Inchtuthil, not yet completed, was systematically dismantled in 85–86, leaving nothing for the natives to pilfer. Unused pottery and glassware was broken and pounded into a gutter, drains were blocked, stone walls dismantled and timbers carted away. The excavators found a hoard of 875,000 nails of all sizes, weighing nearly 12 tons, buried in a pit under the workshop (samples of the nails can be seen in Edinburgh's National Museum).

Inchtuthil lies on a plateau on the N. side of the Tay River near its conjunction with the Isla. The remains of a temporary camp, used during the construction of the fortress, have been traced W. of the fort, later crossed by a defensive outer ditch; and a senior officers' camp S. of the fort, occupied by the constructors and possibly by Agricola himself. The fortress covered 53 acres, protected by a rampart faced with stone. Within the fort the remains of timber buildings were uncovered—four timber gateways, 64 barracks buildings, colonnaded streets with storerooms behind, four senior officers' houses, six granaries, a huge hospital, a drill hall, a workshop and the headquarters building. The commander's house had not yet been built. Of all this, today on private land, only the outer ditch on the E. side and the mounds of the rampart on the S. are visible. A visible enclosure in a wood to the E., called the Redoubt, may have been a stores compound. To the NE of this complex the remains of a long boundary line earthwork called the Cleaven Dyke, now difficult to find, may have delimited the area under military control.

IONA ISLAND
(Inner Hebrides/
Strathclyde)

Famous tiny island off the SW tip of the island of Mull, reachable by ferry and steamer. Here St. Columba landed from Ireland with 12 companions in 563 AD to found a monastery and begin the conversion of Scotland. Of the original monastery only traces remain. The vallum, or bank and ditch surrounding its precinct, can distinctly be seen paralleling the W. side of the modern road from the pier. Excavations at the site in 1979 revealed traces of wooden buildings and found exceptionally well-preserved objects of wood and leather, including leather shoes of the type shown in the *Book of Kells*, the illuminated gospel manuscript that may have been written here before the 9th-cent. Viking raids forced the community to return to Ireland. The excavations also suggest that the original monastery may lie under the cemetery called Reilig Odhrain, or Tombs of the Kings, SW of the present abbey church, rather than under the church itself.

In this cemetery, lying around the Romanesque St. Oran's Chapel, the kings of the Dark Ages and later were reputedly buried (including Macbeth!). Here and within the precinct were once many high crosses, of which three survive, now standing just outside the abbey church. They date from the period of the *Book of Kells*. The sculpture on St. John's cross (a replica, the original fragments are in the site museum in the Nunnery) is remarkably close to the ornamentation of that masterpiece, and both cross and book attest to the artistry of the early monks. St. Martin's cross is magnificently complete, standing over 15 ft. high and richly decorated in Celto-Northumbrian style. Of St. Matthew's cross only the lower part survives. Finally, on a hillock called Tor Abb just W. of the abbey church are the reputed remains of St. Columba's cell. It contained a rock-cut bed and stone supports for a seat.

ISBISTER
(Orkneys, South
Ronaldsay)

Neolithic chambered tomb on the SE tip of the island, discovered by the local owner of the land in 1958 and excavated by him, with the help of experts, thereafter. The tomb held a long central chamber divided into a number of stalls, three small chambers opening off it, and the entrance passage at right angles to it. What set this tomb apart from other Orkney "stalled cairns," however, was the discovery of some 16,000 bones stuffed into it—human and animal. There were human skulls and piles of bones on the sides of the main chamber and in the side chambers, but never a complete skeleton. In the center were bird, fish and animal bones. Altogether at least 342 individual people were represented—their bodies allowed to decompose outside, their jumbled bones then moved inside. The tomb was in use for some 800 years, from about 3150 BC to 2400 BC, and from these bones much valuable information was obtained about these ancient people whose "temple" and burial place this monument had been—their diseases, their average height (surprisingly tall). The prevalence of the bones and talons of the white-tailed sea eagle has suggested that this bird was the totem of the sub-tribe who built the tomb. The fish and meat bones were apparently remnants of offerings. The bones are now in the Tankerness House Museum, Kirkwall. See also *Midhowe*.

**JARLSHOF
(Shetlands, Mainland)**

Remarkable, many-layered site revealing over 3,000 years of habitation, period by period, at the very southern tip of Mainland Island, between the airport and Sumburgh Head. The 3-acre site lies on the E. side of the shallow bay between the two peninsulas at the bottom of the island that form a fine harbor. Behind it lay rich arable and grazing land. The massive ruins were first exposed after a great storm in 1897 and were excavated by the famous V. Gordon Childe in the 1930s, then by J. R. C. Hamilton in 1949–52. The site is now in state care, with a small museum that is useful in disentangling this complex site, which ranges from the Late Neolithic or Bronze Age to the Iron Age, the Viking and medieval periods and ends with the ruins of a 17th-cent. Scottish laird's house (named "Jarlshof" by Sir William Scott in one of his novels).

The earliest houses here are a cluster of round stone-built huts with rough piers inside to hold a roof. The stone tools found with the houses place them in the Neolithic or Early Bronze Age period, but under the houses earlier middens were detected, bringing the site back to perhaps 1800 BC or earlier. "Dwelling 3" of the cluster, with three rooms opening off a court, is the best preserved and can now be viewed from a wooden platform. By its entrance on the S. a large grain-grinding quern can be seen where it was found. Dwelling 2 apparently housed a prehistoric cow, once tethered to a visible whalebone ring on the wall, the floor hollowed to catch the liquid manure. House 3 was used in the late 8th or 7th cent. BC by a bronze smith whose molds were found in the floor. There were molds for axes, swords, a sunflower pin. Still later, perhaps in the 5th cent. BC, Iron Age people built rather more substantial houses, again with roof piers, over the earlier ones. Today one can look down into the remains of House 4 of the earlier village under the floor of the Iron Age house built over it.

This settlement was deserted and covered in windblown sand when new people arrived early in the 1st cent. AD to build themselves a round-towered broch (see *Broch of Mousa*) with an unusual walled yard attached to it. Part of the broch and half of the yard have been washed into the sea, and a seawall now protects the remainder. But one can still see part of a mural cell and the guardhouse of the broch inside its wall, and a well or water tank in the courtyard. After about 200 AD when the broch had fallen out of use, substantial wheelhouses—compact drystone round houses with tall piers radiating inward to make separate paved bays around a court—were built inside it and its walled yard. The concept grew in stages: first a round house without piers was built in the yard; free-standing piers were later added, making it an aisled wheelhouse. Part of this was later incorporated into a true wheelhouse, then another was built, a third inside the old broch and a fourth to the SE. See also *Barpa Langass*; *Kilphedir*.

The Norse, or Viking, settlement along the N. side of the site, by far the most complete in Britain, grew eventually (from the 9th to the 13th cents.) to eight bow-shaped longhouses or farmsteads with their outbuildings, leaving on the site a complex of building and rebuilding that is difficult to understand today. The earliest farmstead, No. 1, dated to the early 9th cent., was centered on a long hall with kitchen and outlying bathhouse, smithy and other buildings. Finds in the house and a scratched picture of a ship on its walls suggest the builders came directly from a certain locality in far northern Norway. In the 13th cent. a medieval farmstead, now partly preserved, was built just E. of Norse house No. 1 and on top of the Late Bronze Age village. The farm was in use for the next 300 years. And so we come to the shell of the laird's house, built in 1604–05, that dominates the site today. One corner of it lay over part of the broch. Finds from Jarlshof are in the Shetland Museum in Lerwick.

KEILLS CROSS
(Argyllshire/Strathclyde)

See *Kilmartin.*

KILDALTON CROSS
(Inner Hebrides, Islay)

Superb high cross of the 8th or 9th cent. AD in a graveyard next to a ruined chapel. It can be found a few mi. NE of Ardbeg village on the southern coast of Islay, 7 mi. (11.25 km.) NE of the ferry at Port Ellen. There are full-scale replicas of the cross in Edinburgh's National Museum and Glasgow's Art Gallery and Museum for those who can't reach Islay. The wheeled cross is complete and stands 9 ft. high, with biblical scenes on its front face, Northumbrian-style interlace decoration around the base and a lower panel of Celtic curves and spirals. The back is similar, with beasts and serpents. The cross is thus an interesting mixture of Anglian and Celtic (Irish) influences. Another cross at Kilnave in northwestern Islay, in an old burying ground on the western shore of Loch Guinart, is earlier (about 750 AD) and much weathered. Its sculpture, on one face, is purely Celtic in character. See also *Abercorn Cross; Iona; Ruthwell Cross.*

KILDONAN DUN
(Argyll/Strathclyde)

Iron Age fort, 6.5 mi. (10.5 km.) NE of Campbeltown near the bottom of Kintyre peninsula, overlooking Kilbrannan Sound; excavated in 1936–38 and somewhat restored. Triangular in shape, with walls 12 ft. thick and doubled, there is a double stairway inside the two walls, presumably leading up to a parapet on a low wall-head; a gallery in the wall S. of the wide entranceway (with door checks and bar hole); and another cell opposite it—all suggesting aspects of the later brochs (see *Broch of Mousa*). The fort is dated between 100 BC and 200 AD. The finds are in the Campbeltown museum.

KILMARTIN
(Argyll/Strathclyde)

One of Scotland's richest archaeological areas, ranging from the Neolithic into the Early Christian, can be found near this village, chiefly in the Kilmartin valley from Lochgilphead to Kilmartin. From ancient times the region was crossed by travelers moving N. or S. along the indented coastline or E. from Ireland, bringing settlers, trade and new ideas into this fertile region. The sites include, for instance, the Dark Ages fortress of *Dunadd*, already discussed, or the Keills Early Christian cross outside a medieval chapel 16 mi. (26 km.) SW of Lochgilphead at the end of a remote peninsula. The blue slate cross here is remarkably similar to the Kilnave cross on Islay to the SW (see *Kildalton Cross*).

The principal sites on the road to Kilmartin begin with the two areas of exposed rock on a hillside, 2 mi. (3.25 km.) N. of Lochgilphead and just outside Achnabreck village. They are covered with cup and ring marks and spirals. More cup and ring marks, those mysterious prehistoric symbols, are to be found at Cairnbaan, 2.5 mi. (4 km.) to the NW. Another Bronze Age inscribed rock is off the main road N. at Kilmichael Glassary, 4 mi. (6.5 km.) N. of Lochgilphead. The main road to Kilmartin now leads past *Dunadd* fort to the Ballymeanoch standing stones, about 1.5 mi. (2.3 km.) S. of Kilmartin, a strange alignment of six stones, some bearing cup and ring marks. Just SW of the stones are the weathered bank and ditch, with two entrances, of a very ancient henge circle, about 130 ft. across. Two cists in the interior, one with a Beaker burial, show that it was in use for many years. Farther N. is the large, circular Bronze Age cairn of

Dunchraigaig, with a chambered tomb beside it bearing a huge capstone 13 ft. long.

Moving on toward Kilmartin we come upon the small, isolated stone circle of Temple Wood in a copse, 13 stones out of 20 still standing, its interior filled with cobbles and a cist enclosed in low slabs. Excavated in 1929 and from 1974, it has recently been restored. The northern stone of the circle is incised with two most unusual double spirals reminiscent of the designs on the *Boyne Valley* tombs in Ireland. Just SE of the circle is the Nether Largie x-shaped alignment of five much larger standing stones, the central stone 9½ ft. high and covered with cup and ring and cupmarks. Astronomical uses have been suggested for the circle and alignment together.

The most spectacular sight in the valley is the "linear cemetery" of Nether Largie, five cairns stretching for almost 3 mi. (4.75 km.) in a deliberate line from Kilmartin southwards, the only example in Scotland, though such lines are common in the *Stonehenge* region in England. The oldest is the fourth down, the Neolithic Nether Largie South, just across a lane from Temple Wood circle; the others are Early Bronze Age, attesting to the continuity of tradition, over a thousand years, in this region. This cairn is the focus of the group. Cleared out in 1864 and now somewhat restored, it is a gallery grave of the Neolithic Clyde group with a chamber 20 ft. long roofed by giant capstones and divided by sills into four segments.

S. of it at the end of the line is the dilapidated Ri Cruin cairn of piled-up stones with three cists; an end slab of one cist shows a number of carvings of bronze axe heads of Irish type. N. of Nether Largie South is Nether Largie Mid Cairn, a circular cairn covering two cists, excavated in 1929. Nether Largie North is a large round cairn, excavated in 1930, containing one large cist that can now be entered by a ladder. The underside of its capstone is ornamented—for the eyes of the dead alone—with axes again, and cupmarks. The most northerly, the Glebe Cairn, is again a round tomb, explored in 1864, with one cist covered by a massive capstone. It contained an inhumation burial with a food vessel.

In Kilmartin itself the parish church contains a fine collection of medieval and Early Christian carved stones, especially an early slate cross standing near the entrance path. Finally, about 6 mi. (10 km.) N. of Kilmartin, at Kintraw near the head of Loch Craignish, is a round kerbed cairn, excavated in 1959–60, covering one cist and with a standing stone, leaning over, close by it. Above the cairn was found a man-made viewing platform on the hillside from which, apparently, the midwinter solstice could be observed over the standing stone and a post that once stood on the cairn.

KILMICHAEL GLASSARY
(Argyll/Strathclyde)

See *Kilmartin*.

KILNAVE CROSS
(Inner Hebrides, Islay)

See *Kildalton Cross*.

KILPATRICK
(Inner Hebrides, Arran)

See *Machrie Moor*.

KILPHEDIR
(Outer Hebrides, South Uist)

Remains of a wheelhouse of the early cents. AD, near the southern end of the island, on the coast 2 mi. (3.25 km.) W. of the main road. Sunk into the dunes, it is 30 ft. across with a long entrance passage. Remnants of the internal radiating piers can be made out. See also *Barpa Langass; Jarlshof*.

KINTRAW
(Argyll/Strathclyde)

See *Kilmartin*.

KIRKMADRINE CROSSES
(Wigtownshire/Dumfries and Galloway)

Early Christian stones, 8 mi. (13 km.) S. of Stranraer, set into a glassed-in recess on the wall of Kirkmadrine church, 1.5 mi. (2.3 km.) SW of Sandhead. The three important stones here date from the earliest Celtic conversion of Scotland, just after the end of the Roman Empire. All three show crosses in a circle at the top, the circle converted into a chi-rho monogram. The oldest (5th cent. AD) includes a well-lettered Latin inscription: "Here lies the holy and chief priests, Ides, Vaventius and Mavrovius," suggesting that the site had once been an important center of the early Celtic church. The second stone appears to be late 5th cent. The third, inscribed from Revelation, "The beginning and the end," is dated around 600 AD. See also *Catstane; Iona; Whithorn*.

KIRKWALL
(Orkneys, Mainland)

Long-standing capital and principal town of the Orkneys. Aside from the handsome St. Magnus cathedral and the Bishop's palace, a charming 16th-cent. merchant's house, Tankerness House, has been restored and converted into a museum of Orkney life and history, with displays from the prehistoric until recent times.

KNAP OF HOWAR
(Orkneys, Papa Westray)

Remarkable find of a stone-built farmstead with two structures, dating from the Early Neolithic, the period of the fine chambered tombs of the Orkneys (see *Blackhammer; Knowe of Yarso; Midhowe Cairn; Taversoe Tuack*). These are undoubtedly the earliest known stone-built houses in Britain. They are well-preserved, having been protected by a blanket of sand like the somewhat later, Neolithic settlement of *Skara Brae* on Mainland Island. The houses, on the western shore of Papa Westray, W. of Holland House, were first excavated in the early 1930s and were thought to be Iron Age in date. However, new excavations in 1973 and 1975 found through radiocarbon-dating that they had been inhabited between 3500 and 3100 BC. The houses, their walls still standing around 7 ft. high, are set side by side and are roughly rectangular, with rounded ends, and are beautifully built of close-fitting drystone masonry. They are divided inside by upright slabs—like the "stalled cairns"—into two compartments for the larger house (No. 1) and three for the smaller, which seems to have been a working and storage area for the larger house. It was linked to No. 1 by a small passage through both walls and had cupboards in its walls. Both houses are entered through passages at the NW end, with door checks, and probably had timber-framed roofs covered with turf or slats. The farmers probably lived on seafood and raised stock. See also *Holm of Papa Westray; Rinyo*.

KNOWE OF YARSO
(Orkneys, Rousay)

One of the smaller passage tombs of the Orkney-Cromarty type, excavated in the 1930s and now in state care, about 2 mi. (3.25 km.) W. of Rousay pier. Rectangular, about 50 ft. long and 25 ft. wide, it was entered by a 13-ft.-long passage at the eastern end, and is divided into four stalls or compartments by

4-ft.-high slabs. The tomb may once have been two-storied. When it was excavated the dismembered bones of 20 adults and one adolescent were found in the interior, 15 of the skulls ranged side by side along the wall. There were also the bones of red deer, some sheep and a dog, and a number of fires had been burned in the tomb. Apparently it was in use for a long time, though built within the range of 3000 to 2500 BC, because while the bones were Neolithic the pottery was of Early Bronze (Beaker) date. See also *Blackhammer*; *Midhowe Cairn*; *Taversoe Tuack*; *Unstan*.

LAWS HILL FORT
(Angus/Tayside)

See *Ardestie Earth-House*.

LEARABLE HILL
(Sutherland/Highland)

Stone alignments, cairns and a stone circle mark a once-sacred area around Learable Hill, about 18 mi. (29 km.) up the Strath of Kildonan from Helmsdale on the coast, just beyond Kildonan Lodge. One can discern five parallel rows of stones and just N. two single rows; also just S. a single standing stone (incised with a later cross), then farther SE a fan-shaped alignment of stones. To the W. are the five remaining stones of a stone circle. Many cairns are to be seen on the hillside. From these scant remains one can only guess at the elaborate ritual activity that took place here so long ago.

LECCAMORE, DUN OF
(Inner Hebrides, Luing)

Typical Argyll dun on this small island, an oval fort or fortified homestead that is a kind of local variation on the brochs that were being built about the same time, the early cents. AD (see *Broch of Mousa*). The fort's 16-ft.-thick wall survives up to 10 ft. high; it has two entrances on opposite sides, one with bar hole and door checks, the other flanked by a guard chamber with corbelled roof giving access to a stairway within the wall. See also *Skye*.

LECKIE
(Stirlingshire/Central)

Broch and fort, about 8 mi. (13 km.) due W. of Sterling, S. off the main road, excavated 1974 on. This site, with others, suggests that the southern brochs at least were often built as a defense against the encroaching Romans; for this broch, on a promontory between two streams, was burned, probably by them, in the late 2nd cent. AD. Traces of the timber-built house of this well-to-do family that preceded their building of the broch have been found under the latter. They possessed many Roman imports and bronze jewelry, as the finds attest, and probably built the broch to protect what they had, only to have it burned by the Romans. Nevertheless, occupation continued on the site until perhaps the early 3rd cent. AD when the family started to build a promotory fort S. of the ruined broch. Then the establishment was again, and finally, destroyed. See also *Edinshall*; *Torwoodlee*.

LERWICK
(Shetlands, Mainland)

Capital of Mainland Island. The Shetland Museum here displays finds and models from all periods of the Shetlands' history and prehistory.

LITTLE DUNAGOIL FORT
(Bute/Strathclyde)

See *Dunagoil*.

LOANHEAD OF DAVIOT
(Aberdeenshire/
Grampian)

Fine example of a Recumbent Stone Circle, 5 mi. (8 km.) NW of Inverurie, in state care. These curious stone circles, a local development and akin also to the earlier *Clava Cairns* to the W., are found in large numbers, mostly in Aberdeenshire in the foothills of the Grampians, and their excavation has provided more information, sometimes quite baffling, on the ritual practices of the time than any other group of circles in Britain. The recumbent circles are impressively large, carefully planned and built on leveled land, and always with distant views. The ring of standing stones is graduated in height toward the SW where a huge supine "recumbent" stone, its top precisely leveled, lies between the two tall "flanker" stones. Inside the circle a ring cairn, the heart of the monument, encloses a central open circle where much burning has taken place and where "offerings," *not* burials, of cremated human bones are interred. Other offerings, often in pits, consist of deliberately broken pottery. There are cupmarks on some of the stones; and obviously astronomical alignments—in this case probably centered on the motions of the moon—are usual. However, these circles are not observatories but ritual centers, temples in which ancestor and fertility ceremonies probably took place with the aid of astronomical sightings. The recumbent monuments were built roughly between 2500 and 1800 BC.

Loanhead, excavated in 1934 and restored, is an early example. About 65 ft. across, it has nine standing stones in its circle and the recumbent, with five outlying stones. Little pits at the base of the circle stones contained offerings of broken pottery, and one stone in the circle was inscribed with five small cupmarks (representing the moon?). A low ring cairn, now hard to distinguish, surrounded the open center. Here, under fire-hardened earth, a thick layer of charcoal was found containing much human bone, including some 50 pieces of the skull bones of very small children (a human sacrifice?). Beaker pottery finds indicated that the circle was in use into the Early Bronze Age. Next to it was an oval-shaped, enclosed cremation cemetery of the succeeding Food Vessel people, containing the remains of some 35 urn burials.

Easter Aquhorthies, 5 mi. (8 km.) S. of Loanhead and 3 mi. (4.75 km.) W. of Inverurie, is another recumbent circle with nine stones in an almost exact circle. The recumbent on the S., with its tall flankers, stands slightly within the circle. The ring cairn here is well preserved. The site has not been excavated. Balquhain, again S. of Loanhead and 3 mi. (4.75 km.) NW of Inverurie, is on private land and is much ruined, with only three of the original 10 stones still standing. Most striking here is a tall quartz outlying stone, as well as a number of cupmarks on the circle stones—notably over 25 on the stone next to the W. flanker. See also *Berrybrae*; *Old Keig*; *Strichen*; *Tomnaverie*.

LOCHHILL
(Kircudbrightshire/
Dumfries and Galloway)

Very early Neolithic long cairn, 6 mi. (9.6 km.) S. of Dumfries near New Abbey W. of Solway Firth. Careful excavation, stone by stone over two years, indicated that the trapezoidal cairn covered a much earlier and elaborate timber predecessor. This was a mortuary chamber, long and narrow, lined on three sides by large granite boulders, with a plank floor. Two massive split timbers stood 6 ft. tall, or more, at either end, with two small ones in the middle. Possibly they supported a mortuary platform in the first version of the chamber, which was found to contain token deposits of human bones—offerings again. The chamber was faced by a curving facade of 16 timber uprights with a porch of four standing stones at the center. At a later stage the whole was deliberately burned, allowing for a radiocarbon date of about 4000 BC. Still later the cairn, with a small chamber, was constructed over the remains and a stone facade, smaller than the original, built farther out. Finally the chamber and facade were deliberately sealed in Neolithic times; Beaker sherds on the cairn, however, indicate that the site was still considered sacred into the Early Bronze Age.

LOCH ROAG STONE
  CIRCLE
(Outer Hebrides/Lewis)

See *Callinish*.

LOCH STEMSTER
(Caithness/Highland)

Or Achavanich Standing Stones; U-shaped setting of 36 tall, thin stones up to 6 ft. high (a few are now stumps), 12 mi. (19 km.) SW of Wick, beautifully sited near the shores of tiny Loch Stemster. The monument is probably Bronze Age in date, and could well have been an astronomical sighting place. There are the remains of a cist on the N. side of the site.

LOUDON WOOD CIRCLE
(Aberdeenshire/
Grampian)

See *Berrybrae*.

LOUPIN' STANES
(Dumfriesshire/Dumfries
and Galloway)

See *Girdle Stanes*.

LUSSA WOOD
  (Inner Hebrides, Jura)

Mesolithic site on a terrace above the Lussa River on the NE coast, near Ardlussa. Here is perhaps the earliest setting of stones in Scotland—three conjoined circles of stones, each about 5 ft. across, probably the interior of a Mesolithic tent site, radiocarbon-dated to the 6000s BC from charcoal found in the rings. Also found inside the rings were bones, red ochre and limpet shells and small flint tools left behind by these hunter-gatherer people. On Oronsay, a nearby island to the W., about six shell mounds, known since the 19th cent. and some huge, have yielded a variety of tools from a later phase of the Mesolithic (about 4500 BC)—tools of stone, bone and antler, including fish hooks, awls, mattocks and what were probably harpoon heads of bone.

MACHRIE MOOR
  (Inner Hebrides, Arran)

Or Tormore. Arran Island has proved to be unusually rich in Neolithic and Bronze Age sites. Preeminent is the complex of Bronze Age circles, cairns and standing stones on the W. coast at Machrie Moor, along the S. of Machrie Water, just inland from Tormore village. Obviously an important cult center for the region, it has been incompletely excavated and is not fully understood. Walking E., one of the most complete of the visible circles is encountered first. Moss Farm Road Circle has a cairn in its interior. Farther on, beyond a cist grave, is a double ring with an outer, egg-shaped circle and inner true circle, both of granite boulders, with a ruined, empty cist at the center. Nearby are the remains of four other circles, one still half-buried under the peat, another with only one tall sandstone slab remaining. It originally had nine and again was egg-shaped. Two cists in the center contained an urn and flints and a crouched burial. Another ring was attractively constructed of alternating granite blocks and sandstone slabs, but with no cist. The final circle has only three tall stones still standing. One of its cists contained flint flakes and a Food Vessel pot, suggesting that the cists within this circle may have been inserted later. All around the circles are isolated standing stones and an occasional cairn. The circles and stones suggest possible astronomical purposes and the use of rather sophisticated geometry in laying out the circles, especially the egg-shaped rings.

  At Tormore and at Kilpatrick, some 4 mi. (6.5 km.) to the S. along the coast, recent surveys have uncovered substantial, round Bronze Age houses associated with field systems—a heavy stone wall with an inner ring of posts to support a thatched roof. A mile or so N. of Tormore, at Auchagallon, there is another Bronze Age round cairn surrounded by a circle of 15 standing stones (these may actually have been the original kerb stones for the cairn). Moving to the S. and E. of the island one finds a series of Early Neolithic, Clyde group chambered cairns, notably the Torrylinn gallery grave just beyond Kilmory Water on the S. coast. Only the side walls of the 21-ft.-long chamber remain, divided into four compartments by slabs. The usual human skulls and bones, in separate groups, were found here in 1900. A similar ruined cairn, the Clachaig cairn, lies to the W. of it. Difficult of access is the best-preserved of these tombs, Cairn Ban, inland at the head of Kilmory Water. Less than 2 mi. (3 km.) E. of Torrylinn is East Bennan cairn, a trapeze-shaped tomb with a forecourt and a chamber divided into five compartments. Near the E. coast, inland beyond Lamlash, is the Monamore cairn with tall portal slabs and a compartmented chamber. A radiocarbon date from charcoal from the buried forecourt seems to bring it back as far as 4000 BC.

From Lamlash one can take a boat to Holy Island and the cave cell of St. Molaise, cleared out in 1908, with medieval runic inscriptions on the walls of this Early Christian site.

MAES HOWE
(Orkneys, Mainland)

The finest megalithic tomb in Britain. Its sophisticated architecture is superbly constructed of close-fitting, dressed sandstone slabs. It is about 9 mi. (14.5 km.) W. of Kirkwall, close to the Ring of Brodgar and the *Stenness Standing Stones*. The monument, now in state care, was perhaps the temple-tomb of a powerful Neolithic Orkneys family. Recently dated by radiocarbon method to about 2800–

The interior of Maes Howe, the magnificent Neolithic passage tomb on the Orkneys' Mainland island. The superb masonry of walls and passage is made of long sandstone slabs, dressed and laid without mortar. The chamber, 15 ft. square, has three burial niches for special people at the sides and the rear, entered by window-like openings. Note the divergence of the walls at the top, where they once continued into a high corbelled roof, and the heavy buttresses, each faced by a huge upright slab, which helped to hold up the roof. The great mound covering the tomb outside measures 110 ft. in diameter. (Courtesy of Historic Buildings and Monuments, Scottish Development Dept.)

2700 BC, it is the culmination of a local building tradition in the Orkneys, though it may owe something to such magnificent passage tombs as New Grange, in the *Boyne Valley* in Ireland, which is slightly earlier in date.

The great grassy mound of Maes Howe, 24 ft. high and 110 ft. across, lies N. of the main road and is surrounded at a distance by a wide ditch. The passage in the SW, over 26 ft. long, has an unusual door check near its entrance and toward the inner end is built of enormous slabs over 18 ft. long. It opens into the central chamber, 15 ft. square, with heavy buttresses at each corner to hold up the once corbelled roof, each buttress faced by an enormous upright slab. The walls still stand over 12 ft. high and show the beginning of the corbelling as they incline toward the center. The roof was destroyed by Viking treasure-seekers and crude 1861 excavations, and is now replaced by a modern concrete dome. Off the chamber three small cells, reached by raised, window-like openings on the N., E. and W., were probably used for favored burials A blocking stone lies on the floor outside each cell. Viking raiders seeking treasure in the 12th cent. broke into the tomb and left 24 enigmatic, runic inscriptions and some scatched drawings on the walls including a beautifully rendered dragon. For other Orkneys tombs of the Maes Howe group see *Cuween Hill*; *Holm of Papa Westray*; *Quanterness*; *Quoyness*.

MAIDEN STONE
(Aberdeenshire/
Grampian)

Beautiful Class II Pictish symbol stone, a red granite slab 10 ft. high, the best-known example in the whole region. In state care, it stands just W. of the village of Chapel of Garrioch, 6 mi. (9.6 km.) NW of Inverurie. The cross on its face, somewhat damaged, is surrounded by panels of sculpture, one probably depicting Jonah and the whale. There are spiral designs at the bottom, elaborate interlace and knotted patterns on the sides, and four panels of Pictish symbols on the back. See also *Meigle*.

MEIGLE
(Perthshire/Tayside)

Village museum in Meigle, 4 mi. (6.5 km.) NE of Coupar Angus, containing 34 interesting Pictish symbol stones and cross slabs. See also St. *Vigeans* for another village museum with a similar collection.

MEMSIE CAIRN
(Aberdeenshire/
Grampian)

Immense Bronze Age round cairn of loose stones, over 20 ft. high, just NE of the village, 3 mi. (4.75 km.) SW of Fraserburgh, in state care. The cairn offers a rare example of the outer coverings of Bronze Age tombs, since most have disappeared over the centuries, leaving the stones of the tomb exposed.

MID CLYTH STONES
(Caithness/Highland)

Or Hill o' Many Stanes. See *Camster*.

MID-GLENIRON CAIRNS
(Wigtownshire/Dumfries
and Galloway)

Two interesting chambered cairns, about 3 mi. (4.75 km.) N. of Glenluce on Luce Bay and a mile or two N. of Glenluce Abbey. A careful excavation in 1963–66 clearly showed for the first time the slow elaboration such cairns underwent over a long period of use—like a medieval cathedral. The *Cairnholy* cairns showed much the same progression. Mid-Gleniron I was a long cairn with three chambers inside it and a curved facade at the N. end. Excavation showed that the original tomb had been an oval cairn with a single chamber, now the rear chamber of the three. In time the two other cairns with chambers and the facade had been added to the first one during the Neolithic 4th and 3rd millennia BC, and the whole incorporated into the one long cairn, then finally blocked up. Later, in the Bronze Age, nine new burials were inserted into the chambers. Mid-Glen-iron II to the SE was also a long cairn with a similar history. See also *Camster*.

MIDHOWE BROCH AND CAIRN
(Orkneys, Rousay)

A fine example of a broch (see *Broch of Mousa*) and a large Neolithic stalled cairn, close together on the northwestern shore of the island, both in state care. The broch, very similar to the *Broch of Gurness* on Mainland Island, still stands about 14 ft. high on a promontory almost surrounded by water, and the neck of land leading out to it is defended by a massive wall with deep ditches on both sides—just possibly built earlier as a promontory fort. Excavated in 1930–33, the broch is 30 ft. across with walls 15 ft. thick at the base; in the walls are ground-level galleries. Access to one gallery is from one of the guard chambers flanking the well-preserved entrance passageway, with its door checks and bar hole. Access to the other gallery and intramural stairway is from an interior doorway 6 ft. up. The interior ledge around the wall, for an upper floor, can also be seen. A later settlement of houses built of huge flagstones (probably 2nd-3rd cents. AD) grew up between the broch and the defensive wall, and the broch itself was partitioned. Some of the houses are still visible.

The Midhowe chambered cairn, the largest known, belongs to the Orkney/Cromarty group of stalled cairns from a far earlier period (roughly 3000–2500 BC) that includes, on Rousay alone, *Blackhammer*, the *Knowe of Yarso* and *Taversoe Tuack* to the E. and *Unstan* on Mainland. This immense cairn, 106 ft. long and 42 ft. wide, contains a narrow central chamber 76 ft. long, with its entrance on the S. end, divided into 12 compartments on each side by tall slabs. The outer wall of the cairn is constructed of drystone masonry in a herringbone pattern. The whole can now be viewed from catwalks above the chamber and under an immense modern shed. Most of the compartments on the E. side have raised floors on which the bones of at least 25 people were found, including six adolescents and two very small children. Strangely, few bones were found in the W.-side compartments. Also uncovered in the tomb were numerous bones of oxen, sheep, voles, many birds and limpet shells. Some of these may have represented tribal totems (see also *Isbister*).

MIDMAR KIRK CIRCLE
(Aberdeenshire/ Grampian)

See *Cullerlie*.

MILTON LOCH
(Kircudbrightshire/ Dumfries and Galloway)

Example of a rather widespread type of prehistoric lake dwelling on an artificial island called a crannog, common in Ireland too. In Milton Loch, 8 mi. (13 km.) SW of Dumfries, one of the two known crannogs was excavated in 1953, revealing that the house and its surrounding "porch" were built on a platform of large logs, about 40 ft. wide, resting on thick mud so that the whole island "shook" when the excavators jumped on it. The platform was surfaced with split alder logs to make a floor. Around the platform numerous piles had been driven into the lake floor to provide additional support for the house walls and the "porch" all around it. A causeway on more piles, probably carrying a corduroy path, led to the shore. There may have been a small boat harbor on the opposite shore. At the center of the house was a hearth of clay on flat stones. The house may have had a central rectangular room with other rooms radiating from it. There were few finds, but these and radiocarbon dates from the platform suggest that the house may have been built as early as the 4th cent. BC and occupied into the early cents. AD.

MONAMORE CAIRN
(Inner Hebrides, Arran)

See *Machrie Moor*.

MONS GRAUPIUS
(Perthshire/Tayside)

See *Inchtuthil*.

MOSS FARM ROAD
CIRCLE
(Inner Hebrides, Arran)

See *Machrie Moor*.

MOTE OF MARK
(Kircudbrightshire/
Dumfries and Galloway)

Dark Ages fortress on a rocky hill overlooking Rough Firth, 7 mi. (11.25 km.) S. of Dalbeattie, associated in legend with the Arthurian King Mark of Cornwall. It was excavated in 1913 and again from 1973. The most visible remains are those of a heavy, timber-laced rampart around the hill that had been "vitrified," or burned (see *Castle Law Hill Fort*). The excavations have indicated occupation of the site from the 6th cent. AD. The finds include evidence of extensive metalworking in bronze and iron as well as glass vessels of the 8th-9th cents. AD and imported continental pottery, all indicating extensive trade. The fort was probably that of a chieftain of the kingdom of Rheged, though there may have been a previous Iron Age fort on the site. The finds are in the Dumfries museum. See also *Dunadd*.

MOUSA, BROCH OF

See *Broch of Mousa*.

MULLACH HILL FORT
(Dumfriesshire/Dumfries
and Galloway)

Near Dalswinton, about 7 mi. (11 km.) NW of Dumfries, an impressive hill fort in Nithsdale, with extensive views. Oval in shape, it has two concentric rings of timber-reinforced stone ramparts, now "vitrified" after burning, as the tumbled remains of the walls show. Never excavated, the fort probably dates from the 8th to the 4th cents. BC.

NESS OF BURGI
(Shetlands, Mainland)

Iron Age promontory fort, in state care, on the western tip of Sumburgh Head at the bottom of the Shetlands, 2 mi. (3.25 km.) S. of the airport and 1 mi. (1.6 km.) W. across the bay from *Jarlshof*. The promontory is defended by a massive wall, still about 7 ft. high with ditches on both sides. Just inside the wall is a heavy "blockhouse" akin to that at *Clickhimin*, apparently a local Shetlands development. A rectangular, freestanding structure pierced by a central entranceway, it has two cells on either side inside the walls (suggesting the later brochs), one giving off the entrance passage, the other entered from the fort area. Traces of a third cell are discernible at the SW end where part of the blockhouse has fallen into the sea. Despite excavations in 1935 the fort is undated, though it is probably early (pre-broch) Iron Age.

NESS OF GRUTING
(Shetlands, Mainland)

There are many oval prehistoric house sites in Shetland. At Gruting, about 14 mi. (22.5 km.) across the island from Lerwick and SE of Bridge of Walls, one of a group of five Neolithic houses has been excavated. The oval house with 10-ft.-thick walls contained a principal room about 20 by 30 ft. and a small annex with rounded walls off it. The finds were abundant and included much pottery—

for this was a potter's workshop—and 28 lbs. of charred barley. The houses were associated with field walls and piles of cleared stones. See also in the Orkneys: *Knap of Howar; Rinyo; Skara Brae.*

NETHER LARGIE CAIRNS
(Argyll/Strathclyde)

See *Kilmartin.*

NEWSTEAD ROMAN FORT
(Roxburghshire/Borders)

The fortress of Trimontium, less than 2 mi. (3.25 km.) E. of Melrose, lay on Dere Street, the principal Roman road from Corbridge (S. of *Hadrian's Wall* in England) into Scotland, and was the heavily fortified kingpin of the early defenses of southern Scotland. Today nothing except a monument marks the site, but exhaustive excavations in 1905–10, with further exploration in 1949, yielded a rich collection of metal weapons, tools, superb cavalry parade helmets of brass and bronze, and elaborate tableware attesting to the splendor of life on this frontier fortress at its height at the end of the 1st cent. AD. These famous finds are now in the National Museum, Edinburgh.

The first fort here was built on the Tweed River by Agricola in 81 AD and named after the three peaks of the Eildon Hills to the SW, the most northerly peak being the site of its predecessor, *Eildon Hill North* hill fort. The Agricolan fort was replaced about 86 AD by a more conventional fortress with massive ramparts, and with external bath house and guest house, that became the major outpost of Roman power in the North until the end of the century. This fort was apparently burned in some sudden catastrophe that prevented the soldiers from removing many possessions. Instead, they were dumped into rubbish pits where the excavators found them. Abandoned in 105 AD, the site was refortified in the Antonine period of Roman advance in two phases, with a new stone-faced rampart and ditches, but was finally abandoned in the middle of the 2nd cent. on the withdrawal to Hadrian's Wall.

NORMAN'S LAW HILL
FORT
(Fife/Fife)

Great hill fort overlooking the Firth of Tay in the N., 5.5 mi. (9 km.) NW of Cupar and about 3 mi. (4.75 km.) NE of Lindores. One ring of tumbled stone walls encircles the summit, with another lower down around the whole hill. Though the fort is unexcavated, these rings were undoubtedly both Iron Age, the higher circuit probably the earliest. Another small oval annex enclosure to the SW, off the lower circuit, with walls 12 ft. thick, may be Dark Ages in date, as are probably the circular hut foundations that in part overlie the earlier ramparts.

NORTH UIST
(Outer Hebrides)

See *Barpa Langass; Udal.*

OLD KEIG
(Aberdeenshire/
Grampian)

Small Recumbent Stone Circle (see *Loanhead of Daviot*) 11 mi. (17.75 km.) W. of Inverurie and 2.5 mi. (4 km.) NE of Alford, on private land. The circle was excavated in 1931 by V. Gordon Childe and is now in poor shape, its stones tumbled, its ring cairn scarcely visible. But it is famous for its huge recumbent stone, over 16 ft. long and weighing 50 tons. Hundreds of men probably dragged it some 6 mi. to its site, where it was pointed roughly on its bottom and propped in its hole with packing stones to make its top exactly horizontal—probably as an observation platform for the rising and setting of the midsummer moon. More ritual is implied by the evidence of a great fire set in the middle of the circle as it was built, after which a deep pit was dug there and filled with broken pottery and the cremated bones of a young adult. See also *Berrybrae*; *Strichen*; *Tomnaverie*.

ONSTAN
(Orkneys)

See *Unstan*.

ORKNEY ISLANDS

For the principal headings, see: *Blackhammer*; *Broch of Gurness*; *Brough of Birsay*; *Brough of Deerness*; *Cuween Hill*; *Dwarfie Stane*; *Fan Knowe*; *Holm of Papa Westray*; *Isbister*; *Kirkwall*; *Knap of Howar*; *Knowe of Yarso*; *Maes Howe*; *Midhowe*; *Quanterness*; *Quoyness*; *Rennibister*; *Rinyo*; *Skara Brae*; *Stenness*; *Taversoe Tuack*; *Tofts Ness*; *Unstan*; *Westness*.

ORONSAY ISLAND
(Inner Hebrides,
Oronsay)

See *Lussa Wood*.

OUSEDALE BROCH
(Caithness/Highland)

About 5 mi. (8 km.) NE along the coastal road from Helmsdale, on the seaward side of the road; this solid-based broch had its interior excavated in 1891 and some of the upper parts reconstructed. The well-preserved entrance on the SW has door checks for double doors (a late feature), and a guard chamber on the right. A mural stair and one cell can be seen in the wall. About 15 mi. (24 km.) farther up the coast road, at the fishing port of Dunbeath, is another similar broch, again with double door checks. It lies just inland up Dunbeath Water. There is a curving guard cell to the right of the ruined entrance, and a mural cell with corbelled roof in the wall, which still stands about 10 ft. high in places. It was excavated perhaps in the 1870s. See also *Broch of Mousa*.

PENNYMUIR
(Roxburghshire/Borders)

See *Woden Law*.

PITCUR EARTH-HOUSE
(Angus/Tayside)

Souterrain, 3 mi. (4.75 km.) SE of Coupar Angus; an underground passage 190 ft. long, with a side passage of 60 ft. opening off it. The original roof, of large lintels, still covers about a quarter of the main passage. See also *Ardestie*; *Culsh*.

PUNDS WATER CAIRN
(Shetlands, Mainland)

An example of a Neolithic Shetlands heel cairn, cleared out in 1930 (with *Vementry* one of the finest of these curious heel-shaped cairns of the Shetlands). It lies in wild moorland near the NW coast of the island, 7.5 mi. (12 km.) NW of Voe, accessible only after a vigorous walk. Unlike Vementry, the whole cairn here, built of white granite boulders and standing about 5 ft. high, is heel-shaped, with an impressive 50-ft.-wide facade at the base of the heel. The passage leads into a clover-leaf-shaped chamber from the middle of the facade; both are now open to the air.

QUANTERNESS
(Orkneys, Mainland)

Neolithic chambered cairn belonging to the Orkney Maes Howe group, 3 mi. (4.75 km.) W. of Kirkwall. The tomb is an early example of the group that includes *Maes Howe* itself, directly W. and in between Wideford Hill and *Cuween Hill* along the same westward road and *Quoyness* and *Holm of Papa Westray* on other islands. Quanterness is also close to the much later souterrains of Grain and *Rennibister*.

Quanterness, first opened in the 19th cent. and intensively studied by Colin

Renfrew in 1972, has now been closed up again and appears as a mound with a flagpole. The passage in this 90-ft.-wide cairn was over 22 ft. long and led into a rectangular chamber (about 22 ft. by 7 ft.) in which, in the later dig, the bones of 157 individuals were found in six cells opening out from it. The bodies had been buried, the bones then broken up into small pieces and placed in the tomb to the accompaniment of fires and possibly feasting—for the bones of sheep, cattle, fish and birds were also found, as well as the bones of a dog, possibly a totem animal (see Isbister). Radiocarbon dates indicated the tomb was built about 3000 BC and was still in use some 600 years later, the bones (possibly of some 400 people originally) representing interments over a long period from a small community of about 20 people, buried without distinction of rank in a period when the village of Skara Brae flourished. The average age of the dead was about 20 years.

QUOYNESS
(Orkneys, Sanday)

Chambered tomb of the Neolithic Maes Howe group (see Quanterness above), on a headland on the S. coast of this northern island, 2 mi. (3.25 km.) SW of Roadside, excavated by V. Gordon Childe in 1952. Now in state care, the oval cairn has been reconstructed to show its three outer retaining walls. The cairn stands on a platform and can be entered by stairs leading from the platform down to the passage, 12 ft. long. The rectangular chamber, with a slightly corbelled roof 13 ft. high, has six small cells opening off it. A cist on the floor of the chamber contained fragments of the bones of at least 10 adults and four to five children. Artifacts found in the excavation linked it with the contemporary Neolithic villages of Rinyo and Skara Brae.

RENNIBISTER
(Orkneys, Mainland)

A typical Orkney type of late Iron Age souterrain or earth-house (underground chambers for storage or refuge), about 4.5 mi. (7.25 km.) W. of Kirkwall. Another souterrain, Grain, can be found about 3 mi. (4.75 km.) NE of it, close to Kirkwall. Unlike the souterrains of eastern Scotland (see Ardestie; Culsh; Pitcur), which were only shallow, covered trenches, the Orkney examples are deeply buried. Rennibister, in state care, lies under a farmyard and is now entered by a trapdoor in the roof. Access to the hexagonal chamber, about 8 ft. by 11 ft., was originally by a narrow sloping passage. Its walls are of drystone masonry and upright slabs, its roof of overlapping lintels supported on four heavy pillars. When it was opened, burials, undoubtedly later ones, were found in the chamber.

The Grain (or Grainbank) souterrain, also in state care and situated amidst buildings in the outskirts of Kirkwall, is very similar, but one must descend a stair and crawl along a low curving passage to enter it. The chamber roof here is of flat slabs, again supported by four pillars.

RESTENNETH PRIORY
(Angus/Tayside)

Early medieval church, 1.5 mi. (2.3 km.) E. of Forfar. The lower 9 ft. or so of its much older, square tower was undoubtedly originally the porch of one of the earliest "Roman" Christian churches in Scotland, built for the Pictish king Nechton about 710 AD by masons sent from Monkwearmouth in Northumbria (ENGLAND). It contains a narrow door topped by a round arch cut from a single, large block of stone. The rest of the tower, except for the 15th-cent. spire, appears to be pre-Norman.

RI CRUIN CAIRN
(Argyll/Strathclyde)

See Kilmartin.

RING OF BRODGAR
(Orkneys, Mainland)

See *Stenness*.

RINYO
(Orkneys, Rousay)

Neolithic settlement in the NE of Rousay, discovered in 1937 and excavated by V. Gordon Childe in 1938 and 1946; he also excavated the famous Neolithic village of *Skara Brae*, on Mainland Island. At Rinyo eight stone-built houses on terraces on the slopes of a hill were uncovered, apparently occupied over a long period. A radiocarbon date in the 3rd millennium was determined. The houses consisted of single rectangular chambers within thick walls, the entrances furnished with jambs and door checks at the outer end. To the left and right of the entrance were stone beds, and a stone dresser opposite the entrance, with a square hearth in the middle. A stone-lined box with a stone lid was set into the floor. In one house a rare oven was found in position. The finds were similar to those of Skara Brae. Today little of interest is visible at Rinyo. See also *Knap of Howar*.

ROUGH CASTLE ROMAN
FORT
(Stirlingshire/Central)

See *Antonine Wall*.

RUTHWELL CROSS
(Dumfriesshire/Dumfries
and Galloway)

Superb Anglo-Saxon (Northumbrian) high cross, one of the finest religious monuments of Dark Ages Europe. Reconstructed and restored after it was smashed by Protestants in 1640, it now stands over 15 ft. high, flood lit, in a special apse built for it in the little Ruthwell church, just N. of that village, 9 mi. (14.5 km.) SE of Dumfries. Dating from the early or mid-8th cent. AD when Northumbria was in control of this part of Scotland, it closely resembles the *Bewcastle Cross* in Cumbria, England. The sculpture, mostly biblical scenes in rectangular panels on each flat side, is of a high order. Latin inscriptions run around the margins. The narrow sides are ornamented with vine scrolls with entrapped birds and beasts, and on these margins is inscribed in runic letters the first 78 lines of the Anglo-Saxon religious poem, "The Dream of the Rood," earliest and most moving of Early English poems. The arms of the cross are modern restorations. The cross may well have been set up to celebrate the Romanization of the Celtic church after the Synod of Whitby in 664 AD. See also *Abercorn Cross*; *Iona*; *Kildalton Cross*.

SAINT ANDREWS
(Fife/Fife)

Ancient cathedral town. In one of the former monastic buildings of the famous cathedral—the "warming room"—a small museum holds an important collection of Early Christian grave and cross slabs from the even earlier, large Celtic monastery formerly on the site (no trace of it survives), as well as the reputed Sarcophagus of St. Andrew, which could well be 8th cent. Its carved panels show an interesting mixture of Pictish and Northumbrian styles. In the St. Andrews University museum there is a small collection of prehistoric finds from the Fife region.

SAINT BLANE'S CHURCH
(Bute/Strathclyde)

See *Dunagoil*.

SAINT NINIAN'S CHAPEL
(Wigtownshire/Dumfries
and Galloway)

See *Whithorn Priory*.

The Ruthwell Cross in Dumfriesshire, now mounted inside a church, is one of the finest of Dark Ages monuments. It is Northumbrian (Anglian) in inspiration, since Northumbria controlled this part of Scotland in the 8th cent. The middle panel of the sculpture, which is one of the best, shows Mary Magdalene washing the feet of Christ; the sides are ornamented with elaborate vine-scroll enclosing birds and beasts, and a Latin inscription runs along the front borders, a runic one on the sides. The latter gives part of the early English poem, Dream of the Rood. The cross was restored after smashing by zealous Protestants. (Courtesy Scottish Tourist Board.)

SAINT NINIAN'S ISLE
(Shetlands, Mainland)

Tiny islet 8 mi. (13 km.) NW of Sumburgh airport, on the W. coast and connected to Mainland Island by a narrow spit of sand. Excavations here by Aberdeen students in 1955–58 uncovered the foundations of a 12-cent. church, still visible, and under it the walls of an earlier, Pictish-period Celtic church, presumably destroyed in Viking raids in the 9th cent. Under the floor of the older church the grave of a 6-ft.-tall man was found, as well as six Pictish stones carved with symbols. Then in 1958 a most remarkable hoard of 28 decorated silver pieces turned up under the same floor—the famous St. Ninian's Isle treasure, now in Edinburgh's National Museum. The treasure had been hastily packed in a larch-wood box along with the jawbone of a porpoise (purpose unknown), obviously buried to escape a Viking raid. The treasure, dated at about 800 AD, includes shallow bowls, hanging bowls, tableware, sword fittings, and brooches of a specifically Pictish type, though other objects show Irish, Northumbrian, even Mercian influences. All are profusely decorated, indicating a sophistication in possessions at the time that contrasts with the simplicity of the architecture. The hoard could have been the treasure of the church, or perhaps that of a Pictish chieftain.

SAINT VIGEANS MUSEUM
(Angus/Tayside)

Village museum, 1 mi. (1.6 km.) N. of Arbroath. Housed in a cottage, it contains a remarkable collection of 32 Early Christian-Pictish carved stones found in and around the nearby church of St. Vigeans. Most interesting of these is the Class II Drosten Stone, a cross bearing three Pictish names in 9th-cent. writing and Pictish symbols, beasts, a stag hunt and, on the back, a bowman.

SEABEGS WOOD
(Stirlingshire/Central)

See *Antonine Wall*.

SHETLAND ISLANDS

For the principal headings, see: *Broch of Burland; Broch of Mousa; Busta; Clickhimin; Jarlshof; Lerwick; Ness of Burgi; Ness of Gruting; Punds Water; St. Ninian's Isle; Stanydale; Vementry.*

SKARA BRAE
(Orkneys, Mainland)

Famous Neolithic stone village on the southern shore of the Bay of Skaill on the island's W. coast, about 7 mi. (11 km.) N. of Stromness. The ruins, deeply buried in the sand dunes, were partially uncovered by a great storm sweeping in from the sea in 1850, a storm as fierce no doubt as the tempest that apparently engulfed the settlement before 2000 BC—so suddenly that the necklace of a fleeing woman broke, scattering the beads behind her as she ran. Since 1850 the site has often been excavated, the first time seriously by V. Gordon Childe from 1927 to 1930, the latest in 1972–73, during which a series of radiocarbon dates were obtained ranging from 3100 to 2450 BC. This is the same flourishing period in the Orkneys that produced the stone circles and the *Maes Howe* series of magnificent megalithic tombs.

The miniature houses of Skara Brae—six to eight of them built and rebuilt over a long period—huddled close together, with alleys and covered walkways in between them. The whole village in the end was buried in piles of refuse from the settlement, contributing warmth as well as smells no doubt, so that it must have resembled a subterranean village. It was then more deeply buried in sand from the great storm, preserving everything to a remarkable extent. Exposed to view, these one-room, rectangular little houses with built-in stone furniture now have the charm of a doll's house. Each was roughly 15 ft. square, with heavy walls and rounded ends. The walls, corbelled near the top, still stand up to 8 ft.

A corner of Skara Brae, the famous Neolithic village in the Orkneys, inhabited for over 600 years and then, before 2000 BC, engulfed in sand from a storm. It was uncovered again after another storm in 1850 and subsequently much excavated. The handful of close-packed houses thus revealed have provided rare and exciting glimpses into Neolithic life at the time of Maes Howe and Stennis. The one-room houses were comfortably provided with built-in stone furniture (a box-bed enclosure is shown), storage space in the walls and floors and, probably, a roof of whalebone and turves. The whole village was once covered deep in piles of its own garbage! (Courtesy Scottish Tourist Board.)

high; the roof was probably made of whalebone rafters covered with turf. A low entrance passage with a bar hole for the door led into the single room with a square hearth at the center. Around it were box beds, two-tier dressers, storage boxes for limpets in the floor, cupboards and storage cells built into the walls (one with a drain used as a latrine) and stone seats, all neatly built of flat stone flags. One house is now covered in glass for easier inspection.

From the archaeological evidence, such as carbonized grain, the inhabitants grew crops but also depended heavily on shellfish, fishing, the breeding of cattle, sheep and pigs. Their varied artifacts of stone, flint, bone, antler and ivory were found at the site in abundance and included stone balls, pottery and pins, all decorated, as well as decorated slabs set into the walls—art forms reminiscent of the passage graves of Ireland. There is a site museum and informative lectures. See also *Knap of Howar*; *Rinyo*.

SKYE
(Inner Hebrides, Skye)

This large island, rich in Scottish historical associations, also displays a wealth of ancient monuments—an Early Christian monastery, Neolithic cairns, a souterrain, Pictish symbol stones, brochs, duns and forts. Most of these monuments are well represented elsewhere and easier to find; but Skye is most notable for possessing the largest number of brochs and semi-brochs in the West. Indeed, according to one theory the broch may have originated on Skye, developing out of the so-called semi-brochs and galleried duns, then spreading to the E. and N. of Scotland. The semi-brochs are forts, not round towers, but they have the same hollow walls and other features of the far more substantial brochs (see *Broch of Mousa*).

An example of the many semi-brochs on Skye is Dun Ringill on the eastern shore of the Elgol peninsula, about 10 mi. (16 km.) SW of Broadford and a few mi. short of Elgol. Very similar to the semi-broch of *Dun Grugaig* to the E. across the Bay of Glenelg, it is a D-shaped fort on a promontory; the straight wall runs along the cliff over the sea and is much thinner than the curving inland walls, which are doubled and include an upper gallery and a corbelled mural chamber within them. The broch-like door checks and bar hole are still visible in the entrance passage, though it was much altered in later centuries. Farther along the E. coast is a second Dun Grugaig, a semi-broch simpler and earlier than Dun Ringill and very difficult to find. Still another semi-broch, Dun Ardtreck, excavated in 1965, lies NW of Ringill on the shores of Loch Bracadale, near the entrance of Loch Harport, a mi. or so from Fiskavaig. This, too, is a D-shaped fort dramatically sited on an isolated knoll over a high sea-cliff. The curving landward wall was built on an artificial platform, with a paved entrance and guard chamber, and galleries running throughout the wall. The fort was violently destroyed by fire, and a radiocarbon date in the 1st cent. BC was obtained from the charcoal.

The best example of a true broch of Hebridean style on Skye is Dun Beag, excavated in 1915, on a hill overlooking Loch Bracadale a mi. or so W. of Bracadale. Its wall, 14 ft. thick, stands up to 12 ft. high and its circular court is 36 ft. across. There is a mural stair and cell, and opposite these a long gallery in the wall. To the NW, a mi. or so beyond Dunvegan Castle, Dun Fiadhairt broch stands on a desolate, rocky knoll on a westward-facing peninsula. Its entrance passage, with door checks, has two guard chambers; again there are doors leading into a mural cell and the stair, and a ground-level gallery in the wall. On clearing it out in 1914 a Roman terracotta model of a bundle of hides or sheepskins was found, suggesting trade from afar. Straight N. (E. of Hallin village on the Vaternish peninsula) is Dun Hallin broch, on private land. Its court is 36 ft. across and it has two guard cells and a stair. Finally, jumping a long way to the NE coast, is Dun Flodigarry broch, recently excavated, near Staffin, 20 mi. (32.25 km.) N. of Portree. It has galleried walls, a single entrance and mural cells. There is a small site museum here.

SOUTH CLETTRAVAL HILL (Outer Hebrides, North Uist)

See *Barpa Langass*.

SOUTH YARROWS (Caithness/Highland)

See *Yarrows*.

STANYDALE TEMPLE (Shetlands, Mainland)

Interesting and unique site near the W. coast, 2.75 mi. (4.25 km.) NE of Walls and 8 mi. (13 km.) NW of Lerwick; excavated in 1949 and in state care. Here is an exceptionally large structure of the Late Neolithic or Early Bronze Age that may well have been a temple—or perhaps a communal meeting place or chief's hall. It is heel-shaped, with the entrance through the incurved facade, the whole oval, enclosing an area of 20 ft. by 40 ft. The thick, 12-ft. walls are well-constructed of large blocks of stone. Opposite the entrance and along the sides are six shallow recesses formed by low, projecting masonry piers, and in the interior the excavators found two stone-lined postholes for massive timber uprights that may have supported a timber and thatch roof, whose sloping roof beams may have rested on the piers. Fragments of spruce were found in the postholes, a tree unknown in the Shetlands at the time, thus perhaps driftwood from America or imported from Scandinavia. The structure was in use over a long period.

It was set among nine (poorly preserved) houses. About 40 ft. to the S. is an arc of standing stones. The whole suggests a most unusual communal or religious center of importance.

STENNESS STANDING STONES (Orkneys, Mainland)

Impressive Neolithic sacred area with two principal henge-circles, Stenness and the Ring of Brodgar, and numerous standing stones and round barrows; about 10 mi. (16 km.) W. of Kirkwall, 5 mi. (8 km.) NE of Stromness. Within the larger area are to be found two well-known Neolithic burial cairns, *Maes Howe* to the E. and *Unstan* to the SE, both dating approximately to the same period as Stenness, as does the Neolithic village of *Skara Brae* 6 mi. (9.6 km.) to the NW.

Of the Ring of Stenness on the shores of Loch Stenness little survives today. It was originally a henge circle with bank and ditch about 200 ft. in diameter, with one entrance. Within this a smaller stone circle was erected, probably with 12 stones, of which only four remain. These, the Standing Stones of Stenness, are tall, thin monoliths up to 17 ft. high. The flat stone table now at the center of the ring is a folly of 1906. Excavations at the site uncovered the remains of a timber mortuary house just within the henge entrance, and from it a cobbled pathway led to the center where there was a rectangular stone "hearth" (on which no fires had been lit), which contained bits of bone and pottery and burnt seaweed as offerings. A towering timber post seems to have been set at its center, while to the S. five pits contained offerings of nuts, barley, seeds and fruit. Radiocarbon dates from the henge averaged 2950 BC.

One can see its companion, the stones of the Ring of Brodgar, about 1 mi. (1.6 km.) away from Stenness NW across the neck of land separating lochs Stenness and Harray. Between them, just this side of the Bridge of Brodgar, stands a huge monolith nearly 19 ft. high, the Watch Stone. It may have been part of another, lost circle, or perhaps of a processional way between the two circles.

The Ring of Brodgar on Mainland, the Orkneys, the largest stone circle in Scotland, set in a dramatic landscape. It is fully 360 ft. across. Of its 60 original stones, 27 still stand up to 16 ft. tall. Actually the Ring was a henge with a deep encircling ditch (just visible behind the stones) and two causeway-entrances. The ditch was hewn out of bedrock at vast labor. There was probably no bank. About a mile away is a companion henge and circle, probably earlier, the Stones of Stennis, of which only four tall uprights still survive. The whole area was another religious complex like Callinish in the Hebrides and Stonehenge in England. (Courtesy of British Tourist Authority, New York.)

The Ring of Brodgar is the largest and finest stone circle in Scotland, and in its setting of water, sky and wild moorland one of the most beautiful in all of Britain. It, too, was a classic henge (see *Avebury* in England), a huge circle 360 ft. across. Around the perimeter was a deep ditch, 30 ft. wide, laboriously hewed out of the rock (it took an estimated 80,000 man hours!) and still well-preserved. Two wide, opposing causeway-entrances ran across the ditch and bank (the latter has almost disappeared). The ring itself, a perfect circle, originally consisted of 60 stone uprights up to 16 ft. high—tall, thin, elegant slabs of flagstone, their flat faces turned inward, of which 27 survive today. Four of the stones bear later inscriptions—in ogham and runes—a cross, and an anvil. A single stone, the Comet Stone, stands alone well outside the circle. Brodgar was probably later than Stenness, erected perhaps around 2500 BC or subsequently. Much inconclusive study has gone into its possible astronomical implications, for instance, lunar sightings across nearby barrows or via the cliffs of Hoy to the SW. The mathematical accuracy of the setting of the stones, however—exactly 6 degrees apart—is indisputable.

STONES OF STENNESS

See *Stenness*.

STRICHEN CIRCLE
(Aberdeenshire/ Grampian)

Recumbent Stone Circle, dramatically sited on the crest of a hill S. of the road from Strichen to New Deer, .5 mi. (1 km.) from Strichen. This unfortunate circle was destroyed by a farmer in the 1830s, crudely reconstructed, then destroyed again in 1965. It has since been properly reconstructed and is open to the public. It lies 7 mi. (11.25 km.) SW of *Berrybrae*, another recumbent circle. For details on these circles, see especially *Loanhead of Daviot*.

SUENO'S STONE
(Morayshire/Grampian)

One of the most remarkable of Dark Ages carvings, a very late (Class III) Pictish stone of the 9th or 10th cent. AD, standing 23 ft. high in the northeastern outskirts of Forres, in state care. A sandstone slab, much weathered at the top, its front shows a wheel cross with interlace decoration below it. On the sides Anglian vine scrolls enclose beasts and men, but on the back there are four panels closely packed with martial scenes—soldiers and horsemen in combat and decapitated bodies. What looks much like a broch is in the background of one scene. It is thought that the stone commemorates a great victory of the Picts, in the last days of their power, over the invading Vikings somewhere near this spot; or, less likely, it may celebrate an earlier (8th cent.) victory of the Picts over the Scots of Dalriada invading from the W. (see *Dunadd*).

SUNHONEY CIRCLE
(Aberdeenshire/ Grampian)

See *Cullerlie*.

TAVERSOE TUACK
(Orkneys, Rousay)

Rare "apartment house," two-storied Neolithic passage grave or stalled cairn on the S. coast of the island. It is one of a group of stalled cairns of the W. on Rousay, including *Blackhammer*, *Knowe of Yarso* and *Midhowe*. Excavated in 1937 and now in state care, Taversoe stands less than a mile W. of Brinyan pier on a commanding bluff over the sea. It was originally covered by a round cairn with a kerb, 30 ft. across, now replaced over the remains of the upper chamber by a protective concrete dome. The sunken lower chamber was entered from the S. at right angles by a sloping passage and is divided by slabs into four compartments. On the line of the passage a drain or trench leads ahead outside the cairn to a small rock-cut chamber only 3 ft. high, with stone-lined walls, a slab roof and a sloping entranceway. Neolithic pottery was found in it, so it may have been an odd subterranean "earth-house." The walls of the upper chamber, apparently built at the same time and supported on the roof slabs of the lower chamber, now stand only a few ft. high. It was entered from the N. by a shorter passage, and its chamber has two rounded compartments on either side and a small recess at the far end. A trap door now connects the upper and lower chambers.

TEALING EARTH-HOUSE
(Angus/Tayside)

See *Ardestie Earth-House.*

TEMPLE WOOD CIRCLE
(Argyllshire/Strathclyde)

See *Kilmartin.*

TOFTS NESS
(Orkneys, Sanday)

Early Bronze Age settlement of dwellings, fields, and cairns, excavated 1986–87. The principal find in this settlement, occupied during the little-known period of about 2000 to 1500 BC, is an elaborate round house of stone, discovered covered over in wind-blown sand, probably during the Bronze Age itself (like the earlier Neolithic village of *Skara Brae*, also in the Orkneys). Again like the houses of Skara Brae, this Bronze Age house boasted built-in stone furniture—five snug box-beds against the wall—with a stone-flagged hearth at the center. The refuse midden next to the house yielded a wealth of environmental materials—plant remains, animal bones, tools of bone and stone and sherds of pottery—that are now being studied at the University of Bradford, which carried out the dig.

TOMNAVERIE CIRCLE
(Aberdeenshire/
Grampian)

Recumbent Stone Circle, its outer ring of stones still visible around a circle 56 ft. across; 9 mi. (14.5 km.) NW of Kincardine O'Neil, 1 mi. (1.6 km.) SE of Tarland. Inside is a circle of smaller stones, probably the kerbs for the usual ring cairn. The large recumbent stone, over 10 ft. long, lies on the SW. See also *Berrybrae* and especially *Loanhead of Daviot.*

TORHOUSKIE CIRCLE
(Wigtownshire/Dumfries
and Galloway)

A well-preserved Bronze Age stone circle 3 mi. (4.75 km.) W. of Wigtown, in state care. A flattened circle 60 ft. in diameter, built on a platform, it consists of 19 upended granite boulders, the largest at the SE, with three others in a line at the center. There are other standing stones nearby, some of which may be the remains of another circle.

TORMORE
(Inner Hebrides, Arran)

See *Machrie Moor.*

TORRYLINN CAIRN
(Inner Hebrides, Arran)

See *Machrie Moor.*

TORWOODLEE BROCH
(Selkirkshire/Borders)

One of the few brochs in SE Scotland, about 6 mi. (10 km.) W. of Melrose, built into an Iron Age hill fort on a ridge. Cleared out in 1891, more carefully excavated in 1950, it was found to be filled with, and built upon, quantities of broken Roman glass and pottery. Unusually, it was encircled by a ditch. The broch was systematically destroyed and the ditch filled up not long after the latter was dug, so that only a few ft. are left of the broch's circular wall, over 16 ft. thick; though one can trace the usual features—entrance with door checks, door to the stairway, an intramural cell—in the remains. The broch was built partly over the ditches of the hill fort, also filled up. All of this seems to mean that the hill fort was taken in the Roman advance under Agricola about 80 AD, that the broch was then built after the Roman withdrawal about 100 AD, then destroyed in the usual thorough fashion by the Romans as they again advanced about 140 AD. The Roman material would then have come from the nearby fort of *Newstead*, abandoned about 100 AD. For other southern brochs see also *Edinshall* and *Leckie*.

TRAPRAIN LAW
(East Lothian/Lothian)

Scant remains of a fort on a huge isolated hill, 10 mi. (16 km.) W. of Dunbar, 2 mi. (3.25 km.) S. of East Linton. In Roman times it was the capital of the Votadini, a friendly tribe, but overall was occupied from the Bronze Age into the Dark Ages, undergoing four major phases of fortification. All that is visible now is an impressive, 12-ft.-wide, stone-faced turf wall dating from the mid-5th cent. AD. A quarry intrudes on the NE. At its height, perhaps in the 1st cent. AD, the oppidum covered 40 acres and was, with *Eildon Hill North*, one of the two largest in Scotland, and it was filled with native huts. A series of excavations from 1915 to 1921 recovered numerous finds, including rare Late Bronze Age metalwork and the finest hoard of late Roman silverware, over 100 pieces, ever found in Scotland. The finds are now on view in Edinburgh's National Museum. But the early excavations neglected the stratigraphy of the site and how it related to the finds, thus negating the archaeological results from this important site.

TRIMONTIUM
(Roxburghshire/Borders)

See *Newstead Roman Fort*.

TRUSHEL STONE
(Outer Hebrides, Lewis)

Huge monolith, presumably Bronze Age in date, standing 19 ft. high and the tallest in Scotland. It is 13 mi. (21 km.) NW of Stornoway, just SE of the village of Balantrushel, and was probably one of a group of standing stones.

TWELVE APOSTLES
CIRCLE
(Dumfriesshire/Dumfries and Galloway)

Huge open stone circle, 3 mi. (4.75 km.) NW of Dumfries and S. of Holywood. Probably dating from the Late Neolithic-Early Bronze Age period of circle building, it had 11 stones in a flattened circle, only five still standing.

UDAL
(Outer Hebrides, North Uist)

Important dig of the 1970s and 1980s of a long-lived settlement on a sandy peninsula on the northern Atlantic coast of the island. The fertile, sandy soils on the coastal machair obviously attracted settlers to the region. Current archaeological findings indicate that the settlement at the Udal goes back at least to the dawn of the Bronze Age and extends through the Iron Age, the Pictish period, the Norse and beyond, and into the Middle Ages. In the 7th to early 9th cents. AD there was a group of houses, presumably Pictish, much like those at Buckquoy in the Orkneys (see *Brough of Birsay*) though less sophisticated, including a figure-of-eight type of main house. In the 9th cent., just as at Buckquoy, the Vikings took over and built their rectangular long houses in the ruins of the earlier settlement. About this time a strongly-defended enclosure was built on the highest point of the village, either by the natives or the Norse. The excavations have also uncovered the grooves made by Viking ploughshares at this time—a rare discovery, much like that at Lindholm Høje in Denmark. See also *Jarlshof*.

UNSTAN
(Orkneys, Mainland)

Or Onstan. Neolithic chambered tomb just S. of the Loch of Stenness, about 3 mi. (4.75 km.) NE of Stromness, and not far from the *Stenness Standing Stones* and the Ring of Brodgar. The tomb, in state care, lies under a round cairn about 45 ft. in diameter, now replaced at the top by a concrete dome with windows to facilitate viewing the long chamber below (11 ft. by 5 ft.) whose walls still stand up to 7 ft. high. It is divided into five compartments on each side by tall flagstone slabs, and a small cell opens off the center on the W. The passage enters the main chamber at right angles. The cairn around the chamber was built up with two concentric retaining walls. When excavated in 1884 the tomb yielded burnt and unburnt human bones, flint arrowheads and tools and sherds of at least 22 pots of a distinctive, local Neolithic type now classified as Unstan Ware. The tomb belongs to the group of passage graves, or stalled cairns, found in the Orkneys and in Caithness on the mainland, dated roughly from 3000 to 2500 BC and including *Blackhammer, Knowe of Yarso, Midhowe Cairn* and *Taversoe Tuack* on Rousay Island, and *Isbister* on South Ronaldsay.

VEMENTRY
(Shetlands, Vementry)

Finest of the Shetlands Neolithic heel cairns (see also *Punds Water*). It stands at the N. end of the small uninhabited island of Vementry, just off the W. coast of Mainland Island, on Muckle Ward, the highest hill. The round cairn sits on a heel-shaped platform, with a slightly concave, great facade of upended boulders, 36 ft. wide, forming the base of the heel and built right across it, actually sealing the passage into the cairn behind. For this reason it is thought that the cairn was built first, the heel-shaped platform with its facade later, perhaps when the tomb was closed. The passage, 12 ft. long, led into a chamber under the cairn, with three recesses in a clover-leaf design.

WAG OF FORSE
(Caithness/Highland)

See *Yarrows*.

WATLING LODGE
(Stirlingshire/Central)

See *Antonine Wall*.

WESTNESS
(Orkneys, Rousay)

Viking farmstead of the 9th cent. AD on the SW coast, opposite Mainland Island. The foundations of a Norse long house or hall were uncovered here, and the family graveyard nearby as well. The grave goods of these warrior-farmers included their weapons.

WHITE CATERTHUN
(Angus/Tayside)

See *Caterthuns, The*.

WHITESIDE HILL FORT
(Peebleshire/Borders)

Prominent and well-preserved Iron Age hill fort on a hill 1,200 ft. high overlooking the valley of the Lyne Water from the E. It is about 6 mi. (10 km.) in a direct line NW of Peebles. Though never excavated, studies of the fort show that it went through four phases of fortification. Its original rampart enclosed an area of about 300 ft. in diameter. This was soon enlarged with two more ramparts after which, contrary to the usual pattern, the fort was reduced in size, having now only a single stone wall. Finally it contracted again, to a small, walled enclosure in the E. corner of the earlier fort. Traces of hut circles probably date from the period of its maximum expansion.

WHITHORN PRIORY
(Wigtownshire/Dumfries
and Galloway)

Ruins of a medieval priory church, long associated with St. Ninian, a Romanized Briton who became bishop of Whithorn in the 5th cent. AD and reputedly built the first church in Pictland here—called by Bede, "Candida Casa." In 1949 and 1965 excavations just outside the E. end of the church did indeed uncover the rude walls of an Early Christian structure that could be St. Ninian's church—though more likely a 7th-cent. church, perhaps built on the site of the earlier one. The later excavation also uncovered associated graves that may well date from St. Ninian's time.

New excavations near the priory in the 1980s have discovered two houses under the medieval cemetery that appear from finds to be part of a prosperous, 12th-cent. community of the Norse Vikings. More is to come.

The site museum and interpretive center outside the entrance to the churchyard displays a fine collection of Early Christian crosses and monuments from the site. The earliest is the "Latinus Stone," the oldest known in Scotland, a rectangular gravestone dating from the mid-5th cent. The "Peter Stone," with a dedication to St. Peter, dates from the 7th cent. There are also boulders carved with crosses from St. Ninian's Cave, on the shore 2 mi. (3.75 km.) SW near Glasserton, a cave traditionally thought to be St. Ninian's hermitage. More crosses were later scratched on boulders at the cave and on its walls by pilgrims. See also *Catstane*; *Iona*.

WIDEFORD HILL
(Orkneys, Mainland)

See *Cuween Hill*.

WODEN LAW
(Roxburghshire/Borders)

Iron Age hill fort on a high summit in the wild, bare hills of the border country, about 10 mi. (16 km.) SE of Jedburgh. The fort, partially excavated in 1950, began with a single stone wall enclosing an oval area. Presumably, when the Romans were first moving N. into Scotland this was hastily reinforced by two outer ramparts with a ditch in between; but soon afterwards the fortifications were destroyed as the Romans under Agricola, having subdued the fort, were building Dere Street close to it, one of the two main Roman roads into Scotland. The raised causeway of Dere Street can still be seen just SE of Woden Law. Farther S. on Dere Street were the Roman camps of *Chew Green*, only 3 mi. (4.75 km.) S., and *High Rochester* (see England for both). Woden Law's third phase of fortification was a heavy boulder and rubble wall built within the earlier ramparts in post-Roman or Dark Ages times.

Once in control of the area the Romans apparently used the abandoned native fort for siege and artillery practice works. For the native ramparts are faced on the E. with lines of ditches and banks, built in sections and never completed and all about 70 ft. away, discreetly out of the usual range of native weapons. Further practice lines, one at right angles to the rest, are visible farther down the hill. Some of the banks have been flattened and reinforced, obviously as artillery platforms. The troops under training here must have come from the *Pennymuir* camps, only 1.5 mi. (2.3 km.) to the N. See also *Birrens*.

YARROWS
(Caithness/Highland)

A broch and other ruins on the Loch of Yarrows, inland from the main coastal road from Thrumster and Ulbster, accessible by a farm road. The broch's thick, round wall still stands high enough so that the galleries, cells and stairway are visible within it at ground level. It was excavated in 1866–67. Around it are the remains of a post-broch settlement of long rectangular houses, probably of Pictish date (and possibly influenced by Scandinavian models), that includes a figure-of-eight house similar to those found at Buckquoy (see *Brough of Birsay* and *Udal*). A secondary wall inside the broch dates from the same time.

SW of the nearby farm are the two South Yarrows Neolithic long barrows, excavated in 1865. Both had hornworks at either end. The southern cairn, the largest, is about 245 ft. long and has two chambers, the other cairn one chamber within. No doubt both were built up out of individual round cairns over a long period, like the *Camster* cairns about 5 mi. (8 km.) W. across country.

At Wag of Forse, inland from the main road between Latheron and Lybster and to the SW of Yarrows, one finds a massive circular drystone dun, over 45 ft. across inside its walls, which contain a mural cell. A lintelled passage leads in from the N. with a guardroom on one side, a stair on the other. A settlement of later long houses like those of Yarrows (above) was built over and around the dun, which may be pre-broch in date.

YARSO

See *Knowe of Yarso*.

IRELAND

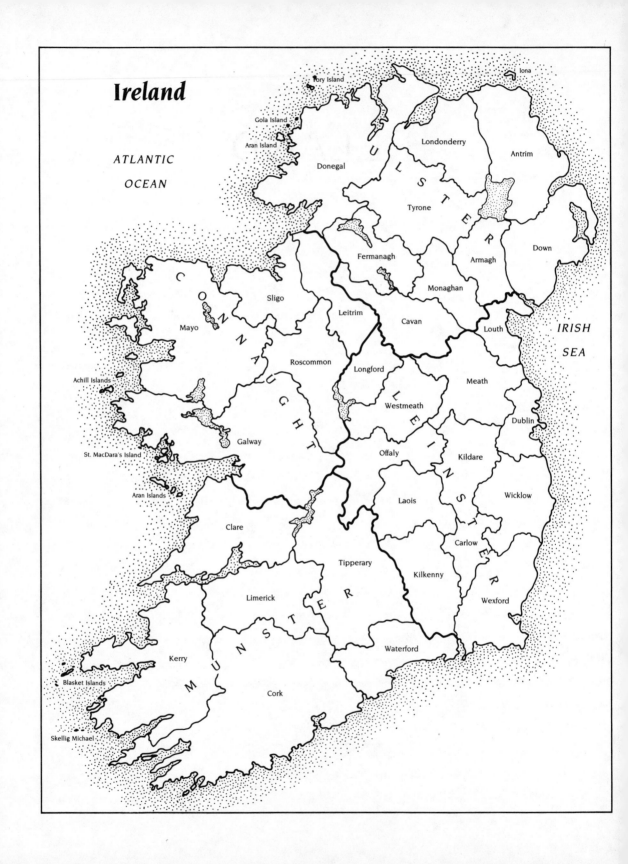

The
Archaeology
of Ireland

Although far off and on the outer edges of the continent of Europe, Ireland displays an astonishing profusion of archaeological sites and monuments. This is in part because Ireland has always been and largely still is a rural, agricultural country where a greater number of monuments and sites have survived than in more industrialized countries. Most of these sites are small, but some—like the great passage tombs of the *Boyne Valley*—are among the finest of their kind in Europe. Though most early Irish monuments are variations on those found elsewhere in Europe, here and there one finds distinctive Irish developments, like the graceful, tapering round towers and superb, sculptured high crosses of the Early Christian period, as well as the steep, corbelled stone roofs of the early oratories and churches.

Despite the number of Irish monuments, comparatively few of them (compared, for instance, with England) have been investigated with modern scientific precision. One result is that dating is often a problem in Irish archaeology, and educated guesses must often suffice for lack of radiocarbon dates or other reliable information. Moreover the exceptional continuity of Irish culture means that the same sites might have been used over and over again for thousands of years. Bronze Age people often buried their dead in or over earlier megalithic tombs to preserve their sanctity. Or the hilltop site of a Neolithic passage tomb or Bronze Age cairn might later be used for an Iron Age enclosure or hill fort, which in turn would become the seat of an Irish king or chieftain in the Early Christian period, and which finally might become a local "place of assembly" and remain so until very recent times. Hilltop pagan enclosures were also liberally taken over by the early monks as Christian centers (see, for example, *Downpatrick*). All in all, Ireland presents a difficult though rich and almost virgin field for the determined archaeologist.

For the purposes of this guide "Ireland" of course includes Northern Ireland as well as the Republic—the whole island—for archaeology is no respecter of modern boundaries, except for the purposes of location. Chronologically the guide ranges from the Mesolithic, beginning about 7000 BC (there is so far no reliable evidence for the Paleolithic in Ireland) through the Early Christian period, ending with the Anglo-Norman invasion and the coming of Romanesque styles in the 12th cent.

The whole question of successive invasions of peoples, bringing with them their own distinctive cultures is, in modern archaeological thinking, very much open to discussion. The tendency today is to emphasize indigenous development, the local people simply absorbing and modifying cultural influences from abroad. These could come through trade, travel or other means short of actual invasion.

Certainly the earliest Mesolithic hunter-gatherers and perhaps even some of the first Neolithic farmers did come from Britain or parts of Europe; but were there subsequent invasions of megalith builders, Beaker Folk bringing metals, or the so-called Celts? When did the Celts, or their culture, actually arrive? Were the Beaker Folk the first Celtic-speaking Irish? Such questions are really irrelevant in a guide such as this, which largely describes what can be seen on the ground, not necessarily how it got there.

Though, as stated, the conventional terms of Mesolithic, Neolithic, Bronze Age, Iron Age, are used for convenience, these are arbitrary divisions of time. The latest, and probably most effective way of looking at Irish prehistory is to note the actual changes, sometimes very gradual, indicated by the archaeological findings—the introduction of farming and new domestic animals (cattle and sheep and later the horse); the changes in tool kits, weapons, pottery, ornaments; the increasing use of metals (copper, bronze, then iron); the differing ritual and burial practices; the types of megalithic tomb; the building of stone circles and henges.

There are obviously close parallels among the different types of megalithic tomb in France, England, Scotland and their counterparts in Ireland—for example, the Irish wedge tombs and those in France. But do these result from invasions or simply the dissemination of ideas and techniques from abroad? It is now thought that most of these differing tomb types, and the presence of various artifacts such as the Beakers, represent different cults that may have spread from one country to another—or have developed locally.

Quite recently a number of Mesolithic sites have turned up, especially Mount Sandel in Derry, and others will be found. The Mesolithic in Irish archaeology is very much an unfinished chapter.

The Neolithic

There are approximately 1,200 known megalithic tombs in Ireland, meaning, simply, tombs constructed with large stones. These were built not only for burials (after all, the bodies could have been buried in the ground, quite simply, as we do today) but were also for display, probably representing an ancestor cult, and as a symbol of the cohesion and continuity of the local group that built them. Almost all occur in the Neolithic period (roughly 4000 to 2000 BC), though not in the earlier part of that period. There is also much evidence, as there is in Britain, for the rebuilding and enlarging of the tombs, often over a long period. The tombs are sometimes roughly divided into two main types, structurally speaking: gallery tombs (stone-walled and roofed burial galleries for the dead, usually subdivided into several chambers and possibly covered by a large mound or cairn of stones) and passage tombs (burial chambers under a mound entered through a long passage). The former are divided in Ireland into three main types:

Court Tombs: These are traditionally thought to be the earliest type, and are gallery tombs under a trapezoidal mound or cairn, bordered by a kerb of heavy stones, and entered from an unroofed ceremonial court in front for ritual purposes; usually semicircular. The chamber often has a corbelled roof. Variations are the full court tomb with a fully-enclosed court in front with its own entrance; double court tomb with a court and its gallery at both ends of the cairn; and the center court tomb, a single court in the center with galleries opening off both sides of it. In some court tombs subsidiary chambers are found, entered from the long sides of the cairn. About 370 court tombs are known in Ireland, but only about one-eighth of these have been excavated. They are found almost entirely in the northern half of the country, especially in the NW.

Portal tombs: These are the showiest, most dramatic of the gallery tombs. A single huge capstone, rakishly tilted up and forward over the portal stones, covers a single chamber with side slabs and an end stone and the two tall portal stones. A closing slab often stands between the portal stones. The huge capstones can weigh up to 100 tons (see *Browne's Hill*). Portal tombs may once have had rudimentary courts in front, and in fact may have been derived from court tombs, their distribution again being largely in the northern half of the country, but with an extension down the E. coast. There are 165 such tombs known in Ireland (only about 20 have been excavated), and similar portal tombs are found in Cornwall and Wales. They may have been covered by cairns (the evidence is inconclusive), but it is doubtful if the whole monument was covered; the huge capstones, so provocatively thrusting upward, seem unlikely to have been deliberately buried under a mound!

Wedge Tombs: These are the most common type (450 are known), with a wide distribution over most of the country, especially in the W. and S. Again, only about 20 have been excavated. Generally the wedge tombs have a main chamber enclosed by tall stones and roofed by slabs. The chamber is higher and wider in front—hence, wedge-shaped. In one type the chamber is entered through a portal of tall stones with a flat facade of stones flanking it, and around the chamber, at some distance, a U-shaped setting of stones. The chamber may have a rounded inner end with a small closed chamber inside that. The whole tomb was once covered by a cairn, sometimes with a kerb. In another type the chamber is enclosed within a double wall of stone uprights and there is often a small burial chamber at its W. end, and perhaps another small, square closed chamber at the eastern end. This type seems to have been covered with a round or oval cairn, sometimes also with a kerb.

Passage Tombs: Around 150 to 200 passage tombs—the second of Ireland's two main types of megalithic tomb—have been identified in Ireland, and there may be more. They are rather different from the three types of gallery tomb, the best of them perhaps the finest of the type found all through Europe—an imposing mound, with a kerb, covering a chamber deep inside it that's reached by a long narrow passage through the mound. The tombs are almost always built on conspicuous hilltops with wide views, are often found together in cemeteries; and nearly 40 of them are decorated with elaborate, non-representational "passage grave art"—spirals, circles, lozenges and other geometric motifs, sometimes in quite intricate patterns. The classic form of the chamber is cruciform, with subsidiary chambers at the sides and back, though there are many variations. In the finest and largest of the tombs (see *Boyne Valley*) the central chamber is roofed with tall, magnificent corbelled vaults; in the smaller tombs the chamber is roofed with horizontal slabs, as are the passages in all the tombs. Passage tombs are mostly found to the E. and to the N. of Ireland's central plain.

It now seems possible that all four types of megalithic tomb may have, to an extent, overlapped in time, during roughly the same mid and late Neolithic period, rather than representing any sequence of development—each type reflecting a different cult rather than being the product, as once thought, of waves of different invaders. Occasional hybrid tombs with features borrowed from different types support this view. Most of the tombs were used for collective burials, with cremation the dominant practice, though unburned skeletons have also been found. The bones of over 65 people were found in the passage tomb at *Fourknocks*, for instance, while the three giant tombs dominating the *Boyne Valley* cemetery seem to have been reserved for an elite. The grave goods, where found, consisted of various types of Neolithic pottery and weapons and utensils of flint and stone. Only in the passage graves were the weapons—arrow- and spearheads—virtually absent. Instead the emphasis was on personal ornaments such as stone beads and pendants, stone pins, as well as enigmatic stone spheres or "marbles." Though characteristic Beaker pottery was discovered in a small number of wedge tombs, there is not enough evidence to prove that the tombs were actually built as late as the Early Bronze Age.

Neolithic houses, built of posts with walls of similarly perishable materials and thatched roofs, have seldom survived, though the remains of a number of examples, round and rectangular, with stone footings, have been found, notably at *Lough Gur* and at *Ballyglass*. Recently, a type of Neolithic communal gathering place called the Causewayed Camp, well-known in southern Britain and western Europe, has for the first time been identified in Ireland and excavated at *Donegore*, being dated roughly to the mid-Neolithic; more examples will probably turn up. Another, later type of Late Neolithic ceremonial enclosure, again known from Britain, is called a henge—a circular enclosure surrounded by a ditch with a bank *outside* it (thus not for defense), and sometimes with a stone circle inside the bank. About 50 to 60 henge sites are now known in Ireland, though few have been excavated. Starting in the Late Neolithic, they seem to have continued into the Early Bronze Age.

The Beaker Period

A relatively short period centering around 2000 BC, marking the transition between the Late Neolithic and the Bronze Age. The Beaker culture is identified by the distinctive large pots called beakers. Possibly there actually were Beaker People in England and Ireland, with a distinctive cult and culture, who moved from the continental Lowlands into southern England. But their actual presence in England and especially in Ireland is debatable, since only locally-made Beaker pots—and no other aspects of the culture—have been found in "squatter" habitation sites in Ireland, specifically New Grange. Thus again, the Beaker was probably a cult and culture influenced from abroad but developed locally in response to changes in the society and environment in Ireland. Whatever it was, the Beaker period is definitely marked by the introduction of metals—gold, copper and bronze—and also, probably, by a change to a seminomadic culture, with emphasis on herding, and the introduction of the horse into Ireland. Thus Beaker pottery is found not only in a few wedge tombs but also on henge sites, in stone circles and in cairns. The shadowy culture of the Food Vessel people is identified from their pottery, which is found buried in cists; it was coexistent with the Beaker and a little later.

The Bronze Age

Neolithic ways lasted in Ireland until about 1800 BC, gradually shading into the Bronze Age. The Early Bronze Age is characterized by burials in pits, or in cists (simple stone boxes) found under cairns sited on hilltops. Sometimes the cairns are found together in cemeteries. Many burials were also inserted into older monuments (see *Tara Hill*). Later the ashes began to be placed in urns, and bronze objects and gold ornaments are increasingly found in burials. As the building of large megalithic tombs died out, the megalithic impulse went into the erecting of stone circles, stone alignments and single standing stones.

The stone circles, of which about 200 are known, occur in two main groups. The first group is in southwestern Ireland (Cork/Kerry) and is divided about equally between small five-stone circles and larger multi-stone circles, usually with a low axial or recumbent stone on the SW, opposite the portal stones. Often sited on high ground with extensive views, these circles may well have been aligned on important lunar or solar events. They are often accompanied by cairns and short alignments of three to six stones, as well as boulder burials, a type found only in this area (a large boulder raised on small stones to cover the grave). Simple cremation burials have been found on many sites, with sparse grave goods. Only a half dozen of the 100 or so southwestern stone circles have been excavated.

The other main group of about 100 sites is in central Ulster. These circles, often occurring in groups or pairs, are very different, being made up of many small stones (about half of them have over 45 stones). Long alignments, again of small stones, often ray out from the circles. The best-known site is at *Beaghmore* in Tyrone, dated to the mid or late Bronze Age. Also found in the Bronze Age are petroglyphs or rock art on boulders, outcrops or standing stones. The designs are pecked out, like the earlier passage grave art, but are far simpler, the most common motif being the cupmark, a round hollow encircled by a ring or rings, possibly representing the sun. These are also found in Scotland and northern England. The designs also include wavy lines and arcs. Since Bronze Age habitation sites are scarce, the thousands of Fulachta Fiadha, or cooking sites, found all over Ireland are considered as temporary communal cooking places, identified today by a heap of cracked, burned stones. Heated stones were thrown into a trough of water to heat it, and the meat, wrapped in straw, was boiled in the water. Modern experiments found the method quite successful (see, for instance, *Ballyvourney*; *Drombeg*). These sites date from about 1700 BC into the Iron Age.

The Late Bronze Age, from about 1350 BC on, is marked by cremation burials in urns and a far wider range of metalwork—bronze axes, daggers and spearheads, and later rapiers—as well as many exquisitely worked gold ornaments. Much of this material has been found in buried hoards. After 1000 BC the sword was introduced, and in this period sheet metal working became common—cauldrons, buckets, and trumpets, blown at the end or at the side. It is probable that a warrior aristocracy had begun to develop, with ownership of cattle as a mark of wealth, while at the same time the end of the period saw more intensive farming of arable land. Substantial houses are now known, again discovered at *Lough Gur*, and in the earlier phases of *Navan Fort*. From the Late Bronze Age comes the earliest evidence for large hill forts—tribal centers or sometimes ritual enclosures—with one or more circuits of ramparts.

The Iron Age

We have reached the borders of the Iron Age (roughly 500 BC to 500 AD), a period characterized by the full development of the hill forts, by crannogs, artificial islands in lakes for safe habitation, and the smaller defended farmsteads called ring forts, all of which continue without a break into the succeeding Early Christian period. The large forts, usually stone-built in the W. and with earthen ramparts in the E.—as well as promontory forts, a neck of land on an inland promontory or over the sea, cut off at the base by defensive ramparts—are exceedingly difficult to fix in time and may date from the Bronze Age into the Early Christian period. Many of these larger forts and the ring forts (stone-built "cashels" in the W., "raths" in the N.) may have souterrains under them, partly rock-cut underground chambers and passages, used for storage and probably for refuge too. Burial rites in the Iron Age, according to the archaeological evidence, seem to have been of far less importance than before. In the Early Iron Age iron objects of the European Halstatt type are scarce in Ireland, and bronze-working continued as before.

A fully iron-using society did not develop until after 300 BC, and this was a reflection of the latest European Iron Age phase, the La Tène. The warrior aristrocracy, now distinctively Celtic, continued to develop with its warrior bands and cattle raids—as reflected in the Ulster heroic sagas—and tribal confederations centered on the larger hill forts appear to have been forming proto-kingdoms, as suggested by the many long, linear defensive earthworks such as those guarding the southern boundary of Ulster (see *Dorsey Enclosure* and *Navan Fort*). Beautifully carved ritual stones (see *Turoe Stone*) and strange, carved stone figures, some perhaps Early Christian (see for instance *Boa Island* and *White Island*) are found, as well as Ogham stones. These are stones, often standing stones, inscribed with an Irish script of straight strokes along a guiding line, based on the Latin alphabet. They are found from the Late Iron Age into the Early Christian period. The later part of this period is precisely that of the Roman occupation of Britain, and although there is no evidence of Roman occupation of Ireland, the numerous Romano-British finds (see New Grange in the *Boyne Valley*) could have reached Ireland through trade, Irish raids on Britain, "tourists," refugees fleeing Britain or similar causes.

The Early Christian Period

The period extends roughly again from the 5th cent. AD until about 1000 AD. This is, above all, the period of the ring forts, or raths in the N.—self-sufficient farmsteads of the wealthier members of the community. In eastern Ireland the ring forts are enclosed in one or more earthen ramparts, not so much for defense as for protection and social prestige. In the W., where stone is more easily available, a single rampart is built of stone, as are the buildings inside. There are well over 40,000 of these farmsteads in Ireland—the most common form of field monument. The period is also characterized by the remains of numerous monastic communities, which are usually very similar to the ring forts, though dedicated to religious purposes and probably wealthier. From the 7th cent. on these religious enclosures, mostly monasteries, became the important cultural centers of the great, early Irish Renaissance, their skilled craftsmen copying books, producing the lovely, early illuminated manuscripts, such as the *Book of Kells* and the *Book of Durrow*, as well as intricately ornamented chalices and reliquaries. Scholar-monks presided over the schools attended by students from many countries, veritable "universities" that also sent out missionary teachers all over Europe to found other monasteries and spread learning far and wide. Yet these accomplished monks lived in the crudest of enclosed settlements built of earth and timber, and little survives today on the ground from this early period; what does survive dates from when stone began to be used in the 8th cent.

Today many of these early sites are marked by a later church and perhaps a graveyard with a few early cross slabs in it. There may be a round tower and perhaps remnants of an early enclosure, some ruined stone oratories or churches, and maybe a high cross or two. For a representative monastic site, see *Nendrum*. Much more is to be seen, of course, at the large monastic centers such as *Clonmacnoise* and *Glendalough*. Long after the original missionary impulse, which had done so much to raise Europe out of the Dark Ages, had withered away, the monks went on to produce the superb high crosses so typical of Ireland; to build from the 10th to the 12th cents. the slender round towers; and finally in the 12th cent. to decorate their churches with the profuse sculptural ornamentation of the early Romanesque.

There are over 65 round towers surviving in Ireland in various states of preservation, most of which have been included in this guide. They all follow a similar pattern and were probably erected by roving teams of specialist builders. Essentially an upward extension of the Irish clochán or round, corbelled stone hut found in the interior of many early monasteries (see *Skellig Michael*)—mortar bonding and rubble infill in the lower parts borrowed from the Roman tradition—the towers were remarkably shallowly based, yet tapered inward as they rose, giving them their long-lasting stability. At the top was a conical stone cap, corbelled on the inside. The towers could rise as high as 100 ft. and there were usually six or seven floors (of wood), a few windows, especially around the top, and a doorway raised well above the ground to promote stability of the tower as well as the security of the monks. The towers were used as belfrys, as safe storage for the church treasures, as lookouts, as refuges during raids, whether Irish or Viking, but above all as symbols of the aspiration toward God in His heaven above—like the Hindu temple-mountains.

The earliest extant high crosses date from the 7th cent. (see *Fahan*), the cross itself made up of interlaced ribbons, with a few stiff figures, very much like those on the Pictish symbol stones of Scotland. But the remarkable development of these masterpieces really began in the 8th cent. when high crosses, obviously translated into stone from the earlier portable crosses of wood and metal, began to appear. From their predecessors these crosses retained the bosses, now decorative, and the distinctive open circle around the cross itself, once functional but now also decorative (see *Ahenny*). These crosses were exuberantly decorated with Celtic spiral and interlace designs, and figured scenes now began to appear, but usually only on the base of the cross. Some were biblical, but others showed strange scenes of hunting and processions—probably symbolic, though also harking back to pagan Celtic motifs. Carved cross slabs and grave slabs were usually found in conjunction with the high crosses on the same site, many of which survive today (see *Clonmacnoise*).

The next step is represented by the transitional crosses of the 9th cent. (see, for instance, *Castledermot* and *Moone*), which are still intricately ornamented. But now the biblical scenes, in panels, begin to dominate the whole cross, on the arms and shaft. For these high crosses were not used as grave markers; they were preaching crosses, the "poor man's Bible" in a largely illiterate country. They were also used as a focus for meditation and prayer. The finest of the high crosses were erected from the late 9th into the 10th cent., exemplified by the wonderful high crosses at *Kells*, *Monasterboice* and elsewhere. Thereafter decline set in until the last type of high cross appeared in the 12th cent. These featured, instead of biblical scenes, figures carved in high relief of Christ, of abbots and bishops (see *The Burren*, Kilfenora).

As time went on the larger monastic centers grew wealthier and more crowded, belying their ascetic origins (in fact, there was a reformation in the 12th cent. in an effort to return to the simple monastic life, and anchorite communities were founded, especially in the W.). The richer monasteries, of course, became prime targets for the Viking raiders of the 9th and 10th cents., who were after plunder. Large settlements grew up around them, with many lay people attached to the monastery, so that these conglomerates became in effect the closest thing to towns that rural Ireland had seen before the coming of the Normans.

But it was actually the Norse Vikings, beginning to settle down in Ireland instead of raiding, who founded the first real proto-cities in the country. These began as trading posts on the far-flung Viking sea routes, then by the 10th cent. began to develop into commercial cities. Among them were Cork, Limerick, Waterford, Wexford, and above all *Dublin*. As the Viking population was gradually absorbed into Irish society they contributed their own Scandinavian beast designs to the melange of Irish art. Then in the 12th cent. came the Anglo-Norman invasion, and we enter the Middle Ages.

AGHADOE
(Kerry)

Stump of a round tower, much reconstructed, in a commanding position on a ridge 3 mi. (4.75 km.) NW of Killarney, remnant of an early monastery. Near it is a ruined church of the 12th–13th cents. The tower, one of some 65 known in Ireland, now stands only about 22 ft. high, and is not a very good example of these lovely towers. They were used as belfrys or bell towers, as safe storage for the monastery's treasures and as places of refuge—and as an emblem of the towering aspiration toward God above. Aghadoe belonged to one of the earliest groups, but its date, and that of most of the round towers, is uncertain. It could date anywhere from the mid-7th to the 10th cents.

AGHAGOWER
(Mayo)

Another round tower, preserved up to the 4th floor (about 52 ft. high), 4.5 mi. (7.25 km.) SE of Westport on the lower Mayo coast. The tower, next to a 12th–15th cent. church, is itself probably 12th cent. Its original, round-headed raised doorway is supplemented by a modern ground-level doorway. Round tower entrances were generally raised to provide security and also to enhance the stability of these tall, tapering towers.

AGHANAGLACK COURT TOMB
(Fermanagh)

See *Boho*.

AGHAVILLER
(Kilkenny)

Stump of a round tower, 2 mi. (3.25 km.) SW of Knocktopher, still standing about 40 ft. high, with a recent ground-level doorway inserted into it. Near it is a ruined rectangular tower, a former church later fortified, and a holy well.

AGHNAHOO SOUTERRAIN
(Tyrone)

See *Leitrim*.

AGHNASKEAGH
(Louth)

Two overgrown cairns of considerable interest, 50 yds. apart, a little over 4 mi. (6.5 km.) N. of Dundalk, on a side road running W. off the Dundalk-Newry road at Feede. The larger, egg-shaped cairn has been excavated, yielding a roofless portal tomb at one end, with four cremation burials and late Neolithic objects, and at the other end six later, Bronze Age cist burials as well as an Iron Age iron-smelting, paved area on the N. side. The smaller, circular cairn covered four separate Neolithic chambers. On the NE is a ring fort of earth. About 2 mi. (3.25 km.) S. lie the *Proleek* tombs, and 2.5 mi. (4 km.) SE the *Kilnasaggart* pillar.

AHENNY
(Tipperary)

Two of the earliest decorated high crosses of stone in the country, 5 mi. (8 km.) N. of Carrick-on-Suir and only a few mi. N. of the *Kilkieran* crosses. Richly ornamented in a style recalling the famous *Book of Kells*, they are thus possibly 8th cent. in date. Both are about 12 ft. high and carry unusual stone caps. The shafts and arms are decorated with spirals, interlacing and geometrical designs, some obviously deriving from earlier portable wooden crosses overlaid with metal. Figured panels on the bases (best on the N. cross, much worn on the S. cross) depict various biblical scenes, and a curious funeral depiction of a headless man and a chariot procession (N. cross), suggesting pagan rituals. See also *Dromiskin*; *Killamery*; *Kilree*.

AILECH FORT
(Donegal)

See *Grianan of Aileach*.

The North Cross at Ahenny, Tipperary. The two crosses here are among the earliest in Ireland. They probably derived directly from the earlier, portable wooden crosses covered in decorated sheet metal. Even the nail bosses have been translated into stone. The geometric ornamentation at Ahenny is so close to that of the Book of Kells *that the crosses probably date from the 8th cent. Both carry strange caps, and only on the bases are there figured scenes, some biblical, others enigmatic scenes that seem to hark back to pagan rituals. On the base of the North Cross, here, a man is shown under a palm tree, with animals. (Courtesy of Irish Tourist Board, Dublin.)*

AILLEMORE COURT TOMB (Mayo)

A megalithic tomb 5 mi. (8 km.) SW of Louisburgh on a ridge near the coast overlooking a river valley. Its cairn, well over 50 ft. long, still rises to the top of the stones of the two-chambered gallery and conceals, along with a modern fence, the court in front. Behind the gallery is another small chamber. The tomb is noteworthy for the remaining corbelling of the large slabs of the gallery roof, particularly on the N. side.

ALTADAVEN (Tyrone)

See *Clogher.*

ALTAGORE (Antrim)

Stone fort, over a mi. (1.6 km.) N. of Cushendun, W. of the coast road to Ballycastle. The walls of this fort survive to a height of about 9 ft. and enclose an area of about 45 ft. across. There are traces of steps that led up to a terrace. It was probably built in the Early Christian period.

ALTDRUMMAN (Tyrone)

Portal tomb 3.5 mi. (5.6 km.) NW of Carrickmore (also called Termon Rock) and N. of Lough Macrory in central Tyrone, in an area rich in megalithic monuments. Called "Cloghogle," the tomb has an enormous capstone nearly 9 ft. long and garlanded with grasses on top, resting on relatively small supporting stones. To the NE .75 mi. (1 km.) is a fine example of a wedge-shaped tomb with four out of five roofstones still in position and a tree growing out of it. Like many tombs it is called "Dermot and Grania's Bed." A half mi. (.75 km.) NE is a large court tomb about 75 ft. long with remains of two chambers in its SE end. The kerb stones of the original cairn are still visible. Both the latter tombs are in Loughmacrory townland.

ANNAGHMARE CAIRN
(Armagh)

One of the finest court tombs in the north of Ireland, excavated in the early 1960s. Called the Black Castle, it is about 2 mi. (3.25 km.) N. of Crossmaglen. The cairn of piled-up stones, over 62 ft. long, covers a burial gallery with three segments. At the back (N.) end two more chambers were added later. The impressive horseshoe-shaped court to the S. and the facade are built of tall stone uprights filled in with fine drystone walling. The excavation yielded both burned and unburned human bones, Neolithic pottery, a flint javelin and bones of ox and pig. The *Dorsey* enclosure lies not far to the N. of this site.

ANTRIM
(Antrim)

Round tower, now in a suburb of Antrim, .5 mi. (.75 km.) N. of the town. It belonged to a renowned Early Christian monastery and was probably built in the 10th or 11th cent. It is well-preserved, standing about 96 ft. high, with a raised doorway with a cross on its lintel, eight small windows and a restored cap.

ARAN ISLANDS
(Galway)

Group of islands at the mouth of Galway Bay. Only the three largest are inhabited—Inishmore, about 8 mi. (13 km.) long, and the smaller Inishmaan and the still smaller Inisheer. Culturally and geologically the islands have more in common with *The Burren* in Clare to the SE than with Galway. The three islands not only preserve some of the traditional Irish culture but are also littered with ancient remains from different periods, many now in state care—small ring forts, chamber tombs, hut sites, crosses and the remnants of many early Christian monasteries, and the imposing prehistoric drystone forts typical of the islands. A detailed tourist map of the islands is available at Kilronan on Inishmore, the port of entry, and on the boats and ferries from the mainland. Some of the more important earlier monuments are described below. Few if any have been accurately dated.

The dramatic, great stone forts, traditionally built by the legendary Firbolgs, can date anywhere from late BC to early medieval. They have been extensively and often inaccurately restored. The famous Dun Aengus (or Dun Angus) for instance was completely rebuilt in 1881. It is spectacularly sited on the edge of a tall, sheer cliff in Kilmurvy townland, Inishmore. Originally it had four irregular half circuits of drystone walls, ending on the cliff edge and enclosing 11 acres, with a wide field of *chevaux de frise*—limestone spikes set upright to deter the enemy—in the large space between the third and fourth walls. The inner citadel, 150 ft. across, is enclosed in walls 16 ft. thick and 13 ft. high, with wall chambers and a fine lintelled entrance passage. A bronze fibula of the early Iron Age was found in its walls in 1839.

The equally spectacular and overly restored Dun Oghil (Inishmore), roughly round, with two ramparts, once had stone huts in its interior. Also on Inishmore are the circular Dun Onaght with a single wall and three house sites within, and Dun Doocaher (Dun Chathair, or the Black Fort), a restored promontory fort with a massive stone rampart across the promontory, restored stone huts inside it,

Tighlagh Eany, a typical early church on Inishmore, largest of the Aran Islands off Galway Bay. Note its fine rounded window and doorway. The church harbors the grave of St. Eany and, traditionally, that of St. Enda, a famous 5th-cent. missionary. (Courtesy of Irish Tourist Board, Dublin.)

and remnants of *chevaux de frise* outside the wall. On Inishmaan is Dun (or Caher) Conor, a D-shaped fort with one massive (restored) wall with terraces behind and wall chambers, and restored house sites in the interior. On Inisheer is the Creggankeel fort, irregularly shaped. An unusually large oval stone hut, Clochán na Carraige, stands on Inishmore. It has a S. window and doorways E. and W.

There are many remnants of the early Christian monasteries on the islands. In the 5th cent. AD St. Enda was supposed to have founded one of the earliest Irish monasteries on Inishmore, sending his disciples out to found other great monasteries like *Clonmacnoise*. Several early churches, often rebuilt or extended in later times, survive. These are usually simple rectangular structures of stone like Temple Benen on Inishmore, a little oratory only 7 ft. by 11 ft. with a flat lintelled doorway and enormous side-wall stones. There are vestiges of a cashel and huts around it, and inside and outside, as with most of these churches, early cross slabs and other remnants. There is also the stump of a round tower at Temple Benen.

At Temple Brecan, much altered in medieval times, there is a curious gravestone dedicated to seven Roman saints, as well as the reputed grave of St. Brecan. Temple MacDuagh, near Dun Aengus, is again built of large stones with a flat-headed doorway, and inside it one finds the figure of a horse. St. Enda himself is reputed to be buried at Tighlagh Eany, a fine early church with rounded E. window and later additions, as well as fragments of a high cross (12th cent.?), and St. Eany's grave within it. These are all on Inishmore. On Inishmaan one might mention Kilcanonagh, a small stone oratory, and on Inisheer Kilgobnet (church of St. Gobnet), another small oratory. Close to the landing place is an early, circular graveyard called Knockgrania.

Among a number of Neolithic chambered tombs on the islands a wedge tomb W. of Dun Oghil on Inishmore, called as usual Dermot and Grania's Bed, shows three overlapping capstones on top of a long burial gallery. On Inishmaan, about 1 mi. (1.6 km.) NE of Dun Conor, another Dermot and Grania's Bed, also a wedge tomb, has a capstone over 10 ft. long resting on two uprights.

ARBOE CROSS
(Tyrone)

High Cross, the sole survivor, with a ruin called Arboe Abbey, of an early Christian site of great antiquity; on the western shore of Lough Neagh, 5 mi. (8 km.) E. and a little S. of Coagh, close to Arboe Point. This is the best of a group of mostly fragmentary northern crosses. Probably dated to the 10th cent., the cross is a veritable "poor man's Bible," showing many scenes from the Old and New Testaments carved on all four sides of the shaft and on the cross. These high crosses were not memorials or grave-markers but focal points for preaching, praying and meditation.

ARDGROOM OUTWARD
CIRCLE
(Cork)

A fine example of the axial or recumbent stone circles typical of the Cork/Kerry group, a striking monument of long, thin, surviving stones up to 6 ft. high, commanding wide views over Bantry Bay and Ardgroom, 4.5 mi. (7.25 km.) SW of Lauragh Bridge. In these circles the portal stones (usually the tallest) face an axial stone, lying on its side, across the axis of the circle, usually to the SW (compare the Recumbent Stone Circles of Scotland). In this case, unusually, the axial stone stands upright. There is an outlying standing stone to the E. of the circle.

ARDMORE
(Waterford)

One of the most beautiful and best-preserved of the Irish round towers, a late example, 95 ft. high, with a fine, round-arched raised doorway and the original conical roof. It stands 5 mi. (8 km.) E. of Youghal in a field overlooking the sea. The tower is divided into four stages by string courses and has an unusually pronounced inward lean or batter. It dates from the late 12th cent. as does the "Cathedral," the ruined church close by, which exhibits arcades of quaint Romanesque sculpture on its front, much weathered but obviously biblical in subject. Inside the church are two Ogham stones; one reads, simply, "beloved." Nearby St. Declan's oratory, restored, is a much earlier building and in its interior is the reputed grave site of St. Declan who founded the original monastery here (5th cent. AD?). In the 12th cent. Ardmore was the seat of a bishop, and later was owned for two years by Sir Walter Raleigh.

ARMAGH
(Armagh)

A very ancient town. The Protestant cathedral here was built on the site of St. Patrick's principal church and a later monastery with an important monastic school. Before that the site was one of the sacred enclosures of pagan Ireland, and one can still trace two rings of the ramparts. Inside the cathedral there is an interesting group of figures from this ancient site. Of these carved stone figures about half a dozen are considered "Celtic" (i.e., well before the 6th cent. AD). These include three bears, two stone heads, a figure of the Celtic sun god with rayed headdress, and a grinning horned figure, probably the war god Nodens (called the "Tandragee Figure"); another figure shows bared breasts and a skirt. In the excellent Armagh County Museum are three more probable Celtic heads (see also *Boa Island, White Island*). Fragments of one of the northern figured high crosses can be seen in the W. end of the cathedral (see *Arboe Cross*). The Armagh Public Library displays one of the earliest Christian stones known, from Drumconwell, carved with a crude cross and an Ogham inscription. Not far from Armagh is the great Ulster fort of *Navan*.

The beautiful round tower at Ardmore, Waterford, a late example (12th cent.) that differs from earlier towers in its pronounced batter and the string courses that divide it into four sections. Very well-preserved, it has its original conical roof. The ruined church behind it dates from the same century. (Photo: courtesy of Irish Tourist Board, Dublin. Photo: the author.)

ARMOY
(Antrim)

Stump of a dilapidated round tower, over 90 ft. high, in a modern churchyard ENE of Armoy village in northern Antrim. Its raised, tapering doorway is reputedly the narrowest in Ireland, and is topped by a heavy monolith with an arch carved out of it. About 1 mi. (1.6 km.) ENE from the tower, at Tullaghora, are two interesting standing pillars up on a slope above the road—one in the rough shape of a cross, the other, taller one with a shape suggesting a phallus, with a curious scissors-like design incised into it. They may not be as old as they look; on the other hand, white quartzite pebbles are scattered on the ground around them, usually an indication of pagan magic, and they may very well be part-Christianized, pagan standing stones.

ARRAGLEN
(Kerry)

See *Dingle Peninsula*.

ATHGREANY
(Wicklow)

A fine stone circle, 1.5 mi. (2.3 km.) S. of Hollywood village off the road to *Baltinglass* (about 11 mi. or 17.75 km. to the S.). Known as "The Piper's Stones" because of an outlying stone (the piper piping to his ring dancers), its 14 stones—both boulders and pillars—enclose a circle over 90 ft. across. It is probably Bronze Age. About 6 mi. (9.6 km.) S. is another stone circle at *Castleruddery*.

ATHLONE
(Westmeath)

The Castle Museum here holds some interesting Early Christian survivals. The *Bealin Cross* stands outside Athlone, which is a convenient center for visiting *Clonmacnoise*.

AUDLEYSTOWN CAIRN
(Down)

Good example of a double court tomb, near the southern shore of Strangford Lough, .75 mi. (1 km.) W. and N. of Strangford; discovered in 1946, excavated in 1952 and now preserved inside fences. The trapezoidal cairn is revetted with drystone walling, and shallow courts at either end lead into galleries with four chambers opening off each. The jumbled remains of 34 skeletons, only some of them burned and all apparently reburied here, were found in the excavations. The whole tomb suggests the influence of the Severn-Cotswold type of British late Neolithic tomb across the sea.

BALIX LOWER COURT
TOMB
(Tyrone)

See *Clogherny*.

BALLA
(Mayo)

Round tower in central lower Mayo, in a graveyard. Only the stump, about 32 ft. high, remains—up to the third floor, including the raised doorway with rounded top. The tower alone survives from a monastery founded here in the 7th cent. AD. About 3 mi. (4.75 km.) to the S. is the tiny hamlet of Mayo, which gave the county its name, site of an even more famous 7th-cent. monastery founded by English monks after the Synod of Whitby in 663 AD. Only fragments of ecclesiastical buildings and traces of the circular enclosure wall are left.

BALLINLOUGHAN
(Louth)

Good examples of Bronze Age petroglyphs abundant in Louth and Monaghan, and not too hard to find—5 mi. (8 km.) WSW of Dundalk and 1 mi. (1.6 km.) N. of Little Ash, NE of the road to Iniskeen (in Monaghan). The designs include rare examples of small cup marks within a cup and ring design. See also *Derrynablaha* (Kerry).

BALLINEETIG STANDING
STONE
(Kerry)

See *Dingle Peninsula.*

BALLYBARRACK
(Louth)

Fine and elaborate examples of underground souterrains, just outside Dundalk, discovered in 1977. They are very late (13th cent.) but are typical of a class of monument found in Ireland, many dating from the Viking period or earlier and very similar to the *fogous* of Cornwall in England. Like others, these were built inside a ring fort, undoubtedly for storage. The chambers here are partly rock-cut, with the rest constructed with corbels supporting heavy lintel stones.

BALLYBRACK
(Dublin)

Portal dolmen or tomb, fenced in for protection, 9 mi. (14.5 km.) SE of Dublin and just E. of Laughlinstown. Some of its stones are missing, but the heavy, tilted capstone is impressive. It bears a prominent cup mark.

BALLYBRIEST
(Londonderry)

A ruined double court tomb called Carnanbane, on Lough Fea, about 7 mi. (11.25 km.) NW of Cookstown. The two forecourts, E. and W., leading into two-chamber burial galleries can still be discerned. Excavated in 1937, the tomb was constructed over the remains of an earlier Neolithic settlement or ritual site, with wooden structures. Across the road to the E. are the remains of what appears to be a large wedge tomb, and another, smaller one lies just to the S. To the NE 1.25 mi. (2 km.) are the Corick Circles, uncovered from under the peat— five circles, one with a standing stone at the center, and three alignments.

BALLYEDMONDUFF
(Dublin)

Impressive example of a large wedge-shaped tomb, assigned to about 1700 BC in the Early Bronze Age. This "Giant's Grave" is magnificently sited at over 1,000 ft. on the SE slope of Two Rock Mountain, a little over 2 mi. (3.25 km.) SW of Stepaside, W. of the Glencullen road. Its rectangular double-walled gallery is divided into three sections like the tomb at *Labbacallee* in Cork and is set within heavy kerb stones. On excavation the tomb yielded pottery and cremated bone.

BALLYGANNER SOUTH
(Clare)

See *The Burren.*

BALLYGLASS
(Mayo)

Center court tomb, one of 27 in the area, excavated 1968–72. It lies .75 mi. (1 km.) NW of the resort village of Ballycastle near the N. coast. Close access is unfortunately discouraged. Two-chamber burial galleries run off at either end of an elliptical center court entered from the side. Of chief interest here was the discovery of the remains of a large, earlier Neolithic wooden house under the NW end of the tomb, radiocarbon-dated at around 2620 BC. The tomb was obviously somewhat later.

BALLYGROLL
(Londonderry)

Interesting prehistoric complex, 6 mi. (9.6 km.) ESE of Londonderry town and 4 mi. (6.5 km.) NE of Claudy, up a long lane to a hilltop. Here, partly peat-covered, are over a dozen small, round cairns, several stone circles around 9 ft. across (which may be the kerb-stones of cairns), a barrow, at least two wedge tombs, a court tomb, and stretches of prehistoric field walls. The barrow was excavated in 1978–79. The monuments are probably Neolithic to Early Bronze Age.

BALLYHEAGHBOUGHT
(Kerry)

See *Dingle Peninsula.*

BALLYKEEL
(Armagh)

Fine example of a portal tomb, 4.5 mi. (7.25 km.) SW of Carnlough on the western slopes of *Slieve Gullion*, with the remains of a long cairn stretching behind the portal stones (a burial cist was found in the far end of the cairn). The tall portal stones, with a blocking stone between them, support a huge capstone sloping down to the back stone. The tomb, excavated in 1963, yielded from its main chamber and the cist quantities of Neolithic pottery.

BALLYKINVARGA FORT
(Clare)

See *The Burren*.

BALLYMACALDRACK
(Antrim)

An unusual egg-shaped court tomb cairn called "Dooey's Cairn," .75 mi. (1 km.) SE of Dunloy, about 10 mi. (16 km.) NW of Ballymena, excavated in 1935 and 1975. Its U-shaped court, apparently built on to the tomb about 500 years after its initial construction in about 3000 BC, is in fine shape, lined by uprights chinked with small stones. Beyond the court there is one chamber under the kerb-lined cairn, and behind that again a curious passage with three cists dug into the floor. One cist contained the cremated bones of six adults.

BALLYMACDERMOT
(Armagh)

A fine court tomb, possibly very early in the sequence, 2 mi. (3.25 km.) SW of Newry on the southern slope of Ballymacdermot Mountain. The trapezoidal-shaped cairn, about 90 ft. long, has an almost circular forecourt of low stones at the N. end leading into an antechamber and two chambers in the gallery. Some of the corbelling of the chambers is still visible. Excavated in the 19th cent., the tomb was reexcavated in 1962, yielding the usual flints and Neolithic pottery. It is safe to assume that the tomb is about 4,800 years old.

BALLYNAGILLY
(Tyrone)

Interesting Neolithic settlement site, now unfortunately quarried away, near Cookstown. On a low sandy hill the remains of a substantial timber-built house, almost square, were found. Postholes in the interior indicated roof supports, and there were two hearths as well as a refuse pit filled with sherds and domestic debris. The house had burned down, and radiocarbon dates indicated a period well before 3000 BC for the house. In higher strata sherds of Early Bronze Age Beaker-type pottery turned up, and above that evidence of the Food Vessel people.

BALLYNAHATTY
(Down)

Remarkable Late Neolithic enclosure called "The Giant's Ring," 4 mi. (6.5 km.) S. of Belfast center, about half way between the M-1 and A-24 roads, on a terrace above an ancient crossing of the Logan River. A bank, up to 15 ft. high, encloses a ritual center of seven acres, with the remains of a small passage grave of five uprights with a capstone near the center. It appears that this ritual enclosure may be a henge like those in England and Scotland. Of the five gaps in the bank, at least three may be original. The site was excavated in 1954.

BALLYNASTAIG
(Galway)

See *Crannagh*.

BALLYNOE
(Down)

Stone circle, called by Aubrey Burl "one of the finest megalithic rings in the British Isles"; 2.5 mi. (4 km.) S. of *Downpatrick* and only 2 mi. (3.25 km.) N. of Dundrum Bay on the E. coast. From here the W. coast of England is only about 80 mi. across the water; and on the trading route between Ireland and the Lake Country in England is a remarkably similar ring, *Swinside*, at the head of Duddo

Sands, suggesting a close relation between the two rings. Ballynoe was a large open ring, a true circle of over 50 closely-spaced boulders about 110 ft. across with two large portal stones standing outside the ring on the WNW. Opposite them, within the ring, is a crescent of five stones. Other low outlying stones stand outside the circle. Thousands of years after it was constructed, Bronze Age people, utilizing a still sacred site, built an earth-covered cairn inside the eastern side of the ring with a stone kerb. Limited excavations in 1937–38 found two cists within it containing cremated burials. One sherd of pottery found in the original ring helped to date it to the Late Neolithic. Obviously Ballynoe was a central gathering place for the Neolithic people whose settlement remains have been found along the shore to the S.

BALLYREAGH (Fermanagh).

Double court tomb in the remains of a very long cairn over 330 yds in length, 1.75 mi. (2.6 km.) NW of the village of Tempo, and about .5 mi. (.75 km.) SW of Lough Mulshane. There are forecourts at each end leading into galleries with two chambers each. The entrance on the W. is unusually fine with a curious sill stone; that to the E. is made of larger stones (up to 6 ft. high). The western part of the tomb was reused for urn burials in the Late Bronze or Early Iron Ages. See also *Boho* (Aghanaglack) and *Ballywholan*.

BALLYVOURNEY (Cork)

Early Christian site, 8.5 mi. (13.75 km.) W. of Macroom and S. of the main road to Killarney from Macroom. W. of the parish church about .75 mi. (1 km.), is the site of a nunnery founded perhaps in the 7th cent. by St. Gobnat, a virgin figure with fertility and healing powers whose 13th-cent. wooden statue is preserved in the church. At the nunnery site are the ruins of a medieval church incorporating remnants of an earlier church, as well as St. Gobnat's House (a National Monument), actually the ruins of a circular drystone hut once used by iron smelters and bronze workers in the Early Christian period, as excavations have shown. Under it the remains of an even earlier rectangular timber house was found, used for the same purpose. Pilgrims still perform a "pattern" in the area, which is obviously a very ancient site, especially around the parish church where the stations include St. Gobnat's Grave in the old churchyard; a low mound; the Priest's Grave just outside the parish church; a holy well; and St. Abban's Grave, a small cairn with a cist in it and three Ogham stones around it; and various crosses incised on stones, gateposts, boulders. A half mile (.75 km.) NE of Ballyvourney church at Killeen is a very early cross pillar, St. Gobnat's Stone, with Greek crosses in double circles on it and on one face a small carved figure recalling those in the *Book of Durrow*. It was found at the site of a dried-up holy well nearby.

At Ballyvourney, also, Prof. Michael O'Kelly discovered and excavated a *Fulacht Fian*, a cooking site of a type used in Ireland as far back as the Early Bronze Age, with a stone-lined pit, a wood-lined trough, hearths and the remains of a hut. Here stones were heated and thrown into water to make it boil and cook meat wrapped in straw. O'Kelly actually reconstructed the site and cooked a 10-pound leg of mutton in the boiling water—with success!

BALLYWEE (Antrim)

A ring fort or rath and associated structures, excavated in 1974, 4.5 mi. (7.25 km.) ENE of Antrim town. Like most raths the site belonged to the Early Christian period, and included a low circular bank (not for defense) enclosing an area about 180 ft. across containing a rectangular stone-paved house with central hearth, approached by cobbled paths, and elsewhere three souterrains for storage and three outbuildings. Much domestic rubbish was retrieved, especially from the house area. Nothing is now visible except the earthen bank.

BALLYWHOLAN
(Tyrone)

A well-preserved double court tomb, 3.5 mi. (5.6 km.) SE of *Clogher*. This small tomb, called "Carnagat," is still embedded in its 60-ft.-long cairn. Forecourts at either end led into galleries of two chambers each, with tall stones around the NE court. To the NW 1.5 mi. (2.3 km.) is another tomb, much overgrown, with a similar cairn, called "Carnfadrig." This is a hybrid type, for at the E. end is a wrecked portal tomb and rectangular chamber, while at the W. end a transverse gallery with no obvious entrance is divided into a number of sections. Both were partly excavated in 1899. See also *Ballyreagh* and *Boho* (Aghanaglack).

BALTINGLASS HILL
(Wicklow)

A hill affording magnificent views 1 mi. (1.6 km.) NE of Baltinglass village with its ruined medieval abbey. The hill, much built over, initially held three small passage tombs, two single-chambered tombs, a cist burial and other features, Late Neolithic or Bronze Age, all under a huge cairn of which only the double retaining walls remain. Farther down the hill are the double stone ramparts of the great Iron Age hill fort of Rathcoran. A third massive wall around the hill seems to be of more recent date. The earliest of the passage tombs (Tomb I) was largely destroyed by the building of the large cairn and kerb of Tomb II. Beside Tomb I is a beehive-shaped structure, probably contemporary with the tomb. The second surviving tomb, to the N. and much larger, had a central chamber and five side chambers with a short passage. The third tomb to the S. had a single circular chamber that contained a large, decorated stone basin, as in the larger passage tombs in the *Boyne Valley*. Some of the roof stones of its passage can still be seen. Tomb I also held a basin, much smaller. About 600 yds. NW of the hill is another hill fort, Rathnagree, again with two circuits of ramparts. Six stones scattered around Baltinglass Hill show passage grave decorations.

BAURNADOMEENY
(Tipperary)

A fine, large wedge tomb, excavated and now conserved in an almost round circle of kerb stones, .5 mi. (.75 km.) NE of Rear Cross, which is 7 mi. (11.25 km.) SE of Newport. The tomb itself, sitting in the midst of the remainders of its cairn, has a large chamber over 12 ft. long and a long antechamber separated from it by a septal slab and still covered with a roof of capstones. There were five cremation burials in the antechamber and 16 others in cists and pits under the area of the cairn, about 45 ft. in diameter. There are crude decorations of incised lines and pockmarks on some of the stones. Many Neolithic potsherds were recovered.

BAUR SOUTH TOMB
(Clare)

See *The Burren*.

BEALIN CROSS
(Westmeath)

Fine early cross on a hill N. of Bealin post office, over 2 mi. (3.25 km.) ENE of *Athlone*. Found in Bealin, it has been moved to Twyford Demesne. An inscription by a bishop of *Clonmacnoise*, where it was probably made, dates it to about 800 AD. The cross is beautifully ornamented with spirals, interlace and animals, and shows on its N. face a hunter with spear, dog and a deer, very similar to Pictish reliefs from Scotland. In the time of these early crosses biblical figured scenes had not yet come into fashion.

BEENALAGHT
(Cork)

Best known of many alignments in an area rich in megalithic monuments; 8.5 mi. (13.75 km.) S. of Mallow on a hill W. off the Coachford road near Bweeng. Called *An Seisear* (The Six), one of its original six stones, up to 9 ft. high, has fallen. One mi. (1⅔ km.) S. by W. is a fine stone ring, Gowlane North, a perfect circle of eight stones, two fallen, 21 ft. across with an entrance on the N. Two outer portal stones at the entrance face a rectangular recumbent stone across the axis of the circle.

BEENBANE FORT
(Kerry)

Stone fort 1 mi. (1.6 km.) NE of Waterville. Called Lisoven, it is a horseshoe-shaped fort facing on to Lough Currane, with a shallow souterrain inside it. Outside it are the ruins of a large beehive hut with walls 7 ft. thick, and in the fields to the N. are the remains of huts, houses, pillarstones and two small chamber tombs.

BEAGHMORE MONUMENTS
(Tyrone)

Well-known site with stone circles, alignments and cairns on the gentle slopes of the Sperrin Mountains; 8.5 mi. (13.75 km.) NW of Cookstown, off a minor road. A major Bronze Age ritual center, Beaghmore is the finest of many monuments of the type in Tyrone and Fermanagh, all made of quite small stones closely positioned. Peat-cutting at Beaghmore in 1945–49 and 1965 has uncovered seven circles of varying size, often paired, and 10 alignments and over a dozen small stone cairns associated with the circles—and more will be found as the cutting proceeds. The cairns, some containing burial cists, may be earlier than the stone monuments, which were probably not all erected at the same

Some of the stone circles, alignments and a cairn at the Bronze Age ritual center of Beaghmore, Tyrone. These curious circles of Northern Ireland are typically composed of small stones and, as shown, are often paired. The unusual large circle in the background is filled with close-set stones, for reasons unknown. (Crown copyright: Historic Monuments and Buildings Branch, DOENI, Northern Ireland.)

time, the site being quite late and dated from the late 2nd into the early 1st millennia BC. One of the largest circles is inexplicably filled with close-set boulders. The finds, of pottery, skull fragments and other items, were scarce. Faint traces of Neolithic field boundaries underlie the monuments, indicating earlier use of the land as arable. Indeed the monuments may have been built as desperate propitiary offerings to stem the gradual loss of the arable land under the peat.

At Davagh Lower 2 mi. (3.25 km.) NE of Beaghmore, another site, in Davagh Forest, offers a double circle, part of a single circle, a possible alignment, a wedge tomb and another collapsed tomb. Another impressive wedge tomb lies 2 mi. (3.25 km.) S. of Beaghmore at Dunnamore.

BELFAST
(Antrim)

Industrial port and capital of Northern Ireland. The Ulster Museum here is well worth a visit. Outside the museum a fine court tomb, originally from Ballintaggart in Armagh, has been reerected. It has a shallow forecourt and four burial chambers.

BELTANY STONE CIRCLE
(Donegal)

Large Bronze Age circle, in state care, on the summit of Tops Hill in eastern Donegal, about 2 mi. (3.25 km.) S. of Raphoe and about 3 mi. (4.75 km.) N. of Castlefinn. The stones are small, as is usual in the north, except for a few taller ones on the W. and E. sides. Sixty survive out of many more originally. One of the stones is covered with cupmarks, thought to be symbols of the sun, and the name Beltany recalls Beltane, the Celtic May Day festival of the sun. In the interior of the circle is a ruined cairn, and the circle may actually have been its kerb. One stone stands outside the circle to the SE.

BERRYSFORT
(Tyrone)

Example of the many standing stones in Ireland, whose purpose is seldom clear. Berrysfort, less than a mi. (1.5 km.) SE of Castlederg, stands on a rise just S. of the Derg River. The conspicuous stone is about 7 to 8 ft. high and is considered, like most such stones, to date from the Bronze Age. In state care.

BLASKET ISLANDS
(Kerry)

See *Dingle Peninsula*.

BOA ISLAND
(Fermanagh)

Celtic carved stone figures on an island in Lough Erne, 3.25 mi. (5 km.) SW of Pettigoe, linked to the mainland by a bridge. They stand in Caldragh graveyard, and probably date from the Iron Age, 8th cent. or earlier. These crude statues are probably pre-Christian. The principal one shows a male and female back to back, legless, with stick-like arms and pointed chins, the man showing a prominent phallus. There is a deep depression between the heads, probably for libations. Crude zigzags incised on one side may represent hair. The other, smaller statue, the "Lusty Man," was brought here from Lusty More island and may represent the Celtic Badhbha, the Divine Hag, origin of the name Boa. See also *Armagh; Devenish; White Island*.

BOHO
(Fermanagh)

Early cross in the graveyard of the Catholic church in Toneel, 1.5 mi. (2.3 km.) NW of Boho and 7.5 mi. (12 km.) W. of Enniskillen. The base and shaft of this 9th–10th-cent. cross, surviving from an ancient monastery on the site, shows fine scenes of Adam and Eve and the baptism of Christ set in interlace decoration. About .75 mi. (1 km.) to the W. of the graveyard are the six Reyfad Stones, large boulders now in front of a bungalow, five of them covered with cup and ring designs. They probably date from the Bronze Age. Two mi. (3.25 km.) SW of the Boho cross is a splendid, though nettle-filled, double court tomb at Aghanaglack. Back to back galleries at either end, with two chambers, are faced with the two courts, one set well askew. Excavations uncovered only one burial in each gallery and suggested a Late Neolithic date. See also *Ballyreagh; Ballywholan.*

BOHONAGH
(Cork)

The principal structure here is a fine, large stone circle, .5 mi. (.75 km.) E. of Ross Carberry and to the NW of the Ross Carberry-Clonakilty road, close to the southern coast. Of the 13 original large stones four are missing and three were reerected after the 1961 excavation of this Bronze Age complex, which included a rectangular timber house and a boulder burial. The two portal stones of the circle are set radially across from a large recumbent or axial stone on the W. side, the axis pointing to the equinox sunsets. In the center of the ring was a cremation burial. The boulder burial, 60 ft. E. of the circle, is one of over 50 of a local variant of the megalithic chambered tomb known only in the Cork/Kerry region. The heavy boulder capstone rests on three out of the four original small boulder supporting stones, two of which are of quartz, which had magical significance. The capstone has cupmarks on its top, as does a loose slab nearby. The tomb contained a cremation burial but no grave goods.

BOVIEL
(Londonderry)

Fine example of a Neolithic wedge tomb, with a double-walled chamber and an antechamber; 3 mi. (4.75 km.) ESE of Dungiven. The tomb is called Cloghna-galla.

THE BOYNE VALLEY
TOMBS
(Meath)

Set into a wide curve of the Boyne River, 6 mi. (9.6 km.) W. by S. of Drogheda and about 26 mi. (32 km.) N. of Dublin, is a remarkable group of Neolithic monuments, a cemetery and sacred area above a sacred river, dominated by the

The great Neolithic passage grave mound of New Grange rises majestically above the Boyne valley on its commanding hilltop. Within sight of New Grange are two other huge mounds, Knowth and Dowth, each on its hill, and many lesser monuments are scattered about on this once sacred ground. New Grange is 260 ft. wide and contains a magnificent passage and a high-roofed burial chamber within. The controversial quartz facade around the entrance, reerected by the excavator, can be clearly seen. (Photo: the author.)

three huge passage grave burial mounds of New Grange, Dowth and Knowth, in commanding positions on hilltops within sight of each other. This central sacred area is comparable to *Stonehenge* in England, though the three great tombs are considerably older than the monument we see at Stonehenge today—and older by some 700 years than the Great Pyramids of Egypt, being currently dated at about 3200 BC. In an area of some 3 sq. mi. (4.75 sq. km.) around the three great mounds is a scattering of satellite passage tombs, some 30 to 40 in all, many of the smaller tombs nestling close to the great mounds. Here and there a considerable number of small henge sites, standing stones, barrows, and possible hut sites have been identified. This extraordinary ritual site is one of the great monumental areas of Europe and needs to be better known.

Only a very prosperous community of Neolithic farmers, tilling the fertile, 20-sq. mi. (32.25 km. sq.) lands of the Boyne basin as the local people do today, could have amassed the wealth and commanded the manpower to build these enormous tombs—probably under the direction of a priest-leader and the compulsion of an overriding cult of the dead. The complexity of these great tombs, revealed by recent excavation, the sophistication of planning, the immensity of labor that went into them, suggest a highly cultured community, possessing skilled craftsmen, engineers and artisans—and artists too, for the Boyne is distinguished from Stonehenge and other early sites by the abundance of non-representational art on the stones of the tombs. Only in Britanny in France does one find such art, which, however, is no longer considered directly related to that of the Boyne.

New Grange, excavated and partly rebuilt by Prof. Michael O'Kelly of the University College, Cork between 1962 and 1975, is now open to the public, with guided tours and a display center. It has been known since 1699, and long before that figured in Irish mythology as a place of special importance. The flat-topped mound is 260 ft. in diameter and about 36 ft. high, and is held in place by 97 huge contiguous kerbstones, many of them elaborately ornamented, es-

The reconstructed entrance to New Grange, with the elaborately decorated entrance stone before it. Above the entrance to the passage is the "roof box" through which, on the winter solstice of Dec. 21st, the rising sun strikes over 60 ft. deep into the tomb to illuminate the entire burial chamber for a brief interval. (Photo: the author.)

pecially the magnificent entrance stone with its complex design of spirals and lozenges, and another stone diametrically opposite it on the other side of the mound. Ornamentation also appears on the orthostats of the passage, in the tomb chamber—especially in the right hand burial niche—and elsewhere. The passage into the mound is 62 ft. long, its roof rising in the interior to meet the corbelling of the chamber. It leads into the roughly circular central chamber with its magnificent corbelled roof rising 20 ft. above its floor—still intact after 5,000 years. There are two burial niches at the sides and one at the back, making a cruciform chamber.

To stabilize the passage (now inside an invisible concrete tube) Prof. O'Kelly took down the mound to the roofs of the passage and chamber, and in a controversial move built up the entrance front with a retaining wall faced with glittering white quartz (scatters of the quartz were found all over the ground around the entrance). The quartz facing gives the mound as reconstructed an oddly "modern" appearance. The mound, he found, was built largely of water-worn boulders, mostly small, but also with layers of turf that thickened toward the interior to help to stabilize the whole. It has been estimated that there are 200,000 tons of stone in the tomb. To keep the interior dry, water channels, O'Kelly found, had been ingeniously cut in the roof slabs of the passage and the gaps had been plugged with hardened burned turf. Why this effort to keep the tomb dry? Obviously it was a communal tomb, but just as obviously only a few "special" people were buried here, probably the priests. Lesser people were buried in the smaller satellite tombs.

There are flat stone basins in all three niches of the burial chamber, two in the right-hand niche, one inside the other, the upper one beautifully shaped of granite. Here, one surmises, the burned and unburned bones of the "special ones," carefully washed, were laid with offerings, perhaps in yearly rituals. A unique feature of New Grange is the roof box, a rectangular opening above the passage entrance, its lintel decorated. Carrying out a bold surmise, O'Kelly found that on December 21st (the winter solstice) the rising sun struck through the roof box and down the upward-sloping passage into the burial chamber, shining onto the basin at the far end and brightly illuminating the whole chamber for exactly 17 minutes! Perhaps each year at the winter solstice the blocking stone (still outside the entrance) was removed and in a solemn procession the revered bones were carried down the passage into the chamber as the sun bathed the whole ceremony in its light—an awesome thought!

In soundings around the great tomb remnants of at least four satellite passage tombs have been located, and under the slippage from the mound that had covered the kerb stones evidence was found of Late Neolithic Beaker squatters (about 2100 BC)—flints, a bronze axe, a hammerstone and fragments of beakers. It was probably at this time, it is now agreed, that a huge stone circle was erected around the mound (already considered an ancient holy site) at some distance from it, in diameter one of the largest circles in the British Isles, enclosing about two acres. Only 12 of the possible 35 to 38 original monoliths survive.

In explorations around the southern side of the tomb O'Kelly uncovered a strange arc of many large pits. Later, in 1982 and 1983, Sweetman discovered more pits and postholes in brief cuttings that appeared to join with those found by O'Kelly to form a large, circular, henge-like monument. The cuttings indicated the probable existence of a huge circle almost 300 ft. across, made up of a circle of heavy free-standing posts with arcs of pits inside the posts; and there was posthole evidence within the circle for some apparently temporary huts. A number of flints were scattered about and from the huts came sherds of Beaker pottery and Late Neolithic Grooved Ware, while charcoal from the pits yielded radiocarbon dates (uncalibrated) of around 2000 bc. The pit circle lay to the S. of the great tomb, not around it like the stone circle, and a careful analysis of the complex evidence indicated that the pit circle and temporary huts belonged to a comparatively brief time of intense ritual activity early in the Beaker period. The great stone circle, however, was almost certainly erected later in the Beaker period and was contemporaneous with the "squatter" habitation sites uncovered by O'Kelly.

If this great post and pit circle was a henge, it was a most unusual one, for there was no bank or ditch enclosing it, though two large standing stones outside the circle suggested an entrance. Moreover the arcs of pits, up to six deep, were unique. Most contained charcoal and animal bones—ox, pig, dog and deer—both burned and unburned, while in some of the outer, clay-lined larger pits there was evidence of intense burning, animal parts apparently cremated directly within the pits in some arcane ritual offering. It is possible that the bones were burned in the clay-lined pits and then distributed, or "buried" in the smaller inner pits. There is no parallel for this pit circle in all the known henges in Britain and Ireland. All one can say is that the pit circle and its succeeding stone circle dramatically indicate the continuing sacred nature of the great New Grange tomb, centuries after it was built. In later centuries, too, New Grange continued to be an object of awed attention. Roman coins and ornaments from all the centuries of the Roman occupation of Britain have been found there, dropped by "tourists" or left as offerings; and in later Celtic mythology the mound became the work of the chief god, Dagda the Good.

Knowth, the second of the three great mounds, is very similar in dimensions to New Grange; however, its stones inside and out are far more profusely ornamented, and it has not one but two burial chambers inside it, entered from the E. and the W., so that the two chambers are almost back to back inside the mound. The eastern tomb has the longest entrance passage in all of Europe (where there are many passage tombs). It is 134 ft. long, while the western passage is also very long, at 114 ft. Since 1962 Professor George Eogan of Dublin has been carrying out season after season of meticulous excavation at Knowth—about 25 seasons in all, funded by the state's Office of Public Works. When the tomb is finally prepared and opened to the public in a few years it will undoubtedly outshine New Grange as a tourist attraction.

Its great mound, covering an acre and a half, is differently constructed from that of New Grange, with successive layers of sod, boulder clay, cobbles and shale. Originally there were 127 kerb stones, each up to 6 ft. long, transported from at least 8 mi. (13 km.) away and most beautifully decorated. Around the tomb 18 satellite tombs have been discovered. These were of two types, with either simple or cruciform chambers, and contained successive burials. Two of them predated the great mound. In the great tomb itself the western tomb chamber, discovered in 1967, was little more than an extension of its passage, separated from the passage by a sill stone, and was almost entirely roofed by a single huge capstone. But the eastern tomb, discovered the next year, boasted a cruciform chamber with three burial niches like that of New Grange, with a magnificent ornamented stone basin in the right-hand niche. Above the chamber a corbelled roof as fine as that at New Grange rose up to 21 ft. high.

Knowth was not abandoned after the Neolithic period. Soundings around the great mound discovered the remains of an Early Bronze Age settlement as well as a large Neolithic house about 36 ft. long. And there seems to have been activity there up into the Late Iron Age, up to about 200 AD. Then in the Early Christian period, in the 9th and 10th cents. AD, there was a large rural settlement on the site with evidence of metal-working, fields and the grazing of cattle and sheep, and the great mound itself was riddled with the passages of the village's souterrains. The settlement seems to have been the seat of the kings of Northern Brega. Finally the mound itself was used, up into the 14th cent., as the motte of a Norman castle.

The third mound, Dowth, is of about the same size but has been cruelly used. A great crater, result of a misguided 1847 excavation, disfigures its top, and much of the western side of the mound, over the tombs, has been destroyed. Only some of the kerb stones are now visible—many ornamented—and inside there are again two tombs on the W. side and a later souterrain. The northern tomb passage is 27 ft. long, leading into a similar, three-niche cruciform chamber, roofed by slabs rather than corbelling, and with a two-compartment annex chamber leading off the right-hand niche. A large stone basin occupies almost all the floor space of the main chamber. The southern tomb is simpler, with a short passage, slab roof, and only one recess, to the right. Many of the stones in both tombs were decorated, though the designs are inferior to those of the other mounds. It is possible that Dowth was the earliest to be built of the three. Access is difficult, including climbing over stones and down a ladder.

In closing it is obvious that the rich economy of the Boyne valley people must have been immensely stimulated, during the 500 years or so when the site was in use, but also strained to the utmost, by the enormous effort of designing and building three such huge tomb-temples, not to mention all the lesser tombs—with only stone tools to hand. There is some evidence pointing to a depression in later centuries. No wonder!

BROWNE'S HILL
(Carlow)

Or Mt. Browne Dolmen, a collapsed portal tomb 2 mi. (3.25 km.) E. of Carlow in Kernanstown (Ballykernan), famous for its huge 100-ton capstone, reputedly the largest in Europe. The huge stone rests on three short uprights in front and on the ground in the rear, with a fourth upright close by in front.

BURREN
(Cavan)

A fine wedge tomb, the "Giant's Grave," in a forest clearing due S. of Blacklion village, which lies between the Upper and Lower Lough Macneans. The tomb is difficult to find but is worth the trouble. The gallery, over 20 ft. long, is covered by five capstones and is entered through a triangular portal in the facade, made by two leaning uprights. The gallery, much like those in northern France, is divided by a slab into a long antechamber and a main chamber. Parts of the outer walls survive. To the S. on a ridge are the ruins of a court tomb as well as another, smaller and more orthodox type of wedge tomb.

BURREN, THE
(Clare)

Remarkable limestone plateau in northern Clare, with a rich concentration of archaeological sites. It is a bare, craggy, haunting "moonscape" of a region, unlike any other. Its "karst" geology is fascinating; so is its profusion of flowers

Browne's Hill Dolmen, a portal tomb in Carlow well-known for its huge tilted capstone, estimated to weigh 100 tons and probably the heaviest in Europe. It must have been a daunting job for the ancients to raise it. (Courtesy of Irish Tourist Board, Dublin.)

A box-like wedge tomb, typical of many found in The Burren, a haunting, craggy limestone plateau in Clare with its own special flora and fauna and many archaeological monuments. Of the more than 400 wedge tombs known in Ireland, about one quarter are in The Burren. (Photo: the author.)

and plants (as well as fauna), mixing Arctic, Alpine and Mediterranean types. The Burren proper lies roughly around and N. of Kilfenora and Killinaboy, and the earlier sites include many megalithic tombs, hundreds of stone forts, and numerous Early Christian sites, often marked only by later churches. Of the over 400 wedge tombs known in all of Ireland, nearly 100 are in The Burren; these are, however, of a simplified type, box-like and with a single chamber. With such a profusion of monuments only a few of the more obvious ones can be described here. Besides, detailed maps and guides are available in most shops, and there is a Burren Display Center in Kilfenora.

Of the many wedge tombs, that at Derrynavahagh is one of the best, sited with magnificent views 5 mi. (8 km.) W. of the resort of Lisdoonvarna, and about 3.5 mi. (5.6 km.) SW of Ballyvaughan. The typical thin slabs of The Burren here enclose a chamber about 11 ft. long, covered by a broken capstone at its western end. The E. end is closed and that to the W. partly closed. Equally fine is Baur South, 5 mi. (8 km.) SSW of Ballyvaughan on the edge of a plateau. Its capstones covering the chamber are complete and, unusually, in the back part of the chamber is a chamber within a chamber, sharing the same backstone. Ballyganner South, 3 mi. (4.75 km.) ENE of Kilfenora and a mile from Lemaneh Castle, is the largest of Burren's wedge tombs, two immense slabs forming the sides of the chamber, which is partly closed in front. Some slabs of the huge roof, shattered by a celebration bonfire in 1955, still cover the W. end of the chamber. There are other wedge tombs nearby. At Parknabbinia, a little over a mi. (about 2 km.) NNW of Killinaboy, are a number of wedge tombs. At the "Giant's Grave" the sides of the chamber are again formed by single slabs, and parts of the long roofstone and the surrounding cairn survive. Finally at Caheraphuca, .5 mi. (.75 km.) SW of Crusheen, a wedge-shaped tomb consists of five uprights and two capstones. A recent wall built against it spoils its symmetry.

Two other graves of different types worth seeing include an often-illustrated portal tomb at Poulnabrone, 5 mi. (8 km.) S. of Killinaboy and 2 mi. (3.25 km.) S. of Gleninsheen. The striking, thin capstone of this "Druid's Altar" tilts back from two imposing portal stones with a sill between. It stands in the remains of a low round cairn. Recently excavated, it yielded burials and flints. One mi. (1.6 km.) SSW of Caherconnell crossroads at Poulawack is a quite different site, an Early Bronze Age cairn 60 ft. across on top of a hill, excavated by the Harvard University expedition in 1934; it contained a number of cist burials (stone-lined boxes), including the remains of 18 people, mostly young and none over 35. The two principal cists, side by side at the center of the cairn, contained four individuals, apparently a family. The finds included food vessels and urns and one sherd of a beaker. The cairn, made largely of stones, was contained within a circular stone wall.

A few of the major stone forts would certainly include Caherconnell, about .5 mi. (.75 km.) S. of Poulnabrone portal tomb. This was probably an Iron Age fort that was reused in the 15th and 16th cents. A mi. or two (2 to 3 km.) to the NW is another large fort, Cahermacnaghten, also reused in medieval times, as the gateway attests. About 100 ft. in diameter, it is almost round, and the high ground level inside suggests a long period of occupation. The foundations of rectangular buildings can still be seen. One of the most complex of the forts is Cahercommaun, about 1.5 mi. (2.3 km.) S. on the road from Carron, then a rough 15-minute walk E. across The Burren. Dramatically sited on a cliff edge over a valley, the fort has three concentric walls, the inner, largest rampart almost circular, the outer two ending at the cliff edge. Excavated by the Harvard expedition of 1934, the inner wall was found to contain three wall chambers and the fort's interior about 12 stone buildings, their foundations now largely lost in new growth. At least two of these had souterrains underneath them, one including an escape passage down the cliff. There was also a guard house and sentry post. A silver brooch found in the ruins showed that the fort was already in use in the 9th cent. AD, which gives some indication of the date of the other forts.

Two very different types of prehistoric tomb in The Burren. Poulnabrone, a portal tomb, is well-known for its thin but striking capstone tilted high over the burial chamber. The large, Early Bronze Age cairn of Poulawack, crowned by a standing stone, was built on a high hill with wide views all around. Excavated in 1934, it yielded the cist burials of 18 people. (Photo: courtesy of the Irish Tourist Board, Dublin. Photo: the author.)

Ballykinvarga, nearly 2 mi. (3.25 km.) ENE of Kilfenora, is a huge fort. More correctly Caherballykinvarga, it has two circuits of ramparts well built of limestone blocks and nearly 18 ft. thick in places. Around much of the wall is a *chevaux de frise*, as in some of the *Aran Islands* forts, a belt of thickly strewn upright stones about 45 ft. deep. Hut remains, built up against the inner wall, can be seen in the interior. Finally there is the remote fort of Caherdooneerish (or Caherdoonfergus) high up behind Black Head overlooking Galway Bay at the

Among a scattering of Early Christian remains in The Burren are a number of high crosses just outside the village of Kilfenora. All are late (12th cent.), including this slender cross with lovely geometrical ornament standing in a field outside the local church. (Photo: the author.)

very top of Clare, about 4.5 mi. (7.25 km.) WNW of Ballyvaughan. The fort, built of Burren limestone, affords magnificent views and interesting Burren flora as one climbs up to it. It is D-shaped, with walls still about 12 ft. high and almost as thick in places, a terrace, and the remains of steps. Remnants of the narrow gate are on the E. side.

There are few Early Christian survivals in The Burren, though many sites once belonged to earlier monasteries. Most are 12th cent. or later, like the crosses in the Protestant cathedral churchyard just W. of Kilfenora village. There are two complete 12th-cent. high crosses here, the shaft of another with interlace decoration, and in a field W. of the church a tall slender cross. Chief of these crosses is the ''Doorty Cross'' with an unpierced ring, bearing remarkable high relief sculptures typical of the late period. A fifth cross was moved to *Killaloe* in 1821. Another 12th-cent. cross is built into the church at Killinaboy (or Kilnaboy), once a monastic site like Kilfenora. The stump of a round tower marks the site of the monastery.

CAHERAPHUCA
(Clare)

See *The Burren.*

CAHERBALLYKINVARGA
(Clare)

See *The Burren* (Ballykinvarga).

CAHERCALLA FORT
(Clare)

See *Magh Adair*.

CAHERCOMMAUN FORT
(Clare)

See *The Burren*.

CAHERCONNELL FORT
(Clare)

See *The Burren*.

CAHERCONREE
(Kerry)

See *Dingle Peninsula*.

CAHERDANIEL
(Kerry)

A fine stone fort .5 mi. (.75 km.) W. of the hamlet of Caherdaniel on the Ring of Kerry road, 8.75 mi. (14 km.) W. of Waterville. Its heavy walls, still standing nearly 15 ft. high, are 12 ft. thick and overlook Kenmare Bay, following the craggy lines of a stony outcrop. Built of small flat stones, they enclose an area about 83 ft. across, with the entrance on the S.

CAHERDOONEERISH
FORT
(Clare)

See *The Burren*.

CAHERDOONFERGUS
FORT
(Clare)

See *The Burren*.

CAHERGAL FORT
(Kerry)

See *Leacanabuaile Fort*.

CAHERMACNAGHTEN
FORT
(Clare)

See *The Burren*.

CAIRNBANE EAST and
WEST
(Meath)

See *Loughcrew*.

CALLAUN
(Tipperary)

See *Timoney Hills*.

CARNANMORE
(Antrim)

Or Carnlea; passage grave in the extreme northern end of Ireland, 1.5 mi. (2.3 km.) SW of Torr Head. The round cairn, with a good deal of quartz mixed into it, sits on top of Carnanmore Mtn., a walk of over half a mi. up from the coast road. The rectangular chamber inside has a corbelled roof and one of the higher stones in the roof shows traces of passage grave designs (see *Boyne Valley*).

CARNDONAGH
(Donegal)

Or Cardonagh, Early Christian carved stone pillars, standing by the road across from a church at the W. end of Carndonagh town in northern Donegal. The principal monument here, St. Patrick's Cross, is a cross slab, one of the earliest types of stone cross, with interlace designs forming a cross on one side, with two Pict-like crude figures, and on the other side more such figures with interlace. Two small slabs with figures and curvilinear ornament stand on either side of the cross slab. In the graveyard of the church behind is another slab with two figures flanking a schematic marigold and stem on one side and a crucifixion on the other. There are unusual Byzantine-like roundels on this slab, which may date from the 8th cent. The cross slab may be as early as the 7th cent., or perhaps the 8th, and the two small flanking slabs perhaps later. See also *Fahan*.

CARNFREE
(Roscommon)

See *Rathcroghan*.

CARRAIG AILLE I and II
(Limerick)

See *Lough Gur*.

CARRICK EAST
(Londonderry)

Megalithic tomb in Carrick East, about 4 mi. (6.5 km.) SE of Limavady, possibly a center court tomb, though the court gives no access to the chambers on either side. The chambers still have their capstones, and there are traces of the cairn.

CARRICKGLASS
(Sligo)

Fantastic portal tomb with an immense capstone crowned with thick foliage, resting precariously on two tiny portal stones and a backstone. The capstone weighs about 70 tons and is 15 ft. long. Locally called The Labby, the tomb stands in the corner of a field at Carrickglass, 1 mi. (1.6 km.) NE of Ballindon with its ruined friary, not far S. of Lough Nasool—or 4.5 mi. (7.25 km.) NW of Ballyfarnan. (See also *Browne's Hill*.) In Heapstone, 1.5 mi. (2.3 km.) to the W. at the top of the lake near the road N. to Rivertown, is a huge cairn of stones with large kerb stones around it, about 180 ft. in diameter and almost 20 ft. high. Though unexcavated, it must cover a passage tomb. See also *Knocknarea*.

CARRIGAGULLA
(Cork)

Fine example of the large Cork-Kerry stone circles, 7 mi. N. of Macroom and 1.75 mi. (2.6 km.) N. by E. of Ballynagree up toward the mountains. Sixteen of the original 17 stones are still in place, the largest next to the portal stones set radially, with the rather high recumbent or axial stone across the circle. A boulder sits at the center of the ring. See also *Drombeg*.

CARROWCROM
(Mayo)

Well-preserved, small wedge tomb 4.5 mi. (7.25 km.) ESE of Ballina and 3 mi. (4.75 km.) NE of Attymass. Its 6-ft.-long capstone is in place and most of its cairn is intact. There is a high facade of four uprights and a sill stone, and some of the walling of the single chamber can still be seen.

CARROWKEEL
(Sligo)

Large passage grave cemetery on the top of the limestone ridges of the Bricklieve Mtns., just W. of Lough Arrow and about 9 mi. (14.5 km.) NE of Boyle. The tombs are scattered over several townships (Carrowkeel is only one of them) and there are about 14 passage tombs and two cist tombs in the main cemetery. Extensive peat overlies some of the cairns. On a lower ridge to the NE are nearly 50 round hut circles, called "The Village," which may be the huts or tent shelters of the tomb builders, though there is no evidence to show that they are contemporary. The tombs vary enormously in size and arrangement, but usually have a cairn with a heavy kerb around it; however, there is no passage grave art at Carrowkeel or at the other cemetery nearby at *Carrowmore*. Some of the tombs cannot be entered; others are unexcavated. The classic passage grave type, as in the *Boyne Valley*, is represented by tombs E, G and K with passages leading into cruciform chambers with corbelled roofs and fine double-lintelled entrances. Probably tombs C, M and N are of the same type. The fine cairn F has two chambers on each side of the main chamber, while cairns A and P contained no tombs at all, and cairns H and D only box-cists. Finally tomb E, under a long cairn, combines a court at one end with a blocked cruciform chamber. It seems to be a rare fusion of court and passage tomb in an area of overlap. Finds from the cemetery were sparse, mostly cremation burials with ornaments and sherds of "Carrowkeel" ware.

CARROWMORE
(Donegal)

See *Clonca*.

CARROWMORE
(Sligo)

Largest megalithic cemetery in Ireland, 2 mi. (3.25 km.) SW of Sligo, the tombs generally near the road. It lies about 15 mi. (24 km.) NW of its sister passage grave cemetery of *Carrowkeel* (above). The cemetery again extends to several townlands and is dominated by the vast, unexcavated cairn of "Maeve's Lump" on the very top of Knocknarea Mtn. with magnificent views all around. The cairn, undoubtedly containing a passage tomb, is nearly 200 ft. in diameter and 34 ft. tall and is surrounded by heavy kerb stones. There are satellite tombs around it, one of them the only passage grave with a cruciform chamber as in the *Boyne Valley* tombs. Late Neolithic small huts have also been found on Knocknarea— possibly hunters? The others generally have short passages and small chambers roofed by horizontal slabs. The cemetery proper consists of a number of small passage graves and a few chambered tombs, probably all originally covered by stone cairns with a kerb. There are also stone forts and standing stones intermixed with the tombs. Originally there were 100 or more tombs, but the cemetery is badly neglected and is still subject to quarrying, and now only about 32 tombs remain, though 60 have been identified. The largest and most prominent is Listoghil at the center of the cemetery, overlooking the others. The cemetery was extensively "excavated" in the mid-19th cent., but in 1979–80 four tombs were more carefully excavated, and recent dating indicates a date for the cemetery in the 4th millennium BC. Once thought to be late in the passage grave sequence, the cemetery may well be among the earliest. There is no passage grave ornamentation at Carrowmore. Curvilinear ornament on a roofless small tomb at Cloverhill to the S. is now thought to belong to the Iron Age, or even Early Christian period.

CASHEL
(Tipperary)

St. Patrick's Rock, or "Cashel of the Kings"—once an early stone cashel or fortress, then capital of the king-bishop of Munster—is one of the most evocative sites in Ireland and perhaps in the whole of Europe. It was visited by St. Parrick in 450 AD, and later was presided over by the famous Brian Boru, king of Munster in the 11th cent. AD. While admittedly late for this guide, it has many interesting aspects reflecting earlier times. An excellent guidebook is available at the site.

The picturesque group of buildings on this rock looming over the plains

The famous rock of Cashel in Tipperary rises dramatically above the plain, carrying its evocative cluster of ruins: a 12th-cent. round tower, the shell of the medieval cathedral with the archbishop's tower behind it and, set at a curious angle, the fascinating little Cormac's Chapel with its steep stone Irish roof, flanked by two towers. The rock, called "Cashel of the Kings," did indeed once hold a cashel, a long vanished, stone-built fortress of ancient times. (Courtesy of Irish Tourist Board, Dublin.)

include the roofless shell of the 13th-cent. cathedral, with a perfectly preserved round tower (10th to 12th cents.) attached to one side, and the tiny Cormac's Chapel, consecrated in 1134 AD, nestling into the other side at a curious angle and flanked by two tall towers. Cormac's Chapel, a masterpiece of Romanesque building influenced by the churches of the Rhineland, nevertheless has a steeply pitched stone roof deriving straight from the earlier beehive huts and oratories and early, small churches of Ireland. The lavish decorative use of human heads on the N. door, in the nave, the chancel and on the chancel arch may well hark back to the Celtic cult of the severed head. Inside the chapel is a striking broken sarcophagus, found originally in the cathedral, beautifully ornamented with a strong design of interlaced serpents in the Scandinavian manner, attesting to the Viking influence in Ireland.

Near the tourist entrance looms St. Patrick's Cross, probably of the 11th cent. It stands on a massive base ornamented with weathered interlace designs and reputed to be the coronation stone of the kings of Munster, though it does appear to have been constructed with the cross itself. The round tower, nearly 92 ft. high, with the usual conical cap and raised, round-headed doorway, undoubtedly indicates the former presence of an earlier church. Before the cathedral was built the tower could have been seen from Cormac's Chapel. Three windows above the tower's entrance door and four more at the top light the interior.

CASHELKEELTY STONE CIRCLE (Kerry)

See *Shronebirrane*.

CASTELNALAGHT
(Cork)

A fine example of an alignment about 4 mi. (6.5 km.) N. of Bandon, which lies SW of Cork city. The four stones, aligned in a high field, increase gradually in height. In the next field to the N. is a boulder burial typical of the Cork-Kerry region, a large round boulder resting on four small support stones.

CASTLEDERMOT
(Kildare)

Round tower and high crosses in the churchyard of a modern church, about 16 mi. (25.75 km.) S. of Kildare, in the Barrow valley. The round tower, built in 919 AD, and the crosses date from an important early monastery in Castledermot, once a larger walled town. The top part of the tower and its battlemented parapet are medieval. The two superb granite crosses are transitional in style (9th cent.), like the wonderful cross at *Moone*, 5 mi. (8 km.) to the N., meaning that for the first time crude but lively figured biblical scenes now cover most of the cross—on one side of the S. cross and on both sides of the N. cross—rather than just on the base as on the earlier crosses at *Ahenny*. A crucifixion is also at the center of one face of the S. cross. However, there are still many areas of geometric and wave-like designs on both crosses. In the churchyard are also two holed standing stones, one the "Swearing Stone," a cross slab; as well as

The high crosses at Castledermot, Kildare. With the round tower, these mark the site of an important early monastery. Both crosses are transitional (9th cent.), combining intricate geometrical designs with, for the first time, biblical scenes on the shaft and cross. Such scenes cover only one side of the South Cross, seen here head-on with a crucifixion at the center and on the base the animals going to the Ark. The North Cross, seen from the side, is richly ornamented with geometric designs. (Photo: courtesy of Irish Tourist Board, Dublin. Photo: the author.)

the only Scandinavian-style decorated hogback gravestone in Ireland in the shape of a long house, attesting to the Viking influence. The monastery here was twice sacked by Viking raiders in the 9th cent. There is also a reconstructed Romanesque doorway from an earlier church on the site and an ancient church foundation.

CASTLERUDDERY LOWER STONE CIRCLE (Wicklow)

The circle lies 2.5 mi. (4 km.) SW of Donard near the Wicklow Mtns. Lost in hawthorn and tall grass at the top of a hill, this neglected and unexcavated enclosure, 100 ft. across, is really a stone-lined Early Bronze Age henge or ritual meeting place, similar to the great Lios circle near *Lough Gur*. There is a circular bank, once lined with small stones on the outside and large boulders around the inside—up to 30 of them of all sizes, some lying flat, others upright, still others scattered about haphazardly inside the circle. The entrance, exactly on the E., is flanked by two huge portal stones of white quartz (of magical significance); a scatter of stones outside the circle suggests a ceremonial entrance avenue from the E. The passage graves of *Baltinglass* are 5 mi. to the SW and another circle is at *Athgreany* about 6 mi. (9.6 km.) N.

CASTLESTRANGE
(Roscommon)

Beautifully decorated, small rounded stone; an Iron Age cult object, probably phallic, a companion piece to the larger *Turoe* stone in Galway. It is protected by railings beside a private avenue in Castlestrange, 4 mi. (6.5 km.) SW of Roscommon and NW of Athleague. Probably dating from the 1st cent. BC, its flowing curvilinear designs are incised and are pure La Tène Celtic in style.

CASTLETOWN AND
GLINSK
(Offaly)

High cross, in the garden of the 19th-cent. Castle Bernard, now a Forestry Training Center, 3 mi. (4.75 km.) NE of Kinnitty village and about 7 mi. (11.25 km.) E. of Birr. The battered and repaired cross, possibly 10th cent., is sculptured on one side with a fine scene of Adam and Eve amidst interlacing and geometric ornament, and on the other with a crucifixion and another scene. Seir Kieran, about 5 mi. (8 km.) S. and 6 mi. (9.6 km.) SE of Birr, just S. of Clareen, is the site of an early monastery. Its ancient earthen walls and ditch can still be traced in part. Inside them is a modern church, with fragments of cross slabs in its walls and around it; the foundations of an older church; the base of a round tower; and the figured base of an early high cross, perhaps of the 10th cent. According to tradition a sacred fire burned here in pagan times.

CAVE OF THE CAT
(Roscommon)

See *Rathcroghan*.

CHURCH ISLAND
(Kerry)

Ancient monastic site on a tiny island off Beginish Island near Valentia Island, on the Ring of Kerry route; access only by hired boat from Caherciveen. The remains consist of a rectangular corbelled stone oratory, possibly 8th cent. or later, a round stone hut and a square house. Excavations uncovered the remains of an earlier wooden oratory and hut and yielded a fine, incised early cross slab with a later Ogham inscription, now in *Cork*. The monastery wall is a later addition. There is another Church Island in Lough Currane—on the same route—with Romanesque ruins, cross slabs etc.

CLAGAN
(Londonderry)

See *Tireighter*.

CLOCHAN NA CARRAIGE
(Galway)

See *Aran Islands*.

CLOGHANMORE
(Donegal)

See *Glencolumbkille*.

CLOGHBRACK
(Antrim)

See *Tievebulliagh*

CLOGHER
(Sligo)

There is an impressive stone fort here called "Cashelmore," in the Coolavin Estate, amidst trees on a hill overlooking Lough Gara, about 4 mi. (6.5 km.) NE of Ballaghaderreen in Roscommon. Restored in the 19 cent., it is built of stones that are largest at the bottom. Three sets of steps lead up to the ramparts, with three wall niches in the walls and two souterrains.

CLOGHER
(Tyrone)

Once a bishopric, now a small village on the Dungannon-Enniskillen road. Earlier it was the site of a monastery founded by a follower of St. Patrick, near the royal seat of the ancient kingdom of Airgialla. The Protestant cathedral lies within a large Celtic hill fort, probably of the 4th–5th cent. AD, that may have been the "royal seat." The fort's earthen ramparts and external ditch can still be traced. Much Bronze Age occupation evidence was found near the top of the hill. Several crosses remain from the former monastery; one is 2 mi. (3.25 km.) W. of the cathedral, possibly 9th or 10th cent. and reconstructed in 1912, and another earlier cross is in the cathedral's N. porch. An interesting site 4 mi. (6.5 km.) ESE of Clogher, at Altdaven in a forest, is "St. Patrick's Chair and Well." The chair is a huge stone block shaped like a chair, possibly on purpose, on top of other big boulders; the "well" is an open chamber with another boulder above it. Cup marks on some of the large stones suggest that the location was originally a pagan inauguration site or ritual center.

CLOGHERNY
(Tyrone)

Composite wedge tomb and circle, 2 mi. (3.25 km.) N. of Plumbridge, E. off the Plumbridge-Dunnamanagh road, E. of Strabane at Meenenigal Rocks. The tomb, in a low cairn, is enclosed in a circle of 17 low stones with a diameter of about 60 ft. (stone circles are common in this area). One roofstone and the facade of the tomb survive; the closed chamber is divided internally by jambs. A mi. (1.6 km.) farther N., on a hillside at Balix Lower, is a court tomb with a V-shaped court in front opening into a chamber in a long cairn.

CLONCA
(Donegal)

An attractive, early high cross standing very tall near a 17th-cent. church, 1.5 mi. (2.3 km.) SE of Culdaff, close to the northern coast of Donegal. Small figured panels on one side depict two men with folded arms and mythical beasts, and on the other two seated men. Tight geometric patterns cover the rest of the cross. The church, on the site of an ancient monastery, incorporates a carved lintel from an earlier church. One mi. (1.6 km.) S., at Carrowmore, more crosses stand on either side of the road, a tall narrow cross pillar, another cross pillar and a carved pillar stone. See also the early crosses at *Cardonagh* about 5 mi. (8 km.) to the W.

CLONDALKIN
(Dublin)

Fine round tower, 84 ft. tall with its original cap, about 5 mi. (8 km.) W. of the center of Dublin city, one of the few that can be climbed to the top to see the inside corbelled construction of the cap. In the nearby graveyard are two granite crosses and a font. With the round tower, these are the only reminders of the 7th-cent. monastery here. One cross is ringed, the other shows faint signs of carving.

CLONES
(Monaghan)

Round tower in a graveyard at the lower end of Clones, about 15 mi. (24 km.) SW of Monaghan town. It rises to about 75 ft. but is capless. The doorway and windows are square-headed. In the market in the center of town is a high cross, put together from two different fragments found originally near the round tower. The cross, probably 10th cent., shows figures on both sides. These are relics of a monastery founded here in the 6th cent.

CLONFERT
(Galway)

St. Brendan's Cathedral with a famed Romanesque doorway, exuberantly carved and the finest achievement of the Irish Romanesque; 9 mi. (14.5 km.) SE of Ballinasloe and SW across the Shannon River from *Clonmacnoise*. Probably 13th cent., its six orders and triangular pointed hood are richly carved with a profu-

Romanesque doorway of St. Brendan's Cathedral in Galway. This extraordinary composition, with its unique, tall hood and profusion of strange beasts and human heads, is justly famous as the finest example of Romanesque design in Ireland. The numerous human heads remind one irresistibly of the ancient and persistent Celtic cult of the severed head—for instance, the panel of carved heads at Entremont in southern France, a pagan temple destroyed by the Romans in the 2nd cent. BC. (Courtesy of Irish Tourist Board, Dublin.)

sion of animal heads and foliate and geometrical design—and especially with numerous human heads. Although the cathedral and its doorway are late for this guide, they should not be missed, and the numerous heads probably reflect, like those on Cormac's Chapel in *Cashel*, the ancient Celtic cult of the severed head.

CLONMACNOISE
(Offaly)

Famous Early Christian monastic center overlooking the Shannon, some 8 mi. (13 km.) S. of *Athlone*; founded by St. Ciarán in 548–49 AD and a major center of learning and the arts in the pre-Norman period. Within the enclosure are five churches, the roofless cathedral, two round towers and a number of high crosses. Of great interest to the student of the early Irish church is a large collection of sandstone grave slabs dating from the 8th to the 12th cents., grouped by types on the walls of a long gallery to the left of the entrance and displaying every type of elaboration on the theme of the cross. Of particular interest are two very early slabs in the gallery, one with a vigorous design of intertwined monsters, the other showing a deer in a trap. At the end of the gallery is the principal round tower (12th cent.), now about 60 ft. tall, once perhaps twice the height, with a handsome arched doorway. The six churches are mostly Romanesque and

The superbly carved Cross of the Scriptures at the well-known Early Christian site of Clonmacnoise in Offaly, with its numerous ruined churches, two round towers, and cross slabs and high crosses. The west face of the cross, probably 9th or early 10th cent., shows some of the many biblical scenes that cover it, surrounding a crucifixion. (Courtesy of Irish Tourist Board, Dublin.)

medieval, though Teampull Connor may date a bit earlier, and there is a tiny round oratory where St. Ciarán was reputedly buried. A small and perfect round tower next to Teampull Finghin was built, unusually, as part of the church.

The worn South Cross, S. of the cathedral, is an example of a 9th-cent. transitional cross like those at *Castledermot*, covered with ornament but with figured panels and a crucifixion. The damaged North Cross is of the same type. W. of the cathedral is the glorious Cross of the Scriptures, somewhat later, with many figured panels, one apparently showing St. Ciarán erecting his first wooden church here, and a weathered hunting scene on the base. The Twyford Cross at *Bealin*, 2 mi. (3.25 km.) ENE of Athlone, undoubtedly came from Clonmacnoise.

CLONTYGORA
(Armagh)

An impressive but much damaged court tomb 4 mi. (6.5 km.) S. of Newry, built of huge slabs. Called "The King's Ring," it was excavated in 1937. A U-shaped court led into a three-chambered gallery, with some of the capstones now still in position. The finds included cremation burials, pottery and flints.

CLOYNE
(Cork)

Handsome round tower almost 100 ft. high, with a later battlemented top; across from Bishop Berkeley's cathedral in Cloyne, 7.5 mi. (12 km.) E. of Cobh. As usual, it marks a vanished monastery. Windows light all of the floors.

COHAW
(Cavan)

A very good example of a double court tomb, excavated in 1949, standing in a rectangular cairn of stones about 83 ft. long, with a kerb. Semicircular courts at either end lead into two-chambered galleries, with a fifth chamber between them.

CONG
(Mayo)

Site of an ancient monastery and now of the attractive ruins of a 12th-13th-cent. abbey. From the monastery came the superb wood and metal cross of Cong, now in Dublin's National Museum. To the NE of Cong, 1.5 mi. (2.3 km.), are four stone circles close together, of different kinds.

CORK
(Cork)

Large southern city. Its Municipal Museum in Fitzgerald Park contains interesting local collections from Cork city and old Munster.

CORRICK STONE CIRCLES
(Londonderry)

See *Ballybriest*.

CRAGGAUNOWEN
(Clare)

In the grounds of Craggaunowen Castle, near Bunratty and Shannon airport, is the Craggaunowen Project, which includes a full-scale reproduction of a Bronze Age crannog (artificial island) with two round thatched huts equipped with replicas of original Bronze Age tools, furniture and utensils. There is also a reconstructed stone ring fort of the Early Christian period with a souterrain and, more recently, a replica of St. Brendan's leather boat, which was sailed to America in 1976–77. See also *Knocknalappa, Lough Gara, Lough-na-Cranagh*.

CRAIGAROGAN
(Antrim)

Neglected passage tomb called Carn Greine, or "Granny's Grave"; 2.5 mi. (4 km.) ESE of Templepatrick, between Belfast and *Antrim*. A low roofed passage about 27 ft. long leads toward a polygonal chamber, curiously sealed off from the passage, roofed by a single slab. It was once surrounded by a stone circle or a kerb.

CRAIGS
(Antrim)

A fine court tomb on the western side of Long Mtn., 3 mi. (4.75 km.) N. of Rasharkin and about 12 mi. (19 km.) NW of Ballymena, requiring a long hard walk. The so-called "Broad Stone," once a popular assembly place, is disguised by a loose capstone propped recently against the entrance, but the court can

A reconstructed crannog, or artificial island, at Craggaunowen in Clare near Shannon airport. The round huts are furnished with authentic replicas of Bronze Age implements and furniture. Other sites at the archaeological park at Craggaunowen include a reconstruction of a cashel or stone ring fort of the Early Christian period. (Courtesy of Irish Tourist Board, Dublin.)

be seen leading into the three chambers in the gallery, all set within a long stone-lined cairn. SW across the road, less than a mi. (about 1 km.), is "Craig's Dolmen," seven uprights supporting a capstone from a former passage grave.

CRANNAGH
(Galway)

A portal tomb at one end of a long cairn, called as usual "Dermot and Grania's Bed"; between Kinvarra (about 4 mi. or 6.5 km.) and Gort (about 3 mi. or 4.75 km.) near Caherglassaun Lough. Its tall portal stones manage to support a tilted capstone about 11 ft. long. Well to the S. is a wedge tomb at Ballynastaig, its single large capstone still intact. The lovely *Kilmacduagh* round tower is to the WSW of Gort, again about 3 mi. (4.75 km.).

CREEVYKEEL
(Sligo)

Magnificent large court tomb, E. of the Sligo-Bundoran road and about 6 mi. (9.6 km.) SW of Bundoran, set in the remains of a wedge-shaped rubble cairn, about 180 ft. long, held in by large kerb stones, doubled on the S. The enclosed oval court, nearly 50 ft. long and bounded by large uprights, is entered from a short paved passage on the eastern or broad end. The chamber, about 10 to 30 ft., is roughly divided into two, and is entered through a facade of eight larger uprights at the western end of the court. At the back of the cairn three subsidiary chambers—two entered from the N. and the third, the best-preserved, through a short passage from the S.—were apparently built at the same time as the tomb proper. Excavated by the Harvard expedition in 1935, the tomb yielded four cremation burials, flints, polished stone axes and Neolithic pottery. A small kiln for iron smelting in the NW corner of the court dates from the Early Christian period. To the WSW some 650 yds. are the remains of another chambered tomb.

A fine example of a megalithic court tomb at Creggandevesky in Tyrone, as cleaned up and restored after recent excavation. Set in the remains of its cairn of stones, the semicircular court (no doubt used for mortuary ceremonies) faces the entrance with its heavy lintel, leading into three burial chambers. Some of the inward-leaning corbel stones that supported the roof slabs can be seen. Flints, cremated human bone and Neolithic pottery were found in the chambers. (Crown copyright: Historic Monuments and Buildings Branch, DOENI, Northern Ireland.)

CREGDUFF
(Mayo)

Remarkable enclosure, undoubtedly a prehistoric ritual site, though unexcavated; it lies just N. of the Shrule-Kilmaine road, 1. mi. (1.6 km.) S. of Kilmaine village. The huge enclosure, about 270 ft. in diameter, is surrounded by two sets of banks and ditches with a wide formal entrance on the E. On the edge of the outer bank up to 340 close-set, low stones were placed, of which 135 still remain (best on the S.). The banks and ditches enclose a central area about 90 ft. across that must have witnessed elaborate ceremonies. Its nature and siting preclude its being a fort, as sometimes stated.

CREGGANCONROE
(Tyrone)

See *Creggandevesky*.

CREGGANDEVESKY
(Tyrone)

A very well preserved court tomb on a hillside W. of Lough Mallon, W. of the Pomeroy-Creggan road, 2.5 mi. (4 km.) NE of Carrickmore. The whole area is rich in chambered tombs and other megalithic monuments. Before excavation from 1979 to 1982 it was still buried in its wedge-shaped cairn. The tomb now shows a semicircular court leading into three burial chambers with some roof corbelling still in place as well as parts of the drystone walling of the cairn. In the interior the usual cremation burials, flints and Neolithic pottery were found. A few mi. to the NE another court tomb is to be found at Cregganconroe on a hill S. of Cam Lough, 3 mi. (4.75 km.) NW of Pomeroy. Unexcavated, this is an impressive pile of huge stones. A shallow court opens between tall portal stones into the 18-ft.-long chamber, divided into two. Behind this again two other chambers were reached by entrances on either side of the cairn. One huge capstone, askew, still survives and a lintel has fallen among the portal stones.

CREGGANKEEL FORT
(Galway)

See *Aran Islands*.

CROAGHBEG
(Donegal)

See *Shalwy*.

CRUACHAIN
(Roscommon)

See *Rathcroghan*.

CULLEN VILLAGE
(Tipperary)

See *Longstone*.

CURRAN, THE
(Antrim)

See *Larne*.

DANE'S CAST
(Armagh)

See *Lisnagade* (Down) and *Navan Fort* (Armagh).

DAVAGH LOWER
(Tyrone)

See *Beaghmore Monuments*.

DEERPARK
(Sligo)

See *Magheraghanrush*.

DERRY
(Down)

Ruins of two small, early stone churches, 1.5 mi. (2.3 km.) NE of Portaferry, E. of the road; excavated and consolidated in 1962. Both churches, simple rectangular structures, probably of the 10th to 11th cents., were built of slabs bonded with clay (now replaced), and had typical projecting antae of the side walls beyond the gables. Beneath them an Early Christian graveyard was uncovered, with long, stone-built graves of the 7th or 8th cent., as well as the foundations of a possible earlier church of stone and timber under the smaller S. church. A simple grave slab with Latin cross, probably also of the earlier period, is set in the present N. church. A church similar in date and construction can be found at nearby *Saint John's Point*.

DERRYINVER
(Galway)

Fine alignment of six stones on a peninsula in Connemara; ENE of the road around Tully Mtn., about 9 mi. (14.5 km.) N. of Clifden. The alignment stands out boldly, about 36 ft. long, running E–W, with the tallest stone nearly 6 ft. high.

DERRYNABLAHA
(Kerry)

Extensive group of Bronze Age petroglyphs, 2 mi. (3.25 km.) S. of the remote Ballaghbeama Gap on the Iveragh peninsula, about 10 mi. (16 km.) WNW of *Kenmare*. Over 20 inscribed rocks, hard to find, are scattered on the hillsides on both sides of the road. They are covered with cups, cup and ring, circles and grooves. See also *Ballinloughan* in Louth.

DERRYNAVAGH
(Clare)

See *The Burren*.

Devenish Island, a monastic site in Lower Lough Erne in Fermanagh. Originally a monastery founded in the 6th cent. AD, it was later the site of a medieval priory. The fine round tower, only 75 ft. high, is nevertheless complete even to its original conical cap. (Crown copyright: Historic Monuments and Buildings Branch, DOENI, Northern Ireland.)

**DEVENISH ISLAND
(Fermanagh)**

Monastic site with a fine round tower; on an island in Lower Lough Erne, the most important of many in the lough, about 2 mi. (3.25 km.) N. of Enniskillen, reached by ferry or boat. The monastery, founded by St. Molaise in the 6th cent. AD, was later the site of the parish church and of St. Mary's Augustinian priory in the Middle Ages. The earliest building here is the ruined St. Molaise's House near the tower, a small oratory of stone that was once roofed in stone. Both church and tower are of the 12th cent., decorated in the Romanesque manner, the round tower having on its cornice, under the original stone cap, a head under each of the four top windows. The tower, though complete, is only 75 ft. high. It may be climbed to the top. The foundations of an earlier tower have been found nearby, and the little church we see today may have replaced St. Molaise's original wooden church. In the graveyard around the lower church (13th cent.) an early recumbent grave slab lies among other stones, still in its original position. Other stones are displayed in a small thatched museum. See also *Boa Island; Inishmacsaint; White Island.*

**DINGLE PENINSULA
(Kerry)**

The western end of the peninsula, around the town of Dingle, and the offshore western islands exhibit an astonishing number of ancient sites and monuments, most now in state care and almost all impossible to date with any degree of accuracy. There are many large stone forts and ring forts, many clocháns or stone huts—single, double or multiple and in groups or inside enclosures (especially around Glanfahan). There are souterrains, standing stones, Ogham stones, cross slabs or cross pillars, monastic sites and stone oratories, petrogylyphs and a number of wedge tombs as well as other sites. Only a brief selection can be given here; detailed information is easily available elsewhere.

To begin with the stone forts: Dunbeg is perhaps the best known. It is dramatically sited above tall cliffs on a promontory 3 mi. (4.75 km.) SW of Ventry and is defended on its landward side by a massive (reconstructed) drystone wall with terraces behind it and four outer earth ramparts. A fine lintelled entrance passage leads into it, with guard chambers, a long souterrain under it and a large stone hut (round on the outside, square within) in the interior. SE of Dingle another fine promontory fort looks S. over Dingle Bay with great views. Doonmore, or "The Doon," covering 80 acres, is defended by a deep ditch and rampart and a stone-faced wall 10 ft. high. The interior is divided into three wards, with three huts and a souterrain. Two mi. (3.25 km.) NNW of Dingle is the great stone fort or ring fort of Ballyheaghbought with two lines of ramparts, the inner one stone-faced. Inside it are the remains of two clocháns with a souterrain under them.

Near the Gallarus oratory (see ahead), S. of and overlooking Smerwick Harbor, is Emlagh East, a neat round fort with two circles of ramparts and an outer ditch. Finally, the least accessible and most magnificent of the forts is Caherconree, dramatically sited 2,050 ft. high on a spur of Slieve Mish at the eastern base of the peninsula, 4 mi. (6.5 km.) SW of Tralee, accessible only by a path and a long walk up the steep mountain. An inland promontory fort, it is protected by cliffs on two sides and at the back by a curving stone wall 14 ft. thick and 350 ft. long, with a ditch. There were chambers and passages in the wall, which appears to have been terraced.

Of the many single stone pillars, an example of a presumably prehistoric standing stone is to be found at Ballineetig, about 2 mi. (3.25 km.) E. of Dingle.

Known as Gallaunmore, it is 15 ft. high. A great many other standing stones are pillars with Ogham inscriptions and often bearing a cross. An example lies not far S. from Ballineetig, near a golf course and sited just above high water mark; it is called Emlagh East Ogham Stone—presumably because it was found (the first to be so discovered) at that locality and was reerected here. It is called "The Priest's Stone." Another curious monument is a large boulder, about 1 mi. (1.6 km.) N. of Ventry, at Maumanorig on the ancient monastic site of Kilcolman. Incised into the boulder is an equal-armed cross within a circle, a smaller cross, and a late Ogham inscription naming "Colman the Pilgrim."

The finest Early Christian monument on Dingle is of course the famed Gallarus oratory with a fine early cross pillar near it, 4 mi. (6.5 km.) NW of Dingle overlooking Smerwick Harbor. This is a large, perfectly preserved example of the rectangular stone oratories of Dingle, with walls sloping inward like an upturned boat. It is beautifully constructed, with a lintelled doorway and a round-headed E. window. Though it looks very ancient, it could be as late as the 12th cent. and probably was a product of the ascetic reform movement in the church at that time and earlier. For the adventurous, the ruins of another oratory, of the famous St. Brendan the Navigator, can be seen on the way up the "saint's road," a path up to the top of Ireland's third highest mountain, Mt. Brandon. Within traces of a cashel wall are the rectangular oratory, St. Brendan's Well, and several clocháns of the anchorites who lived here. Farther N. along the mountain ridge one comes to a remote monument at Arraglen on a slope at a height of over 2,000 ft. This is a fallen Ogham stone with an inscription (naming a priest) and incised maltese crosses.

Remains of another anchorite community may be found at Ballymoreagh, 3 mi. (4.75 km.) WNW of Dingle. Teampull Geal (The White Church) or St. Manchán's Oratory is a stone structure of the same type as Gallarus, with a lintelled

The Gallarus Oratory on the Dingle Peninsula, Kerry, largest and finest of Kerry's curious Early Christian oratories—shaped like upturned boats. The masonry of Gallarus is outstanding and there is one small round-headed window at the back. Gallarus looks very old and is remarkably well-preserved, but it may be as late as the 12th cent., a period of ascetic revival and many anchorites. The oratory was obviously the lonely refuge of an early Christian hermit. (Courtesy of Irish Tourist Board, Dublin.)

A typical Dingle scene of fields and wide water with the Blasket Islands offshore. Like many of the numerous offshore islands around the peninsula, the Blaskets harbored Early Christian communities, though they are now uninhabited. (Courtesy of Irish Tourist Board, Dublin.)

doorway and an Ogham-inscribed cross pillar opposite it (the Latin inscription on it is probably a fake); also present are St. Manchán's Well and St. Manchán's grave with other small cross slabs and stones near it.

These Early Christian anchorites also took refuge on many of the islands around the peninsula. Most are difficult to reach. Perhaps the easiest site to reach is on Illauntannig, largest of the Maharee islands W. of Tralee Bay and 1 mi. (1.6 km.) N. of Rough Point at the top of Dingle. A community founded here by St. Senan is enclosed within a massive wall, and includes a small stone oratory, the ruins of another with a white cross over the doorway, remains of three clocháns, three burial monuments and a cross-inscribed slab. The uninhabited Blasket islands lie in the Atlantic SW off the peninsula and on the largest of the group, Great Blasket, are the ruins of an early church, age unknown. Two of the smaller islands also held anchorite communities. On Inishtooskert are the ruins of an oratory, four clocháns and three cross slabs. On Inishvickillane again there was an oratory, several clocháns and some cross slabs and grave stones.

Back on the peninsula at Kilmalkedar, 4.5 mi. (7.25 km.) N. of Dingle, one of the most attractive Early Christian sites, N. of Gallarus, is a lovely 12th-cent. Romanesque church marking the location again of an early monastic community. With beautifully carved decorations, the church once was roofed by stone corbelling with a barrel vault beneath, linking it closely with Cormac's Chapel at Cashel. In the churchyard are an early decorated sundial, a large cross and an Ogham stone. Inside the church is the interesting Alphabet Stone, showing a Latin cross and the alphabet in half-uncial letters. Finally at Reask, about 1 mi. (1.6 km.) ENE of Ballyferriter, another ancient monastic walled site has long been marked by an exceptionally fine early cross pillar engraved with a cross-in-circle, spiral designs and the letters DNE (for Domine). Recent excavations

An interesting Early Christian cross-pillar still standing within the remains of a walled monastic enclosure at Reask on the Dingle Peninsula. The letters DNE on one side stand for Domine. The notch high up on the same side was traditionally used by lovers to plight their troth by holding fingers across it, a very ancient practice. Recent excavations on the site uncovered the remains of a small oratory, double huts, two smaller cross-pillars and a number of early graves. (From Henry Françoise: Irish Art in the Early Christian Period *[1947], by permission of the publishers, Methuen & Co.)*

here have uncovered the remains of the monastic community—a small rectangular oratory, groups of double clocháns, two small cross pillars, and very early lintelled graves. The site was later used as a cemetery.

DISERT OENGHUSA (Limerick)

Round tower at Carrigeen, a few mi. (about 3 km.) NW of Croom, next to a roofless medieval church. The tower, though truncated, still rises 65 ft. high. The doorway, exceptionally high above the ground, has a decorative molding over its arch.

DONAGHMORE (Down)

Unique high cross in the Protestant graveyard of Donaghmore, 6 mi. (9.6 km.) NNE of Newry, on the Banbridge road. It marks the site of an ancient monastery.

The weathered cross, probably 9th or 10th cent., is unique because its biblical figures are not, as usual, framed in separate panels, and it is smaller than most, only about 9 ft. high.

DONAGHMORE SOUTERRAIN (Louth)

Fine example of the many souterrains in the region, underground chambers used for storage or refuge; 3 mi. (4.75 km.) W. of Dundalk. The drystone walls of this elaborate souterrain, built into a previously dug trench, consist of five low passages and chambers running in different directions, in all almost 230 ft. long. The roof is of flat lintels, supported on a course of corbelling. There is a trap to foil intruders, a secret passage, and ventilation. Probably it was used for refuge in Viking times when the Norse raiders were active here. It can be visited, with the aid of modern stairs.

DONAGHMORE (Meath)

Round tower and church, just NNE of Navan. The truncated tower, next to a 15th-cent. church, was restored in the 18th cent. without its conical cap and upper windows, thus losing its proportions. As usual, it marks the site of an ancient monastery. Its raised doorway shows heads on either side and a curious crucifixion carved on several stones over its arch. There are some Early Christian grave slabs in the churchyard.

DONEGORE (Antrim)

A Neolithic causewayed camp, a meeting place defined by circuits of ditches with causeways across them as found in England; but so far this site is unique in Ireland. It lies close to Donegore Motte, about 4 mi. (6.5 km.) E. by N. of Antrim, itself probably a prehistoric burial mound used for a castle by Anglo-Normans. The camp was discovered by aerial survey and crop marks in 1982 and then excavated, revealing a double, possibly triple line of ditches around the hill, interrupted by causeways, with a round house and hearth inside them. The finds included over 30,000 sherds of mid-Neolithic pottery, tools, flints and other occupation rubbish. The site has been radiocarbon-dated 3000–2200 BC. Donegore lies about 4 mi. (6.5 km.) NW of the Neolithic enclosure at *Lyle's Hill*.

DOOEY'S CAIRN (Antrim)

See *Ballymacaldrack*.

DOON FORT (Donegal)

Strikingly sited oval stone fort, extremely well-preserved (though restored), covering an entire small island in Lough Doon on a western peninsula of Donegal; about 5 mi. (8 km.) NNW of Ardara. The tapering walls, enclosing a maximum area of about 135 ft. in diameter, contain wall passages like those in the *Grianan of Aileach* fort, also in Donegal, and are terraced on the inside, with steps up to the wall.

DOONMORE FORT (Kerry)

See the *Dingle Peninsula*.

DORSEY ENCLOSURE (Armagh)

Or Dorsy. Huge 300-acre Iron Age enclosure long and narrow, probably defending Ulster to its N.; about 4 mi. (6.5 km.) NE of Crossmaglen, at Drummill Bridge. Its E-W dimension covers about a mile. The enclosure is defined by two banks, the inner one larger, and a ditch—about 39 yds. wide in all. On boggy ground the ramparts are based on oak pilings with horizontal beams. There were traces of a wooden guardhouse at one entrance. By tree-ring chronology and comparison with *Navan Fort* about 17 mi. (27.5 km.) N., it can be dated to around the 3rd or 2nd cent. BC.

DOWNPATRICK
(Down)

Cathedral town and ancient site, 21 mi. (33 km.) S. of Belfast. To the SW of the Protestant Cathedral Hill, which rises above the town, traces of the ditch and bank of a very large hill fort, Rath Celtchair, can be seen. This was probably a royal enclosure of about 1000 AD, or perhaps, originally, Late Bronze Age. Neolithic materials and extensive evidences of Bronze Age occupation have been turned up here, showing that the site is indeed very ancient. An Early Christian monastery was deliberately founded inside the hill fort—according to legend by St. Patrick himself—from which a round tower and other buildings survived until an enlargement of the Cathedral in the early 19th cent. Recent excavations have uncovered some of these foundations; and fragments of early crosses from the site have been built into the Cathedral's Chapter Room. Also, a much weathered, figured high cross, probably 9th or 10th cent. and assembled from fragments, stands outside the Cathedral. The Downpatrick Mound, 1.5 mi. (2.3 km.) NW of the town center, is a huge earthwork ringed by a bank and outer ditch, with another small mound with a ditch in its SE corner. Reputedly this was the motte and bailey of a castle built by de Courcy, the Norman who seized Downpatrick in 1177. The enclosure, however, may well be a reused pre-Norman site, as investigations in the 1980s may show.

DOWTH
(Meath)

See *Boyne Valley.*

DROMBEG STONE CIRCLE
(Cork)

One of the largest and best of the Recumbent Stone Circles typical of the area, excavated 1957; 1.5 (3 km.) E. of Glandore, near the coast. It stands on a previously prepared platform on a slope with wide views. The 17 standing stones enclose an area of about 30 ft. across, with the recumbent or axial stone on the

One of the finest and largest of the Bronze Age stone circles of Cork, in a lovely situation near the coast. Drombeg is about 30 ft. across. Its 17 stones stand on a previously prepared platform, with the long, low recumbent stone, marking a sacred direction, at the back. The two large portal stones in the foreground stand opposite it. Though probably built in the Bronze Age, there is evidence from the excavations that the site was venerated as sacred for thousands of years. (Photo: the author.)

W. and the others graded in height toward it. Two large portal stones stand on the NE. The circle probably dates from the Bronze Age, but was in use over a long period since a cremation burial in an urn at the center has been dated to between 150 BC and 130 AD, in the Iron Age. Two joined round huts were found 60 yds to the W. of the circle, the smaller one containing a baking oven. From them a stone-paved causeway led to a cooking place or *fulacht fian* with hearth, well and a trough in which water was boiled for cooking with hot stones. Its dating to the 5th cent. AD indicates that seasonal ritual meetings at this circle may have taken place here for thousands of years.

DROMBOHILLY UPPER STONE CIRCLE (Kerry)

See *Shronebirrane*.

DROMISKIN (Louth)

Round tower and high cross demarking the site of an early monastery, about 11 mi. (17.75 km.) S. of Dundalk. The tower, near the ruins of a medieval church, is 55 ft. high with a modern cap and upper windows. Its Romanesque, round-headed doorway and large windows suggest a rebuilding of an older tower in the 12th cent. Near it is the mounted top part of a high cross, carved in the 8th cent. manner with Celtic spirals on one side, beasts in a wheel on the other and two figured panels, one of a stag hunt the other of a strange procession with a headless corpse on a horse, like that on the North Cross at *Ahenny*. Memories of the Celtic cult of the severed head?

DROMORE (Down)

Ancient weathered high cross of granite (9th or 10th cent.?), smashed in the 17th cent. and later reassembled, restored and reerected by the Lagan Bridge at Dromore, SW of Belfast, near the present cathedral. It belonged to an ancient monastery at Dromore.

DRUMBO (Down)

Stump of a round tower, about 30 ft. high, in the Presbyterian churchyard at Drumbo, 1.5 mi. (2.3 km.) SW of Belfast.

DRUMCLIFF (Clare)

Ruined round tower, about 25 ft. high, 2 mi. (3.25 km.) NW of Ennis. It has fallen away on one side so that one can see its interesting internal construction. It stands in a cemetery next to a medieval church. See also *Kilmacduagh*.

DRUMCLIFF (Sligo)

Stump of around tower and a high cross amidst lovely rural scenery, marking the site of an ancient monastery founded by St. Columcille (Columba), 4 mi. (6.5 km.) N. of Sligo. The tower, hit by lightning in 1396, is now only about 25 ft. high. On the path to the Protestant church, where W.B. Yeats is buried, is a fine, late (11th cent.?) high cross of white sandstone, intricately carved with many biblical scenes amidst strange beasts and monsters and interlace ornament.

DRUMENA (Down)

Substantial stone cashel or fort in an upland meadow 2.25 mi. (3.75 km.) SW of Castlewellan, signposted off the main road. The oval cashel, clearly a farmstead enclosure of the Early Christian period, has walls up to 10 ft. thick. It was excavated in 1925–26 and partly reconstructed. A T-shaped souterrain, about 45 ft. long, lies under the interior and can be explored (through a modern entrance).

A *magnificent high cross of white sandstone at Drumcliff, Sligo, probably 11th cent. With the stump of a round tower it is a survival from an early monastery founded here by St. Columba. The cross, with biblical scenes and elaborate geometric decoration, stands near the grave of the poet, William Butler Yeats. (Courtesy of Irish Tourist Board, Dublin.)*

DRUMLANE
(Cavan)

Round tower, about 6 mi. (9.6 km.) SW of Belturbet and E. of the main road, relic of a monastery founded here in the 6th cent. AD. The lower part of the tower, standing now about 36 ft. high, rises next to a medieval church. It probably dates from the 12th cent. There are weathered carvings of birds about 6 ft. up the tower.

DRUMSKINNY
(Fermanagh)

Attractive stone circle, easily accessible, 4.5 mi. (7.25 km.) N. of Kesh. It is similar to many other Bronze Age circles in this region, and is of the small-stone type found especially at *Beaghmore* (Tyrone). The 39 smallish stones enclosed an area some 40 ft. across. Excavated in 1962, a compact cairn with kerb stones was found at the NW side of the circle, with an alignment of 24 small stones running away from it for about 25 ft.

DUBLIN
(Dublin)

Outstanding in this capital city is the National Museum of Ireland with its important collections of prehistoric and Early Christian exhibits. Trinity College Library nearby displays the famous 8th-cent. illuminated manuscript of the *Book* of *Kells*, as well as other illuminated manuscripts such as the *Book of Durrow*. Archaeologists from the National Museum have also been responsible for the recently-completed Wood Quay excavation of Viking and early medieval Dublin (1974–81), one of the largest as well as earliest of urban digs in Europe. This ambitious project, along with the recent, very similar large-scale excavation of Viking *York* in England and other excavations in Scandinavia, has rehabilitated our image of the Vikings. No longer just ferocious raiders, they are now seen as traders, merchants, artisans and superb explorers—heralds of the reawakening of Europe in the early Middle Ages.

Invading Norse Vikings, after raiding Ireland from 795 AD, founded Dublin as a small fortified settlement, a ship port and winter base, on the S. bank of the Liffey in 841 AD—and in the following cent. established similar settlements at Wexford, Waterford, Cork and Limerick. These were the first real towns in Ireland. By chance in the 19th cent. a series of richly-furnished graves of Viking warriors and their women (now destroyed) was discovered upriver from central Dublin at Islandbridge and Kilmainham, a cemetery of the first Norse settlers. Their original river port may have been close by. However, Dublin as a commercial city in its own right developed only after the start of the 10th cent., in an area within the limits of the medieval walled town of Dublin proper, now centered around Christchurch Cathedral, and the streets leading down to the Liffey. This area has been the focus of a series of recent excavations in advance of redevelopment that has explored the remains of early Dublin from the early 900s up to about 1400 AD. No remains of the earliest settlers have been found here.

Viking Dublin began as a Scandinavian outpost of Norse settlers under a dynasty of Danish kings, a way station on the far-flung northern trade routes of the Vikings; but after 954 AD when Viking York fell to the English, Dublin in turn became one of the principal trading towns of Europe, a wealthy cosmopolitan center with increasingly stronger links with Anglo-Saxon England, France and the Irish hinterland as well as Scandinavia. King Sigtrygg Silkbeard, half Viking, half Irish, established the first mint in Dublin about 997 AD. Thereafter, until the Anglo-Norman conquest of the late 12th cent., Dublin continued to prosper, though increasingly enmeshed in the western European commercial and cultural spheres rather than the Scandinavian.

After some preliminary explorations, the series of National Museum excavations in central Dublin began in 1962 under A.B.O. Riordáin on several different sites and continued well into the 1970s. The results were spectacular—though now, of course, nothing is on view except the finds. Packed habitation layers of wood and wattle houses with their outhouses, workshops, garbage pits, fences and pathways, all well-preserved in the waterlogged conditions, were uncovered as well as over 100,000 objects of all kinds, also well-preserved. However, this pioneering series of urban excavations was merely preliminary to the latest Wood Quay series of 1974–81, which revealed nine different waterfronts on the Liffey, from the simple bank of the early 10th cent. to later, more elaborate earthen ramparts that encircled the whole town. A group of living plots bounded by fences were also explored, each containing over a dozen levels of superimposed house sites—a new house usually built over the leveled remains of the previous house about every 20 years.

The finds again were staggering in their variety—coins, metal tools, artifacts of bone and stone and richly carved wooden objects, imported glasswares, pottery, silks, amber and walrus ivory. Daily life was illustrated by the well-preserved remains of wooden chairs, of dishes, spoons, spades and shovels, bronze pins and combs of bone, figurines and gaming boards. Reused ships' timbers had been built into the waterfronts, showing that the standard ship, up to the 12th cent., was still the Viking keel boat with high prow and stern, a single mast and a steering oar. Boat models confirmed the findings. Finally a rich haul of animal and fish bones, seeds and pollen, grain and insect remains from the houses and pits, is still being studied, revealing a detailed picture of the diet and the environment of these ancient Hiberno-Scandinavian Dubliners.

DUN AENGUS
(Galway)

See Aran Islands.

DUN AILINNE
(Kildare)

Large ceremonial hill fort on Knockaulin, .75 mi. (1 km.) NW of Old Kilcullen. An earthen rampart, up to 15 ft. high, encloses a hilltop area of about 20 acres. A wide ditch *inside* the wall indicates that the site was ceremonial rather than defensive. It has been identified as Dun Ailinne, the ancient seat of the kings of Leinster, and recent excavations determined that it had been in use from the Bronze Age (and probably earlier) up to as late as 1800 as a ceremonial meeting place, and in more ancient times as a sacred enclosure. Traces of a large timber building like that at *Navan Fort* were found in the interior. See also *Rathgall; Tara.*

DUNBEG FORT
(Kerry)

See *Dingle Peninsula.*

DUN BHALAIR
(Donegal)

See *Tory Island.*

DUN CHATHAIR
(Galway)

See Aran Islands.

DUN CONOR
(Galway)

See Aran Islands.

DUN DOOCAHER
(Galway)

See Aran Islands.

DUNGLADY
(Londonderry)

A very large ring fort, probably of the Early Christian period, 4 mi. (6.5 km.) NE of Maghera, 1 mi. (1.6 km.) from Culnady. It is in state care. Three circuits of ramparts enclose the fort, the outer ones much obscured by vegetation.

DUNLOE
(Kerry)

Ogham stones, inscribed in the ancient Irish writing, 2 mi. (3.25 km.) N. of the well-known tourist Gap of Dunloe route and 5 mi. (8 km.) W. by N. of Killarney. These eight stones were moved here from elsewhere—seven of them had been used as roofing in a souterrain.

DUNNAMORE
(Tyrone)

See *Beaghmore Monuments.*

DUN OGHIL FORT
(Galway)

See Aran Islands.

DUN ONAGHT FORT
(Galway)

See *Aran Islands.*

DUN RUADH
(Tyrone)

Unusual Neolithic-Bronze Age multiple cist tomb, exceedingly rare in Ireland, 2 mi. (3.25 km.) NE of the village of Sheskinschule, SW of The Six Towns. A huge oval cairn of stones, about 90 ft. long, much robbed but still impressive, surrounds a central cobbled court defined by 17 uprights and dry walling, with an entrance into it from the SW. There is no kerb around the cairn; instead it is bordered by a ditch and low bank outside the ditch in the manner of a henge. Some 13 box-like burial cists were found in the cairn, some well-built, others makeshift, containing Late Neolithic pottery. The *Beaghmore* stone circles lie only about 4 mi. (6.5 km.) to the E.

DUNSEVERICK FORT
(Antrim)

Dramatically sited promontory fort on a bold rock over the sea, with the remains of a later castle; 4.5 mi. (7.25 km.) NE of Bushmills and about 3 mi. (4.75 km.) E. of the Giant's Causeway. The original fort probably dates from the Early Christian period. See also *White Park Bay.*

DUNTRYLEAGUE
(Limerick)

A fine passage tomb lost in an encroaching state forest, 1.5 mi. (2.3 km.) W. by N. of Galbally, about 8 mi. (13 km.) SW of Tipperary. Its long covered passage leads into a cruciform chamber expanding toward the back and roofed by three overlapping stones. If the tomb was covered by a cairn, it has disappeared.

DURROW
(Offaly)

Site of the ancient monastery of Durrow, founded by St. Columba about 553 AD and source of the fine, illuminated, 7th-cent. *Book of Durrow*, now in Trinity College Library, *Dublin.* Durrow Abbey is about 4 mi. (6.5 km.) N. of Tullamore, W. of the road to Kilbeggan. The old monastery is marked only by its fine high cross next to an essentially modern church. Of the 10th cent., the cross displays varied biblical scenes on all four sides. Near the cross are some early gravestones with intricate designs of the *Clonmacnoise* type and a fragment of another cross with interlace design.

DUVILLAUN MORE
(Mayo)

See *Mullet Peninsula.*

DYSERT O'DEA
(Clare)

Round tower and cross at the site of an 8th-cent. monastery 4 mi. (6.5 km.) S. of Corofin. The stump of the ruined round tower, only about 45 ft. high, is of the 12th cent. as is the fine Romanesque carved doorway, displaying a profusion of human and animal heads, built into the much-altered church (see also *Cashel; Clonfert*). The high cross, in a field E. of the church, is of the same period, rather late in the series of crosses. Biblical scenes have disappeared; instead a crucifixion and the figure of an abbot, both carved in high relief, are on one side; the rest of the cross is given over to interlace and geometric designs with some figures. Clare's famous *The Burren* region lies just to the N.

EIGHTERCUA
(Kerry)

Stone alignment on the Ring of Kerry route, 1 mi. (1.6 km.) SSE of Waterville. Four standing stones, up to 9 ft. high and running E-W may be associated with a nearby cairn, or were perhaps part of its tomb facade.

EMAIN MACHA
(Armagh)

See *Navan Fort.*

EMLAGH EAST
(Kerry)

See the *Dingle Peninsula*.

FAHAN
(Donegal)

Ancient crosses, relics of a monastery founded by St. Mura early in the 7th cent.; 4.5 mi. (7.25 km.) S. of Buncrana. St. Mura's enshrined staff is now in the National Museum. A 7-ft.-high cross slab, St. Mura's Cross, stands in the graveyard. This is a truly outstanding and rare survival from the 7th cent. Each side is adorned with crosses of intricately interlaced ribbons, two figures standing beside the one, two birds above the other. There are faint inscriptions in Irish and Greek, the first a blessing, the other the "Gloria Patri." Built into the graveyard's outside wall is another early cross slab showing a ringed cross in a square.

FEERMORE, RATH OF
(Galway)

See *Turoe Stone*.

FERTAGH
(Kilkenny)

Also Grangefertagh. Round tower on a monastery site, 7 mi. (11.25 km.) NW of Freshford, N. of the road to Durrow. Originally the tallest tower in Ireland, it was burned in 1156 and has lost its cap, though it is still a slim 100 ft. high with eight floors. Its doorway is not the original.

FORE
(West Meath)

Ruins of the Early Christian church of St. Feichin, probably 9th or 10th cent., 3 mi. (4.75 km.) E. of Castlepollard. The church is all that remains of a once flourishing monastery founded by the saint in the 7th cent. It was burned or pillaged 12 times between 771 and 1169 AD. The ruin stands in the western graveyard above the road and a medieval chancel and E. windows have been added to the original simple rectangular building with steep pitched roof and projecting antae (side walls). Its original doorway, topped by a massive lintel carved with a Greek cross, is its most distinguishing feature. Nearby are the impressive ruins of Ireland's only medieval Benedictine priory.

FOURKNOCKS
(Meath)

Impressive example of a large passage tomb. 17 mi. (27.5 km.) N. of Dublin, about 6 mi. (9.6 km.) E. by S. of Balbriggan. Its unusually large cruciform chamber and passage filled most of the original mound of turf, held in by a kerb. The tomb had collapsed and has been reconstructed with a modern concrete dome that skillfully illuminates the uprights and drystone walling of the large chamber and three small side chambers. It is thought that the main chamber, too large to be covered by the usual slabs or corbelling, was roofed by timbers resting on some courses of corbelling and a central post to hold it up. The carefully packed bones, cremated and unburned, of over 65 bodies were found in the chamber and passage. They had been put in the tomb all at once and the tomb then sealed; later burials, in cists and urns, were inserted in the mound. Twelve of the tomb's stones are decorated with typical passage grave art (see *Boyne Valley*) and one shows an unmistakable sketch of a human face. Another mound nearby to the E. was found to have been used to cremate the bodies in a special trench before burial in the main mound.

GALLARUS ORATORY
(Kerry)

See *Dingle Peninsula*.

GALLAUNMORE
(Kerry)

See *Dingle Peninsula*.

GALLEN PRIORY
(Offaly)

In the grounds of a modern priory here, .5 mi. (.75 km.) S. of Ferbane, is a rich collection of Early Christian grave slabs and cross slabs, comparable to those displayed at *Clonmacnoise*, dating probably from the 7th to the 11th cents. Many of them were found in excavations on the site of a 5th-cent. monastery here. Some are built into the gables of a medieval church, one is in the center of the church, and others on the grounds outside it. The exuberant decoration of the stones includes interlacing, fret patterns, a Celtic whirl, animal and human heads, deer and serpents.

GAULSTOWN
(Waterford)

Two very fine portal tombs close to each other. Gaulstown is 5.5 mi. (9 km.) S. of Waterford and the other tomb, at Knockeen, 4 mi. (6.5 km.) to the SW and 2 mi. (3.25 km.) E. of Gaulstown. A single huge capstone, about 13–14 ft. long, covers the six uprights of the Gaulstown tomb, the two portal stones jutting forward to form a kind of porch, with a closing slab between them. Knockeen is very similar but has two capstones, the larger one overlapping a smaller one.

GIANT'S RING
(Down)

See *Ballynahatty*

GLANFAHAN
(Kerry)

See *Dingle Peninsula*.

GLENBALLYTHOMAS
(Roscommon)

See *Rathcroghan*.

GLENCOLUMBKILLE
(Donegal)

Village in a remote valley in far southwestern Donegal, close to the Atlantic, 7 mi. (11.25 km.) NW of Carrick. (One of the village's attractions is a folk park of old cottages.) Here, over thousands of years, the prehistoric and Early Christian periods meet in a present-day "pattern" (*turas*) or pilgrimage still performed on June 9 in honor of the great St. Columcille (St. Columba), who in tradition vanquished some demons here. There are 15 stations over a three-mile route that is marked by cairns of stones, almost all of them topped by Early Christian cross slabs with rectilinear designs—survivors, it seems, of an Early Christian monastery here, probably Columban. Moreover, the pilgrimage starts from the remains of a megalithic court tomb just W. of the Protestant church (which has a well-preserved souterrain near its doorway) and ends at the church again. Near the 9th station are the scant remains of a huge center court tomb with the largest court in all of Ireland; it has two-chambered galleries at either end and perhaps four subsidiary chambers. The tomb is called "Munnernamortee Cave."

The area is indeed rich in megalithic monuments, attesting to its sanctity since prehistoric times. (What, one may ask, were those demons vanquished by St. Columba?) Near Malin More, 3 mi. (4.75 km.) SW of Glencolumbkille, are a number of tombs, including a portal dolmen and two court tombs. One of these, called Cloghanmore, 43 yds. long and much reconstructed, is in state care. It has a full court with entrance at the E. end, subsidiary chambers off each side of the court and two galleries at the far W. end, each segmented into two chambers. Slabs at the entrances of the side chambers bear rare incised designs similar to passage grave art (see *Boyne Valley*); but these could just as well date from the Iron Age or Early Christian periods. Less than a mi. (about 1 km.) W. of the court tomb are six megalithic tombs in line, probably once covered by a single immense cairn. Those at each end are large portal tombs.

Early Christian cross slab standing on a cairn in Glencolumbkille in remote Donegal. Many such slabs mark the "stations" of a pilgrimage or "pattern" carried out here every June in honor of St. Columba. The slabs apparently came from an ancient monastery dedicated to St. Columba, and the rectilinear patterns are typical of the cross slabs found along the western and northern coasts of Ireland. There is also a concentration of megalithic tombs around Glencolumbkille, a sanctified region for thousands of years. (Courtesy of Irish Tourist Board, Dublin.)

GLENDALOUGH (Wicklow)

Famous monastic site in a lovely wooded valley clustering around two lakes high in the Wicklow Mtns; 1 mi. (1.6 km.) W. of Laragh and some 30 mi. (48 km.) S. of Dublin. With *Clonmacnoise* it ranks as one of Ireland's most popular tourist attractions. Founded by St. Kevin in the 6th cent. around the upper lake, it grew into one of Ireland's major religious centers, and to gain space was moved down the valley, probably in the 8th cent., to the present site of most of the buildings E. of the lower lake. The numerous remaining buildings were heavily and not always happily restored in the 19th cent. and again in the early 20th. An informative guidebook is available.

The central group of buildings clusters around the elegantly proportioned round tower, soaring 100 ft. above them. Its cap was rebuilt in 1876; otherwise it is complete. The buildings, lying behind the medieval arched gatehouse (it had a second story, and is the only surviving example in Ireland), center around the cathedral, whose large nave and lintelled W. doorway are probably 10th cent., the chancel and sacristy probably 12th. Next to it stands St. Kevin's church (or "kitchen"), probably of about the same earlier period, a rectangular building notable for its steep-pitched Irish-style stone roof with a later belfry, much like a small round tower, growing out of it. There is a fine 12th-cent. cross inside the church and other relics. To the W. is another church, St. Mary's, originally

St. Kevin's Kitchen, or church, in the lovely vale of Glendalough, high in the Wicklow Mtns. S. of Dublin. Here are the numerous ruined churches and other monuments of a monastery founded by St. Kevin in the 6th cent. AD. These include a well-proportioned round tower. Glendalough is now a favored tourist haven. The "Kitchen," probably 10th cent., has a typical Irish steep stone roof with a small, round tower-like belfry topping it. (Courtesy of Irish Tourist Board, Dublin.)

perhaps 10th or 11th cent. but with a Romanesque chancel added to it. A cross is carved on the lintel of its flat-headed W. doorway. In between it and St. Kevin's in the midst of a graveyard, is a little Romanesque building called the Priests' House, perhaps a mortuary house. Over its N. door is a broken but interesting crude panel of three figures, probably earlier in date.

Moving E. down the Laragh road one finds another church, Trinity, a nave and chancel church, perhaps 11th or 12th cent. A round tower at the church was blown down in 1818. Still farther E. and across the river is St. Saviour's priory. The church, 12th cent. and later, boasts a profusion of Romanesque decoration. In the opposite direction, beside a path up to the edge of the upper lake is the site of another church, a stone fort (the "Caher") and four high crosses. On the other side of the path is the interesting, tiny Reefert church, possibly 11th cent., with flat lintelled W. doorway, round-headed windows, chancel arch and corbels at the outside corners that once supported rafters. There are early stones and crosses in the graveyard.

A path from the church takes one up to "St. Kevin's Cell," the ruins of a round stone hut, rare in these parts. The probable site of the original monastery on the lakeside can only be reached by boat. Here by the lake is Temple na Skellig, a small rectangular church, probably on the site of St. Kevin's original church, and W. of it a walled enclosure in which, it is thought, the original wattle and daub huts of the early monastery once stood. On the way to it one can stop and climb a cliff to a narrow, man-made cave, "St. Kevin's Bed." It is more likely a far older Bronze Age burial cave. All around the site of Glendalough as a whole are more stone crosses and cross slabs, many inside the various churches, as well as the foundations of other buildings.

GOWARD
(Down)

A megalithic portal tomb in an area containing many other tombs, W. of Newry and 2 mi. (3.25 km.) NE of Hilltown. Called Cloughmore, or more quaintly "Pat Kearney's Big Stone," the grave's huge capstone over the chamber, now slipped to one side, is estimated to weigh about 50 tons.

GOWLANE NORTH STONE
  CIRCLE
  (Cork)

See *Beenalaght.*

GRANGE CIRCLE
  (Limerick)

See *Lough Gur.*

GRANGEFERTAGH
  (Kilkenny)

See *Fertagh.*

GREENGRAVES
  (Down)

See *Kempe Stones.*

The famous Grianan of Aileach, a huge stone fort in Donegal, typical of the larger stone forts of western and northern Ireland and of the Aran Islands, in particular. Topping a hill near Londonderry city, the round stone fort was largely rebuilt in the 19th cent. on foundations dating from the Early Christian cents. Whether authentic or not, the fort is still impressive. (Courtesy of Irish Tourist Board, Dublin.)

GRIANAN OF AILEACH
(Donegal)

Or Ailech; renowned stone fort on the border of Londonderry and Donegal, 5 mi. (8 km.) WNW of the city of Londonderry. The huge circular fort on a hilltop, seat of the Northern Uí Néill with magnificent views over Loughs Foyle and Swilly, consists of a heavy stone rampart, now over 17 ft. high and 13 ft. thick, enclosing an area 77 ft. across. The wall is backed up by three terraces with ascending steps, and there are remains of three more concentric earthen ramparts, probably much older than the stone wall around the hill; and there are two galleries within the main wall. The massive fort, its stone wall dating from the early cents. AD was unfortunately rebuilt, and most inaccurately, in 1870 on the base of the original wall, then only about 6 ft. high; nevertheless the rebuilt fort makes a fine show.

GURRANES ALIGNMENT
(Cork)

See *Knockdrum*.

GURTEEN CIRCLE
(Kerry)

See *Kenmare*.

HAROLDSTOWN DOLMEN
(Carlow)

A fine granite portal tomb on the banks of the Deneen River, S. of Accuan Bridge, 4.5 mi. (7 km.) NE of Tullow. Here are two capstones resting on 10 uprights, forming a large chamber with a closing slab between the two portal stones. In fact the tomb is so complete that it was used as a dwelling in recent times. Deep grooves on the larger capstone may have been deliberately cut.

HARRISTOWN
(Waterford)

Finest of a local group of passage tombs, on top of a hill near the coast with wide views; 2 mi. (3.25 km.) N. and slightly W. of Dunmore East. These tombs, often called Entrance Tombs, closely resemble those found on the *Scilly Isles* off England. In these tombs the long passage and the chamber at the end are one. The discovery in a cremation burial at Harristown of a polished stone axe amulet, identified with the Scilly Isles, confirms the connection. On the other hand the slightly wedge-shaped chamber end of the passage ties these tombs to the common Irish wedge tomb. Two cremation burials were found in the tomb and eight later Bronze Age burials, three of them in urns. Only two of the roofstones are still in place and the remains of a cairn surround the tomb. Another good example of the type is found at Mathewstown, about 9 mi. (14.5 km.) to the W. (1.5 mi. or 2.3 km. N. of Fennor and about 4 mi. or 6.5 km. W. of Tramore). Here three capstones still cover 10 uprights, and some of the kerb stones of the vanished cairn survive.

HEAPSTOWN
(Sligo)

See *Carrickglass*.

HIGH ISLAND
(Galway)

Ruins of an ancient monastic community on an uninhabited island 2 mi. (3.25 km.) offshore in the Atlantic, reached by hiring a boat at Cleggan. The monastery is probably to be dated to the 7th cent. AD. The chief building is a small rectangular church with a (possibly later) flat-headed doorway—for the lintel is a reused grave slab. Around the church are more cross slabs with intricate decorations, and beyond the wall around the church are the clocháns or huts and other buildings of the community, again within a wall. A final wall cuts off the monastic end of the island.

HILL OF WARD (Meath)	Ancient communal meeting place, a hill fort 1 mi. (1.6 km.) E. of Athboy, formerly called Tlachtga, where on Samhain (October 31st) there was a great annual gathering of the Irish to mark the beginning of winter. Far earlier the hill seems to have been a pagan Celtic shrine of the sacred fire. Today the site shows disturbed traces of the four banks and ditches that enclosed the platform on top of the rise. See also *Tara* and *Teltown*, also in Meath.
ILLAUNTANNIG (Kerry)	See *Dingle Peninsula*.
INCHBOFIN (Longford)	See *Inchclauran*.
INCHCLAURAN **and INCHBOFIN** (Longford)	Two of the islands with monastic remains in the large Lough Ree on the borders of Westmeath, Roscommon and Longford. They can be visited together by boat from Lanesborough (Longford) at the northern end of the lough, or from near *Athlone* (Westmeath) at the lower end. Both were sites of monasteries founded in the 6th cent. AD, and both have interesting early cross slabs and grave slabs. There are the ruins of six churches on Inchclauran and two on Inchbofin, all largely medieval except for the tiny Tempall Diarmúid on Inchclauran, a rectangular building with antae (projecting side walls) and a lintelled doorway. On Inchbofin a piece of 10th-cent. Viking bronze work was found, probably a relic of a known Viking raid on the island in 922 AD.
INISFALLEN (Kerry)	See *Innisfallen*.
INISHCALTRA ISLAND (Clare)	Or Inis Cealtra, or Holy Island; in Lough Derg, not far from its western shore in eastern Clare. The remains of a monastic community here, with a round tower, can be reached by boat from Mountshannon, 1 mi. (1.6 km.) NE. The monastery was founded by St. Caiman in the 7th cent., and the earthen ring enclosure of the monastery can still be seen around the ruined buildings, which include five churches of uncertain date, apparently mostly Romanesque and "restored" in the 19th cent. St. Mary's is the largest. St. Brigid's and St. Caiman's have Romanesque doorways. Ruined St. Michael's was a tiny oratory in its own enclosure, while the equally tiny "Church of the Wounded Men" is set in the Saint's Graveyard, which has been excavated, with gravestones dating from the 8th cent. and later. There is also the "Anchorite's Cell," another tiny structure in an enclosure. It may have been a shrine or tomb. Preserved inside St. Caiman's, supposedly built by Brian Boru, are several early crosses and gravestones and part of a high cross, called the "Cross of Cathasach," decorated with two panels of figures and interlacing. The Holy Well was the start of a "pattern" or pilgrimage held here from the 17th cent. The round tower, still standing about 79 ft. high, has lost its top story and cap. It has a round-headed doorway.
INISHGLORA (Mayo)	See *Mullet Peninsula*.
INISHKEA NORTH (Mayo)	See *Mullet Peninsula*.

INISHMACSAINT
(Fermanagh)

Island just off the W. side of Lower Lough Erne, near Blaney, 7.5 mi. (12 km.) NW of Enniskillen and 5.5 mi. (9 km.) NW of *Devenish Island*; site of a 6th-cent. monastery. The W. end of the ruined church here is of the 10th or 11th cent., with a blocked W. door; the rest is Romanesque and medieval. Near the church stands a plain cross, 13 ft. high, without decoration or ring. It probably also belongs to the earlier period. See also *White Island*.

INISHMURRAY
(Sligo)

Ancient monastery on an island about 4 mi. (6.5 km.) off the western coast of Sligo at Streedagh; a 9 mi. (14.5 km.) trip by hired boat from Mullaghmore harbor. Though difficult to reach and confused by rather extensive "restorations" in 1880, the monastic enclosure here gives one a good idea of the appearance and layout of an early monastery—most of which were built of wood, except here in the stony west. The monastery, founded by St. Molaise in the 6th cent., is enclosed by an oval, heavy stone wall up to 13 ft. high and 175 ft. across at its widest. It is divided into four sections by lower stone walls. There are cubicles and passages in the main wall—some of them possibly inaccurate "restorations."

Inside the largest section is the Men's Church with projecting antae and a flat-headed doorway. Also in this sector is the tiny St. Molaise's Church, very early with reconstructed stone roof and a cross on the lintel over the doorway with its sloping jambs. Here also are a number of standing pillar stones and three square outdoor "altars" or *leachts* topped by slabs with crosses on them. One, said to harm one's enemies if directed toward them, was turned toward Hitler's Germany by an Englishwoman during World War II! In the small NW sector is a large, round corbelled beehive hut with low entrance and one small window, called The Schoolhouse for a later use of the hut. Next to it is the medieval House or Church of the Fire. Outside it a perpetual fire once burned, possibly pagan in origin. To the NW outside the wall stands the Women's Church and graveyard. Inside and outside the whole enclosure are some 50 slabs engraved with crosses and beautiful designs. These marked a postmonastic "pattern" or pilgrimage. One is a holed stone; it was once frequented by expectant women. See also *Nendrum*.

INISHTOOSKERT
(Kerry)

See the *Dingle Peninsula*.

INISHVICKILLANE
(Kerry)

See the *Dingle Peninsula*.

INNISFALLEN ISLAND
(Kerry)

A monastic community in Lough Leane, just SW of Killarney. It can be reached by boat from Ross Castle. Founded in the 7th cent., the monastery flourished as a center of learning in the 12th and 13th cents. Consequently the remains, an oratory and abbey, are Romanesque and later. *The Annals of Innisfallen*, written here around 1215, is an important source for early Irish history. The western end of the abbey, with projecting antae and a flat-headed doorway, belonged to an earlier church. Even this was probably 12th cent. There are also two Romanesque oratories.

ISLAND
(Cork)

A very good example of a small wedge-shaped tomb, excavated in 1957 and partly restored, 5.5 mi. (9 km.) SE of Mallow, .75 mi. (1 km.) E. of Burnfort. The

The wedge tomb of Island, County Cork, a typical example of the type, excavated in 1957 and somewhat restored. The chamber, about 18 ft. long, is faced by the two tall portal stones in a facade, and is enclosed within double walls. Some roof slabs are still in place. Not visible are the extensive remains of the original cairn, edged by kerb stones. (Courtesy of Dept. of Archaeology, University College of Cork.)

gallery-chamber, about 18 ft. long, is enclosed by the usual double wall with a rounded back end and two tall portal stones at the center of the flat facade in front. The roofstones, very thin, are still in place. The whole is set within a heel-shaped cairn, bordered by a kerb and still filled with cairn material between kerb and gallery. In front of the entrance was a semicircle of low stones. A few cremation burials, with flints, were found at the end of the gallery.

ISLANDBRIDGE
(Dublin)

See *Dublin.*

KEALKIL STONE CIRCLE
(Cork)

Miniature circle of five stones, magnificently sited on a hill overlooking Bantry Bay, just SE of Kealkill (sic) village, 12 mi. (19 km.) W. of Dunmanway. This is an axial or recumbent circle and the four stones are graded in height up to the fifth, recumbent stone set at the exact N. To the E. of the circle is a small ring cairn surrounding a circle of low stones, and in between circle and cairn are two tall, thin standing stones, one 12 ft. high though broken and originally about 18 ft. high. The circle, excavated in 1938, yielded within it two cross trenches originally holding timbers, probably the support for a standing pole, like a totem pole, in the middle of the ring.

KELLS
(Meath)

Remains of the former monastery in this town include a round tower, an oratory and a number of high crosses; but the monastery, traditionally founded by St. Columba in the 6th cent., is chiefly remembered for the famous *Book of Kells*, a beautifully illuminated and decorated folio now in the library of Trinity College, Dublin. The book may have been produced at Kells, or perhaps at Iona in Scotland, also a Columban foundation, whence the monks fled from Viking raids to Kells in 807 AD. Certainly the manuscript was at Kells thereafter for many centuries, though it was stolen in 1007 and finally recovered with its gold cover missing. It was given to Trinity in the 17th cent. by a bishop of Meath. The monastery at Kells was also raided three or four times by the Vikings, and later many more times by the Irish; nevertheless it managed to survive for some time.

The round tower, capless, still stands 90 ft. high by the S. gate of the graveyard of the Protestant church, which occupies the site of the ancient monastery enclosure. The tower dates from before 1056 when an Irish chieftain, according to ancient records, was murdered at the tower. Four of the crosses stand in the graveyard: the South (or Tower) Cross, dedicated to Sts. Patrick and Columba, stands near the tower. Probably 9th cent., it is an early transitional cross with intricately carved surfaces shared by interlace and vine scroll designs, with birds and animals, a hunting scene, chariot procession, panels of biblical scenes, a crucifixion and a Christ in Judgment. The ornamentation on the cross is remarkably similar to that in the *Book of Kells*. The stump of the West Cross nearby, originally perhaps 18 ft. high, shares biblical scenes with geometric decoration. Only the ornamented base of the North Cross survives, while the East Cross, with a cricifixion, appears to be unfinished, its panels waiting to be carved. N. of the Protestant church is the bell tower of a medieval church with interesting older fragments, grave slabs and a sundial, set against its wall.

NE of the graveyard, at the center of the town, stands the much-weathered Market Cross, showing biblical scenes, beasts, and a battle scene on its base. NW of the graveyard is St. Columba's (or Columcille's) House, a traditional 12th-cent. stone oratory with a steeply-pitched roof (held up from within by a small chamber above the vault). The main chamber, originally entered from the W., is now high off the ground, the ground level having been lowered, and one enters the basement by a modern door.

KEMPE STONES
(Down)

Portal tomb in Greengraves 1.5 mi. (2.3 km.) E. of Dundonald, which in turn is the same distance E. of Stormont entrance gate, Belfast. This fine small tomb has a huge capstone resting at a slant on a portal stone in front and on a smaller roofstone at the back.

KENMARE
(Kerry)

In this resort town at the head of Kenmare River (an inlet), a stone circle worth noting stands 600 yds SW of the 17th-cent. Cromwell's Fort. Originally there were 15 stones set in an oval ring almost 50 ft. across; at the center is a boulder burial consisting of a boulder capstone set over three small supporting stones. There are many other circles in this region (see *Shronebirrane*); for instance, 7 mi. (11.25 km.) to the E. and 2 to 3 mi. (3 to 5 km.) S. of Kilgarvan is another stone circle at Gurteen on a ridge. It is over 30 ft. in diameter and its 11 stones include the large axial or recumbent stone. Two leaning portal stones on the E. are faced with two more outside the circle to emphasize the formal approach. A large boulder in the middle presumably covers a cist grave.

KILBENNAN
(Galway)

Round tower in the village graveyard, 3 mi. (4.75 km.) NW of Tuam. The tower still stands nearly 50 ft. high but one side has fallen away. It marks the site of an ancient monastery founded by St. Patrick's successor at *Armagh*. There was a Romanesque church on the site, but the present church is that of a 15th-cent. monastery. The tower, burned in 1114, has a roundheaded doorway. NW of the church is a Holy Well where a pattern or pilgrimage was held into the 19th cent.

KILCANONAGH
(Galway)

See *Aran Islands*.

KILCLOONEY MORE
(Donegal)

Behind Kilclooney church, 4 mi. (6.5 km.) N. of Ardara, there are two portal tombs set into the remains of one long cairn. One tomb is quite small, the other dramatically huge, its great mushroom-like capstone, 18 ft. across, set aslant on portal stones nearly 5 ft. high in front and on a backstone. The small tomb, roofed with a single slab, consists of side stones, backstone and only one portal stone. Nearby is a court tomb with only one of its two capstones still surmounting the gallery.

KILCOLMAN
(Kerry)

See the *Dingle Peninsula*.

KILCULLEN
(Kildare)

See *Old Kilcullen*.

KILDARE
(Kildare)

Round tower and a plain granite high cross in the churchyard of Kildare's medieval cathedral. The site is a very ancient one. St. Brigid founded a famous monastery here, for both men and women, in the 6th cent. on the spot where the sacred fire of her pagan predecessor, the goddess Brigid, was kept alight. Apparently the sacred fire continued to be tended here with no interruption through the Middle Ages—a commentary on pagan and Christian in Ireland! The round tower stands 106 ft. high; the lower 9 ft. are of fine granite masonry, above that of local limestone, suggesting that in the 12th-cent. period of reform a new tower was erected on the stump of an earlier, derelict tower. The unusual doorway, of red sandstone, high up in the later part and much reconstructed, has four 12th-cent. Romanesque orders framing it and the remains of a triangular hood molding above it. The tower's conical cap was replaced in the 18th cent. with a battlemented top. The windows are also unusual—narrow slits on the outside splaying outwards on the inside up to round arches. The tower can be climbed—for a fee.

KILDREELIG
(Kerry)

Ruins of a neat little monastery within a circular cashel or ring fort, 2 mi. (3.25 km.) SW of Ballinskelligs and about 5 mi. (8 km.) W. of the Ring of Kerry route. In the interior of the cashel is a ruined stone oratory of the Gallarus type (see *Dingle Peninsula*), also two stone huts or clocháns (one with a souterrain under it), two rectangular structures and two cross pillars. Another ruin outside the wall may have been a small oratory. Well up the slope to the NE is an alignment of four stones, from 3 ft. to about 8 ft. high, commanding a fine view. Across Bantry Bay from it is the better-known alignment of *Eightercua*. See also *Killabuonia*.

KILFEAGHAN
(Down)

Portal tomb with an enormous 40-ton boulder capstone resting sideways on smaller stones; about 4 mi. (6.5 km.) SE of Rostrevor, N. of the Kilkeel road. It is set in the N. end of the faint remains of a very long cairn. It was excavated early in the 20th cent.

KILFENORA
(Clare)

See *The Burren*.

KILGOBNET
(Galway)

See *Aran Islands*.

KILKENNY
(Kilkenny)

Pleasant cathedral and market town that grew up around an ancient monastery; survived only by the round tower, just S. of St. Canice's cathedral. It stands 101 ft. high, with six windows at the top and medieval battlements replacing the original conical cap. The tower can be climbed to the top.

KILLABUONIA
(Kerry)

Monastic site on three terraces looking out from the mountainside toward the Skellig Islands; about 4 mi. (6.5 km.) NW of Ballinskelligs and 8 mi. (13 km.) SW of Cahersiveen, well W. of the Ring of Kerry route. On the top terrace is a small oratory of the Gallarus type (see *Dingle Peninsula*), some graves, a cross pillar, and a shrine-shaped tomb called The Priest's Grave. It has a round hole in the W. gable. There were nine clocháns or huts on the middle terrace up to the mid-19th cent.; now there are only two, and two rectangular structures. St. Buonia's Well and Cross and a double clochán are off in a field. Pilgims still visit the well and the Priest's Grave. To the E. of the site is a ruined wedge tomb. Another monastic site, *Kildreelig*, is several mi. to the SE.

KILLALA
(Mayo)

Well-preserved round tower, 84 ft. high, in Killala at the NE top of Mayo on Killala Bay. It stands on a plinth, with its doorway 11 ft. off the ground. It was struck by lightning and repaired in the last cent. The tower is a remnant of an ancient monastery traditionally founded by St. Patrick in the 5th cent. In the graveyard is a complex souterrain with two rectangular and one corbelled round chamber and a passage.

KILLALOE
(Clare)

The Protestant cathedral in this town at the lower end of Lough Derg, about 15 mi. (24 km.) NE of Limerick, was built on the site of an early monastery founded here by St. Molua. There was a later Romanesque church on the site whose ornate doorway is preserved inside the cathedral. On the grounds is the interesting, 12th-cent. oratory of St. Flannan who succeeded St. Molua as abbot of the monastery in the 7th cent. The oratory also has a fine Romanesque doorway and an Irish-style stone roof, supported by a small chamber over the vault. Near the Romanesque doorway in the cathedral is a unique stone with inscriptions in both Ogham and Norse runes. Its maker was one Thorgrim. Near it is a cross removed from *Kilfenora* showing a crucifixion and geometric and interlace ornament. Farther up the hill, on the grounds of the Catholic cathedral, is another interesting early building, St. Molua's Oratory, rescued from an island in the Shannon now submerged under a reservoir. The little church, with nave and later stone-roofed chancel and flat-headed doorways, is certainly in origin older than the 12th cent.

KILLAMERY
(Kilkenny)

An important transitional high cross (9th cent.) in a graveyard off the road S. from Callan (5 mi. or 8 km.) to Clonmel and Carrick on Suir. It is a survivor from an early monastery. The cross is richly decorated with geometric designs, serpents and other beasts, and stylized marigolds. Figured panels depict a chariot procession, a hunting scene, a crucifixion, etc. Its cap, typical of these early crosses, is much worn because it was formerly used as a cure for headaches! Near the cross in the graveyard are an Ogham stone and some cross pillars. Not far off are other examples of these 9th-cent. transitional crosses, at *Ahenny*, *Kilkieran* and *Kilree*.

KILLARY
(Meath)

Stump of a high cross in a graveyard at Killary, just W. of Lobinstown, ornamented with geometrical decoration and biblical scenes on its shaft very similar to those on the West Cross at *Kells*, only 10 mi. (16 km.) to the SW. It is probably 10th cent. In the NE corner of the graveyard the base and arm of a cross may belong to this shaft.

KILLEANY
(Galway)

See *Aran Islands*.

KILLEVEY CHURCHES
(Armagh)

Two roofless churches, linked by a later wall, marking the site of a once important early nunnery; 3 mi. (4.75 km.) SW of Newry on the lower slopes of *Slieve Gullion* mountain where there is a passage tomb. The nunnery was traditionally founded about 450 AD with a wooden church, was several times raided by Viking Norsemen, and survived until 1542. At one time there was a round tower on the site. Of the two churches, the smaller W. church is of great interest because it is certainly pre-Romanesque (10th cent.?). Its W. doorway is made of huge finished blocks of stone, including a massive lintel stone. There is a small round-headed E. window. The larger church seems to be medieval.

KILLINABOY
(Clare)

See *The Burren*.

KILLKIERAN
(Kilkenny)

Or Killkeeran, 3.5 mi. (5.6 km.) N. of Carrick on Suir. Here are three 9th-cent. early high crosses of the same type as those at *Ahenny*, only a mi. or so to the N. The West Cross is elaborately decorated with geometric, spiral, interlace and animal designs. On the base eight horsemen appear. The East Cross is the same type, though undecorated, possibly unfinished. Both have caps on top of the shaft. The North Cross, or Tall Cross, is a unique "sport" on a circular base with very short arms, no ring, and traces of decoration on it as well as four strange hollows, outlined by molding. A fourth "cross" consists of fragments put together with cement on a pillar. See also *Killamery*; *Kilree*.

KILMACDUAGH
(Galway)

Round tower, about 3 mi. (4.75 km.) WSW of Gort. At over 100 ft. it is now the tallest and one of the best-preserved in Ireland; remnant of a monastery founded in the 6th or 7th cent. It leans slightly, like the famous tower at Pisa. Around it is a fine collection of five ruined buildings. Closest to the tower is the cathedral with a blocked-up lintelled W. doorway of the 11th or 12th cent. St. John's church is possibly 12th, the other buildings 13th and later.

KILMAINHAM
(Dublin)

See *Dublin*.

KILMALKEDAR
(Kerry)

See the *Dingle Peninsula*.

KILMALLOCK
(Limerick)

Small market town, 20 mi. (32.25 km.) S. of Limerick. At the SW end of the ruined medieval Collegiate church here is a very much rebuilt round tower that served as its belfry. It was apparently a survivor of a monastery founded here in the 7th cent.

The lovely round tower at Kilmacduagh, Galway, the tallest in Ireland, marking the site of an ancient monastery. Around it are the remains of four early medieval churches and a house. Largest is the cathedral, close and to the right of the tower. (Courtesy of Irish Tourist Board, Dublin.)

KILMOGUE
(Kilkenny)

Excellent example of a portal tomb, in a field up a private farm lane, 7.5 mi. (12 km.) NE of Carrick on Suir and about 1 mi. (1.6 km.) NW of Milltown. Known as Leac an Scáil, it is hidden in a hollow. Its capstone, tilted dramatically upward, projects over portal stones nearly 12 ft. high, and at the back and lower end rests on a small capstone covering part of the irregular-shaped chamber. A closing stone is in position between the two portal stones.

KILNASAGGART
(Armagh)

The oldest securely dated cross slab known in Ireland, 1.75 mi. (2.75 km.) S. of Jonesborough and about 6 mi. (9.6 km.) N. of Dundalk, close to the Louth border. It stands in a field in a modern enclosure, marking an Early Christian graveyard excavated in 1966 and 1968 that once belonged to a monastery. Close by, one of the great early Christian roads ran N. from Drogheda. The stone, which originally may well have been a pre-Christian standing stone, is carved with three crosses on one side and 10 on the other, most of them simple equal-armed crosses in circles. On the S. side is a dedicatory inscription in Irish by one Ternohc, who died in 714 or 716 AD, thus placing the cross roughly at about 700 AD. A few crude cross slabs and grave markers lie around it.

KILREE
(Kilkenny)

Round tower and cross on the site of an early monastery, 1.5 mi. (2.6 km.) S. of *Kells*. The round tower, 96 ft. high, has lost its cap. Next to it is a ruined early church with heavy lintelled doorway, projecting antae (side walls) and later medieval additions. The much-worn high cross, off in a field, appears to date from the 9th cent. and resembles the crosses at *Ahenny*, *Killamery* and *Kilkieran* not far off to the SW. The biblical scenes, amidst geometrical designs, are hard to distinguish. There is a chariot procession, a hunting scene, and curious decorated bosses at the center.

The oldest known cross slab in Ireland, standing in an Early Christian graveyard at Kilnasaggart, Northern Ireland. Bearing a total of 13 crosses on its two sides, it may well have been a prehistoric standing stone reclaimed for Christianity. The dedicatory inscription in Irish securely dates it at about 700 AD. (Crown copyright: Historic Monuments and Buildings Branch, DOENI, Northern Ireland.)

KILTIERNAN
(Dublin)

A visit to this huge portal tomb, about 7 mi. (11.25 km.) S. of Dublin, involves a side road, a private avenue and a path across three fields. It lies .5 mi. (.75 km.) W. of Golden Ball. The great granite capstone, 22 ft. long and estimated to weigh 40 tons, has displaced some of the stones of the large chamber beneath it.

KILTIERNEY DEERPARK
(Fermanagh)

A complex site, 3.5 mi. (5.6 km.) NNW of Irvinestown, N. of Lower Lough Erne. It includes a passage tomb with 22 small ring cairns around it as well as an incomplete stone circle of eight surviving stones on a raised platform. On top of the cairn of the passage tomb are six large stones, one showing passage grave geometric art (see *The Boyne Valley*). Iron Age cremation burials have been inserted into the earlier cairns.

KING'S STABLES
(Armagh)

See *Navan Fort*.

KINNEIGH
(Cork)

Round tower, about 3 mi. (4.75 km.) NW of Enniskean, W. of Bandon, as usual marking the site of an early monastery. Topless and now 68 ft. high, it is an unusual tower in that for the first 18 ft. it is hexagonal or six-sided, the rest the usual circular construction. There are also the remains of slate-paved floors, for the whole tower is built of slate and rests on a slate outcrop. The doorway is flat-headed and the top of the tower (now reached by an internal ladder) was altered later to make it into a church belfry.

KNOCKAULIN
(Kildare)

See *Dun Ailinne.*

KNOCKDRUM
(Cork)

Stone fort, restored in the early 19th cent., .75 mi. (1 km.) W. of Castletownshend and just to the S. above the road to Skibbereen. The thick circular walls enclose an area 95 ft. across with a roofless square building in the middle. A three-chamber rock-cut souterrain runs from one corner of the building. Inside the fort's entrance, with a small guard chamber to the right, is a cross pillar presumably moved here from somewhere else, and outside it is a large recumbent slab with about 40 Bronze Age cup marks on it. Conspicuous on a ridge across the road is the Gurranes alignment, the striking "Three fingers," three tall slim stones remaining upright from the once five-stone alignment; a fourth stone has fallen nearby and a fifth has been moved to a garden in Castletownshend.

KNOCKEEN
(Waterford)

See *Gaulstown.*

KNOCKGRANIA
(Galway)

See *Aran Islands.*

KNOCKIVEAGH
(Down)

Remnants of a Neolithic round cairn on the summit of this mountain (788 ft. up) with wide views; in Edenagarry townland, 3.5 mi. (5.6 km.) NNW of Rathfryland. The bank and ditch enclosure suggests that this was a very early henge monument, and pits in the interior filled with refuse were probably similar to the ritual pits found in many places, such as the Aubrey Holes at *Stonehenge* in England. The enclosure has been dated at about 3700 BC, several hundred years earlier than Newgrange and the Neolithic cemetery in the *Boyne Valley.*

KNOCKMANY
(Tyrone)

Passage tomb, called "Annia's Cove," 1.75 mi. (2.6 km.) NW of Augher. Access is through a forest up to a hilltop with magnificent views over the Clogher valley. The tomb is normally locked (try the Clogher police station) and has been covered with a modern roof to protect it from vandals. The small tomb, with no passage—common in the N.—was under a round cairn of stones and earth with a kerb. Three of the stones of the chamber are decorated with typical passage grave art—spirals, circles, zigzags, cupmarks. A similar tomb can be found at *Sess Kilgreen*, also in Tyrone to the NE.

KNOCKNALAPPA
(Clare)

Typical Late Bronze Age crannog, or artificial island, in Lake Rossroe NE of Newmarket on Fergus; formed by peat and stones piled inside an oval ring of hazel stakes set in the shallow lake bottom. It was not long occupied, perhaps having been flooded out. Excavations found the remains of a wooden structure and many bones of ox, sheep, pig and horses. It was dated to the same period as the hilltop settlement of *Rathgall* in Wicklow. See also *Craggaunowen; Lough Gara, Lough-na-Cranagh.*

KNOCKNAREA
(Sligo)

See *Carrowmore*.

KNOCKONEILL
(Londonderry)

Court tomb, 2.5 mi. (4 km.) WNW of Swatragh, reused in the Bronze Age; a very well-preserved monument with a forecourt (about 21 ft. across) and two chambers and an antechamber in the gallery running off the court. Behind this is still another chamber entered from the side of the cairn. When excavated, it appeared that the court had been reused for burials in the Bronze Age, at which time its far end had been closed with a line of uprights and the whole tomb covered by a round cairn. At Tamnyrankin, 1.5 mi. (2.3 km.) to the NE, is a similar court tomb just NW of the village; this is one of the largest in the country, sited at 650 ft. The partly preserved cairn, about 36 ft. long, still rises up about 9 ft. and there is a fine, U-shaped court. The gallery contains two chambers, and a third behind it extends the length of the cairn, divided into two by a sill stone. Even a few of the corbel stones at the top of the gallery survive.

KNOWTH
(Meath)

See *Boyne Valley*.

LABBACALLEE
(Cork)

Largest wedge-shaped tomb in Ireland, 1.2 mi. (2 km.) SE of Glanworth and about 4 mi. (6.5 km.) NW of Fermoy. A large rectangular gallery, triple-walled, and smaller one at the back, divided from it by a slab, are covered by three huge capstones sloping away from the higher and broader front end. At the very front is a kind of unroofed portico, broader than the gallery. The whole may have been covered by the wedge-shaped cairn with a kerb. Excavated in 1934, the tomb yielded Late Neolithic-Early Bronze Age pottery, animal bones and at least five burials, one of a woman, in the smaller chamber at the back, whose skull had been removed to the larger chamber. It is possible that the small chamber and its burial were earlier than the larger extension to the W.

LARNE
(Antrim)

The Curran, a sickle-shaped tongue of land just S. of the town, has yielded from ancient raised beaches thousands of worked flints from the late Mesolithic period—axes and small tools (microliths) made by the Larnians, probably the second wave of men to reach Ireland (there is as yet no reliable evidence for Paleolithic man in Ireland). These hunter-gatherers apparently arrived by boat from Scotland around 8000–7000 BC in search of the rich deposits of flint found most profusely in Antrim, and from there spread S. and W. See also *Mount Sandel*.

LEACANABUAILE FORT
(Kerry)

A fine, round, stone ring fort on a massive rocky hill, 2 mi. (3.25 km.) NW of Cahersiveen near the Ring of Kerry tourist route. The walls are up to 10 ft. thick and reconstructed to about 4 ft. high. Inside there are two terraces on the NE with 10 sets of steps leading up to them. Originally there were three round hut remains in the interior, but only one survives. A square house was later added on to it, built over the remains of the other two huts. A souterrain leads over 30 ft. underground from the surviving hut to a chamber in the wall, and there is another wall chamber. A culvert runs from the square house to the fort's entrance. Yields of domestic objects from the excavations dated the fort to the 9th or 10th cent. AD. A few hundred yards to the SE is another fort, Cahergal, similar to the well-known stone fort of *Staigue*, with stairs leading up to terraces inside

The largest wedge tomb in Ireland at Labbacallee, Cork, viewed from the back; and the interior of its long gallery. A smaller chamber at the rear, separated by a slab, may have been an earlier tomb. In it was found the headless skeleton of a woman. Her skull had been removed to the larger front chamber. At least four other burials were found in the tomb, and pottery of the Late Neolithic-Early Bronze Age period. (Photos: the author.)

the heavy wall. In the interior, about 90 ft. in diameter, are the remains of an oval stone house and a rectangular house built up against the fort's wall.

LEGANANNY DOLMEN (Down)

Famous portal tomb, 4 mi. (6.5 km.) S. of Dromara on the slopes of Slieve Croob, equally striking for its shape and for the fine view of the Mourne Mtns. from the site. The heavy sloping capstone, about 9 ft. long, perches 5 ft. high on three

A fine round fort at Leacanabuaile on the Ring of Kerry in western Ireland, somewhat reconstructed and dated by the finds to about the 9th or 10th cent. AD. The walls, backed by terraces and steps, are up to 10 ft. thick and contain chambers within them. Huts and a large souterrain occupied the interior. (Photo: the author.)

The well-known Legananny Dolmen, a strikingly bizarre portal tomb in Northern Ireland. Its huge sloping capstone, about 9 ft. long, has rested precariously on the three spindly supporting stones for about 4,000 years, and is still an amazing site. (Crown copyright: Historic Monuments and Buildings Branch, DOENI, Northern Ireland.)

unusually tall, thin supporting stones. There are traces of its large cairn around it.

LEITRIM
(Tyrone)

Impressive portal tomb, 3.5 mi. (5.6 km.) SW of Castlederg and 1 mi. (1.6 km.) WSW of Killen village. Called "The Druid's Altar," it is enclosed in a fence. Its huge tilted capstone, resting on portal stones only about 3 ft. high, contains nuggets of white quartz, always magic to the ancients. At the top of Leitrim Hill to the NW of the tomb is a dilapidated stone fort well over 300 ft. in diameter. About the same distance to the N., at Aghnahoo, is a large souterrain about 45 ft. long, with a passage and a polygonal chamber roofed with lintels and partly rock-cut. It is in state care.

THE LIOS
(Limerick)

See The Grange Circle in *Lough Gur*.

LISNAGADE
(Down)

Spectacularly large circular ring fort or rath, 3 mi. (4.75 km.) SW of Banbridge, between it and Scarva. The rath has three heavy earthen banks and ditches and a small subsidiary rath to the N., linked to the main one by more banks and ditches. It was excavated shortly after 1950. Lisnagade is probably the largest rath in Ireland, and is surrounded by over a dozen other strong raths. One of these is the oval ring fort of Lisnavaragh, 500 yds. to the W. of Lisnagade, with three banks and (at present) two ditches—a third was probably obliterated. Close by Lisnagade to the S. runs a section of the Dane's Cast defenses of Ulster (see *Navan Fort*). Both the Dane's Cast and the raths probably date from the Early Christian period, perhaps 4th cent. AD.

LISNAVARAGH
(Down)

See *Lisnagade*, above.

LISSYVIGGEEN
(Kerry)

A strange and unique, small stone circle, 2.5 mi. (4 km.) E. of Killarney and .25 mi. (.5 km.) N. of the Killarney-Cork road, after Woodford Bridge. Like other circles to the E., seven boulders enclose an area of about 12 ft. across, with a broader stone at the W. apparently representing the axial or recumbent stone typical of these circles. It stands opposite the largest of the boulders. Outside the circle are two far larger standing stones. In between these and the circle is a most unusual irregular enclosing bank with two entrances (no ditch), much like a henge. The circle and its outliers may well be Late Bronze Age, and the henge bank even later.

LISTOGHIL TOMB
(Sligo)

See *Carrowmore*.

LONGSTONE
(Tipperary)

Complex burial mound, excavated 1973–76, about 7 mi. (11.25 km.) WNW of Tipperary. The mound was erected over a Beaker period (Early Bronze Age) habitation site, and in it were three cremation cist graves. Later in the Bronze Age the mound continued to be used for many other cist burials, which yielded food vessels, urns and miniature cups. Later, in the Iron Age, a ring cairn was built on the SE side of the mound with a cremation burial in it. Still later an enclosure about 225 ft. across, with bank and ditch, contained up to 30 cremation burials. Then in the early centuries AD the site was used for a platform ring fort.

The site takes its name from an 8-ft. standing stone on top of the mound. Nearby, at Cullen village NE of Longstone, a small bog yielded in the 18th and 19th cents. a variety of objects, mostly Late Bronze Age, possibly thrown into a former lake here as votive deposits; included were gold artifacts and 300 swords.

LONGHASH
(Tyrone)

Wedge grave, 4.75 mi. (7.6 km.) ESE of Dunnamanagh and 4.5 mi. (7.25 km.) SSW of Claudy in Derry. The "Giant's Grave" here, a National Monument, is a complex wedge tomb with a vestigial forecourt like a court tomb. It has a double portal to the antechamber and a main segmented chamber with two compartments behind it—five sections in all. The chambers are double-walled, and one roof slab remains. There was a circular cairn around it surrounded by a ditch—possibly a remnant of an older monument. It has been excavated. SE of it is a small circle with an alignment known as "Cashelbane," yielding cremation burials and Bronze Age and Beaker artifacts. A similar wedge tomb, the Windy Hill "Giant's Grave," is much overgrown. It lies 2.5 mi. (4 km.) W. of Dunnamanagh.

LOUGH BOORA
(Offaly)

See Mt. Sandel.

LOUGHCREW
(Meath)

Neolithic passage grave cemetery called "Slieve na Calliagh," 3 mi. (4.75 km.) SE of Oldcastle and 10 mi. (16 km.) W. by N. of Kells. It lies some 30 mi. (48 km.) W. of the great passage grave cemetery in the Boyne Valley. There were over 50 tombs in this cemetery but now only about 24 are left, and some of these have not been opened while others do not appear to have had internal chambers. Thirteen of the tombs are ornamented with a local variation of the geometric motifs known so well from the Boyne Valley tombs. The tombs at Loughcrew are grouped around two principal hills. Cairn T on Cairnbane East is the largest of the tombs, a huge mound 120 ft. in diameter sited at the top of the hill, with a fine incurving facade at its entrance. It is usually locked. The tomb is profusely ornamented with circles, zigzags, and especially flower motifs. Inside it has a large cruciform chamber with side chambers, and around it are grouped six smaller satellite tombs, also decorated. On the other hill, Cairnbane West, the largest mounds are Cairn G, apparently without a chamber, and Cairn K, a fine decorated tomb with a large chamber and five side chambers. A standing stone, probably of phallic significance, stands inside the chamber. Seven smaller satellite tombs surround these two, of varying designs according to the age of building. A third hill to the E., Patrickstown, carries less accessible remnants of four other tombs, remainders from perhaps 25 originally. Many of the tombs are surrounded by white quartz stones, probably used as facing as at Newgrange in the Boyne Valley. Whether the Loughcrew tombs were a development from those in the Boyne Valley or were earlier precursors of the type is still hotly debated among scholars. See also Carrowkeel; Carrowmore; Fourknocks.

LOUGH GARA
(Roscommon/Sligo)

Small lake, about 6 mi. (9.6 km.) SW of Boyle. Extensive drainage works here in 1952 lowered the lake level and revealed the remains of over 300 crannogs, or artificial islands. Of these, two were excavated in 1953–55 by Dr. Raftery. The most interesting of the two proved to be in Rathtinaum, Sligo, a crannog built up of brushwood and peat inside a ring of piles. It had been occupied in the Late Bronze Age, then after a period of desertion, again in the Iron Age (about 150 BC). Finally a large circular house was built on the island in the Early Christian period (radiocarbon dates around 320 AD), yielding among other finds well-preserved goods of leather and textiles. From the scanty evidence indicating occupation there appeared to have been 10 houses on the island in the earlier period, each with a hearth set into clay-plastered wicker. The finds included pottery, amber beads and objects of bronze and gold. The later period also produced various iron implements as well as bronze and pottery. See also *Craggaunowen*, *Knocknalappa*, *Lough-na-Cranagh*.

LOUGH GUR
(Limerick)

There is a remarkable grouping of ancient sites around this small lake 12 mi. (19 km.) SSE of Limerick, 2.5 mi. (4 km.) N. of Bruff. They date chiefly from the Late Neolithic but range into the Early Bronze Age and into the medieval. Apparently the light limestone soils and sparse forestation attracted the early settlers to the area. It is one of the few sites in Ireland where the remains of a number of Neolithic houses have been discovered, in extensive excavations by Ó Ríordáin in the 1940s (see also *Ballyglass* in Mayo, *Ballynagilly* in Tyrone and *Lyle's Hill* in Antrim). The houses, round, rectangular and irregular in shape, included one isolated, rectangular, aisled timber-post dwelling, and a number of round houses, sometimes in groups. Around some of the houses are traces of ancient field systems. Though their footings were of stone, the house walls were probably of timber or wattle, with thatched roofs, and some were enclosed within stone walls. In them were found Neolithic, Food Vessel and Beaker pottery, and many animal bones, 95% of them of oxen. Though by now the remains of these houses are hard to find or have disappeared, this was the most important discovery at Lough Gur in terms of the archaeological record.

Many other types of sites are scattered in and around the lake and on the hills above it. There is a Lough Gur Interpretive Center at the site, and the locations of the sites worth seeing can be found here and in detailed guidebooks. The sites include a well-preserved wedge-shaped tomb, the best of a number here in which over a dozen burials were found; several standing stones;

The entrancing little lake of Lough Gur in Limerick. Around it is an astonishing profusion of ancient sites: Neolithic house foundations, megalithic tombs, Bronze Age burial mounds, stone circles, crannogs and early stone forts, as well as medieval castles. In other words the lake has been favored by settlers of all periods since prehistoric times. (Photo: the author.)

Among the many sites at Lough Gur is this double-walled dwelling enclosure in the hills above the lake. Its interior was occupied by houses from the Neolithic into Bronze Age times. The most archaeologically significant finds at Lough Gur, hardly visible now, were the remains of a number of Neolithic houses, few of which have been found in Ireland. (Photo: the author.)

a circular Neolithic burial enclosure inside a double stone wall with a standing stone within it; a large Neolithic-Bronze Age dwelling enclosure surrounded by a well-defined double wall; a Bronze Age burial mound (a flat-topped cairn, surmounted by a stone circle, which yielded urn burials of about 1500 BC); and next to it a fine stone circle with a ditch in the interior and a bank on the outside faced with stone on both sides. There are several other stone circles here, one a small circle of large stones, another the remnants of a similar monument.

The best of the stone circles is in Grange townland S. of the lake and near the road to Limerick, often called The Lios. This is one of the largest and most impressive circles in Ireland, and is much like *Castleruddery* in Wicklow. An area over 150 ft. across, surfaced with packed clay for the elaborate, large rituals that must have taken place here, is surrounded by a ring of contiguous stones set against a high bank 30 ft. wide, making it into a henge. Twelve large boulders, two flanking the narrow entrance on the E., two more opposite it, and the rest interspersed with smaller upright stones to contain the bank, make up the circle. The monumental entrance is stone-paved, and on excavation in 1939 quantities of smashed Late Neolithic-Beaker ware were found under the clay of the interior, probably ritual offerings. The whole resembles the enclosure at *Ballynahatty* in Down. To the N. and NE of the circle is another smaller circle of large stones, a standing stone, and remnants of another circle.

Other sites include at least one ring fort close to the lakeside, and two strong stone forts, Carraig Aille I and II, oval and circular, with drystone walls 15 ft. thick in places. Both forts show house foundations, round and rectangular, both inside and outside the forts, and steps that once led to parapets. They were occupied from the 8th to 11th cents. AD. Excavations uncovered six tons of animal bones, again mostly oxen, and in one was found a 10th-cent. hoard of Viking silver. From this period, too, dates the site called "The Spectacles," two round hut foundations close together, with adjacent field systems. Finally, there were several crannogs, artificial islands, in the lake. One is now Bolin Island; the remains of another lie close to the shore with a bit of marsh now connecting it to the mainland. The larger Garret Island was also proved to have been artificially raised in Neolithic times by means of a platform of boulders.

LOUGHMACRORY
(Tyrone)

See *Altdrumman.*

LOUGH-NA-CRANAGH
(Antrim)

One of the finest surviving examples of a crannog, an artificial island in a lake, though unexcavated to date. It lies in a lough on the summit of Fairhead amidst wild moorland scenery rising to steep cliffs over the sea, at the very top of Antrim, about 4 mi. ENE of Ballycastle. The striking oval island is entirely contained within heavy drystone walls. See also *Cragaunowen; Knocknalappa; Lough Gara.*

LOUGH NA SHADE
(Armagh)

See *Navan Fort.*

LUSK
(Dublin)

Fine early round tower in a churchyard, all that remains of a monastery, about 14 mi. (22.5 km.) N. of Dublin center. The tower is built into the corner of a heavy, square tower of a former church of the 15th-16th cents., which has three smaller round towers, built later onto the other corners to match the original tower. About 68 ft. high, with five stories and its original conical cap, the tower has an excellent early-style lintelled doorway now not far off the ground—since the ground level around it has risen.

LYLE'S HILL
(Antrim)

On this hilltop, about 8 mi. (13 km.) NW of Belfast and 6 mi. (9.6 km.) SE of Antrim, is an enclosure of about 12.5 acres surrounded by a bank of earth, revetted with boulders, about 20 ft. wide. It is apparently of Neolithic construction, and may possibly be a causewayed camp. On the summit was a low tumulus containing a burial under a cairn dating from Late Neolithic times. The cairn seems to have been built over a somewhat earlier Neolithic settlement, for under it and around it were found thousands of Neolithic potsherds, flints, axes of porcellanite from the *Tievebulliagh* axe factory, greenstone beads, a hone, as well as a burnt area with human bones. More sherds were found buried in pits. The cairn was bounded by a kerb (one kerb stone from the "entrance," now in the Ulster Museum, Belfast, was decorated with chevrons and hatched triangles). The single disturbed cremation burial under the cairn was that of a young person interred with flints and Neolithic and Food Vessel pottery. Three later cists containing cremated remains, food vessels and a Bronze Age urn had been inserted in the cairn.

About 4 mi. (6.5 km.) to the NW is the *Donegore* Neolithic causewayed camp.

MAGH ADAIR
(Clare)

A flat-topped mound with bank and ditch and other earthworks marks the inauguration site of the kings of Thomond, including the famous Brian Boru, everybody's ancestor. The site is 3.25 mi. (5.3 km.) SW of Tulla and was obviously a place of ancient sanctity, for there is also a cairn and a standing stone. Only about 500 yds to the SW is the large stone fort of Cahercalla with triple defenses. See also *Moghane.*

MAGHERA CHURCH
(Londonderry)

To the S. of Maghera town in eastern Derry is a ruined church of many periods. It marks the site of an early monastery; later it belonged to a medieval bishopric and then became a parish church. It is well known for its elaborately decorated, 12th-cent. Romanesque W. doorway, with a crucifixion. The nave, however, built of large stones, may be as early as the 10th cent. In the large graveyard is a prominent, much-worn early cross pillar. NW of the town (1.5 mi. or 2.3 km.) is the well-preserved ring fort or rath of Tullyhearan on a hill, enclosed within two banks with a ditch between them.

MAGHERABOY
(Antrim)

"The Druid's Stone," a passage grave on a hill less than a mi. SW of Ballintoy, which is about 6 mi. (9.6 km.) W. of Ballycastle on the N. coast; a simple polygonal tomb set in the remains of a round cairn with many of its kerb stones surviving. Five heavy uprights support a massive capstone and there are traces of a passage on the NE. In Ballintoy itself there are more passage tombs.

MAGHERAGHANRUSH
(Sligo)

Or Deerpark; a splendid court tomb on top of a hill, 4 mi. (6.5 km.) E. of Sligo. The view is magnificent but will soon be obscured by recently planted conifers. There is an oval center court, 50 ft. long, entered from the S. From the court two galleries extend to the E. and one to the W., each with two chambers, making a length overall of about 90 ft. A lintel still rests over the entrance to one of the E. galleries. Nearby are the ruins of a wedge tomb, a stone fort with souterrain; and a stone circle.

MALIN MOOR
(Donegal)

See *Glencolumbkille.*

MATHEWSTOWN
(Waterford)

See *Harristown.*

MAUMANORIG
(Kerry)

See the *Dingle Peninsula.*

MAYO
(Mayo)

See *Balla.*

MEELICK
(Mayo)

A very fine round tower, prominent on a ridge in open country, 3 mi. (4.75 km.) SW of Swinford near Bohola; testimony as usual to the site of an early monastery. It stands over 70 ft. high but has lost its conical cap. However, there is a good round-headed doorway and windows with both pointed and lintelled tops. At its foot is an early grave slab with an interlace cross and border and an inscription. Another round tower is 8 mi. WSW at *Turlough.*

MILLIN BAY CAIRN
(Down)

An interesting cairn 2.25 mi. (3.6 km.) SE of Portaferry on the Ards peninsula overlooking Millin Bay. Today, it is just a long, sandy grass-covered mound; when excavated in 1953 it proved to be a complex Late Neolithic monument with a long cist of slabs and another cist set within an oval of stone slabs around it and a kerb. There was a bank outside the oval. Between bank and oval were seven more cists, some with cremated burials. The main long cist, however, contained the bones of at least 15 people, neatly sorted and stacked. The area within the oval was finally filled with shingle and slabs and the mound piled over it all. Many of the stones were decorated with pecked and incised designs in the passage grave tradition. Perhaps the monument showed influences from northern England, not far off across the sea.

MOGHANE
(Clare)

Huge stone hill fort with three circuits of banks and ditches, the largest in Ireland. It lies 4.25 mi. (7 km.) SW of *Magh Adair* and about 7.5 mi. (12 km.) SW of Tulla. The fort is so large and so overgrown that it is difficult to see on the ground. It is best viewed from the air. It can be dated roughly to the Early Iron Age, that is late BC or early AD.

MONASTERBOICE
(Louth)

Monastic site, 5 mi. (8 km.) NW of Drogheda, with two simple rectangular churches, ruined and of little interest, a round tower, some early grave slabs, a decorated sundial, and the famous high crosses. The round tower marks the site of the original 6th-cent. monastery that was briefly taken over by Viking freebooters in 968 AD and was abandoned in 1122. Although the tower has lost its upper parts (it was burned in 1097) it still stands about 90 ft. high and can be climbed to the top. Its doorway is round-headed.

But the two high crosses are the glory of Monasterboice. They belong to the early figured style of the 9th cent. and one of them, Muiredach's Cross, named for an inscription on its shaft, is possibly the finest high cross in Ireland. The carving of scriptural scenes is superb and full of interesting detail, and the cross is also distinguished for its intricate ornamental motifs of many kinds. Its slightly later companion, the much-weathered West Cross or Tall Cross, stands an unusual 21 ft. 6 in. high and again is crowded with figured panels. Both crosses are topped by caps in the shape of shingle-roofed churches with finials on their gables. A third high cross stands in the NE corner of the graveyard, with a crucifixion on one face.

MONEYGASHEL
(Cavan)

Stone ring forts or cashels, about 4 mi. (6.5 km.) S. of Blacklion, a village between the upper and lower Lough Macnean. The central fort, with walls about 9 ft. thick, encloses an area 80 ft. in diameter with a blocked souterrain. It has two stairways inside the walls and, unusually, another external stairway. The entrance bears a lintel. A smaller cashel S. of it has a later, freestanding corbelled sweathouse (a kind of sauna) just inside the entrance.

MOONE HIGH CROSS
(Kildare)

In an abandoned graveyard .5 mi. (.75 km.) W. off the main road from Dublin to Carlow, at Moone in the Barrow valley. It is on the site of an ancient monastery. The cross, 17 ft. high, is one of the earliest of the transitional, 9th-cent. figured crosses to show biblical scenes, and it is unique. Its particular charm lies in its naively crude figures in flat relief, the logical ordering of the scenes, and the rightness of its composition within these limitations. Such crosses were the illiterate man's Bible. Note the fetching figures of the 12 apostles lined up frontally four by four above each other. The decorations of the cross include many strange animals, showing Scandinavian influence, for this was the period of the Viking raids and settlements. The granite cross was restored in the 19th cent. from fragments found buried here, and there are fragments of other crosses in the graveyard and in the roofless church close by. The whole site, with its church and manor house, is most attractive and is well worth a visit. See also the two other transitional crosses at *Castledermot* a few mi. to the S.

Among the most attractive of all the high crosses in Ireland is the Moone Cross, Kildare, an early transitional cross (9th cent.), one of the first to include biblical scenes on the cross itself as well as the base. The simple scenes are in flat relief (note the apostles four by four on the base) and the charm of the cross lies in the ordering of the scenes and the attractive composition of the whole. Moreover, the 17-ft. cross rises against an evocative background of a ruined tower house and a roofless church with its ancient yew. (Photos: the author.)

MOUNT BROWNE
(Carlow)

See Browne's Hill.

MOUNT GABRIEL
(Cork)

A commanding mountain in southern Cork about 14 mi. W. of Skibbereen. Copper mines of the Early Bronze Age were found here high on the slopes of the mountain when the peat was removed, and brief excavations were carried out in 1966. The 25 mines found were small holes quarried into the rock no deeper than 30 ft. Abundant charcoal in the holes showed that the miners lit fires in them, threw cold water on the rock to shatter it, then pounded out the copper ore with beach cobbles, often shaped, that were found scattered about the site.

MOUNT SANDEL
(Londonderry)

Important Mesolithic site just S. of Coleraine on the estuary of the Bann River. Here on the bluffs overlooking the river, close to the NE end of Mt. Sandel Fort (a huge man-made mount, possibly Anglo-Norman) P. C. Woodman excavated, from 1973 to 1977, what appears to have been a rare, Mesolithic seasonal habitation site with the postholes and a succession of hearths of a hut—the earliest

dated "house" in the British Isles and probably in Europe—and others around it. The radiocarbon dates ranged from 7000 to 6500 BC. The circular hut measured 19 ft. 6 in. across and was probably constructed of saplings. Uncovered were also rubbish pits, flint-knapping floors and numerous finely-worked microlithic flints, as well as two small, polished axe heads. Other finds of animal, bird and fish bones, especially of hazelnut shells, and of seeds of apple and water lily, attested to the inhabitants' hunter-gatherer economy. These people were probably among the first immigrants to come over from northern England, possibly at first over a land bridge, later by boat. Similar finds, but without the huts, have been excavated at a Mesolithic site at Lough Boora in Offaly. The excavation area of Mount Sandel has been fenced and the site preserved for visitors.

MOYLISHA
(Wicklow)

Wedge tomb, 6 mi. (9.6 km.) SE of Tallow and 3.5 mi. (5.6 km.) W. of Shillelagh village. This tomb, inside a modern enclosure, is unusual in that its long chamber widens toward the back in a reverse wedge-shape. There is an antechamber and the whole is set within a U-shaped row of stones; beyond that lie the remains of a cairn of stones 42 ft. long.

MOYTIRRA
(Sligo)

Here on a ridge NE of Lough Arrow, about 7 mi. (11.25 km.) NE of Boyle and 1 mi. (1.6 km.) N. of Kilmactranny, are several tombs in an area rich in megalithic remains. At Moytirra East there is a court tomb, the "Giant's Grave," with a semicircular forecourt and a long burial chamber behind it divided into four compartments. At Moytirra West is a wedge tomb set within the remains of a round cairn. Excavation here in 1884 yielded the inhumation remains of at least four adults and a child, and with them four bell beakers. These were the first found in Ireland.

MULLET PENINSULA
(Mayo)

Islands with early monastic remains off the remote Mullet Peninsula in westernmost Mayo. They can be visited by boat, but in good weather only, from Blacksod Point with landings by curragh. Among the islands is Inishglora, with a

An Early Christian cross slab on one of the two Inishkea islands off the Mullet Peninsula in western Mayo. On many of these islands were early anchorite communities now marked by ruined churches, beehive hut foundations and many such cross slabs. (From Henry Françoise: Irish Art in the Early Christian Period [1947], by permission of the publishers, Methuen & Co., London.)

monastery founded in the 6th cent. by St. Brendan the Navigator. The ruins include three churches, the oldest being St. Brendan's Oratory, rectangular, with a steep roof and lintelled doorway; also three beehive huts in an enclosure, remains of the monastery walls, a number of early cross slabs, and seven pilgrims' "stations." On Inishkea North, with its deserted village, there was also a monastery from which one church survives, St. Columba's (Columcille) church, a rectangular drystone building with a lintelled doorway. On a large conspicuous sand dune called Bailey Mor the remains of beehive huts and rectangular houses with corbelled roofs (probably recent) were found along with early cross slabs and pillars, one showing a primitive, incised crucifixion. Numerous purpura shells were also found, used by the monks to make a blue dye for manuscript illuminations. Most difficult to reach is the tiny island of Duvillaun More with very similar remains of an anchorite community. Several cross slabs have been removed from the islands to the National Museum in Dublin.

NAVAN FORT
(Armagh)

Legendary capital of the kings of Ulster, Emain Macha, renowned in early Irish literature. On a prominent hill with wide views, 2 mi. (3.25 km.) W. of Armagh city, is a circular enclosure of about 18 acres with a ditch *inside* the bank, in the manner of the English henges. Thus the site was undoubtedly an important ritual center as well as the seat of kings, but never actually a fort. Inside the enclosure were two mounds. The larger one, nearly 150 ft. wide, was meticulously excavated from 1963 to 1971 and a fascinating story was revealed. (The mound has now been reconstituted.) The earliest finds were Neolithic; then about 680 BC, in the Bronze Age, a large round timber house or temple was built, with attached stockade, and rebuilt eight times over three to four centuries. Other round houses joined it on the site some centuries later. Finally, in the Iron Age, around 465 BC, all was leveled and a hugh circular ceremonial structure over 130 ft. in diameter was raised over the whole area—indicated by five rings of postholes. The outer ring was doubled, undoubtedly to support the weight of a roof. An entrance led through a passage among the posts to the center of the building where a tall, free-standing oaken post towered up like a totem pole—over 36 ft. high, it has been estimated. The heavy stump of the post was found in the ruins.

Obviously this huge "temple" was the focus of a sacred area of some size that extended all around it, like *Stonehenge* in England. Two "sacred lakes" for instance have been identified nearby. One was Lough na Shade, E. of the hill, in which four superb decorated bronze trumpets used in Celtic rituals (1st cent. BC) were discovered in the 18th cent. Only one now survives. These were undoubtedly thrown into the lake as ritual offerings. To the W. of the hill a pond at the site called the King's Stables was found to be artificial, and many sacrificial animals had been thrown into it. Part of a human skull was also found in it.

Roughly in the same period in which it was built the huge temple structure seems to have been deliberately destroyed, probably for obscure ritual reasons. First it was filled with cobbles, packed around the posts while they were still standing. The outer wooden structure (which probably included flammable siding of some kind) was then set alight and burned down about 265 BC, and after the conflagration had died a huge mound of turves and soil was erected over the cairn. That was the end; there is no indication of any activity on the hill after about 100 BC. But the sacred importance of the hill was not forgotten. It

Navan Fort near Armagh city in Northern Ireland, traditionally the site of Emain Macha, early capital of the kings of Ulster. Long before this period it was an ancient cere- monial center, as seen when excava- tion of the larger mound within the spacious hilltop enclosure revealed re- mains going back to the Neolithic period. Most astonishing was the dis- covery of the post-holes of a huge Iron Age timber structure, 125 ft. across, a ritual center that was later deliberately filled with cobbles, burned down about 265 BC, then covered by a mound of earth and turves in some arcane ceremony. Only much later did the site become the spiritual and temporal capital of the old king- dom of Ulster. (Crown copyright: Historic Monuments and Buildings Branch, DOENI, Northern Ireland.)

A hypothetical reconstruction of the great Iron Age timber building at Navan Fort, probably a temple, with a procession, led by trumpeters, is- suing from it. It was constructed with five rings of heavy posts holding up the roof and a giant oaken "totem pole" freestanding at the center. The whole structure was ritually burned down while the posts were still stand- ing. (Illustration by Stephen Conlin; Courtesy of Ulster Archaeological Society and Queen's University of Belfast, Dept. of Archaeology.)

became the seat of the Ulster kings and as late as the Middle Ages it was the site of regular assemblies and fairs.

That Emain Macha was indeed both the spiritual and political capital of pagan Ulster is further suggested by the huge defensive enclosure of *Dorsey* in

Armagh to the S., which seems to have been part of the southern defenses of the kingdom. Tree-ring chronology has dated Dorsey to the same period as the great Iron Age structure at Navan. More defenses known as Dane's Cast—a ditch and bank built in vulnerable areas—are still traceable about 4 mi. (6.5 km.) S. of Navan and in Down county, where part of the defenses run just S. of the great fort of Lisnagade.

Today, and for many years previously, Navan Fort has been threatened by an ever-encroaching quarry works that has edged right up to the hill and has almost engulfed Lough na Shade. Let us hope that it will be closed down before it is too late. See also Tara Hill.

NENDRUM
(Down)

One of the best examples of an early Irish monastery, on a glacial hill on Mahee Island in Strangford Lough (now linked to the mainland by bridges), about 6 mi. (9.6 km.) SE of Comber. Three concentric rings of drystone masonry surround the hill, with the church and round tower inside the inner ring. The monastery was founded in the 5th cent. AD, but nothing is known about it until about the 7th cent., and it disappeared from history about 976 when the abbot was burned in his house. The site was extensively excavated in 1922–24 (and again in 1954) and parts of the church (little more than foundations), the stump of the round tower and the walls were restored. Little that could be dated earlier than the 8th cent. was found. Cross slabs and a sundial were inserted into a wall of the reconstructed church, and the monastic graveyard next to it was also investigated. Inside the second ring a number of round hut foundations were uncovered, one a bronze foundry, and a rectangular building, known as the "schoolhouse" because inside it were found about 30 tablets of slate or stone with drawings and Celtic designs inscribed on them—probably trial pieces from the monastic school or workshop. The interior of the large outer ring has not been investigated. The extensive finds from the 1920s excavations are in the Ulster Museum, Belfast, and include a bell, the slates, and a rare bit of stone inscribed with a name in Runic (Viking) letters. See also Inishmurray.

NEW GRANGE
(Meath)

See Boyne Valley.

OLD KILCULLEN
(Kildare)

Round tower and high crosses remaining from an ancient monastery; W. off the main road to Carlow, about 2 mi. (3.25 km.) S. of Kilcullen. Here on a hill are a stumpy ruined round tower with a round-headed doorway, the remains of a Romanesque church, and parts of three ancient high crosses; the worn shaft of one, the base of another and the West Cross, again only a shaft remaining but with good transitional, biblical scenes carved on one face, with interlace decoration. The exceptionally fine early cross at Moone is about 11 mi. (17.75 km.) farther down the road to Carlow, and the crosses at Castledermot a few mi. beyond that.

OSSIAN'S GRAVE
(Antrim)

See Tievebulliagh.

OUGHTERARD
(Kildare)

Round tower, about 8 mi. (13 km.) SSE of Maynooth, SW of Dublin, on a hill beside a ruined church and in a graveyard. Marking the site of a monastery, it still stands 34 ft. high and has an unusual, early round-headed doorway.

PARKNABINNIA (Clare)	See *The Burren*.

PORTAVOE STANDING
STONE
(Down)

A striking monument close to the sea, standing over 8 ft. high on the western side of the Bangor-Donaghadee road, 2 mi. (3.25 km.) NW of Donaghadee. The sandstone pillar has been reinforced with cement.

POULAWACK CAIRN
(Clare)

See *The Burren*.

POULNABRONE DOLMEN
(Clare)

See *The Burren*.

PROLEEK
(Louth)

Good example of a portal tomb, on the grounds of the Ballymascanlon Hotel 3.5 mi. (5.6 km.) NE of Dundalk. Called "The Giant's Load," its 40-ton granite capstone rests on three uprights, the two front ones portal stones over 9 ft. high. The chamber probably had no side stones. If you throw a pebble on to the capstone and it stays, you'll be married within a year! (But suppose you're already married??) On the path to the tomb is a ruined wedge tomb with two roofstones. About 3 mi. (4.75) ESE is an interesting court tomb at Rockmarshall. Its court leads into four large chambers with massive side stones, curiously separated from each other by gaps and blocking stones.

PUNCHESTOWN
(Kildare)

Standing stone, 2.25 mi. (3.75 km.) SE of Naas, just S. of Dublin, near the Naas racecourse. This graceful, tapering granite monolith stands over 20 ft. high, among the tallest in Ireland. When it fell in 1931 (and was reerected) an empty Bronze Age cist was found at its base. There are other tall standing stones in the neighborhood and remnants of stone circles, megalithic tombs and henges.

RATH CELTCHAIR FORT
(Down)

See *Downpatrick*.

RATHCORAN FORT
(Wicklow)

See *Baltinglass Hill*.

RATHCROGHAN
(Roscommon)

A remarkable and mysterious group of at least 100 ancient monuments of all periods, covering several square mi., is centered around Rathcroghan crossroads and Glenballythomas, 3 mi. (4.75 km.) NW and SSW of the village of Tulsk. The area is associated with Cruachain, the traditional seat and inauguration site of the kings of Connacht. (The name is also used for the great limestone plateau of northern Roscommon, and is perpetuated as well in the "croghan" of Rathcroghan.) Obviously the whole region is one of great and ancient sanctity, predating the inauguration of the kings. The actual inauguration hill is supposed to be the small stone-faced cairn named Carnfree (itself possibly a prehistoric burial mound) in the SE sector of the area. It was in use up to the 15th cent. The whole region is dotted with monuments: burial mounds, ring barrows, standing stones, numerous ring forts (probably Iron Age), and linear earthworks "avenues" like the so-called "Banqueting Hall" at *Tara*, often connecting one ring barrow with another. There is a circular enclosure called "The Cemetery of the

Kings," and near Carnfree a small ring fort with a 7-ft. standing stone in its center called Knockannagorp, or King Dathi's Grave, said to be the burial place of "the last pagan king of Ireland." Some of the burial mounds may date from the Bronze Age, or may be even earlier passage tombs, and at Glenballythomas is a court tomb. There are also other ruined megalithic tombs to the S. of the main monuments. A final unique and mysterious site is the Cave of the Cat, or Oweynagat, a deep limestone fissure, the legendary entrance to the Otherworld. It is entered through a circular ring, perhaps Iron Age, and through a dry-stone souterrain, with two of its large lintel slabs bearing Ogham inscriptions.

RATHGALL
(Wicklow)

Large ceremonial hill fort 3 mi. (4.75 km.) E. of Tullow, excavated by B. Raftery in 1969–75 and 1978. The site, traditionally the seat of the kings of South Leinster, dates from the Bronze Age but was in use for some 2,000 years and there is extensive evidence for Bronze Age, Iron Age and Medieval activities. The ridge top covers 18 acres and was enclosed within three circular ramparts, the two outer ones prehistoric with external ditches, the third a stone wall of medieval date, a kind of citadel enclosing the inner core of the fort. Excavations here uncovered the remains of a large, circular, Bronze Age post-built structure (about 980 BC?) 48 ft. across, with some 1,500 postholes. The burned bones of an adult—a rare Late Bronze Age burial with the remains of a funeral pyre—were recovered at the center. It was surrounded by a wide ditch, in part now overlaid by the medieval wall, and outside the ditch to the E. were the remains of a large late Bronze Age bronze workshop inside a post-built structure. Much later, in the Early Christian cents., iron-working was carried out on the site of the Bronze Age workshop. The foundations of a medieval house were also found. See also *Clogher* (Tyrone); *Downpatrick*; *Dun Ailinne*; *Navan Fort*; *Tara Hill*.

RATHLIN ISLAND
(Antrim)

Large island off Ballycastle, the northernmost end of Ireland. Here in Brockley townland are remnants of a Neolithic axe factory—bits and pieces of unfinished or discarded axes of porcellanite, a hard rock that outcrops here and around *Tievebulliagh* in Antrim, where a similar axe factory has been found. Polished axes were widely exported from both locations and have been found on many sites from northern Scotland to southern England of around 2500 BC. These axes enabled Neolithic man to chop down large trees, build houses such as those found at *Lough Gur*, and otherwise master his environment.

RATHNAGREE FORT
(Wicklow)

See *Baltinglass Hill.*

RATHTINAUM
(Sligo)

See *Lough Gara.*

RATTOO
(Kerry)

Round tower in a graveyard next to a 15th-cent. church, 14 mi. (22.5 km.) N. of Tralee and 7 mi. (11.25 km.) W. of Listowel at the top of Kerry. The tower, nearly 90 ft. high, well-preserved—and restored—probably dates from the 12th cent. It has a round-headed doorway with a curvilinear design above it, and inside an upper window a carved figure that cannot be seen (a cast is in the National Museum, Dublin). As usual the tower is on the site of an obscure early monastery.

REANASCREENA SOUTH
(Cork)

Circle of 12 large stones, including the two portal stones and an axial or recumbent stone opposite them; 4 mi. (6.5 km.) NW of Ross Carbery. It is surrounded by a bank and ditch making it into a henge. There are other circles nearby, and *Bohonagh* axial circle and another fine one at *Drombeg* are not far off.

REASK
(Kerry)

See the *Dingle Peninsula*.

REYFAD STONES
(Fermanagh)

See *Boho*.

RING OF KERRY
(Kerry)

See *Beenbane; Caherdaniel; Church Island; Eightercua; Kenmare; Kildreelig; Killabuonia; Leacanabuaile; Skellig Michael; Staigue Fort*.

ROCKMARSHALL
(Louth)

See *Proleek*.

ROSCAM
(Galway)

Round tower in a monastic site, next to a medieval church, 4 mi. (6.5 km.) E. of Galway city, S. of the road to Oranmore. The round tower, only about 30 ft. high, may never have been completed because the scaffolding holes were never filled in. The semicircular churchyard wall obviously incorporates some of the old monastic cashel wall, with a curious passage in it with a pointed roof. To the NE about 500 yds. is a standing stone, the Long Stone.

ROSCRAE
(Tipperary)

Round tower and church just outside Roscrae, the modern Dublin-Limerick road cutting right through the ancient monastery of St. Cronan (6th-7th cents.) and leaving the round tower on one side, the remaining W. facade of the 12th cent. Romanesque church of St. Cronan on the other. The round tower, now about 60 ft. high, was reduced 20 ft. in height by the English in 1798 when one of their men was shot from the tower's top. About 25 ft. up the tower there is a relief of a ship inside a window. Beside the church is a damaged 12th-cent. cross with a crucifixion on one side, St. Cronan on the other, and two other figures in the typical bold relief of the period, as well as interlace designs. Close to the succeeding Catholic church is an early pillar stone.

ROSDOAGH
(Mayo)

A fine double stone circle in far NW Mayo, 6 mi. (9.6 km.) NW of Glenamoy village, overlooking Broad Haven. The "Druid's Circle" has two concentric stone rings, the outer (54 ft. across) of 33 stones, the inner of 16 stones.

SAINT BRENDAN'S
ORATORY
(Kerry)

See the *Dingle Peninsula*.

SAINT BRENDAN'S
ORATORY
(Mayo)

See *Mullet Peninsula*.

SAINT DECLAN'S
ORATORY
(Waterford)

See *Ardmore*.

SAINT JOHN'S POINT
CHURCH
(Down)

Early church, 1.5 mi. (2.3 km.) SW of Killough, near Ardglass and close to the end of the Lecale peninsula. This simple rectangular stone church probably belonged to an early monastery. It is very typical of the earliest stone-built churches of the 10th-11th cent. (earlier ones in this area were usually of wood), and is similar to the churches at *Derry* to the N. The doorway, with sloping jambs, is topped by a heavy lintel; there are antae (projecting side walls and gables) and one window. Its steep roof was probably thatched or covered with shingles. There was undoubtedly an earlier wooden church on the site, and some excavation in 1978 discovered earlier burials under the N. wall. There is a holy well on the site.

SAINT MACDARA'S
ISLAND
(Galway)

Ancient stone church on an island 6 mi. (9.6 km.) S. of Roundstone (SE of Clifden), part of an early monastery. It can be reached by boat from Carna near Mace Head. MacDara was a much-venerated saint of the 6th cent., and the island was long a place of pilgrimage. Several pilgrims' stations remain today, marked by cross slabs, and there is a holy well. The church, which has been restored, was undoubtedly based on wooden prototypes. It is built of very large stones, there is one window, and its projecting antae or side walls continue steeply up the gables to meet at the top. Some of the roof stones, obviously imitating wooden shingles, still survive, and there was a carved finial on the roof, discovered on the ground nearby. This is the only surviving church of a type depicted in miniature as caps on some early crosses (such as those at *Monasterboice*).

SAINT MANCHÁN'S
ORATORY
(Kerry)

See the *Dingle Peninsula.*

SAINT MEL'S CHURCH
(Longford)

Early church in Ardagh village, about 6 mi. (9.6 km.) SE of Longford. The broad stone church, somewhat restored, commemorates St. Mel who traditionally founded a monastery here in the 5th cent. It has projecting antae and a flat-headed doorway. Traces of a timber church, possibly 8th cent., were found beneath it in 1967 excavations. Tradition has it that St. Mel is buried in the church.

SAINT MOCHTA'S HOUSE
(Louth)

Ancient oratory in Louth village (which gave its name to the county), 7 mi. (11.25 km.) SW of Dundalk. St. Mochta, a disciple of St. Patrick, founded a church here, precursor of an early monastery on the site. The sole survivor of the latter is the simple, rectangular stone oratory, much restored and probably late 12th cent. in date. The door and windows are modern. Inside, the main vault is surmounted by a vaulted upper room, reached by narrow stairs, that serves to support the stone roof.

SAINT MULLIN'S ABBEY
(Carlow)

Monastic site with ruins of a medieval abbey, site of an early monastery founded by St. Moling (7th cent.); 4 mi. (6.5 km.) SSE of Graiguenamanagh, on the E. bank of the Barrow River. The earliest known plan of an Irish monastery in the 7th-cent. *Book of Mullin* shows a circular monastic wall with 12 crosses inside it and outside it. (For an example of such a monastery, see *Nendrum* in Down.) Remaining from the monastery today, among later buildings, is the stump of a round tower, a tiny oratory (St. James' Chapel), a small, damaged granite high cross with a crucifixion and heads on one side and interlace and wavy decoration, and St. Moling's Well.

SANDHILL SITES
(Antrim)

See *White Park Bay.*

SAUL
(Down)

Traditional site of the barn that became St. Patrick's first church, close to the site of his landing in Strangford Lough, which later became an important monastery. Today all that is left are several engraved slabs and a cross pillar preserved in the modern church of St. Patrick on the site, W. of the village—one slab has six ringed crosses on one side—and a few more worn slabs in St. Patrick's churchyard. In the churchyard also is an early stone-roofed tomb-shrine.

SCATTERY ISLAND
(Clare)

Island in the Shannon estuary S. of Kilrush, with a round tower; reached by boat from Cappa pier. St. Senan founded a monastery here in the 6th cent.; though suffering from Viking raids, it lasted as an ecclesiastical establishment until Elizabethan times. There are five churches, mostly late in date and some much ruined. The cathedral has antae (projecting side walls), a flat-headed doorway and later windows. Another is an oratory. There is a holy well, some cross slabs, and remnants of the cashel walls of St. Senan's monastery. The round tower, almost 80 ft. high, is of interest because it has an unusual round-arched doorway at ground level. This and the small windows and heavy masonry indicate an early date for the tower, when the advantages of a raised doorway (structural as well as for security) had not yet been realized. The cap is complete inside but appears truncated because it was never finished on the outside. One may step inside the door and look straight up at the cap (the floors are gone), an impressive sight.

SEEFIN
(Wicklow)

An imposing passage tomb sited on the top of Seefin Mtn., 3.5 mi. (5.6 km.) S. of Kilbride, SW of Dublin and a few mi. (about 3 km.) E. of Blessington. An entrance passage leads through the kerb of a massive stone cairn, over 70 ft. in diameter and 9 ft. high, and into a main chamber, now roofless though once with a corbelled roof. There are two lesser chambers at each side of the main one, and one at the back. Stones near the entrance and in the passage bear diamond-like designs and another design of fine lines. An Early Christian cross is engraved on one of the roof stones, suggesting that the tomb has been open for a long time.

SEIR KIERAN MONASTIC
SITE
(Offaly)

See *Castletown and Glinsk.*

SESS KILGREEN
(Tyrone)

Passage grave ("The Fort") less than 2 mi. (3.25 km.) WNW of Ballygawley, in the direction of Omagh. Like nearby *Knockmany* it is roofless and is a degenerate tomb with no passage (common in the N.). Two of its stones are decorated with lozenges and circles, linking it with passage tomb art. A highly decorated slab, probably the capstone of a tomb, lies neglected in the next field .

SHALWY AND
CROAGHBEG
(Donegal)

Two fine full-court tombs not far apart though in different townlands; 2 mi. (3.25 km.) ESE of Kilcar in the direction of Killybegs, in western Donegal overlooking Donegal Bay. Shalwy is called "Muinner Carn," Croaghbeg the "Portabane Carn."

Both have heavy portals with massive lintels and two-chambered galleries, and much of their cairns survives. The galleries are roofed with heavy slabs resting on corbels. Croaghbeg's court, to the SW overlooking the bay, is impressive, its heavy side stones increasing in height toward the entrance. On the court's N. side is a subsidiary chamber.

SHRONEBIRRANE STONE CIRCLE (Kerry)

This and several other circles are grouped around Lauragh Bridge, S. of the Kenmare River. Shronebirrane, 3 mi. (4.75 km.) to the SW, has eight tall stones (out of a possible 13) set close together, with one remaining tall portal stone opposite an axial or recumbent stone with a flat top. The circle is over 20 ft. in diameter. Drombohilly Upper stone circle is 1.5 mi. (2.3 km.) to the NE of Lauragh Bridge. On the top of a hill with magnificent views, it is even larger, with nine pillar-like slabs out of a possible 11 still standing, the two portal stones set radially. The recumbent stone is missing. At Cashelkeelty, 2 mi. (3.25 km.) WSW of Lauragh Bridge, are the remains of a five-stone circle with an outlying alignment, about 20 ft. long, to the S. of it. Another possible alignment lies to the W., and there are traces of ancient Late Bronze Age field systems around the circle.

SKELLIG MICHAEL (Kerry)

Famous early island monastery, isolated on Great Skellig, a paradise for bird watchers and a sheer island rising to two sharp pinnacles, 7 mi. (11.25 km.) W. of Bolus Head. It can be reached by boat from Valentia or from Cahersiveen pier—a wonderful voyage, worth the trip in itself. The monastery ruins, extremely well-preserved in the mild climate, are chiefly situated in a saddle between the peaks, about 550 ft. above sea level. They cannot be dated except to say that they are 12th cent. or earlier, since it is known that the monks abandoned the site for the mainland in the 12th or 13th cent. Access was originally up three different, precarious flights of steps (depending on the weather), meeting at the central "Christ's Valley," a terraced site. The modern path follows a different route. In the valley and in front of a modern wall, there are six large stone huts or clocháns—round on the outside, square inside, with corbelled roofs and no windows but little wall cupboards in the interiors and tiny garden plots around them. Here, also, is one of the two small oratories of the Gallarus type (see the *Dingle Peninsula*), though smaller and not as well built; also the ruined St. Michael's church (probably 12th cent.) and the cemetery with 22 early gravestones. To the N. is the smaller of the two oratories built on an artificial platform over the sea. There is also a blocked souterrain, a latrine, the "Monks Garden," and many grave slabs and early cross slabs here and there, as well as a monolithic cross. For other early monasteries see also *Church Island*; *Inishmurray*; *Nendrum*; and Reask (*Dingle Peninsula*).

SLIDDERYFORD DOLMEN (Down)

Striking portal tomb at Wateresk, 1.5 mi. (2.3 km.) SSW of Dundrum. A huge capstone, 9 ft. by 3 ft., rests on three large upright stones, with a fourth bearing no weight. It is difficult to discern any chamber.

SLIEVE GULLION CAIRNS (Armagh)

Two cairns on the prominent ridge of Slieve Gullion, about 4 mi. (6.5 km.) SW of Newry. The South Cairn is a passage grave in a cairn of stones nearly 90 ft. in diameter with a heavy kerb of stones laid flat. The passage, roofed with lintels, leads in from the SW to an octagonal chamber, once corbelled but now crudely roofed in concrete, with one small recess at the back. All is made of drystone walling except this back chamber, which is lined with orthostats. There are indications that a side cairn was added to the main one in the Bronze Age. The North Cairn, at the northern edge of the ridge near the summit, is a true Bronze Age cairn. It has no kerb. Excavations in 1961 uncovered two cists, one with bits of Food Vessel pottery and burned bones. The date is probably Early Bronze Age.

SLIEVE NA CALLIAGH
(Meath)

See *Loughcrew*.

SRAHWEE
(Mayo)

A wedged-shaped tomb called "Tobernahaltora" is attractively sited beside the road, 6 mi. (9.6 km.) S. of Louisburg and NE of Lough Nahaltora (named for it). The tomb is a fine specimen, its gallery double-walled and over 12 ft. long, almost covered by a large single roof stone, rather thin. There are traces of a cairn around it. For some reason the locals venerated the tomb as a holy well.

STAIGUE FORT
(Kerry)

Magnificent drystone fort, about 2 mi. (3.25 km.) W. of the main Ring of Kerry tourist road and about 10 mi. (16 km.) SW of Sneem village. The restored fort, at the head of a valley opening downward toward the sea, is about 90 ft. across on the inside with massive walls about 16 ft. thick at the base and tapering up to a height of 18 ft. There is a lintelled entranceway and passage through the walls and a complex of stairways, terraces and passages, and two corbelled chambers in the wall. A wide ditch and low bank surround the fort. It probably dates from the early (pre-Christian) Iron Age. See also *Doon Fort* and the *Grianan of Aileach* in Donegal and Dun Aengus and the other stone forts on the *Aran Islands*.

SWORDS
(Dublin)

A fine if battered round tower at the NE end of Swords, 10 mi. (16 km.) N. of Dublin on the Belfast road. It stands nearly 80 ft. high next to a 14th-cent. square steeple and near the Protestant church; its short conical cap is surmounted by a cross, with four large, round-headed windows just below it. The lintelled doorway is now almost at ground level. The tower is the only relic of a once important monastery and archbishopric, with the remains of the manorial palace nearby. The round tower at *Lusk* is only 5 mi. (8 km.) to the N.

TAGHADOE
(Kildare)

Round tower in a graveyard beside a 19th-cent. church. It stands over 60 ft. high but has no windows at the top and may never have been completed. There is a molding around the arched doorway and a much-worn head carved above it. Little is known about the monastery it belonged to.

TAMLAGHT
(Londonderry)

A fine portal tomb just W. of Coagh beside the road to Moneymore. Called "Cloghtogle," its huge capstone is made of quartzite, its supporting stones of basalt.

TAMNYRANKIN
(Londonderry)

See *Knockoneill*.

TARA HILL
(Meath)

Famous site, the Tara of the High Kings, a swelling hillside commanding wide views with a church in a grove of trees at the back and only some vague earthworks to interest the visitor today. It takes some imagination to realize the ancient importance of the hill, though tradition, legend and history, combined with archaeological findings, amply confirm its former sanctity. It was the site of a passage tomb in prehistoric times, later became the seat of priest-kings before the arrival of Christianity, and finally was the inauguration site of the High Kings of the northern half of Ireland until it was abandoned in 1022 AD.

The most prominent feature of the site, and the oldest, is the Mound of the Hostages (the fancy names were given by 19th-cent. antiquarians). On excavation this proved to contain a modest passage tomb with a narrow passage leading into a small chamber of seven orthostats, roofed by two remaining capstones. One of the upright orthostats bore examples of passage grave geometrical designs. The chamber and cairn over it contained masses of cremated bones (of at least 100 persons) and inserted burials of Food Vessel people. Later, about 1400 BC, Bronze Age people put down a layer of clay in which to insert their own inhumation and urn (cremation) burials. These yielded fine bronze knives and daggers and the body of a youth (a boy king?) wearing a valuable necklace of bronze, amber, jet and faience beads.

The Mound of the Hostages stands within a vast, oval Iron Age enclosure, 800 ft. by 950 ft., the "Royal Enclosure," with its ditch *within* the bank, suggesting that it was a ceremonial site rather than a hill fort. Near the center of the enclosure are two ring forts with double ramparts (the Royal Seat and Cormac's House). The latter, and larger, ring fort is built around a flat-topped mound that may originally have been an Early Iron Age burial mound, and its outer rampart bulges to enclose a Bronze Age burial mound. On its top is a granite pillar, the Lia Fáil, a phallic stone that originally stood near the Mound of the Hostages. On it, traditionally, the High Kings were crowned.

Moving outside the Royal Enclosure there is another large rath or ring fort to the S. named after Laoghaire, the king of Tara in St. Patrick's day. To the N. is the mutilated Rath of the Synods, messed up by some fanatical Englishmen in 1899 looking for the Ark of the Covenant—and later reexcavated in 1952–53. This proved to be another ring fort (these were individual seats of chieftains) with three ramparts, built in four phases from the 1st to the 3rd cents. AD. The ramparts bore palisades on the top, and post holes in the interior belonged to many wooden houses with palisades. Cremation and inhumation burials indicated prolonged occupation of the site. Roman glass, pottery and a lock and a seal helped to date the occupation.

Still farther N. is the so-called Banqueting Hall, a long rectangular hollow, 750 ft. long by 75 ft. wide, bordered by banks. This evoked dreams among the antiquarians of drunken royal orgies in a vast, long banqueting hall. It was more likely a ceremonial entrance roadway to the ancient site. NW again are three more mounds, ring forts or burial mounds, Grainne's Fort (with a mound in its middle), and two sites called the Sloping Trenches, N and S. About .5 mi. (.75 km.) to the S. of Tara Hill is another earthwork on a hill, Rath Maeve, an Early Bronze Age henge, 650 ft. across with a bank and ditch. In the graveyard next to the Rath of the Synods stands another small phallic pillar stone, and another stone bearing a much-worn figure in high relief, "St. Adamnán's Pillar," possibly a depiction of the Celtic god Cernunnos. See also *Baltinglass; Dun Ailinne; Hill of Ward; Moghane; Navan Fort; Rathgall; Teltown.*

TEAMPULL GEAL
(Kerry)

See the *Dingle Peninsula.*

TELTOWN
(Meath)

Ancient place of assemblies and games where the Lughnasa festival was held at the beginning of August under the Uí Néill confederation, the last time in 1168. Little is known about the site except from old Irish literature. A number of earthworks are scattered over a wide area, probably centering on Rath Dubh, The Black Fort, a circular earthwork about 50 yds. across that has lost half its bank. It is situated 1.5 mi. (2.3 km.) W. of Dunaghpatrick church, about 4 mi. (6.5 km.) W. of Navan. Teltown has been described as originally a pagan cemetery, and in later years only the king of *Tara*, which lies about 10 mi. (16 km.) to the SE, could preside over the assembly. Across the road the "Crockans," a large long mound, is associated with the "Teltown marriages," perhaps a survival from the ancient festival, in which a couple could separate if they wished after a year and a day. Just NE of Rath Dubh are two parallel ancient earthworks of unknown origin. Obviously the site could bear careful investigation.

TEMPLE BENEN
(Galway)

See *Aran Islands*.

TEMPLE BRECAN
(Galway)

See *Aran Islands*.

TEMPLEBRYAN NORTH
(Cork)

Stone circle and monastic site, about 2 mi. (3.25 km.) N. of Clonakilty. Five large flat stones of the 30-ft. circle (out of a probable nine) survive, including the recumbent stone and one of the portal stones opposite it. In the center of the ring is a white quartz boulder—always a magical color. Some ways to the N. is a large, ruined monastic enclosure with the remains of a square oratory, a well, a souterrain, graves, and a tall tapering monolith about 11 ft. high, probably associated with the stone circle as an outlier, on which the monks had engraved a cross and a faint Ogham inscription.

TEMPLE MACDUAGH
(Galway)

See *Aran Islands*.

TIBBERAGHNY CROSS
(Kilkenny)

Remarkable cross slab, a remnant of an ancient monastery, perhaps the shaft of a cross, standing in an old cemetery 1.25 mi. (2 km.) E. of Carrick-on-Suir. It shows many different animals, real and fanciful, undoubtedly all symbolic, including a centaur holding two axes, and on the E. side a deeply cut spiral design as well as swans and ducks. It may date as early as the 9th cent. The crosses at *Kilkieran* are 4 mi. (6.5 km.) to the NW.

TICLOY
(Antrim)

Portal tomb, 5 mi. (8 km.) SW of Carnlough, W. of the road to Ballymena. On Ticloy Hill, this tomb is part portal, part court tomb. There are the remains of a long cairn, and at one end is a small chamber roofed by two capstones, and in front of it a shallow court, defined by five large uprights. There were two portal stones fronting the chamber; one has fallen. At the other end of the cairn was another small chamber.

TIEVEBULLIAGH
(Antrim)

Neolithic axe factory high on the slopes of Tievebulliagh, a prominent mtn. near Cushendall on the NE coast of Antrim; first identified around 1900. Here and elsewhere in Antrim, and particularly on *Rathlin Island* to the N., there are outcrops of porcellanite, a hard volcanic stone eminently suitable for fashioning the polished axes that were used by the first Neolithic immigrants to Ireland and their successors. Here at Tievebulliagh and on Rathlin the axes were roughed out and exported as far as northern Scotland and southern England, where many have been found, while other roughs were taken down to the sandy shore at the Sandhill sites on *White Park Bay* for finishing and polishing. At Tievebulliagh a thick deposit was found consisting only of rejected or unfinished roughouts for the axes. A cairn on top of Tievebulliagh is probably Bronze Age. Many of the polished axes are found in Irish court graves, and a good example of such a tomb is found again on the slopes of Tievebulliagh 22 mi. (35.5 km.) WNW of Cushendall. Cloghbrack, or Ossian's Grave, has a semicircular court and a two-chambered gallery set in a short oval cairn.

TIGHLAGH EANY
(Galway)

See *Aran Islands*.

TIMAHOE
(Laois)

Round tower, 7 mi. (11.25 km.) SE of Port Laois on the edge of the village of Timahoe, remnant of a 7th-cent. monastery that survived into the late Middle Ages. The tower, remarkably fat, stands 96 ft. high and is noted for its Romanesque doorway about 15 ft. up, with four orders and decorated with human heads with their hair intertwined. There is also a Romanesque window at the third floor. Differences in stonework indicate that the tower below the doorway is far earlier and the upper part was built onto it, probably in the 12th cent.

TIMONEY HILLS
(Tipperary)

Large group of nearly 300 standing stones, here and in Callaun, 5.75 mi. (9.3 km.) SE of *Roscrae*. Except for 16 stones that form a circle, none of the stones appear to be in any coherent order.

TIREIGHTER
(Londonderry)

Wedge tomb, 5.5 mi. (9 km.) SE of Claudy, off the Dungiven-Londonderry road, S. of the hamlet of Park; an exceptionaly fine tomb with an imposing facade of uprights, an antechamber, and a main chamber about 12 ft. long. The double walling is clearly visible. The chamber and antechamber are partly filled with stones from the cairn and a massive fallen roof stone at the back. Over 2 mi. (3 km.) NNW at Clagan (3 mi. or 4.75 km. ESE of Claudy) are three large standing stones, one fallen, another reset at an odd angle after being overturned in 1770. The field here is littered with white quartz pebbles, always a magical color.

TIRKANE
(Londonderry)

See *Tirnony*.

TIRNONY
(Londonderry)

A fine portal tomb, 1 mi. (1.6 km.) NW of *Maghera*, with a tilted capstone over a square chamber. A tall stone stands alone beside one of the portal stones. At Tirkane, 1 mi. (1.6 km.) to the WNW, there is a typical sweathouse, well-preserved and easily accessible. These sauna-like communal bathing houses, perhaps introduced in Viking times and in use in the northern counties until recent years, are fine examples of primitive stone building styles. This one is typically built up against a bank for strength and has a stone-paved floor, but instead of the usual corbelled roof it has one of flat stones with a small smoke-hole in one corner. Water from a nearby well served to cool the sweaty bathers.

TLACHTGA (Meath)	See Hill *of* Ward.

TORY ISLAND
(Donegal)

Ruined round tower in West Town on this remote island 7 mi. (11.25 km.) off the NW coast. With the scant remains of two churches, several crosses and two early grave slabs it is all that remains of an early monastery founded by St. Columba (Columcille) in the 6th cent. The round tower, built of heavy granite boulders, is broken off above the round-headed doorway and one window. On the E. end of the island is a promontory fort, Dun Bhalair, with four-fold defenses and many hut sites within it.

TUAM
(Galway)

Late but interesting Romanesque remains, a good example of the pervasive Viking influence in Ireland in the 12th cent. Tuam, site of an early monastery, became the ecclesiastical center of the O Conor kings of Connacht. The 19th-cent. cathedral here incorporates a Romanesque survival, a superb wide chancel arch from the 12th-cent. church, which is highly decorated with strange human masks and beasts, and interlace in the Scandinavian "Urnes" style. More of the same is found on three round-headed Romanesque windows in the chancel's E. wall and on a 12th-cent. cross preserved in the S. aisle. In the center of town, behind railings, another 12th-cent. cross, the Market Cross, assembled from fragments of several crosses, also bears Urnes style decoration on its shaft and base.

TUAMGRANEY CHURCH
(Clare)

A church 2 mi. (3.25 km.) SW of Scarriff in eastern Clare. Its western section, with lintelled doorway and projecting sides (antae), dating from an ancient monastery founded here by St. Cronan in the early 6th cent., is reputed to have been rebuilt by an abbot in 969 AD and further repaired by Brian Boru about 1000 AD. The eastern end of the church is 12th cent. Inside it is an early gravestone and Romanesque fragments from *Killaloe*.

TULLAGHOGE FORT
(Tyrone)

Circular enclosure commanding a hilltop with views all around, 2.5 mi. (4 km.) SSE of Cookstown; the inauguration site of the northern Uí Néill from the 11th cent. AD. But it was undoubtedly in use from Early Christian times until its buildings and the stone inauguration chair, which stood on the hilltop to the SE, were destroyed by an Elizabethan general in 1601–02. Inside the circular bank, and separated from it by a wide space, is a polygonal banked enclosure where the houses stood. The O'Neill inaugurations continued here until 1593.

TULLAGHORA STANDING
STONES
(Antrim)

See *Armoy.*

TULLAHERIN
(Kilkenny)

Round tower, 5 mi. (8 km.) SW of Gouran, on the site of a former monastery, now lush pastureland. It stands 73 ft. high next to the ruins of a nave and chancel church of different periods but with an Early Christian nave. The tower, of substantial masonry of an early type, had a new parapeted top added to the original shaft. Half ruined, only four of the original eight windows of the parapet survive. The raised doorway of the tower has been torn out and the opening is now supported by a pillar. Near its base is a fragment of a worn Ogham stone.

TULLYHERAN FORT
(Londonderry)

See *Maghera Church*.

TULLYLEASE
(Cork)

Monastic site in far northern Cork 2 mi. (3.25 km.) SW of Drumcolliher in Limerick. In the church here, of various dates, are a number of Early Christian grave slabs built into the walls, including an exceptionally fine cross slab fastened on to the inside of the E. gable. Its incised carving, beautifully executed, and a Latin inscription in honor of the Saxon saint Berichert who founded the monastery here, so much resemble a page of the *Lindisfarne* gospels (ENGLAND) that it has been confidently dated to the 8th cent.

TULLYSKEHERNY
(Leitrim)

Remarkable pair of court tombs, The Giants' Graves, in a wild limestone landscape reminiscent of *The Burren*, 3 mi. (4.75 km.) S. of the border town of Manorhamilton. Built of the same limestone, the two tombs, only about 15 ft. apart, lie back to back on the same axis, both smothered in the remains of their cairns. The more northerly one is distinguished by no less than six subsidiary chambers opening onto the long sides of the cairn, all of them behind the main two-chambered gallery and antechamber. There was a long narrow court in front of it. The other tomb has the usual two-chambered gallery and the remains of a court, all set in a large oval cairn over 70 ft. long.

TURLOUGH
(Mayo)

Round tower, about 4 mi. (6.5 km.) NE of Castlebar, below Lough Conn. Complete at only about 70 ft. high, this tower is squatter than most and its doorway has been blocked up. Otherwise it is well preserved and, like the *Meelick* round tower 8 mi. (13 km.) to the NE, has both flat-headed and pointed windows.

TUROE STONE
(Galway)

Outstanding Iron Age cult stone, in a field near a house NW of the village of Bullaun, 3.75 mi. (6 km.) NNE of Loughrea town. The granite stone, now set in concrete, is 5 ft. 6 in. high and rounded, with superb, flowing La Tène-style designs in relief on its upper part above a band of Greek-key decoration. It originally stood next to a nearby Iron Age ring fort, the Rath of Feermore, which on excavation proved to belong to the late cents. BC. The stone, obviously a ritual centerpiece for important ceremonies, probably phallic, must date to the same period. It is one of three of four such stones surviving in Ireland, including the Killycluggin Stone in the National Museum and the stone at *Castlestrange* in Roscommon with similar designs, though incised.

TYNAN CROSS
(Armagh)

Several times removed, the worn Village Cross now stands W. of the Tynan village church, 7 mi. (11.25 km.) W. of Armagh, probable site of an early monastery. It is made up of pieces from two crosses, with weathered, figured scenes, interlace decoration and an open ring decorated with large bosses. Another cross from the monastery is in the Demesne of Tynan Abbey to the SW. This Terrace Cross is decorated with raised moldings and diamond and circular patterns. The Demesne also holds other early crosses from the region.

USHNAGH
(Westmeath)

Place of assembly, pagan sanctuary and hill fort on a commanding hill 5 mi. (8 km.) E. of Ballymore. This is one of those vague sites with a long and complex history, a place where people assembled on May Day, probably reflecting the earlier pagan fire cult of the Beltane festival celebrated on that day. The hill,

The beautifully carved Turoe Stone, preserved in Galway. Somewhat over 5 ft. high, the stone was apparently a ritual centerpiece, probably phallic, for pagan Iron Age ceremonies, and is dated to the late cents. BC. The lovely flowing designs of the upper part are pure La Tène style, a flamboyant motif developed in the late European Iron Age. A number of similar stones have been found in Ireland, although this is the finest. (By permission of The Commissioners of Public Works, Republic of Ireland.)

These curious Celtic figures now stand against a ruined church on White Island in Lower Lough Erne, Northern Ireland. Their origin is a matter of much speculation, but since they stood within the enclosure of an ancient monastery they are considered by most as Christian in intent, representing Christ as warrior, David the psalmist and the like. But they certainly embody earlier Celtic traditions of carving, known elsewhere in Ireland. Since each figure has a socket on top of its head, they may have served a structural purpose. (From R. Cavendish: Man, Myth and Magic [1970], Marshall Cavendish BPC Publishing, New York.)

poorly excavated in 1925–28, displays numerous earthworks, ring forts, ring barrows, burial mounds, the "Cat Stone," a natural boulder within a low earthen ring said to mark the center of Ireland, a prostrate pillar stone, a sacred well, "St. Patrick's Bed," a rectangular platform of stones, and the prominent "fort" inside which several houses had been built. See also *Tara Hill.*

WHITE ISLAND
(Fermanagh)

Island near the eastern shore of Lower Lough Erne, 2.5 mi. (4 km.) S. of Kesh, reachable by boat from Castle Archdale. Here, within the enclosure of an early monastery, is a small, ruined Romanesque church and set against its wall are seven crude, strong carved figures and a head, with sockets on top of the figures' heads. They probably belonged to an earlier church on the monastic site and may have served some structural function. Their meaning and purpose, however, have provoked much controversy; but they seem to be Christian in intent and probably date from the 9th or 10th cent. AD, though reflecting earlier pagan Celtic traditions (see also *Armagh; Boa Island*). Three pairs of the figures with interesting details reflecting early costumes seem to represent symbolically Christ as warrior, David as psalmist and so forth. On the other hand some think they may represent mythical or historical Irish characters. Recently a stone with a carved cross has been found set into the church. See also *Devenish* 9 mi. (14.5 km.) to the S. and *Inishmacsaint,* another monastic island in Lower Lough Erne.

WHITE PARK BAY
(Antrim)

A stretch of beach and coastland between Ballintoy and the Giants Causeway, preserved by the National Trust. The area was much frequented by Neolithic man (worked flints and sherds are abundant), and at the Sandhill Sites many axes of porcellanite brought down from *Tievebulliagh* mtn. have been found. They were worked and polished here with sand and water. Near the center of the stretch, on a low hill, is a grassy cairn with a stone kerb over 30 ft. in diameter. See also *Dunseverick Fort* nearby.

APPENDIX

APPENDIX

Contents

England
and Wales

Avon
Bath
Bristol
Stanton Drew
Stoney Littleton Long Barrow
Worlebury Hill Fort

Bedfordshire
Five Knolls

Berkshire
Alfred's Castle

Buckinghamshire
Taplow
Wing

Cambridgeshire
Barnack
Cambridge
Flag Fen
Great Paxton
Stonea Grange
Wandlebury
Water Newton

Cheshire
Chester
Eddisbury Hill Fort
Maiden Castle
Sandbach Crosses

Cleveland
Huntcliff Signal Station

Clwyd
Caer Drewyn
Eliseg's Pillar
Pontnewydd

Cornwall
Bodmin Moor
Boscawen-un
Carn Brae
Carn Euny
Castle-an-Dinas
Castle Dore
Chun Castle
Chysauster
Gurnard's Head
Halligye
Lanyon Quoit
Men-an-Tol
Merry Maidens
Nine Maidens
Pennance Megalithic Tomb
St. Just
Tintagel Head
Tregeare Rounds
Trevelgue Head
Zennor Quoit

Cumbria
Ambleside
Banks East, Banks Burn
Bewcastle Cross
Castlerigg Stone Circle
Gosforth Cross
Hadrian's Wall
Hardknott Castle Roman Fort

Long Meg and Her Daughters
Maryport Roman Fort
Mayburgh
Pike of Stickle Axe Factory
Swinside

Derbyshire
Arbor Low
Cresswell Crags
Mam Tor
Melandra Castle Roman Fort
Minning Low
Repton
Stanton Moor

Devon
Dartmoor
Exeter
Grey Wethers
Grims Pound Village
Hembury Castle
Kent's Cavern
Martinhoe

Dorset
Badbury Rings
Blandford Forum
Cerne Abbas Giant
Chalbury
Dorchester
Eggardon Hill Fort
Hambledon Hill
Hengistbury Head
Jordan Hill
Maiden Castle

Nine Stones
Wareham
Woodcuts Settlement

Durham
Binchester Roman Fort
Bowes
Durham
Escomb
Piercebridge Roman Fort
Rey Cross Marching Camp

Dyfed
Carmarthen
Castell Henllys
Dolancothi Gold Mines
Gors Fawr
Newport
Pen Dinas
St. David's Head

East Sussex
Cadburn, The
Combe Hill
Holtye Roman Road
Itford Hill
Pevensey
Whitehawk Camp
Wilmington Long Man

Essex
Bartlow Hills
Bradwell-on-Sea
Colcester
Greensted Saxon Church
Mersea Mount Mausoleum
Mucking

Glamorgan
Carn Llechart

Gloucestershire
Belas Knap
Blackpool Bridge
Chedworth Roman Villa
Cirencester
Claydon Pike
Crickley Hill
Dean Hall
Deerhurst

Gloucester
Great Witcombe Roman Villa
Hetty Pegler's Tump
Lodge Park
Lydney
Nympsfield Long Barrow
West Tump Long Barrow
Woodchester Mosaic

Greater London
Keston
London
Orpington

Greater Manchester
Manchester

Gwent
Caerleon
Caerwent
Usk

Gwynedd
Anglesey
Barclodiad y Gawres
Bryn Celli Dhu
Caer Gai
Caer Gybi
Caernarvon
Caer y Twr
Capel Garmon
Carn Fadrun
Castell Odo
Dinas Emrys
Din Lligwy
Dyffren Long Barrow
Moel Goedog
Penmaenmawr
Tomen Y Mur
Trefignath Chambered Tomb
Tre'r Ceiri

Hampshire
Beacon Hill
Braemore
Broom Hill
Bury Hill
Butser Hill
Danebury
Meonstoke

Old Wincester Hill
Portchester
Quarley Hill
Silchester Roman Town
Southhampton
Winchester

Hereford and Worcester
Arthur's Stone
Bredon Hill
Credenhill Camp
Croft Ambrey
Herefordshire Beacon
Midsummer Hill Camp
Sutton Walls

Hertfordshire
Harpenden Roman Mausoleum
St. Alban's
Welwyn
Wheathampstead

Humberside
Arras
Barton-on-Humber
Great Driffield
Hull
Rudston

Isle of Wight
Brading Roman Villa
Newport Roman Villa

Kent
Aylesford
Bigbury
Canterbury
Dover
Lullingstone Roman Villa
Lympne Castle
Oldbury Hill
Reculver
Richborough Roman Fort
Rochester
Stone-by-Faversham
Swanscombe

Lancashire
Halton
Heysham
Ribchester Roman Fort

Leicestershire
Breedon-on-the-Hill
Burrough Hill
Great Casterton
Leicester

Lincolnshire
Ancaster
Caistor
Horncastle
Lincoln
Rothwell
Skegness
Stow Anglo-Saxon Church

Mid Glamorgan
Gelligaer Roman Fort

Norfolk
Arminghall
Brancaster Roman Fort
Burgh Castle
Caister-by-Yarmouth
Caistor-by-Norwich
Cockley Cley
Grimes Graves
Haddiscoe
North Elmham
Warham

Northamptonshire
Brixworth
Earls Barton
Northampton
Raunds
Stanwick Roman Villa

Northumberland
Blawearie Cairn
Bywell
Chew Green
Hadrian's Wall
Hexham
High Rochester
Lindisfarne
Risingham
Walltown
Whitley Castle Roman Fort
Yeavering

North Yorkshire
Ailcy Hill
Aldbrough
Cawthorn
Devil's Arrows
Duggleby Howe
Hovingham
Ingleborough
Malton
Middleton Crosses
Ripon Cathedral
Scarborough Head
Stanwick Hill Fort
Star Carr
Thornborough Moor Henges
Whitby
York

Oxfordshire
Chastleton
North Leigh Roman Villa
Oxford
Rollright Stones
Wallingford
White Horse of Uffington

Powys
Brecon
Brecon Gaer
Breiddin Hill
Caersws
Castell Colon
Cerrig Duon
Ffridd Faldwyn
Ty Isaf Chambered Tomb

Shropshire
Mitchell's Fold
Old Oswestry
Wrekin, The
Wroxeter

Somerset
Brent Knoll
Charterhouse
Cheddar
Glastonbury
Ham Hill
South Cadbury Castle

South Glamorgan
Cardiff

South Yorkshire
Carl Wark
Sheffield

Staffordshire
Wall Roman Station

Suffolk
Hoxne
Sutton Hoo
West Stow

Surrey
Abinger Common

Tyne & Wear
Hadrian's Wall
Jarrow
Monkwearmouth

Warwickshire
Lunt Roman Fort

West Glamorgan
Coelbren
Goat's Cave
Maen Ceti
Neath Roman Fort
Parc Cwm Chambered Tomb

West Sussex
Bignor Roman Villa
Bosham
Boxgrove
Chanctonbury Ring
Cissbury Ring
Devil's Dyke Camp
Fishbourne Roman Palace
Sompting
Trundle, The
Worth

West Yorkshire
Almondbury
Blackstone Edge
Ilkley
Ledsham

Wiltshire
Avebury
Battlesbury and Scratchbury
Bradford-on-Avon
Cricklade

Devizes
Figsbury Rings
Knap Hill
Littlecote Roman Villa
Marden Henge

Ramsbury
Salisbury
Stonehenge
Woodhenge
Yarnbury Castle

Scotland (Counties)

Aberdeenshire
Barmkin of Echt
Berrybrae
Broomend of Crichie
Cullerlie
Culsh Earth-House
Dyce
Loanhead of Daviot
Maiden Stone
Memsie Cairn
Old Keig
Strichen Circle
Tomnaverie Circle

Angus
Aberlemno Pictish Stones
Ardestie Earth-House
Brechin
Caterthuns, The
Finavon
Pitcur Earth-House
Restenneth Priory
Saint Vigeans Museum

Argyll
Achnacreebeag
Gallachroy
Dunadd Fort
Dun Skeig Forts
Eilach-an-Naoimh
Kildonan Dun
Kilmartin

Banffshire
Cullycan

Berwickshire
Edinshall

Bute
Dunagoil

Caithness
Ackergill
Camster Chambered Tombs
Loch Stemster
Ousedale Broch
Yarrows

Dumbartonshire
Bearsden

Dumfriesshire
Birrens
Girdle Stanes
Mullach Hill Fort
Ruthwell Cross
Twelve Apostles Circle

East Lothian
Chesters
Traprain Law

Fife
Balfarg
Norman's Law Hill Fort
St. Andrews

Inner Hebrides
Dun Mor Vaul
Glenvoidean Chambered Tomb

Iona Island
Kildalton
Leccamore, Dun of
Lussa Wood
Machrie Moor
Skye

Invernessshire
Clava Cairns
Corrimony
Craig Phadrig
Dun Grugaig

Kircudbrightshire
Ardwall Island
Cairnholy
Castle Haven Dun
Lochill
Milton Loch
Mote of Mark

Lanarkshire
Glasgow

Midlothian
Edinburgh
Elginhaugh Roman Fort

Moray
Burghead
Elgin
Sueno's Stone

Orkneys
Blackhammer
Broch of Gurness
Brough of Birsay
Brough of Deerness
Cuween Hill
Dwarfie Stane
Fan Knowe
Holm of Papa Westray
Isbister
Kirkwall
Knap of Howar
Knowe of Arso
Maes Howe
Midhowe Broch and Cairn
Quanterness
Quayness
Rennbister
Rinyo
Skara Brae
Stenness Standing Stones
Taversoe Tuack
Tofts Ness
Unstan
Westness

Outer Hebrides
Barpa Langass
Callinish
Dun Carloway
Kilphedir
Udal

Peebleshire
Deva Craig Hill Fort
Whiteside Hill Fort

Perthshire
Abernethy
Ardblair
Ardoch Roman Fort
Castle Law Hill Fort
Croft Moraig
Dun Fallandy Stone
Fowlis Wester
Inchtuthil
Meigle

Ross and Cromarty
Dun Lagaidh

Roxburghshire
Bonchester Hill
Borthwick Mains Pictish Stone
Eildon Hill North
Hownam Rings
Newstead Roman Fort
Woden Law

Selkirkshire
Torwoodlee Broch

Shetlands
Broch of Burland
Broch of Mousa

Busta
Clickhimin
Jarlshof
Lerwich
Ness of Burgi
Ness of Gruting
Punds Water Cairn
Saint Ninian's Isle
Stanydale Temple
Vementry

Stirlingshire
Leckie

Sutherland
Carn Liath Broch
Dun Dornadilla
Farr Stone
Learable Hill

West Lothian
Abercorn Cross
Cairnpapple Hill
Catstane, The

Wigtownshire
Ardwellbroch
Barsalloch Point
Kirkmadrine Crosses
Mid-Gleniron Cairns
Torhouskie Circle
'Vhithorn Priory

Scotland (Regions)

Borders
Bonchester Hill
Borthwick Mains Pictish Stone
Deva Craig Hill Fort
Edinshall
Eildon Hill North
Hownam Rings
Newstead Roman Fort
Torwoodlee Broch
Whiteside Hill Fort
Woden Law

Central
Leckie

Dumfries and Galloway
Ardwall Island
Ardwell Broch
Barsalloch Point
Birrens
Cairnholy
Castle Haven Dun
Girdle Stanes
Kirkmadrine Crosses
Lochhill
Mid-Gleniron Cairns
Milton Loch
Mote of Mark
Mullach Hill Fort
Ruthwell Cross
Torhouskie Circle
Twelve Apostles Circle
Whithorn Priory

Fife
Balfarg
Norman's Law Hill Fort
Saint Andrews

Grampian
Barmkin of Echt
Berrybrae
Broomend of Crichie
Burghead
Cullerie
Cullycan
Culsh Earth-House
Dyce
Elgin
Loanhead of Daviot
Maiden Stone
Memsie Cairn
Old Keig
Strichen Circle
Sueno's Stone
Tomnaverie Circle

Highland
Ackergill
Camster Chambered Tombs
Carn Liath Broch
Clava Cairns
Corrimony
Craig Phadrig
Dun Dornadilla
Dun Grugaig
Dun Lagaidh
Farr Stone
Learable Hill
Loch Stemster
Ousedale Broch
Yarrows

Lothian
Abercorn Cross
Cairnpapple Hill
Catstane, The
Chesters
Edinburgh
Elginhaugh Roman Fort
Traprain Law

Strathclyde
Achnacreebeag
Ballachroy
Dunadd Fort
Dunagoil
Dun Skeig Forts
Eilach-an-Naoimh
Glasgow
Kildonan Dun
Kilmartin

Tayside
Aberlemno Pictish Stones
Abernethy
Ardblair
Ardestie Earth-House
Ardoch Roman Fort
Brechin
Castle Law Hill Fort
Caterthuns, The
Croft Moraig
Dun Fallandy Stone
Finavon
Fowlis Wester
Inchtuthil
Meigle
Pitcur Earth-House
Restenneth Priory
Saint Vigeans Museum

Ireland

Antrim
Altagore
Antrim
Armoy
Ballymacaldrack
Ballywee
Belfast
Carnanmore
Craigarogan
Craigs
Donegore
Dunseverick Fort
Larne
Lough-na-Cranagh
Lyle's Hill
Magheraboy
Rathin Island
Ticloy
Tievebulliagh
White Park Bay

Armagh
Annaghmare Cairn
Armagh
Ballykeel
Ballymacdermot
Clontygora
Dorsey Enclosure
Killevey Churches
Kilnasaggart
Navan Fort
Slieve Gullion Cairns
Tynan Cross

Carlow
Browne's Hill
Haroldstown Dolmen
Saint Mullin's Abbey

Cavan
Burren
Cohaw
Drumlane
Moneygastel

Clare
Burren, The
Craggaunowen
Drumcliff
Dysart O'Dea
Inishcaltra Island
Killaloe
Knocknalappa
Magh Adair
Moghane
Scattery Island
Tuamgraney Church

Cork
Ardgroom Outward Circle
Ballyvourney
Beenalaght
Bohonagh
Castelnalaght
Cloyne
Cork
Drombeg Stone Circle
Island
Kealkil Stone Circle
Kinneigh
Knockdrum
Labbacallee
Mount Gabriel
Reanascreena South
Templebryan North
Tullylease

Donegal
Beltany Stone Circle
Carndonagh
Clonca
Doon Fort
Fahan
Glencolumbkille
Grianan of Aileach
Kilclooney More
Shalwy and Croaghbeg
Tory Island

Down
Andleystown Cairn
Ballynahatty
Ballynoe
Derry
Donaghmore
Downpatrick
Dromore
Drumbo
Drumena
Goward
Kempe Stones
Kilfeaghan
Knockiveagh
Legananny Dolmen
Lisnagade
Millin Bay Cairn
Nendrum
Portavoe Standing Stone
Saint John's Point Church
Saul
Slidderyford Dolmen

Dublin
Ballybraek
Ballyedmonduff

Clondalkin
Dublin
Kiltiernan
Lusk
Swords

Fermanagh
Ballyreagh
Boa Island
Boho
Devenish Island
Drumskinny
Inishmacsaint
Kiltierney Deerpark
White Island

Galway
Aran Islands
Clonfert
Crannagh
Derryinver
High Island
Kilbennan
Kilcanonagh
Kilmacduagh
Roscam
Saint Macdara's Island
Tuam
Turoe Stone

Kerry
Aghadoe
Beenbane Fort
Caherdaniel
Church Island
Derrynablaha
Dingle Peninsula
Dunloe
Eightercua
Illauntannig
Inishfallen Island
Kenmare
Kildreelig
Killabuonia
Leacanbuaile Fort
Lissyviggeen
Rattoo
Shronebirrane Stone Circle
Skellig Michael
Staig Fort

Kildare
Castledermot
Dun Ailinne
Kildare
Moone High Cross
Old Kilcullen
Oughterard
Punchestown
Taghadoe

Kilkenny
Aghaviller
Fertagh
Kilkenny
Kilkieran
Killamery
Kilmogue
Kilree
Tibberaghny Cross
Tullaherin

Laois
Timahoe

Leitrim
Tullyskeherny

Limerick
Disert Oerghusa
Duntryleague
Kilmallock
Lough Gur

Londonderry
Ballybriest
Ballygroll
Boviel
Carrick East
Dunglady
Knockoneill
Maghere Church
Mount Sandel
Tamlaght
Tireighter
Tirnony

Longford
Inchclauran and Inchbofin
Saint Mel's Church

Louth
Aghnaskeagh
Ballinloughan
Ballybarrack
Donaghmore Souterrain
Dromiskin
Monasterboice
Proleek
Saint Mochta's House

Mayo
Aghagower
Aillemore Court Tomb
Balla
Ballyglass
Cong
Cregduff
Killala
Meelick
Mullet Peninsula
Rosdoagh
Srahwee
Turlough

Meath
The Boyne Vally Tombs
Donaghmore
Fourknocks
Hill of Ward
Kells
Killary
Loughcrew
Slieve na Callaigh
Tara Hill
Teltown

Monaghan
Clones

Offaly
Castletown and Glinsk
Clonmacnoise
Durrow
Gallen Priory

Roscommon
Castlestrange
Lough Gara
Rathcroghan

Sligo
Carrickglass
Carrowmore
Clogher
Creevykeel
Drumcliff
Inishmurray
Lough Gara
Moytirra

Tipperary
Ahenny
Baurnadomeeny
Cashel
Longstone
Roscrae
Timoney Hills

Tyrone
Altdrumman
Arboe Cross
Ballynagilly
Ballywholan
Beaghmore Monuments
Berrysfort
Clogher
Clogherny
Creggandevesky
Dun Ruadh
Knockmany
Leitrim
Longhash
Sess Kilgreen
Tullaghoge Fort

Waterford
Ardmore

Gaulstown
Harristown

Westmeath
Athlone
Bealin Cross
Fore
Uisnagh

Wicklow
Athgreany
Baltinglass Hill
Castleruddery Lower Stone Circle
Glendalough
Moylisha
Rathgall
Seefin

Index

354